The Child
Development Through Adolescence

The Child
Development Through Adolescence

Bernadine Chuck Fong
Foothill College

Miriam Roher Resnick

The Benjamin/Cummings Publishing Company, Inc.

Menlo Park, California • Reading, Massachusetts
London • Amsterdam • Don Mills, Ontario • Sydney

Sponsoring Editor: Larry J. Wilson
Developmental Editor: Linda Baron Davis
Production Editor: Madeleine Dreyfack
Cover Designer: Michael Rogandino
Cover Illustrator: Katy Rogandino
Book Designer: Michael Rogandino
Photo Researcher: Kay James
Artist: Doreen Masterson

Copyright © 1980 by The Benjamin/Cummings
Publishing Company, Inc. Philippines copyright 1980
by The Benjamin/Cummings Publishing Company,
Inc.

August 14, 1987

Library of Congress Cataloging in Publication Data

Fong, Bernadine Chuck.
    The child: development through adolescence.

    Bibliography: p.
    Includes index.
    1.   Child psychology.   2.   Child development.
I.   Resnick, Miriam Roher, joint author.   II.   Title.
BF721.F574   155.4   79-19793

ISBN 0-8053-9010-3

ABCDEFGHIJ-HA-83210

The Benjamin/Cummings Publishing Company, Inc.
2727 Sand Hill Road
Menlo Park, California 94025

Preface

- A child development book that treats children as *real live people*, rather than as abstract objects of investigation

- A child development book that *integrates* the advantages of *age–stage* progression with the advantages of *topical* and thematic treatments

- A child development book that weaves together the products of *scientific research* with *practical applications* to parenting, teaching, child-care, and social policy

- A child development book that discusses the *latest issues* of concern to students and professionals alike

- A truly effective textbook that is *interesting* and *enjoyable* for a one-semester or quarter course in child development

This is the kind of book we have tried to write. Although these goals may seem abstract, we have adopted specific strategies to achieve each of them.

Real-life Examples

The study of child psychology can easily succumb to conceptual abstraction. Of course, concepts are essential if the student is to appreciate and understand developmental processes. Still, the ultimate subject matter of child psychology is human beings, real people. Therefore, for illustrative purposes, we have taken frequent advantage of the lives and experiences of real people. Abigail Jane, who is introduced in Chapter 2, is a real child who was born while this book was being written. Every such human example makes a developmental point. Students will realize over and over that child development is really all about themselves and individuals they know. It is a *human* science.

The Integrated Topical and Chronological Approach

Topical treatment lends itself to the study and research of child development. But the chronological (age–stage) method provides a familiar framework for beginning students of child psychology. We have written this text largely because others' efforts to use both of these avenues have not always been successful. One of the chief reasons for this book's existence is to make a serious attempt to harness the "energy" from both of these approaches and to integrate them so that they support and complement each other. *The Child: Development Through Adolescence* never loses sight of chronological progress while also fully describing the topical framework. We believe this dual approach makes sense for teacher and student alike.

How do we carry out this integration? We have divided the text into 12 chapters of roughly equal length. Each chapter contains three main sections. A typical chapter begins with a section on theory, is followed by a chronological treatment of development, and ends with a section on special influences, both environmental and genetic. Therefore, within each topical area a full sense of chronological development is created when applicable. For example, the chapter outline below illustrates a typical chapter structure, which fully treats age-stage development within the overall topical framework.

Typical Chapter Organization

Chapter 5 Cognitive Development

Theory
{
What is Cognition?
  A universal developmental sequence
  Theorists of cognition
Piaget's Theory
  From egocentrism to relativism
  Schemes
}

Age–Stage
{
Stages of Cognitive Development
  Four major periods
  Infancy–toddlerhood: the sensorimotor period
  Preschool years: preoperational thought
  Early school years: concrete operational thought
  Adolescence: formal operational thought
  Comparison of the theories of Bruner and Piaget
}

Special Influences (Individual Differences) {	**Individual Differences**
	    Effects of education
	    Effects of intelligence
	    Differences in cognitive style
	    Sex differences
	    Family influence on cognition

Chronology review	**Summary** **Chronological Overview** **Applying Your Knowledge**

Treatment of Research

In preparing this textbook, we have scoured the research literature in child development. We have used both the latest research results and also the classical studies. But it was not our purpose to present each scientific investigation only because of its methodological significance. We have avoided presenting research study after research study. Rather, we have extracted and synthesized the chief results and researchers' methods, and arranged the material logically, so that the results can be assessed for their applications to the classroom, the home, and the professional setting. A comprehensive range of research is made attractively accessible to students, without the usual side-effects that stultify the interest of beginning students with no desire to become researchers. Since it is in the nature of psychological research and theory to be somewhat controversial, we have exposed the pros and cons of many issues. Thus, it is made clear that the field of child development is a growing and changing body of knowledge.

Treatment of Issues

This book not only includes the latest research and some of the controversy surrounding it but devotes several pages per chapter to in-depth treatment of particularly stimulating problems and issues. These "boxes" are separated from the text by color background. They are intended to provide topics to enliven classroom discussion and to show that there are many problems and issues yet to be solved by inquiring students of child development. For example, "Piaget: Development of a Psychologist," in Chapter 5 (page 164), is a brief history of Piaget's life. "Problems of Teenage Sexuality," in Chapter 10 (page 428), suggests why modern adolescents may get into sexual trouble. Most chapters include one or more in-depth descriptions of important investigations.

As a Textbook

Our definition of a successful textbook is one that makes learning not only possible but enjoyable and efficient. To accomplish this, we have used some proven strategies in writing and organizing the material. We have made a conscious effort to keep sentences short and to use a simple and vivid vocabulary. It is important, we believe, that beginning students, who come to the study of psychology with varying abilities and backgrounds, should not be put off by the manner of presentation. Therefore, the use of jargon has been minimized, and all definitions are given at the first use of a technical word. These definitions are highlighted in the margins for easy study and review.

Students who use this book will not miss the important points. Vital information is emphasized in many different ways by the format and design of the book.

1. **Chapter outlines** precede each chapter and prepare the student and the teacher for what is to come.
2. **Important terms** are set in a colorface within the text and defined in the margin alongside the paragraph where they are first introduced.
3. **Chapter summaries** freshly synthesize the main points of the chapter.
4. **Chronological overviews** reinforce the age–stage aspects set forth in the chapter.
5. **Applying your knowledge** features questions to focus student attention on how to use what has been learned—in teaching, parental, and research settings.
6. **Further readings** provide brief but helpful descriptions of books students might enjoy if they wish to pursue the subject further.
7. **Charts** and **illustrations** are used frequently to summarize long-term trends and other data.
8. **Photographs** have been carefully selected to reinforce the important messages and the *real life* quality of the text.

9. A **glossary** summarizes all technical terms for easy student reference.

10. A **bibliography** of all research sources used in the text provides the scientific underpinning of the book and is a comprehensive reference for future study.

11. **A student guide to psychological research** in the **Appendix** provides basic statistical concepts and a sample consent form for courses emphasizing the experimental nature of child psychology research.

Organization

The book is organized into five major parts. Part 1, which includes the first chapter, tells what child development is all about and how the study originated historically. It gives a simple explanation of how modern research is conducted.

Part 2 deals in three chapters with the biological and physical foundations of development. Chapter 2 is personalized in such a way that it tells an interesting story, while at the same time covering genetics, conception, prenatal development, delivery, and birth. Chapter 3 gives a lucid explanation of perception and sensory development, utilizing the most recent research. And Chapter 4 includes a strong presentation of genetic and environmental influences on physical and motor development, including discussion of the secular trend and the effects of early deprivation.

Part 3 covers the development of intellectual and communication abilities. The treatment of cognitive development in Chapter 5 is comprehensive but at the same time clearly understandable. Chapter 6, on language development, contains a great deal of information about the young child's understanding of the meanings of words at various stages of development, particularly useful for adults who work or live with children. Learning and intelligence, treated in Chapters 7 and 8, include learning theory for the particular benefit of teachers as well as a thorough airing of the pros and cons of intelligence and other types of testing.

Part 4, which includes Chapters 9-11, discusses the development of the social person. This section covers personality development, socialization, and motivation and achievement. Current issues are fully explored, among them the influence of sexism in American society, working mothers, absent fathers, day care, deprivation at all levels of society, and adolescent sexuality. The varying "recipes" for bringing up children are discussed within the framework of research to date.

The final section, Part 5 (Chapter 12), examines abnormal development: the kinds and causes of psychological, emotional, genetic, and cognitive problems that may be encountered among children, plus a survey of treatment methods.

Supplements

The text is accompanied by three thoughtful sets of materials:

1. *Student Study Guide:* features self-test quizzes and answers.
2. *Films and Projects Guide:* offers many ideas and sources for course enrichment.
3. *Test Item File:* is available for easy testing of overall aspects of child development paralleling the text.

Acknowledgments

Every large enterprise, particularly one dealing with the study of people, depends on the contributions of many individuals. The subject matter of any textbook is, by its very nature, derived from the work of others: the investigators, researchers, and thinkers who have created the discipline that is being explained. The authors are grateful to these scholars for the knowledge and insight they have provided. We are also indebted to the many students who have given suggestions and honest reactions.

Extremely helpful prepublication reviews and advice came from the following colleagues: Donalene Andreotti, El Camino College; Phyliss Blumenfeld, University of Michigan; Libby Byers, California State College, Rohnert Park; Doreen Croft, De Anza College; Janet Fritz, Colorado State University; Robert D. Hess, Stanford University; Dennis MacCombie, Kent State University; and Tom Spencer, San Francisco State University.

Joy Liberty and Phyllis Dolloff, who are both friends and colleagues, provided the initial encouragement that launched the two authors on this project. Larry Wilson, our sponsoring editor, contributed foresight and faith. Linda Baron Davis was our able and enthusiastic developmental editor.

We would also like to acknowledge Madeleine Dreyfack, who coordinated the entire production team and contributed greatly to ensuring quality copy editing, maintaining the schedule, and controlling the myriad of details involved in producing this text. Others who added their special talents include Alice Klein, copy editor; Michael Rogondino, designer; Kay James, photo researcher, and Doreen Masterson, illustrator.

Paul Raymond, Suzanne McCarroll, Susan Liu, and Larisa Fong served as research assistants. Janice Hall was our major typist and a research assistant as well. The necessary research was expedited by Dolly Prchal, now retired as head librarian at Foothill College, and her staff.

Many friends and relatives have naturally found a place in this book. They know who they are and that we appreciate them. We name only one, Abigail Jane, whose birth was simultaneous with this book's "birth." Our gratitude goes to our respective husbands, who endured, were supportive in times of crisis, and on many occasions uncomplainingly acted as couriers for "important material."

Bernadine Chuck Fong
Miriam Roher Resnick

About the Authors

This book is the product of an unusual collaboration between a psychologist and a professional writer. Bernadine Chuck Fong is a member of the department of psychology and child development at Foothill College, Los Altos Hills, California, and director of Foothill's Palo Alto Satellite Center. A psychologist with degrees from Stanford University and years of teaching experience, she has also been coordinator of the child development program at Foothill College, taught at Stanford University's Bing Nursery School, published in *Child Development*, and served on the Committee of Examiners on Human Growth and Development for the Educational Testing Service. She has twice won the teaching excellence award for superior classroom instruction and technique at Foothill College.

Miriam Roher Resnick, whose social science training was gained at Barnard College (Columbia University), Northwestern University, and the University of California, is a professional writer. For many years her specialty has been "translating" technical social science material into attractive, accessible English prose. She is the author of textbooks, numerous articles and many government publications.

Photo Credits

Contents

PART 3 Intellectual and Communication Processes

PART 5   Abnormal Development

PART 1

Overview

Chapter **1**
Introduction

Not long ago, an investigator reached a group of Chicago parents by writing and phoning the first name on every fifth page of the city telephone directory. An astonishing proportion—94%—of these people from all walks of life (who had telephones) reported that they had read books or articles about child-rearing while their own children were young. Almost every one of the individuals questioned had hoped to learn from their reading "more about *child development* ... how babies grow and change ... develop physically, mentally, socially, and emotionally ..." (Clarke-Stewart 1978, page 366).

Child development: the physical, mental, emotional, and social growth of the child

The Subject Matter and Its Early History

Who is interested

Parents are not the only ones who seek guidance, wherever they can get it, about how their children develop and how to cope with them while they are young. Teachers, nurses, doctors, social policy-makers, and administrators, among others, all want information about the range of "normal" behavior of children at various ages. They also would like to know what conditions could create individual differences.

Many mothers and fathers would be pleased to be able to bring up daughters and sons who are bright, creative, motivated, talented, loving, obedient, happy, and popular with the "right" kind of friends. Other parents would like their children to be able to fulfill their "ultimate potential." Teachers would be delighted to know the secret of producing a class full of pupils who learn readily, ask the right questions, strive to do well, and are never unruly. Nurses and doctors would be glad if they could precisely diagnose all behavioral and psychological problems brought to them and prescribe sure cures. And a utopia for social policy-makers would be a store of hard information enabling them to set up schools and programs to transform all the children in the United States into well-educated, prosperous, informed voters.

Early ideas

Researchers who study human behavior would probably be happy to help everyone fulfill these assorted goals. For at least three centuries some individuals have been trying systematically to understand the conditions that could influence the minds, personalities, and behavior of children. Earlier, in the Middle Ages,

In earlier times, children were treated like small adults.

infants were generally looked upon as unimportant creatures who required only physical care. As for children, they were treated like small adults who needed correction when they did not meet grown-up standards. This attitude began to change in the seventeenth century, when certain intellectual leaders asserted that children were not ready for adult life and needed schooling to prepare them for their roles in society. Families also began to be recognized as molders of bodies and souls. Both are concepts that we share today (Aries 1962).

John Amos Comenius was an influential seventeenth-century philosopher who pioneered the notion that material used in

Picture books are specifically designed for a child's ability and interest.

school should be on the level of the pupils' ability and interest. He was the creator of one of the first picture books for children. He thought, as modern scholars also do, that children learn through their senses. Another of today's ideas that first came from Comenius is that children should not and cannot be forced to learn. Rather, they must *want* to learn. Therefore, he did not believe in punishing a child for failing to learn. He thought it was the teacher's responsibility to create the desire to learn and that a pleasant atmosphere is an important motivator.

John Locke, slightly later in the seventeenth century, may have been the earliest "environmentalist." He wrote that experience is the source of reason and knowledge. He believed that the child's mind is blank at birth and that *environment*—people and

Environment: all the conditions and forces that surround and influence the individual

The schoolroom is where the fate of civilization is decided, according to John Dewey.

surroundings—provides ideas. Locke's theories led to our current conviction that children should be treated as rational individuals.

Jean-Jacques Rousseau, an eighteenth-century thinker really "discovered" children. He wrote: "Nature wants children to be children before they are men. If we deliberately pervert this order, we shall get premature fruits which are neither ripe nor well-flavored, and which soon decay." He was the first intellectual leader to express concern about children's well-being and to urge consideration for the young. Rousseau rejected the idea of original sin. He thought children are born with natural goodness.

An intellectual descendant of Rousseau was Friedrich Froebel, a nineteenth-century German educator. He invented the kindergarten. There children as young as a year old could be encouraged to act spontaneously. By following their own interests, they would be able to "unfold" their "inner essence."

Some believe that Charles Darwin's mid-nineteenth century work, *On the Origin of Species*, was the real beginning of the science of child behavior. Darwin originated the notion that human development can be understood only by a study of origins, and the origins of men and women are the children they once were (Kessen 1965).

John Dewey may have had the most profound influence on the study of children in the twentieth century. He contributed the idea that schools are society's most important institutions, places where civilization's fate is decided (Drake 1955).

Earliest studies

Along with early theories about the nature of children came attempts to find out what children are like and how they develop. Perhaps the first systematic study was the diary kept by a doctor to record the development of King Louis XIII of France, born in 1601. It contained 9000 entries, covering his first 26 years (Marvick 1974).

A later, slightly more sophisticated kind of investigation was the "baby biography." The first was published in 1774 by Johann Pestalozzi, a Swiss educator, who observed his own baby son. He theorized about the nature of the child and how and why he grew as he did. Similar biographical studies followed, written by Dietrich Tiedemann, an eighteenth-century German philosopher, and Charles Darwin, among others.

Unfortunately, by modern scientific standards, these early investigations were seriously flawed. The material was gathered by no particular system. The authors' samples were limited to a single well-loved child. Each observer had his own pet theory to promote. But the baby bios were important because they were forerunners of later scientific investigations of how children develop and the conditions that create individual differences.

Current Ideas and Research

Goals

The study of child development has come a long way since the diaries of two or three hundred years ago. Today, investigators follow rigorous, scientific standards in attempting to learn the facts about human behavior. They have two major goals: to catalog and describe how children act at various ages and to understand why they behave as they do. Since all adults were once children, to understand children is also to gain an understanding of the grown-ups they become.

Nevertheless, *developmental psychology* will probably never match the physical sciences in terms of precise answers to precise questions. Human behavior is inevitably full of uncontrollable exceptions and variables. Individuals are (by definition) different from one another; therefore behavior is full of differences. Thus, "laws" of behavior can only be generalizations that apply to most people most of the time. As in any scientific effort, the purpose of the study of child development is to gain a fuller understanding of the world and the people in it. The practical goal is to describe; the theoretical goal is to explain.

Developmental psychology: the branch of psychology that studies the processes of growth and maturation and the effects of experience

Leading theorists

The first influential modern theorist and investigator in the field of child development in this country was G. Stanley Hall. Late in the nineteenth century, Hall began to study children in a systematic way. He believed that his work would lead to a better understanding of adults. His particular contribution was the use of questionnaires to be answered by large groups of children and parents.

Sigmund Freud, Jean Piaget, Erik Erikson, Abraham Maslow, and Carl Rogers are some of the major authors of current theories relating to stages of emotional and cognitive development. As a result of their work, it is now generally accepted that human development progresses in biologically based stages, linked in a continuum. What happens to an individual in one stage can influence behavior in subsequent stages. Modern investigators try to discover the behavior that is characteristic of particular age spans.

Arnold Gesell was a pioneer in working out behavioral *norms*—levels of behavior that seem to describe how most children act most of the time under given conditions. Norms are characteristic of a group but they are not necessarily true for every individual in the group. Thus, individual differences might also be normal.

Norms: standards or measurements of behavior or development

B. F. Skinner, a spiritual descendant of John Locke, is an enormously influential advocate of environmentalism, a dominant theory in modern developmental psychology. Environmen-

This boy is being tested to determine where he ranks according to Gesell's norms.

talists believe that human behavior is shaped by outside influences we encounter in the course of our lives. Most of today's research attempts in one way or another to discover exactly how child behavior is affected by environment: the conditions under which children are conceived and born and under which they are reared and educated; the mores of the group to which they belong; the family's life-style and relative poverty or wealth; the very air they breathe.

These are only some of the important names and dominant theories in modern child development research. The work of these leaders and other investigators will be described in later chapters. All the researchers have something in common: the systematic way in which they conduct their studies, in contrast to the informal and unsupported theorizing of past centuries.

Issues and trends

No one should leap to the conclusion that the last word on child development has been said by any one theorist or investigator. Psychology is a young science and the study of child development is an even younger branch of the discipline. Like the physical sciences, psychology continues to evolve. Some of today's laws may be dismissed as myths tomorrow. Several major issues enliven and motivate the contemporary study of child development.

For example, the evolutionary theory upon which some early studies of child development were based is now being questioned. In the early part of the twentieth century, Darwin's theory of evolution led to the belief that every person goes through the same stages of development as the people of the world have done through the ages. In other words, *ontogeny* recapitulates *phylogeny*—the development of the individual repeats the evolution of the species. Thus, babies begin as savages, become barbarians in childhood, and go through a nomadic period in adolescence (Hall 1904). While this concept is still influential, it is no longer universally accepted.

Ontogeny: the development of the individual

Phylogeny: the development or evolution of the species

A widely publicized current issue is the *nature–nurture* controversy. How much are children's behavior and developmental characteristics influenced by the *genes* they inherit, and how much by parents, home, and community environment? The contention of some scholars that intelligence level is determined by racial inheritance has become a serious social issue.

Nature: inherited characteristics

Nurture: environmental factors

Genes: the elementary units of heredity

A related question concerns the causes of behavioral differences among various groups in the population. Sex differences have become a burning issue, particularly influenced by the women's movement. Is the psychological development of a girl different from a boy's because of her biology or because of the way she is brought up? Many studies focus on this question. Other aspects of the group differences problem are the effects on children's development of race, socioeconomic class, ethnicity, and culture. A great deal of research has focused on attempts to sort out the characteristics and origins of such behavioral variations among different groups in this country and in the world.

How much can biology teach about child development? Current animal research by some child developmentalists is based on the theory that the nature of children is linked to evolution and to our animal ancestry. Documented changes in human growth patterns over the years throughout the world seem to suggest that biological evolution plays a part in human psychological development. Biology also underlies considerable current research on the effect of heredity on child development. For example, it is now possible to identify before birth children who will suffer from certain abnormalities due to unusual chromosomal combinations.

To be able to predict how children will turn out is the dream of many who work in the field of child development. The obvious practical reason for prediction would be to enable parents, teachers, or other agencies to intervene in time to protect, foster, or prevent (as the case may be) the predicted behavior. Not long ago one public figure urged the federal government to adopt a program of screening in order to single out prospective delinquents while they were very young (see Chapter 12). But the science of child development is still too inexact to make it possible to make accurate forecasts.

At a meeting of the Society for Research in Child Development, a lawyer complained, justifiably, about the scantiness of data available to help public policy-makers who must decide issues involving foster care, child custody, treatment of delinquents, and care of neglected or abused children. He pleaded for better guidance so that the consequences of different policies could be known beforehand. He said:

> We need developmental psychologists who are willing to participate with lawyers in facing the hard questions involved in drafting a specific statute. They must be willing to apply existing data to help define those conditions that justify state intervention. Moreover, they must be willing to do the additional research needed to provide answers to the questions we cannot answer at present (Wald 1976, page 4).

Unfortunately, it is one thing to ask for simple answers to such questions but it is quite another matter to provide those answers. Nevertheless, researchers in the field of child development are trying to solve such problems. This book reflects and summarizes those investigations.

Research Design

How does an investigator carry out research in the field of child development? The basic research design in this branch of social science is not very different from research design in the physical sciences, although the "materials" are human beings.

Setting up the experiment

The problem is the reason for a research project in the first place. What do we want to know? For example, Albert Bandura (and his colleagues, 1961, 1963*a*, 1963*b*), wanted to find out whether children who watch violence on television are influenced to become aggressive. Based on his prior knowledge of how children learn, he formed an appropriate *hypothesis,* a proposition to be tested. His hypothesis was that children will be likely to imitate aggression if they have seen such behavior either on film or in real life. The proposition was based on the *theory* that learning is acquired from *models,* people who are imitated. Bandura's theory, like other theories, was a general principle explaining the relationship of a set of facts.

Hypothesis: a proposition that must be tested to determine its validity

Theory: a general principle that attempts to explain the relationship of a set of facts or behaviors

Model: someone who exhibits any kind of observable behavior

To test his hypothesis, Bandura set up an experiment using four separate groups of nursery school children, each of which was subjected to a different experience. One group viewed a film that showed a cartoon figure (a model) hitting a doll. Another group saw a film of a real child assaulting a doll. The other two groups were shown examples of neutral behavior. One of these groups saw a live model behaving nonaggressively, and the other was not exposed to any model. The first two groups were *experimental groups:* they were exposed to conditions testing the hypothesis (aggressive models). The latter two were *control* groups, not subjected to experimental conditions.

Experimental group: subjects exposed to conditions whose effect is to be tested

Control group: subjects not exposed to special conditions

In comparing the subsequent play behavior of the four groups, the investigator found that cartoon models caused as much imitation as live models. Moreover, aggressive models were imitated more frequently than nonaggressive models (Bandura, Ross, and Ross 1961). Thus, Bandura tested his hypothesis and confirmed a relationship that has serious practical implications with respect to children's television watching.

Sample: a group of people, representative of a larger group (population), who are studied in order to gain information about the entire population

Determining who will be chosen to participate in a study is an important element of research design. The nature of the *sample* those persons who are representative of the group, or *population,* about which the investigator would like to generalize, has a great deal to do with the study's outcome. The population Bandura chose to study was nursery school children. The four groups of children he selected were all comparable in age, sex, and level of education. In this way, Bandura was making sure there were no important *variables* or differences that would affect the results: the groups were basically the same.

Population: the entire group of people under study, from which a sample is taken

Variables: influencing factors in a given situation

Economic and social background are two more variables that investigators usually control in setting up their samples. In Bandura's study, the children were all from the same socioeconomic level because he did not want that variable to affect his results. However, for some types of investigations—such as public opinion polls, which study the behavior of very large and mixed populations—the *subjects* are chosen to include representatives of all social and economic groups, and the sample includes the same proportion of each group as in the population as a whole.

Subject: person being studied

Other types of investigation use *random* samples. A random sample is one in which everyone in the population from which the sample is to be drawn has an equal chance of being selected.

Random: drawn by chance

A good research design provides *descriptive statements* relating to all the elements in the study. This permits later generalizations that go beyond the characteristics of the individuals and the conditions being tested. For example, Bandura carefully defined the various kinds of aggression being investigated and the meaning of *modeling* in his experiment.

In the Bandura experiment, data were collected by trained observers, who watched the playground behavior of the four groups of children immediately after they had seen the films. The observers used predetermined *rating scales,* in order to make sure their observations were *uniform* and *systematic.* Other studies might use *interviews,* carefully structured to cover the same points with each subject. Written *questionnaires* are often used as well. For public opinion polls, for example, the interviewers are rigorously trained and the questionnaires carefully worded so that neither the questions nor the questioners unwittingly bias the answers.

Studies may be either *experimental* or *correlational.* Bandura's was experimental because certain conditions devised by him were imposed on his subjects. They were not conditions that would necessarily have occurred in exactly the same way in the normal course of life. In contrast, correlational investigations may compare similarities or differences among two groups that occur without imposing any experimental conditions. An example would be a comparison between the intelligence quotients of children and their parents.

Correlation: degree of similarity or correspondence between two or more variables

A number of other types of investigations are also used in studying child development, depending on the kind of information the researcher is seeking. For example, some research is *clinical:* studying the behavior or histories of selected individuals to find out how they act or have acted in the past. Bandura might

Clinical: involving investigation of background factors, family relations, and test results for a diagnosis

have interviewed children or parents about their television-viewing habits and their actions, but for better proof of his hypothesis he was able to set up an experiment. However, some kinds of human behavior, like sexual activity, do not usually lend themselves to experiments.

Field studies, observing children at home, in school, in other everyday situations, are another research instrument, which may precede formal research. Such studies often provide ideas for hypotheses. Field studies might also test the conclusions of formal research. But field studies cannot stand alone because conditions are not controlled. Throughout this book, examples from real life are used for illustration. Abigail, Jon, Steve, and other children cited are real people. The anecdotes are like field studies, but they have no status as research.

Applied research attempts to answer a specific, practical question. For example, the attorney mentioned earlier would presumably be pleased to hear about a definitive study outlining the special circumstances under which children would be better off in their fathers' custody. Another example of applied research would be a study of the most effective way to teach a particular school subject.

Phylogenetic research studies the behavior of nonhumans in order to draw conclusions about humans. A practical reason for doing such research is that experimental conditions are used that would be impossible to impose on people. For example, some experimenters have reared monkeys under artificial conditions to see the effects of different kinds of mothering.

Longitudinal studies examine the behavior of a particular group of subjects over a long period of time. Usually the purpose is to determine how the variables under consideration change with the increasing age of the subjects. For example, Bandura or another researcher might have decided to follow up a group of child television-viewers over a period of years, to see how aggressive they turned out to be. The advantage of the longitudinal approach is that data can be gathered about the same subjects at various developmental stages. The result is a profile of human development and the conditions that affect it. But such studies are costly. They require a long-term staff and constant efforts to follow the subjects. Over the years, the sample may suffer from attrition: subjects may be lost because they have moved out of reach or died or because of poor record-keeping.

Another useful form of research is to make a *cross-sectional* analysis by comparing the behavior of members of a group who

Phylogenetic research: study of nonhuman behavior in order to relate findings to humans

Longitudinal research: periodic study of a particular group over a long period of time

Cross-sectional study: comparison of behavior of individuals in a group similar in all except one characteristic

are basically similar except in one characteristic, like age, social class, or education. All other important variables are presumably controlled. Thus, Bandura might have studied the effects of seeing filmed violence on children of various ages, to determine whether older children are more or less susceptible than younger children.

A variation of this method of study is to compare the behavior of two or more large groups or *cohorts*, for example, each born in a particular period. Each group constitutes a cross-section of people who have experienced historical and sociological conditions that are different from the experiences of those born at another time. A researcher might come to conclusions about the effects of the groups' differing experiences.

Cohort: a group of individuals with a certain factor in common, such as age

Another variation is the *cross-cultural* approach, comparing the patterns of development of different cultural groups. The purpose is to find out which behavior is *universal*—true for all people in all cultures—and which behavior is specific to certain groups, presumably because of cultural factors. Perhaps Bandura might have tried his television experiment on American children and on Chinese children, to see if they reacted the same way.

Cross-cultural: relating to the differences among peoples in the world

Universal: common to all persons or cultures or groups

Analyzing the data

The hypothesis, the beginning of any scientific investigation, is also the end of the study. It is either confirmed by the data, eventually rising to the status of theory, or it is refuted. In the latter case, a theory may also be made, although in a negative way. In any case, all results and conclusions depend on statistical analysis of the data, which have been collected and organized according to established statistical procedures.

Suppose a research project has been dealing with more than one variable, and the goal is to discover the correlation between the two variables. For example, in a study to discover the relationship between parents' and children's IQs, a perfect positive correlation would be $r = +1.0$. That would mean that the intelligence scores of each parent–child pair are exactly the same. (Perfect correlations in the behavioral sciences are rare.) A perfect negative correlation would be $r = -1.0$, meaning that a high IQ for a child is linked to a low IQ for the parent, or vice versa. If the correlation is zero, it means the variables are unrelated. Correlations are also useful in cases where the relationship between two different characteristics in a group is being studied, such as race and IQ, or in comparing paired subjects, like twins.

It is important to realize that a correlational relationship between two variables does not necessarily imply a cause-and-effect relationship. One must apply common sense in interpreting the results of investigations of human behavior. This point was made by someone who said he made a survey of women five feet tall to ask them if they liked chocolate. The correlation was +1.0. The facetious conclusion was that chocolate stunts a girl's growth. (See Appendix, page 528, for more information on methods used in psychological research.)

Observing through a one-way window is a common way of studying children.

Ethical and Practical Considerations

Studying children is complicated. Any experiment involving human beings is more difficult than dealing with things, which do not think or feel. Objects will do exactly what you make them do with no harm to anyone except possibly the experimenter.

Also, investigators must be extremely ingenious if they want to measure hard-to-capture human qualities like aggression or affection or attachment. Besides, although they are humans themselves, researchers must try to be inhumanly objective, to discard personal bias, which might influence their observations and interpretations. Those who work with infants, who cannot express their feelings, have an additional problem. They must be extremely inventive in trying to work out ways of discovering what, if anything, their subjects are thinking or feeling. Investigators also have to be diligent and persuasive in trying to find children and care-givers who will be appropriate and willing subjects.

Finally, researchers face serious ethical and moral problems in any study affecting human subjects. Those who study children are particularly obligated to make sure they are not harming them. This caution relates not only to physical damage but also to psychological consequences, such as pain, anxiety, fear, and frustration. Another consideration is whether investigators have a moral right to observe individuals, either with or without their knowledge or consent. They must be careful not to invade the privacy of individuals or families.

Consent

A major prerequisite in psychological research is obtaining subjects' consent. Anyone who is a research subject must agree to take part in the project. But when the subjects are children, the ethical and legal problems are complex. Children are especially susceptible to harm because of their immaturity. Therefore, the courts have ruled that documented consent is essential in biomedical or behavioral research, and that the written consent form must be readily understood by the subject. (See Appendix, pages 529–530.)

But at what age may children responsibly give consent? There is no general agreement on this matter in either the scientific or the legal community. Courts have set varying age limits in different cases and varying circumstances. State laws also differ. Some lay down specific ages of consent. Others use the "emancipated minor" rule—roughly, anyone who is self-supporting and living independently is deemed able to give informed consent (Glantz, Annas, and Katz 1977).

Generally, however, it is up to the parent to consent to experimentation involving a child, although at this writing, there are no decided cases or state laws dealing specifically with this point. However, the courts appear to be expanding their responsibility to protect the best interests of children (Glantz, Annas, and Katz 1977). They have been extremely conservative in their rulings on the permissibility of experimenting on minors in situations that do not clearly benefit the subjects.

In the meantime, federal agencies that give grants to support behavioral research have stepped into the breach. The agency that lays down the rules for informed consent is the Department of Health, Education, and Welfare, which finances a great deal of medical and behavioral research, provided researchers follow HEW procedural regulations.

A typical project

A project recently proposed by a university professor and a postdoctoral fellow illustrates the safeguards that conscientious researchers must use before they start a study involving children. This particular investigation was to deal with the development of attachment: the bonds between mothers and their babies.

Details of the proposed project were set before a standing committee of physicians and laypersons. These were people who had accepted the responsibility of serving as a "human subjects committee" for the review and advance approval of medical and behavioral research projects undertaken in the geographical area in which the university was located. The committee had been set up in accordance with federal regulations and state law.

The investigators proposed to test the assumption that not until the age of five-to-seven months will babies become upset if strangers try to comfort them or if they are separated from their mothers. The researchers planned to observe the reaction of even younger infants subjected to the stress of a doctor's examination. Some babies were to be held by a stranger, while others were to be held by the mother. The test of stress was to be a drop of plasma drawn from the infant's heel, since stress may be measured by the condition of the blood.

The investigators described their project in detail to the human subjects committee. They also provided a consent form that was to be signed by the mothers of the babies they wished to use as subjects. The consent form explained the proposed study in simple language. The practical value of the results was described: the research might answer the question of how early it is advisable to place babies in day care or with an unfamiliar babysitter. The consent form promised to provide the parent with a copy of the results of the study. Complete confidentiality was assured—no names would be used, and each child would be identified by number only. The parent was told that the small heel prick was harmless and only momentarily uncomfortable.

The consent form specified the right of the subject (represented by the parent) to withdraw consent and discontinue participation in the study without prejudice to future medical care. The parent was told whom to call if not satisfied with the manner in which the study was conducted or if dissatisfied in any other way. In addition to the parent's signature, the consent form required signatures of a witness, of the baby's doctor, and of another physician who certified that the parent was competent to give informed consent for the child's participation in the study.

Only after the human subjects committee approved the research and the consent form would the investigators have the right to proceed with their research. In this case, the committee requested a number of changes, both in the research plan and in the consent form.

This research project on the subject of infant attachment and stranger anxiety is typical of the thousands that have been undertaken, particularly over the past 50 years, to add to the store of knowledge of how, and by what timetable, human beings develop, physically and psychologically. It is the stuff from which the following chapters are made.

Summary

The study of child development deals with the growth and maturation processes of children—physical, mental, emotional, and social. The subject is important to all those involved with children—parents, teachers, medical professionals, and social policy-makers, among others—as well as to anyone interested in understanding people in general.

Theories about the nature of children have undergone much change, especially in the last three centuries. Some of the most influential thinkers in this area were Comenius, Locke, Rousseau, Froebel, Darwin, and Dewey. Because of the ideas of such people, we no longer accept the medieval view of children as miniature adults, but appreciate children for themselves. We generally agree that they require special care and education and that they are deeply influenced by their environment, especially their homes and schools.

The earliest studies of children were biographies of specific babies—not very scientific according to modern standards. Current child development research has two major goals: to catalog and describe *how* children behave at various ages, and to understand *why* they behave the way they do. Modern investigators conduct their research in a systematic manner, using methods similar to those used in the physical sciences.

Some of the major issues and trends in current studies relate to these questions:

Does individual development repeat the stages of the evolution of the species?

What are the relative influences of heredity (nature) and environment (nurture)?

What causes behavioral differences among various groups?

What is the relationship between animal behavior and human behavior?

Can human behavior be predicted?

Research design usually involves formulating a hypothesis, devising relevant variables, selecting experimental and control groups, choosing subjects who will be a sample of the population to be studied, and devising appropriate methods of accumulating data. Studies may be experimental, correlational, clinical, applied, done in the field, phylogenetic, longitudinal, cross-sectional, cross-cultural. Correlations, important products of research, are statistical findings that measure the degree of correspondence between variables in the experiment.

Many legal and ethical problems must be confronted by human development investigators. Experimentation with human beings involves the special difficulties of preserving them from harm, obtaining their informed consent, and protecting their privacy. When the subjects are children, who are particularly vulnerable because of their age, parents' consent is essential. Despite these difficulties, a great deal of significant research has been accomplished, particularly in the past 50 years. These investigations provide the foundation of current knowledge of child development.

Applying Your Knowledge

1. In what ways might writing a baby biography be useful to a parent?

2. To what uses could teachers put knowledge of the child's developmental norms at various ages? Is it possible that such knowledge would be detrimental? How?

3. Since there are always exceptions to the generalizations derived from the study of humans, why are those generalizations still useful?

Further Readings

Anderson, Barry F. *The psychology experiment*. 2nd ed. Belmont, Calif.: Brooks/Cole, 1971. A helpful book for understanding the scientific method and how to conduct an experiment. Paperback.

Aries, Phillippe. *Centuries of childhood*. New York: Knopf, 1962. A thorough account of the changing attitudes toward childhood over the years.

Blalock, Hubert M., Jr. *Social research*. Englewood Cliffs, N.J.: Prentice-Hall, 1970. Explains the nature of some of the basic issues encountered in research in the social sciences. Paperback.

DeMause, Lloyd (ed.). *The history of childhood*. New York: Psychohistory Press, 1974. A survey of historical views of childhood over the last two thousand years.

Kessen, William. *The child*. New York: Wiley, 1965. A collection of essays on childhood by noted philosophers and child observers from the eighteenth to the twentieth centuries.

Medinnus, Gene R. *Child study and observation guide*. New York: Wiley, 1976. A guide to observing children under different conditions and using different observational techniques. Also includes a series of observation projects. Paperback.

Quanty, Carol, and Davis, Anthony. *Observing children*. Sherman Oaks, Calif.: Alfred, 1974. Guidelines for observing preschool children under different conditions. Paperback.

Wright, Herbert F. *Recording and analyzing child behavior.* New York: Harper and Row, 1967. An example for studying children in naturally occurring situations rather than under experimental conditions.
Paperback.

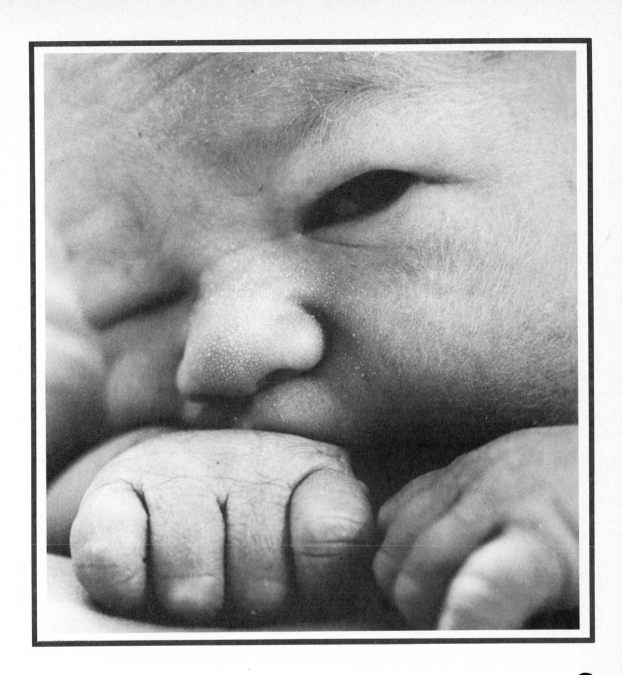

Part 2

Biological and Physical Foundations

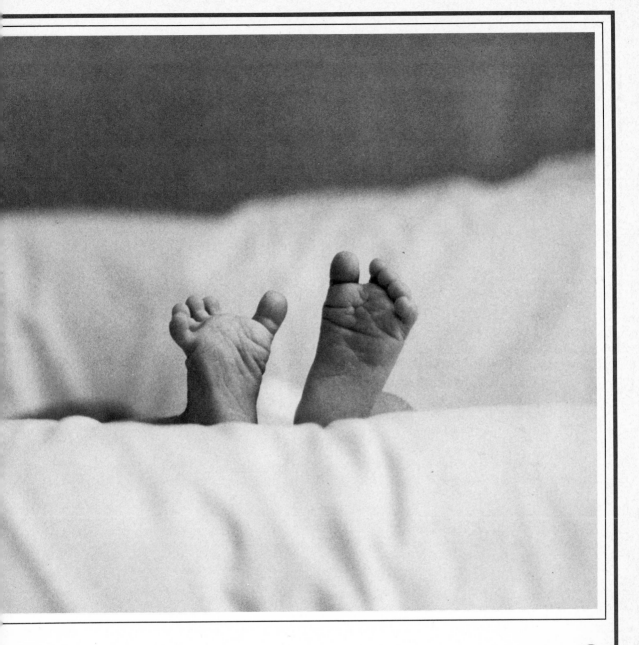

Chapter **2**
Prenatal Development and Birth

On the last day of July, a six-pound baby girl named Abigail Jane was born in a university hospital. By happy coincidence, on that day a member of the infant's family was beginning work on this book. With the permission of Abigail's parents, we will use her as a living example of two major principles of human development: first, growth and maturation proceed in the *same* fashion for all of us; second, we all behave *differently* and look different from everybody else.

How is it possible for Abigail to grow up to be both the same and different? What biological and psychological processes are at work? For this child, as for all others, the story of development begins not at the time of birth but long before.

Genetic Influences

How heredity is transmitted

Abigail (like everyone else) is the product of a long line of human ancestors, stretching farther back than even the most avid genealogist could trace. When, approximately nine months before the infant's birth, Abigail's father's *sperm* cell penetrated her mother's *ovum*—egg cell—the sperm and the ovum were already carrying the elements that would determine Abigail's uniqueness. So the story of human development rightly begins with the cell, the fundamental unit of life.

Sperm: male sex cell
Ovum: female sex cell

The cell A *cell* is the smallest living entity capable of reproducing itself. It is the basic structural and functional unit of living organisms. With a microscope we can see that each cell is encased in a membrane and contains a number of recognizable structures, including the nucleus, which we shall describe below. (See Figure 2–1.) All living bodies are made up of cells; the human body contains trillions.

Cell: the basic unit of life, capable of reproducing itself

Scientists still do not fully understand the remarkable process whereby cells divide and reproduce themselves. Even less understood is the process of *differentiation*, or specialization, that cells undergo during the development of a new human being from a fertilized egg. By the time of birth, there are many different types of cells. Each type performs a different, specific function. For example, a sex cell does a different job from a body cell or a brain cell. They also look different from one another.

Differentiation: specialization of cell functions

A cell's reproductive ability depends on certain structures contained in its *nucleus*. These structures include the chromo-

Nucleus: a subunit of the cell that carries the structures of heredity

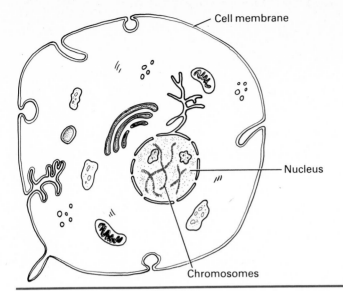

Cell membrane

Nucleus

Chromosomes

FIG. 2–1 The cell. Encased in a membrane, the human cell contains a number of structures, including the nucleus.

somes. Within the chromosomes are the genes, which transmit unique hereditary characteristics from ancestors to descendants like Abigail.

Chromosomes, genes, and DNA All human cells, except the sperm and ovum, have 46 *chromosomes* in their nucleus. (The sperm and ova cells have 23 chromosomes, as will be explained below.) Chromosomes are rodlike structures that contain *genes*, the elementary units of *heredity*. A gene is made up of *DNA* (deoxyribonucleic acid).

The huge DNA molecule is constructed like a spiral ladder, the famous double helix. (See Figure 2–2.) A single DNA ladder has millions of rungs, but there are only four different types of rungs. An individual's unique heredity is determined by the sequence of the four kinds of rungs on the DNA ladder.

Gene is the name given to any sequence of rungs that determines a specific hereditary characteristic, but usually more than one sequence work together to transmit hereditary traits. For any child, Abigail included, sequences of as many as a thousand rungs determine features like the shape of a nose. The work of mapping out which sequence of rungs determines which traits is only beginning, although much is already known about the operation of our hereditary machinery.

Chromosomes: rodlike structures that contain the genetic material of cells

Gene: elementary unit of heredity

Heredity: characteristics passed on from parents to children

DNA: a double-helix structure in chromosomes that carries the genetic code

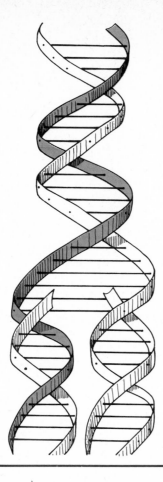

FIG. 2–2 DNA. When the two strands of DNA separate, each provides the model for the synthesis of a new identical strand.

How many genes are contained in each human cell, scientists still do not know. But they estimate around a million. Because human characteristics are so numerous and complex, it is no wonder that so many genes are necessary to program a single individual. These genes constitute the total inheritance each of us has received from our ancestors, the accumulated bank of genetic information that influences our development. Some of the information passed on by those genes makes for the similarities in human development. But some of the genetic information makes us different from everybody else.

How can we account for the similarities we share and the differences we see? At least a partial answer lies in two processes of cellular reproduction: mitosis and meiosis.

Mitosis   *Mitosis* is the process of cell division that makes it possible for a human body to grow, develop, and maintain itself. As we have already noted, each cell in the human body contains 46 chromosomes. However, there are only 23 *types* of chromosomes. The normal cell has two of each type, 23 from a person's father, 23 from the mother.

In mitosis, a process that goes on throughout human life, each chromosome duplicates itself through an extraordinary process whereby the DNA of the chromosome separates at each rung of the ladder. As the long strands of DNA come apart, their exact counterparts are formed at the rungs of both separated strands, thereby forming two new DNA strands identical to the original ones. (See Figure 2–2.) Since the chromosome is largely composed of DNA, the chromosome has, in effect, duplicated itself.

Next, in a series of cellular phases, each set of doubled chromosomes separates so that 46 chromosomes move to one region of the cell and 46 to an opposite region. Each new set of 46 chromosomes is just like the original 46. Shortly after the chromosomes have separated, the cell divides into two (identical) "daughter" cells. (See Figure 2–3.) Thus, the process of mitosis makes it possible for all animals to maintain basic biological functions: through mitosis, new cells grow and dead cells are thus replaced.

Mitosis explains why a baby like Abigail grows and develops from a union of only two cells into a six-pound infant and eventually into a full-grown young woman. But what makes her different from every other person? Meiosis, the other cell reproduction process, is the reason why children are never identical to their parents nor to their brothers or sisters, even though they share some family characteristics. This process is like a game of chance, although far more remarkable than any dice game in Reno or Atlantic City.

Meiosis   *Meiosis* is the process whereby *germ cells* divide to produce either sperm (in a male) or ova (in a female). The end result of meiosis is that each sperm and each ovum contain only 23 chromosomes, instead of the 46 contained in the germ cells and other body cells. So when the sperm and ovum join to create a new individual, the result is a cell with the requisite 46 chromosomes. Only germ cells undergo meiosis.

Meiosis depends on the fact that each chromosome in the germ cell has a "partner" chromosome, one partner from the individual's mother, the other partner from the individual's

Mitosis: cell reproduction into "daughter" cells, identical to the parent cell, with 46 chromosomes each; the key to growth and development

Meiosis: cell division into either sperm or ova, containing 23 chromosomes each; the key to sexual reproduction

Germ cell: cell from which a sperm or ovum is generated

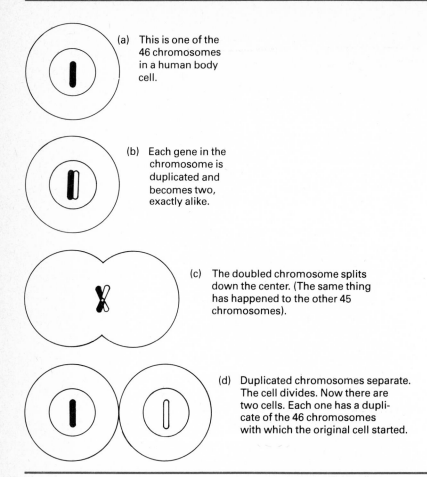

FIG. 2–3 Mitosis.

(a) This is one of the 46 chromosomes in a human body cell.

(b) Each gene in the chromosome is duplicated and becomes two, exactly alike.

(c) The doubled chromosome splits down the center. (The same thing has happened to the other 45 chromosomes).

(d) Duplicated chromosomes separate. The cell divides. Now there are two cells. Each one has a duplicate of the 46 chromosomes with which the original cell started.

father. The total comes to 46 chromosomes, which are divided into 23 types, identified as pairs. These pairs are numbered 1 through 23. Each pair, or set of partners, contains hereditary information relating to the same group of traits. During meiosis, these partner chromosomes (which have already doubled) come together and *cross over*, each chromosome exchanging some genes (and parts of genes) with its partner.

After crossing-over, the pairs separate into four groups. Each group carries only one partner chromosome of each of the 23 doubled pairs. This partner could be from either father or mother. The new groups form the genetic nuclei of new cells: the sperm or ova, each containing 23 chromosomes. (See Figure 2–4.)

Crossing-over: process that mixes the genetic content of chromosomes

(a) This is the father's germ cell, containing *his* 23 pairs of chromosomes. The dark ones come from his father (the future baby's grandfather); the light ones come from his mother (the future baby's grandmother).

(d) Again the cells divide. Now there are four cells. Each of the four receives *one* chromosome from each pair.

(b) The chromosomes pair. During pairing the chromosomes cross-over. Then each doubles. The doubled pairs line up at the center of the cell. Then the doubled pairs separate. Each goes to opposite sides of the cell.

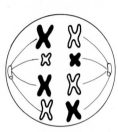

(e) The four cells, each with 23 single chromosomes, separate from one another. The chromosomes go into the head of the cell, while a tail forms. These are sperm.

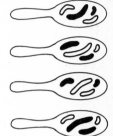

(c) Now the cell has divided into two cells. Each cell contains one doubled member of each pair. But the chromosomes from the grandmother and the grandfather are mixed by chance.

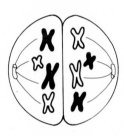

(f) The four sperm cells, each with a different variety of chromosomes, now acquire even longer tails.

This is the father's side of the story. A similar process happens to the mother's cells, but only one of the four parts becomes an egg; the rest are sloughed off.

Thus, through pairing and crossing-over, a remarkable genetic mixing has occurred. The process has produced many different genetic possibilities in each sperm and each ovum—no two sperm and no two ova alike.

How many different chromosomal combinations are possible for Abigail or any other infant? Even without crossing-over, genetic variance would have been guaranteed.

The possible combinations of father and mother chromosomes from the 23 original pairs is two (each pair) to the twenty-third power (2^{23})—or over eight million for the sperm alone.

FIG. 2–4 Meiosis. Cell division process reduces chromosomes to half the normal number before the cell divides into two.

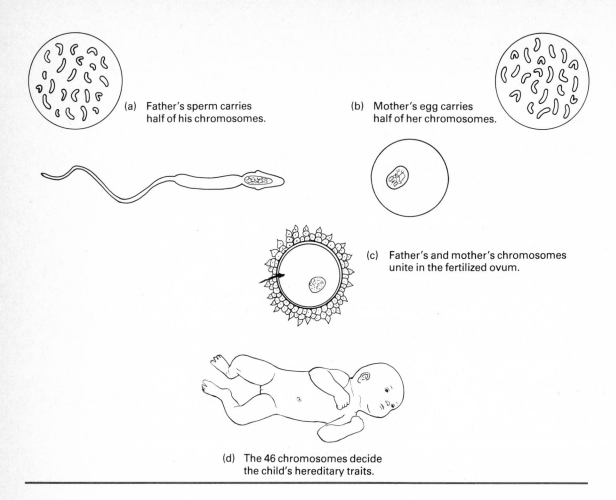

(a) Father's sperm carries half of his chromosomes.

(b) Mother's egg carries half of her chromosomes.

(c) Father's and mother's chromosomes unite in the fertilized ovum.

(d) The 46 chromosomes decide the child's hereditary traits.

FIG. 2–5 How chromosomes are passed on: 23 from father and 23 from mother.

Combine that with the possible combinations of chromosomes in the ovum. The total number of possible combinations for the united sperm and ovum reaches over 70 trillion. Add to this the effects of crossing-over. The number of possible chromosomal combinations is staggering. No wonder each of us (except identical twins, as we shall see later) has a unique genetic inheritance. Abigail is not one in a million. She is one in some incomprehensible number (See Figure 2–5.)

Dominant and recessive traits   Meiosis is not by any means the end of the biological dice game. Several other factors come into play. One of them is the fact, already noted, that because of meiosis each human inherits two *different* sets of chromosomes, one set of 23 from the father's sperm and one set of 23 from the mother's ovum. Together they provide the new individual with 23 pairs of chromosomes, each pair carrying genes for the same group of traits. The question naturally arises: what determines which particular genes within each of the 23 partner chromosomes will determine the attributes of the new individual? And which will lie undetected within his or her cells? To use a common and easy example, what color will Abigail's eyes be? Her forebears included both blue-eyed and brown-eyed individuals. But both her parents have brown eyes. Will she have blue eyes or brown eyes?

An explanation of how such traits are "determined" for each individual was worked out nearly 150 years ago by Gregor Mendel, an Austrian monk. He experimented with plants to determine the basic principles of *dominant* and *recessive traits*. It is now known that certain genes will prevail over certain other genes, if they happen to appear with one another in the particular pair of chromosomes an individual inherits from parents. Thus, brown-eye genes are dominant; blue-eye genes are recessive. A child who has inherited both kinds of genes will be brown-eyed. But suppose the vast mixing process of meiosis and fertilization has turned up two blue-eye genes in the chromosomes of a "new" individual? That person will have blue eyes, even though brown eyes have frequently appeared in the individual's ancestry. So it was with Abigail. She became a blue-eyed baby, in spite of the fact that her parents have brown eyes. (See Figure 2–6.)

Mendel worked out complex mathematical tables to illustrate the chances of dominant–recessive inheritance, given a known ancestry of traits. Calculating these chances was easier to do with the plants he was studying than it is with humans. Still, Mendelian principles have made it possible to forecast the inheritability of many human traits.

Because it is relatively easy to detect traits with readily observable physical manifestations—eye color, hair color, shape of nose, dimples, blood type, allergies, diabetes—geneticists know a great deal about the patterns of dominance and recessiveness for such traits. They can predict the chances for blue eyes or brown eyes, given a particular hereditary history.

More important, geneticists can also predict mathematically the chances of passing on certain serious diseases that are genetic in origin. Some of these diseases are *congenital*, present at birth. Others will show up only in later life.

Dominant traits: governed by genes that ordinarily prevail over recessive genes, producing an individual's observable characteristics

Recessive traits: governed by genes that produce an observable characteristic only when a dominant gene for the same characteristic is not present

Congenital: present at birth

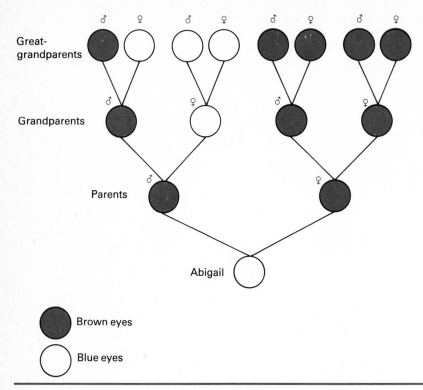

FIG. 2–6 Eye color: dominant–recessive.

Great-grandparents

Grandparents

Parents

Abigail

● Brown eyes

○ Blue eyes

Gene dominance–recessiveness is only one more aspect of the story of human inheritance. We must still account for the process—also dependent on chance—whereby a new individual is conceived and whereby that individual receives the maternal–paternal package of inherited traits.

Conception Every one of us is a product of the process of *fertilization,* when a sperm penetrates an egg. Normally, a mature woman *ovulates*—releases one mature egg, or ovum—once a month. (In the infant Abigail, as in all normal females, all the egg cells are stored in the ovaries in an undeveloped state from the time of birth.) Only if the sperm meets the egg during the few days of the month when it is still viable can it be fertilized. *Conception* occurs when the sperm has fertilized the ovum to produce a single new cell, called the *zygote*

But which particular egg, carrying which particular genetic characteristics, will be released? And which sperm will penetrate

Fertilization: the penetration of the ovum by the sperm
Ovulation: release of a mature egg from the ovaries

Conception: the union of the sperm and ovum to produce a zygote
Zygote: the single cell produced by conception

the available egg? Some 300–500 million sperm are present in the normal male ejaculation. After *one* penetrates, for a reason not yet understood, no other can do so. With penetration, fertilization has been accomplished; the hereditary code unique to that future individual has been passed on.

Sex determination At the moment of fertilization, another fateful biological decision is made: the sex of the future baby. That decision depends on the sperm, which is uniquely responsible for sex determination. The reason lies in one of those same gene-carrying chromosomes that pass on all other inherited characteristics.

Sex is determined by the number 23 chromosome pair. Each of a woman's two number 23 chromosomes is normally an X chromosome, carrying (among other types of genes) genes for the traits of femaleness. Each ovum produced through meiosis therefore normally carries an X chromosome. But each of the male's number 23 chromosomes is different: one is an X and one is a Y. Each sperm produced through meiosis therefore carries either an X or a Y for its number 23 chromosome. If the particular sperm that penetrates the ovum carries an X chromosome, then the zygote will have two X chromosomes, one from the father's sperm and one from the mother's ovum. This determines that the child will be female. If, however, the sperm bears a Y chromosome, the zygote will have one Y and one X chromosome. The XY combination results in a male offspring. (See Figure 2–7).

Why, then, do boys outnumber girls? Statistics for Caucasians not only in the United States but also in other societies show that 105–106 males are born for every 100 females. For blacks, the numbers are a little different: 102–103 males for every 100 females. However, the ratio of boys to girls decreases with later pregnancies and in cases where twins or triplets or other multiple births occur (Rubin 1967). Recent research discovered that males not only produce more Y-carrying sperm than X-carrying sperm, but also that the sperm with the Y chromosome are smaller, move faster, and are thus more likely to find the maternal target than sperm with the X factor (Rorvik and Shettles 1970; Schuster and Schuster 1972).

However, while sperm with Y chromosomes are faster, they are less hardy than sperm with X chromosomes. Studies of stillbirths have established that there is an average of 120 male conceptions for every 100 female conceptions, but that only

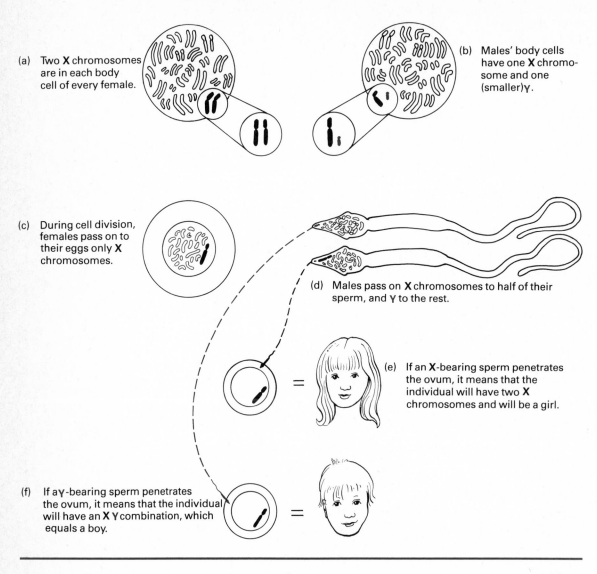

(a) Two **X** chromosomes are in each body cell of every female.

(b) Males' body cells have one **X** chromosome and one (smaller) **Y**.

(c) During cell division, females pass on to their eggs only **X** chromosomes.

(d) Males pass on **X** chromosomes to half of their sperm, and **Y** to the rest.

(e) If an **X**-bearing sperm penetrates the ovum, it means that the individual will have two **X** chromosomes and will be a girl.

(f) If a **Y**-bearing sperm penetrates the ovum, it means that the individual will have an **X Y** combination, which equals a boy.

FIG. 2—7 Boy or girl?

105–106 males survive to be born (Spencer 1957; Shettles 1961). The male fetus is evidently frailer than the female fetus.

Though some individuals would like to tamper with the sex ratio, efforts to do so have had generally poor success. But more important than assuring oneself of a boy or a girl is to try to produce a healthy baby. In this area the child's sex may sometimes be an important factor. It is the female child with her X chromosomes who is most likely, in some families, to carry on to the next generation a variety of genetic peculiarities, like color blindness. Some are merely inconvenient, but some may be serious, as we shall see in Chapter 12.

Using genetic knowledge

Most of us need not fear giving birth to children who are retarded, deformed, or otherwise disabled. Abigail Jane, for one, was a normal baby, with the requisite number of arms and legs and facial characteristics. So were the 15 other infants who were in the hospital nursery at the same time. And yet, it is obvious to proud relatives elbowing for a place outside any hospital nursery window that, even at a day or two old, all newborn infants look very different. These differences, already apparent at birth, are most likely to be genetic. An alert observer might perceive psychological differences as well.

Genetic counseling The profession of genetic counseling, recently come into being, deals with the problems of inherited characteristics. Its practitioners are still not numerous, and they cannot yet work all the miracles we might wish for. Nevertheless, they can often be helpful in advising how to avoid passing on to a new generation problems that are genetic in origin. Therefore, genetic counseling before pregnancy is important for couples who believe, for any reason, that a child of theirs might incur some risk.

Chromosomal studies and family history provide the clues that guide a qualified counselor to advise no pregnancy at all or to prescribe a procedure called *amniocentesis*. This test may be performed by a physician as early as the twelfth or thirteenth week of pregnancy, and no later than the sixteenth week. Since the fetus normally sloughs skin cells into the amniotic fluid in the sac surrounding it, the specialist can examine those cells by extracting a small amount of amniotic fluid. Analysis of the chromosomes in the skin cells makes it possible to determine whether or not an abnormality exists. (See also Chapter 12, page 484.)

Amniocentesis: medical procedure that extracts amniotic fluid from the uterus to test for chromosomal abnormality

Ability to predict From the developmental psychologist's point of view, it would surely be useful to know in advance the prob-

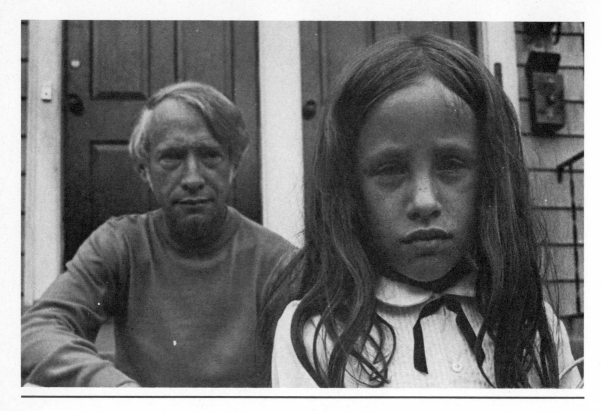

Unmistakably, her father's daughter.

ability of passing on to children the genes responsible for psychological characteristics, such as temperament, personality, creativity, intelligence, or disorders like schizophrenia. In these matters some knowledge does already exist, increasing as experimentation and research continue.

But the ability to predict or even to isolate such traits is still not very far advanced. And the influence of environment on these psychological characteristics is so pervasive that it is virtually impossible to separate out genetic and environmental influences. One cannot yet point to an adult or even to a young child and say with assurance: "There! She's her nutty grandmother's granddaughter, all right!" Or: "No doubt about it—that one is the sick product of a bad home."

Still, we do unmistakably inherit our physical selves from our parents and others who came before us in the family. Investigators confirm that an individual's genes can be responsible for motor skills, physique, rate of maturation, and for the functioning of the autonomic nervous system (Jost and Sontag 1944). For example, one study determined that children's growth rate and the timing of their bone development followed the body build of their parents (Garn et al. 1960).

One whimsical footnote on the effects of heredity came from a mother who wrote to a magazine that her husband married her because she could throw a ball. She said she tried to pass on that throwing ability to her two daughters, but was successful only with one. "My five-year-old shows absolutely no aptitude. . . . Meanwhile, my number two daughter at 10 months holds a . . . ball in one hand with the cool of a Globe Trotter" (Kivowitz 1976).

Twin studies Studies of twins have been an excellent source of information about which characteristics people inherit from their genes and which traits are probably environmental. One way of doing this is to compare groups of fraternal twins with groups of identical twins. Identical—*monozygotic*—twins are the single exception to the uniqueness of human inheritance. They result when a fertilized ovum splits and becomes two zygotes. Thus the twins have identical genes.

Monozygotic twins: developed from one zygote

In contrast, fraternal—*dizygotic*—twins have a separate genetic background because they result from the fertilization of two eggs by two different sperms. (See Figure 2–8.) Fraternal twins are no more apt to be alike, genetically, than any other brothers and sisters in the same family, although they do share the same intrauterine environment.

Dizygotic twins: developed from two zygotes

Investigators get an extra bonus by studying and comparing identical twins who, for some reason, are brought up in different homes. Obviously, the characteristics still shared by identical twins reared apart are more likely to be caused by genetic factors than by environmental factors.

Studying both kinds of twins, one investigator reported a probable genetic cause for the phenomenon occasionally reported in newspaper stories: identical twins who die within a short time of each other, even though physically far away, leading quite different lives. On the average, the difference in the life span of identical twins who died after the age of 60 was found to be only about three years. But the average difference in the life span of fraternal twins was more than twice that much. The physical similarities of identical twins are equally striking throughout their life spans: how fast they become feeble, the rate at which their hair grays or thins, their wrinkles, even the way their eyes

FIG. 2–8 How twins are produced.

MONOZYGOTIC TWINS

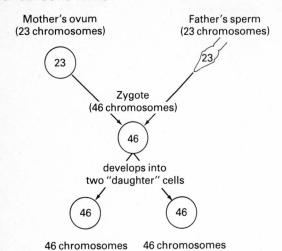

Mother's ovum
(23 chromosomes)

Father's sperm
(23 chromosomes)

Zygote
(46 chromosomes)

develops into
two "daughter" cells

46 chromosomes   46 chromosomes

DIZYGOTIC TWINS

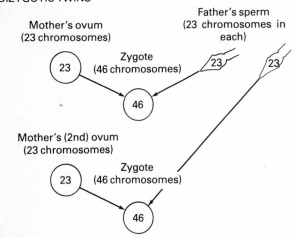

Mother's ovum
(23 chromosomes)

Father's sperm
(23 chromosomes in
each)

Zygote
(46 chromosomes)

Mother's (2nd) ovum
(23 chromosomes)

Zygote
(46 chromosomes)

and teeth deteriorate as they grow older (Kallmann and Sander 1948).

Twin studies demonstrate that heredity seems to play a role in a number of developmental traits, such as life span, aging, intelligence, personality, and emotional disorders. These investigations confirm the impression of parents with more than one child that "they came out *different* from the first moment."

Studies comparing identical twins with fraternal twins show that even though both types of twins share the same uterus, the identical twins are far more alike in their feeding and sleeping patterns (or problems), their activity level, how much they smile, and how they react to strangers. Thus we seem to owe a great deal of our nonphysiological selves to our genes, as we shall see in subsequent chapters.

Genetic engineering   Some people have speculated about the possibility of influencing the inheritance of genes. Mendel and plant geneticists did it, to produce new and hardier species. Turkeys, cattle, and dogs are deliberately bred to emphasize desirable genetic characteristics and to "lose" the undesirable ones. Why not breed humans to create a super-race? This is what the Nazis advocated.

Obviously, our system of morality does not tolerate this kind of human experimentation. Nevertheless, it *is* beginning to be possible to alter the genes, the mechanism of inheritance. These developments are so new and their moral implications so awesome that it is impossible at this juncture to guess where they will lead. However, we already have available entirely legitimate ways of foreseeing certain kinds of genetic problems and of preventing them by socially sanctioned means. It is important to be on the lookout for the diseases and weaknesses that seem to "run in the family." Then, it is up to medical science and our own willingness to cooperate.

Prenatal Development

Nature and nurture: an interaction

Abigail Jane, our "textbook example," was born with at least one possible hereditary "taint": her families are full of allergies. Does this doom her to hay fever, no matter what? Must she be forever deprived of the pleasure of having a cat or a dog?

Not necessarily. She and all the members of her generation will benefit from the work of the many specialists who are trying to mitigate problems that have a genetic origin. Not all genetically-based illnesses and weaknesses are currently curable, but there is progress. It is also important to realize that Abigail is more than the sum of her genes—her "nature." She is also greatly influenced by her environment—her "nurture." And another whole battery of specialists is active in attempts to understand the effects of environment and to deal with those aspects that might harm children's development. Among these experts are psychologists, psychiatrists, physicians, teachers, social workers, even politicians.

In considering Abigail's development, therefore, we must consider the way her parents treat her while she is growing up. We must think of her future relationships with siblings, baby-sitters, grandparents, neighbors, teachers, friends, lovers, mate(s), and her own eventual children and grandchildren. How will she be affected by future scientific achievements, by political and social changes, by wars, natural or man-made calamities, or other environmental threats? In short, environment is where we are, what we eat, whom we deal with, the events and accidents the world thrusts upon us. Combined with our inherited characteristics these influences make us what we are at any given time in our lives.

Most psychologists have pretty much revised the old *nature–nurture issue*, a proposition like "which-comes-first-the-chicken-or-the-egg?" The general consensus is that human development is the result of an interplay of nature (genes) and nurture (environment). This interaction goes on throughout our lives. It begins at the moment of conception.

Nature–nurture issue: the problem of deciding the relative influences of heredity and environment on development

Environmental influences before birth Abigail Jane had a place to live—an environment—right after her father's sperm entered her mother's ovum. During the ensuing nine months, like any other fetus, Abigail was almost literally bombarded by her environment, by her mother's body and everything that affected it: by what her mother ate, by her moods and attitudes, by the work she was doing, by her exposure to illness, by the very air she breathed, and by the sounds in the air as well.

Even Abigail's father indirectly contributed to her prenatal environment. His pleasure at the prospect of fatherhood, the daily concerns stemming from his work, his interaction with his wife and their four parents—all inevitably had an effect on his relationship with his pregnant wife. In turn, her resultant moods and behavior influenced her unborn child.

A leading researcher sums it up this way: "The level of hormones in the mother's blood, the presence of drugs or toxins . . . food elements . . . sounds or mechanical pressures . . . and such maternal factors as emotional state, physical activity, fatigue . . . represent an environment as complete and probably fully as important as the . . . environments of infants or children" (Sontag 1941, page 996).

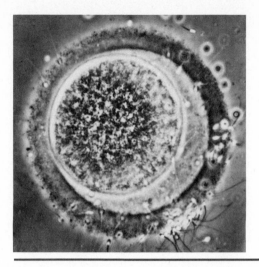

FIG. 2–9 A fertilized ovum at the moment of conception.

Stages of prenatal development

By the time she emerged in the hospital delivery room, Abigail Jane had already survived three important stages of her life. The Chinese are perhaps more realistic about this matter than Americans: they figure that a newborn child is starting the second year, not the first. The prenatal stages are the period of the ovum, the first two weeks after conception; the period of the embryo, two weeks through eight weeks; and the period of the fetus, the last seven of the nine months.

Ovum—zygote Abigail began as a single fertilized ovum, or zygote. (See Figure 2–9.) Her "address," at that instant, was one of her mother's two fallopian tubes. The first two weeks of pregnancy, the period of the ovum, is not perceptible to the woman in whom the person-to-be has taken up residence. But it is a fateful time, during which both environment and genetics are operating. (See Figure 2–10.)

Within three or four days after conception the ovum moves two inches into the uterus and becomes attached in another week or so to the uterine wall (Thoms and Blevin 1958). From conception till the sixth day the cells have been dividing slowly inside the fertilized egg, and now total about 100 cells. But the total volume seems the same, and the "baby" is no more than a dot. Then, as the first week ends, the cluster of cells begins to separate

[Handwritten margin notes: "fertilized ovum in the fallopian tube", "(conception)", "within 3/4 days after concept", "uterus - attached to the uterine wall", "immediately"]

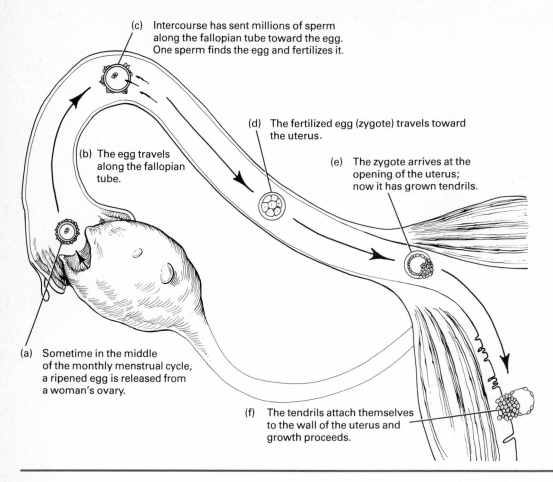

(c) Intercourse has sent millions of sperm along the fallopian tube toward the egg. One sperm finds the egg and fertilizes it.

(d) The fertilized egg (zygote) travels toward the uterus.

(b) The egg travels along the fallopian tube.

(e) The zygote arrives at the opening of the uterus; now it has grown tendrils.

(a) Sometime in the middle of the monthly menstrual cycle, a ripened egg is released from a woman's ovary.

(f) The tendrils attach themselves to the wall of the uterus and growth proceeds.

FIG. 2–10 A baby's conception: period of the ovum.

into two layers. One of those layers will become the child's body; the other will be the source of the child's nourishment. *(to the zygote to survive there's many)*

Many a fertilized egg aborts for one reason or another during these early days. Sometimes the mother's thyroid and pituitary glands do not produce enough hormones to prepare the uterine wall, thus keeping the zygote from attaching itself to the source of nourishment. Another cause might be insufficient yolk in the egg to nourish it while it is traveling toward the uterus. Should the ovum fail to survive, it will be eliminated with the menstrual flow, and probably neither mother nor father will have any idea that they have lost a potential child.

Embryo The second period of Abigail's development—the *embryo* state—began with the second week and lasted until the eighth week. (See Figure 2–11.) The rapid increase in Abigail's size during this period resulted from mitosis (the duplication of cells described earlier), which is the basic biological process of growth and renewal that continues throughout human life.

In the embryo stage, Abigail already had the rudimentary physical characteristics of a human being. Her rapidly increasing cells were differentiating into the possibilities for bodily features: lungs, brain and spinal cord, diaphragm, esophagus, and circulatory and nerve systems. The broader end of the embryo would become her head. The upper end of a kind of tube down the embryo's length would develop into her brain; the lower end would become her spinal cord. Then, as growth accelerated, the embryo would double up in order to still fit into the uterine cavity.

During this period, the growing embryo is nourished by a system of fragile, rootlike interconnections—villi—between the embryo and the nutrition to be found in the pregnant woman's uterine wal. Around the beginning of the fourth week, those villi had their own blood vessels, a beginning of the child's circulatory

Embryo: fertilized ovum in the second to eighth week of development

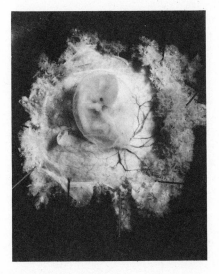

FIG. 2– 11 The embryo.

system. The heart began to beat, and the blood circulated in increasing volume. The system was carrying oxygen and food from the mother to the child.

Arms and legs also began to grow during this stage. They started as "buds," turned into "fins," and soon would be recognized as arms and legs. Rudiments of hands and feet, fingers and toes appeared. Also, from the fourth week to the end of the seventh week, eyes and ear emerged, as well as the elements of the face—nostrils, eyelid folds, and a bump for a nose. By the time this period was over, the head had become noticeably larger.

Miscarriage—spontaneous abortion—is a possibility during the embryo stage. Some miscarriages are thought to be nature's means of eliminating a child who would be grossly defective. The causes of miscarriage at this stage are generally environmental. There may not be enough maternal *progesterone*, an essential hormone during pregnancy, to keep the uterine walls from contracting and pushing the embryo away from its source of nourishment. The mother may not be supplying enough thyroid hormone or vitamin E, both of which are also vital. A starving or seriously undernourished mother may also miscarry.

Miscarriage: death of the embryo

Progesterone: a female sex hormone that inhibits muscle contractions in the uterus during pregnancy

However, the effects of environment during this period may fall short of miscarriage and still be immensely serious for the developing baby. Nature has decreed a definite timetable for the development of the individual's body in the embryonic stage. Thus, particular environmental insults at critical times appear to have specific results. For example, one environmental hazard at this stage is German measles (rubella). Blindness, deafness, and mental deficiency are the possible results for her baby if a woman gets the disease during the first three or four months of pregnancy, when the embryo's head is developing. After the ninth week, when the embryonic period ends, the illness may have only small consequences (Greenberg, Pelliteri, and Barton 1957).

Another example of the effect of enironmental disturbances during critical periods is the birth of children without limbs to mothers who took the drug thalidomide from the third to the sixth week of pregnancy. This is a critical period for the development of arms and legs. The point is that it is not the environmental insult alone that is important, but its timing. A condition that might kill or maim the developing infant at one period may have little or no effect at another time.

It should be noted that much of the evidence of environmental harm to the embryo from a mother's illnesses or drugs is circumstantial. Such connections are hard to prove conclusively,

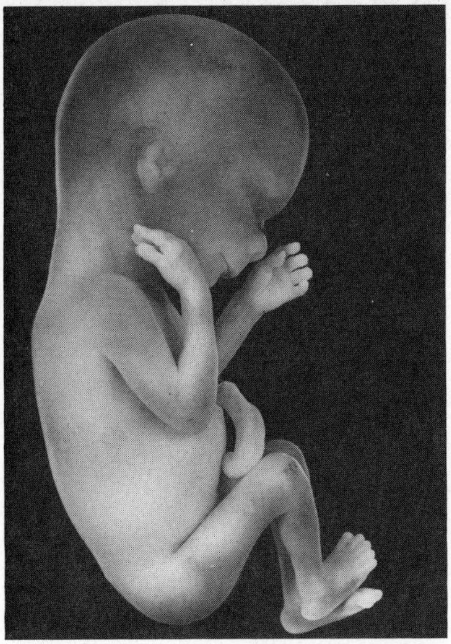

FIG. 2–12 The fetus.

since the data come from correlations between the illnesses or drugs and the condition of the newborn infant. As we noted in Chapter 1, correlations do not necessarily show a cause-and-effect relationship. But there seems to be no alternative way of determining cause and effect unless animal subjects are used. We cannot conduct potentially dangerous experiments on pregnant women.

Fetus Abigail Jane spent the longest portion of her prenatal nine months as a *fetus*—seven months. (See Figure 2–12.) The baby-to-be is a fetus when, at the age of eight weeks, floating in a watery *amniotic sac*, she has acquired a new system of nourishment, the *placenta*, to which she is attached by a cord. (See Figure 2–13.) The placenta is a crucial body of tissue, for it metabolizes the food drawn from the mother, processing it into simpler form suitable for the baby's unsophisticated digestive system.

From the placenta, via the cord, Abigail took from her mother oxygen, hormones, nourishment, and everything else required to sustain life and to grow to her eventual six pounds. And through the cord she expelled to the placenta most of the metabolic wastes from her body. Her blood and her mother's blood never mingled during this time. Instead, all transactions between mother and fetus took place through these remarkable intermediaries, the cord and the placenta. All the while, the am-

Fetus: unborn child from third through ninth month

Amniotic sac: fluid-filled sac that surrounds the fetus

Placenta: an organ that nourishes the fetus by transmitting food products and metabolic wastes between the blood of the mother and the fetus

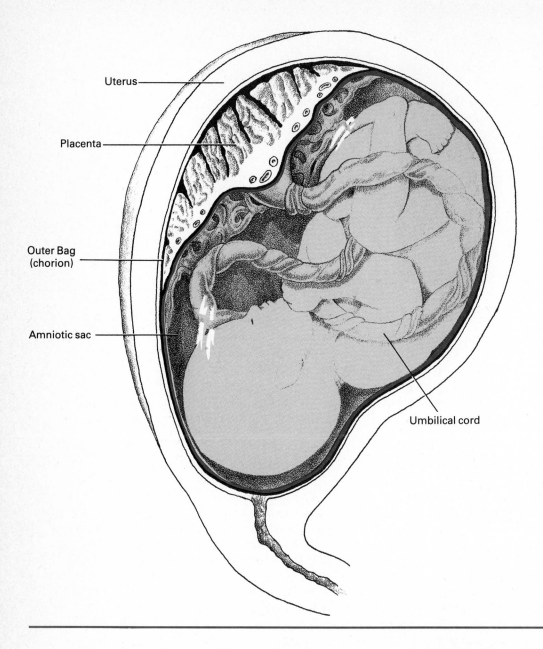

Uterus

Placenta

Outer Bag
(chorion)

Amniotic sac

Umbilical cord

FIG. 2—13 A baby in the amniotic sac. The mother's
bloodstream is normally not
directly connected to the baby,
nor are the mother's nerves.
But maternal blood cells, antibodies, or chemicals may
sometimes pass through the
placenta and reach the baby.

niotic sac cushioned her from the shocks of the outside world in which her mother was living. These seven fetal months were devoted primarily to the growth and development of the human features already formed in the earlier weeks.

This does not mean that the fetus who became Abigail was immune from danger or maternal influence during those six months. What happened to her mother, her mother's diet, activities, and emotions could all have had subtle or marked effects on the dependent fetus, whose sole lifeline and buffer were the maternally-fed placenta and the maternal uterus. The hazards of the fetal stage could possibly have been so extreme as to cause miscarriage, premature birth, or complications during delivery. More likely, the environmental influences on the fetus would be more subtle: peculiarities of personality; bad teeth, perhaps; behavioral problems in later life. Research in recent years has taught us a little about the later consequences of life in the uterus. In time to come, we will probably know more.

Maternal influences

If Abigail's mother had made a special point of listening to great music while pregnant, could she have produced a musical prodigy? Not likely. The "musical heredity" on both sides of that particular family is weak. Scientists have disproved most of the old wives' tales about a mother's ability to "mark" or influence her baby prenatally by deliberate acts or through witnessing accidents. Nevertheless, there is now very little doubt that a mother can exert enormous influence on her baby through diet, exercise, and emotions, and even as a result of her age at the time she becomes pregnant.

Mother's age The best age for a candidate for motherhood would be neither very young nor very old. Abigail's mother, at 26, was in the ideal range. The statistics show that abnormalities are "significantly" more frequent in children born to mothers over 35. Younger mothers, under 23, also are more prone to problem pregnancies and to producing stillborn or defective babies.

Investigators speculate that inadequate development of the reproductive system, poor prenatal care, and perhaps bad diet are at fault in the case of the younger mothers. The older mothers, it is believed, probably have endocrine deficiencies (Montagu 1950; Drillien and Richmond 1956).

Diet People used to believe, and perhaps many still do, that if a pregnant woman's eating habits are poor, or if she doesn't get enough to eat when she is "eating for two," the "selfish" unborn baby will take what it needs for itself, so that the mother alone would be damaged by malnutrition.

Research seems to prove pretty much the opposite. The fetus may actually suffer more (Burke et al. 1943). Inadequate maternal nutrition may be associated with miscarriages, stillbirths, prematurity, malformation, brain damage, and susceptibility to illness during infancy (Ebbs et al. 1942; Burke et al. 1943; Tompkins 1948). These maternal conditions, more frequent among poor and ill-informed people, could possibly affect their children throughout their lives.

A British study of the myelinization of the brain, the process by which brain fibers develop, suggests that poor maternal nutrition during this extremely vulnerable period could cause brain damage. What is the critical timing? The investigator's educated guess is the last few months of intrauterine life (Davison and Dobbing 1966).

Fetal *anoxia*—oxygen starvation—could be another consequence of the mother's malnutrition or anemia. The infant's blood and oxygen level is a function of the mother's state of health. Breathing difficulty after birth is seen three times more often in children born to malnourished mothers than in children who come from more fortunate circumstances. According to one finding, the rate among poor children was ten times as great as for middle-class children (Montagu 1964). Severe anoxia could cause permanent brain damage. Women who are in poor health may also be candidates for premature delivery, which is related to anoxia.

Anoxia: oxygen deficiency

Drugs Recent research continues to stress the dangers of drugs taken during pregnancy. No newspaper reader in recent years can have missed learning the results of studies that indicate prenatal damage from drugs and cigarette smoking. The widely publicized "thalidomide babies" in the 1960s drew the attention of scientists to the question of what happens to the children of mothers who have used a whole spectrum of nonfood substances. Chromosomal defects, miscarriage, brain damage, illness, and behavioral peculiarities in the newborn infant are among the results that have been found.

Tranquilizers (thalidomide was one) are a common danger. In 1976, the federal Food and Drug Administration ordered the drug industry to warn doctors not to prescribe popular tranquilizers like Valium, Librium, Miltown, and Equanil for women in the first three months of pregnancy. These drugs have been tentatively linked by recent studies to various infant malformations, such as cleft lip.

Drugs taken by mothers for their psychic effects have also been shown to endanger their unborn infants. LSD may result in chromosomal abnormalities. Morphine and heroin cause newborn babies to have "withdrawal symptoms of restlessness, irritability, tremors, convulsions, sleeplessness, fever, gastroenteritis, yawning and sneezing." Even aspirin taken by a woman prior to delivery could cause brain damage in her baby (Brazelton 1970, pages 96–97.)

Barbiturates and similar drugs given during labor have been blamed for cutting down the fetus's supply of oxygen. The result could be asphyxiation and either permanent brain damage or some degree of mental impairment (Hughes, Ehmann, and Brown 1948).

It must be stressed that all these consequences of maternal drug-taking are the exception, not the rule. Timing is an important element. For example, the embryonic period is a particularly critical time because the infant's body is being formed. Drugs like thalidomide seem to have little or no effect during the fetal period, when the baby is simply attaining full size.

Fertility drugs may be a mixed blessing. They do often work, but they may work too well. A WHO report (World Health Organization 1973) stated that fertility drugs increase the normal pregnancy rate from 4 to 35%, depending on which drug is used. But the multiple pregnancy rate is 1.5–20% above the normal occurrence. Multiple births—an overly crowded womb—may result in prematurity, sometimes a severe problem, as we shall see a little later.

Alcohol and cigarettes "Will it hurt my baby if I smoke or drink?" The answer to this common question is probably "Yes!"—if the mother indulges heavily.

Nobody has yet shown that *moderate* social drinking is a threat to the unborn. But a detailed study by four doctors in Seattle indicated that babies born to alcoholics suffered from much lower birth weight than normal; they were shorter than average; and even by the time they were a year old, they had failed to regain these losses. The problem does not appear to be the malnutrition from which alcoholics often suffer. The doctors studied children whose mothers were malnourished but not alcoholic. These children did not have the pattern of other defects that were found in the alcoholics' children: small head size, joint and heart defects, and underdeveloped jaws (Jones et al. 1973).

Some consequences of heavy smoking during pregnancy have been documented by a 1979 report issued by the U.S. Department of Health, Education, and Welfare. They are a higher rate of miscarriage; smaller babies, who may never catch up; greater risk of infant death at birth or soon afterward, otherwise unexplained; more complications during labor and delivery, including a higher rate of prematurity; and a greater incidence of neurological abnormalities in the baby.

The report suggests that heavy smoking during pregnancy may even affect the child in later life. These children may score lower on psychological tests than other children. They are more likely to be hyperactive, and thus to have learning problems, and their intellectual and physical growth may be slower. According to the study, children whose mothers smoked half a pack or more a day when they were pregnant tended to be shorter than other children at the age of 11. And at the same age they lagged from three to five months behind other children in their ability to read and do arithmetic.

The cause of this potential damage, says the report, seems to come from a shortage of oxygen during the fetal period. Carbon monoxide from cigarette smoke replaces oxygen in the blood, so that by smoking two packs a day, the pregnant woman may reduce the fetus's oxygen supply by 40%. But there is a ray of hope: If the smoker stops when she becomes pregnant, the risks are greatly reduced (*Smoking and health*, 1979).

Pollutants The world can be a dangerous place. Even the unborn child is not exempt from the mother's environment, often outside the mother's control. Air pollution, traces of insecticides and chemicals in commercially processed food, radiation from X-rays might all, in excess, hurt the unborn baby.

Although knowledge about these common hazards is far from complete, enough is known about their effects on the embryo and fetus so that experts feel there is a possibility in some instances of poisoning or oxygen insufficiency (Montagu 1964).

Mental retardation of the child was the most frequent result of the exposure of pregnant women to the atom bomb in Hiroshima toward the end of World War II (Plummer 1952). However, a study of children conceived in the years *following* their parents' exposure to the fallout showed very little radiation effect (Awa et al. 1968). Whether X-rays cause chromosomal damage is still open to question. Caution is a good idea, even for nonpregnant individuals. People should not subject their sex glands to X-rays if they can avoid it, to prevent possible damage to their chromosomes and their future offspring (Spencer 1957). A recent study suggested that perhaps older women are more likely than others to give birth to infants with Down's Syndrome (see Chapter 12) because they have been exposed over a longer period of time to environmental radiation (Apgar and Beck 1973).

Air pollution can be dangerous, too, though not to the same degree as radiation. A pregnant woman who is breathing polluted air has less oxygen in her blood and therefore less to pass on to her unborn child (Montagu 1964). Pesticides and other chemicals that a pregnant woman may absorb seem to pass through the placenta and thus into the body of the fetus. They have also been found in mothers' milk. How much damage they can do is not yet known, but it is reasonable to assume that there may be danger. Even continued loud and agitating noises have some effect on the unborn, investigators believe (Sontag 1941).

Emotions From the day she was brought home from the hospital (aged about 36 hours), Abigail Jane was an obviously contented baby. She gained weight rapidly and slept well. Genetic differences aside, researchers now strongly suspect that such infants are born to mothers who really wanted their babies and whose pregnancies were without undue emotional stress. Maternal emotions appear to have a chemical effect on the fetus. Stress is "transmitted" to the fetus via hormones passing through the placental barrier. The results, for good or ill, sometimes show up in how the baby acts.

While investigators are becoming more and more convinced that maternal emotions can have these effects, they emphasize that mere maternal "impressions" or "psychological states" cannot be transmitted as such, as superstitious gossip would have us believe. Rather, it is thought that the unborn child is affected only by "gross chemical changes" communicated through hormones in the mother's bloodstream and passed through the placental barrier (Montagu 1950). Their origin is severe emotional distress, not fleeting thoughts or impressions, during the later months of pregnancy (Sontag 1941, 1944).

One study, comparing pregnant women whose anxiety level was low with "highly anxious" women, revealed that the children of the latter group did less well than the children of low-anxiety women on tests of intellectual development and emotional adjustment (Davids 1968). The same researchers linked delivery room complications to a woman's emotional problems during pregnancy (Davids, De Vault, and Talmadge 1961).

Caution: What these investigators were dealing with were the effects of unusually severe emotional problems. In contrast, not dangerous at all, except perhaps for the pregnant woman herself, are the varying emotional states experienced by most pregnant women. In the course of a pregnancy, many women will experience what are considered "normal" kinds of stress. They may have feelings of anxiety, suffer often from "the blues," cry unexpectedly, have nightmares. They may even be not quite as "sharp" intellectually as they were before becoming pregnant (Colman and Colman 1973). Normal hormonal changes characteristic of pregnancy may be responsible. Other reasons that make sense are a woman's natural concern about her baby's welfare, fear that she may not be a good mother, marital conflict, and a sense of her body's entrapment by a process over which she has no control.

According to a husband-and-wife psychological team who studied the experience of pregnancy, women characteristically have three different sorts of psychological reaction during the three trimesters of pregnancy (Colman and Colman 1973). During the first three months, when the pregnancy is not yet visible, many women suffer from ambivalence. They think: "Do I really want this baby? I'm stuck with this. I hate this nausea. My breasts ache. I feel sleepy—ugly—hungry all the time." And at the same time they may be thinking what a wonderful thing has happened to them, what a lovely secret they are harboring, what a joyous achievement. and what a wonderful outcome is in store.

In the second trimester, feeling the baby move is the dramatic highlight. Many women (and their husbands, too) are overwhelmed with wonderment and delight.

In the last three months of pregnancy, according to the psychologists, almost every women has lost her negative feelings about the coming child. The reality of the imminent birth is inescapable. She is burdened by physical awkwardness and discomfort. Every little ache or contraction makes her worry and wonder (especially if this pregnancy is her first). But she may well enjoy the special status and extra attention given to the very obviously pregnant. Whatever fears she suffers are likely to be only the ones related to the forthcoming delivery.

The reality of the imminent birth is inescapable.

Not every pregnant woman reacts in the manner just described. Every pregnant woman tells a slightly different story about her experiences. And sometimes the story changes in retrospect.

Testing

One concern runs through almost every woman's mind all through her pregnancy. Often it is the subject of dreams, possibly nightmares. *Will my baby be all right?* Fortunately, medical science is making appreciable strides in answering that question *before* birth—sometimes long, long before the ninth month.

Premarital tests for maternal syphilis (which could be deadly to the fetus) are a long-established medical routine, usually required by state law. But the unmarried can be both syphilitic and

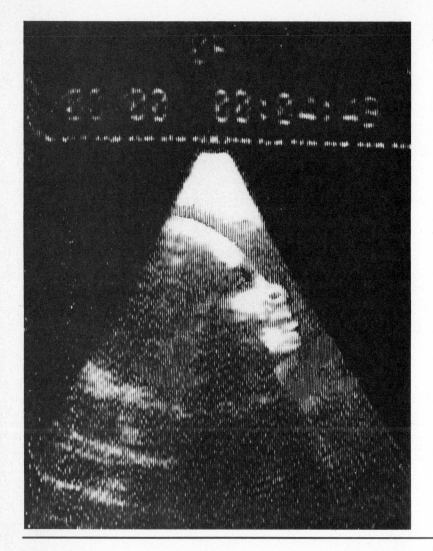

Five-month-old fetus portrayed by ultrasound.

pregnant. And it is also possible for a woman to acquire syphilis after becoming pregnant. Fortunately, syphilis in a pregnant woman can be detected by a simple blood test and effectively treated. But the treatment must come before the sixteenth to eighteenth week of pregnancy. Even if the mother is cured later, the child may still suffer damage: problems with bones, teeth, hearing, and vision (Apgar and Beck 1973).

Amniocentesis is a recently developed technique used to test for suspected chromosomal defects (see page 39). An even newer technique, with other applications, is *ultrasound*. Ultrasound is something like the sonar used at sea: sound waves reflect the shape and the heartbeat of the solid object (the fetus) in its watery amniotic sac. One of the best aspects of ultrasound is that it seems to carry little risk.

Ultrasound: technique using sound waves to detect the size, shape, and position of the fetus

Using this technique, it is possible to "hear," as early as the eighth week, the beating heart of the fetus. Ultrasound can also determine very early whether there will be a multiple birth. More important, ultrasound can guide the needle used in amniocentesis so that no vital organ is pierced.

Ultrasound can make an actual "picture" of an embryo or fetus; it can monitor the fetal heartbeat; and it can detect certain physical abnormalities (not all), early in the pregnancy.

The most frequent use for prenatal diagnostic testing during pregnancy is when there is some reason to suspect a problem. What to do about any problem that is detected is, of course, another question. Ending the pregnancy is sometimes an obvious alternative, unacceptable to some. But an advantage stressed by at least one investigator is that couples who know they have been exposed to genetic or environmental risk can now chance a pregnancy, assured that they will know in plenty of time whether or not to end it (Kingsley 1975).

Effects of the Birth Process

A fateful period

Nine months have passed. The baby (Abigail) has been born. The new father, phoning everyone he can think of in the middle of the night, is drunk with the experience and the triumph. He was in the delivery room. He saw the baby come out. He keeps describing the wonder of it all.

The infant's mother, who had very little sedation during labor and delivery, as is the common practice these days, is also on the phone shortly after the baby's arrival.

"It wasn't too bad, then?" her mother asks.

"Well," she retorts, "it was no fun!" But her voice is deeply tinged with satisfaction.

As for the baby who has just come into the world, she expresses herself only with a mewling sound something like that of a kitten. What, if anything, is she thinking or feeling? No one really knows, although some psychiatrists maintain that the experience of birth is relived and remembered one way or another by all of us.

In any case, no one denies that the process of being born can be both psychologically and physically fateful for a child. A difficult birth can maim the body. Oxygen deprivation or clumsy use of instruments can damage the mind.

Birth can be traumatic for the mother, too, depending on the physical difficulties she encounters as well as the attitudes she has been building up during the preceding nine months. The way she is treated in the hospital by attendants and physicians can also be physically or psychologically hurtful. Some investigators speculate that a difficult labor and delivery may be reflected later in the mother's attitude toward her child.

On the other hand, a birth that is happy and supportive can send both mother and child off to a wonderful start. A woman who has been well-prepared, psychologically and physically, and is supported by people who attend the birth sympathetically and ably, can orchestrate a grand overture to life's opera for her newborn child. The father also can benefit from a successful birth, since it can enhance his future relationship to his child, especially if he has had a role in the preparation and the delivery.

Labor and delivery

The last days The physical process of birth can be summarized very simply. By the ninth month, the fetus has taken over almost the entire abdomen of the mother. (See Figure 2–14.) The organs that normally occupy that space are consequently squeezed, although still functioning, so that heartburn, digestive discomfort, a need to urinate frequently, and the burden of more than a dozen extra pounds of weight all in one area combine to make a woman feel at least slightly miserable most of the time.

There is no comfortable way to sleep. If the pregnant woman is sharing the same bed with her husband, his physical nearness can be a great comfort. But because of her uncontrollable restlessness, he loses sleep too. Add to that the early uterine contractions, which make a woman (especially a *primipara*) keep wondering if the moment of birth has not at last arrived. It's a fairly unpleasant and uncertain few weeks.

Primipara: a first-time mother

Just before labor begins, the baby's head, which has been moving down in the last weeks, becomes wedged between the mother's pubic bone and the sacrum. The plug of mucous and blood vessels that has been a barrier between baby and cervix may give way. The pressure of the baby's head may break the bag

FIG. 2-14 Fetal development.

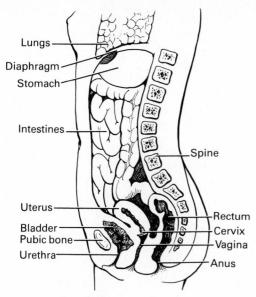

Lungs
Diaphragm
Stomach
Intestines
Spine
Uterus
Bladder
Pubic bone
Urethra
Rectum
Cervix
Vagina
Anus

(a) Nonpregnant uterus.

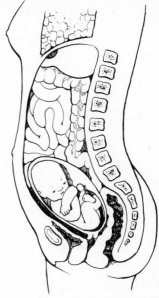

(b) Fifth month: fetus is in the abdominal cavity, pressing somewhat against mother's diaphragm and lungs.

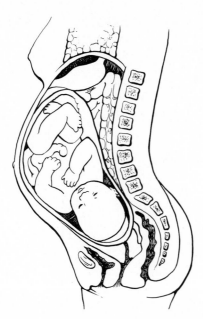

(c) Ninth month: baby fills mother's whole abdominal cavity.

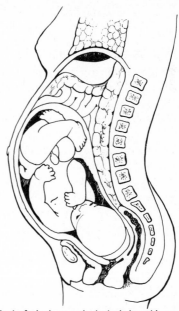

(d) End of ninth month: baby's head is wedged between mother's pubic bone and sacrum.

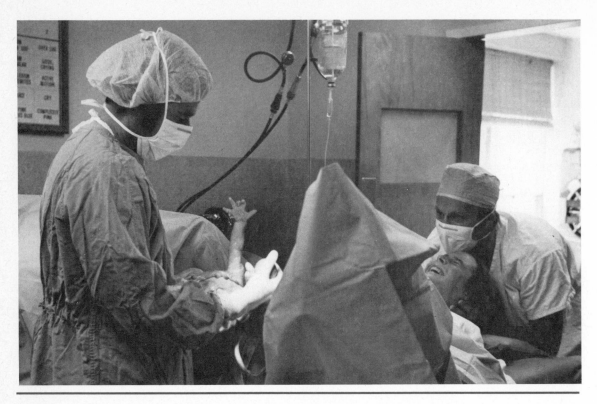

Birth.

of water in which the fetus has been floating for the past several months (Bing 1969). A discharge of mucous or the breaking of the water bag may signal that labor is imminent. Sometimes neither happens without assistance from the doctor or attendant, or they may occur spontaneously.

Birth process Shortly before or shortly after these events, labor begins: uterine contractions brought on by any of several factors relating to hormones and the size and position of the fetus. The contractions come closer and closer together. Their effect is to dilate (open) the cervix enough to make room for the baby to be pushed through the opening and into the world. (See Figure 2–15.)

In a normal birth, the head, the largest part of the baby, comes out first. That is by far the hardest part. Labor is well named, for it is hard work for the mother to push. Many have likened the process to an enormous bowel movement. The pushing is really quite similar, but usually much, much more difficult.

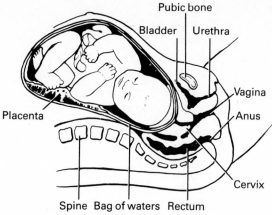
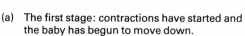
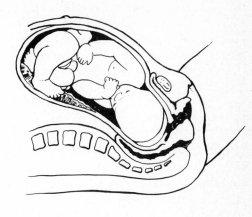

(a) The first stage: contractions have started and the baby has begun to move down.

(b) The cervix begins to dilate.

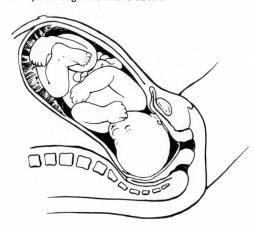
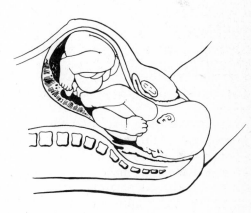

(c) The cervix is fully dilated, and the baby's head is entering the stretched vagina.

(d) The baby is pushed through the birth canal.

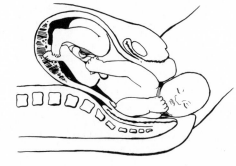

(e) The head rotates at the time of delivery to let the shoulders and arms emerge. Then the rest of the body follows, and the child is born.

FIG. 2–15 Stages of labor.

The amount of pain depends on several factors: the size of the baby's head compared to the size of the vaginal opening; how relaxed the mother is between contractions; the mother's general health; whether this is a first baby; and any unusual conditions.

Normal labor and delivery average 8 to 14 hours. Labor is longer for a first baby (Montagu 1964). If the baby is in the normal head-first position, labor and the subsequent passage down the four inches of the birth canal will probably be easiest.

Drugs during labor   Much has been written about the dangers of drugs to the newborn, and about the joy of a mother who is awake and able to witness the excitement of her child's arrival. No wonder, then, that some doctors and pregnant women have become extremely reluctant to use pain-relieving drugs except when absolutely necessary and in the smallest doses possible.

A generation ago, drugging women into insensibility was routine. In contrast, Abigail's mother was told by her obstetrician when labor began that a drug had been prescribed but would be administered only if and when she felt that she needed help. During the course of the labor, she did ask for that assistance, but never was she "out cold." As a result, she had the incomparable satisfaction of being entirely conscious when her baby was born.

It is now known that at least a portion of the drugs given to a mother will enter into the maternal blood circulation, pass through the placenta, and enter the fetus (Aleksandrowicz 1974). The placenta is evidently not the completely protective barrier it was once thought to be, at least when birth is imminent. The present belief is that most drugs are transferred from mother to child in this way, depending on the chemical nature of the particular drug (Aleksandrowicz 1974).

The litany of ills attributed to overuse of drugs during labor and childbirth is depressing. Subsequent mental and motor problems may result. One study found a "significant relationship" between the use of certain drugs during labor and infants' attentiveness in their first few days. These researchers feel there is good reason to believe that the effects last much longer than that, perhaps even for a few years (Stechler 1964a). Other studies have shown that newborns suffering from anoxia (lack of oxygen during delivery)—a common result of drugs given to the mother and passed on to the infant through the cord—were, at the age of three, intellectually harmed and perhaps "more infantile, negative, distractible, impulsive" than other children (Ernhart, Graham, and Thurston 1960). Still another study found that seven-year-olds who were anoxic at birth were at least minimally impaired in abstract verbal ability, perceptual skills, and social competence (Corah et al. 1965).

Doctors have noted that mothers heavily sedated with barbiturates and other drugs often give birth to babies who also appear sedated, "even to the point of severe respiratory depression" (Hughes, Ehmann, and Brown 1948, page 626). One study found abnormal brain waves lasting for three days in such infants. Another detected drug effects in babies several days and even months after their birth (Aleksandrowicz 1974).

As for the long-term effects of maternal use of drugs at birth, research is still too scant to prove much, if anything. However, enough is known about the adverse immediate consequences to warrant a "Caution!" sign in every delivery room. And current medical practice seems to be observing that caution.

Natural childbirth Perhaps partly because of all these drug-related problems, new ideas about how to give birth have emerged in recent years. People tend to have strong opinions on the subject, and almost everyone is interested. After all, every one of us was born at one time or another, and most of us father or mother at least one child. Some notions may be just fads; others prove themselves.

Some people believe that childbirth is so natural a process that a woman should be able to deliver her infant without pain at all, "by the side of the road" like the "noble savage" of literature, and then go about her normal business of cooking the evening meal or returning to her daily work. Others stress the biblical injunction that "in pain shalt thou bring forth" as a sort of payment for Original Sin. A third very popular opinion is that a woman and the baby's father should both be involved in childbirth, in a "natural" setting, using "natural" aids for labor and delivery.

Natural childbirth is not exactly a side-of-the-road procedure. But it does stress that maternal exercise and advance psychological preparation of both father and mother can minimize, if not eliminate, the need for drugs during labor and delivery. Thus, danger to the infant is reduced and labor may be shortened.

Some enthusiasts would like to do away with the hospital setting altogether and, if possible, the doctor as well. They advocate home births, with only the baby's father, the couple's friends, and perhaps a midwife in attendance. The unequal distribution of obstetricians, they argue, would be offset by more frequent use of midwives who also have more time to spend with their patients. Midwives can also help the doctor in the hospital if they are not allowed by law to substitute for him (Blankfield 1968; Klusman 1975).

A variation on this idea is the homelike labor–delivery room now available in some hospitals and some doctors' offices. It looks just like a conventional bedroom, and anyone involved in the event, including older children, may be present. But all the hospital facilities and personnel are available at all times, just outside the door. (See Box 2–1.)

Box 2–1   Letter from a New Mother

Dear Friends,

As you can see by the card, we've just had a little girl baby—Tracy Joelle. The delivery was planned for our doctor's office, and it was such an exciting experience that we'd like to try and share some of it with you.

First, the best part was being together after Tracy arrived. She was born at 7:10 P.M., Friday. Carl and I were together through labor and after delivery on a comfortable double bed in a birth room decorated as an early American bedroom. Carl massaged and stroked me and gave lots of verbal encouragement throughout labor. When it came time to push, he helped to physically pull me into the right position. Pushing was hard, hard work, but having Tracy emerge and immediately rest on my bare stomach was such an emotional high. Ryan (our three-year-old) and Grandma Joanie (my Mom) were also in the room,

along with a midwife, a nurse practitioner, and a close friend who was taking pictures for us. We put a blanket over Tracy to keep her warm and spent the next half-hour watching her every move and talking about how wonderful she was, while the doctor stitched me up. Sometime during the first hour we cut a cake and sang happy birthday to Tracy. I moved from the bed to a rocking chair and nursed Tracy.

Ryan's involvement and responses during the birth experience were all that we'd hoped for. During my labor he was mostly interested in playing in the waiting room with Grandma Joanie. He did come in three or four times to check on how things were going and to ask for juice. The one time he caught me in the middle of a contraction, he got on the bed and helped Carl rub my back. After Tracy came out, it didn't take Ryan long to touch her slippery body and help

Lamaze   Currently in great favor is almost drugless childbirth, with the father coaching the mother in both labor and delivery. (This was the method chosen by Abigail's parents.) Originally suggested by Grantly Dick-Read in 1933 and elaborated by Russian investigators in the 1950s, the procedure was brought into its current form by a Frenchman, Fernand Lamaze, in 1951. *Lamaze* childbirth education classes for pregnant parents can now be found almost everywhere.

Lamaze: childbirth method using relaxation exercises

The first step in Lamaze training is to demystify pregnancy and childbirth by explaining to both parents the physiological

make her warm. When I nursed her in the rocking chair, he climbed on my lap and helped feed me some cake. Then he sat in a bean-bag chair and held her and talked with her. By about 10 o'clock we were all home to be together as a family.

In selecting this method of delivery, the question of medical risk was of course very important to us. Our doctor helped us with this throughout our pregnancy. First of all, the large majority of births are "normal" and trouble-free. However, having an office delivery is not just a matter of taking your chances. The doctor estimates that 10% of the parents that apply for an office birth are turned down on the basis of prior medical history that indicates any potential for difficulty. Another 10% accepted in the program wind up birthing in the hospital due to risks that develop during pregnancy. Of course, during and after labor, if a problem were to develop, a transfer would be made immediately to the hospital a few blocks away. Additionally, the office staff is excellent and quite used to working together should a problem develop. The extra staff attention that is afforded each birth in the office was a definite plus for us. All in all we feel that for normal deliveries the office birth has extremely little if any medical risk over hospital deliveries.

A common justification for hospital deliveries is to provide the mother with two or three days of rest. Our experience was that both mine and Tracy's needs could be better met at home by a caring family. It's really essential to have someone holding the house together, and Grandma Joanie performed this thankless task for a week while we spent time getting to know each other and Tracy and our new roles as a result of her joining our family.

facts and what they may therefore expect to happen. This alone, the Lamaze people believe, eliminates much of the pain and tension. Then, as the birth approaches, the two parents are taught tension-relieving exercises, not only to minimize the physical stress of late pregnancy but also to prepare for the actual birth.

When the time for birth comes, the father-to-be accompanies the prospective mother into the labor and delivery rooms, encouraging her to breathe correctly during contractions and to push during delivery. Because of the relaxation training and the elimination of fear, Lamaze parents report less pain during labor, have shorter labors, and feel more "involved" in the experience (Cronenwett and Newmark 1974). The doctor also has a cooperative patient. The mother is awake and alert and able to appreciate her achievement. The father becomes an integral part of the climax to a process in which he was an essential partner from the beginning. He has the added bonus of viewing his child even before the mother sees it. And the child gains most of all, because the threat of damage from excessive drugs and prolonged labor is diminished.

Lamaze childbirth seems to be the wave of the future. It was even featured over a series of weeks on one of the most popular television series of the 1970s, "All in the Family".

Benefits for father   Not every hospital allows the father-to-be in the delivery room. Some even banish him from the labor room. But Abigail Jane's father believes his presence was a high point in his life, and the baby's mother was happy to have him there (though she dryly remarks that the labor was, after all, hers alone). The obstetrician was evidently not inconvenienced; she even invited Abigail's father to have a close look at the birth canal. One researcher notes that "this is a positive emotional experience for a man and in most cases ought to be encouraged" (Hazlett 1967).

There appear to be later benefits, too. With his more clearly defined role and greater participation in the birth process, the father subsequently becomes more involved in the rearing of his child. A study of 19 couples, of whom all fathers except one were present during labor and delivery, showed that these fathers took a far greater part than average in caring for the newborn infant (Parke, O'Leary, and West 1972).

Several psychologists have studied the father's role in pregnancy, childbirth, and the early weeks of infancy. As one might expect, there are many individual differences. But there is no question that it is a crucial period for the father, as well as for the mother. "It is a time when feelings about separation are intensified while infantile conflicts between the father and his own parents are reactivated and dependency needs are heightened," writes Beatrice Liebenberg in a study of 64 "normal" fathers. In concluding, she quotes comedian Bob Newhart: "A man goes through a little hell, too. You may wonder how the world ever got overpopulated" (Liebenberg 1969, page 276).

Special situations

Delivery complications Any delivery may have complications. Sometimes nobody can foresee them. If the pelvic opening is too small to permit passage of the baby's head, a *Caesarian section* will have to be performed. This is an operation involving an incision in the mother's abdomen and the surgical removal of the baby.

Caesarian section: delivering the baby through an incision in the mother's abdomen

Other difficulties may require *forceps delivery:* assistance by a special surgical instrument. Normally no harm is done, but in some rare instances the forceps may inflict damage on the baby's delicate head, with either temporary or permanent harmful consequences.

Forceps delivery: using a surgical instrument to ease the newborn out of the birth canal

The baby may never have maneuvered itself into the head-down position, so that at birth the infant is in the *breech position,* trying to be born buttocks or feet first. This endangers the child's oxygen supply. Sometimes an attending doctor can move the baby around to the "right" position, but this is a delicate and possibly time-consuming procedure. If it takes too long, the baby may suffer from anoxia or other physical problems.

Breech birth: when the newborn emerges feet or buttocks first

Breathing problems and the possible negative effects of drugs used during labor are possibilities that must be carefully monitored because of their far-reaching consequences. Anoxia, a lack of oxygen, comes from any one of a number of possible causes: separation of the baby from the placenta too soon; drugs administered to the mother that have passed through the umbilical cord and affected the fetus; prematurity and consequent general physical immaturity; the effects of poor maternal diet or smoking; an overlong labor; or medical bungling.

Apnea, the temporary cessation of breathing, can lead to behavioral disorders, mental retardation, learning problems, and a variety of neurological defects. However, in many cases these difficulties gradually disappear within the first two or three years (Stechler 1964*b*).

Apnea: temporary cessation of breathing

The Rh factor   One problem that could culminate at birth is Rh incompatibility. The *Rh factor* is a substance in most people's red blood cells. Those who have it are called Rh positive; those without it are Rh negative. Neither condition is dangerous, except when an Rh negative woman and an Rh positive man conceive an Rh positive child. (If the situation is reversed—an Rh positive mother and an Rh negative father—there is no possible danger.) An Rh negative mother's blood type might be incompatible with that of her Rh positive child. For example, a person with Rh negative blood, if transfused with blood containing the positive factor, would react in the same way the body reacts to a virus: antibodies would be manufactured to combat the invasion. But few of the baby's blood cells ordinarily reach the mother's bloodstream, because the circulatory system of the fetus is separate. During childbirth, however, this mixing is more likely to occur, especially if the birth is difficult. In such a case, the mother's antibody mechanism goes into action.

Rh factor: substance in most people's red blood cells that may cause neonatal problem when mother alone lacks it

With a first baby, neither mother nor child is usually harmed by the blood type discrepancy. But in a later pregnancy, the antibodies already developed in the mother's blood can have dire effects on her baby; they may get into the baby's circulation and lead to anemia, heart failure, jaundice, brain damage, cerebral palsy, and perhaps death. These problems appear at birth, but their basic cause is prenatal (Apgar and Beck 1973).

There are now remedies for all the possible consequences of Rh incompatibility. Tests before conception and during pregnancy can show whether threatening conditions exist or are likely to develop. If there is trouble ahead for either mother or child, preventive injections, vaccines, or transfusions are available (Apgar and Beck 1973). Rh incompatibility is one problem from which nobody needs to suffer if the proper medical advice and aid are at hand.

Prematurity   *Prematurity* is one of the major hazards to the physical and psychological health of the newborn. It can also be a psychological problem for the parents of a baby who starts life with this handicap. Premature infants—babies of low birth weight—run a higher than average risk of developmental and psychological problems.

Prematurity: when a newborn weighs less than 5 pounds

A baby cannot live at all unless it is born after 20 weeks of gestation and weighs at least 400 grams (less than a pound) (*Stedman's Medical Dictionary* 1972). But any baby who is born weighing less than five pounds, no matter how long it has lived in

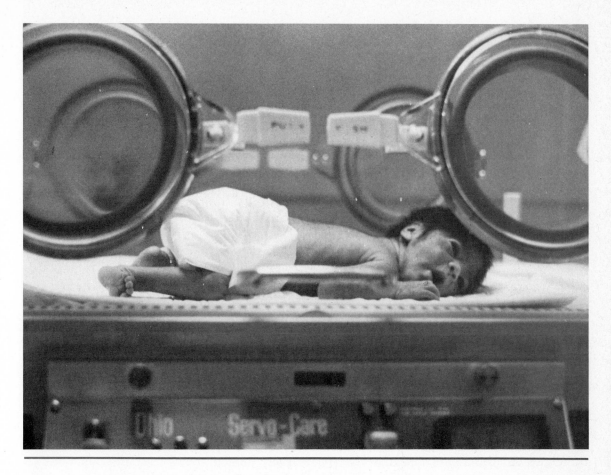

A premature infant in the protection of an isolette.

the uterus, could be prone to a variety of dietary disorders, infections, and cerebral and neurotic damage (Montagu 1964). None of these problems are inevitable. Still, they occur often enough for scientists to view prematurity with caution.

Compared to babies of normal birth weight, premature, low-birth-weight babies run a higher risk of having lower than normal intelligence. A disproportionate number are among the mentally retarded. Many are found among those who are institutionalized for various problems as well as among high school dropouts. Studies show that premature children are more likely to envince "deviant behavior," such as autism. They have more childhood accidents than full-term babies. Their language development, reading, and academic achievement may be below normal. Their growth, weight gain, motor behavior, and neurological functioning may be affected (Caputo and Mandell 1970). They seem to have more than the usual number of personality problems (Drillien and Ellis 1964).

There are some interesting differences in the degree to which prematures are affected in later life. Prematurity is more serious for boys than for girls. Premature boys seem to be more vulnerable than girls because males' developmental rate is slower. More of the boys fail to survive at birth. Of those who do live, their physical and psychological ills are worse than those of premature girls (Braine et al. 1966). Children brought up in homes of higher socioeconomic status seem to suffer the consequences of prematurity less than the extremely underprivileged (Braine et al. 1966; Drillien and Ellis 1964), very likely because their parents have the means to take exceptionally good care of them.

Later emotional handicaps may also result from the fact that underweight "preemies" are kept isolated for unusually long periods in hospital nurseries. They may miss early cuddling and affection, which are important for forming attachment bonds to a

Box 2–2 How Sensory Stimulation Helps "Preemies"

Some babies, even those whose parents are wealthy and well-educated, may be environmentally disadvantaged from the moment they are born. These are "preemies," who have missed days or weeks of the sensory stimulation that the fetus normally gets while inside the mother's uterus. The prenatal environment provides a variety of "experiences" just like massaging and stroking, which are essential to normal development. Thus, the premature infant often starts out with a handicap in terms of future development.

Ruth Rice (1977) determined to see what would happen if mothers of preemies deliberately replaced their infants' missed sensory stimulation. She chose 15 "experimental" infants and 14 "control" infants, all premature, all from similar backgrounds, and all born in the same hospital. The mothers of the experimental group were taught to give their babies special stimulation for 15 minutes, four times a day, for one month, starting on the day the baby came home from the hospital. The special treatment was begun in the hospital by nurses, with mothers assisting or watching. The babies were stroked and massaged over their entire bodies. After each stroking treatment, the mother rocked, held, and

mother figure. It has been shown that greater physical stimulation and care may offset some of the negative effects of a premature birth (Leifer et al. 1972; Kennell et al. 1974; Rice 1977). (See also Box 2–2.)

An open question is whether the problems of the premature start long before their birth, during the most vulnerable period of pregnancy, perhaps because of insults suffered by the embryo or fetus. As we have previously noted, adverse influences during prenatal development could cause both prematurity and other damage that might show up later regardless of birth weight.

The normal neonate

Prospective parents could easily feel overwhelmed and intimidated by widely publicized information about the possibility of producing a baby who is damaged in some way. Still, people go on having children. How substantial, actually, is the chance of giving birth to a defective child?

cuddled her baby for another five minutes. The control group got no such unusual treatment, and those mothers received no special instructions about providing sensory stimulation.

The payoff was evident after four months, when both groups of babies were brought back to the hospital for testing. Those who received the extra tactile–kinesthetic stimulation had made significant progress in weight gain. They had lost various reflexes that are normally gone by that age but that do not usually disappear in prematures. They also acquired new reflexes that are normal at four months for full-term babies. Their mental development also progressed, in contrast to the nonstimulated infants.

A result that could not be measured scientifically was the reaction of the mothers who took part in the program. They reported enthusiastically that "the baby likes being stroked and held," a plus for the mother–child bond, which is important for personality development.

Chance of defects   According to medical authorities, a birth defect is an anatomical or metabolic disorder present at birth, resulting from either heredity or damaging influences during pregnancy (Apgar and Stickle 1968). Every year, about 500,000 babies die at birth because of these disorders, while another 62,000 die from such problems while they are still infants.

About ten million people in this country have birth defects. They are born with them and they live with them all their lives. Among this group, the major problems and the number affected are: diabetes, four million people; mental retardation, three million people; orthopedic (bone) problems, one million people; seriously impaired vision or blindness beginning at birth, half-a-million people; congenital heart disease, 350,000 people; and speech defects, 100,000 people (Apgar and Stickle 1968).

Nevertheless, *"about 93 percent of the time, a new mother can be reassured that her just-born infant is wonderfully normal and obviously healthy"* (Apgar and Beck 1973, page vii).

The Apgar score   The reassuring statement above comes from the preface to a book co-authored by Dr. Virginia Apgar. She is the originator of a widely used scoring system that rates the physical condition of *neonates* (newborns) on a scale of zero to two for each trait. Scores are assigned at one minute, and again at five minutes after birth. A total of ten is a perfect score. The rating indicates how normal and healthy the baby is. The scale measures five vital signs: *a*ppearance or coloring; *p*ulse; *g*rimace; *ac*tivity; and *r*espiration. The initial letters of these criteria form the acronym APGAR.

Neonate: newborn baby

Like the overwhelming majority of infants, Abigail Jane was normal and healthy. Her APGAR rating was 8–9 at one minute, and 10 at five minutes. APGAR ratings between 7 and 9 denote infants who are "significantly less attentive" than those rated 10, and those differences seem to be apparent throughout the first year of life (Lewis et al. 1967).

After the first gasp or cry, newborn babies characteristically behave very much like newborn animals. They sniff. They move their heads from side to side. They open and close their eyes in a rather jerky manner. They startle spontaneously and exhibit the "Moro reflex"—flinging their bodies in such a way that their arms and legs are outspread. They suck, chew, purse and smack their lips, swallow, grimace, root about, and chew their fingers. Their tongues protrude. Their hands and feet tremble, and so does their diaphragm. They cry briefly and cry out again. They

Newborn.

are not, by ordinary standards, very beautiful, especially when covered with the characteristic whitish substance with which they emerge (Desmond et al. 1963). But to the mother and father, each newborn is always unique and beautiful.

Early characteristics   Those who maintain that their children were "different" from the moment of birth have been shown, by at least one research project, to be correct. Babies two to three days old were photographed. Their mouthing, hand–face contacts, hand–mouth contacts, and finger sucks were noted The investigators reported that "hand–mouth contacting stands out as the most highly individual and reliable trait" (Korner, Chuck, and Dontchos 1968, page 1158).

   This study discovered consistent differences in the manner in which the babies found their mouths with their hands. Some infants had more success than others in reducing tensions by sucking their hands. The researchers theorize that these early behavioral differences probably indicate temperamental differences and may foreshadow later development.

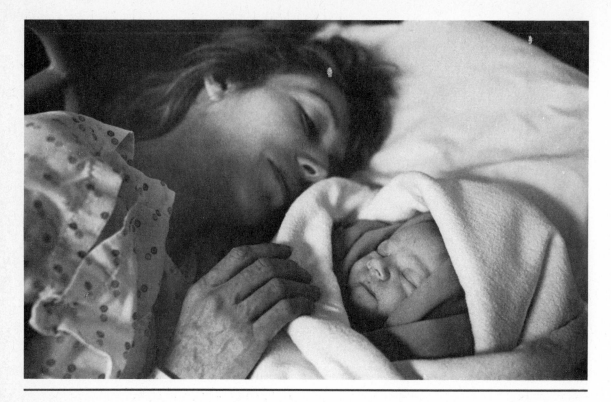

Perhaps weaning will be more difficult for babies with a strong need to suck. Infants with greater oral needs, but a greater capacity for satisfying them, might depend less on Mother's comforting presence later on (Korner, Chuck, and Dontchos 1968). It may be that such genetic predispositions could have a long-term effect on the relationships between parent and child. A dependent infant may be a child who will always look to parents for comfort. An independent infant might develop a much cooler relationship with the mother and father.

Another study suggests that the more and the sooner mothers are able to spend time with their babies, the better it bodes for mother–child relationships one month and even one year after birth (Kennell et al. 1974). The implication is that the average hospital procedure, which gives babies to their mothers only for brief periods during the day, may not be a good idea in the long run.

"Rooming in," permitted as an alternative in some maternity hospitals, may be one solution. The baby is kept in the mother's

The sooner mothers spend time with their babies, the better it bodes for mother–child relationships.

room most of the day, which allows the two to get used to one another. Shorter hospital stays could be another solution. A third alternative is home delivery, with no separation at all between baby and mother. These new ideas may be the wave of the future, even if only to save on hospital bills.

Summary

At conception, when the male's sperm penetrates the female's ovum, we are each the product of our ancestry. Physical and psychological traits are carried from generation to generation by genes, the mechanism of inheritance.

Each human cell contains all of a person's genes, carried by 46 chromosomes, two sets of 23 chromosomes each, one set from father and one set from mother. The chromosome pairs are matched for characteristics, but the genes they carry are not identical, because of their separate parental origins. A long series of chances determines which of the genes is passed on to the infant. Thus, no two individuals are precisely alike, except identical twins, who are the product of the splitting of a single fertilized ovum. These twins inherit the same chromosomes. Fraternal twins, in contrast, are the product of the fertilization of two different female ova. Their genetic inheritance is no more alike than that shared by other siblings. Psychological experimentation has benefited by comparing identical and fraternal twins, and by comparing identical twins who have been reared in different environments.

An individual's environment begins immediately after conception. The period of the zygote is the first of three prenatal stages. It lasts two weeks, during which the zygote moves along the fallopian tube. The second embryo stage lasts until the end of eight weeks. The embryo is attached to the uterus by villi, which draw nutrition from the uterine wall. In this stage, the rudiments of all human organs are developed and the embryo is most vulnerable to disease and to other interior and exterior environmental disturbances that could cause permanent damage. In the third stage, the stage of the fetus, the unborn baby is receiving its nourishment from the placenta, via the umbilical cord. Influences during these final months of pregnancy include the mother's diet, drugs, medicines, illnesses, gross psychological condition, exercise, and environmental conditions in the world outside.

The developing infant and its parents may also be affected by the birth process itself. A difficult delivery can have permanent adverse effects. A happy, relaxed labor and delivery can be beneficial to all three participants. One of the most serious by-products of a difficult delivery can be lack of oxygen. Prematurity and drugs are other possible hazards. By the time a baby is born, its basic psychological and physical makeup has already been determined and its developmental course has been launched.

Chronological Overview

Prenatal Development

First 2 weeks	period of the zygote (ovum)
	zygote moves from fallopian tube to uterus
2nd to 8th week	period of the embryo
	cells begin to differentiate into features of the human body: brain, spinal cord, circulatory system, and nerve system
3rd month to birth	period of the fetus
	fetus floats in amniotic sac, attached to placenta by umbilical cord
	growth of all organs
	all nourishment transmitted through the placenta
Birth	labor begins when baby's head moves between mother's pubic bone and sacrum
	uterine contractions dilate cervix to allow baby's passage out of uterus

Applying Your Knowledge

1. Why is the physical and psychological health of a pregnant woman so important?
2. Without frightening potential parents, how might educators inform them about the precautions they should take to prevent harm to their offspring?

3. Describe the possible ethical and political problems that could arise when an investigator attempts to study malnutrition in pregnant women.

Further Readings

Apgar, Virginia, and Beck, Joan. *Is my baby all right?* New York: Simon and Schuster, 1974. A very complete account of possible prenatal problems and birth defects and the progress of medical science in treating them.
Paperback.

Colman, Arthur D., and Colman, Libby Lee. *Pregnancy: the psychological experience:* New York: Seabury Press, 1973. A very readable introduction to the experience of pregnancy for an individual and as a family event.
Paperback.

Gaddis, Vincent, and Gaddis, Margaret. *The curious world of twins.* New York: Hawthorn Books and Warner Paperback Library, 1972. A fascinating compilation of data on twins: facts, case histories, photographs.
Paperback.

Montagu, M. F. A. *Life before birth.* New York: New American Library, 1964. A detailed account of prenatal development and the effects of heredity and environment.
Paperback.

Rorvik, David, and Shettles, Landrum B. *Your baby's sex: now you can choose.* New York: Dodd, Mead, and Co., 1970. An interesting description of one investigator's theory on sex determination.
Paperback.

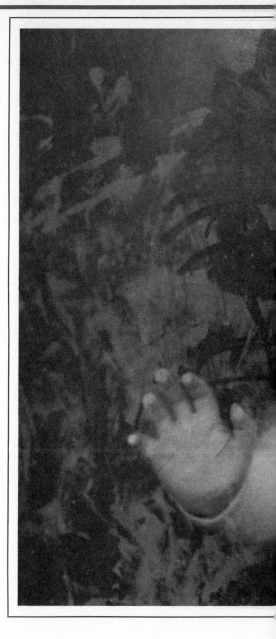

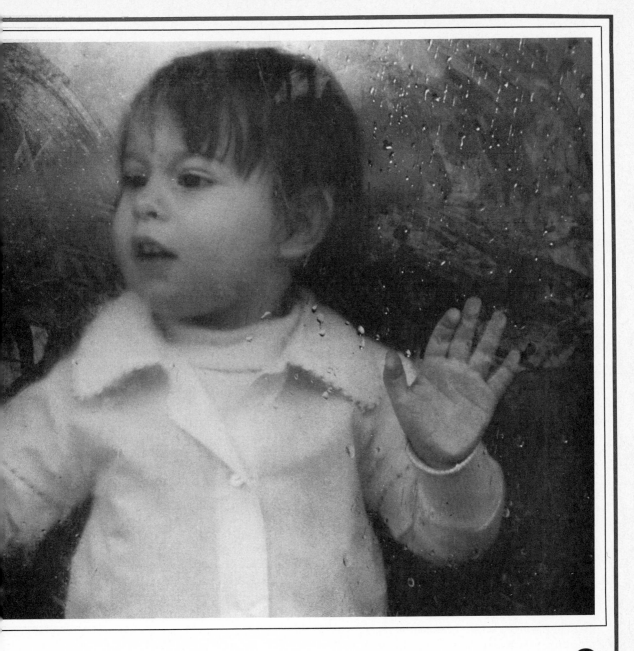

Chapter **3**

Perceptual and Sensory Development

When Abigail Jane was four weeks old, she committed her first act of outright rebellion. Until then, she had been fed alternately by breast and bottle. A summer baby, she was being prepared by her parents for late September, when her mother would return to work and would be obliged to close up the maternal commissary. But on this particular day, Abigail flatly refused her bottle. Even though she was hungry, she pushed it away with her fist, turned her head away, and cried bitterly.

Could a child so young rebel like an adolescent? Obviously not. And yet Abigail's show of independence did illustrate an important capability of the very young. Investigation has shown that normal infants are born with a full set of sensory capabilities. They can see, hear, feel, taste, and smell. When Abby refused the bottle, what she may have meant was: "My mother's breast feels good. Her milk smells good. It tastes good. This bottle is not nearly so delightful. I want to nurse!" In other words, her senses probably told her when she had a good thing going.

Theory of Perceptual Development

Neither Abigail nor any other infant can make her senses work for her as usefully as those of a grown-up. She sees, but the meaning she receives from what she sees is limited. She hears, but does not understand what she hears. Her *perception*—the ability to organize and interpret *sensory* experiences into meaningful events—is limited.

Perception: ability to organize and interpret sensory stimulation in the light of previous experience

Sensory: pertaining to the sense organs

Perception: from global to differentiated

Perception is based on the use of the senses, which are *innate* (present at birth). One is born with vision, hearing, and the senses of touch, taste, and smell. But both maturation and learning are required before an individual may fully perceive. *Maturation* is the physical growth and development of mind and body. *Learning* is a change in behavior due to experience and stimulation from the environment (Gibson 1963*a*).

In other words, while sensations are felt at birth, perceptive ability improves as the body grows and matures and as experiences with people and things accumulate. Throughout our lives, we experience our world through our senses. All types of perception supply the foundation for thinking, for coping, for enjoying, for self-expression, for physical safety. Thus, perception is *developmental;* it builds with maturity and experience.

Innate: present at birth; inborn

Maturation: physical and mental growth and development, governed by heredity

Learning: acquisition of knowledge, skills, or habits through experience

Developmental: related to maturation and experience

The neonate—the newborn in the first week of life—is a living illustration of the reverse of the old cliché about not being able to see the forest (the whole) for the trees (the parts). In contrast, the newborn cannot yet perceive the trees, only the forest. The adult perceives details; the neonate gets only a general impression.

A more formal way of describing the development of perception is to say that, at first, perception is *global*, or *holistic*: the total or "whole" event is considered, rather than its parts. Later, with age and greater maturity, perception becomes *differentiated* (Werner 1957). For example, when a newborn sees a face, what is perceived is a form. Very soon, the infant begins to notice the features—eyes, nose, mouth, eyeglasses, earrings, mustache. This developmental pattern seems to hold true not only for vision but also for all the other senses. Young children tend to focus on general outlines of a figure, a problem, or a picture, instead of paying attention to the details (Wolhwill 1960). Time and experience give them the ability to perceive both the parts and the whole (Elkind, Koegler, and Go 1964).

Global, holistic: relating to the whole, or entirety, rather than the parts

Differentiated: separated into finer parts; discriminated into parts

Role of environment, maturation, learning

Investigators have followed the course of perceptual development throughout life, tracing the effects of maturation, stimulation, practice, and training. The most extensive work has been done with vision, which is the most complex sense and the dominant mode for receiving information. Infants are aware of form—like the human face—from almost the very beginning of life (Fantz 1961). Normal individuals have many perceptual abilities, not just vision, ready to develop and work for them from the moment of birth. And changes can be noticed almost immediately thereafter, particularly if the senses are stimulated: by the sounds of human voices, by the sight of color and movement and light, by the feel of a breast against the skin, by the taste of milk.

Training and practice help a child to notice *distinctive features*, cues that differentiate one event from another (Gibson and Gibson 1955). You do not suddenly "see" the difference between *O* and *C;* you have to learn to look for the "distinctive feature" that distinguishes otherwise similar letters of the alphabet. And you can be taught only when your mind and body are ready.

Distinctive features: attributes or characteristics essential for discriminating one object from another

Some forms of visual perception, such as noticing that there is a difference between Mother and a stranger, develop in the ordinary course of experience. But for some kinds of perception, teaching is necessary. Perceptual development consists of learning to make fine discriminations; through experience a child learns to pay attention to the critical, or distinctive, features of a *stimulus* (Gibson 1963a,b). A child must be taught to see the differences between a horse and a cow, because the visual cues in this case are so similar.

Stimulus: something that provokes a response

Not all the senses develop at the same rate. For instance, touch—*haptic perception*—develops more slowly than visual perception. It takes more time and experience to discriminate between different kinds of "feelies" (Gibson 1963a).

Haptic perception: perception through touch

How the Senses Mature

Visual development

What, if anything, did Abigail Jane see at the moment she was born in the delivery room of the hospital? Is there any way to know what she saw?

Innate ability Neonates perceive form, color, and changes in illumination and are aware of persons and objects. Studies have been made of the eye movements of newborn infants, not only through simple observation but also by elaborate photographic procedures. We can make a number of educated guesses about Abigail's earliest visual experiences. She probably saw the obstetrician's face (Haynes, White, and Held 1965), though she would not have focused on it very long (Lipsitt 1966). Nor would her eyes have been working together as efficiently as they would only a few weeks later (Slater and Findlay 1975).

A change in the level of lighting in the delivery room would have been apparent to her (Hershenson 1964). Possibly at the hour of birth, but certainly within a few days, she would have been aware of color and have color preferences (Bornstein 1976). As early as her fifth day in the outside world, she would probably be aware of people or objects moving near her. Babies have been shown to stop sucking for a moment when that happens, which indicates that they have noticed a change in the environment (Haith 1966).

An infant's position may influence its perception. Most caregivers have learned by trial and error that even the youngest infants "forget to cry" for at least a little while when they are put up on a shoulder where they can see the world around them. Infants are visually able to capture and follow an object much

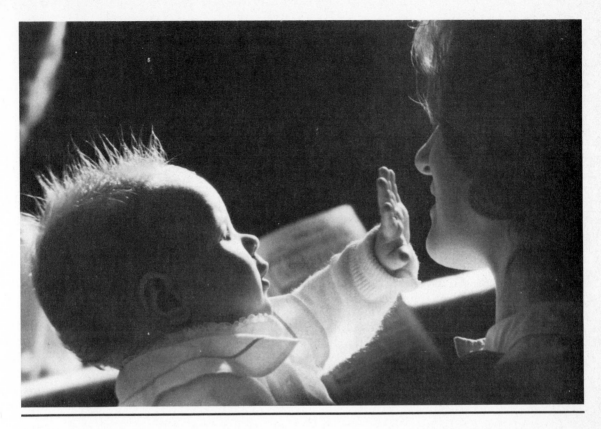

Discovery and learning
through perception.

better in that position than when lying down or held "sitting up" (Fredrickson and Brown 1975; Korner and Thoman 1970).

Visual discovery of parts of the body begins in the neonatal period. Two- to three-day-old infants seem to make a visual connection between their hands and their mouths. The discovery and learning process has already begun. One study showed that young babies who happened to find their hands near their mouths gave a clear visual response, a sort of "what is it?" And when the hand "lost" the mouth, the eyes moved in a "where is it?" fashion. This kind of "alerting" was apparent from their wide-open, bright, shiny eyes (Korner and Beason 1972).

Consider a rather unusual experiment in which baby pacifiers were fitted with tiny sensors, which measured the pressure of the child's lips and the vacuum caused by sucking. By linking the pacifiers to a computer and also to a screen capable of flashing differing visual patterns, the experimenters found that infants actually exercised the power of choice over visual stimuli. They varied their sucking patterns to enable them to look at the visual patterns they liked best (Alexander 1970). (See Box 3–1.)

The implications of this kind of study, offbeat as it may sound, are remarkable. It would appear that individuals, no matter how young, can use their innate faculties, like seeing and sucking, to pursue personal goals or objectives. It has been given to all of us, from our earliest moments, to have an effect through our sensory equipment on how the world treats us.

Never underestimate an infant. It matters to babies where they are put, what is done to them, what they have to see, hear, feel. The child is "all there," waiting only for further maturation and the stimulation and learning provided by care-givers and teachers.

Early maturation To grandparents who saw her only every couple of weeks, Abigail changed remarkably with each visit. Even though they had no special knowledge about child development, they knew from her gaze that she was noticing more things all the time. They would have been even more impressed if

Box 3–1   Infants at the Movies

Jerome Bruner and his associates at the Harvard Center for Cognitive Studies discovered that eight-week-old infants can enjoy movies enough to learn how to turn on the picture. The researchers rigged up a wired pacifier that measures the pressure of the baby's lips and the vacuum caused by sucking. The whole thing was tied into a computer programmed to respond by changing the patterns created by colored lights or by making a slide or movie projector go into action.

The infants learned to put their minds and their senses to work in order to enjoy the available sights. By sucking, the babies were able to make a picture appear on a screen and bring it into focus. Since they could not suck and concentrate on the picture at the same time, they learned to look away while sucking a picture into focus, and then to look fast before the picture went out of focus.

The psychologists' conclusion was that even very young children can use their senses and their limited physical ability to control and enjoy the environment. They are not passive creatures but active participants in the world (Alexander 1970).

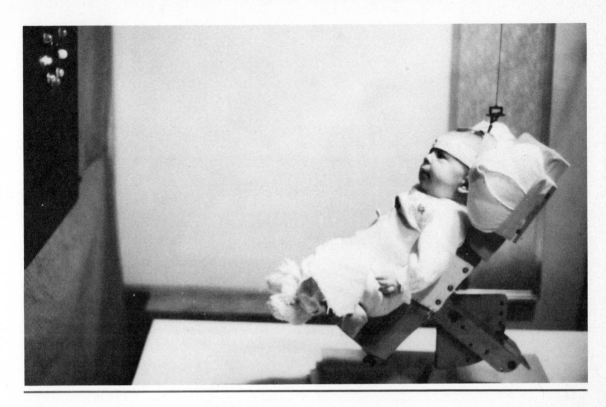

An infant at the "movies."

they had realized just how sophisticated she was quickly becoming. Recent studies have confirmed that infants' eyesight can be as sharp as adults' vision as early as the first four to six months of their lives. In effect, their visual *acuity* —their ability to discriminate detail—is as good then as it ever will be.

Acuity: sharpness of perception

At birth, though able to see light and color, an infant cannot fixate on any object for an appreciable length of time. But within only a week there is an increase in visual attentiveness. In Abigail's case, a mobile had been hung over her crib soon after she came home. For a while, the baby gave no sign that she noticed it. But by about ten weeks, she was clearly inspecting the moving colored disks above her. At the same age, it was clear that when one person was holding her and somebody else approached, she would "track" the newcomer with her eyes, as if to say, "There's something and it's moving."

Abigail first reached for and made momentary contact with an object at three months. It was her father's wristwatch, only a

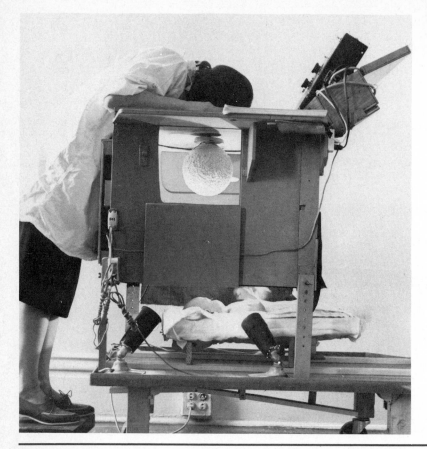

A Fantz experimenter explores an infant's perceptive ability.

few inches away from her. But not until she was about five months old had her visual and motor abilities matured sufficiently for her to grasp successfully for things that came her way: a child, a cracker, the car keys. Thus Abigail demonstrated the research-confirmed fact that reaching attempts by three- to seven-month-olds are controlled mostly by what they see, rather than by what they happen to touch (Field 1977).

"Looking time" research Most studies of infant vision use the length of time a baby looks at a stimulus as an indication of the child's ability to discriminate among different stimuli. Looking time is also a clue to the looker's perceptual preferences.

Robert L. Fantz's (1961) classic experiments sought the answers to several crucial questions: How much form perception is inborn? Is there a critical age at which visual perception begins to operate? What are the relative influences of native ability and experience on what we perceive with our eyes? Fantz showed infants from 1 to 15 weeks old four pairs of test patterns that varied in both form and complexity. They were shown horizontal stripes and a bull's-eye design; a checkerboard and two different-sized plain squares; a cross and a circle; and two triangles exactly alike.

The babies' eye movements were observed once a week through a peephole in a board above their cribs. By studying the babies' retinal images, the investigator measured the total time the infants looked at the various pairs and found noticeable differences. The more complex pairs interested the babies the most: they gave the most attention to the horizontal stripes–bull's-eye combination, a little less to the checkerboard–square combination, and least of all to the plainer figures. When the parts were separated, the bull's-eye won out over the stripes, and the checkerboard won over the plain square. What this means is that human beings are apparently born with a preference for viewing complex patterns over simple ones. (See Figure 3–1).

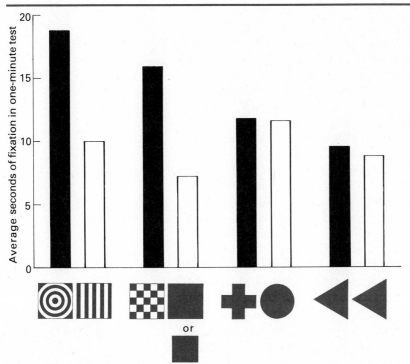

FIG. 3–1 Interest in form in infants. These are the patterns that were used in Fantz's tests. The bars indicate "looking time," illustrating how interesting the babies found each pattern compared to the others. *Source:* R. L. Fantz, The origin of form perception, *Scientific American,* 1961, *204* (5), 70.

Other studies support this conclusion. The more elements, angles, and other "information" in patterns shown to infants under six months old, the more interest they show, as demonstrated by longer looking time (Fantz and Fagan 1975). It also appears that two- to four-month-old infants respond visually to patterns with both interesting contour and variable elements (Greenberg and Blue 1975). By the time they are four to six months old, they prefer angles to straight lines (Ruff 1976).

It has been shown that longer looking time is associated with style of scanning—that is, what an infant looks at and how. Smaller eye movements and longer looking time are associated with more attractive stimuli (Pipp and Haith 1977). It has been suggested that looking time is also related to the difference, or discrepancy, between a new visual stimulus and a familiar one. The more the new stimulus differs from the familiar one, the more interest the infants show. But at a certain point, when the discrepancy between the objects is too great, the infants' interest begins to decrease. For example, as long as there is a certain resemblance between two stimuli, the less familiar one will get more attention. But when the differences are too great, the infants' attention decreases (McCall, Kennedy, and Applebaum 1977).

Vision can be a source of pleasure for an infant, as it is for any child or adult. Attention to objects begins at around two weeks of age. Newborns look in all directions, up and down and across, and appreciate forms as narrow as a quarter-inch stripe a foot away (Miranda 1970). After two weeks, babies start to show interest in mobiles and similar decorative items (Ruff and Turkewitz 1975). Preference for complexity increases with age, and substantial changes are apparent from 3 to 14 weeks (Brennan, Ames, and Moore 1966). Infants are also attracted to color and contrast (Fagan 1974; Bornstein 1975). It has been shown that three-month-olds can discern colors. (*Baby vision is highly developed* 1979).

All this might be an argument against a bland pink or blue nursery. Red designs chasing across a white wall might be more likely to get high marks from an infant critic. A Miro poster in a home she was visiting proved totally fascinating to three-month-old Abigail—it was full of greens, blues, reds, and fanciful shapes. Various other studies suggest that the unvarying preference of inexperienced infants for pattern is the base that nature has provided for their later ability to accumulate knowledge through the use of their eyes (Fantz 1961).

By the time babies are three-and-a-half months old, they have become choosy about what they look at. Designs shown repeatedly lose their attention. The babies stop looking. *Habituation* has set in: a decline in responsiveness and sensitivity as a result of repetition.

Habituation: adaptation to a stimulus so that it no longer elicits a response

Three-dimensional perception Infants evidently perceive all forms as being solid (Bower 1971). A moving object coming toward a baby, even if the "object" is no more than a shadow, causes the child to react as if it were solid and thus dangerous. Babies from 2 to 11 weeks old responded to such threats by widening their eyes, withdrawing their heads, and raising their arms (Ball and Tronick 1971). We seem to be born with the need to defend ourselves, and our eyes are important in detecting approaching danger.

A recent study detected evidence of depth perception in month-old babies. They paid more attention to recessed L shapes than to similar two-dimensional figures, indicating that they were able to detect a difference (Pipp and Haith 1977).

By two to three months, the infant is beginning to pay attention to three-dimensional objects, such as a rattle, a mobile, a teddy bear. Even though the baby is still unable to grasp any of these, an observer can tell that the child's eyes are fixed on the toys. By the age of six months, infants can tell the difference, visually, between a three-dimensional wooden object and a picture of the object (Rose 1977).

The most dramatic illustration of a baby's awareness of three-dimensionality comes from studies that demonstrate the early awareness of danger. It is interesting that this development becomes evident about the time when most infants are beginning to move around on their own and are thus apt to put themselves into the path of harm. In the classic study by Gibson and Walk, done in 1960, the experimenters built a "visual cliff" using boards and clear glass. The board was placed across the middle of a sheet of heavy glass, supported more than 3½ feet above the floor. To make the glass look as solid as it actually was, the investigators put a sheet of patterned material against the underside of the glass, on one side of the board. On the other side, the same material was placed on the floor. Thus, the edge of the board looked like a dropping-off place, the "cliff." (See Figure 3–2.)

Crawling infants from 6 to 14 months old were placed on the center board. When their mothers called to them from the other

side of the cliff, almost all cried, backed away, or refused to move. But when called from the other direction, where safety was apparent to their innocent eyes, they showed no hesitation.

The investigators do not claim that this experiment by itself proves that the human infant's perception of the cliff, and avoidance of it, are necessarily innate. Very early learning may be partly or even entirely responsible. By the time these infants were old enough to participate in the experiment, they might have learned about the dangers of a fall in the course of their daily experiences. But the investigators do suggest that some other experiments with a variety of infant animals may support the conclusion that depth perception is innate or learned very early. In general, the animals avoided the cliff at ages suitable to their own developmental needs.

The investigators add a caution for parents inclined to test their own babies with a real drop. Even though the babies in the study were aware of the cliff, some were too awkward to avoid the

FIG. 3–2 This is the visual cliff constructed by Gibson and Walk.

Developmental task: skills, achievements, or competencies that are considered important at certain ages for normal development

"danger." Children's visual ability comes before their motor ability (Schaffer and Parry 1969). If there had been a real precipice, a few would have fallen off.

Later experimenters added an interesting postscript to the cliff study. They measured both five- and nine-month-old babies' heart rate and blood pressure in such a situation. Evidently, the perception of danger is related only to visual attentiveness at five months. There was no physical evidence of fright. But by nine months, physiological measurements showed that a cautious response had changed to outright fear. Probably, physical maturity played a part, but learning through experience must have been an element as well (Schwartz, Campos, and Baisel 1973). Depth perception is a universal *developmental task*, an achievement that individuals in all cultures master on the way toward maturity. Infants everywhere develop depth perception at about the same age (Jahoda and McGurk 1974).

Recognizing faces Very early awareness of and preference for the human face over pictures of objects is another important universal characteristic (Sellers et al. 1972). Fantz tested infants with three different drawings, each the size and shape of a head. (See Figure 3–3.) On one was painted in black the important elements of a face. The background was pink. On another, the eyebrows, eyes, nose, and mouth were shown, but scrambled in a way not resembling a person. The third pattern contained a solid

FIG. 3–3 Preference for faces and pattern (a) Fantz showed that infants prefer a real-looking face to a scrambled face, but they like either one better than just an oval shape. The graph shows looking time for each. (b) Babies like pattern even better than color or brightness, according to Fantz's experiments. Six disks were shown to infants: the bottom three were plain red, white, and yellow disks; the top three were a face, printed matter, and a bull's-eye. The black bars represent looking time for two- to three-month-olds. The gray bars represent looking time for babies older than three months. *Source:* Robert L. Fantz, The origin of from perception, *Scientific American,* 1961, *204* (5), 72.

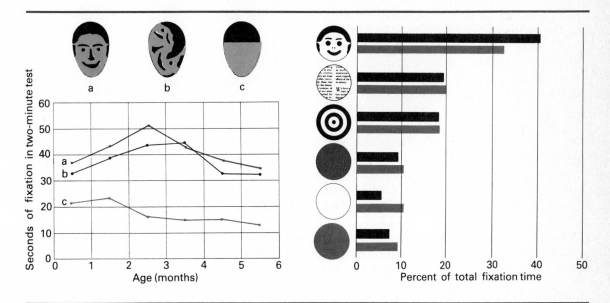

black area and an equal area with the elements of human features. Babies from four days to six months old were shown the three designs, which were paired in all possible combinations.

Up to the ages of three to four months, Fantz found, the infants looked longest at the pattern that most resembled a real face. This happened most conspicuously among the youngest babies. It may be that babies are born with an appreciation for the form that is most meaningful for their survival: the human face (Fantz 1961).

Thus, the sight that is almost always most interesting to a baby is the face of the care-giver. This is true throughout those all-important first six months when a child's visual acuity is developing (Woodruff 1972). Moreover, four- to six-month-old infants can discriminate between facial expressions. It makes a difference if the face is happy or frowning. They look longer at faces expressing joy than at angry faces (La Barbera et al. 1976). The adult's mood can come across in these ways even to an infant.

Another interesting finding is that babies make comparisons between familiar faces and strange ones. In the early months of a

Babies look longer at faces expressing joy.

child's life, parents are usually the first sources of sensory stimulation. In fact, the basis of *attachment* to parents is sensory: the baby's taste, touch, smell, vision, and hearing are all involved. (See also Chapter 9.) The infant is repeatedly exposed to the care-givers' faces, their expressions, their voices, their particular ways of handling the baby. This is the foundation for the child's recognition that the care-giver is special. Thus, it is not surprising to discover that babies are sensitive to the difference between familiar and unfamiliar faces.

Attachment: emotional dependence on or attraction to a particular person

One study demonstrated that infants only a month old do seem to recognize the difference between Mother and a stranger (Maurer and Salapatek 1976). The amount of time babies fixed their gaze on Mother was measured against the amount of time they gazed at the stranger. Using videotape and special cameras to follow eye movements, the investigators were able to discover exactly what the babies were looking at, and for how long. The unfamiliar faces got more attention. Perhaps this was a "who in the world is that?" kind of response. However, there were age differences. The one-month-olds looked less at the stranger's face than babies a month older. The younger ones concentrated more on facial outlines, while the older babies demonstrated differentiation: they paid more attention to eyes.

By four months, infants respond to the overall configuration of a face and not just to facial outlines or specific features like eyes (Haaf and Bell 1967; Haaf 1977). Four-month-olds (like one-month-olds) also pay more attention to a photo of a stranger's face than to their own mothers' photos (Bernard and Ramey 1977).

By six to eight months, most children have developed a demonstrable ability to recognize faces to which they have been frequently exposed. An early memory of a familiar face has probably been stored in the mind as a mental formula—*scheme*—of that face. The reaction to a strange face may be prolonged looking or anxiety, most commonly around the eighth month. The infant may show it by crying or pulling back in alarm (Greenberg, Hillman, and Grice 1973).

Scheme: fundamental unit of images, thoughts, or actions; an outline or mental sketch

Older children may react less strongly to strangers. Ten-month-olds confronted by both Mother and a stranger tended simply to move toward Mother. The stranger's presence produced more looking than crying (Corter 1976). The older child appears more curious than fearful, demonstrating continued discriminatory ability but also increasing adaptability to the new situation.

The appearance of *stranger anxiety* may be considered a sign

Stranger anxiety: apprehensive or fearful response to strangers that a child's perceptual development is progressing "on schedule." In fact, this ability to tell the difference between what is familiar and what is not may reflect the early ability to think—*cognitive ability.* (See also Chapter 5.)

Cognitive ability: ability to think, reason, understand

Environmental influences Awareness of the faces that have meaning in their lives is part of an infant's awareness of the surroundings in general. Investigators have some interesting things to report about the effects of the environment on a child's visual progress. Would it enhance Abigail's perceptual progress to fill her room with pictures, mobiles, rattles, stuffed animals, and other things to look at or touch? What would be the effect of leaving the room plain and relatively sterile?

Some aspects of perceptual development can be influenced by manipulating an infant's visual environment. One study provided ten normal five-week-old infants with two colorful, bright, immovable patterns of tassels and flowers hung at the head of each bassinet. A control group of ten normal infants of the same age had nothing hanging over their cribs. All 20 babies were tested weekly for eight weeks to determine the age at which they acquired a *blink response* to a dropping ball.

Blink response: involuntary (reflexive) shutting and opening of the eyes as a result of a stimulus

The investigators found that the "stimulated" babies acquired the blink response within two weeks on the average. But the babies who had no such "training" in looking did not begin to blink at the ball until several weeks later. Since the blink response seems to be based on *visual accommodation*—efficient use of the eyes to focus on near and far objects—those babies with the enriched environment really did benefit.

Visual accommodation: changes in the lens of the eye to focus on near or far objects

But the experimenters also found that the unstimulated babies began to catch up with the experimental group by about ten weeks of age. By then, the investigators reason, the babies were all spending more time out of their bassinets and in the world around them, where there is plenty to look at (Greenberg, Uzgiris, and Hunt 1968).

This study and several others demonstrate that an infant's development may, indeed, be influenced by environmental stimulation. More than 150 years ago, the pioneer German educator Friedrich Froebel, who founded the kindergarten system, urged mothers to hang colorful paper birds over their babies' cribs. He said it would give them a chance to "exercise their God-given power of looking as soon as this power emerged" (Greenberg, Uzgiris, and Hunt 1968, page 172).

Modern investigators add a caution that "enrichments" should be provided in such a way that the infant can take them or leave them (Greenberg, Uzgiris, and Hunt 1968). A baby might be overwhelmed by too much stimulation. A really complicated stabile (a nonmoving construction, as opposed to a mobile) placed over babies' cribs when they were little more than a month old caused them to look less and cry more. But an experiment in which a simpler object was placed to the side of the crib, giving the baby a choice of looking or not looking, proved to be not at all upsetting (White and Held 1966).

On the other hand, infants seem to become habituated and to lose interest when they see the same things all the time. Fantz demonstrated that two- and six-month-olds recognize patterns and stop looking if they see them too often (Fantz 1964). One child development textbook suggests changing the infant's position from one end of the crib to the other every few days so that the "view" may be varied (Lugo and Hershey 1974). True, up to about six weeks, familiar things are what babies appear to like (Weizmann, Cohen, and Pratt 1971); but by ten weeks a change begins to be appreciated (Wetherford and Cohen 1973).

Some children become habituated more quickly than others. Looking-time studies of 11-week-old babies demonstrated that babies get used to a particular sight and thus lose interest at different rates. The quicker babies may have the ability to process information faster (Greenberg, O'Donnell, and Crawford 1973).

Early reading   Even though a baby appears to be a rapid information-processor, it is probably unwise to leap to the conclusion that the child will be ready to read exceptionally early. Some ambitious parents, however, try to teach reading to very young children. The question is whether they are wasting their efforts or harming the child in some way.

Studies have repeatedly shown that early teaching will not necessarily promote earlier maturation of ability. Maturation governs the time in children's lives when they will have the ability to *discriminate* one letter from another. Both mind and eye must have grown up to the right stage. Forms are perceived from birth, but the ability to perceive subtle differences between forms is at least partly developmental, as well as the result of explicit teaching.

While stimulation from parents does play a certain role in developing a child's skills, there is evidently a limit to how far

Discrimination: ability to perceive differences, to make distinctions

ahead any care-giver can push the developmental timetable. Discrimination of complex forms, such as letters, seems to begin around age three-and-a-half, as a result of maturation. Form discrimination is crucial for dealing with any symbols, not only words but also numbers and the signs used for higher mathematics.

Preschool children seem to be aware of differences in the shape of forms but not differences in *orientation*. One test asked preschoolers to tell whether various geometric figures were different or the same. The shape of a figure and whether it was open or closed appeared to be the controlling factor in the judgments made by these young children. But they were not yet sensitive to the number of sides in a figure nor to whether one was upside down compared with another (its orientation) (Taylor and Wales 1970).

Orientation: position in space

Form perception and discrimination are obviously necessary for reading readiness. For example, it is not easy for a child to tell the difference between O and U—one is open, the other is closed. Nor is it easy to tell the difference between b, p, and d. Consider, too, the problem of discriminating between W and M. The shapes are the same, but one is an upside-down version of the other. The ability to judge orientation in space is usually beyond the power of the average three-year-old. The greatest increase in the ability to make such judgments occurs between the ages of three to six (Abravanel 1968).

People who deal with preschoolers often wonder why it is so difficult for these children to tell the difference between 3, S, and 5. The problem is maturation. By four or five, most children have developed to an appropriate level and are receptive to being trained to see the distinction. Therefore, they are ready to learn to read at about five. One experimenter was successful in teaching five-year-old children the differences between b and d and between p and q. Effective training involved clear and repetitive visual demonstrations of the differences between similar letters and similar geometric forms. What was important was the way the letters and forms were presented (Koenigsberg 1973).

Both showing and telling are helpful. Four- to six-year-olds learn the orientation of forms best if the instructor tells them in advance what kinds of clues are important—what to watch for (Caldwell and Hall 1970; Koenigsberg 1971). Children must be explicitly told, for example, "Pay attention to where the tail of the letter is—is it above the line, or below the line?"

Form discrimination increases with age (maturation) and learning (experience). The famous "scribbles experiment" shows how important a role learning plays in perceptual discrimination. Six- to eleven-year-old children were given a stack of cards, each card showing a different scribble. The children were asked to go through the deck and look for those cards that matched a standard previously shown to them. (The standard was not visible during the "test.") They were given additional chances to see the standard and then retake the test. Their accuracy in identifying the cards that matched the standard increased with repeated runs through the shuffled deck. This is an example of the effects of practice and learning on tasks that rely on visual judgment (Gibson and Gibson 1955).

Using *graphemes*—letterlike forms—one of the same investigators asked children between the ages of four and eight to match identical forms. The ability to avoid errors climbed significantly as the age of the children increased. The improvement appeared to be the result of learning to distinguish the graphemes' distinctive features—those crucial characteristics that differentiate one object from another. For example, caricatures accent the distinctive features of celebrities (Gibson 1969). By the age of eight, children have become more sensitive to small differences among very similar shapes. By that age, of course, most children have had considerable training in reading, which involves the specific visual skill that was tested (Gibson et al. 1962).

Graphemes: nonsense forms that resemble letters of the alphabet

Reading in school Most of us take for granted the idea of starting the first grade at the age of six. But is it really the best time to start serious schooling? When are children's eyes and minds actually working together well enough to master not only reading but also all the other basic disciplines necessary in our society?

Studies of how well children perceive the parts and the whole of drawings give interesting answers to how much a teacher or a parent can expect of a child in the early school years. The ability to perceive both the parts and the whole of a picture does not develop until eight or nine years; prior to this age, children perceive pictures in terms of parts *or* wholes.

A group of investigators showed some pictures to 195 children from the ages of five to nine (Elkind, Koegler, and Go 1964). (See Figure 3–4.) The children were told: "I am going to show you some pictures one at a time. I want you to look at them and tell

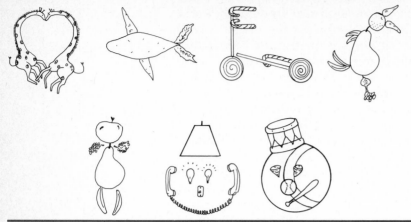

FIG. 3–4 Part–whole perception. These are the drawings that were used by Elkind's group to test part–whole perception. *Source:* D. Elkind, R. R. Koegler, and E. Go, Studies in perceptual development, *Child Development,* 1964, *35,* 84. © The Society for Research in Child Development, Inc.

me what you see, what they look like to you." If either parts or whole had been missed, the next question was: "Do you see anything else?"

Almost all the youngest children saw parts only.

"Two giraffes."

"Anything else?"

"No."

This was age five.

By age six, a few children saw the whole, but uncertainly, and retreated to the parts alone when questioned.

"A man, I mean fruit."

"Can you show me the man?"

"No."

At the next stage, usually ages seven to eight, children saw both whole and parts but did not seem to put them together.

"Some fruit. Oh! A clown."

The investigators call the logic "slow motion," indicating that the child of this age still does not realize the contradiction of giving two different meanings to the same picture.

In a final stage, not reached until eight or nine, children put the parts and whole together at a glance. Ben, aged eight, saw "a man made of fruit." And Ed, aged nine, saw "a scooter made of candy."

The point of this study is that part–whole perception is an important element of *perceptual logic* —the ability to add up the parts (of anything) to make a whole (Elkind, Anagnostopoulou, and Malone 1970). A youngster still deficient in part–whole perception would have trouble learning to read. The child would be

Perceptual logic: ability to add up parts (of anything) to make a whole

unable to add up the letters to make a word and to add up the words to make a sentence.

Reading, however, is not merely visual; it also depends on the information and experience that the reader brings to the printed page. Familiarity with content and concept is crucial if the reader is to make sense of the ink-marks on the page (Smith 1975). The written words are merely parts; the whole is supplied by the reader through experience.

Another factor, besides inexperience, that hampers visual perception in the very young child is inability to pay attention to what is important. *Selective attention* increases with age. The ability is evidently developmental. Second graders and sixth graders were shown pairs of colored animal forms in a viewer and asked to say which were alike and which were different. In some cases, they were asked to pair the animals for color likeness; in other cases, for form likeness. The older children were much better at the job than the younger ones (Pick, Christy, and Frankel 1972).

Selective attention: focused attention

A slightly different illustration of the same principle comes from a study with students from the sixth, eighth, and eleventh grades. A new element in an otherwise unchanged picture attracted their attention. But introducing a large number of new objects reduced the effect. The students were less able to discriminate what was new and different (Wolf 1971). The implication for teaching strategy appears to be that, regardless of the age of the pupil, new visual stimuli attract the most attention when not lost in an overly complex field.

Another study with implications for teaching showed that actual objects elicit more responsiveness in young children than pictures do. Teachers who bring in real apples or oranges to teach early-graders to add are more likely to be successful than if they just use pictures of fruit. Five-year-olds and nine-year-olds were tested for their responses to objects and pictures. The younger group did better with objects than pictures; the older group showed a much greater ability to respond to both picture and object (Klapper and Birch 1969). Evidently, the older the child, the better he or she is developmentally able to understand pictorial symbols.

In sum, the development of visual perception is shown by an individual's increasing ability to discriminate and attend to relevant cues. A remarkably varied number of clues must be attended to: shape, size, orientation, color, texture, and depth. Visual perception is an ability that depends both on the natural course of a person's development from the time of birth and on experience and learning. (See Box 3–2.)

Auditory sensitivity

Especially to first-time parents, a crying infant—particularly one who has just recently been fed—can be very upsetting. No one has yet found a means of interviewing babies to find out why they sometimes cry without apparent reason. But anxious mothers and fathers often stumble on ways of stopping the "meaningless" distress.

Abigail Jane's parents accidentally invented a new method. They put her bassinet next to their fish tank. The tank's pump was sending out a steady buzzing sound, and the monotony of it, it seems, put the baby to sleep.

Discrimination   The experience with the fish tank illustrates the results of several recent experiments that show that a human infant not only hears from the time of birth (and probably before)

Box 3–2 Seeing Requires Concentration

Dr. Bill Harrison used to be a pretty good baseball pitcher in high school and college. Not good enough for the majors, he went on to become an optometrist and eventually used his professional knowledge to make a special study of the role played by vision in athletic success.

He found that although plenty of athletes have "perfect vision," some of them can see much better than others and therefore can hit the ball better. Harrison believes that vision depends on concentration and that people can be trained to "see" better by learning to concentrate better (Distel 1976).

Harrison's theory appears to suggest that what an adult perceives is governed pretty much by the same principles as what a child perceives: it's a matter of learning to pay attention. But concentration may sometimes be more difficult for adults than for children. The complications of life give adults more to distract them from perceiving what is before their eyes—be it a golf ball or a husband's haircut. On the other hand, they have long practice in using visual cues to make perceptual discriminations (Barclay and Comalli 1970).

This principle of visual concentration applies to more than sports. For example, a person who is interested in automobiles can easily tell one make from another and can even identify the year of a car that has just passed by at 55 miles an hour. He or she has learned the cues. But people who don't care about such things can barely distinguish a hardtop from a sports car.

---

but also discriminates one sound from another. Auditory discrimination in infants is shown by different types of responses to different sounds. Heartbeat, movement of the eyes and other parts of the body, and breathing have been monitored by various researchers with some interesting results. The sound of a loud heartbeat, for example, appears to have a pacifying effect, while a regular tone of a similar nature does not (Roberts and Campbell 1967). Certain sound frequencies (that fish tank, for instance) are soothing, while others are upsetting (Kearsley 1973). A baby less than two days old may react to the sound of another newborn's cry by joining in. And even so young an infant can tell the difference between a real cry and a synthetic one; the real thing is more likely to elicit more of the same (Sagi and Hoffman 1976).

Localization   Infants can also tell where a sound is coming from. *Spatial localization*—locating a sound (or other event) in space or anticipating where a sound will come from—appears very early. In one experiment, eight infants as young as 30 days old were obviously upset when they saw Mother speak to them in one place while her voice came from another part of the room (Aronson and Rosenbloom 1971). Babies turn in the direction of a sound when they are around four to five months old. They can determine the precise source of a sound when they are a few months older. One investigator showed and sounded a bright, gold-colored bell for an infant audience. Then the bell was hidden behind a screen and sounded again. The babies who moved the screen to look for the bell were judged to have made a connection between sound and its source. They did this most frequently between the ages of eight and ten months (Freedman et al. 1969).

Spatial localization: locating an object or event in space

By eight months a baby has connected Mother's face to Mother's voice to form a definite concept of this important person. Any discrepancies can be recognized. Babies aged five months and eight months were tested with recordings of voices that were synchronized with lip movements. Mother spoke with Mother's voice; Mother spoke with a stranger's voice; stranger spoke with stranger's voice; and stranger spoke with Mother's voice. The infants' visual responses to the incongruous combinations were measured. "Searching" responses came from the older babies; some even cried as if distressed (Cohen 1974).

Accuracy and selective attention   "You're not listening!"
Parents say this to children. Teachers say it to students. Wives say it to husbands—and vice versa. Are they complaining

about wilful inattention, or is there something developmental they ought to know about?

Compared with the considerable body of work on visual ability, there are few studies of auditory perception. But the investigations that have been done show that listening accuracy is, indeed, developmental. Young children often do not seem to hear small words or contractions. Preschoolers are not necessarily being contrary when on being told, "Don't close the door!" they do exactly the opposite. They simply fail to attend to the "don't" (Feldman 1969).

Listening accuracy continues to develop up to about the age of nine (Mecham 1971). The increase in an individual's ability to sort out one verbal message from several may not necessarily come from better hearing but from more experience with language (Maccoby 1967). Adults who travel in foreign countries discover this truth for themselves. Armed with high school French, at first a visitor is in trouble in a French village. But after several days' exposure to the language, experience pays off. The physical ears are no better, but the "ear" for French is apt to be vastly improved.

Just like visual perception, *selective* auditory *perception*— the ability to tune out distractions—is a result of development and practice. The younger the child, the more difficult it is to ignore the whispering going on in another part of the classroom and pay attention to what the teacher is saying. The distraction of TV while homework is supposed to be done can also be very real.

Selective perception: focused perception

The potential for auditory overstimulation seems greater than for visual overstimulation. An infant cannot usually be overstimulated by having too much to look at; the child can simply close its eyes. But it is impossible to shut the ears to noise (Bower 1976). Adults know how upset infants can become when exposed to the social babble of a lot of strangers. Children brought up in surroundings that are always full of conflicting sounds may possibly be affected in ways not yet demonstrated.

Innate Sensory Ability

While vision and hearing seem to be by far the most important of the innate perceptual abilities of the human animal, a small galaxy of other sensory gifts is bestowed on the child even before it is placed in the cradle. Among these gifts are a sense of time and rhythm, *tactile ability* and the ability to feel pain, and the senses

Tactile ability: ability to perceive by sense of touch

of taste, temperature, and smell. All are present at birth or before, and all are useful to the developing individual.

Motion and sleep

When Abigail's parents discovered that she could be quieted by the buzz of the fish tank motor, they were inadvertently proving more than her ability to hear. Steady, continuous stimulation of all kinds, notably rhythmic sound and motion, has a marked pacifying effect on infants. It decreases heart rate, motor activity, and crying, and increases quiet sleep (Brackbill 1971). Other parents have found that the hum of a vacuum cleaner or the sound of running water operates in the same way as the fish tank did for Abby.

Sense of time and rhythm   This apparently innate appreciation for auditory rhythm may be connected to infants' preference for rhythmic motion. Probably even cave-dwelling humans rocked their babies. Experiments show that there is an optimum rocking rhythm; one might rock too slowly or too fast to comfort a baby (Ter Vrugt and Pederson 1973).

Of course, the rocking response may be something other than an appreciation for rhythm: perhaps an infant's feeling that a care-giver is present and thus all is well with the world (Van den Daele 1970). Steady movement is also rather boring and thus sleep-inducing. A trip from home to market in an automobile was a sure thing for putting infant Abigail to sleep; she also always succumbed to the rocking motion of a baby swing.

Similarly, it has been shown that infants only ten weeks old can get used to and thus stop reacting to visual stimuli given to them on a regular clockwork basis. A mobile over a crib, set to move automatically on a fixed schedule, might put a baby to sleep and would certainly lose the power to stimulate (Vietze, Friedman, and Foster 1974).

An infant's sleep–wake cycle may be the result of some kind of body rhythm, an innate time mechanism. Newborn infants appear to spend nearly equal amounts of time sleeping and waking, regardless of whether the parents attempt to impose a regular feeding schedule or follow the feeding-on-demand system (Gaensbauer and Emde 1973).

"States" in an infant's day   Like older children and adults, newborn babies also seem to dream. At least, they spend a third of

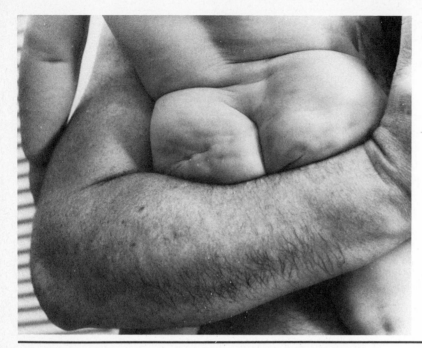

At birth, the most highly developed sense is touch.

their day, equivalent to half their sleeping time, in the kind of sleep characterized by rapid eye movements—REM sleep. It is known that such REM sleep in adults is dreaming sleep. The high ratio of REM sleep in the infant drops gradually as the child grows older (Roffwarg, Muzio, and Dement 1966).

A study of very young babies, less than five days old, distinguished several *states:* regular sleep, irregular sleep, drowsiness, alert inactivity, waking activity, and crying. These emotional and physical conditions seem to be related to what the infants are told by their senses: whether they are hungry, physically uncomfortable, or affected by any number of stimuli in the environment. In other words, a baby's state is a sensory response (Wolff 1966).

State: a person's mental, emotional, or physical condition

Tactile sense and pain

Nine-month-old Stacey (Abigail's older cousin), given a bowl of Jello for the first time, responded this way, according to her mother, a fascinated observer of her child's development: "She watched me dip it out with a spoon. Quite willingly, she took the bite into her mouth, slowly and very quietly. Then she reached for the dish to feel the Jello. Slowly at first, she touched it. She tried to pick it up. Finally, she succeeded—then was disappointed when it dropped out of her hand."

Tactile communication   The most highly developed sense at the time of birth may be the sense of touch. A person's skin—the whole body, but in particular the lips, mouth, and other body openings—meets the environment continually. The eyes and the skin work together from the earliest weeks of life. To be aware of this interesting partnership is to be less surprised that blind people "see" with their fingers. To some extent, all of us do.

Harry Harlow's classic experiments showed the importance of touch in infant monkeys. The animals were fed not by their own mothers but by wire "mothers," each with a bottle attached. But in their cages were terry cloth "mothers" as well. To whom did they rush for comfort? To the cloth mothers, who apparently felt good to them (Harlow 1959). (See also Chapter 9). According to the researcher, tactile comfort—bodily contact and the security it represents—is the source of an infant's attachment to its care-giver, more important even than food. Love for mother, at least in the early stages, is a matter of touching and feeling. Why does a baby stop crying when picked up? One ready explanation is that it feels good.

Various studies have shown that early development does not progress normally unless a baby's sense of touch is stimulated. Just to feed an infant and keep it clean are far from enough. The act of feeding has to be accompanied by the feel of a breast or an arm and a body. If a machine could change a baby's diaper or give it a bath, it would not serve the same purpose as the mother, father, or care-giver who tends the child. Hugs and cuddling and kisses seem to be crucial to a baby's growth.

The tactile sense is also important for learning. The Montessori schools for preschoolers make extensive use of cones and pyramids to teach children form perception. Children not only see these forms but can feel them with their hands. This strategy of manipulative activity is supported by various studies. One investigation showed that three- to four-year-olds were helped to learn the differences between printed letters when given three-dimensional wooden letters to play with (Thornburg and Fisher 1970; Kraynak and Raskin 1971).

Tactile perception continues to improve in the early school years. During the period from kindergarten to third grade, children get better and better in feeling differences in texture,

A Montessori pupil blind-folded to help her develop sense of touch.

although there does not seem to be any age trend in discriminating shapes by feeling (Gliner 1967).

Pain in infancy   Do infants feel pain? Investigators studying crying and withdrawal movement determined that sensitivity to pain or discomfort is evident in earliest infancy. Some kinds of stimuli affect a baby more than others. Circumcision does not seem to cause an infant much, if any, discomfort (Merskey 1975); but a baby quickly informs a care-giver about a stomachache by crying and thrashing. Sensitivity to pain increases during the first few days after birth (Smart and Smart 1973). It is possible that as we mature we learn to feel pain, but there is not yet conclusive evidence to prove this (Merskey 1975).

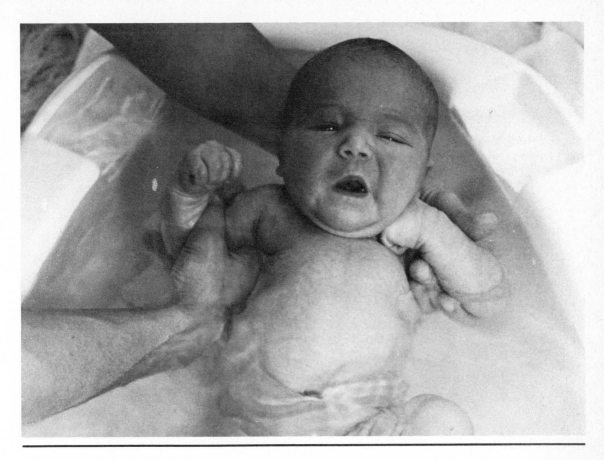

Newborns are sensitive to heat and cold.

Taste, temperature, smell

Candy eaters might feel less guilty to know that we are all born with a taste for sweets. Infant formulas rely on the fact that a baby prefers sweet things (Desor, Maller, and Turner 1973) and is less likely to accept anything salty, bitter, or sour. Babies also prefer a sweet solution to plain water (Engen, Lipsitt, and Peck 1974).

A three- to four-day-old infant can tell the difference between milk and a dextrose solution and make it clear that milk is preferred (Dubignon and Campbell 1969). Canestrini, experimenting in 1913, concluded that the sense of taste is the best developed of the infant's senses (Jensen 1932).

Nelson found that newborn babies are also sensitive to heat and cold, though they react less strongly to temperatures warmer than their bodies than they do to colder temperatures (Jensen 1932). As for the sense of smell, infants can definitely discriminate one smell from another. It has been shown that even one- to three-day-old infants react to various odors, like anise oil and spices. But they can also become habituated to a smell and stop paying attention to it. The study tested attention by measuring changes in breathing (Engen and Lipsitt 1965). One of the few investigators in the field of smell has discovered that this sense is vulnerable to allergy and can be lost after the flu or a bad cold or a blow to the head, as well as a result of more serious illnesses (Henkin 1976).

Special Influences

Abigail's mother excels at putting together toys that come disassembled. Her sense of spatial relationships is superior. But the baby's father is upset even before the box is opened; he has an unfortunate record for putting the pieces in the wrong slots.

These two people illustrate the fact that we are not all exactly alike in our ability to use our senses. Even though the general course of development appears to be the same for all normal people, we all seem to be at different levels in our ability to use each of the perceptual skills needed for daily life. Form perception, *spatial visualization*, auditory discrimination, sensitivity to pain, even whether we have an extra-strong taste for sweets—all these (and all other perceptual abilities and sensitivities) seem to vary from one person to another.

Spatial visualization: forming a mental picture of an object in space

The natural question is: why the differences? Is it a matter of intelligence, heredity, sex, environment, some developmental accident or flaw? Research does not have all the answers yet, but there is evidence that all these influences sometimes play a part.

Effects of heredity

If Abigail, at birth, were removed to a different family, would she nevertheless have a chance of being as visually acute as her parents, and thus as accomplished as they are in arithmetic and spelling?

Twin studies In one study, those ideal research subjects—twins, both identical and fraternal—were given a battery of standardized tests designed to study their spatial ability, which is important in reading, arithmetic, science, and many professions. The twins' ages ranged from 12 to 20. All were students in public and private high schools in Kentucky and Indiana. By comparing results for identical twins with results for fraternal twins, investigators found that there is a hereditary component in perception of form and perspective. The identical twins, who have the same heredity, had a higher correlation in this kind of perception than the fraternal twins, whose genes are different. But there is a smaller correlation in tests that require ability to move objects around in one's mind. The conclusion was that different perceptual abilities are influenced to different degrees by heredity. Heredity may play a role in the ability to perceive form and perspective, but it is less influential in the ability to visualize objects in space (Vandenberg 1969).

Sex differences For a society rightly concerned with the question of the *real* differences between girls and boys, men and women, researchers have so far provided only a few studies on the perceptual and sensory abilities of males versus females.

There is some evidence that boys are better at perceptual organization and spatial visualization than girls. Third- and fourth-grade boys and girls were asked to copy patterns, first by drawing and then by "walking" the patterns. They had to do this in three different places: in a large empty school cafeteria, on a nine-foot-square linoleum mat, and in a nine-foot-square sandbox. Significant sex differences emerged, reflecting different styles of perceptual organization. The boys were better at the task, especially when more visual cues (like edges) were available to both sexes. It appeared that boys paid more attention to those cues (Keogh 1971). However, it is important to question whether environmental influences were not already at work in this group of subjects.

Some sensory differences between the sexes do appear to be present at birth. Tests of newborns with different feeding formulas established that females are more responsive to sweets than males (Nisbett and Gurwitz 1970). The same study reported that boys are more willing to "work" for their formula when sucking is made more difficult. Also, newborn girls seem to have greater sensitivity to pain than do newborn boys, another finding that may give some support to the notion of innate differences (Lipsitt and Levy 1959). It is unlikely that sex-role learning would have played much, if any, part in any of these findings.

Environmental deprivation

How well would a privileged child like Abigail do if she were brought up in a deprived environment? Investigators have made a number of attempts to measure the effects of deprivation, both material and spiritual, on the development of the senses. The findings suggest that harm is possible. Still, not enough studies have been done so far to conclude without a shadow of a doubt that disadvantaged children are permanently damaged.

Low socioeconomic level Adolescents from lower-income homes seem to demonstrate less selective hearing attention than their middle-income counterparts, possibly because of lack of practice. One study showed that low-economic-level high school graduates were poorer in their ability to distinguish certain sounds in a standard hearing test, even though they had no actual hearing loss. The subjects were 226 recent high school graduates selected for a federal hearing evaluation project. The criteria for selection were strong intellectual potential for academic achievement in college and a culturally and economically limited background. The investigators speculate that these young people were brought up in homes where there was a great deal of noise, which interfered with the opportunity to practice selective attention (Goldman and Sanders 1969).

Similarly, auditory and language discrimination are poorer for children coming from poor homes than for middle-class children. Children from homes where a second language is spoken also have difficulty in this area. One study indicated that children from a Mexican-American background with low socioeconomic status were worse in language listening discrimination than poor Anglo-American children who spoke only one language (Arnold and Wist 1970). Perhaps the children from homes where English was a second language were confused by hearing one tongue at home and another in school. They had problems of auditory discrimination of English word sounds because of insufficient exposure to English. (See Chapter 6 for a fuller discussion of language development.)

Institutionalization One of the severest sensory deprivations is to be deprived of a home—a real home—with a mother or father (or somebody who acts like a parent). A child's psychological development relies on adequate sensory stimulation and environmental support. A baby born blind but brought up in a normal household, hearing the normal sounds and being nurtured in

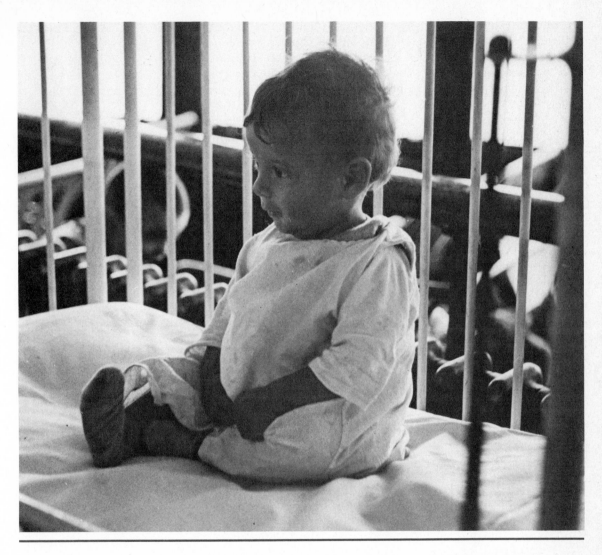

Institutionalized infants get little or no sensory stimulation.

a normal fashion, and also allowed to move around like any other baby, will probably develop a personality much like that of a person who has normal vision. In contrast, institutionalized infants and others who get little or no sensory stimulation in their early months grow up with psychological and personality abnormalities.

Doctors are beginning to realize that there may be psychological danger in the customary isolation of underweight, premature babies. One experiment provided prematures with various stimuli—toy birds hanging in isolettes (incubators), handling, exposure to faces and voices. These babies showed more "looking" behavior than preemies who received no such stimulation. The "advantaged" preemies looked at the faces of the nurses who fed them. They reacted like normal babies to handling and to voices, both of which could quiet them when they cried. These low-birth-weight infants, who were further handicapped because they came from poor homes, were given special help not only in the hospital nursery but throughout their first year. The mothers were regularly visited at home by social workers who taught them how to give the children various kinds of sensorimotor stimulation. The program paid off both biologically and socially as these babies were able to overcome their early deficits (Scarr-Salapatek and Williams 1973).

We have already seen that infants who are visually stimulated beginning at five weeks of age acquire a blink response earlier than children who have no such stimulation (Greenberg, Uzgiris, and Hunt 1968). Perhaps this is more evidence of the way development is affected by early deprivation. However, research in this area is still inconclusive. This does not mean that what we know so far is unimportant. It is certainly vital to realize that from the very beginning of life, none of us can be considered a passive organism.

Summary

Perception—the ability to organize and interpret sensory experiences into meaningful events—is based on the use of all the senses: vision, hearing, taste, touch, and smell. All are innate. But both maturation and learning are necessary for full development of perceptual ability.

Although perception is developmental, the various senses do not develop at the same rate. At first, perception is global: the whole event is considered. Later perception becomes differentiated, and parts are perceived. Eventually, time and experience provide the ability to perceive both parts and the whole.

Vision is the most complex sense and the dominant mode for receiving information. Newborns perceive form, color, and changes in illumination and are aware of persons and objects. Even very young babies can use their visual ability to pursue personal objectives. Infants are attracted to pattern, and this is the basis for the later ability to accumulate knowledge. They also seem to be born with an attraction to complexity and form. Babies like color and contrast, too, but can become habituated to visual stimuli presented too often.

A sense of three-dimensionality is apparent by two to three months of age. By about six months, infants are aware of depth and seem to be wary of the danger of a drop (as demonstrated by experiments with a "visual cliff"). But outright fear does not appear until nine months.

Infants react most to the human face, which has crucial significance to an infant's welfare, and they are aware of the moods they see in faces. By six to eight months, most babies recognize faces to which they have been frequently exposed. A strange face may provoke anxiety.

Developmental factors limit reading readiness before the age of six or seven, but early stimulation may increase visual skills somewhat. Three-and-a-half appears to be the earliest age at which a child can make accurate judgments about differences in form, a skill that is necessary for dealing with symbols. Part–whole perception develops slowly through the school years.

At birth, human infants hear and can discriminate sounds. Some sounds are more soothing than others. Spatial localization of sound begins to appear at about one month and becomes progressively refined. Listening accuracy is developmental up to about nine years, when it becomes stable. Selective attention is a result of both development and experience with language.

Sense of time and need to sleep are innate. Sleeping time may also be the result of innate body rhythm. Sleep can be brought on by steady continuing stimulation, which has a pacifying effect on infants.

The sense of touch may be the most highly developed sense at birth, so bodily contact is important. Early development depends partly on touch stimulation by a care-giver. The sense of touch also works with the visual sense to promote learning. Tactile perception improves through the early school years.

Sensitivity to pain, minimal at birth, increases early. The senses of smell and taste appear to be innate.

Perceptual ability varies among individuals, and differences may exist between the sexes, perhaps due to heredity. But environmental factors, such as lack of stimulation or overstimulation, may create individual differences too. Nurturing by a care-giver is necessary for the full development of perceptual ability.

Chronological Overview

Newborn   perceives form, changes in illumination, and color

unable to fixate on an object for any length of time

hears and discriminates among sounds

sense of time and rhythm

sense of touch; feels pain

sense of taste temperature, and smell

Infancy

1st week: makes visual connection between hands and mouth

increased visual attentiveness

tracks objects and individuals

1–6 months: attracted to contrast, contour, and three-dimensional forms

attentive to faces

turns in direction of a sound

visual acuity almost like adult's

depth perception

7–12 months: fear of depth that appears dangerous

recognizes familiar faces

strange sounds evoke anxiety

Preschool

3½ years: discriminates letters but not sensitive to orientation

4–6 years: learns orientation of letters

first signs of reading readiness

Childhood

6–8 years: perceives picture either in parts or whole, not both

8–9 years: perceives both parts and whole

Applying Your Knowledge

1. What kinds of environmental stimulation could parents provide to facilitate perceptual development in their infants?
2. Suggest methods of helping to distinguish the letters *b, p,* and *d* for children who are learning how to read.
3. How could habituation confuse the results of a research project intended to measure visual discrimination by length of looking time?

Further Readings

Bower, T. G. R. *Development in infancy.* San Francisco: W. H. Freeman, 1974. A technical but fascinating account of research on infant perception.
Paperback.

Brazelton, T. Berry, M.D. *Infants and mothers.* New York: Dell, 1969. A month-by-month description of development during the first year. A highly readable book.
Paperback.

White, Burton L. *The first three years of life.* New York: Avon, 1975. A practical guide to infant development. Includes suggestions for activities to facilitate infant perception.
Paperback.

Willemsen, Eleanor. *Understanding infancy.* San Francisco: W. H. Freeman, 1979. Contains two clearly written chapters on infant perception.
Hardbound.

Chapter 4

Physical and Motor Development

At ten weeks, to her parents' immense relief, Abigail slept through the night three nights in succession. In that brief period since her birth, she had grown from 6 to 11 pounds and attained the ability to eat morsels of solid food (although inefficiently). Her body was growing. Simultaneously, her personality was developing. She was looking at a mobile with apparent interest, tracking her mother as she passed by, "enjoying" the sound of her father's typewriter, and was noticeably happier as soon as she was held in someone's arms.

Abigail was no different from most other infants. Her physical growth and development, especially the maturation and organization of her nervous system, were obviously the basis for learning and accomplishment. Like all children, she was becoming increasingly ready for the demands of a human lifetime. *Development*—as reflected through behavior—is an interaction of the processes of physical maturation and learning.

Development: growth and behavior that reflect maturation and learning

Nature of the Maturation Process

A patterned progression

Growth and *maturation* take place in a relatively orderly and predictable sequence. Study after study has shown that a kind of inborn computer begins to operate at the moment of conception. It governs the growth and maturation of every human being throughout pre- and postnatal life. The body, site of individuality and personality, develops in a predetermined order. Consequently, many kinds of physical and motor behavior can be foreseen, and *norms*—developmental timetables—may be worked out as a descriptive guide to development.

Maturation: physical and mental growth and development, governed by heredity

For example, a baby normally will begin to suck even before birth. An infant—be it male or female, black or white or yellow—will raise its head within the first several weeks, but it will not be able to sit until four to six months later. Creeping and standing come before walking. In short, the development of the body's capacities—the maturation process—is something that happens by pattern in a certain order to all human beings who are normal.

Norms: standards or measurements of behavior or development

Maturation versus growth Is maturation the same as growth? Not exactly. Investigators who have studied maturation and growth draw a clear distinction between the two processes. A child grows *quantitatively:* he or she puts on pounds and adds inches. But *maturation is qualitative*, the nature of the child's

Quantitative: related to measurable portions

Qualitative: related to distinctive traits or activities

activity changes: the baby sits, then stands; the arms flail about at first, while later the baby is able to grasp an object using the fingers in a truly sophisticated way. Maturation and growth happen together, and together they provide the potential for learning.

The direction of growth   Why does turning over happen first, then sitting, then standing, then walking? The order in which humans grow is *cephalocaudal*—from head to toe. The head grows fastest, which is why the fetus is proportionately half-head, half-body. By adulthood, our heads constitute only one-seventh of our bodies. Throughout our growing, we are developing downward. Thus, an infant's earliest major physical accomplishment is the ability to support its head. Then the child is able to sit up when the trunk has grown enough to support its weight. The legs develop later, so standing comes afterward.

Cephalocaudal: head-to-toe

Development, however, is also *proximodistal*—from the center of the body outward. First the larger parts in the center of the body develop: trunk, chest, and shoulders. Later the arms, legs, fingers, and toes develop sequentially. So babies a few months old can reach with their arms toward that attractive toy, but they are not yet adept enough with their hands to pick it up, until later, at around five or six months.

Proximodistal: from the center of the body to fingertips or most distant points

These developmental principles matter to all those who are involved with children. They must know what to expect, and when, and not to look for the impossible. A baby cannot be hurried to sit or stand. The body must reach the stage when sitting or standing is maturationally possible (Shirley 1933). Nor will a teenage boy be able to sing bass until the growth spurt of adolescence has been completed. This is a sequence of events that comes at some time to every teenager, but the precise timing differs from person to person and from girl to boy (Tanner 1964). Obviously our genes are partly responsible for the differences in how we look and grow and in our eventual physical attainments.

Influence of environment and learning

Does nature's developmental timetable require us to allow children to grow up like weeds? Can we assume that genetic inheritance, maturation, and growth will take care of everything? Obviously not. Indeed, the environment (including teaching and training) determines the outer reaches of the maturational process.

Maturation depends on support from the environment. Without at least a minimally supportive environment—care, feeding, teaching of one kind or another—nobody would grow up at all. It is the environment that determines the ultimate result of the maturational process: whether a girl or boy becomes a long-distance runner or just a person with pretty good endurance. Food, instruction, and human care and concern are all crucial. The youngster is physically ready to read at around six but will not become a reader until taught by somebody. Future Olympic champions develop the potential for greatness as they grow from childhood to adolescence, but they will never grasp the gold medal unless they are rigorously trained.

The secular trend Better training alone is certainly not responsible for the feats of today's athletes—all the shattered Olympic records. There is strong evidence that other influences are at work, notably the so-called *secular trend*, patterns of evolutionary growth. The secular trend is related to both heredity *and* environment. All over the world, children's physical growth has been faster and greater than it used to be. Physical maturity has come earlier. Nearly all of us are taller and heavier than our ancestors. Although the secular trend is now leveling off, Abigail may yet grow up to be a bigger woman than her mother, may begin to menstruate earlier, and may attain her full height at a younger age than her parents and grandparents. (See Box 4–1.)

Secular trend: patterns of evolutionary growth related to heredity and environment

The consensus appears to be that improved nutrition is among the important environmental causes of the secular trend. The secular trend seems to stop, and may even be reversed during hard times when food is scarce or unemployment widespread (Tanner 1968).

Better health care may also contribute to the trend. Decline in family size is another possible factor. Children from smaller families tend to be bigger and to mature earlier than children from large families. Other positive environmental elements are better housing and a generally higher standard of living.

There may also be an environmental basis for a suggested genetic cause of the secular trend. Improved means of transportation, starting early in the nineteenth century, made it possible for people to seek mates far from home. This outbreeding and mixing of the gene pools may be related to the trend toward increased height (Tanner 1968).

Several studies show how the secular trend has operated in this country. Height statistics for North American and European boys and girls from 1905 to 1965 clearly show a rise over the years, and this seems to be true for all racial groups and in varying geographic areas (Meredith 1963; Tanner 1968). (See Figure 4–1.)

Basic studies of maturation and growth

Wide-ranging studies, some carried on over a period of many years, have provided the data that demonstrate the basic principles of physical growth and development. These investigations have taken place not only in the United States but also in other countries with different cultural and environmental conditions.

Gesell and Thompson: twin studies   Studies show that training may hasten the maturational process, but only within the limits of heredity. A classic investigation that has served as the foundation for what we know today about developmental timetables (norms) was begun by Arnold Gesell and Helen Thompson in 1929 and not

Box 4–1   Age of First Walking

Reference	Age of first walking in months	Approx. date	Nationality
Macrobius	28	400 A.D.	Roman
Federico d'Este	14	1501	Italian
James VI	60	1571	Scotch
Anne of Denmark	108	1575	Danish
Anne Clifford's child	34	1617	English
John Hamilton	14	1793	American
Augustus Hare	17	1834	English
Marianne Gaskell	22	1836	English
H. Taine's son	16	1860	French
Tricksy du Maurier	12	1865	English
W. Preyer's son	15	1880	German
Franklin Roosevelt	15	1884	American
G. Dearborn's daughter	15	1900	American
Amer. Inst. Child Life	12–17	1913	American
Univ. of Minn.–23 babies	15	1931	American

Source: Lloyd DeMause, The evolution of childhood: a symposium, *History of Childhood Quarterly,* 1974, *1*(4), p. 552;

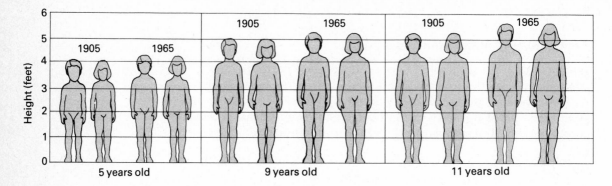

FIG. 4-1 Height over the years. In 1965, five-year-old boys and girls from average economic circumstances were two inches taller than children 50 years ago. Nine-year-olds were about three inches taller. Eleven-year-olds were four inches taller. Measurements were made in the United States and Europe. *Source:* J. M. Tanner, Earlier maturation in man, *Scientific American,* 1968, *218* (1), 21.

completed until more than a decade later. Two girls, identical twins (and thus with identical heredity), were followed from the time they were a few weeks old until they were 13.

When the twins were ten months old, the investigators undertook to teach them to climb stairs. But one was given more training than the other, and somewhat earlier. So at one year of age, the trained twin knew how to climb stairs while the other did not. But then training began for the second twin. Four weeks later, both twins were almost exactly equal in speed and agility in stair climbing (Gesell and Thompson 1929). Retesting at intervals during the next couple of years showed occasional fluctuations in ability between the two; but by the age of three, the speed and timing of both girls were virtually the same. This experiment, and others with the same pair of twins, demonstrated that, in general, the internal developmental clock cannot be made to run faster over the long term, regardless of attempts by parents or teachers to push it ahead by training.

Gesell and his associates, who were responsible for the basic work on maturation, done at their Institute for Behavioral Research at Yale, also established norms for *what* happens *when* in a child's development. This timetable, elaborated by other investigators, is still a bible for parents anxious to know whether their children's growth is "on schedule." The norms are also a valuable guideline for teachers, pediatricians, and curriculum planners, who must be aware of the probable capacities of children at various ages.

Hungarian, Israeli, and American studies   Research has established that the maturational sequence is the same for all children, irrespective of ethnic and cultural differences and specific learning experiences. In a notable investigation of the motor development of 736 normal children raised in an institution in Budapest, Hungary, the children were all given total freedom to develop their motor abilities but were not taught or helped in any way. The norms of maturation were clearly demonstrated: they all turned from back to side, sat up, crept, kneeled, and walked in the same order and at roughly the same ages (Pikler 1968).

Still another investigator tested 361 Israeli infants, some reared in kibbutzim (communities where children are brought up collectively), some in institutions, and some in middle-class homes. Eye-hand coordination, manipulative ability, and walking developed in the same sequence in all three groups, and the progression matched the development of American babies, in spite of differences in culture, style of care, and diet (Kohen-Raz 1968).

Within the United States, motor behavior was tested in 12 different metropolitan areas, with about 1500 infants aged 1 to 15 months. They all matured in the same sequence, regardless of sex, race, birth order, geographic location, or parental background (Bayley 1965).

These and other studies demonstrate that maturation—the internal clock—determines the sequence of human motor and physical development, and that the same sequence applies to all humans, no matter where they live or who their parents are. When, as a developing infant, Abigail turned herself from stomach to back at four-and-a-half months, her parents were delighted by the accomplishment. Seeing the baby struggle to do it again, her mother was tempted to help her. But the aid was unnecessary. The time simply had come for Abigail to be able to turn over, just as the time will come when she is able to learn to ride a bicycle. Everywhere else on earth, babies turn over at approximately the same age.

The word *approximately* is important. While developmental and maturational achievements happen in a universal sequence, the precise ages at which they occur differ with each individual. To say that children begin to walk at a year is to give an average. Some are early walkers, some are late. But almost all have walked *after* they sat, and all have rolled over *before* they sat. In normal children, the sequence of developmental stages does not vary very much.

Norms

Observing a baby's growth can be more than casually interesting. How Abigail—or Stevie or Susie or Greg—changes with the passing days, weeks, months, and years may give parents important clues to abnormality or retardation or other kinds of psychological as well as physical trouble. Determining whether the child is growing according to the norms, which are now well established, and doing something about it early if the discrepancy is too great can make all the difference in the eventual outcome of an individual's life.

Significance of norms

But psychologists warn that norms must not be accepted as absolute truths. Individual differences, which are also normal, must be taken into account. Pioneer Helen Thompson wrote in 1954: "Norms are not criteria for optimal growth. They are statistics for basic comparisons. They are mathematical devices to avoid the error of generalization from isolated cases. . . . What is normal for one individual is not normal for another" (pages 296, 297).

It is essential to be aware that growth and development norms may differ from one racial group to another, from one generation to another, and from one family to another. Note, too, that a child who grasps, sits, or walks at an earlier age than most children is not necessarily going to be a more physically agile or adept adult. Conversely, those who develop more slowly will eventually grow up just the same as children whose timetable is advanced (Johnston 1964). Nor are infants who weigh more than the average necessarily retarded in sitting, standing, or walking (Peatman and Higgons 1942). With these cautions, norms can still be useful in detecting a child who is obviously out of phase in maturation and growth.

The neonate

Birth weight and APGAR score Birth weight is an important indicator of prenatal growth and development and a good predictor of future development. Birth weight considerably below five-and-a-half pounds might be an early warning sign of serious difficulties. Extensive international studies report that birth weight and *gestation period*—how long the fetus was in the womb before delivery—reflect the course of the infant's development before birth and predict the potential for physical and intellectual handicaps in the future. A variety of behavioral patterns, not only growth rate and intelligence, seem to be related to birth weight. Infants with low birth weight account for a disproportionately large number of those who have neurological and mental abnormalities (Hardy 1973).

Gestation period: length of prenatal development

A newborn's probable development, and possible problems that may require attention, can be judged by means of the APGAR score. As we saw in Chapter 2, the APGAR score is an assessment of physical and physiological development at birth. It is based on physical signs: heart rate, breathing, muscle tone, reflexes, irritability, and color. Infants rated 0–2 (on a scale of 10) have turned out to have lower mental and motor scores by the age of eight months than babies rated 7–10 (Edwards 1968; Serunian and Broman 1975). This is interesting evidence of the continuity of developmental trends, beginning even before the cradle.

Reflexes Many of the infant's first motor responses are *reflexes:* unlearned motor activity. The baby comes fully equipped from the womb with a set of spontaneous reactions to certain physical stimuli. These reactions—reflexes—are among the indices in the APGAR rating. Babies who will develop normally have these reflexes. Some of them are precursors of basic motor abilities vital to the mature individual.

Reflexes: unlearned motor responses

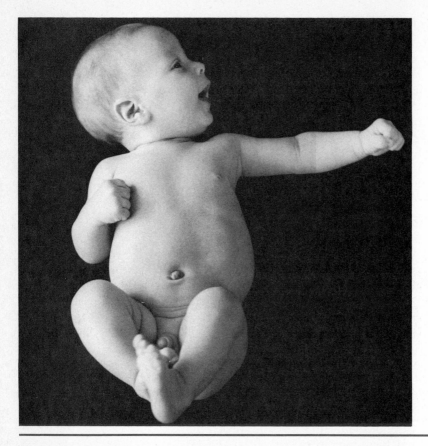

Tonic neck reflex.

Some reflexes serve a useful developmental function. Turn a newborn baby's head to left or right, and the infant will extend the arm on the side toward which the head was turned and flex the opposite arm. This is the *tonic neck reflex,* which seems to be present even before birth. It is useful in the child's primary mission—to find food—since it is a good position for breast-feeding.

The tonic neck reflex has a function for the future, too. This is the beginning of looking, a means of perceiving the possibilities in the baby's world. The same reflex "finally figures in innumerable adult acts of skill, aggression, and extrication," according to Gesell (1954, pages 353–354).

The *Moro reflex,* a startle response, is the neonate's reaction to loud noises or any other sudden strong happening. The newborn baby flings out arms and legs, may cry, and then will draw back into the customary huddled position. One study found a high correlation between children's mental and motor proficiency at four years and their Moro reflex rating at birth (Edwards 1968).

Rooting and *sucking* are related reflexes, crucial if the baby is to be nourished. Sucking has been observed even before birth (Bruner and Bruner 1968). Rooting is turning the head toward a stimulus and opening the mouth. Sucking follows. Especially when a baby is hungry, even the slightest touch will bring on the sucking reflex. In fact, there would be no infant thumb-suckers without the sucking reflex (Benjamin 1967).

Stepping and *placing* are other inborn reflexes. An infant who is tilted to one side while being moved forward makes a reflexive stepping movement. Lightly touching the bottom of the foot while a very young baby is held erect with leg extended causes the child to flex at the knee and hip, thus "placing" the leg in a semblance of walking. Normally, after three or four months, these reflexes disappear.

One group of investigators gave infants daily walking exercise. They not only succeeded in preventing the reflexes from disappearing at the usual time but also caused their subjects to walk earlier than usual (Zelazo, Zelazo, and Kolb 1972).

The *Babinski response*—when a newborn's foot is stroked in the middle of the sole, the toes come up and out—seems to have little utility, except as one of the signs that an infant is normal. The reflex disappears later in infancy. Afterwards, touching the bottom of the foot gets exactly the reverse response: the toes go down, instead of up.

The neonate's fingers also *grasp* reflexively. It has been reported that during the first few weeks an infant is able to reach out to touch an object and might even succeed in grasping it. The ability disappears by about four weeks and does not reappear until several months later. The newborn's toes will also grasp if touched at the base of the toes, an opposite response from the Babinski reflex, which comes from stimulating the sole.

Withdrawing from a painful stimulus and *blinking* the eyes in response to visual stimulation are also infant reflexes. Hold a baby horizontally, with a hand on its middle, and the child will make *swimming* movements, still another reflex. Some people have "taught" very young babies how to swim, using this reflex as a basis.

Infancy

An adult rarely stops to think about what a remarkable act of dexterity it is to pick up a fork or a pair of chopsticks to eat dinner. But that everyday act is really an important feat, founded on proximodistal development early in infancy.

Sensorimotor coordination Coordination of the senses with motor activities begins at two to three months. By that time, children are able to do something about what their sense of touch tells them (Rubenstein 1974). Eye–hand coordination, a manifestation of *sensorimotor* ability, begins to be successful. Attempts are made to grasp what is felt—a hand, a toy—although, as in Abigail's case, success may be minimal at the beginning. In the attempt to grasp a rattle at two-and-a-half months, she threw her whole body in the direction of the toy. But by three months, she succeeded in getting a firm grasp on her father's shiny wristwatch. However, her system was inefficient at best.

Sensorimotor coordination: the harmonious working together of sensory and motor responses

By the critical age of about 28 weeks, the baby has developed the four essentials for zeroing in on a target. First, it is located with the eyes; second, it is approached with the hand; next, it is grasped; and finally, the child may do any one of many things with it (probably try to put it in the mouth). The hand has replaced the forearm and body as the instrument of control. The child reaches, uses the index and middle fingers instead of sweeping with the whole "paw," and grips not with the palm but by using the essential thumb (Halverson 1931). The feat is an illustration of proximodistal development, too, showing the development of outer extremities after the development of the parts closer to the body.

Jerome Bruner (1973), a leading developmental investigator and theoretician, analyzed what happens when a baby sees an object and wants it. First, there is looking. Then mouth, tongue, and jaws move, because that is where the baby will put the object. Then the fists are clenched and the arms move, perhaps inefficiently. Eventually the object is captured. Practice, says Bruner, is crucial, but all the basic movements first emerge through physical maturation.

Observe your own infant—or someone else's. To see the grasping stages emerge on schedule is a fascinating experience. Place an attractive object in a one-month-old baby's field of vision. The infant will stare at it but make no attempt to grab it. By about two-and-a-half months, the baby will swipe at it but will be far off target. By around four months, the child will raise a hand in the general area of the object, look at hand and object alternately, gradually shorten the gap between hand and object, and may even succeed in touching it. By five to five-and-a-half

Triumph: he can stand.

months—triumph!—the baby will reach for the object and make contact on the first try (White and Held 1966).

Most parents, at least with a first child, painstakingly record another maturational sequence, the eruption of teeth. Generally, the first baby tooth arrives at six or seven months. Teeth come at various intervals after that, until by two a child generally has a mouthful—all of which, of course, will be lost later on as permanent teeth push their way through (Thompson 1954).

Developmental stages   Gesell and his co-workers (1940) recorded the stages of a baby's motor development, beginning with head control and ending with the exciting finale: walking. Here is the progression. Ages are approximate.

Sitting

At birth: little control of head movements

16 weeks: rotates head from side to side and raises it

24 weeks: supports self on extended arms, head erect

28 weeks: holds trunk erect for short time

36 weeks: holds trunk erect for considerable time; leans forward, reaches, then sits up straight again

44 weeks: sits up from a prone position or can reverse the procedure

Standing (baby held in standing posture by adult)

16 weeks: head is erect and compensates for baby sway

20 weeks: supports some body weight for just a moment

32 weeks: supports all body weight for short intervals

36 weeks: supports own weight and stays standing when held under arms, though may bend forward at the hips

40 weeks: pulls self to knees and stands holding on

48 weeks: supports weight on one foot for short time; pulls self to standing position while holding on

Walking

20 weeks: rolls over on side

28 weeks: gets into crawling position, supports upper part of body with arms

32 weeks: gets moving: crawls using arms to pivot

36 weeks: gets into creeping position

10–11 months: creeps forward on hands and knees; gets around upright, using support

10–12 months: walks alone; stands still, but with balance problems

20 months: stands on one foot with help

2 years: picks up objects, holds them, runs, walks up and down a few stairs

Walking and standing are easy by age three, graceful and even athletic by four, and by five a child can do complicated things like hopping! (See Figure 4–2.)

FIG. 4-2 Learning to sit and walk.

0 month

Fetal posture

1 month

Chin up

2 months

Chest up

3 months

Reach and miss

4 months

Sit with support

5 months

Sit on lap   Grasp object

6 months

Sit on high chair Grasp dangling object

7 months

Sit alone

8 months

Stand with help

9 months

Stand holding furniture

10 months

Creep

11 months

Walk when led

12 months

Pull to stand by furniture

13 months

Climb stairs

14 months

Stand alone

15 months

Walk alone

Toddler and preschooler

A period of rapid growth A child who is walking has not, by a long shot, become a "big girl" or a "big boy," although he or she seems like a totally different creature from the fairly helpless inhabitant of the playpen. Growth and maturation are amazingly rapid in the first 21 months (Bayley 1935). Then, between two and three years, a child grows about five inches; and three or four inches in the following year. After that, growth tapers down to two or three inches a year, until the growth spurt that is characteristic of puberty (Whipple 1966).

Motor development and body build are only slightly related. One investigator has noted that extremely stocky or extremely thin children may have a slight handicap in motor scores, and long-legged children may have a minor advantage. But, in general, body build is not an important factor in motor development (Bayley 1935). In a normal environment, gross motor skills like creeping, crawling, sitting, standing, and walking appear even when a child has no teaching whatever (Pikler 1968).

Toilet training After 24 months the child is physically ready for toilet-training. An overeager parent with an aversion to dirty diapers may sometimes try to toilet-train earlier. But in this case, the one who is being trained is really the care-giver, who learns the times when a child is apt to have a bowel movement. Ability to control the sphincter, the muscle involved in elimination, depends on maturation. Sphincter control is not normally possible for a child until about 20 months, sometimes later for boys than for girls (Sears, Maccoby, and Levin 1957; Azrin and Foxx 1974). Only after that development is toilet training truly effective. (See also Chapter 7, pages 282–283.)

Developmental norms During the preschool years, from two to five, physical prowess is impressive. At two, a child can turn the pages of a book, build a tower six or seven blocks tall, put a spoon into his or her mouth without turning it upside down, hold a glass in one hand, make a circular stroke on a page like Mommy does, and maybe put on a jacket without help. The two-year-old can run well and walk up and down stairs alone.

Test a youngster at three and notice the striking new achievements. Now the tower the child constructs is nine blocks tall, and there may be a bridge, too. The child can catch a ball with arms straight, use a spoon without spilling or only spilling a

little, and pour from a pitcher. The three-year-old can unbutton a sweater, put on shoes, copy a full circle, and draw a straight line as well. The boy or girl can walk on tiptoe now, jump down a step 12 inches high, stand on one foot, hop with both feet, and ride a tricycle.

By four a child is able to cut on a line with scissors, make designs and crude letters, and dress without aid. The girl or boy gallops, might do stunts on the tricycle, and walks down steps (short ones) like a grown-up, alternating feet.

With the five-year-old one can see that school is now a distinct possibility. Children this age are able to copy designs, letters, and numbers. They can button their clothing, fold paper into a double triangle, walk a straight line, skip, and hop on one foot.

How children use their bodies seems to be related to other aspects of behavior. A study of the activity level of identical and fraternal twins from the ages of one to four compared the more active twin with the less active one. Differences showed up at four as they had at one. The more active twin had a shorter attention span, walked earlier, but had less manual dexterity than his or her co-twin (Matheny and Brown 1971). (See also Box 4–2.)

Growth in spurts

The norms illustrate an important truth: human beings grow in spurts. Physical development takes place in uneven increments for different parts of the body. Some periods are typically slow; others are much faster.

A study of bone and muscle widths during the childhood years reveals a rapid increase in infancy and a slower growth rate during childhood. Then follows an accelerated increase during adolescence, known as the adolescent growth spurt. Thus, not only is growth uneven, but it is often unpredictable. The chubby infant may turn out to be a thin adult, and vice versa. Usually there is very little relationship between childhood and adolescent physical configurations (Maresh 1966). The best measurement of

Box 4–2 Checking Learning Readiness by Testing Motor Skills

Teachers have discovered that their young pupils' readiness to learn has a close connection with basic physical and motor skills. Some primary grade teachers use the Davies Perceptual–Motor Profile Test, designed for ages four to seven, to discover their pupils' weaknesses in this area.

Balance is tested by having the child slowly walk a balance beam, watching a target ahead. The child is also asked to stand on one foot for two seconds and to hop in place with arms relaxed.

Upper–lower coordination is assessed by having the pupil jump forward into a series of boxes, taking off and landing with both feet. A related test is to jump or hop along a path, landing on designated spots.

Visual–motor coordination is rated by having the child watch a bean bag and grab it when it is dropped. The children are also asked to imitate a series of arm movements done by the teacher. Another test of visual skill is having the child follow a moving target with his or her eyes.

Auditory–motor coordination is checked by the ability to follow instructions quickly, such as putting hands on head or ears and lying down face up. Teachers find out if the child can carry out instructions relating to moving different parts of the body in a particular fashion.

All these motor and perceptual abilities, it is now known, contribute to some of the differences between an able learner and a child who cannot keep up with the class. Usually, training can remedy deficiencies.

physical maturity in a child is skeletal age. Using X-ray, hand–
wrist–bone development is compared with the average for each
sex at various chronological ages (Eichorn 1968).

The rate at which an individual matures often has social and
psychological consequences. The child who matures earlier than
average is apt to be not only an earlier walker but also an earlier
reader. He or she may also be seen by peers as "strong" and as a
"leader." Thus, the early bloomer has a social advantage over the
other children (Garn 1966). To have a head start gives a person
feelings of self-confidence and thereby improves his or her ability

to deal with social relationships. In contrast, below-par physical growth, seen in schoolboys studied over a ten-year period, was related to continually poor scholastic achievement (Hopwood and Van Iden 1965). Maturational differences between males and females may be especially fateful. But all individual differences may be psychologically meaningful, and investigators have tried to find out why and how they happen.

Individual Differences

To a casual friend of the family (and a non-baby-lover), three-month-old Abigail looked pretty much like any other baby— somewhat plump and given to gurgling and cooing. Not so to her nearest and dearest. Claimed resemblances to her mother at the age of three months, and to her father at the same age, were the subject of serious family debate. Close relatives know that each baby is unique, and yet delightfully like half a dozen other family members.

Genetic influence

Twins' similarity   That there are genuine genetic influences on physical and motor development is borne out by many investigations. Studies of twins provide evidence of the role heredity plays in the maturation process. They show how the genes cause differences and also, in some cases, similarities in the body development of individuals.

* Pioneer developmental psychologist Arnold Gesell provided a particularly striking example of the genetic controls of development in his famous study of identical twin girls (Gesell and Thompson 1929). He and his collaborator made a photographic record of the twins' every gesture when they were offered cubes and pellets. This was done at various intervals in the twins' first year of life. Their reactions were uncannily alike. The way they used their hands and fingers progressed according to an identical pattern. Some 612 comparative ratings of behavioral items were made. No less than 513 were identical or nearly so.

This "overwhelming parity of behavior patterns," says Gesell, proves the existence of a maturational schedule that is genetically determined. "How," he asks rhetorically, "can the environment, even of twins, accomplish such architectonic [structural] miracles?" (page 26).

Physical features and growth   Other studies also show the importance of genetic factors in individuals' maturational schedules. Eventual body weight has been demonstrated to be under genetic control (Bakwin 1973). Identical twins, it has been established, are more similar in birth weight than fraternal twins of the same sex. (Yet the first-born identical twin usually weighs more, and the heavier twin is more likely to be heavier when he or she is 6 to 12 years old. This indicates that some environmental influences are also at work, since the heredity of the twins is the same.) There is a demonstrated relationship between the height of parents and the length of an infant. Short parents will have short children; tall parents will have tall children (Wingerd 1970).

The shape of a person's body may be even more under genetic control than its size. Identical twins are apt to be shaped so much the same that it could be impossible to tell one baby from the other, except that one may be slightly larger than the other.

Further evidence of the relationship between heredity and body shape comes from a study of Japanese children reared in California. The American-born children grew larger than those initially brought up on the poorer diet of Japan, which shows the effects of environment on growth. Nevertheless, there was no change in the characteristic Japanese facial and trunk–limb proportions, which seem to be genetically determined (Tanner 1973).

Still another twin investigation revealed that identical twins resembled one another more than fraternal twins in physiological traits, such as blood pressure, heart rate, pulse, and respiration rate. Even in the functioning of the autonomic nervous system there appears to be genetic influence, though there are other influences too (Jost and Sontag 1944).

Motor abilities and activity level   Motor abilities and activity level seem to be under genetic control. Identical twins are strikingly alike in motor development. When they were tested repeatedly on a standard scale, the motor performance of each twin varied no more, from one to the other, than if the same child had done the same test more than once (Wilson and Harpring 1972). Fraternal twins, in contrast, showed distinct motor differences.

Likewise, overactivity in a youngster may be the result of genes, rather than a consequence of what the mother and father have "done to the child." Joy, pregnant with twins, identified the one "on top" as by far the more vigorous kicker. During the infancy of her fraternal twins, Erik, the "bottom" twin and first-born, turned out to be a placid baby, while Heather, active in the uterus, continued to be more easily agitated and harder to deal with. Since twins share the same intrauterine environment, the difference is more likely genetic than environmental.

A recent study supports Joy's experience. The activity levels of identical and fraternal twins were rated by their parents. The children were observed at play, doing homework, watching TV, wiggling, talking, handling objects, and sleeping. General restlessness was also rated. The activity level of the identical twins was highly correlated; but the fraternals were no more alike than any other brothers and sisters (Willerman 1973).

The study suggests that conscientious parents should feel less guilt-ridden about somehow being the sole cause of some kinds of childish misbehavior. Children, in some respects, do indeed often seem to have been "born that way." (See also Box 4–3.)

Box 4–3   The Consequences of Being a Lefty

Preliminary findings by Theodore Blau, a psychologist who tested hundreds of children in a private outpatient clinic, suggest that the psychological development of left-handed children may be different from that of children who are right-handed (Schaar 1974).

Lefties seem to be more likely to have behavioral difficulties before the age of five. They may have more preschool and first-grade behavior and adjustment problems. Their intellectual performance appears to be more variable, and they may be less likely to live up to their potential. Bedwetting may continue for a long-time. Often more imaginative and creative, lefties also may exhibit more socially unacceptable behavior.

Blau thinks "mixed cerebral dominance" has something to do with the traits he found in lefties. While all people are influenced by both lobes of the brain, right-handed people are dominated, more than lefties, by the left hemisphere. The left hemisphere determines analytic, logical thinking. The right hemisphere is mostly responsible for creativity, imagination, and artistic and musical ability.

Some lefties are converted to right-handedness by their parents or their school. Possibly the traits Blau found are related to this environmental influence. He did discover that both lefties, and those righties who had "mixed dominance," possibly as a result of being converted, all demonstrated the behavioral traits he outlined as being typical of lefties.

Sex differences

Perhaps it is too obvious to put into words—but one of the most important determinants of human development depends on the simple fact that there are two sexes. They develop not only in different ways but also according to different calendars. Size and shape and physical capabilities of males and females are different. And, of course, males and females have separate though complementary reproductive development, which makes for enormous differences in their respective psychological development. What may not be so obvious is that a great many of these developmental differences are apparent from the day of birth (or even before).

Developmental patterns   Girls develop earlier than boys. This is a documented difference that continues throughout the developmental years. Other developmental motor differences between males and females can be easily cataloged.

To begin with, infant mortality rates are higher for males than for females. Although boys are larger, heavier, and more active than girls at birth (Thompson 1954; Knop 1946), girls' bone structure matures faster than boys' (Acheson 1966; Tanner 1964).

As early as 20 weeks after conception, male development (qualitatively) is two weeks behind female development. Newborn boys are four weeks behind girls' development at birth, two to three years behind in reaching puberty (Eichorn 1968). This is probably why girls tend to walk earlier than boys.

Boys are generally larger than girls in bone and muscle widths (Maresh 1966), but girls tend to be fatter (Garn 1966). Boys are usually taller than girls, except during the period between ages 11 and 14, when girls are taller. Boys are also heavier than girls, except during the years before *puberty* (Horrocks 1954). Between the ages of 10 and 14, girls seem to grow more than in other periods. Boys grow the most between 12 and 16 (Maresh 1966).

Puberty: period when reproductive organs first become functional, till onset of adulthood

Motor performance   Notable differences between the sexes appear in motor performance too; some of the causes may be cultural and/or genetic. Preschool girls are superior to boys in manual dexterity; but boys are superior in large-muscle coordination. Is this a genuine physiological difference or a culturally induced condition? Another possible cultural difference is boys' superiority over girls in activities involving strength and endurance, such as kicking, running, and throwing (Govatos 1959). Perhaps males excel in these areas because that is what they are trained to do.

It is during adolescence that differences in physical strength between men and women first appear. Motor performance improves until ages 17 through 18 for boys, but only until 15 for girls. Again, the cause may be partly physiological, but there are undoubtedly sociological aspects. This is the age when many girls are turning to more sedentary pursuits (Horrocks 1954).

Norms All these differences between the sexes are reflected in the year-by-year developmental norms described by Gesell and his associates (Gesell, Ilg, and Ames 1956). The most notable distinctions begin at about the age of ten. Though boys and girls are about the same height at that age, many girls are just beginning to mature sexually. Nipples begin to project, a small amount of pubic hair is visible, and bodily form and features are beginning to round and soften.

At age 11, generalizations about girls' growth are no longer possible. Some girls are still childish; others are already beginning to look like women. The average girl has now reached nine-tenths of her eventual height.

Boys this age are much more alike. Few have begun the adolescent growth spurt. The average 11-year-old boy is 80% as tall as he will be as an adult. This may be a "fat period" for some boys, which will probably end around age 14. Many boys do increase in bone structure now, especially in the chest area.

At 12 years old, an average girl is experiencing the fastest increase in height and weight: height first, weight a little later. She will achieve her greatest strength gain around 12½, a full two years before the average boy. It is at this period that sex-related changes appear.

Sexual development

It would be impossible to separate general physical development from sexual development once adolescence begins. Human sexuality is as much a part of physical development as are bones and fat, muscles and nerves. In fact, sexual influence begins at the instant of conception; sexual characteristics begin to develop from that moment on.

Adolescent changes Girls tend to mature before boys. By age 12 or 13 many girls begin to menstruate; also their breasts fill out and their nipples darken. Twelve-year-old boys have begun to be very different among themselves, more so than ever before. Some are maturing fast, some hardly at all. Different parts of a boy's body may show different stages of maturity. For instance, genitals may seem to be developing, but other physical parts may look the same as they did the previous year.

By 13, some girls may be slowing down. Most are filling out, and more are reaching *menarche*—the first *menstruation*—marking the beginning of the reproductive cycle. During the same year, boys are beginning to catch up. Most are acquiring pubic hair and experiencing rapid genital growth. Voices are beginning to change. By the end of the year, about half have reached the fastest rate of height growth and will have their first *seminal emission*—involuntary release of sperm.

Many girls have become womanly in appearance by age 14. They have nearly reached adult stature, their breasts and pubic hair are mature, and their overall features are stronger and better defined. In contrast, boys at 14 are usually still in transition. Most boys experience their most rapid height growth between the ages of 13½ and 15. Their muscles also become heavier. Sexual characteristics are developing: their faces are looking stronger, they have more body hair, they perspire much more, most have experienced *ejaculation*, and their voices are definitely deeper.

Girls of 15 are usually completing their development, while boys are looking increasingly manlike. The average boy of 15 has reached about 95% of his eventual size; his strength is increasing. Sexual features are nearly mature. His head and face look smaller, compared to his new filled-out size, and he has a prominent Adam's apple.

At 16, girls appear not much different from the previous year, although some continue to grow. Physiologically, they are close to the young adult. As for boys, some 16-year-olds are still adding many inches, but most have reached 98% of adult size. Their bodies are now firmer, more "put together." Some are shaving regularly.

Adolescence is thus characterized by a growth spurt that is unique for each individual. Development comes in fits and starts, although the whole period is a spurt compared to the growth that has preceded it in childhood. Typically, growth first accelerates six months before puberty (Horrocks 1954), with girls usually in the lead. Thus, girls are developmentally older than their male classmates for several difficult years.

Boys reach puberty between the ages of 10 and 18. Some are finished with pubertal growth by 16, others not until 20 or 21

Menarche: first menstruation
Menstruation: discharge of blood and uterine material in monthly cycles

Seminal emission: involuntary release of sperm, usually during sleep

Ejaculation: release of sperm, usually in intercourse or masturbation

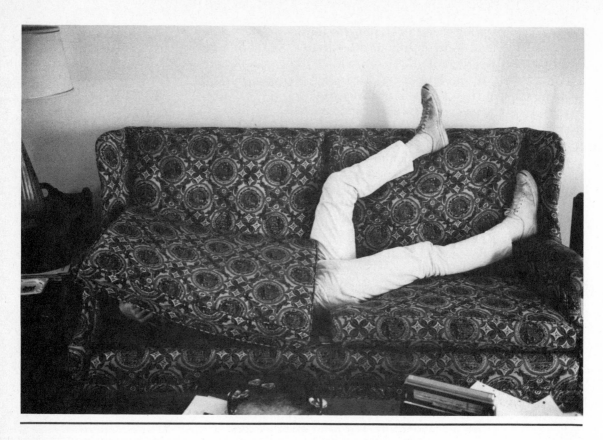

Privacy.

(Schonfeld 1943). During the senior high school years, students of the same age have a range of at least six years in maturational age (Eichorn 1968).

Adolescent problems These differences in adolescent growth rates—among girls, among boys, and between the sexes—almost inevitably lead to difficulties for individuals. And therein, some psychologists believe, lie the seeds of many adult problems.

Many seventh-grade girls are daydreaming about dancing and dating, and some are becoming sexually active. At the same time, the boys who are their contemporaries are apt to be thinking about baseball or soccer. However, not a few seventh-grade girls are still preoccupied with doll collections, while some seventh-grade boys may be perplexed by "wet dreams" or may already be experimenting with sexual intercourse. Thus, youngsters who are in school together and are the same chronological age may be experiencing widely differing biologically based urges.

Many girls and boys have adjustment problems because social and cultural standards presume equal development and conformity. Peers, parents, teachers, and society as a whole unrealistically expect everyone the same age to have similar interests, to look basically the same, and to do the same things in the same fashion (Dwyer and Mayer 1968–69). Therefore, personality and self-esteem are affected by whether a boy matures early or late: either way, he sees himself as "different" from others (Mussen and Jones 1957).

Boys who mature earlier than average appear poised and responsible and seem to lack neurotic symptoms. Their picture of themselves is good. They become the class leaders. In their school yearbooks they are apt to be tagged "most likely to succeed."

An investigation of a group of boys who were followed from adolescence to maturity showed that, by age 33, the physical differences between the late and early maturers were no longer evident. But the psychological effects remained. The early maturers still scored well in "good impression" and "socialization." Some had made "exceptional progress" in their vocations. As for the later maturers, they were still looking for attention, and some were still vocationally unsettled (Jones 1957).

The culture—TV, movies, magazines, peers, parents—compounds adolescent difficulties by laying down an "ideal" feminine or masculine physique that few young people can live up to. One study confirmed that the chief areas of youngsters' dissatisfaction are their height, their weight, and their physique (Clifford 1971). During adolescence, boys and girls are constantly concerned with their physical appearance (Cobb 1954) and their complexion (Frazier and Lisonbee 1950).

Girls are more concerned about being overweight; boys are more worried about being thin. Height is a problem to tall girls and short boys (Frazier and Lisonbee 1950).

Menstruation   A particular problem for girls is the age at which they "get their period." Some fear it may never happen. Others, young at menarche, are terrified, embarrassed, and miserable at being different. In any case, menstruation is usually viewed with at least a degree of distaste.

A questionnaire study of 54 young adolescent girls (both pre- and postmenarcheal) and boys of the same age revealed that all had acquired definite and mostly negative ideas about menstruation, its symptoms, and its effects on daily activities. And their experiences conformed to those expectations. The investigators suggest that the responses reflect cultural stereotypes. Evidently, at least some girls approach physiological maturity with a clear set of unpleasant expectations. And some boys share those opinions. So the negative experience of menstruation could be a self-fulfilling prophecy (Clarke and Ruble 1978).

Effects of the secular trend   Another potential source of problems for adolescents and their parents is the secular trend (see p. 122). Young people are starting the adolescent growth spurt sooner than the previous generation and are reaching sexual maturity earlier (Horrocks 1954). Contrast the average age for the onset of menstruation now—12½—with 17, the average age a century ago (Maddock 1973). (See Figure 4–3.) Also, both sexes are reaching adult height and sexual maturity earlier than ever before, and their eventual size is apt to be greater than that of their mothers and fathers. According to one estimate, an American boy may well be an inch taller and ten pounds heavier than his father. An average girl is a half-inch to one inch taller and two pounds heavier than her mother, and she will begin to menstruate almost a year earlier (Muuss 1970).

The result is that young people are ready at a younger age than the previous generation for sexual give-and-take, but their parents may not be willing to concede their readiness.

Concerning the additional social and psychological implications of sexuality in adolescence, and the attendant problems, more will be said in Chapter 10. But it is important to note here that while there are certainly cultural aspects, a basic source of these problems is physiological.

Special Influences on Physical Development

Fateful as the universal developmental clock may be to each of us, whose bodies mature according to its ticking, other influences also have lasting developmental consequences. These influences include our race and ethnic background, the environment in which we are reared, and poverty or other kinds of deprivation.

Racial and ethnic influences

Racial and ethnic differences are not discussed lightly in our egalitarian society. Nevertheless, the statistics demonstrate that

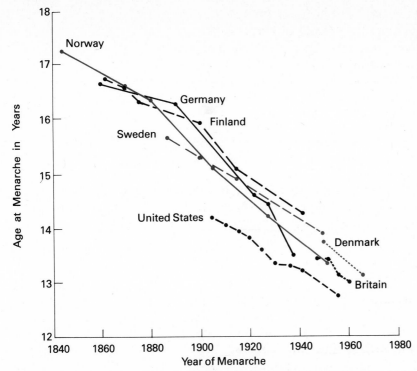

FIG. 4–3 Age of menarche. Girls now begin menstruating 2½ to 3½ years earlier, on the average, than they did 100 years ago. *Source:* J. M. Tanner, Earlier maturation in man, *Scientific American,* 1968, *218* (1), 26.

the extent of physical and motor development differs somewhat among the various races, although the maturational timetable is universal. Some of the differences may be caused by cultural factors; others appear to be biological.

Motor superiority of blacks The motor skills of black people tend to be superior to those of whites. As early as 12 weeks of age, black infants surpass white infants in motor development (Walters 1967).

One investigator administered tests of mental and motor development to 1409 infants, aged 1 to 15 months, in 12 metropolitan areas. The babies were drawn mostly from hospital well-baby clinics, but their parents' education (and probably their socioeconomic status) was about the same as for the American population as a whole. Black and white children scored the same in the mental tests, but the black children were consistently superior to the whites on the motor tests (Bayley 1965).

Black babies weigh less at birth than white babies, but they gain weight faster (Shaw, Wheeler, and Morgan 1970). There is even evidence of racial difference in skeletal growth as well as differences in adult body build. Black babies in America surpass white norms in sitting up, crawling, and vocalizing, and their permanent teeth come a year earlier. All these differences seem to be genetic (Tanner 1961).

Variations worldwide Cross-cultural studies also demonstrate differences in body size of children in different parts of the world (Meredith 1968), even under similar nutritional conditions (Meredith 1970).

These biologically ordained differences may seem impressive, but there is equally impressive evidence that other influences, environmental in nature, can also have consequences in terms of an individual's physical and motor development.

Environmental influences

Within genetic limits, it seems to be within the control of parents, teachers, and society at large to benefit (or harm) children's physical and motor development. We have already noted at length that the intrauterine environment provided by a mother has a great deal to do with the health, well-being, and normal development of her baby (see Chapter 2). Environmental influence continues after birth, with demonstrated effects on motor development. An enriched environment that provides loving, handling, stimulation, and good nutrition is essential if a child is to realize its fullest physical and motor potential. Early training is also effective in promoting some motor skills.

Aiding the premature If they are handled by caring people, instead of being totally isolated in their aseptic hospital cribs, premature infants gain weight faster, are healthier, grow better, and have better motor coordination (Solkoff et al. 1969). Handling preemies, talking to them, using mobiles, rocking—any sort of positive stimulation—will result in better sensorimotor and motor development (Cornell and Gottfried 1976). (See also Chapter 2, pages 72–73.)

That food is not the only requirement of babies is demonstrated by an experiment involving 30 infants with low birth weight, born to disadvantaged mothers. Half the babies were included in an experimental program during their first year of life. They were given visual, tactile, and kinesthetic stimulation dur-

ing six weeks in the hospital nursery. Afterward, their homes were visited every week to teach the mothers or care-givers ways of stimulating their infants. Tests at four weeks and intelligence scores when the babies were a year old showed that the experimental group, compared with the 15 who had no help, had made greater developmental strides and had greater weight increase (Scarr-Salapatek and Williams 1973).

The baby's motor development may be accelerated: as the mother moves, the infant is forced to adjust.

Value of enrichment Such attentiveness is important to all babies throughout infancy. Five-month-old infants whose mothers talked to them, looked at them, and touched and held them were more apt to touch and manipulate interesting new objects put in their paths (Rubenstein 1966). The more enrichment in the environment, the more a baby will look and reach out for what is available (White and Held 1966).

An interesting comparison of Zambian and American babies revealed that the motor development of Zambian babies is faster (Goldberg 1972). This may be because Zambians get more and earlier stimulation. In Zambia, babies are carried everywhere in a sling on their mothers' backs. Only at night do they lie horizontally. As the mother moves, the baby adjusts its position reflexively; the infant is, in effect, forced to use its motor equipment. These babies are "constantly receiving kinesthetic and tactile stimulation," without any special effort on the part of the mother (page 80). However, it is not certain whether Zambians are also genetically superior to Americans. The case for an environmental cause is not clear-cut.

Effect of training   Deliberate training, even of young infants, can sometimes have an effect on motor development. We have already seen that exercising infants to maintain the stepping reflex leads to earlier walking (Zelazo, Zelazo, and Kolb 1972). Training in creeping is also effective in developing later motor skills.

Older children, aged four, are capable of learning complicated gymnastic skills. All that is necessary is to train them (Leithwood and Fowler 1971). As we have seen, normal abilities do develop without training, provided that the environment offers no hindrance. But the "extras" come from added environmental stimulation.

Early development of motor skills can be helpful in the development of social skills (although psychological problems might also be created). Those who are physically competent may develop confidence that stands them in good stead in areas having nothing to do with one's muscles (Lagerspetz, Nygard, and Strandvik 1971).

Deprivation

If a good environment will promote motor development—and it seems to do so—it follows that a poor environment might have an adverse effect. Considerable research has shown that it is possible to harm a child or young person by lack of stimulation, by poor diet, or by outright malnutrition, particularly during critical periods of physical growth.

Faulty nutrition   Evidence abounds on the importance of nutrition in motor development (Thompson 1954; Garn 1966). Illness and disease can retard motor development, and poor nutrition makes a child susceptible to illness.

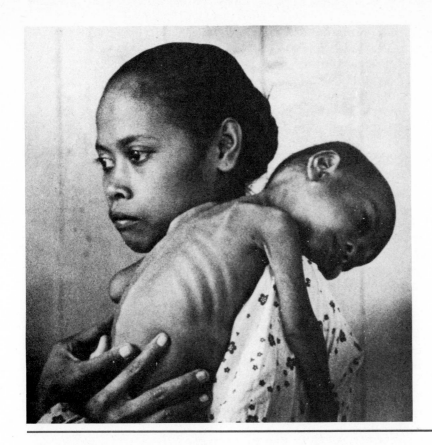

Undernourished—and perhaps permanently harmed.

It has been demonstrated that children are harmed, not only physically but also perceptually, and perhaps permanently, if they are not well fed. Different crying sounds of year-old infants can be distinguished, depending on how well they have been nourished. The ill-fed babies' cries have a longer initial sound, a higher pitch, and are weaker and less rhythmic. All these characteristics are also true of the cries of brain-damaged babies. Perhaps malnutrition affects the central nervous system, since poorly fed infants are also less responsive to sounds (Lester 1976).

Protein malnutrition is the greatest threat to physical development. Not only does it leave a baby prey to debilitating illness, but it can have devastating effects on the course of growth. The first four months of life are critical. Undernourished babies, although hospitalized and treated, were still shorter, weighed less, and had inferior motor ability than a control group when measured three and one-half years later (Chase and Martin 1970).

However, some environmental repair is possible. Severely malnourished Korean orphans adopted before they were three years old by middle-class American families were followed through elementary school and compared with moderately malnourished and well-nourished Korean children adopted into similar homes. None of the parents knew their children's nutritional history. Over one hundred children were followed for at least six years.

The investigators found that even the severely malnourished children eventually exceeded Korean height and weight norms. Only a small difference in height remained between the most deprived and those who had not suffered at all from malnutrition. School achievement for all three groups was about the same as what can be expected of normal children in the United States. The improvement in the status of these adopted children may reflect the special character of the adoptive parents and the superior environment in which these children were brought up.

Still, the study reported statistically significant differences between the previously malnourished and the well-nourished children in terms of intelligence and achievement scores. Could those differences be permanent? The answers are, of course, not yet available. It is worth noting that none of the groups of Korean adoptees in the study reached the mean height and weight of American children of the same age. This may reflect a genetic difference or perhaps several generations of undernutrition in Korea (Winick, Meyer, and Harris 1975).

Lack of stimulation Adequate environmental stimulation may be as important as food to the motor development of infants. In the first year of life, a child's development seems to happen in normal fashion even without any special stimulation. But this occurs only if a baby is not prevented from doing what comes naturally. Development takes place as long as the opportunity for learning is there. A baby will turn over eventually, and will laugh aloud, with or without stimulation (Dennis 1941). The classic experiment that demonstrated this principle was done with twins who were cared for but left unstimulated. They nevertheless followed the motor timetable for babies in the first year (Dennis 1941).

A later investigation (Dennis 1960) studied institutionalized babies in Iran who never had a fair chance to develop. Reared under crowded conditions with minimal care and no toys, and confined to cribs or placed on a piece of linoleum on bare floors, these infants became unmistakably retarded. They were deficient in sitting, creeping, standing, and walking.

In a follow-up study infants transferred in their early months from this substandard orphange to a better institution were tested. The new housing had more attendants, the babies were held when fed, their position in the cribs was changed from time to time, they were propped up, put into playpens, and given toys. And their care-givers were trained. The dramatic result: the babies, far below normal on arrival, attained normal weight within a few months. Their eventual behavior was much less retarded.

These findings do not necessarily contradict research showing that motor abilities develop without training (Pikler 1968). They do emphasize, however, that children will not grow normally unless they are provided with a reasonable living climate in which they are free to develop naturally. Still another study of institutionalized infants found that they were retarded in fine motor coordination, probably because they were not given the kinds of toys that made it possible for them to practice using their arms, hands, and fingers in many different ways (Kohen-Raz 1968).

Evidently, sociocultural factors can change the *rate* of development but not its course. Investigators tested infants from four to seven months old, from institutions, from disadvantaged homes, and from middle-class homes. The babies were rated for their reaching and manipulation responses to a red ring, which either moved or was stationary. At four months, the middle-class children's responses were measurably more developed than those of the other children. Thus, environmental deprivation can be detected early. By seven months, the children who had been tardy in their responses had caught up to the four-month-old level of the others (Slovin-Ela and Kohen-Raz 1978).

Long-term consequences Short-term deprivation can be overcome by increased stimulation. But when deprivation lasts too long, a baby may become indifferent. Six months seems to be a critical age. Normal babies have a particular appetite for novelty then. But institutionalized six-month-olds seemed past caring, even when they were belatedly given the opportunity for play (Rubenstein 1967).

As for the long-term consequences of deprivation, no research is needed to prove, for example, that strong, well-coordinated boys do better at football than clumsy, weaker boys. But there are other effects that are not so obvious, although potentially important to the person who is "different." Perhaps the most significant generalization that can be made about motor development is that all our learning ability—our ability to adjust to the world around us—depends in great measure on the bodies that house us, as we shall see in subsequent chapters.

Summary

Individual development, reflected in behavior, is the result of the interaction of (a) physical growth and maturation and (b) learning. Quantitative growth, such as increases in height and weight, plus maturation, such as qualitative increases in capacity, complement the learning process.

Maturation normally progresses in a fixed developmental sequence, such as: creeping, sitting, standing, and walking; or eye–hand coordination followed by manipulation. These developmental sequences are universal; they always occur in the same order. The maturational sequence resists environmental efforts to change it or speed it up.

The secular trend, an increase in growth rate and maturation rate over historical time, probably reflects a combination of improved nutrition and other environmental factors, as well as increased outbreeding.

Growth charts and norms for physical and motor development are useful as a guide to deviant development and possible correction. But some deviation from the norms is normal for individual children.

Birth weight, motor activity, and general physical condition at birth may foretell future development. Motor activity begins with unlearned, inborn reflexes, essential for feeding, walking, and perceptual awareness. A fast rate of motor development during infancy does not necessarily indicate permanent superiority.

Physical growth occurs in two directions: cephalocaudal and proximodistal. The development of prehension, eye–hand coordination, sitting, and walking demonstrate these trends.

During the school years, physical growth occurs in uneven increments. Differences in growth and maturation among individuals are particularly characteristic of adolescence. Girls generally mature earlier than boys. Psychological and social problems are a frequent consequence of adolescent growth differences.

Individual differences in motor development result from genetic factors—including sex differences, race, and possibly ethnic differences—and the environment. Environmental deprivation may be particularly harmful during periods of physical growth. Handling, stimulation, and good nutrition are important to the physical development of infants. Short-term deprivation may be overcome by increased stimulation, and training may be effective in promoting motor skills and in redressing early deficits. Good nutrition is crucial to physical development at all ages.

Chronological Overview

Newborn reflex motor responses, especially tonic neck reflex and Moro reflex

little control of head movements

Infancy

1–6 months: stares at object, makes no attempt to grasp it

coordination of senses with motor activity begins

swipes at object but makes no contact

raises hand in direction of object and may touch it

sits

stands when held by adult

rolls over to side

makes contact with object on first try

7–12 months: looks at, grasps, and manipulates object or brings it to mouth

holds trunk erect

crawls

holds trunk erect for considerable time

supports own weight when held under arms

gets into creeping position

pulls self to knees, stands holding on

creeps on hands and knees, then on hands and feet

1 year: supports weight on one foot, stands for short time while holding on

walks alone

| 2 years: | walks, runs, climbs stairs, holds objects, picks up objects |
| | beginning of sphincter control |

Preschool

3 years:	constructs a block tower, catches a ball with arms straight, uses a spoon, pours from a pitcher, unbuttons clothing, puts on shoes, draws a full circle and a straight line
	walks on tiptoe, jumps down 12 inches, hops with both feet, stands on one foot, rides a tricycle
4 years:	cuts on a line with scissors
	dresses without aid
	gallops
	walks down steps like an adult
5 years:	copies designs, letters, numbers
	buttons clothing
	folds paper into a double triangle
	walks a straight line; skips, hops on one foot

Childhood   Boys taller than girls

Adolescence

Girls:

10–11 years:	begin to mature sexually
11–14 years:	grow faster than boys
	are taller than boys
12 years:	fastest increase in height and weight
	may begin to menstruate
	secondary sex characteristics appear
15 years:	end of improvement in motor performance
	close to complete physical development

Boys:

11–14 years:	are heavier than girls
11–18 years:	motor performance improves
13–14 years:	fastest rate of height growth
	first seminal emission
	secondary sexual characteristics appear
16 years:	close to complete physical development

Applying Your Knowledge

1. Why is it important for parents to pay attention to developmental norms as they observe the growth of their children?
2. Can training facilitate motor development? What are some important limitations on the effects of training?
3. Why is the study of identical twins a good research approach in investigating maturation and learning?

Further Readings

Brazelton, T. Berry, M.D. *Infants and mothers*. New York: Dell, 1969. A month-by-month description of development during the first year. A highly readable book.
Paperback.

Orem, R. C. (ed.) *A Montessori handbook*. New York: Capricorn, 1966. An introduction to the Montessori method of education. Includes the development of motor skills.
Paperback.

Sears, Robert R., and Feldman, Shirley S. *The seven ages of man*. Los Altos, Calif.: William Kaufman, 1973. A survey of human development—body, personality, and ability.
Paperback.

Part **3**

Intellectual and Communication
Processes

Chapter **5**

Cognitive Development

Abigail Jane is not yet old enough to speak English. For the most part, we must guess what she is thinking and why. For an example from daily life, therefore, we turn to Jon, aged five.

Jon was asked where babies come from.

"From stomachs. They come from Mommies' stomachs. And they go to the doctor and get it and bring it home and see what they got."

What Is Cognition?

Jon obviously had been thinking about birth, but in a childlike way. Certainly not like an adult. What was happening in his immature mind? And how soon would his thinking "improve"?

A universal developmental sequence

Psychologists view *cognition* as a process that changes in various ways from the beginning of life to the end of life. Cognition is the ability to think and reason logically and to understand abstract principles. The result of cognitive development is insight, problem-solving, and abstract thought. Like other aspects of human development, in cognitive development there appears to be a maturational sequence common to all people.

In general, insight, problem-solving, and abstract thought are the outcome of more rudimentary, basic forms of thought. Some theorists believe that the developmental process proceeds from reflexive activity and thought, which are linked with concrete objects, to more sophisticated abstract mental representations. Others contend that motor activity is the forerunner of pictorial representations, which later give way to symbolic processes.

Cognition: ability to think and reason logically and to understand abstract principles

Theorists of cognition

Speculation about the nature and development of cognition began with Aristotle, and perhaps even earlier. But only in recent years have child-observers worked out persuasive analyses of the successive stages of thinking that mark a person's development from infant to child to adult.

Piaget's importance Jean Piaget is probably the major theorist on the whole question of cognitive development. (See Box 5–1.) Many compare his importance in the field of child development to Freud's in psychiatry. Major contributions to the theory

Jean Piaget, the major theorist on cognitive development.

of cognitive development have also been made by others, notably Jerome Bruner and Jerome Kagan, both of whom have done major work with children in university workshops in this country.

According to Piaget's theory, developed by observing children at various ages, the way human beings think progresses through four major periods: (a) sensorimotor activities, from birth to 2 years; (b) preoperational thought, from 2 to 7 years; (c) concrete operational thought, from 7 to 11 years; and (d) formal operational thought, from 11 to 15 years. This progression brings a baby from an initial inability to differentiate between itself and its surroundings, to the next period, in which the world and self are seen as separate, although the child cannot yet think either abstractly or in relative terms. In the third period, a youngster can understand symbols and deal with different dimensions of a problem or a situation all at once. Finally, as adulthood approaches, a young person is able to be logical and to think out a problem deductively.

Bruner's theory Bruner's theory of cognitive growth is somewhat similar to Piaget's, but the stages Bruner describes and what they emphasize are different. According to Bruner, a child moves through three stages of cognitive development: (a) *enactive*, characterized by activity (corresponds to Piaget's sensorimotor period); (b) *iconic*, dominated by imagery and visual perceptions (corresponds to Piaget's preoperational period); and

Box 5–1 Piaget: Development of a Psychologist

The life story of Jean Piaget (1896—), the Swiss psychologist who worked out a widely accepted theory of how human thinking develops, shows that the making of a major scientist is also developmental.

Piaget's father was a scholar who, Piaget reports, "taught me the value of systematic work, even in small matters." His intelligent mother was in poor mental health, so Piaget became greatly interested in psychology and psychoanalysis.

By the time he was seven, the boy had developed an interest in birds, fossils, and sea shells. At ten, he had a one-page article published in a natural history journal. After that, he got permission to study birds, fossils, and shells in the local museum of natural history. The director recognized the youngster's promise and made him his twice-a-week assistant. At the age of 15, Piaget began to publish articles on mollusks. Foreign "colleagues" wanted to meet him but Piaget declined: "I didn't dare show myself since I was only a schoolboy." These early studies were valuable in teaching Piaget scientific technique.

The precocious youngster got his bachelor's degree at 18 and began to write down his ideas in many notebooks. He also read extensively in philosophy, psychology, and scientific methodology. In one of his early published articles Piaget presented an idea that was central

(c) *symbolic*, which involves the use of symbols, such as words or mathematical formulas (corresponds to Piaget's concrete operational period). Thus the child's cognitive growth moves from motor activity, to pictorial representations, and finally to symbolic representations.

The theories of Piaget and Bruner help parents and teachers to understand how children think at various ages and stages, at last making sense out of children's "bright sayings" and "foolish" errors.

Piaget's Theory

Show a four-year-old child two identical glasses of water, side by side. Let each contain the same amount of liquid at the same level. Asked to describe the glasses and their contents the child readily reports that the two are alike.

to all his important later work: that action is logical and that it "stems from a sort of spontaneous organization of acts."

Piaget continued his graduate work and received a doctorate in natural science. During a year off, he wrote a philosophical novel, which embodied his scientific ideas. He notes wryly that "no one spoke of it except one or two indignant philosophers."

Years of work in psychological laboratories followed. Most important was the opportunity to deal with young children at the laboratory of Binet and Simon, pioneers in intelligence testing. Here he had a chance to study at firsthand how children think. "At last I had found my field of research." Three articles that stemmed from that work led to his being offered the job of director of studies at the J. J. Rousseau Institute of Geneva. Many books and articles followed, the product of Piaget's work and his collaboration with the Institute's students, including one who became his wife and co-worker. Studies of his own three children came later, after his ideas about cognitive development had already been formulated.

The honors that greeted Piaget's entrance in the scientific world at the time of his first publications as a youth have never stopped. His position as a giant in the field of developmental psychology is now unassailable (Boring et al. 1952).

Testing cognitive level by means of Piaget's water conservation task.

Then, with the youngster watching, pour the water from one of the glasses into another container, taller and narrower than the original. The water level, of course, has become higher. Now ask the child, "Does one have more water than the other?"

The answer will be that the taller, narrower container has more.

Why?

Because the water is "higher"!

Then, if the water in the third, taller glass is put back into the original glass, the child will have a change of mind. Now the young observer will say that the water in the two original glasses is again the same.

From egocentrism to relativism

This classic experiment with water glasses, which was devised by Piaget, reveals an important characteristic in the early development of thinking: egocentrism. Children of preschool age are characteristically *egocentric*. They perceive information or a situation from only one point of view—their own—and they perceive only one aspect of a situation at a time. (Egocentrism in this context does not mean that the child is selfish, only unable to transcend limited cognitive ability.)

Egocentrism Egocentric children pay attention only to the level of water in the containers. Their thinking cannot yet take into account the additional aspect of the diameter of the containers. They are not disturbed by their own obvious (to an adult) illogic. Their thinking is *irreversible*—they do not mentally return the water to the original container (after it has made its appearance in the taller, narrower one). Nor do they realize that the initial amount is still present. They focus only on the present water levels.

Operations Young children's irreversibility is demonstrated by their inability to understand *operations*, or reversible events. Operations are events that have an end point but that can be returned to the starting point. For example, two plus two equals four; four minus two equals two. The water level experiment is another example of a reversible event.

Relativism Now, if a seven-year-old is subjected to the same water level operation, the response will be quite different. The older child agrees that the water in the first two glasses is the same. But the youngster also realizes that the same liquid poured into a differently shaped container continues to have the same volume as before. The child has, in fact, grown into a higher stage of thinking ability, has progressed from egocentrism to increasing *relativism*. Now the youngster begins to *decenter*—to perceive information or a situation from more than one point of view. The child has also achieved the ability to think reversibly: the young mind is able to "put the water back" into the original container and to conclude that it is still the same amount of water.

Is there any practical reason for a parent or teacher to bother with this wardrobe of terms and descriptions? None at all. But it is important to understand the principles behind the terms if a conscientious care-giver would like to be able to communicate effectively with a child. How many adults have been exasperated by preschoolers' squabbles about who has "more" juice, when the

Egocentric: having perceptions based on one's own view, or focusing on only one aspect of a situation

Irreversibility: inability to mentally return a transformed event to its original condition

Operations: events that have an end point but can be returned to the starting point; reversible events

Relativism: perceptions that include several points of view

Decenter: to become aware of other points of view than one's own

glasses just happen to be different sizes and shapes? The children are not being perverse. They think they are seeing a real injustice.

Schemes

What is going on inside children's minds as they develop from egocentric to relativistic thought? Piaget conceives the thought process as being composed of a kind of building block, which he calls a *scheme*.

Scheme: fundamental unit of images, thoughts, or actions; an outline or mental sketch

Schemes are the fundamental units of thought and action. They are mental formulas about how the world works, which can be generalized or changed from one situation to another. For example, a baby forms a mental image—a scheme—of Mother or Father. This is the formula that makes it possible to distinguish friend from possible foe. When a baby's face is screwed up at the sight of a stranger and the child begins to cry, the event may be proof that thought is going on about who is who, based on clear schemes of those who are familiar.

A baby's sucking reflex is an early scheme. Later it can be generalized or applied to other objects—sucking fingers, nipples, rattles, Mama's car keys.

Organization   Schemes may also interact with one another and become *organized*, or combined, into acts. Example: when an infant sucks (a scheme) at the sight of a nipple (another scheme), two schemes are being organized.

Organization: combination of schemes

Equilibration   The key to cognitive growth, according to Piaget, is a process he terms *equilibration*. Equilibration is the tendency to function at a more complex level, to move from one developmental stage to the next. When schemes are organized to produce new, more complicated behavior, equilibration is said to have taken place. Thus, a baby progresses from sucking to drinking from a cup. Or an infant tires of a simple toy and looks for another with more challenge.

Equilibration: tendency to function at a higher, more complex level

Even the handling of the same rattle can illustrate equilibration. First a baby looks at it, then puts it in its mouth, later shakes it and throws it out of the crib. Confronted with new objects or events in the course of daily experience, the child tries to incorporate them into its repertoire of schemes. The result is equilibration—the organization of schemes into more complex behavior in order to meet new situations.

Adaptation   In organizing schemes as a response to new experience, *adaptation* is taking place. Adaptation is the reaction to new experiences through *assimilation* and *accommodation*. Assimilation is adding new information into one's frame of knowledge or schemes. Accommodation is changing one's frame of knowledge to include new information that cannot be assimilated. Accommodation takes place when the new information does not fit into the "old" picture.

For instance, a child sucks a rattle like a nipple. Or, an older child who is familiar with the color blue calls a purple dress "blue." In these cases, assimilation has taken place. But accommodation occurs when the baby realizes that a rattle will yield no nourishment and the child learns that blue and purple are, in fact, two different colors. In both instances, old schemes have been modified to fit new situations and a new state of equilibration has been achieved.

Another example: a baby picks up a pen and sucks on it. That's assimilation: the child has applied an already acquired scheme (sucking) to a new "event" (pen). Then the baby notices that the pen made marks on the play pen pad and makes some more marks on purpose. That's accommodation: the child has modified its behavior to include the new experience. The two processes add up to equilibration—progress from one developmental stage to the next. Thus do maturation and an increasing number of experiences result in continuous adjustment and development and more appropriate responses to the environment.

Many examples of assimilation and accommodation can be found in adult thought processes. Confronted with the task of learning a new language, most of us resist and try merely to assimilate. We seek resemblances between the new language and the one we already know. But we soon learn that we must accept a new kind of grammar and new rules of pronunciation; we accommodate.

Inappropriate assimilation is an act of egocentrism. (It is egocentric to apply the rules of our own language to another tongue.) Accommodation takes place when assimilation fails and some sort of adjustment to the new objects or events is necessary. (We learn the rules of the foreign language.) A child or an adult changes what is already known in order to deal with a new experience.

Another example from a child's world: a child who has a dog may, when first introduced to a cat, call it a "doggie." After being

Adaptation: reaction to new experiences through assimilation and accommodation

Assimilation: inclusion of new experiences into existing repertoire of behavior

Accommodation: modification of one's repertoire of behavior to include new experiences

told it is a cat the youngster has a change of mind, modifies the previous scheme: the child is learning and accommodating. (See Box 5–2.)

Stages of Cognitive Development

Psychologists see thinking as a process that keeps changing in one way or another throughout life. However, Piaget's theory traces cognitive development only from birth through adolescence, the age span that he actually observed and described in detail. His principles are illustrated by what happens in the various stages of mental development.

Four major periods

According to Piaget, as we have seen, cognition develops through four major periods: (a) sensorimotor activities, from birth to approximately 2 years; (b) preoperational thought, from about 2 to about 7 years; (c) concrete operational thought, from around 7 to approximately 11; and (d) formal operational thought, from around the age of 11 to about 15.

Box 5 – 2   Is This What Piaget Means?

A student interviewed a child aged three years and nine months. Note the examples of egocentrism, assimilation, and accommodation in the child's perceptions.

Q: "Where did you come from?
A: "From my house."
Q: "Were you born?"
A: "No . . . when I was in Pennsylvania I was."

Q: "Where does rain come from?"
A: "From the sky."
Q: "How did it get up in the sky?"

A: "Because the clouds make it go down."
Q: "Who do you think made the world?"
A: "God."
Q: "Who's he?"
A: "He flies in the sky all the time."
Q: "Is he an airplane?"
A: "No . . . he flies like a bird. God is just a bird."

A first-grade boy saw a nun wearing a traditional habit. "Sister, is that your hair?" referring to her hairline. He received no reply. "If it's not your hair, then it must be your feathers."

It is important to note that Piaget's norms are not accepted by all psychologists. Many investigators believe that young children are really more advanced than Piaget gives them credit for (Looft and Charles 1969; Ennis 1971). Another contention is that formal reasoning only *begins* to emerge between the ages of 11 and 15 and that not all formal reasoning tasks can be dealt with by 15 (Martorano 1977).

Infancy – toddlerhood: the sensorimotor period

The baby sees itself as the whole world. In the words of one psychologist, this is a case of "radical egocentrism—a complete lack of differentiation between himself and his actions and the characteristics of the given situation" (Looft 1972, page 76). The child will continue to be egocentric in later stages, but in the *sensorimotor period* the sense of self and the surroundings are totally undifferentiated.

Sensorimotor period: developmental level dominated by the senses and movement

Events An infant's thought processes are dominated by *events*. This is Piaget's term for activities involving the senses and movement—looking, hearing, touching, sucking, kicking. A vast amount of preliminary cognitive activity is also taking place, so much that Piaget felt obliged to divide the first two years of life into six stages. Each is characterized by progressively more elaborate arrangements of schemes.

Events: activities involving the senses and movement, according to Piaget

Stage one, reflexive behavior The month after birth is dominated by the infant's reflexes: behavior and ability with which the child came already equipped from the womb. These are the child's first schemes. Prime example: the infant sucks when the lips are touched. This kind of activity is innate, unlearned.

Stage two, primary (first-level) circular reactions At two to three months, the baby's actions, oriented to the body, are becoming repetitive; when an action is completed, it seems to stimulate its own recurrence. These *primary circular reactions* are thus characterized by purposeless, repetitive behavior. Sucking is different now. At the sight of a bottle, the infant sucks for the apparent pleasure of the activity, even if the nipple does not touch the mouth. No longer a reflex, sucking is now a primary circular reaction. It is also a sign that a child has achieved *object recognition*. But according to Piaget, *object permanence* has not yet been achieved: if someone takes the bottle away, the baby

Primary circular reactions: purposeless repetitive behavior oriented toward the body

Object recognition: ability to identify a familiar thing

Object permanence: awareness that a thing continues to exist although not in view

forgets it. Likewise, a toy dropped from the crib is not only out of sight but out of mind. The infant looks at something else.

Piaget's analysis of what happens during this stage has been disputed by other psychologists, who contend that there is evidence that the infant may not really forget or that the forgetting may not be immediate. One experiment showed that infants still reached for objects that went out of sight when lights were turned out (Bower and Wishart 1972). And in another investigation, infants were repeatedly shown a cube, but each time its orientation in space was different. Eventually the babies became just as inattentive as if the cube had been offered over and over in exactly the same place. The researcher's conclusion was that the infants had demonstrated memory; otherwise, each sight of the cube should

Box 5-3 Piaget's Observation of His Daughter in the Sensorimotor Period

I again find Lucienne swinging her dolls. An hour later I make them move slightly: Lucienne looks at them, smiles, stirs a little, then resumes looking at her hands as she was doing shortly before. A chance movement disturbs the dolls: Lucienne again looks at them and this time shakes herself with regularity. She stares at the dolls, barely smiles and moves her legs vigorously and thoroughly. At each moment she is distracted by her hands which pass again into the visual field: she examines them for a moment and then returns to the dolls. This time there is definite circular reaction.

. . . Lucienne looks at her hand with more coordination than usually. . . . In her joy at seeing her hand come and go between her face and the pillow, she shakes herself in front of this hand as when faced by the dolls. Now this reaction of shaking reminds her of the dolls which she looks at immediately after as though she foresaw their movement. She also looks at the bassinet hood which also moves. At certain times her glance oscillates between her hand, the hood, and the dolls. Then her attention attaches itself to the dolls which she then shakes with regularity.

. . . As soon as I suspend the dolls she immediately shakes them, without smiling, with precise and rhythmical movements with quite an interval between shakes, as though she were studying the phenomenon. Success gradually causes her to smile. This time the circular reaction is indisputable.

Source: J. Piaget, *Origins of intelligence in children*, page 158 (New York: W. W. Norton, 1963). Permission by International Universities Press, New York, Delachaux/Niestlé, Neuchatel, Switzerland.

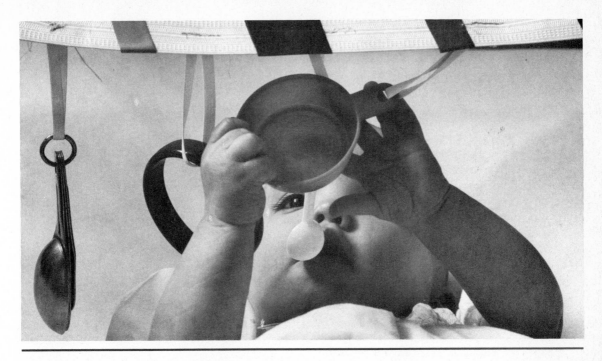

Secondary circular reactions.

have elicited as much attention as when seen for the first time (Bower 1976). The ability to become habituated to stimuli is an early sign of memory.

Mothers and fathers may get their first personal reward from son or daughter at this stage. If they have taken an active role in caring for the child, they will have become "objects" to be recognized. And the baby may smile when they appear. Yet when Father or Mother go out of the room, says Piaget, the baby will not seem to miss them.

Stage three, secondary (second level) circular reactions   At four to eight months the focus of infants' interest moves from their own bodies to the environment. Children are becoming aware that what they do can have amusing consequences. *Secondary circular reactions* are characterized by activities that produce an interesting effect. The child still sucks, but may be doing it to make a nice noise. The baby kicks, not for the sake of kicking, but to move the mobile overhead. Actions remain repetitive, or circular; the same thing will be done over and over again. (See Box 5–3.)

Secondary circular reactions: activities repeated because of their interesting effects

Another advance during this period is a baby's achievement of object permanence, one of the first milestones in cognitive development. As a result, a mother and father will begin to discover a gratifying new consequence of parenthood. The baby not only recognizes them when they appear, but is also starting to remember and miss them when they are out of sight. (This event is apt to take place in connection with the primary care-giver, usually the mother. As more and more fathers play a leading role in their babies' lives, they will also achieve early "father permanence.")

The baby's new accomplishment—missing the prime care-giver—is really an occasion for rejoicing. The child is now able to make use of one more primary building block of thought: there is a scheme to represent an object—father or mother—that is not always present. It is this same ability to retain a scheme for an unseen object that will later enable the child to deal with symbols, words, and mental representation.

Box 5–4 Piaget's Observation of Object Permanence

The universe of the young baby is a world without objects, consisting only of shifting and unsubstantial "tableaux" which appear and are then totally reabsorbed, either without returning, or reappearing in a modified or analogous form. At about five to seven months (Stage 3 of Infancy), when the child is about to seize an object and you cover it with a cloth or move it behind a screen, the child simply withdraws his already extended hand or, in the case of an object of special interest (his bottle, for example), begins to cry or scream with disappointment. He reacts, therefore, as if the object had been reabsorbed. It will perhaps be objected that he knows very well that the object still exists in the place where it has disappeared, but simply does not succeed in solving the problem of looking for it and removing the screen. But when he begins to look under the screen (see Stage 4), you can make the following experiment: hide the object in A to the right of the child, who looks for and finds it; then, before his eyes, remove and hide the object in B, to the left of the child. When he has seen the object disappear in B (under a cushion, say), it often happens that he looks for it in A, as if the position of the object depended upon his previous search which was successful rather than upon changes of place which are autonomous and independent of the child's action.

Source: From The Psychology of the Child, by Jean Piaget and Barbel Inhelder, translated from the French by Helen Weaver, p. 14, © 1969 by Basic Books, Inc., Publishers, New York.

Sixteen weeks is the earliest age for which investigators have experimentally confirmed object permanence (Bower, Broughton, and Moore 1971). Eye movements were observed in a test of infants' ability to track a moving object. At one point, a screen hid the object from view. A baby who had attained object permanence would look at the other side of the screen for the object.

Piaget's work with older infants, also using a screen, revealed a developmental sequence. At six to seven months, babies can find an object partially hidden from view. At eight months, they can find a completely hidden object. However, if a child sees the object hidden at location A and then hidden again at location B, the infant looks for it at A. At nine months, the child searches for the object at the point of its disappearance (Gratch and Landers 1971). (See Box 5–4.)

Stage four, coordination of secondary circular reactions The period from 8 to 12 months is an extension of the previous stage. Earlier, actions were repeated because of their interesting effects. Now we see an even more purposeful sort of activity—to achieve a desired result. Thus, *coordination of secondary circular reactions* involves goal-oriented activities. Because of a new ability to keep an object in mind—to formulate a scheme—the baby can now plan to achieve an end. This ability to seek goals is based on object permanence.

Coordination of secondary circular reactions: goal-oriented activities

Parents now discover they must contend with an individual who has a mind of his or her own. Father is reading a letter with his son in his lap. Baby reaches for the letter; Father puts it in his shirt pocket; Baby reaches into the pocket and takes the letter out. The father puts the paper back into the pocket. But the baby pulls it out as often as the father takes it away. This goal-oriented behavior illustrates one thing more: the child now has a rudimentary understanding of spatial relationships. The baby realizes that there is space in the pocket in which to put the letter.

During this period of a child's life, the concept of persons as permanent objects develops fast. Person permanence is probably one of the first signs of the development of object permanence. To a baby who is 8 to 11 months old, people are even more interesting than pieces of paper or other objects. The child focuses attention more on the care-giver than on inanimate objects (Bell 1970). Person permanence in its earliest form is demonstrated by the infant who motions or moves toward the screen that is shielding a person from view.

Because of object or person permanence, the infant begins to recognize environmental discrepancies, such as strangers or the absence of a care-giver. The obvious clue is how they react to being left with a sitter: the child howls! (Kotelchuck et al. 1975). The worst reaction to being left with a sitter seems to come between 1 year and 15 months. After that, distressed first-time parents may be happy to hear, the baby makes much less fuss (Kotelchuck 1973).

Jerome Kagan (1970), who analyzed these differentiated age responses, believes that they reflect a baby's increasing ability, after nine months, to formulate very simple hypotheses. The child can theorize about what happened to absent parents and whether or not they will come back. A year-old baby can recognize a "different" event, is frightened, and has no idea why such a thing has happened. Later on the child can figure out some answers and is less upset.

Kagan maintains that this sequence is the beginning of cognitive activity. He has some physiological evidence. He points out that an increase in heart rate in older children usually accompanies attentive, thoughtful behavior. Significantly, infants exposed to discrepant events showed a similar increase in heart rate. The most marked increases came between the ages of 9 and 11 months when separation from the parent is an event of profound *cognitive dissonance:* a clash between the child's expectation and the reality of the situation. Kagan therefore concludes that simple cognitive activities begin *within* Piaget's sensorimotor period (0–2 years), not afterward, as Piaget contends.

Cognitive dissonance: conflict between expectation and the reality of the situation

Stage five, tertiary (third-level) circular reactions At 12 to 18 months, the toddler arrives at the trial-and-error stage. *Tertiary circular reactions* involve exploring all the potentialities of objects. The term *tertiary* is used to indicate that children's thoughts have progressed beyond their own bodies (primary circular reactions), beyond the immediate consequences of their actions (secondary circular reactions), to a third dimension. They are now using schemes acquired from previous stages to experiment with the varied possibilities of objects. All the experimentation is acted out. A square peg won't fit into a round hole? The child tries all the holes till one fits.

Tertiary circular reactions: exploratory behavior and trial-and-error experimentation

This is the period when the little one is "into everything"—pots scattered over the kitchen floor, little fingers reaching into the electric light sockets, toilet paper rolls unrolled. Look on the bright side: the baby is merely experimenting with all the wonderful objects in the domestic world, trying them out in all the ways that come to mind.

Piaget lays great stress on these sensorimotor activities. He maintains that they allow the child to interact with physical reality, to learn from and about the environment. A foundation is being laid for later conceptual development. The baby is learning concepts like hard and soft, cold and warm, squashy, round. All this is a veritable voyage of useful discovery.

Stage six, invention of new means through mental combinations   A child aged 18 to 24 months is sophisticated indeed. Through *mental combinations*, the child invents new ways to solve simple problems. It is no longer necessary to rely on trial and error to find the right hole for that square peg. The solution takes place in the mind, rather than through the fingers. The child looks at the peg, surveys the holes, decides what matches by picturing it all in the mind, and then puts the peg into the right hole.

Mental combinations: using the mind to put together ideas (schemes)

Mischief-making of the previous stage, while messy and noisy, is as nothing compared to this new era. Are there cookies on the shelf? The young thinker will look over the situation and figure out a plan: push a chair over to a strategic counter, climb on the chair, climb on the counter, and easily abstract the can of cookies. This naughtiness is just the beginning of mental maturity and problem-solving.

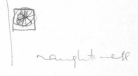

Preschool years: preoperational thought

The age span from two to seven years is termed *preoperational* by Piaget. The sensorimotor period has been left behind through maturation and equilibration. But the preoperational child is still egocentric, and irreversibility continues. The child's world is concrete, absolute. Orientation is *global*. The child is guided mostly by visual cues. Words are becoming important and beginning to stand for objects, but the objects are still more important. Interaction with the environment and with various people has provided the necessary stimulation to propel the preschooler into this new stage. But children this age have not matured sufficiently to deal with the world on any but absolute terms. Abstract concepts and relative terms still escape them.

Preoperational thought: illogical reasoning

Global: relating to the whole, or entirety, rather than the parts

Limitations continue   Piaget's water level experiments reveal the limitations of younger children. They do not yet have the ability to *conserve*, to perceive that transformations in appearance do not alter quantity. Conservation reflects relativistic, re-

Conservation: ability to understand that change in appearance only does not necessarily imply change in quantity

versible thinking. Children whose thought processes are basically egocentric do not conserve or reverse. Nor are children in this age range capable of *classification*, mental division of a category into its component parts. They cannot think of parts and the whole at the same time.

Show preschoolers an array of yellow and green plastic beads, more yellow ones than green ones, and ask, "Which would make a longer necklace, all the plastic beads or just the yellow beads?" They will answer: "The yellow beads, because there are more yellow beads than green ones." The youngster is unable to think of the beads as being both plastic (the whole) and colored (a part of the whole) at the same time.

The beginning of mental maturity and problem-solving.

Classification: division of a category into component parts or the grouping of objects according to a criterion

A four-year-old boy remarked, "I liked oranges when I lived in San Francisco, but not when I was in California." Intellectually, he was too young to grasp the concept of San Francisco and California as belonging to the same time frame.

Relative terms are almost meaningless to children of this age. They think in absolutes. They do not see people or things as darker, lighter, shorter, taller. Objects are dark or light. People are tall or short. Ask a four-year-old which of two tall uncles is taller. The decision is beyond the child.

Relationships are hard to deal with. A four-year-old boy is asked: "Do you have a brother?" "Yes!" "What's his name?" "Jim." "Does Jim have a brother?" "No!" (Phillips 1969, page 61). That he can be his brother's brother is more than he can understand.

Most "bright sayings" date from this period when children are having difficulty understanding classification. They see classes as mutually exclusive:

"Do we eat turkey at Christmas?" "No, at dinner."

"Can you be a Protestant and an American at the same time?" "No—not unless you move" (Elkind 1974, page 24).

"Is a dog an animal?" "No—he's a dog."

Everything is seen from the youngster's own point of view. The child is egocentric in perception as well as in thinking. This was illustrated by an experiment in which three different-sized "mountains" were placed on different parts of a table (Piaget and Inhelder 1956). The child sat in a chair facing one of the mountains. Given some cut-out drawings of what the occupants of each of the chairs might see, from their vantage point, and asked to choose which view would be seen from each chair, the child was baffled. It was difficult to imagine the situation from any other than the child's own point of view. (See Figure 5–1.)

Preoperational children also demonstrate undifferentiated *global behavior*. The most overwhelming impression dominates their thinking, like the higher water line in the glasses-of-water game.

All these absolutes begin to break up between the ages of four and seven. During this transitional period children begin to doubt their previously positive judgments. They start to consider other perspectives. With help from an adult, they can decenter their thinking. At times, they can grasp more than one aspect of a situation. The child is developing logic, and it is getting in the way of what were once clear, if mistaken, perceptions of how things are.

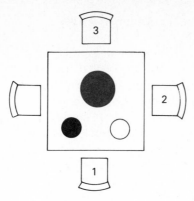

FIG. 5-1 The three-mountains task. *Source:* From *The Origins of Intellect: Piaget's Theory,* Second Edition, by John L. Phillips, Jr. W. H. Freeman and Company. Copyright © 1975.

Influence of language Some people question the validity of Piaget's theories because they wonder what part language plays in children's responses. When children give the wrong answers, isn't it possible that they are simply not understanding words like *more* or *less?* Some experimenters did find that some children used those two words when they were really referring to height and length (Berko and Brown 1960; Bruner et al. 1966). Another investigator found evidence that four-year-olds equate *big* and *tall,* but only semantically. They know what *big* is but often use it to refer to height (Maratsos 1973).

When asked, "Which is bigger?" preschoolers and first and second graders tend to rely heavily on the vertical dimension of objects. Their approach is unmistakably unidimensional (Lumsden and Poteat 1968; Hulsebus 1969; Osgood and Thomas 1971). In judging quantity of liquids, the height of the container is the most salient cue for six-year-olds. In contrast, nine-year-olds also considered the width of the container (Phye and Tenbrink 1972; Miller 1973). Thus, egocentrism decreases with age. Another reason children frequently use height as a standard is that they are often exposed to height standards in daily life: pouring equal amounts of milk or soft drinks into glasses; using measuring cups; standing people back-to-back (Miller, Grabow-ski, and Heldmeyer 1973; Maratsos 1973).

However, some studies have shown that language is not the handicapping factor for children who do not show conservation. Training in the words *more* or *less* does not necessarily improve conservation performance in four-year-olds (Holland and Palermo 1975). Investigators have duplicated Piaget's conservation of quantity experiments without using the two suspect terms. Instead of using jars of water, the experimenters showed children two equal-sized jars of candy. One jar had more candy than the other. Then the smaller amount of candy was poured into a taller, narrower jar so that the level was higher than that of the jar with more candy. The children were asked which jar of candy they would like, and why. Conservers chose the jar that actually contained more, and supported their choice by commenting that there was more candy in it. The ages at which the children demonstrated conservation corresponded to Piaget's concrete operational stage—7 to 11 (Silverman and Schneider 1968). A different study demonstrated that sixth-grade boys who used few hypothetical statements and had poor command of language in general were no less able to think in hypothetical terms, and to demonstrate formal operations ability, than more verbal youngsters (Jones 1972*a*).

While these investigations seem to support Piaget's conclusion that language is not critical to cognitive development (Inhelder and Piaget 1964), the issue is still unresolved. Sixty-six English children around the age of five were given a three-mountains test similar to Piaget's. The children were divided into four groups. Three groups were given three different kinds of training—through movement, visual clues, and verbal clues—to improve their performance. One control group got no extra training at all. The experimenter found that a five-year-old does not necessarily have to occupy another observer's position in order to describe the view from that place. Training procedures that gave the children either visual or verbal information to aid them in visualizing other perspectives were most successful in drawing the right answers from the young subjects (Cox 1977). (Chapter 6, dealing with language, will have more on this subject.)

Conservation of number Even if language is not necessarily crucial to a child's ability to conserve, how about the ability to count? Would not that skill have something to do with a youngster's efficiency in dealing with a set of several objects? Obviously,

The ability to count can facilitate the ability to conserve.

the question is important not only in school but in dozens of aspects of daily life.

The available data suggest that the ability to count does, indeed, have something to do with number conservation. However, being able to count does not necessarily mean that a child has a real understanding of amounts when he or she is still in the stage of irreversibility and is still unable to decenter. Conservation of numbers of smaller sets—two or three objects—is something a four-year-old can do (Winer 1974). But not until the age of six can most children deal with five to six objects.

Try a game with small identical chocolate candies, M&M's, to be found on any grocery shelf, or any objects of identical shape and size, like buttons or beads. Lay two rows of these pellets on a table, the same number in each row. Make two rows of equal length. Because of the global outlook of the egocentric child, the youngster will say there are more if one of the rows is then lengthened by putting greater distance between the pellets.

A two-year-old is not likely to try to count the number of objects in each of the two unequal rows to find out which has more. Three-year-olds may try to do it and make mistakes, like skipping numbers. Four-year-olds who count more accurately are more likely to conserve (LaPointe and O'Donnell 1974).

Concept of time   The idea of time is another concept that eludes a child who is in the preoperational stage of cognitive development. Very young children are "thing"-oriented. Time is not tangible. Therefore little children equate time with distance. They insist on "seeing" it and thus assimilate the concept of time into their understanding of distance and other concrete measures.

For example, try a preschooler with a problem involving two trains moving along the same length of parallel tracks. The child will be sure that it takes the same time for each to reach the end of the course, even though the youngster's own eyes have seen that one train got there before the other. The child cannot yet comprehend that speed and time are somehow related. The reason is that children who are still egocentric and globally oriented can accept only the cues that are meaningful in their own experience. They rely on the most vivid impression: visual cues, in this case.

(Do you want to know what stage a particular child has reached in thinking development? Play one of the games. You might even be surprised to find that the child is in more than one stage at the same time. The youngster could very well understand conservation of number, but might still be preoperational in understanding conservation of volume.)

All the research on what-happens-when fleshes out Piaget's theory and helps explain children's reactions to the events of daily life. It also substantiates the basic hypothesis of the sequence of the stages through which an individual passes in the development of ability to think. However, the ages at which these stages occur may vary from one person to another.

Early school years: concrete operational thought

According to Piaget, the best time to start teaching mathematics to a child who is developing normally is between the ages of 7 and 11. This is the beginning of thinking as we adults understand the process. Children of this age range, in the *concrete operational* stage, are capable of reversible, relativistic thinking. They are more logical than younger children, even though their access to abstract reasoning continues to be limited. They are still basically "concrete," and they rely on objects or what is "real" to help them (Farrell 1969). However, they are beginning to understand the use of symbols—numbers, words—to represent something else. They can mentally retrace steps in an operation, assess a problem relativistically, deal with different dimensions of a situation all at once. They can conserve and classify logically.

Concrete operational thought: logical reasoning

Conservation and classification   School-age children comprehend conservation of volume. In the water level demonstration, they are now able to realize that there is no more liquid in the taller, narrower container than there was in the original container. They can classify by relating to the whole and part of the whole at the same time. They understand that there are two kinds of wooden beads, yellow and green, and that together they constitute a category—plastic beads—that is made up of more than those of either color.

In this new, higher cognitive stage, children have progressed from egocentrism to relativism. They no longer think only in terms of absolutes. They can now perceive a situation from more than one point of view. They have also attained the ability to think reversibly: mentally to return the water to the original container and realize that its volume is unchanged.

Relative concepts are now coming into focus. A child who is short compared to others the same age is ready to be deeply wounded by a teacher who thoughtlessly points out who is the smallest in the class.

Time and speed   And now, because the pupil is able to decenter and can see varied aspects of a situation, it is possible to pose problems involving time and speed. The youngster can grasp the fact that speed is related to both time and movement. When younger, in the preoperational period, if someone had moved object *A* from *a* to *d*, and at the same time moved another object, *B*, from *a* to *b*, the child would have insisted that *A* took longer than *B* (Phillips 1975).

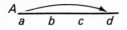   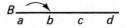

In this early period, the spatial factor dominated everything. But now, in a more mature stage, the pupil thinks more like an adult and can sort out the important factors and realize that the time was equal although the distance covered was unequal. This is the beginning of a grasp of the complex notion of velocity, which depends on both time and space (Flavell 1963).

Limitations on cognitive ability Let us stress the word *beginning*. True, the "average" seven-year-old is beginning to understand complex notions like velocity. But adults must be aware that children's thinking progresses by stages and that each age group has cognitive limitations. Trying to communicate with children in terms they are not yet ready to grasp is a game that both adult and child will lose. The child will not understand, and the adult will be frustrated. Curriculum planners in particular must take into account these developmental limitations.

The reasons for these cautions are illustrated by Piaget's findings about the sequence of conservation concepts. The concepts of conservation are attained in a predictable sequence: number, mass, liquid (volume), weight. Number conservation—the rows of chocolate candies—is the first concept to develop. Six-year-olds will realize they are still seeing the same number of chocolate candies in each row after they are rearranged. Full conservation is not achieved until 11.

Conservation of mass comes later. Show a child two identical clay balls. When one of the balls is rolled into a sausage, the egocentric child will say there is more clay in the sausage because it looks longer. Or, if one ball is flattened into a pancake, the same child will say there is "more" because it is "bigger." An older child who has progressed to the stage of conservation will realize they are the same. But it does not happen until the age of seven or eight at the earliest.

The same clay balls can be used in a game to show whether a child is conserving weight: "Do the balls weigh the same? Does the 'sausage' (or the 'pancake') weigh the same?" Children do not generally give the correct answers until age nine or ten. The age for conservation of liquid, in the famous water-level game, is seven to eight years.

The ability to think hypothetically—"What if . . . ?"—is another stage that does not arrive until around seven. Now the child is able to cope with such problems as: "If I let the dog out, he might run into the street and be hit by a car"; or "If people were born with three ears, would they hear more?"

All normal children will certainly reach this stage of concrete operational thought, which Piaget has described so thoroughly, but the timing will differ from individual to individual. We do not all wake up on our seventh birthday fully equipped to deal with abstract problems.

Adolescence: formal operational thought

Formal operational thought: logical and abstract reasoning

Truth and duty. X equals Y minus three. Photosynthesis. Chemistry lab. Why do I have to be home by eleven?

This bundle of verbal propositions and abstract notions is characteristic of the formal thinking of early adolescence. During the ages of 11 to 15, a person is usually able to think reversibly and relativistically. Boys and girls can formulate and test hypotheses. This means they can also challenge parental authority. They are able to solve problems with a complex array of symbols, to attempt logical deductive reasoning. But they are also ready to question the family's values and beliefs.

Dealing with abstractions The ability to deal with the abstract and the symbolic does not develop all at once. Studies have shown that mass and weight are understood much sooner than volume displacement. In cognitive development, as we have already seen, the ability to deal with the concrete precedes the ability to deal in abstracts.

Moreover, not every kind of abstraction is understood at the same time. Math and science teachers know that volume displacement is one of the last of the conservation concepts that students are able to grasp. For example, let us return to those two balls of clay of equal size, one of them transformed into a sausage (see page 185). Ask: Will they displace the same amount of space? Do they have the same volume? Of a group of 12-year-old pupils who were tested by David Elkind (1961), four out of five had attained conservation of mass and weight, but only one out of three had attained an understanding of displacement. Of a group of 14-year-olds who were tested, more than half had attained conservation of volume displacement. Even by the age of 18, not all—only three out of four—understood volume displacement, although all the students had an understanding of mass and weight.

Elkind provides this caution: the percentages for the later grades may be too high because the students tested were necessarily those who had remained in school; no drop-outs were included. So it seems fair to say that while conservation increases with age, it also seems to reflect the level of schooling (Elkind 1961). But education and maturation do make it possible for a person to attack the volume displacement problem, or any other, by picking out the relevant cues, to realize that volume is the key factor, not weight. (See also Box 5–5.)

Reversible, relativistic, abstract thinking   The density problem is a good example of the reversible and relativistic thinking possible in junior high and high school. Present an early adolescent with a variety of things—a golf ball, a candle, coins, a piece of wood. Ask which will sink and which will float in a tub of water? The preoperational child would make a prediction on the basis of an irrelevancy: "It will float because it is round." The concrete operational child would base a response on a limited perception of the physical property of the object: "The piece of wood will float because wood floats." The child would ignore the importance of the size of the wood and the amount of water (a log will not float in a puddle).

But the formal operational adolescent will have grasped the abstract concepts of density, the relationship between weight and volume, and the answers will be (to an adult, at least) the obvious ones. Nor does the adolescent need to see the wood or the body of water in which it is supposed to float or sink. A description is sufficient.

The thinking of adolescents also becomes more methodical. They are leaving trial and error behind and can, if they wish, make a plan instead of rushing headlong into a project. This is *combinatorial thought*, the ability to combine elements in a systematic, methodical way to arrive at the solution to a problem.

Combinatorial thought: ability to combine elements in a systematic, methodical way

Box 5–5   Grown-up Thinking

Are adults really in the period of formal operational thought?

Ask some adults the following: If you have two equal-sized test tubes filled with equal amounts of water, and you drop a brass cylinder in one test tube, and an aluminum cylinder of equal size in the other test tube, will the water levels rise equally or unequally? Note their responses and reasons! If you want to see if there are sex differences in thinking ability, ask both males and females and compare your results.

Source: "Piaget's Theory: Conservation," Davidson Films, 1967.

Idealistic propositions appeal to adolescents, who are now able to think about what is not and what could be.

For example, give a student several beakers of different colored solutions. Then present a beaker of yet a different color. Ask the pupil to reproduce the color in the last beaker by using any combination.

Adolescents who are using true formal operational thought will approach the problem logically and systematically. They will take Beaker A and combine it with each of the other colors; then B will be combined with each of the remaining colors, and so on, until the sample solution is matched. A younger child, not yet able to think this way, would merely combine A and B, B and C, C and D, or use any other similar approach. The youngster would be unsystematic and would fail to include all the possibilities.

Probability and proportion The absolute world of the child—"My daddy can beat up your daddy because he's the strongest man in the world!"—breaks up during adolescence. The change comes from the newly developing ability to think in terms of *probability*, *possibility*, and *proportion*, another achievement of formal operational thinking.

Example: Before the age of about 11, a youngster making up a list of guests for a birthday party is unlikely to take into consideration just which of the invitees is actually going to show up on the appointed day. But a teenager who is contemplating asking for a date or a job is very much aware of the problem of probability: will I be accepted or rejected? Thus, the age of doubt has arrived: doubt about acceptance by peers; doubt about ability to be independent; doubt about college admission and employment. The world has become an "if" place, often frighteningly so.

This is the period when an individual can get a much more comprehensive hold on "what if" situations. "What if I were adopted?" is a common one. Another is "What if I had no brother or sister?" Or, "What if I *did* have a brother?"

In short, adolescents can think about what is not and what can be, not only in their own lives but in the world. Socialism, communism, back-to-nature-ism—all sorts of idealistic propositions may begin to have an appeal on this newly developing cognitive level.

This new level of cognition—ability to understand proportion and probability—can be further illustrated by how adolescents handle problems in school. An interesting experiment was performed, again involving chocolate candies (Chapman 1975). Various age groups were used. The pupils were shown two containers. Container *BBY* had two brown candies and one yellow candy. Container *BBBYYY* had three browns and three yellows. Asked which container would be more likely to yield a brown candy if one were to dip into it once, 11-year-olds could not cope with the problem of proportions and probability. They were influenced by the total number of candies of the desired color, rather than the probability of drawing the right colored candy, which depends on the proportionate number of each kind. Adolescents did much better than the 11-year-olds. But college students, presumably well into the formal operational mode of thinking, never erred in their choice.

Egocentrism All this certainly does not mean that during adolescence all people come to cognitive maturity, acquire all the equipment for thinking, and that all that remains for them now as adults is to use their ability. Parents and teachers who must

deal with the often maddening, seemingly perverse behavior of adolescents are well aware that adolescents display a unique form of egocentrism that accounts for self-conscious behavior and belief in their own invulnerability.

Elkind writes that "while the adolescent can now cognize the thoughts of others, he fails to differentiate between the objects toward which the thoughts of others are directed and those which are the focus of his own concern . . . since he fails to differentiate between what others are thinking about and his own mental preoccupations, he assumes that other people are as obsessed with his behavior and appearance as he is himself. *It is this belief that others are preoccupied with his appearance and behavior that constitutes the egocentrism of the adolescent*" (Elkind 1967, pages 1029–1030). Inhelder and Piaget (1958) comment on the same egocentric behavior of adolescents.

Adolescents are forever playing to (imaginary) audiences.

Playing to "real" and imaginary audiences . . .

Adolescent egocentrism: they may feel immortal.

They think they are special and may even keep a diary for posterity. Indeed, they feel immortal: death, injury, serious illness can never strike them. They drive dangerously. They take breath-taking risks on the ski slopes. The teenager constructs *"a personal fable,* a story which he tells himself and which is not true" (Elkind 1967, page 1031).

Adolescent egocentrism sounds funny and often is. But it can be tragic—inadvertent pregnancy, auto accidents, a whole catalog of misfortunes can follow in the train of the teenager's egocentric belief that "it can't happen to me."

Another consequence of adolescent egocentrism is a faulty sense of the past and the future. All this self-preoccupation leads teenagers to concentrate on the here and now, disregarding the future. While having a good time at a party, a boy or girl who promised to be home by midnight is unable to envision a parent's worried face. And if a high school student lets grades slip, thereby endangering chances for being admitted to college, it may be because college is too much in the future to be real (Cottle, Howard, and Pleck 1969).

Identity crisis   Reaching the level of formal operational thought may be responsible for the familiar identity crisis of the teenage years. (See also Chapter 9.) "Who am I?" is a question that relies on the newly developed ability to think about probability and possibility ("What if?"). Adolescents can now hypothesize about what they can be like or what they can become. As part of the same quest, they try to separate themselves from family and from society's rules and rotes. They pose questions about the world, moral standards, the status quo in general. This is a traumatic (though, cognitively speaking, normal) period for all concerned. The adolescent is caught between conformity, egocentrism, and formal reasoning. All hypotheses are now subject to testing.

However, psychologists are not entirely agreed that a person who has attained the level of formal operational thinking will necessarily use that ability in all aspects of life. Sixty undergraduate girls, some going through the classic identity crisis, were given a test of logic. The formal reasoning necessary to an identity crisis did not always carry over to the verbal problems on the test. The girls who were in crisis failed to perform significantly better than noncrisis subjects (Berzonsky, Weiner, and Raphael 1975).

Comparison of the theories of Bruner and Piaget

We noted earlier that Jerome Bruner's analysis of cognitive growth, while similar to Piaget's, is still somewhat different. Bruner identified only three stages of cognitive development, instead of Piaget's four. Bruner's three stages represent the steps children take in understanding and conceptualizing events in the real world.

Enactive stage   Like Piaget's *sensorimotor period*, Bruner's *enac-*   *Enactive:* action-oriented *tive* stage involves motor activity, such as biting, sucking, holding, kicking. The enactive stage is characterized by children's activity in dealing with objects in their environment. Children understand the world through their own actions. Since verbal ability has not yet been attained, the world is interpreted in terms of events and activity, rather than through words or symbols. For example, a child understands that a wagon is something with four wheels used for carrying people or things. But the child does not form a concept of a wagon apart from the direct experience of the wagon and does not label or make generalizations about it.

Iconic stage　Where Piaget would refer to *preoperational*, global behavior in the next stage, Bruner terms his second stage *iconic*. It is characterized by imagery. The child's visual perceptions dominate this stage of cognitive development. The water-level experiment, which demonstrates preoperational thought according to Piaget's view, can also demonstrate Bruner's imagery stage. The child who thinks the glass with a higher water level contains more water is demonstrating iconic thought; the image dominates the child's thinking.

Iconic: image-oriented

Symbolic stage　The final stage in Bruner's theory of cognition is the *symbolic* stage. A symbol is something that stands for something else. Thus, symbols are things that carry meaning. Words, numbers, and other abstractions become important in an individual's cognitive process. Now a youngster can understand mathematical formulas, traffic symbols, or any conceptual representation (Bruner 1966). This last of Bruner's stages thus encompasses two stages—*concrete operational thought* and *formal operational thought*—as described by Piaget.

Symbolic: symbol-oriented

　　While there are differences in the way Piaget and Bruner approach the subject of cognitive development, there are many similarities. Both see cognition as a process dominated by maturation, interlaced with an individual's experience with the environment. And both see universal stages of cognitive development from the cradle to maturity.

Individual Differences

We all know that human beings are not stamped out with cookie cutters. Piaget did not rule out the important effect of individual differences on how and when his cognitive stages are attained. Thinking does not happen in a vacuum. How a person thinks is affected by personality, by sex, by family, and by the culture in which the individual is reared.

Research findings that hold true for all cultures are the only clues to those aspects of cognition that are due to maturation. These are the "universals." Everything else about how cognition develops results from influences in the culture, in the environment, perhaps in the genes. Should one wish to tamper with cognitive development, then, the environment contains the elements that might be manipulated.

But can cognition actually be manipulated? And if so, is it desirable? Is there some value in teaching a four-year-old to think like a six-year-old? Should the family, the schools, cultural institutions, the community try to speed up the development of cognition or otherwise make "better" thinkers out of children or adolescents? What are the effects of training, intelligence, language acquisition? What are the effects of other variables, like personality, sex, family, environment, social class, culture, education? Parents and educators, as well as social engineers, would all like to know the answers to these questions.

Effects of education

Can you train a preoperational child to move into the concrete operational stage or turn an average adolescent into a philosopher? Piaget, the father of the theory of cognitive development, says training is effective only when the individual is ready to benefit. He believes that an individual's progress through the stages of cognition depends on the development of mental structures. One grows at one's own pace. While there are differences in growth rate from individual to individual, we all normally pass through most of the stages in our own good time. Training is effective, says Piaget, only when the mental structures have developed. He would not, in other words, try to teach combinatorial thinking, like algebra, in the first grade.

Training experiments: positive effects Other theorists do not entirely agree. Bruner, for one, found that language acquisition training may increase a child's attainment of conservation and logical operations (Bruner et al. 1966). Frank, a member of Bruner's team, trained four- to seven-year-old children to enable them to "conserve" liquids. A variation on Piaget's water-level experiment, this procedure involved two beakers, one taller than the other. The shorter one was filled with water; the other was empty. Both beakers were placed behind a screen with only the tops showing. All the water from the shorter beaker was poured into the taller, empty one. But the water level was shielded by the screen. Asked to predict whether there would be the same amount of water to drink in the second beaker as in the first, all the children except the youngest judged that there was the same amount. The screen "forced" the judgment that "it's only the same water," or "you only poured it."

When the screen was removed, most of the children—again, except the youngest, the four-year-olds—restated the correct judgment: "It looks like more but it is only the same" (Bruner et al. 1966). (See Box 5–6.) Training does help, this seems to say, but only if there is some physical readiness for it (Smedslund 1961; Harlen 1968). The same screen experiment performed by other investigators confirmed Bruner's findings.

Box 5–6 Effects of Training on Conservation Judgment

Percentage of Children Who Made Conservation Judgments

Age (in years)	Pretest— before training	With screen	After training
4	0	50	10
5	20	90	80
6	50	80	100
7	50	100	100

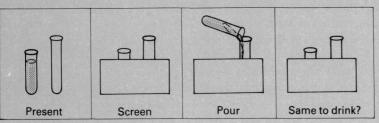

| Present | Screen | Pour | Same to drink? |

Screening procedure used to train conservation.

Source: J. S. Bruner, R. Olver, M. Greenfield, et al., *Studies in cognitive growth,* page 195, page 197 (New York: John Wiley, 1966).

Where do babies come from? "He was just in my mommy's tummy."

Some studies have shown that training can cause children to reach some of Piaget's stages earlier than he predicts. One researcher succeeded in developing the concept of class inclusion in six-year-olds, although the Piagetian age for this cognitive stage is seven to eight years (Sheppard 1973). Training has also been effective in teaching ten-year-olds to conserve density, even though Piaget's assigned age for this is 11 to 15 (Brainerd and Allen 1971).

Training experiments: no effects　Some other studies of children in both Western and non-Western societies have failed to turn up a direct relationship between the development of conservation and schooling. For example, one study found little difference between the performance of schooled and unschooled children in conservation tasks (de Lemos 1969).

In another investigation, children of various ages were interviewed about their knowledge of where babies come from. No matter what the facts (training) their enlightened parents had provided for them, the children gave garbled versions of human reproduction consistent with the way they were thinking and handling information at their particular age (Bernstein and Cowan 1975). (See Box 5–7.) Jon, the five-year-old whose version of reproduction began this chapter, illustrates the point. Children that age, still egocentric, take facts they have been given and adapt them to fit their own experiences.

Using Piaget's theory in school   Not all cognitive development is cast in stone. Children's thinking can be improved by good teaching. Piaget himself never contended that the levels he described are fixed and unchangeable. While he made no specific recommendations to educators, in effect he challenged teachers at all levels to reexamine their teaching methods to make sure they are appropriate to their pupils' level of understanding (Beard 1969). Certainly an adult who understands how a child thinks will be in a far better position to present information to pupils so that they will understand and learn.

Piaget emphasized the importance of exploring children's ideas by questioning them. Inevitably, the youngsters would discover which of their thoughts were inappropriate. Becoming aware of the clash between their ideas and reality produces learning, a process of accommodation.* This does not mean that children should merely be told the right answers. The contrast between right and wrong is what teaches, and the child must discover *why* an answer is incorrect. Thus, logic is taught; it is more important than bare facts.

Some schools have made good use of Piagetian principles. Nursery schools that provide play areas equipped with large toys help children learn to control their actions and to understand spatial relationships. Smaller toys and equipment teach children how to construct, sort, classify, grade, and count. Water, sand,

---

*Taken from a lecture by Eleanor Duckworth at "A Late Summer Institute on Piaget," Stanford University, 1977.

bricks, drawing and painting materials—all are useful ingredients for cognitive growth (Beard 1969).

A good elementary school teaches on three different levels, corresponding to Piaget's successive stages. The youngest children need games and activities involving sand, water, containers. These are unstructured lessons with lots of individual attention from teachers. Later, children may be given more structured activities to help them toward simple concepts and skills. In the next stage, pupils require practice in using the concepts and skills they have acquired and may be exposed to activities that promote conceptual development (Beard 1969).

In the upper elementary grades the activities are similar but more complex. For example, volume may now be taught not with various sizes of boxes but by using cubic inches of water in jars of different shapes (Beard 1969). In junior high school, the pupil is still in the concrete operational stage, and learning goes best when based on concrete experiences, preferably the student's own (Beard 1969).

Box 5–7 Children's Ideas About Getting Babies

Parents' conscientious attempts to teach their young children the facts of life may be doomed to fail unless they take Piaget's cognitive stages into account. This lesson comes from a study by two psychologists who questioned 60 middle-class boys and girls at various age levels. The investigators found that no matter what parents tell the children about where babies come from, the youngsters twist the information to fit their own level of cognition.

The youngest children, three to four years old, in the preoperational stage, unable to understand cause and effect, think babies have always existed. They cannot imagine a world without themselves in it. So a three-year-old's ideas about where a baby comes from tend to be geographical. A baby is somehow made to arrive in the right place. "You go to a baby store and buy one," is a typical reply. Or, "He was just in my mommy's tummy."

At a slightly higher level, around four or five years old, children are still egocentric and can interpret what happens only in terms of their own experience. So their explanations tend to be related to manufacturing. Babies are built, a concoction of skin, blood, bones, and paint.

In a transitional stage, between preoperational and concrete development, children build on their own experiences. "The daddy plants the seed like a flower, except you don't need dirt." Parental explanations are taken literally.

In Oklahoma, a group of researchers and teachers set up a science curriculum improvement study for first graders, to speed up the pupils' ability to conserve. They used direct experiences with real objects, rather than pictures or words. On a higher level the same methods were employed. Eighth- and ninth-grade science courses were designed around the inquiry method. Students conducted their own investigations, rather than depending on textbooks alone. The method seemed to help the pupils move from concrete to formal operation levels. Even in college freshman science courses, the emphasis is on "questioning, classifying, hypothesizing, verifying, restructuring, interpreting, and synthesizing" (Renner et al. 1976, page 127). Formal thought is promoted by "hands on" experience, which encourages students to test presumptions, form hypotheses, and reconcile contradictions.

Those who have made deliberate efforts to use Piagetian ideas in a practical way in the schools emphasize the social aspects of the approach. Student dialogue with peers and teachers

Between the ages of 7 and 10, youngsters may think of the egg as being like the eggs in the refrigerator, know that the penis and sperm are part of the process, but cannot really visualize what happens.

Children 8 to 12 years old are able to think logically, consider past and future, and understand cause and effect. However, in this concrete operational stage most cannot understand the complexities of procreation. They know about intercourse but are apt to think of it as an agricultural operation, like planting a seed.

At a fifth thinking level, around 11 or 12, children have progressed further in their understanding. But some tend to think the baby is in the sperm, which gets food and shelter from the egg. Others believe a miniature person is found in the ovum.

Only in the later formal operational stage are children able to put the whole process together, to understand the physical aspects of conception and birth, and to realize that marriage is not essential for procreation.

The researchers contend that attempts at sex education often confuse children. A book that related the process of human reproduction to animals and eggs, for example, caused a four-year-old to insist that a lady gets a baby to grow in her tummy by going to the store and buying a duck (Bernstein and Cowan 1975, pages 77–91).

is an important part of the learning experience. It allows ideas to be exchanged and hypotheses to be tested. Pupils can also be exposed to other points of view.

Effects of intelligence

Is a child whose thinking ability develops earlier a smarter child? This may seem an obvious conclusion. But the only way we now have of discovering whether the assumption is correct is to use intelligence tests, which merely measure aptitude for doing school work. (See Chapter 8.) So the question must be rephrased: is there a relationship between the level of cognitive development and intelligence as measured on tests?

Some investigators have found that a moderate, though not highly correlated, relationship exists between cognitive development as described by Piaget and intelligence scores (Elkind 1961; Goldschmid 1967; Carlson 1969; Little 1972). There might even be a connection between the age at which a child attains conservation concepts and the child's ultimate intelligence level. Brighter children reach formal operations sooner than average children of the same age (Keating 1975).

However, Piaget and others maintain that the relationship between cognitive development and intelligence test scores is merely superficial. The Piagetian tasks measure only some cognitive functions, *not* overall intelligence. Piaget was more interested in the thinking processes underlying right and wrong answers; he was not concerned with measuring the frequency of different kinds of responses (Furth 1973; DeVries 1974). Little relationship has been found between logical thought and Scholastic Aptitude Test scores or academic performance in high school (Schwebel 1975). Aptitude and academic attainment also rely on other intellectual functions, such as acquisition of knowledge, retention, and information processing. (See also Chapter 7.)

Differences in cognitive style

While intelligence may or may not have a bearing on cognitive development, there seems to be little doubt that there are differences in the way children think. There is such a thing as cognitive style, a particular way a problem is approached, analyzed, and solved. Both children and adults use different ways of organizing in their minds the conditions or situations or problems they encounter. These differences in the way we think appear in childhood and do not seem to change throughout life; they are part of one's personality.

A longitudinal study (Kagan, Moss, and Sigel 1963) followed the same group of people from childhood through their twenties, testing their thinking styles. They found "dramatic and consistent individual differences." Some of the differences seemed to be related to sex; boys and girls actually appeared to organize their thoughts differently. (But see also page 204; these sex differences may be culturally induced.)

Varieties of thinking   Several different *cognitive styles* can be detected among individuals. Some people are *analytic* thinkers; others are nonanalytic, or *global*. An analytic approach breaks down a situation into its component parts in order to look for underlying characteristics. A nonanalytic, or global, approach searches for the most obvious or functional relationships.

Cognitive style: an individual's unique way of thinking or problem-solving

Asked to classify an array of dissimilar objects, an analytic child would look for some common basic attribute. Shown pictures of a watch, a man, a ruler, such a person would say a watch and a ruler go together because both are used for measurement. But a nonanalytic child of the same age would put the man and the watch together because of their functional, conventional relationship—they "go together." Thus, the man wears a watch. Probably one strategy is no better than the other, but they are fundamentally different ways of categorizing experience (Lee, Kagan, and Rabson 1963).

Two other opposing cognitive styles are *reflection* and *impulsiveness*. A reflective approach pays more attention to detail, takes more time, and is usually more accurate. The impulsive approach is less thorough, response time is less, and there is greater probability of error. (See Box 5–8.)

Teachers are all too familiar with children who hurry through tests and make "careless mistakes." They are not necessarily either more or less intelligent than others who take more time to decide on the right answers (Kagan 1966). A timed test might encourage careless mistakes if the pupil is impulsive, so the test becomes a measure of cognitive style, rather than of knowledge.

Reflection and impulsiveness can be measured by the Matching Familiar Figures Test. (See Figure 5–2.) This test shows a pupil a single picture of a familiar object (the standard) and six similar pictures, only one of which is identical to the standard. The subject is asked to select the one that perfectly matches the

FIG. 5−2 Matching Familiar Figures Test. These are examples from the tests of reflexion−impulsivity. *Source:* J. Kagan, L. Pearson, and L. Welch, Conceptual impulsivity and inductive reasoning, *Child Development,* 1966, *37* (3), 585. © The Society for Research in Child Development, Inc.

Box 5−8   Two Children's Cognitive Styles

A striking illustration of the differing cognitive styles of children (and adults as well) comes from a longitudinal study of John and Chris (Kagan, Moss, and Sigel 1963). Both children tested about the same in intelligence. Both came from families with well-educated parents and several brothers and sisters. But each boy had his own unique way of approaching situations that required thought. And that cognitive style did not change from infancy to the early years of school.

"John is a bright, analytic child. . . . During the first three years . . . John was . . . affectionate, placid, and non-aggressive. . . ." At three, in nursery school, "he played quietly with animals or crayons or sat looking at books . . . often sat alone and read, turning the pages diligently, and ignoring the noises that were around him, for he had a very long attention span." At four-and-a-half, he continued to play alone most of the time, ignored distractions, "showed obvious interest in the stories the nursery school teacher read, asking questions about things and listening with rapt attention." At five-and-a-half, observers noted "his outstanding ability to concentrate. . . . When he was working on a hard puzzle or intricate project, he would frequently pay little attention to people near by. . . . He stuck with [the puzzles] until they were done and rarely asked for help."

In contrast, "Chris was hyperactive during the first year ot two of life. He had a very short attention span, he was difficult to control, and he was easily

standard (Kagan 1965). Impulsive children in grades one to four have a mean response time of between 4 and 10 seconds and they make 15 to 20 errors. The mean response time of reflective children is between 30 and 40 seconds, but they make only 2 to 6 mistakes. It would seem that reflection–impulsiveness has something to do with a child's cognitive or *conceptual tempo* (Kagan 1966).

Conceptual tempo: pace in solving problems

As might be expected, reflective children tend to be more systematic and efficient in their problem-solving than impulsive children. Second graders were shown 16 pictures of flowers and asked to select the correct one. They were told to ask questions, which would be answered yes or no, to enable them to select the target picture. Reflective children asked questions that helped them focus on relevant variables and eliminate irrelevant variables. For example: "Is the flower red?" "Are the petals large?" Impulsive children tended to use a trial-and-error approach. "Is it flower *A?*" "Is it flower *D?*" (McKinney 1973).

angered by minor frustrations." At two, it was noted that he "plunged into activity immediately and impulsively. . . . His attention span seemed short, and he played only with simple toys. . . ." At three-and-a-half, Chris showed "very little interest in toys and would often follow his mother through the house bouncing on the bed as she made it. . . . Chris [was] not interested in coloring or pasting and only did such things if someone did it with or for him. . . ." At nursery school, he "seemed very impetuous and usually did whatever the spirit moved him to, regardless of the consequences. . . . If he suddenly got an idea, he would race off to tell someone about it. . . . Chris gave up on tasks that were too difficult for him." Nearly a year later, Chris "often raced down the hall im-

petuously or grabbed forbidden things from the high cupboards. . . . He rarely played by himself . . . didn't stick very long at any one activity and gave up quickly if a puzzle proved too difficult." Similarly, at five-and-a-half, Chris "flitted from one activity to another and had the shortest attention span of the entire group. . . . He never sat down and really worked."

The investigators comment on the striking contrast between John and Chris. "They are of equal intelligence, and there is no difference in the frequency or quality of their language. The major dimensions that differentiate John and Chris involve hyperkinetic impulsive behavior, reflectiveness, withdrawal from social situations, and task involvement."

Implications for education   Reading problems and learning in general are related to cognitive style (Kagan, Moss, and Sigel 1963). One investigator declared that "cognitive styles have two important educational implications . . . the amount of 'structure' that a child prefers in any learning situation and his tolerance of uncertainty" (Smith 1975, page 198). Style differences influence children's learning efficiency, how much information they need in order to make a decision, how much they dare to risk making a mistake (Smith 1975).

Some studies suggest that cognitive style or conceptual tempo may be modified by what happens in the classroom. For example, 1500 three- to seven-year-old Guatemalan children were given picture puzzle tests. Their response times were more highly correlated with the difficulty level of the test items than with accuracy, suggesting that the tendency to be reflective or impulsive may depend more on the nature of the task than on some particular cognitive style unique to an individual (Morrison et al. 1977).

Teachers may be able to curb impulsive children by giving specific instructions emphasizing the importance of accuracy in completing a particular task. One experiment involved 45 kindergartners and an equal number of second graders, who were asked to match familiar figures. On retesting, second graders who were cautioned improved their performance significantly, compared with children who had no such special warning. At least during the early school years, therefore, children can be helped to modify their cognitive style and tempo (Barstis and Ford 1977). Another group of impulsive children did better on the same test when they were cautioned to wait before writing down their answers (Kagan, Pearson, and Welch 1966*a*).

Sex differences

A lively issue in today's world is the question of the "real" differences between men and women, girls and boys. Do the two sexes have different ways of thinking? Does one sex think "better" than the other? And if so, why?

Dozens of recent studies reveal that there are no distinguishing sexual differences in cognitive ability. A review of 45 research studies in the area of cognitive development and sex differences indicated that the two sexes do equally well in conservation tasks appropriate for a particular age group (Maccoby and Jacklin

1974). Studies of more complex operations with both pre-adolescent and adolescent subjects found little or no sex difference (Maccoby and Jacklin 1974).

Studies of cognitive style yielded the same results: no sex differences. These investigations dealt for the most part with children ranging in age from 3½ to 11. The conclusion was that neither sex was more impulsive or reflective than the other (Maccoby and Jacklin 1974).

Thus, earlier reports of cognitive differences between girls and boys in carrying out conservation and classification tasks may have reflected the sociological and cultural climate of those years. Until the last decade or so, girls were taught to concentrate on social relations, while boys were expected to be interested in mechanical and scientific matters. The inevitable result was different opportunities for learning and, consequently, different performance in conservation and classification tasks (Elkind 1961).

Now it appears that times have changed. There is less sex stereotyping in class schedules. Girls take auto shop, boys take cooking, and all of them may be preparing for the same vocational schools, college, and graduate schools.

Family influence on cognition

Family influence begins in the cradle. Parents and older brothers and sisters can significantly influence a child's cognitive progress. A mother who spends a great deal of time with her infant in a warm, close relationship facilitates conceptual development. The baby will recognize relatively early that a person is a "lasting thing" in the environment. At eight months, such a child will be noticeably more advanced in the concept of person permanence than the offspring of a cooler, more rejecting mother (Bell 1970).

A study of 39 babies over a period of a year, from the age of 12 months to 24 months, showed cognitive benefits for those whose home environments were stable, whose care-givers talked to them, and who were given adequate but not intense stimulation (Wachs 1976). In contrast, cognitive development of deprived children seems to be as much as one to two years behind that of middle-class children (Wasik and Wasik 1971; Wei, Lavatelli, and Jones 1971). This seems to say that material things—toys, a home full of things to touch—plus attentive parents, do not "spoil" a child, but make for accelerated cognitive growth. What is significant is a care-giver who questions a child about daily experiences, points out contradictions in the child's reasoning, and encourages curiosity and exploration within the safety of home surroundings.

Brothers and sisters can also influence a child's cognitive progress. Older siblings seem to be a motivating force in the performance of younger siblings. A study of siblings working together showed that the younger child's ability to sort objects according to a classification system improved when working with an older brother or sister. The elder child did not seem to be teaching the younger in this experiment. Apparently the mere presence of an older sibling helps to arouse and motivate the younger child to do well in the task (Cicirelli 1973).

Undoing damage When Piaget discovered that equilibration— the organization of schemes resulting in more complex or sophisticated behavior—depended on the number of new experiences available to a young child, he was explaining that cognitive differences are a function of the quality of a child's experiences in the world. Interesting evidence comes from a study of Guatemalan children raised in a poor rural setting. The young ones showed severe retardation in cognitive development. But the conceptual skills of older children from the same village were equal to those of American children of the same age. Evidently it is not accurate to judge cognitive development only on the basis of how well a child does in infancy. The normal sequence of maturation and interaction with the natural environment seems to help a child catch up to the normal developmental level in later years (Kagan 1973).

Still, the environment does have to provide the necessary stimulation at some time in an individual's development. In some non-Western primitive areas the concrete operations period is never attained by older children or adults (de Lemos 1969; Dasen 1972).

Studies of institutionalized children suggest adverse effects from an impoverished environment. These children were orphaned in the deepest sense: they suffered from inadequate mothering as well as lack of the stimulation that comes from a good home. Fortunately, such damage may be reversible if children are young enough. Children adopted by the time they were 3½ years old had overcome their earlier cognitive deficits by the age of 12 (Taylor 1968, 1970). The new homes provided richer environments, more stimulation, and the children developed more normally.

One experiment trained mothers in disadvantaged homes how to have more and better verbal exchanges with their children. The youngsters' cognitive ability seemed to increase significantly (Levenstein 1970). However, reversal of cognitive damage is not inevitable. No doubt there is a critical period beyond which enriched stimulation would have no effect.

Summary

Jean Piaget originated a comprehensive theory of cognitive development. Other psychologists, notably Jerome Bruner, have also done important studies of cognition. According to Piaget, children progress through stages from egocentrism to relativism. The egocentric child thinks irreversibly when dealing with operations (events that have an end point but that can be returned to the starting point). Later, children are able to think reversibly and to conserve. In Piaget's water-level test, for example, the conserving child understands that pouring water into a different container does not alter the quantity.

Piaget isolated four major periods of cognitive development:

1. The six stages of the sensorimotor period, from birth to 2 years, are reflexive behavior (birth to 1 month); primary circular reactions, involving repetitive actions and object recognition (2 to 3 months); secondary circular reactions, the beginning of object permanence (4 to 8 months); coordination of secondary circular reactions, characterized by experimentation involving the environment (8 to 12 months); and invention of new means through mental combinations (18 to 24 months).

2. The preoperational stage, from 2 to 7 years, is a period of egocentrism and irreversibility. Thinking is global and absolute. The youngster cannot deal with abstract concepts or in relative terms.

3. In the concrete operational stage, from 7 to 11, the child thinks reversibly and relativistically. The child can also conserve, understand symbols, be logical, and deal with different dimensions of a situation all at once.

4. During the period of formal operational thought, from 11 to 15, reasoning is logical and deductive. Thinking is re-

versible, relativistic, abstract, and combinatorial. Elements and complex symbols may be combined in a methodical way to arrive at the solution to a problem. But adolescents are also typically egocentric in terms of their personal lives.

Training or schooling may sometimes help a child attain conservation and logical operations, given minimal physical readiness. However, the age at which a child attains the conservation concept and the ultimate level of intelligence may not be related.

Individual differences in cognitive development may be influenced by family, culture, personality, and socialization of the two sexes.

Chronological Overview

Newborn	reflex activity
Infancy	
1–6 months:	beginning of sensorimotor responses
	object recognition (sucks at sight of bottle)
7–12 months:	object permanence
	engages in activities that produce an interesting effect
	goal-oriented activities
	trial-and-error exploration
1–2 years:	solves simple problems through mental representations
Preschool	beginning of abstract thought
	egocentric: sees world in concrete and absolute terms
	global orientation
Childhood	reversible and relativistic thought
	begins to use symbols to stand for things
Adolescence	propositional thinking
	hypothetical thought
	deals with abstractions
	combinatorial thinking

Applying Your Knowledge

1. How could knowledge of preoperational levels of thinking help parents get along with preschool children?
2. How would it help teachers in the classroom to understand the implications of adolescent egocentrism?
3. How does a child's language ability affect the outcome of Piaget's conservation tasks?

Further Readings

Elkind, David. *Children and adolescents*. Toronto: Oxford University Press, 1974. An introduction to Piaget's theory intended for students of education; not very technical. Paperback.

Flavell, John H. *Cognitive development*. Englewood Cliffs, N.J.: Prentice-Hall, 1977. A thorough but concise overview of the field of cognitive development. Paperback.

Lehane, Stephen. *Help your baby learn*. Jamaica, N.Y.: Spectrum, 1976. A practical guide to Piagetian tasks suitable for children in the first two years of life. Paperback.

Phillips, John L., Jr. *The origins of intellect: Piaget's theory*. San Francisco: W. H. Freeman, 1975. A clear and concise description of Piaget's theory. Paperback.

Piaget, Jean, and Inhelder, Barbel. *The psychology of the child*. New York: Basic Books, 1969. An easily understandable overview of Piaget's theory by Piaget and his chief collaborator. Paperback.

Piaget, Jean, and Inhelder, Barbel. *The origin of the idea of chance in children*. New York: W. W. Norton, 1975. One of the few original works of Piaget that a beginner can read profitably. Paperback.

Characteristics of Language Acquisition
A mysterious process
Language maturational schedule
Unexplained phenomena

Language Theories
Reinforcement: Skinner
LAD: Chomsky
Rule System: Brown
Speech area of the brain

How Language Builds
Early vocalizations
Early speech
Vocabulary growth
Grammar acquisition
Outcome of maturation

Language, Thought, and Learning
Communication
Thinking
Reading

Special Influences on Language Ability
Sex differences
Family influence
Cultural differences
Compensatory programs
Bilingualism

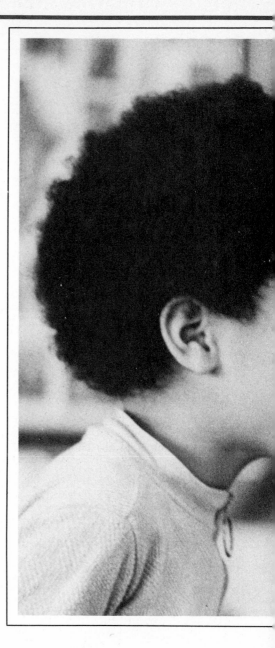

Chapter **6**
How We Acquire Language

When Jon was 11 months old, he was taken on a long automobile trip to visit his grandmother. It turned out to be the kind of expedition parents regret making. Not only was it unseasonably warm and uncomfortable, but the baby showed no inclination to sleep, as he usually did in a car. Instead, he kept crying, "Mi! mi!" He was not yet talking. Still, he was obviously unhappy.

Finally, his agitated mother produced a bottle. Jon drank thirstily. And that was the end of "mi!" for the day. The baby *was* talking. And his word was "milk!" Parents can be astonishingly obtuse. They had seriously underestimated their infant. Young children's first single-word utterances often express complex ideas. Like Jon, they are not just naming objects. Rather, they are trying to express a complete thought.

"Mi!" = "I want milk!"

"Ba" = "Pick up the ball and give it to me."

"Wow" = "The dog is sucking my big toe. Make him stop!"

Characteristics of Language Acquisition

All these communications are early evidence of the importance of language. As we saw in the preceding chapter, even an infant can think, although without words and on a primitive level. But without language the baby cannot express thoughts to others. Language is everybody's bridge to everything and everybody. Words help us learn. Words aid thought. Words are immensely useful for dealing with people and our jobs. Words help us appreciate and deal with the world around us.

A mysterious process

Just as remarkable as the fact that we are able to speak is the way we acquire speech very early in life. The word *acquire* is used deliberately. Of all the human mysteries that psychologists have tried to plumb, language acquisition is one of the most elusive. They dare not dismiss the matter by saying that language is learned. True, it *is* learned. But then again, it isn't. By what mechanism do people speak their native tongue? No one really knows. There are theories, but there is no complete agreement.

Observation of children is the chief means by which psychologists have tried to frame plausible explanations of how human beings acquire the sounds, the words, and the grammar of the language of their own people. They now generally agree that there appears to be a *universal timetable* for language develop-

Ready to talk .

ment. In all cultures, children usually speak their first recognizable words around the end of the first year. Since those words are invariably in the native tongue, learning and imitation obviously must play a role in language acquisition. Still, like other forms of development, the development of language seems to depend on its own peculiar maturational schedule, not related to motor control, nor to cognition, nor to training (Lenneberg 1966). Just what mechanism controls that schedule is still a matter of theory and speculation. (See Box 6–1.)

Language maturational schedule

A twin study years ago proposed that maturation dictates the progress of language acquisition throughout infancy and early childhood (Strayer 1930). Moreover, in language acquisition this readiness factor is only moderately influenced by training or experience. One of a pair of identical twins 84 weeks old (over a year and a half) was given strenuous training in language over a period of five weeks. At the same time, the other was kept in a world without words. By the end of the training period, the child who was taught was far ahead.

But then the second twin received training. Within only four weeks, the language gap between the two had been nearly closed. Months later, with no special further training for either one, they spoke equally well.

This experiment illustrates the importance of maturity.

Box 6–1 In All Cultures, Language Development Is the Same

See doggie.
Book there.
More milk.
Allgone thing.
Not wolf.
My candy.
Big car.
Mama walk.
Sit chair.
Hit you.
Give papa.
Cut knife.
Where ball?

These are examples of two-year-olds speaking. But these children spoke different languages: English, German, Russian, Finnish, Turkish, Samoan, and Luo. The quotations are striking illustrations of the fact that language is (somewhat mysteriously) acquired on the same developmental schedule regardless of culture, regardless of geography, regardless of the particular language that is spoken in the home.

Everywhere a child's first word is usually a noun or proper name relating to something or someone frequently seen. Two words are put together at around the age of two. The meanings of those two-word combinations vary considerably, as the illustrations clearly show. In a short time the grammatical implications of the two-word combinations become fairly elaborate, by means of intonation, word order, and inflection.

By the time the two-word stage is over, most children have mastered a great deal of the basic grammar of their language. So when the three-word stage arrives, the third word is apt to fill in what was implied, but missing, in previous two-word communications.

All the basic elements of grammar seem to be acquired by age four, no matter which language is native to a child and no matter what the social environment. In the years after that, children are merely learning specific details and how to apply the more sophisticated grammatical principles of their native tongue.

It does not seem to matter whether the child's chief language tutor is the mother. Children are programmed by nature to learn language if they are exposed to it (Slobin 1972).

There seem to be critical periods for particular degrees of language skill, depending on anatomical and neuromuscular growth. Speech training can give a push to a child who is not quite ready, but the gain will have very little, if any, permanent value. When a child is ready to talk, the youngster will talk—if there is a normal environment that provides the words and the stimulation to permit learning.

A baby who says "Daddy go!" is able to put the two words together because the maturational schedule makes it possible. But the internal clock must run much longer before the child is able to ask: "Can I go play with Mark? He has a new wagon." Growth occurs in about the same sequence for everybody, though timing may vary (Miller 1951). In fact, even babies who are deaf will coo and babble at the same time as hearing children (Lenneberg 1966).

Sentences are beyond the maturational scope of a one-year-old, whether the child is American or Spanish or Chinese. But everywhere normal children who have reached the age of 18 to 20 months can put two words together.

All people go through similar language acquisition stages no matter what language they speak, no matter what the circumstances of their learning to speak (McNeill 1970). This sequence is similar to the sequences of physical maturation. However, language cannot be acquired by maturation alone. A person who never gets the necessary linguistic experience does not learn to speak.

This much, then, we know: language is acquired by every normal individual in a *predictable sequential fashion*, irrespective of the culture or the language being learned. But the *rate* of language development may well differ from one child to another (Pollack and Halpern 1971).

Unexplained phenomena

"My skin has a hole in it."
"God flies around the sky and is nothing but a bird."
How can one account for the original sentences children speak—sentences they have never heard before? Imitation, learning, and maturational readiness are clearly responsible for infant words and the ability to put words together. But there is obviously more to language than that.

Another language mystery, besides the uniqueness of one's speech, is the acquisition of *grammar* and *syntax*. Even though

Grammar: classes of words and their functions in sentences

Syntax: the way in which words are put together to form phrases and sentences

the differences between verbs, adjectives, and adverbs are not taught to children until well into elementary school (and sometimes not even then), children master tha basic grammar of their native tongue as early as the age of five? This is no mean accomplishment. Linguists estimate that there are at least 2000 different languages now spoken throughout the world, every one of them both complicated and sophisticated.

To understand fully how language is acquired would help everyone who spends time with children. We could know the reasons for children's verbal mistakes. We could avoid misunderstandings when children say what they really do not mean and when we say what they cannot yet comprehend. We could help them to communicate better. We could also facilitate learning, which depends so much on language. The problem is that scholars do not completely agree about how language is acquired. Nor is there any way, yet, to prove one theory over any other.

Language Theories

Reinforcement: Skinner

One early explanation of language acquisition was called the *reinforcement theory*. According to B. F. Skinner, an important learning theorist, a child learns to speak because certain sounds and words that he or she utters are reinforced by whoever spends the most time with the baby—usually the mother. All speech is based on the *universal sounds* common to all languages—sounds that are babbled by all infants. But Skinner pointed out that of all the universal sounds, only the sounds of the mother's language are reinforced. The rest drop out. Thus do children learn to speak a particular language, their mother's native tongue. For example, American babies "forget" babbled sounds that are peculiar to Teutonic languages, but they keep the vowel sounds common to American English. And vice versa for German babies. Similarly, the babbled *ma-ma* sound becomes *mama* in American or the more nasal *maman* in French. A parent need not make an all-out effort to teach these words. When the baby utters the "right" sound the parent just naturally pays attention and thus reinforces the baby in the use of that word.

According to critics, Skinner's reinforcement theory was oversimplified. It is unlikely that a baby babbles all the sounds of the English language, much less of all human languages. Fur-

Reinforcement theory: a response is learned when it is strengthened by a desirable outcome

Universal sounds: sounds common to all languages

thermore, some sounds (like consonant sounds produced at the back of the mouth—*k, g, h*) are more frequent in early babbling than in later babbling or in a child's first words. Therefore, while reinforcement may encourage babbling, it is not the primary reason for how babbled sounds are converted to words (de Villiers and de Villiers 1978). Skinner's theory also made no provision for novelty, the sentences children speak without having ever heard them before. It is also provided no explanation for the spontaneous acquisition of grammar and syntax.

LAD: Chomsky

A more comprehensive explanation of how language is acquired, which was dramatically different from traditional learning theories, came from linguist Noam Chomsky. Rather than concentrating only on the sounds basic to language, he focused also on the underlying structures and rules. Language ability, according to Chomsky, is attained through an innate mechanism he called the *Language Acquisition Device (LAD)*. LAD is a hypothetical model based on the theory that individuals are born with the ability to formulate and understand all types of sentences, even though they have never heard them before.

Chomsky did not deny that imitation and reinforcement of speech sounds are a way of learning language. Imitation does seem to be the means whereby vocabulary is learned. But grammar, syntax, and originality come from the Language Acquisition Device (Chomsky 1957; Whitehurst and Vasta 1975; Slobin 1975).

Thus, using the particular vocabulary, syntax, and structure of one's own native tongue, each person can weave a unique web of language, often generating glories never before heard on earth (Brown 1973). The ultimate result of this human inventiveness can be a letter to Grandma, a poem, a short story, an essay, or a "bright saying" uttered by a three-year-old.

Rule system: Brown

Another important language theorist, Roger Brown, expanded on the LAD. He pointed out that people do not simply acquire a repertoire of sentences. Rather they "acquire a rule system that makes it possible to generate a literally infinite variety of sentences, most of them never heard from anyone else" (Brown 1973, page 97).

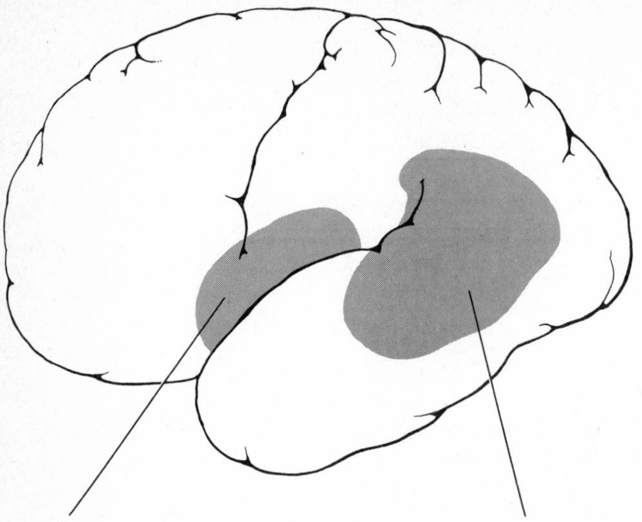

FIG. 6–1 Speech areas in the brain's dominant hemisphere.

Speech area   Speech area

Through *selective imitation*, a child learns new sentence structures without necessarily imitating their content. Imitation starts the process; then creativity takes over (Whitehurst and Vasta 1975). "Johnny do!" insists the little boy. He has the subject and the verb in the right place, but the sentence is one that Mother probably never taught him.

The theories of Skinner, Chomsky, and Brown show how complicated it is to explain language acquisition, to fathom the nature of the mind and its relationship to language. Now we know that it is no longer enough to attribute language to imitation, correction, and reinforcement. Children who rarely imitate, who receive little correction or reinforcement, learn language anyway, just like those who are avid imitators. In the last decade research has taken a new tack. Instead of theorizing about grammatical achievements at each developmental level, investigators are now studying the ways in which language has evolved in order to serve human needs (de Villiers and de Villiers 1978).

Speech area of the brain

If there is, indeed, a Language Acquisition Device, where would we find it? Work with brain-damaged children and adults whose ability to speak is impaired has established that language is almost always controlled by the left hemisphere of the brain. An adult who has an accident or illness that affects that part of the brain will suffer from *aphasia,* a disturbance in the ability to speak or to understand language. But if the other half of the brain is damaged, language is less likely to be affected (Bay 1975). (See Figure 6–1.)

However, if a child who has not yet learned to speak suffers damage to the left hemisphere, the other side of the brain apparently takes over. The individual neither becomes aphasic—loses the ability to use language—nor fails to acquire language in the normal way. Remarkably, a child born with only one hemisphere develops language anyway, with no ill effects (Bay 1975).

Thus it seems to be true that the brain becomes specialized only later in life. For a child, the brain's language acquisition resources are much more flexible and generalized than an adult's. Just how flexible a child's brain is can be illustrated by the remarkable story of how people acquire language, beginning as early as the day they are born.

How Language Builds

Early vocalizations

The birth cry is a human's first communication with the world. But all it means is that we have arrived with the necessary lungs and vocal equipment. A child who has no cerebrum can cry just as well as a child whose brain is intact (Miller 1951).

Sound repertoire   While an infant's cries may have meaning to the child, they have no significance in terms of human language. It is generally agreed that a crying baby tells a parent nothing except that it is crying. It is the parent who guesses that it is a "hunger" cry or a "wet" cry or an "I hurt" cry. But the child's distress may also be psychological, not physical.

However, crying and early vocalizations do show that the basic equipment for speech is present. The same mechanisms used for crying will be used later for speech. In fact, the wave forms of crying (on a graph) have the same characteristics as the sentences uttered by a grown-up (Lieberman 1967).

Babies also make other sounds when they are not in distress—grunts, gurgles, hiccups, snorts—all related to eating, breathing, sleeping, vocal exercise (Miller 1951). The vowel sounds for these noises are not the same as the vowels heard in crying. The differences further illustrate the potentials for later speech (de Hirsch 1970).

Phonemes   Infants have a full sound repertoire in the first year, including vowels and consonants of any language. Close analysis of the sounds made by infants less than ten days old showed that they were already using some of the vowel sounds we need for language (Irwin 1949). The sequence of vocalization is crying, then cooing, then babbling. All the sound production of babies is preparation for words that mean something to the people around them. The infant is getting ready for speech, uttering many of the basic sounds of language, called *phonemes*, both vowels and consonants.

Phoneme: basic language sound

During the first few days after birth, a baby utters eight distinguishable sounds—five vowels and three consonants—about a fifth of the sounds used by adults. By far the most used vowel in crying is *ae*, as in *bat*. Other infant vowel sounds are *i*, as in *bit;* ε, *get:* ʌ, *up; u, food.* Consonants are *h, l,* and a glottal stop, the consonant that results from breath pressured behind the closed *glottis*—for example, the *t* in water or bottle (Irwin 1949). Most of an infant's vowel sounds are made by the front parts of the mouth and tongue, while two of the three consonants are formed by the back of the mouth.

Glottis: the opening between the lower pair of vocal cords in the larynx

In general, the course of development of vocalization is from the front of the mouth and tongue to the back (Irwin and Curry 1941). Back vowels and front consonants begin to be heard during the period of early cooing. This happens around four months, when a baby's cries and snorts are expressions of contentment or pleasure or merely vocal exercise.

Babbling   Finally, babbling brings a full range of the sound elements of language. From about six to nine months, a physically and psychologically normal child is babbling sounds like *ma, da, ba.*

Babbling is different from the earliest sounds, mostly linked to hunger or pain or general discomfort. Now babies seem to be playing with their voices like a musical instrument, having fun with sounds. Some babbling comes when an infant is playing with toys or exploring the surroundings. Some is a response to the care-giver. In fact, whole "conversations" are sometimes held between a mother and a baby. Often the babbling sounds are reduplicated monosyllables—*dada, baba*, and *mama*. These syllables, uncannily realistic, are still meaningless, although they sound much like sentences, complete with the right intonation.

Babbled sounds display a talent that may be partly lost when a child is learning real words. For example, some children who

make the sounds of *l* and *r* when they babble may be unable to produce the same sounds later on for English words like *love* or *rat*. They have to relearn those consonant sounds later (Jakobson 1941).

Grown-ups encourage the right noises.

Remarkably, babies babble in their native language. Compare the babbling of Japanese and American babies. They make the same sounds during the first few months. But by the time they are about nine months old, the Japanese babies have narrowed their repertoire to sounds they will use to speak Japanese, and the American infants are limiting themselves to American sounds (Menyuk 1958).

Thus, now is the time when deliberate reinforcement can begin. The grown-ups consciously teach the baby the language of the household by encouraging the "right" noises. Feedback is important during the babbling period. Deaf infants start to babble, but they eventually stop, apparently because they can hear neither themselves nor anyone else (de Hirsch 1970).

Sensitivity to adult speech *Echolalia*—repeating and imitating their own sounds as well as the sounds heard around them—

Echolalia: repetition and imitation of sounds or words

starts about the time children are ten months old. Say "no-no" to a baby and the child may give it back to you, but may have no idea what "no-no" means (de Hirsch 1970).

But responsiveness to adult speech starts long before ten months. An unusual research project demonstrated that humans are born with a sensitivity to the speech of others. Using cameras and sound tapes, two investigators showed that babies only a few days old moved in a kind of synchronization with the words spoken by adults in their presence. With their body movements, they shared the rhythm of the words, even though the words could not have had any meaning to them (Condon and Sander 1974). Is it possible that this is the basis for the rhythm of our adult speech, and for the gestures we use when we speak?

Even as early as three months old, a baby reacts positively to friendly tones, negatively to angry sounds (Buhler and Hetzer 1935). At five or six months, there are different responses to tones, music, men's and women's voices. All the emotions, major and minor, that are expressed in speech get responses from babies

Box 6–2 When Do Babies Understand?

Adults who talk to infants need not feel foolish. Babies can understand us much earlier than they can make themselves understood—at least in words. Infants respond to intonations and the emotional freight carried by what adults say to them. In the normal course of perceptual development, the mere sound of a human voice has meaning to babies as young as two months old. They pay attention: look toward the speaker or change whatever they are doing.

A study of the heartbeat rates of babies around the age of four or five months showed a distinct response to familiar syllables (Moffitt 1971). Not much later, around six months, some words seem to mean more to a baby than others—maybe *bye-bye* or *bottle*. At a year, a child will react appropriately to various words. For example, many will wave good-bye when verbally prompted.

Children 11 to 15 months old show that they have a definite preference for their mothers' voices as against, say, music, or a stranger's voice (Friedlander 1968). More important, at that age a child knows what "No!" means. The youngster might also be expected to understand some other common warnings, like "Careful!" "Hot!" "Dirty!"

"Give that to Mommy!" might prompt a response by 15 to 17 months, especially if the request is illustrated by a gesture. The game of "Where is your head? Where is your nose?" will get accurate participation soon thereafter (Miller 1951).

long before they understand the words or can respond with words of their own (de Hirsch 1970). (See Box 6–2.)

Early speech

Morphemes First-time parents imagine (beforehand) that they will never forget the moment when the baby utters its first word. But the chances are that the word will go unnoticed—as with Jon's piteous plea for "mi!"—because it sounds like babbling.

Words do tend to merge with babbled sounds toward the end of the first year. Words are composed of *morphemes*, the smallest units of sound that have meaning. A word can be made up of one or more morphemes. In English, *dog* is a morpheme. *Dogs* consists of two morphemes—*dog*, plus the plural, *s*.

Morpheme: Smallest unit of meaningful sound

The babbled sounds of a nine-month-old reappear as words when perceptual ability has developed to the point where the child can imitate what Mother or Grandma or any care-giver is saying over and over. Most likely, it is the mother (or whoever), not the baby, who has chosen these sounds from the child's babbled "vocabulary" and undertaken to "teach" them to the baby (Miller 1951).

Holophrastic speech The child's first word usually is a *reduplicated monosyllable*. *Mama* is one, but it could be *dada, tick-tick, bye-bye*, or something similar. These words are called *holophrases*—one-word sentences. They are truly all-purpose at the beginning. By intonation, by gestures, the baby can turn a single word into a question, a command, or a commentary (Miller 1951).

Reduplicated monosyllable: single-syllable sound repeated to form a word

Holophrase: one-word sentence

Such *telegraphic speech*—a few words standing for a whole world of meaning—suggests that even year-old children are capable of conceiving what might be the equivalent of a full sentence. This would not, of course, be a complicated sentence like an adult's but a generalized notion, "undifferentiated and global" (McNeil 1970, page 1074). These first words often come at the same time as walking (Irwin 1949). It is interesting to note that Jon began to walk at 11 months, the period of the auto trip when he spoke his first word, "mi!" The first word usually appears around the end of the first year, whether it is the English *mama*, the Chinese *ah-ma*—or hundreds of variations.

Telegraphic speech: abbreviated sentences containing only the words essential to convey meaning

Note that a baby's mastery of spoken language is not necessarily linked to ability to think. Anyone who has dealt with babies has marvelled at how much they can understand, even in the *da-da* stage. The gap between the time a baby understands language and the time the child can speak words and sentences may be a few months, even years in some cases.

Vocabulary growth

Parabola of increase   The growth of language varies enormously from one child to another. Floods of words seem to come from some children early in their second year. A few "hardly said a word" till they were two or three, according to the perhaps faulty recollection of their families.

Parabola: a graphed curve that increases along the vertical axis and levels off parallel to the horizontal axis

By two-and-a-half years, 27 is the average number of sounds used by children, two-thirds of the full repertoire used for mature language (Irwin 1949). Most children have now mastered almost all the vowels used in the adult speech of their native tongue, and about two-thirds of the consonant types (Chen and Irwin 1946).

But in general, vocabulary builds unevenly. It begins slowly in the first year (birth to 12 months), increasing in the second year (12 to 24 months), and increasing the most during the third year (24 to 36 months). A graph would show, not a diagonal line rising from age one to age ten, but a *parabola* that peaks at about two-and-a-half (30 months), then slows up considerably in the later years of childhood (Irwin 1949).

From 12 to 18 months, a baby uses only a small number of words. But during the next three months language growth is apt to be remarkable—from about 20 words at 18 months to about 200 words at 21 months. Vocabulary grows to 300–400 words by about 24 months (two years) or soon thereafter. The fastest increase comes from 30 to 33 months. At age three (36 months) or a few months later, a child uses at least a thousand words or more (Lenneberg 1966). (See Box 6–3.)

Articulation problems   By the age of seven, most English-speaking children can pronounce all the sounds of the language. But for many, some of the ability is newly acquired, since three out of four kindergartners (aged five) have difficulty with at least one phoneme. Most of the articulation problems children experience are with *s, l,* and *r.* Children who cannot pronounce these sounds are also apt to have trouble with plurals and other word forms.

Box 6–3 Coordination of Motor and Language Development

Age in months	Vocalization and language	Motor development
4	Coos and chuckles	Head self-supported; tonic neck reflex subsiding; can sit with pillow props on three sides
6 to 9	Babbles; produces sounds such as "ma" or "da"; reduplication of sounds common	Sits alone; pulls himself to standing; prompt unilateral reaching; first thumb opposition of grasp
12 to 18	A small number of "words"; follows simple commands and responds to "no"	Stands momentarily alone; creeps; walks sideways when holding on to a railing; takes a few steps when held by hands; grasp, prehension, and release fully developed
18 to 21	From about 20 words at 18 months to about 200 words at 21; points to many more objects; comprehends simple questions; forms two-word phrases	Stance fully developed; gait stiff, propulsive, and precipitated; seats himself on child's chair with only fair aim; creeps downstairs backward; has difficulty building tower of three cubes; can throw a ball, but clumsily
24 to 27	Vocabulary of 300 to 400 words; has two- to three-word phrases; uses prepositions and pronouns	Runs but falls when making a sudden turn; can quickly alternate between stance, kneeling or sitting positions; walks stairs up and down, one foot forward only
30 to 33	Fastest increase in vocabulary; three- to four-word sentences are common; word order, phrase structure, grammatical agreement approximate language of surroundings, but many utterances are unlike anything an adult would say	Good hand and finger coordination; can move digits independently; manipulation of objects much improved; builds tower of six cubes
36 to 39	Vocabulary of 1000 words or more; well-formed sentences using complex grammatical rules, although certain rules have not yet been fully mastered; grammatical mistakes are much less frequent; about 90 percent comprehensibility	Runs smoothly with acceleration and deceleration; negotiates sharp and fast curves without difficulty; walks stairs by alternating feet; jumps 12''; can operate tricycle; stands on one foot for a few seconds

Source: E. H. Lenneberg, Natural history of language, in Frank Smith and George A. Miller (eds.), *Genesis of Language,* page 222 (Cambridge, Mass.: M.I.T. Press, 1966).

Grammar acquisition

Anyone who pluralizes a word has mastered one element of grammar. Grammar and syntax also involve sentence structure, word order, and "rules" for word usage. To put two words together in the right order—a noun plus a verb—is another element of grammar and syntax. One striking achievement of normal children is that they are already following the rules of grammar and syntax by the latter half of their second year (18 to 24 months), the same age they usually put two words together. A parent who has the time and the interest could make a fascinating diary of the language acquisition of his or her child. Compare diaries with another parent and there will probably be striking similarities.

Word order, plurals, tenses   Children's word order reflects the language structure they hear in their environment. Normal children who are only 18 to 24 months not only combine words but use them in the correct order for their own language. A German child will put the verb after the object. An American child will use the reverse order. A little later in life, children can make plurals (if the language uses plurals—not all languages do) and, where appropriate, form possessives, as well as use the past tense and the third-person singular (Slobin 1973).

One inventive investigator made up nonsense word games to play with four- to seven-year-olds. She told them: "This is a wug. Now there are two of them. There are two _____?"

"Wugs!" the children answered correctly. No one had specifically told them how to make plurals. But they knew anyway (Berko 1958).

Nouns, then verbs   Children learn nouns before any other words. They name the things and people in their lives. Mommy and Daddy, of course. Ball. Milk. Dog. Cat.

Normal children combine two words by 24 months, the end of the second year, and can usually answer simple questions in a simple sentence. Much of the language is composed of _pivot words_—words that are used often and in the same position in a sentence: "See kitty," "See car," "See house." _See_ is the pivot word (Braine 1963; McNeill 1970).

Pivot word: a word used repeatedly in the same position in several sentences

Social talk   By 18 months, children are sensitive to the social implications of other people's conversation. Children this age are less likely to vocalize when adults are talking; they are more apt to talk when adults are not conversing with one another (Fein 1975). By the age of around two (24 months), children are beginning to hold real conversations with adults, responding to both the demands of the listener and the requirements of the situation. In fact, they talk more to adults than to their playmates. They seem to take more care, when talking to adults, to tailor their messages to the receiver's need and to respond to feedback (Wellman and Lempers 1977).

Sentence growth   As children grow older, not only do their sentences become longer, but they also become more complicated. By the time they are three, holophrases are a thing of the past. And after four, the sentences are far more complex.

At five, the average sentence length is around 4.6 words. Basic grammatical rules and the orderly arrangement of words to form a sentence are generally absorbed by ages four to five (Miller 1951). Average children have mastered all the fundamentals of their native tongue by the time they are five. This includes the arbitary signs, each of them with meaning, that we call *words*. It includes, too, the rules for combining those word-signs to express a variety of information and thought. "The acquisition of grammar is one of the most complicated intellectual achievements of children," according to authorities on language (Ervin and Miller 1963, page 116).

Overgeneralization   Many preschoolers carry their grammatical rules too far. The idioms of the language still have to be learned. Children might add *s* for plural on every word—"mans"—if not specifically taught otherwise. A youngster might categorize all women as "mommies." In fact, even a first grader who talks about "gooses" rather than "geese" is merely applying a basic rule of grammar.

The irregular plurals of the English language are beyond a six- or seven-year-old. The child knows about *girls* and *boys*, but that is as complex as plurals can get. Correct use of *-es* for a plural like *classes* does not usually come, right or wrong, until possibly the third grade. Anything even more irregular, like *geese* and *oxen*, is still not a usage most children have assimilated at that age (Graves and Koziol 1971).

Tenses also give little children trouble. The preschool child's grammar has been absorbed only through the environment, which may not yet have supplied idiomatic refinements. And, children could certainly not explain their own "rules." They just "know" (Brown 1973).

How that knowing takes place remains a matter of speculation and experimentation. Children eventually learn subtle differences in syntax by figuring out what meaning a speaker intends to convey. One scholar suggests that the child uses other knowledge, quite apart from language, to understand such grammatical niceties as direct and indirect objects and the importance of the difference between subject and predicate (MacNamara 1972).

Outcome of maturation

Speech development—although not vocabulary—seems to be all finished by about the age of ten. The development of speech coincides with the maturation of the brain, which is relatively flexible or malleable before ten. (See page 219.) By the time puberty arrives, the language maturational schedule is complete. After that, the brain seems to become set in its ways. Basic language skills, like comprehension and grammar, that have not been learned by the mid-teens can seldom be mastered (Lenneberg 1966).

By the end of the first year of life, when language begins, about 60% of the maturation of the brain is already accomplished (Lenneberg 1966). Then the maturation rate slows down. From infancy through adolescence the brain becomes less and less plastic and more specialized. At puberty, the brain is irrevocably committed to language in one hemisphere or the other. The period of primary language acquisition is effectively over. The brain is now mature, and language learning (as in acquiring a new language) becomes a laborious process.

Nevertheless, unlike some purely motor abilities (such as walking), some aspects of language acquisition in one's native tongue are *not* finished early in life. We learn words and new ways of combining them all our lives, although the greatest learning comes during our first 20 years (Miller 1951). After maturation is complete, language acquisition goes on as a result of the bombardment of stimuli from the environment. (Consider all the new slang everyone picks up.) Thus, both maturation and experience produce language (McNeill 1970).

Language, Thought, and Learning

Only a hermit sitting on a mountaintop might deny the importance of language in the daily life of a human being. "Speech . . . is one of the essential means whereby the child finds his bearings in the external world" (Luria 1957, page 116).

Yet even a hermit might need to talk to himself, perhaps to relieve loneliness, perhaps to put his thoughts into order. Language is a vital tool in communication, thought, and learning.

Communication

Egocentric speech   Children often talk to themselves. Piaget (see Chapter 5) found a great deal of such *egocentric speech* among young children—words spoken solely for the children's own benefit or as a means of pulling others into the orbit of their activities. In contrast, children's *socialized speech*, less predominant, according to Piaget, is intended to be part of a give-and-take with the audience. It is an exchange of ideas or an attempt to exert some kind of influence.

Egocentric speech: self-centered speech that shows no concern for the listener

Socialized speech: speech that takes the listener into consideration

On the other hand, George Miller (1951) believes that socialized speech is the more dominant. In fact, he says, children's speech has a primarily social function. Other recent research bears out Miller's contention (Menig-Peterson 1975; Shatz and Gelman 1973).

Semantic difficulties in childhood   Have you ever found yourself in a place where everyone is speaking a language you cannot understand? A dismaying sense of isolation is the fate of many Americans who travel. The feeling of frustration is hard to forget.

Some of that frustration is built into the relationship between adults and children, who are sometimes speaking what amounts to two different languages. Language comprehension involves *semantics*, or word meaning. For those who deal with children, it can be helpful to be familiar with the stages of language development and understanding, to know not only what thoughts a child is trying to convey but also what words a child is capable of understanding. Adults generally do well in avoiding "fancy" multisyllabic vocabulary with children. But they often go astray with the little words. They fail to realize that a small word may signify an advanced concept.

Semantics: meaning in language

Semantic development—learning what words mean—has a close relationship to cognitive development. Both involve the ability to handle concepts. And the development of both proceeds from the concrete to the abstract. There are numerous examples.

What children understand   Preschool children understand *first* and *last* before they understand *before* and *after*. If you tell a child to "move a blue [toy] plane first; move a red plane last," the youngster is more likely to get your meaning than if you say, "before you move a red plane, move a blue plane" (Amidon and Carey 1972, page 421).

The child is also, of course, responding to the word order of the command. Word order will lead to confusion in two statements like: "The girl is helped by the boy" and "The girl helps the boy." To a six-year-old, the same word order in the two sentences will dominate the subtleties of the active and passive verbs.

An adult who really wants to communicate with a first grader must be careful in using adverbs relating to time. *After* is easiest to understand. *Before* is a little harder. *Until* is the hardest (Barrie-Blackley 1973).

Five- to seven-year-olds understand *and then* and *but first* before they understand *before* and *after* (Hatch 1971). Attaining the concepts of *before* and *after* comes in stages. Three-year-olds understand neither word. Gradually, time words are understood (Clark 1971). Anyone who wants to teach a child to tell time had better show, rather than tell. Explanations involving "*before* the big hand reaches the 12" are apt to be misunderstood.

Nor can one count on a preschooler to grasp the difference between *different* and *same*. Until the age of about three-and-a-half, a child usually understands the two words to mean *same*. Slightly older children interpret *different* to mean *another*. Even a little later, children who choose objects correctly still think that *different* requires a certain amount of similarity. It takes a still higher level of language development to understand *different* and *same* as an adult does (Webb, Oliveri, and O'Keeffe 1974).

Preschoolers have a hard time with *negatives*. "No!" is easy, but "Don't close the door!" may create a problem. To the child the *don't* is apt to melt meaninglessly into the sentence. He or she may well close the door instead, particularly since the words *close the door* are the most recent part of the message. Children who were shown blue and red toys and asked to pick up "all the not red things" picked up the red things. A child hears concrete cues like *red*. *Not* is a little word that does not command attention during these early years (Feldman 1969).

Another subtlety that is not understood by young children is *side*. A preschooler comprehends *front* and *back* before realizing what *side* means (Kuczaj and Maratsos 1975).

Cause and effect are hard to grasp. "Don't cross the street because you might get hit by a car." A child might dutifully repeat the warning but might cross the street anyway. The preschooler can verbalize the caution but cannot yet conceptualize it.

Not until almost eight is a child apt to understand the significance of *because* (Kuhn and Phelps 1976). Children have difficulty with connectives straight through the grade school years. *And* is no problem. But *or* is understood later and *if* comes last (Shine and Walsh 1971).

"She's a sweet person." An adult must be careful with such a comment to a first grader. At that age, *sweet* is a taste, not a character trait. Children are very literal. They do understand words like *hard, bright, deep, sweet, warm, dry,* and *cold,* but only as they refer to inanimate objects. A slightly older child might be able to relate those characteristics to people, but only in the physical sense. A person who is "cold" needs a sweater. The psychological use of such words comes much later, when a "cold person" is understood to be someone who is standoffish.

This linguistic progression makes sense when one recalls that cognitive development (and thus semantic development) goes from the concrete to the abstract. It also seems that words connected with the tactual senses—*sweet, warm*—are understood earlier among primary-grade children than visual words, like *bright* and *deep* (Lessor and Drouin 1975).

Certain pairs of terms seem to be understood by preschoolers before other pairs. In fact, there is a definite order of acquisition, which appears to depend on semantic complexity: *big–small; long–short; tall–short; high–low; old–young; thick–thin; wide–narrow; deep–shallow; in front–in back; up–down; in–out; on–off; first–last; over–under; early–late; above–below; ahead–behind; before–after* (Clark 1972). Concrete comes before abstract; the less obvious are the more difficult.

Children seem to *overgeneralize* the meaning of many words. Take the word *cup*. A three-year-old will call all drinking vessels a cup. A few years later, the child will differentiate between a cup and a glass, based entirely on what is seen. Only much later, by

12, will the youngster realize that the boundary between a cup and a glass is really quite vague (Andersen 1975).

Defining words, like understanding words, appears to be developmental. The way a child defines a word proceeds from *functional,* to *concrete,* and finally to *abstract.* A younger child is apt to define a *cup* functionally: "A cup is to drink from." When the youngster is a little older, the definition will be concrete: "A cup has a handle." Last comes the abstract definition: "A cup is a container." The *functional definitions* are most frequent up to the age of nine. By ten, more and more children have reached the abstract (Al-Issa 1969).

Functional: pertaining to use

Concrete: pertaining to a specific instance or object

Abstract: pertaining to a general idea or notion

Obviously, these are all generalizations. Children's understanding differs from one to the other, depending on their individual level of conceptual ability and on many other factors, both genetic and environmental.

Thinking

Private speech   Even very early in life language becomes important to facilitate and organize thinking and problem-solving. Study a preschooler faced with solving a practical problem in the course of play. The child will be silent only until some difficulty crops up. And then the youngster will begin to talk aloud, even if no one is paying attention (Luria 1957). Evidently, according to L. S. Vygotsky (1962), putting one's thoughts into words, even when no one else is there to talk to, helps one cope with problems. Most of us would confess that sometimes we, too, talk to ourselves. That does not necessarily mean we are peculiar. It just seems to help sort things out. Language for young and old alike appears to facilitate the thinking process.

Studies have shown that Vygotsky's notion of "private speech"—talking aloud to oneself—can be taught as an effective tool for rote learning. Most children seem to use this technique without being told to do so, and they resort to it more and more in the early years until they reach the point when such speech goes under cover and becomes thought (Kohlberg, Yaeger, and Hjertholm 1968). But there is some question whether private speech helps thinking or vice versa (Kohlberg 1968).

In any case, no one learns language, written or spoken, without thinking. Words are, after all, symbols for what we see and deal with in the world around us. Language can help thinking, but it can also get in the way of thought. One scholar concluded that once you put your thoughts in writing, or speak them aloud, you have structured your ideas and you have a "record" of what you have said. Thus, in a sense, you have confined your thoughts and limited your own freedom (Carroll 1964).

Concept formation Both language and thought deal with concepts. Conceptual development is facilitated by language and vice versa. A *concept* has been defined as "an internal representation of a class of experiences" (Carroll 1964, page 90). In other words, it is an idea that is usually expressed in words or symbols. Not all concepts need words to give them flesh. A baby has many concepts of people and things that are wordless but nonetheless clear to the child. But words cannot be acquired without concepts, because using a word correctly implies that one is developing or has a concept of what that word represents. (The baby who cried for "mi" had a concept of milk.) Thus, cognitive development is an important factor in language development (Prawat and Jones 1977).

Concept: an idea or notion, usually represented by a word or symbol

Many language concepts are learned without a person's even realizing it. For example, as we have already seen, the basic concepts of grammar and syntax are absorbed, rather than deliberately thought about. But when language is deliberately used as a specific instrument of thought, it is called *reasoning:* if one reasons, one must be able to work out logical steps in terms of language.

Verbal mediation Language helps in every aspect of learning. *Verbal mediation* is the term used to describe the use of language to direct, organize, and regulate behavior. A speaking child has an easy means of communicating with others, which gives the youngster the benefit of their experience. The child can use speech as a way of "organizing" experience and "regulating" action. Thus, what the child does is "mediate" through words (Luria 1957). For example, verbal mediation is being used when elementary school teachers insist that pupils orally repeat the assignments and the plans for what they are supposed to do next. As a result, students are much more likely to do the job right. Their attention has been focused; their memory has been helped.

Verbal mediation: use of language to direct thought and action

An interesting illustration of the power of words came from an experiment with children who were taught to perform a task requiring responses to one of two available cues. Then the experimenters arbitrarily changed the rules: the meaning of the cues was altered. If white started out to be correct, now black was the right cue.

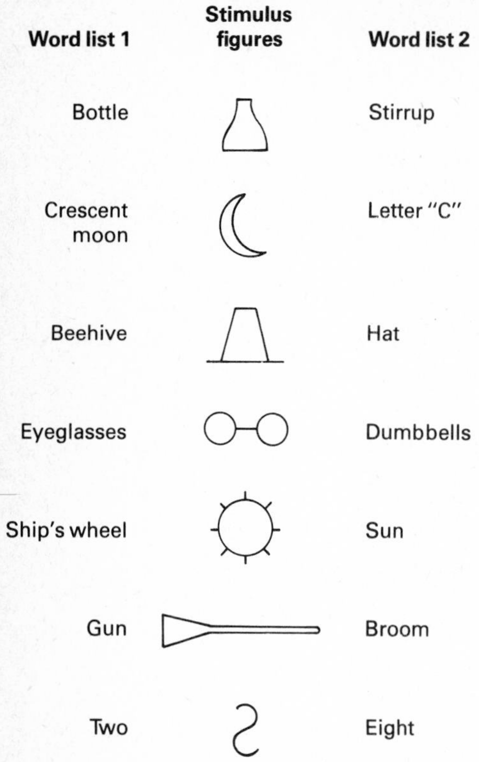

Word list 1	Stimulus figures	Word list 2
Bottle		Stirrup
Crescent moon		Letter "C"
Beehive		Hat
Eyeglasses		Dumbbells
Ship's wheel		Sun
Gun		Broom
Two		Eight

FIG. 6–2 The power of words. In a classic experiment two groups of subjects were exposed to these figures and words and later asked to reproduce them. The reproductions were influenced by which list of labels was given at the time of exposure. For example, the O—O tended to be drawn like O‑O if it had been labelled "eyeglasses." But if the label was "dumbbells," it might be drawn as O‑O. *Source:* L. Carmichael, H. P. Hogan, and A. A. Walter, An experimental study of the effect of language on the reproduction of visually perceived form, *Journal of Experimental Psychology,* 1932, *15,* 73–86.

The testers found that when children between the ages of five and seven were taught to mention the relevant cue—to put it into words—they had an easier time when changing over to the new instructions. However, when older children were faced with the same problem, teaching them to speak the new cues had no extra effect, probably because by now they already were accustomed to using words "in their heads" to help solve problems. Still, if the older children were deliberately taught to mention the irrelevant cue, they made more mistakes (Kendler, Kendler, and Wells 1960).

Another illustration of how wrong words can lead to errors involved colored chips, like those used for poker. A person who put an inaccurate mental label on a color chip—blue instead of lavender, for instance—remembered it later as bluer than it had really been (Brown 1958). (See also Figure 6–2.)

Words can be a help in enforcing discipline, even with very young children. Children as young as two can follow instructions to delay a response until a signal is given (Golden, Montare, and Bridger 1977). And teaching children to say in words that they must not look at attractive toys helped them to resist temptation (Hartig and Kanfer 1973). Impulsive children who were trained to talk to themselves actually were able to become more self-controlled (Meichenbaum and Goodman 1971).

Memorizing   Memorizing certainly depends on words. Some words are easier to remember than others. Rhymes, for example, are very easy to memorize. This may account for the popularity of nursery rhymes and such epics as "The Night Before Christmas."

Many adults use rhyme to jog memory. How about: "Thirty days hath September, April, June, and November. All the rest . . ."? We learn it in grade school and never forget it our whole lives through (Locke 1971). Another good memory device involves semantically similar words. Even three-year-olds do well with related words like *sun, moon, star* (Locke and Locke 1971). (See also Chapter 7, page 278.)

Reading

Readiness   Reading readiness is part of the sequence of language maturation. It seems to come at about six or six-and-a-half. A child can learn to read only after acquiring specific skills in hearing, comprehension, and visual and motor coordination. (See also Chapters 3 and 4.) Therefore, tests to determine whether a child is ready to learn to read rely on several kinds of language skill: how well a child can hear the difference between words and link them to pictures; whether a youngster can remember a story and tell about it; the ability to name objects and classify them (vocabulary); the youngster's ability to answer questions about matters of common knowledge. In addition, reading readiness tests rate visual discrimination, motor control, and understanding of numbers.

The foundation for reading ability is laid during the preschool years, when a child is developing language, seeing pictures, being exposed to books and stories, having attention and curiosity piqued by experiences and various kinds of stimulation. Also important are actual attempts to read. Another way to promote reading ability is to give three- to seven-year-olds visual

orientation training, to help in discriminating letters like *b*, *d*, *p*, and *q* (Spectorman, Shulman, and Ernhart 1977). (See also Chapter 3, page 98.)

Poor readers   Spoken language seems to play a truly crucial role in reading. One might think that *seeing* the words is the only important factor. Evidently that is not so. Poor readers may have a kind of language *hearing* problem. Their memory for sounds may be poor. They are poor in their ability to recall the sequential sounds in words and to make sense of words when the words are presented with some sounds deleted (Golden and Steiner 1969).

Reading difficulties can be fateful to psychological as well as mental development. A poor reader often feels generally inferior and incompetent and may never recover a positive self-image. On the other hand, poor *self-concepts* may actually be the cause of reading disability. Measures of self-concept made in kindergarten seem to be correlated with later reading progress, although the self-concept scores have no relation to intelligence test ratings (Wattenberg and Clifford 1964).

Self-concept: sum total of one's self-perceptions

Specialists seem to agree that children should be allowed to learn to read at their own speed at the age when each is ready. No one should be made to feel like a second-class person because he or she is slower than some others. It is normal for people to differ in their reading ability, just as they vary in their ability to speak, think, and communicate. As to just what are the reasons for language ability differences among individuals, research has provided some answers.

Special Influences on Language Ability

Sex differences

Culture versus genes   Cartoons, living room humor, and television comedy all make much sport with the "talkative female." Is it really true that women talk more than men? Are girls more verbal than boys? And if so, why?

There are, indeed, sex differences in verbal behavior, but these differences may be more cultural than genetic. A study published in 1967, before the public consciousness had been fully raised on feminist issues, took it for granted that girls are naturally more verbal than boys. The investigator found "indications" that language plays a greater part in the early mental development of girls than it does in boys' development. Looking for reasons, it is suggested that "girls may be by nature more interested in communicating, boys investigating the properties of objects. . . . Possibly the characteristically masculine analytic thinking may have its origin in the observation of things, while feminine intuition arises in the process of mentally accommodating to the less predictable behavior of human beings" (Moore 1967, pages 102–103).

This researcher made what might have been perfectly acceptable assumptions about the differences between men and women, without sorting out the possible cultural causes of those differences. Less than ten years later, an entirely different reason for feminine verbalism was proposed by another investigator.

The greater verbal ability of girls . . .

Sex differences were found, but they were attributed to how parents treat their children.

Mothers' influence Mothers seem to use different patterns of verbalization for their sons and daughters. "Girls and their mothers talk more to one another than do boys and their mothers, and mothers encourage verbalization from their daughters more than from their sons. . . . The significant differences observed are all of the mothers' behavior rather than the children's. . . . Mothers of girls are providing a richer language environment compared with mothers of boys." This is the conclusion of one investigation (Cherry and Lewis 1976, pages 280–281).

It is possible, of course, that mothers get more response from their girl-children, and thus talk more to them. Another possibility is that mothers may feel a special closeness to their daughters because they are the same sex and therefore tend to talk to them more. One more factor could be the earlier maturation of girls, resulting in greater responsiveness. This could also encourage a mother to talk more to a daughter.

Even if the greater verbal ability of girls is cultural, rather than genetic, change may come slowly. It may be years—if ever—before mothers start to treat their children alike, regardless of sex. It may also take a long time before fathers share equal time with mothers in raising the young. Should these developments actually take place, what will happen to the stereotype of the verbal woman? No doubt new research will provide some answers.

Family influence

There is a child mental health agency, well-regarded, that does not include fathers in a program whose purpose is to teach first-time parents how to interact with their infants. The reason the agency gives is that no matter how much time fathers give to

The person who rears a child can have a profound effect on language abililty.

their infants' care, they tend to be custodial. They concentrate on changing diapers, providing food at mealtime, making sure that discipline is maintained. But they do not talk much to their children. So training fathers to "interact," according to these experts, would not be as fruitful as training the mothers. Whether the agency is right or wrong, it does seem to be clear that the person who rears a child, and how it is done, can have a profound effect on language ability.

Reinforcement in infancy Skinner's theory that reinforcement, particularly verbal reinforcement, influences language acquisition, is borne out by a study of 24 institutionalized infants three to six months old. Two experimenters tested the relative effects on the babies of food, stroking, and adult vocal imitation whenever the babies uttered sounds. All three stimuli increased the infants' vocalizations, but adult imitation was the most effective (Haugan and McIntire 1972).

Another group of three-month-old babies were studied in their own homes. An adult leaned over some of the infants, smiled, touched the baby's body, and said, "Hi, baby!" Other infants received sessions of continuous eye contact. Both kinds of stimulation were important "releasers" of sounds from the babies (Bloom 1975). The implication is that even in early infancy "speech" depends on how a baby is cared for. The sounds babies make, which are the forerunners of language, are social sounds—and human beings are necessary stimulators, as well as reinforcers.

Mothers, still usually the primary care-givers, have been shown to have enormous influence on their small children's language skills. Their verbal responsiveness to their children, their involvement in childrens' activities, even providing appropriate play materials, are all related to preschool language development (Elardo, Bradley, and Caldwell 1977).

Most mothers seem to tailor their speech to their children's linguistic ability (Snow 1972; Seitz and Stewart 1975; Moerk 1974). Without thinking about it, they simplify, repeat, and otherwise speak on their child's level. However, the fact that a baby cannot answer does not inhibit them. They do as much talking to a one-month-old as they do to three-year-olds (Ling and Ling 1974).

The higher the mother's education level, the greater the language skill of her infant. Apparently better-educated mothers talk much more to their babies than mothers with less schooling.

Mothers also talk more to their first-born children (probably because they have more time). As a result, oldest children in a family may get a better language start (Cohen and Beckwith 1976; Nelson 1973; and Ling and Ling 1974). However, first-born children do not inevitably begin to talk earlier than later children (Lenneberg 1966).

Siblings Contrary to popular impression, having older children in the house does not necessarily help a child learn to speak better. In fact, the effect may be just the reverse. A first-grade teacher reports the case of Billy, who had been in the exclusive care of three older sisters during his preschool years. They anticipated his every need and wish. When he reached school age, he had almost no language; he had never needed words before. But in first grade he made up the deficit in a hurry.

A formal study showed that middle-class children with no brothers or sisters do better in language development than those with several older siblings. This particular study dealt with babies aged 18 to 34 months (Lehman 1971).

Much folk wisdom deals with the language ability of twins. They are said to be late talkers because "they didn't need to talk—they had each other." This belief has some basis in fact. Twins' language development lags as much as six months behind single children, until about the age of three. The reason is not clear. Since twins are usually premature, they may well be developmentally behind singletons (Mittler 1970). But twins may talk later because they have fewer language needs. They may invent their own language. Also, they have companionship from one another without the need to talk (Dales 1969). Whatever the reason, twins' verbal "retardation" is usually only temporary.

Conversation at home While parents' speech may well be the source of a child's sentence structure, correct usage does not necessarily come because parents set out deliberately to teach grammar. In fact, parents usually pay attention to what a child is saying only to correct mistakes in content, not in word order or grammar (Slobin 1975).

"Her curl my hair" got a mother's approval, because the fact was that Mother was curling the child's hair. In contrast, "Walt Disney comes on Tuesday," grammatically correct, was disputed by a parent, because Tuesday was the wrong day (Brown, Cazden, and Bellugi 1968).

It does seem that care-givers need not go out of their way to try to teach children good grammar. Children learn anyway "without explicit tuition" (Slobin 1975). Useful for language learning, perhaps, is "sentence expansion." A parent repeats what a child says and fills in what has been left out (Brown and Bellugi 1964).

Children learn language from the tried-and-true methods: showing a child the pictures in a book and naming the objects; giving a running commentary on what mother is doing as well as what the child is doing; feeding the youngster questions like "What's that? What are you doing?" (Moerk 1974). All these are prime language-teaching techniques.

Parents often complain that they are drowning in "why," "where" and "what" from their young. Is it really worthwhile to try to answer those questions? Evidently the answers are valuable. The feedback and interaction from conversation are important to a child's language development. In fact, it is helpful to deal in "why," "where," "what," and "who" questions even when it is the parent who is asking the child. In either case, children appear to learn language as a result of the conversation, regardless of the "scientific value" of the exchange (Turnure, Buium, and Thurlow 1976; Endsley and Clarey 1975). The question-and-answer technique also has real demonstrated usefulness in passing on information to children (Ross and Balzer 1975).

A word of caution may be in order for overachiever parents who might want to hasten their children's language development by speaking to them on an adult level from babyhood. It has already been noted that for maturational reasons children's understanding of certain kinds of words is limited. Parents run the risk of confusing their children by speaking in abstractions when a child is still at a concrete level. One highly educated mother learned this to her sorrow, when she was having a heart-to-heart session with her 26-year-old son. Throughout the boy's childhood, she had been using the ironic tones and expressions normal to her when speaking to other adults. Now her son told her that he had suffered early emotional anguish because he had the constant impression that his mother disapproved of him. In vain did she now confess that he was actually her favorite child.

Cultural differences

Parent speech   Mother—that familiar scapegoat—is also held to account by some authorities for what may or may not be the "restricted language" in some "deprived" homes. A contrast is shown with the much more elaborate middle-class speech (Bernstein 1962; Hess and Shipman 1965). The language of the child from a lower socioeconomic class may, indeed, be less complex and descriptive than the middle-class child's language.

The differences in speech between children of different economic backgrounds are traced back to the bassinette. According to this view, the middle-class baby gets more vocalization—in response to the baby's own sounds—from the mother. The lower-class mother does much less talking back to her infant (Lewis and Wilson 1972).

According to some analysts (Bernstein 1962; Hess and Shipman 1965), care-givers in lower-class homes (Bernstein's studies were done in England) use language primarily to talk about things and actions. Sentences are short, simple, grammatically uncomplicated. What is said has to do with the here and now and the concrete. Concepts usually have no part in what is talked about. What is said is apt to be a command, not a discussion. "Go to the store and buy bread." "Put on your coat."

In contrast, middle-class speech tends to be individualized, specific, addressed to a particular situation or person, part of a dialogue. It appears to be more differentiated, more precise than lower-class language. Curiosity, questions, "thought" subjects are apt to be encouraged in middle-class homes. "Do you think we ought to have bread or rolls with dinner? Maybe you'd better go to the store and see what they have. Do you think it's going to rain? It might even snow—it seems to be cold enough. You aren't over your cold yet. Better dress warmly."

Middle-class mothers may tend to use longer and more complete sentences when they speak to their children. They may use more adjectives. The differences between middle-class and lower-class speech seem to hold true regardless of race (Bee et al. 1969).

Negative findings A variety of studies present evidence of negative environmental effects on the language of some children who live in crowded conditions full of loud noises and the blaring of radio and television all at once. They seem to have trouble telling the difference between one word and another. They may stop listening altogether. Quite different are the effects of frequent conversation between parents and children as young as a year-and-a-half or two years old, which adds up to stimulation and encouragement (Wachs, Uzgiris, and Hunt 1971).

Because children from some poverty-stricken homes are exposed to only a limited number of places, things, and situations during infancy and preschool years, the result may be at least a temporary cognitive deficit (Kirk and Hunt 1975). A total of 787 kindergartners, divided into high, middle, and low socio-economic groups, were tested soon after starting school and several months later. Language concepts were "significantly" more advanced for the higher socioeconomic group, which also proved to be more advanced in reading readiness (Downing, Ollila, and Oliver 1977).

One study found a significant difference between economically advantaged and disadvantaged first graders in their level of question-asking ability. The advantaged children asked more "why" and "what" questions, while the poverty group children were still operating at the "is it" "ain't it" and "are they" stage (Martin 1970).

Reading difficulties are also a frequent problem of children from deprived homes. Reading involves dealing with written language, which may or may not coincide with one's oral language. One analysis of Head Start children and children with various degrees of reading disability tested how well they translated a sentence into action. Head Start, one of the well-known *compensatory programs* begun in the Johnson era, was dedicated to the proposition that impoverished preschoolers can be helped by giving them the enriching intellectual stimuli they would otherwise miss in their home environment. Both the problem readers and the Head Start children tended to see a string of words, rather than a unified thought. "They seem to lack . . . an appreciation of written language and the rules that govern the relationship of words to words (syntax). . . ." They are "trapped in an oral tradition which is antithetical to the impersonal abstractions of printed language" (Denner 1970, page 887).

Compensatory programs: organized efforts to make up for inadequacies in previous experience

Yet another investigation related the verbal ability of 10- to 12-year-old boys to how much the parents and children talk to each other. The higher the occupational status of the parents (usually correlated with better education) the greater their young sons' language prowess (Jones 1972*b*).

Conclusions questioned How valid are all these findings? Are socioeconomic class language discrepancies genuine or mostly theoretical? It has been argued that the differences are really only a matter of manners and customary ways of behaving. It may be that in lower socioeconomic households, preoccupation with grim daily realities may restrict language use. Another possibility

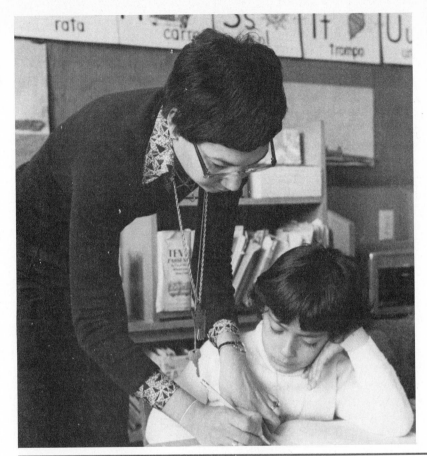

Bilinguals often attain conservation ability earlier than monolingual children.

is that "fancy language" may be associated negatively with school and the whole educational apparatus; thus, in some kitchens, to speak elaborately may simply seem out of place. It has been noted that neither social class nor household problems nor other environmental difficulties have anything to do with the time a child is going to start talking (Lenneberg 1966).

Two language registers The variety of speech and language habits among different cultural groups in our mixed society creates other language problems in school. Scholars are beginning to question an earlier assumption that black children are necessarily deficient in language ability. The evidence seems to show, rather, that they are actually bilingual. At home, in the playground, in their neighborhoods, blacks speak an accepted vernacular. But in the classroom, they are forced to use another English language with which they have had little practice.

A study of black children in rural northern Florida showed that they had at least two language "registers," one for school and one for out of school. The school register was also used when the children talked to people who seemed to be in authority. Only when speaking the school language did the children use short sentences, simplified syntax, strange intonations. What they said was limited and concealed their attitudes, feelings, and ideas.

Out of school, however, the children used their natural language, and in this they were easy, fluent, creative, and even gifted. The language was distinctly nonstandard English; in fact, it was *another* language, with its own grammar. These findings do not support previous assumptions that such children lack the language needed for abstract thinking. People think, with or without language, this investigator argues. The problem may be faulty communication between two different languages (Houston 1970). (See Box 6–4.)

Obviously, the educational system must find ways of coping with the black and white language differences. It might help the problem if teachers became sensitive to their own language variations. They might realize that they speak one way to friends but another way to their supervisors (DeStefano 1972). Then they could better understand how black children deal with authority.

Cultural background, not race, appears to have a great deal to do with the apparent difference in language ability between blacks and whites. White and black children matched for social class and nonverbal intelligence did equally well on standard English sentences. Perhaps black children should be tested using the dialect in which they are skilled, instead of standard English, in order to find out their true language ability. When white children were tested using black dialect sentences, they did poorly indeed (Genshaft and Hirt 1974). (See also Chapter 8, page 339.)

Institutional living Being reared in an institution, even for only the first three years of life, seems to have a serious effect on language development. Children brought up in foster homes, with normal families and normal family interaction, have been shown to be distinctly superior to institutionalized children in language ability. Even when the children from an institution were moved to foster homes, seven months after moving their vocabularies were not equal to those of children reared only in foster homes (Goldfarb 1945a). A comparison of the sounds made by orphanage infants with those of family infants one day to six months old found that the family babies vocalized much more than the orphanage babies (Brodbeck and Irwin 1946). Similarly, institutionalized babies' speech was found to be delayed because of isolation from people who would talk to them (Goldfarb 1943).

However, environment seems to have very little effect on the *time* when children acquire language. As we have already noted, children of all classes begin to speak single words, phrases, and more elaborate sentences at the same age, true to the maturational schedule of all humans. Even children brought up in orphanages, below average at age three, catch up with everyone else by six or seven, as soon as they have a better chance to mix with more people (Lenneberg 1966). (See Box 6–5.)

Compensatory programs

Can the effects of a language-poor environment be overcome by special programs? Cultural deprivation may not consist simply of missing first-hand experiences, but may also involve whether or not someone *talks* to a child about what is happening. For example, middle-class and lower-class children, four to six years old, who had all eaten the same kinds of vegetables, were asked to name them. The middle-class children did better. Perhaps in their homes foods were more often "labeled" than in the lower-class homes (Wight, Gloniger, and Keeve 1970).

A group of four-year-olds in Head Start were compared with children in a middle-class nursery school. The Head Start children seemed to have benefited from the program, but they were still inferior in certain forms of semantic mastery. The conclusion was that they had suffered clear linguistic harm from the conditions of their upbringing (Hunt, Kirk, and Volkmar 1975). This suggests that this particular compensatory program may be only moderately successful in overcoming language deficits.

However, a "crash" language tutoring program might help deprived children make up what they have missed (Karnes et al. 1968). One experimental program chose 22 children in a nursery school in a deprived New York area. A teacher worked with them intensively on simple problems that forced them to understand and use language. Children were required to compare objects and make verbal choices; to make simple decisions; to imagine future courses of action or events; to use language silently and then to express it upon request. They were given commands that required them to repeat, before carrying out what they were told to do. Questions about weather were asked and answers expected.

Box 6–4   The BITCH Test (Black Intelligence Test of Cultural Homogeneity)

	A	B	C	D
1.				
2.				
3.				
4.				
5.				
6.				
7.				
8.				

1. *Hawk*
   (a) Rain
   (b) Sunshine
   (c) Water
   (d) Cold wind

2. *Heavy cat*
   (a) fat
   (b) arrogant
   (c) depressed
   (d) intelligent

3. *Hit on*
   (a) Beating someone
   (b) Trying to make a girl
   (c) Making someone cry
   (d) To discover

4. *H.N.I.C.*
   (a) He Never Intended Colored
   (b) Head Nigger in Charge
   (c) Have Nothing in Common
   (d) He Nodded in Consent

5. *Hog*
   (a) Bad person
   (b) A car
   (c) Animal
   (d) A whiskey still

6. *Horn*
   (a) Loud boom
   (b) Musical instrument
   (c) Shrill singing
   (d) Protuberance

7. *To hot comb*
   (a) To press
   (b) To curl
   (c) To wave
   (d) To set

8. *I know you shame*
   (a) You don't hear very well
   (b) You are a racist
   (c) You don't mean what you're saying
   (d) You are guilty

9. *Jackleg Preacher*
   (a) A preacher with a wooden leg
   (b) A preacher from the South
   (c) A preacher from the North
   (d) A preacher without a church

9. _____

10. *Jack Up*
   (a) Hold up
   (b) Tease
   (c) Make up with
   (d) High

10. _____

11. *Jaws are tight*
   (a) Hungry
   (b) Excited
   (c) Angry
   (d) Frightened

11. _____

12. *Jive*
   (a) very important
   (b) worthless
   (c) old
   (d) social

12. _____

13. *Jump Sharp*
   (a) Well dressed
   (b) Angry
   (c) Bitter
   (d) Get the point

13. _____

14. *LD*
   (a) car
   (b) drug
   (c) drug addict
   (d) lay dead

14. _____

15. *Later*
   (a) That's too bad
   (b) To leave
   (c) Leave him alone
   (d) Don't stop now

15. _____

This is a section taken from the BITCH test.
Test directions: These are some words, terms, and expressions taken from the Black experience. Select the correct answers and put a check (√) in the space provided on the right of the test sheet.
Test answers: 1 D, 2 D, 3 B, 4 B, 5 B, 6 B, 7 A, 8 C, 9 D, 10 A, 11 C, 12 B, 13 A, 14 A, 15 B.

Source: From the BITCH Test (Black Intelligence Test of Cultural Homogeneity) by Robert L. Williams, Ph.D., 1972.

The children were taught to categorize common objects. They were encouraged to make suggestions to the teacher and to discuss possible courses of action. All these efforts were intended not to teach language as an end itself, but as a tool for problem-solving and relating to others.

Even among the children who had been doing relatively well, there was distinct improvement. Intelligence scores rose for all the pupils. (See also Chapter 8, page 336.) Besides, the children were strikingly joyful over what they had learned. They seemed to have a feeling of mastery. Perhaps simple exposure to new materials, to school, to an interested adult is not enough. Enthusiasm and real progress may depend on showing a child how to become actively involved in the learning process. Children from middle-class homes, who have already learned verbal skills, can profit automatically from school. But children from impoverished environments may have to be expressly guided to make use of the stimulation and new experiences that school offers (Blank and Solomon 1968).

Box 6–5 A Case History in Language Development

A bizarre true story about a man named Larry strikingly confirms two developmental principles: that the surroundings in which a person is brought up can seriously stunt language development; that, regardless of environmental deprivation, normal individuals can and do develop some language ability.

At 31, Larry was transferred from a private home for the mentally retarded, where he had lived all his life, to a state hospital. There he was examined by a clinical psychologist who was struck by the fact that Larry had none of the outward physiological characteristics of retarded people. Still, the young man was silent, colorless, his handshake clammy and limp. He had a blank expression and didn't look his interviewer in the eye.

But when the psychologist gave Larry an oral intelligence test, he found that this "retarded" 31-year-old's vocabulary was not only normal for an adult, but superior. Larry even explained the meaning of words like *shrewd, bewail,* and *piscatorial.* In further interviews, the amazed investigator discovered that Larry could read very well, even though he had never gone to school.

"I just picked reading up by myself," he said, explaining that he had spent hours looking at books haphazardly left in the mental hospital by visitors. The staff never noticed. They evidently

Bilingualism

Can a bilingual background also cause English language deprivation? Many Americans can trace their descent from a bilingual or a foreign-language household. For some, the two-language or foreign-language home is as recent as a generation ago. It might even be happening right now. It appears that such a situation is not necessarily harmful to a child's English language development.

Our own personal recollection or family history may bear out this conclusion. Formal research confirms it: bilingualism not only does not hurt, it can help. It may facilitate cognitive as well as linguistic growth. Bilinguals often attain conservation ability earlier than monolingual children. They tend to be intellectually superior and to have higher grades in school (Liedtke and Nelson 1968).

One example is Eberardo, a preschooler with an Anglo mother and a Chicano father. Eberardo spoke both English and Spanish from the time he could talk. To his mother he spoke

thought he was just "holding on to an object."

Persistent investigation by the psychologist revealed the reasons why Larry had been dumped into the institution in the first place. The teenager who was his mother went to enormous trouble to conceal her pregnancy and the birth from her parents and her fiancé. She fell into the hands of an unscrupulous doctor who was running the retarded home for profit. He let her understand that the baby was, indeed, retarded, and he blackmailed her for the child's support until he sold the institution. At that point, Larry came to the state hospital. Later, the psychologist drew the story from the mother (who had never visited her son all during his 31 years).

This true story seems to have had a relatively happy ending. Larry flourished under the understanding sponsorship of the state hospital psychologist. He came out of his "retarded" shell, learned about the real world, and left to take a job working for a landscaping firm. Asks the investigator: "What manner of man might he have become had he enjoyed the benefits of a normal home and a loving family? How many other Larrys are there in the world, who don't even know they are normal people?" (McQueen 1970).

English; to his father, Spanish. Even when he was little more than an infant, he was sensitive to various individuals' language differences. When his grandparents came to visit, no one had to tell him what language to use. He addressed his mother's parents in English, and his father's in Spanish.

Learning two languages at once may increase intellectual potential and help a child form concepts. Growing up bilingual may even speed up the normal process of mental development. An investigator tested two groups of bilingual children and two groups of monolingual children, all with equivalent family backgrounds. In spite of their smaller vocabulary, the bilingual children seemed to be more advanced in perceptual and cognitive skills than the children who spoke only one language (Ben-Zeev 1977). (It is ironic that some people think being bilingual is a handicap, rather than an asset, in areas of this country where many children come from Spanish-speaking homes.)

A strong case has been made for teaching a second language early, in elementary school, because of the ease with which preschoolers acquire languages. Learning another language is easier for the young than for adults because of the early plasticity of the physical apparatus used for language. The brain may contain an "uncomitted cortex" area available for language learning, which by adulthood may be committed to other functions.

Some experimentation has suggested that one way to teach foreign language to children is informally, in a setting as much like home as possible, if possible providing an easy give-and-take with other children who speak the second language. Teaching a second language very early also takes advantage of the fact that children do not seem to transfer their native accent to a foreign language (Politzer and Weiss 1969).

Another recommendation, based on experimentation with fifth to eighth graders and adults, is to duplicate the process whereby children develop understanding of the first language. For example, the instructor used spoken commands that manipulate physical behavior, like "Give Mommy a big kiss!" or "Look at the bird in that oak tree!" Not only was spoken Spanish successfully taught to the groups in that manner, but there was a positive effect on their written Spanish (Asher 1977).

Perhaps this is a practical solution to the language problems of children reared in homes where only one language—not English—is spoken. Bringing these children of recent immigrants early into nursery schools may be the best means of introducing them to English as a second language. It might be a real help in alleviating learning problems in the school years ahead.

Summary

How language develops is not yet entirely understood. Language is acquired in stages, the same for all people in all cultures, and thus depends on maturation. But some aspects of language are acquired through imitation and reinforcement, a learning process. There may also be a mechanism within the brain that governs language acquisition, which is partially linked with the development of cognition.

Individuals acquire the language, grammar, and syntax of their own people through environmental stimulation. But the language-specific maturational schedule is not materially changed by environment or training.

Skinner's reinforcement theory holds that only the sounds of the language spoken in the infant's household are reinforced, while other sounds drop out. Chomsky suggests that the underlying structures and rules of language are acquired through an innate mechanism called the Language Acquisition Device (LAD).

Speech is based on universal sounds common to all language. Elemental speech sounds—phonemes—include vowels and consonants. Infant cries, coos, and babbles are the beginnings of speech. Words begin to emerge from babbled sounds toward the end of the first year. Words are composed of morphemes, the smallest units of sound that have meaning. Baby's first word is usually a reduplicated monosyllable.

About 60% of language maturation is accomplished by the end of the first year, and the fundamentals of an individual's native tongue are mastered by four. Complete acquisition of grammar is finished at about ten, but vocabulary acquisition continues throughout life. Knowing what words mean is closely related to cognitive development. Thus, children have trouble understanding or speaking in abstract terms.

Cultural, educational, and economic differences in children's homes cause differences in language development and restrictions in the speech of "deprived" children. Some children are bilingual, a culturally based condition that may cause difficulty in middle-class-oriented classrooms. Lack of environmental stimulation, particularly among children who are reared in institutions, may cause delayed language development and poorer than average language ability. Special language tutoring may help deprived children improve the quality of their language.

Teaching a second language early may be advantageous. One theory maintains that in the early years the brain contains an uncommitted cortex area available for language learning, which makes language acquisition easier for children than for adults.

Chronological Overview

Newborn   first few days: utters eight
distinguishable sounds

cries; spontaneous vocalizations

has basic equipment needed for speech

Infancy

6–9 months:	babbles
by 1 year:	acquires full sound repertoire
1 year:	first word, a reduplicated monosyllable
	one-word sentences
12–18 months:	uses small number of words
18 months:	uses about 20 words
21 months:	uses up to 200 words

Preschool

2 years:	uses 300–400 words
2½ years:	uses ⅔ of full repertoire of sounds for mature language, including all vowels of adult speech
3 years:	uses 1000 or more words
3½ years:	can understand *different* versus *same*
	word definition understanding proceeds from concrete to abstract

Childhood

5 years:	difficulty using irregular verbs and plurals
	average sentence length: 4.6 words
	follows basic grammatical rules
5–7 years:	understands *and then* and *but first* before *before* and *after*
6–6½ years:	has most reading skills—hearing, comprehension, visual and motor coordination
7 years:	produces all sounds of the language
8 years:	*because* is understood
10 years:	speech development complete but vocabulary still growing

Applying Your Knowledge

1. How can parents facilitate their children's language development?
2. Why would knowledge of psycholinguistics be important to reading teachers?
3. What are some baffling questions still unanswered by language researchers?

Further Readings

deVilliers, Jill G., and deVilliers, Peter A. *Language acquisition.* Cambridge, Mass.: Harvard University Press, 1978. An introductory text to study of language acquisition.
Hardback.

McNeill, David. *The acquisition of language.* New York: Harper and Row, 1970. A good overview of studies in psycholinguistics.
Paperback

Pflaum-Connor, Susanna. *The development of language and reading in young children.* Columbus, Ohio: Charles E. Merrill, 1978. A very readable text for teachers; includes a series of activities to promote language development in the classroom.
Paperback.

Smith, Frank. *Comprehension and learning: a conceptual framework for teachers.* New York: Holt, Rinehart and Winston, 1975. A review of the child's mental processes that underlie learning how to read and write.
Paperback.

Eisenson, Jon. *Is your child's speech normal?* Reading, Mass.: Addison-Wesley, 1976. A practical book that traces speech development from cooing and babbling to first words and sentences.
Paperback.

Gould, Toni S. *Home guide to early reading.* New York: Penguin, 1978. A guide to teaching reading and use of reading readiness games for the preschool child.
Paperback.

Chapter **7**
How Children Learn

David, an infant, learns to smile at Mother. Judy, in junior high, learns that the area of a circle equals πr^2. Ted, a beginning driver, learns not to drive through red lights. Baby Abigail learns that Mama always comes back. Jon, aged five, learns from TV that a certain dry cereal is delicious. All these are examples of learning. Learning happens throughout life as a result of the interaction of a developing individual with his or her environment.

What Is Learning?

A day-to-day process

Learning is the acquisition of knowledge, skills, or habits through experience. In fact, learning is *any* change in behavior that results from experience. Learning is inextricably related to maturation. Much learning relies on cognition: ability to think. Some learning depends on language: ability to understand and use words. Learning may often depend on motivation: desire to learn.

Learning: acquisition of knowledge, skills, or habits through experience

Learning is a cumulative process, a piling up of responses acquired from the time in the womb throughout life. Some learned information is forgotten, but much of it remains at our disposal to make up the sum total of what we know and can use in dealing with our lives.

It is almost impossible to imagine a day in anyone's existence when learning does not play a part. Everything we do or say, we have learned at one time or another. And in the course of almost any day, we learn something new, by the very fact that we are alive and functioning in the world.

Importance of environment

There is a difference between what we learn and what we do as a result of our instincts. Only behavior that is modified by the environment is considered to be *learned*. Behavior that is present in the individual without any learning experience is deemed to be *innate*. An infant's cries are an example of innate behavior. But the child's response to the mobile above the crib is learned. And also learned, of course, is reading. So learning is very much dependent on the environment, as well as on an individual's age, intelligence, or species (animals also learn).

Even an unborn baby can learn. Taking advantage of the fact that the fetus is known to react to loud noises (it will kick or move), researchers have shown that the fetus can learn to kick as a response to a different stimulus, a vibrator applied to the mother's stomach. All that is necessary is to give the fetus several "practice" experiences with both vibrator and loud noise used simultaneously. The "lesson," once learned, lasts at least until the infant is born (Spelt 1948).

While this particular example of learning may have little practical use, it shows the remarkable ability of human beings to learn from their environment. A child learns from mother, father, other care-givers, the home, then the neighborhood and the school. Adults learn from their associations at work and at leisure. The more exposure, the more one learns. Without exposure, without stimuli, learning does not happen.

Learning theories differ

Some learning theorists, of whom B. F. Skinner is a prominent example, believe that almost all human behavior can be explained by a person's learned *responses* to *stimuli* in the environment. They discount the role of genetics or maturation as a major factor in learning. Learning, they assert, is not solely a matter of being ready or mature enough, but largely a question of acquiring new connections through exposure to the outside world.

Response: any behavior or psychological reaction produced by a stimulus

Stimulus, stimuli (plural): something that provokes a response

This view of learning as a product of interaction with the environment differs from the perspective of many psychoanalysts. They argue that people's learning is based primarily on the need for sensual gratification. Thus, they believe that *motivation*, rather than environment, is most crucial to learning.

Motivation: incentive to goal-directed behavior

Another approach is Piaget's. He maintains that maturation is the critical element in learning. A child is unable to benefit from the environment, according to Piaget, until the appropriate level of cognitive development has been reached. (See also Chapter 5, especially pages 162–165.)

Despite these different viewpoints, all learning theorists agree that environmental influence is a major factor in how people learn. But the scholars have different explanations for just *how* the environment produces learning. These varying theories, some of which will be described and discussed in the following pages, are not necessarily mutually exclusive. In fact, when they are considered together they are complementary and provide a comprehensive view of the learning process and its development as we grow from infancy to maturity.

How Learning Occurs

Several major types of learning have been described by different theorists. They include:

1. *Classical conditioning*, learning that results when an individual is repeatedly exposed to a new stimulus together with the one that originally produced a reflex (unlearned) response. An example is the one cited above, when the fetus learned to kick in response to the vibrator.

   Classical conditioning: learning elicited by associating a neutral stimulus with a stimulus that produces a reflex (unlearned) response

2. *Operant (instrumental) conditioning*, learning that results when a person is rewarded in some way for responding in a particular fashion to environmental stimulation. A simple example is a child learning that two plus two equals four. The teacher rewards the right answer by saying: "Yes, that's right."

3. *Social (observational) learning*, learning by imitation. For example, children often copy their parents' mannerisms, speech, and habits.

4. *Information-processing* and *memory*, storing (remembering) information, retrieving it, and reacting to it through structures inside the brain, when the senses are stimulated in certain ways. The theory behind this idea is that the brain is like a computer.

Classical conditioning

Classical conditioning is probably the earliest and simplest form of learning for any human being, although it can take place throughout life. The fetus that responded to the vibrator was demonstrating classical conditioning—the pairing of a new stimulus with one that originally produced a response, usually a reflex (unlearned) response. The fetal kick discussed before is a reflex response to a loud noise; it can be elicited by a different stimulus, provided the new stimulus has been repeatedly paired with the original stimulus. By pairing the vibrator with the loud noise, eventually the fetus learned to kick when exposed only to the vibrator. In other words, in classical conditioning, behavior becomes more complex because of new associations between stimuli and a response.

Pavlov   Early in the century, a Russian, Ivan Pavlov, illustrated classical conditioning in a famous experiment with dogs. He knew that a dog will salivate reflexively (without learning) when there is food in his mouth. So he presented food and a loud bell simultaneously to his dogs. Eventually the bell alone caused the dogs to salivate. The *unconditioned* (unlearned) stimulus was food; the unconditioned (unlearned) response was salivation. The *conditioned* (learned) stimulus was the bell. After a series of pairings, the response, now conditioned (learned), was salivation. But now it appeared after stimulation by the bell alone. The important process in this form of learning is the pairing of the unconditioned stimulus with the one to be learned (the conditioned stimulus). (See Box 7–1.)

Unconditioned: unlearned

Conditioned: learned

Intelligence or cognitive ability has little or nothing to do with classical conditioning. It happens "automatically": the learner is the more or less helpless "victim" of the teacher, who manipulates stimuli to produce the desired response. Thus, problem drinkers can be counterconditioned: along with his martini the alcoholic is given a drug that causes temporary violent sickness when combined with a drink. He "learns" to be sick at the very sight of an alcoholic beverage. (See also Chapter 12, page 514.)

All of us carry within us the effects of early classical conditioning. For instance, try putting your hand on the burners of an unheated range. It takes enormous effort to do it. As a child, you

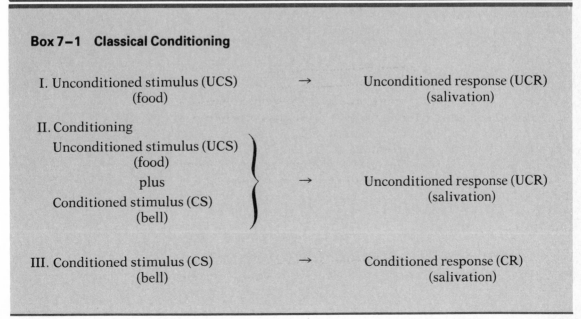

Box 7–1   Classical Conditioning

I. Unconditioned stimulus (UCS)   →   Unconditioned response (UCR)
        (food)   (salivation)

II. Conditioning
    Unconditioned stimulus (UCS)
            (food)
            plus   →   Unconditioned response (UCR)
    Conditioned stimulus (CS)   (salivation)
            (bell)

III. Conditioned stimulus (CS)   →   Conditioned response (CR)
        (bell)   (salivation)

must have learned to associate intense heat with those burners and your reflexive reaction was withdrawal. Now the burners alone, without heat, can cause you to pull back. You were conditioned to avoid touching a burner. You had learned to connect a new stimulus (burners) with heat.

Operant (instrumental) conditioning

When Jon was four he was nipped by a neighbor's nervous toy poodle. After that, he ran in fright at the very sight of a small dog. This common combination of events is an example of *operant*, or *instrumental, conditioning*. This is a form of learning that relies on the *reinforcement* of a particular response. Jon's running away was reinforcing; it took him away from the unpleasant stimulus.

Operant (instrumental) conditioning: learning through reinforcement

Reinforcement: anything that increases the frequency of a response

Examples of operant conditioning, according to Skinner and his followers, are early forms of language learning. As we saw in Chapter 6, a baby utters sounds spontaneously and at random. But the parents reinforce those sounds by repeating and responding with pleasure when the infant babbles. Consequently, babbling is encouraged. According to operant conditioning theory, children learn those responses that are reinforced. The reinforcement acts as a stimulus to produce the response again. But initially, the responses may have been spontaneous, random, or even produced by a variety of stimuli. (See Box 7–2.)

Primary and secondary reinforcers While reinforcement is always an object or event that increases the frequency of a re-

---

Box 7–2   Operant Conditioning

Random responses:

Response 1

Response 2

Response 3

Response 4 → reinforcement → Response 4

Response 5

---

sponse, there are two kinds of reinforcers, primary and secondary. *Primary reinforcers* are those things or events—like food, water, safety from harm—that satisfy basic physiological needs. *Secondary reinforcers* are those things or events that are satisfying but not essential to survival. They might be praise, approval, money, and recognition, among others.

Reinforcement may be either positive or negative. *Positive reinforcement* is usually in the form of a reward, like a gold star for the right answer. *Negative reinforcement* is escape or relief from an unpleasant or painful situation, like obeying a strict parent and avoiding punishment. The reinforcement is negative in the sense that something unpleasant did not happen. Successful avoidance of the punishment or of threatening stimuli is the negative reinforcement. Such reinforcement strengthens the behavior that prevented or avoided the punishment.

The learning that is produced by operant conditioning sometimes happens by accident. For example, when Jon was four, he innocently repeated a four-letter word heard from an adult. His parents gave the child instant attention: "Don't you say that bad word again!" Unfortunately, Jon evidently enjoyed the attention and he used the word repeatedly. Thus, the reinforcement made it more likely that the offending term would become part of the child's vocabulary.

Extinction Since reinforcement increases the frequency of the response that is reinforced, withholding reinforcement can have the reverse effect. If reinforcement is no longer associated with a given response, the frequency of that response begins to decline. *Extinction* is taking place. Thus, adults who are unperturbed when a young child says a "bad word" can probably cause such linguistic misbehavior to undergo extinction by ignoring the whole thing and thus withdrawing reinforcement. (The presumption is that the child will not be reinforced by others.) (See Box 7–3 and Figure 7–1.)

Sometimes adults think they are extinguishing undesirable behavior when they are actually reinforcing it. For example, some children seem to be constantly trying to win disapproval and succeeding only too well. Many teachers and many parents have had sad experiences with youngsters who persist in giving the wrong answers or repeating annoying behavior. Often extremely deprived children seem to act this way. Perhaps any attention at all seems like a reward to them. Indifference is what they cannot bear (Tharp and Wetzel 1969).

Primary reinforcers: things or events that satisfy survival needs

Secondary reinforcers: things or events that are satisfying but not essential to survival

Positive reinforcement: a reward

Negative reinforcement: escape from or avoidance of unpleasantness

Extinction: gradual decline in rate of response because reinforcement is withheld

100% versus partial reinforcement How does one go about eliminating learned behavior that is "bad" or "wrong"? It depends on how thoroughly that behavior was reinforced. The frequency of reinforcement influences the rate of learning. Interest-

---

Box 7–3 Learning Not to Cry

It is never too early to use learning theory, according to experimenters who worked out a way of teaching infants not to cry unnecessarily for attention. The technical term for this procedure is *extinction with reinforcement.*

Barbara Etzel and Jacob Gewirtz (1967) maintain that operant crying—crying on purpose to get attention—is something babies often learn by the time they are only six weeks old. They determined that such behavior can be stopped—extinguished—by refusing to reward babies with attention when they cried. However, when the babies in their investigation smiled, they gave them a reward—reinforcement. Thus they also reduced the chances of crying, since a baby cannot smile and cry at the same time.

Two infants were used in the 30-day study. William was 20 weeks and 3 days old when it began. Anthony was 6 weeks old. During the training periods, once a day each baby was put in a seated position in a plastic baby seat, which was placed in a baby carriage. For the next 15 minutes the children were not handled at all. When they cried, fussed, or frowned, they got no response at all from the experimenter. But when they smiled, the experimenter would say, "Good boy, William (or Anthony)," and nod vigorously.

Figure 7–1 shows the percentage of total time spent by William in crying, smiling, fussing, and frowning. The baseline period consisted of the first several days, when neither reinforcement nor extinction efforts were made. Then came the reinforcement period when, by using several stimuli, the baby was encouraged to smile and then rewarded by the experimenter's approval. The final days, called the extinction phase, were the same as the baseline phase. Neither crying nor smiling was rewarded.

Anthony smiled rarely and cried a good deal during the baseline period, and he made eye contact with the experimenter less than half the total time. During the reinforcement period, however, the baby cried much less and he stopped altogether during the last three days. Smiling increased dramatically, making Anthony an "accomplished smiler," who looked at the experimenter most of the time. When the reinforcement was withdrawn, the baby cried more during the first days. But then the staff of the nursery where he was being cared for stopped rewarding his crying and he resumed the "good" behavior of the reinforcement period. But William's experience was different. The nursery failed to stop rewarding his crying. So, during the "extinction" period, he reverted to his original behavior.

---

ingly enough, behavior that was reinforced at each occurrence (100%) is easier to extinguish than behavior that was only intermittently or partially reinforced. The individual on a 100% "schedule" readily recognizes the change in the reinforcement

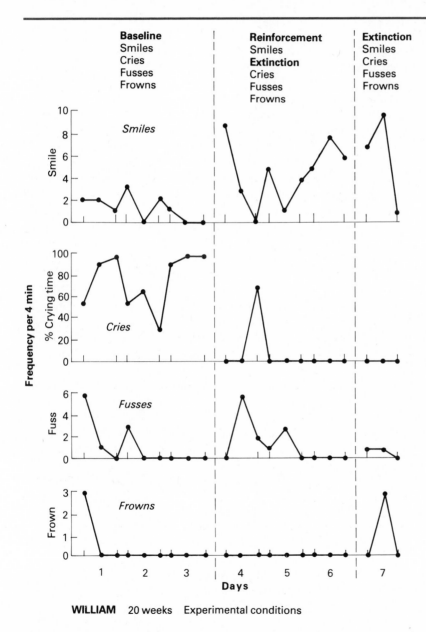

FIG. 7−1 Four concurrent response curves are graphed under three experimental phases for William, age 20 weeks, whose crying was being reinforced in the nursery environment. *Source:* B. C. Etzel and J. L. Gewirtz, Experimental modification of caretaker-maintained high-rate operant crying in a 6- and 20-week-old infant (Infans tyrannotearus): extinction of crying with reinforcement of eye contact and smiling, *Journal of Experimental Child Psychology,* 1967, *5,* 311.

WILLIAM   20 weeks   Experimental conditions

schedule when reinforcement is withheld. The behavior stops promptly. In contrast, someone who is conditioned on an intermittent schedule of reinforcement does not recognize as quickly that there has been a change and that reinforcement is being withheld. So the behavior is apt to continue, at least for a while.

A common example of partial reinforcement is gambling or games of chance. A man who feeds nickels into a slot machine has learned that the machines sometimes pay off if the right symbols show up on the reel. He received intermittent reinforcement in the form of a trickle or, occasionally, a stream of coins. But he does not know just when those nickels will pour out. So he keeps on playing in the hope of seeing those rewarding symbols. It will take a while, putting coins into a "cold" machine, for him to give up in disgust. And he will probably not really stop altogether. Very likely he will just go to a different slot machine.

A baby learns very quickly that crying will often lead to being picked up. Occasional failure to be rescued will not change the "lesson." Similarly, a college professor who does not like note-taking in class will have a hard time enforcing the prohibition. Students superstitiously think the very act of note-taking is somehow related to good grades, because it seems to pay off *sometimes.*

Comparison with classical conditioning Operant conditioning is a more common learning process than classical conditioning. Operant conditioning goes far beyond the limited number of reflex reactions to an infinitude of reinforced, learned responses that enable people to get along better in the world. Thus, operant conditioning results in *adaptive behavior,* critical in everything we do, from dealing with our wives, husbands, children, parents, employers, to mastering our jobs, to enjoying leisure. Moreover, adaptive behavior is subject to change as the environment changes.

Adaptive behavior: behavior that helps an individual adjust to the environment

As a result of operant conditioning, we learn through reinforcement, from babyhood on, the ways of our society and how to react to all the situations of daily life. And in school we learn the elements of the culture and eventually a vocation or a profession. Of course, we may also learn to be antisocial, with disastrous personal results and harm to society as well. We may learn fears, too, harmful to ourselves, if to no one else.

Through reinforcement we learn the responses that are proper for each situation. We learn to change those responses when the environment changes and they are no longer appropriate and no longer reinforced. We make a variety of voluntary responses to any given situation until one is effective (reinforced), whereupon we learn it and make it part of our repertoire. In fact, the things we learn this way have a tendency to spread out, through a process called *stimulus* and *response generalization*. For example, the child who feared one dog learned to fear *all* dogs. Thus, a stimulus that is similar to the original stimulus produces the same learned response. Likewise, responses similar to the originally learned response are produced by the same stimulus. For example, a baby is attracted by a rattle. The infant responds by reaching. After that, the toy brings on other similar responses—grasping, grabbing, and other attempts to reach the toy by using arms and body.

Stimulus generalization: stimuli similar to the original stimulus that caused a learned response produce the same response

Response generalization: responses similar to the originally learned response are produced by the same stimulus

One criticism of this *behaviorist* idea of learning (operant conditioning theory) is that it does not give enough emphasis to the thoughts and observations that might also lead to learning. Therefore, the social (observational) learning theory has also been proposed by scholars.

Behaviorism: explanation of human actions in terms of learned responses to the environment

Social (observational) learning

Recently three-year-old Michael Ward decided to go to school. He took his dog, got into his parents' automobile, and eased out of the driveway. Michael managed to drive two miles before the car turned over, without injuring either the child or his dog.

> The sheriff of the rural area where Michael lives said, "He wasn't going so fast, but he sure knew how to drive. He'd get down on the floor and operate the pedals, then get back up in the seat, once he got the vehicle moving, and steer it. His dad would like us to give him a ticket, and then he'd hand it to him when he's 16 years old. He said the only driving lessons he ever gave him were on the lawn mower."*

Bandura Michael is a too-good-to-be-true example of *social,* or *observational, learning:* learning from *models* and through imitation. (The incident apparently really happened.) Albert Bandura is one of the leading exponents of this theory of how learning takes place. He and other psychologists hold that observation is a major source of the learning of children and adults. (Also see Chapter 10.)

Social (observational) learning: learning from models

Model: someone who exhibits any kind of observable behavior

Much observational learning is incidental, even accidental (like Michael's learning how to drive a car). The lessons are absorbed by observing parents, friends, associates, television, movies. Some of this learning could be anything but desirable.

---

* Reprinted by permission of United Press International.

Bandura's subjects.

But the principle of observational learning can be used as an important method of formal teaching, too.

Bandura guided his research by asking himself, in effect: if children see a particular kind of behavior in someone else, will they learn that behavior themselves? If so, what kinds of behavior are children likely to imitate? Also, does the nature of the model influence the model's effectiveness? For example, would a live model, a film model, or a cartoon model be equally useful for teaching?

To answer these questions, in one of many experiments Bandura exposed nursery school children to both live and filmed models who were playing with (or assaulting) a large plastic doll. Rather frighteningly, Bandura found that film and cartoon models caused as much imitation by the children as the real-life model. Moreover, he discovered that aggressive models were imitated more frequently than nonaggressive models. A nonaggressive, neutral sort of model was used with a control group. This model was imitated too, but much less so (Bandura, Ross, and Ross 1961, 1963a).

Rewards and punishments   Imitation of aggression can be increased if aggression is seen as rewarding. Bandura tested the effect on children when they saw aggressive behavior rewarded: an aggressive model in a film got all the other child's toys. Another group of subjects saw a film in which a model's aggression was punished: a child turned on his attacker and prevented the theft of the toys. It developed that the children were much more apt to imitate the aggressor who departed with all the spoils, even though they piously criticized what he had done. Evidently, the likelihood of a payoff or reward can conquer the learner's supposed value system (Bandura, Ross, and Ross 1963b).

In a similar situation, when the aggressive model was punished, the children seemed to learn aggressive behavior anyhow, though they were reluctant to show it immediately. Their inhibitions disappeared when they were offered an attractive incentive (toys) to behave just like the aggressive model (Bandura 1965a). All this seems to bear out the cynical cliché that every man—or woman—has his price.

Modeling plus reinforcement   Bandura showed that behavior may be taught best through a combination of modeling and reinforcement. Six- and seven-year-old girls were asked to choose the toys they preferred from a number of paired pictures. Children who witnessed an adult's choices, which were approved by another adult, learned readily to choose the same toys. When the adult model's choices were disapproved and thus "punished" by the other adult, the girls learned to choose the item that was not disapproved. The model-plus-reward principle provides an effective teaching strategy: not only to use an adult model but also to make it clear that the model is gaining approval or some other reward for behaving that way (Liebert and Fernandez 1970).

In fact, children's learning from models is affected even if they only *think* there might be a punishment or a reward in store. Third and fourth graders saw a videotape in which an adult either encouraged or forbade a model's play with toys. The children got the point: they later avoided doing what the model presumably would have been punished for (Dollinger and Thelen 1975).

"Appropriate" models Observational learning is influenced by how appropriate the model is for the behavior to be learned. Children discover very early what they should learn as a male or a female. An aggressive male model has been shown to be a more powerful stimulus for learning aggression than an aggressive female model. Clearly, in our society aggression has been more appropriate for boys than for girls. Both boys and girls in Bandura's experiments said of the male, "He's a good socker!" But about the female model, "Ladies are supposed to act like ladies." Yet girls imitated the "male" behavior (Bandura, Ross, and Ross 1961, page 581).

The effectiveness of modeling on observational learning is influenced by the age, beliefs, and developmental level of the learner. The younger the child, the more likely he or she is to imitate adults (Fein 1973). "Patty-cake" and "bye-bye" are two common examples of how babies learn by imitating the behavior of adult models. As a child grows up and moves into the broader world, the number of available models increases. In general, high-status models are imitated to a greater extent than low-status models (Bandura 1971). A second grader will be more likely to imitate an adult than a classmate (Nicholas, McCarter, and Heckel 1971).

Observational learning is a particularly powerful form of learning because it cannot always be controlled. It often works without reinforcement and without conscious effort on anyone's part. And even when effort is exerted to provide a "good" model for a child, there is no telling just what will make an impression.

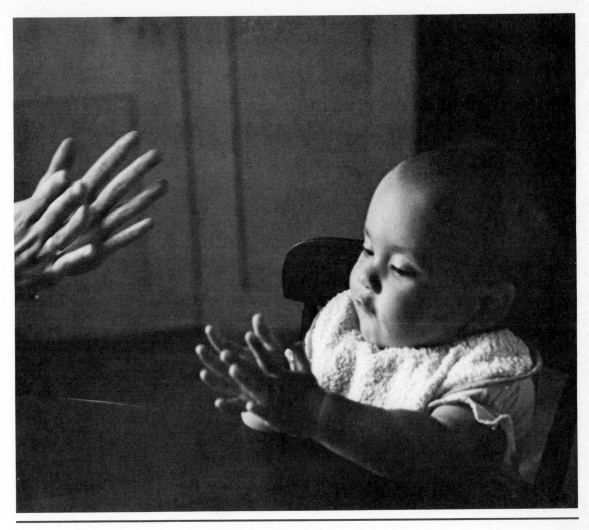

Babies learn by imitating adults.

A parent's bad language may impress a son or daughter, while regular tooth-brushing may be an example that cannot be communicated.

While observational or social learning theory is generally accepted as an important explanation of how people learn, it does not entirely satisfy a group of thinkers who have been influenced by the computer era. They have developed a different theoretical approach, which draws analogies between computers and the human mind.

Information-processing and memory

The *information-processing* theory of how people learn suggests that experiences are received in an individual's mind, stored (remembered), and translated into behavior when appropriate. The process is said to be somewhat like the way computers acquire, store, and retrieve information. Humans are thought to learn and remember in a similar fashion. Thus, information-processing is a theory that is concerned with the internal structures of the mind that are involved in learning and *memory*.

According to this theory, individuals receive sensory stimulation, which leads to certain activities in the brain. The stimulus impinges on the senses, leading to arousal because of discrepancy, similarity, familiarity, complexity, ambiguity, or the incongruity of the stimulus. Thus, the attention of the organism (the individual) is drawn to the stimulus and the information is therefore received into short-term memory. (See Figure 7–2.)

Short-term memory either decays and is forgotten, or it remains, depending on the saliency or meaningfulness of the information. Should the information be sufficiently meaningful, coding, rehearsal strategies, mnemonic devices, and mediational strategies (like verbal labeling) are brought into play, and the memory is stored for the long term. There it is available for retrieval and output as needed.

Short- and long-term memory   Memory theory relies on the distinction between *short-term memory, STM*, and *long-term memory, LTM*. Short-term memory refers to the process by which information is retained for very short periods of time, a few seconds or a few minutes. This sort of memory storage is useful because it prevents our minds from being cluttered up with bits of trivia. For instance, it would be a distinct nuisance if we remembered every telephone number we have ever dialed.

All information that is entered into memory is thought to go through the short-term phase. Then, if the information is not called for over and over, or is not committed to memory through obvious rehearsal, it is forgotten.

But meaningful information becomes long-term memory by deliberate design on the part of the individual. Almost everyone is aware of making an effort to commit to memory a phone number that will be needed repeatedly in the future.

There is evidence that long-term memory involves biological changes in the brain. It is also thought that long-term memory

Information processing: the mind accepts experiences as input and translates the data into behavior (output) and/or memory

Memory: ability to retain and recall learned material

Short-term memory (STM): storage of information for a few seconds or minutes

Long-term memory (LTM): storage of information for an indefinite period of time

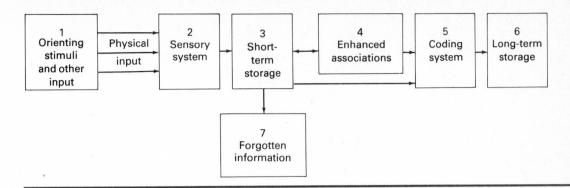

FIG. 7-2 How memory is created by information processing. Source: N. L. Gage and D. Elkind, *Educational Psychology,* p. 136 (Chicago: Rand McNally, 1979).

holds much more information than an individual can readily recall. Given the proper stimulation and cues, however, that "lost" information can be retrieved.

For the transition from STM to LTM to occur, it is important that there be a minimum of interference or anxiety during the short-term phase. Interference interrupts the process. Using the telephone number analogy again, if you look up a phone number and prepare to dial and are distracted by someone asking a question, you forget the number and have to look it up again.

Habituation   Human memory is in working order right from birth. If an infant hears a noise or is subjected to a new odor while sucking, the stimulus will ordinarily cause the baby to stop sucking. But if the same stimulus is encountered repeatedly, the infant will no longer stop sucking. This is evidence that the sound or smell has been remembered (Lipsitt 1967). In fact, the baby has become habituated. *Habituation* is one of the first signs of memory: remembering a stimulus so well that an infant stops reacting to it because it is no longer novel. Children's ability to remember or memorize depends partly on their developmental and cognitive level, partly on motivation, and partly on the strategies they use—or the strategies their teachers use.

Habituation: adaptation to a stimulus so that it no longer elicits a response

Encoding strategies   A child of five is less able to remember than an adult. One major reason for this difference is that memory depends upon the ability to use *encoding* strategies to help learning and retention: to transform information into a set of cues.

Encoding: transformation of information into a set of cues

Some strategies may be beyond the cognitive ability of a pre-schooler (Haith 1971). Young children are less likely to look for particular cues or devices to assist their memory.

Children's memory can be judged by their ability to recall significant events or to recognize television characters. They may remember certain commercials because encoding is made easy by a combination of catchy music, rhyme, pictures. "Sesame Street" watchers remember Big Bird and the Cookie Monster, thanks to repetition, the attractiveness of the characters, and their voices.

Visual versus auditory memory Remembering concrete material is easier than remembering abstract material. Thus, a pre-schooler more easily remembers a picture than a word. Research has shown that young children make use of mental images to remember (Corsini 1969). However, young children are fully able to remember, both pictorially and verbally, simple pictures and the names of the pictures (Tversky 1973). Even by the time a child is in the sixth grade it is easier to remember objects than words. The same is generally true of adults (Kossuth, Carroll, and Rogers 1971). For all ages encoding strategies are more apt to be pictorial than verbal (Haith 1971).

Children's pictorial memory has been shown to be remarkably reliable. Fifth graders who were shown 40 slides of landscapes and city scenes in rapid succession, none of them very remarkable and all unfamiliar, recognized them quite accurately a week later (Entwisle and Huggins 1973). A similar test using 60 pictures from American magazines was given to 11-year-old American city children and to Guatemalan children living in remote villages. The two groups remembered equally well; familiarity evidently had nothing to do with their ability to memorize. These demonstrations suggest that words are not always essential to fix an experience in the mind (Kagan, Klein, and Haith 1973).

Of course, using words as cues can also be helpful in remembering. Even without any particular coaching, younger children do a certain amount of verbal encoding, but not nearly so much or as efficiently as older children or adults (Mowbray and Luria 1973). Preschoolers' ability to remember can be helped if a deliberate attempt is made to give them both verbal and nonverbal clues, a combination of demonstration and description. Groups of three-and-a-half to five-and-a-half-year-olds and seven- to eight-year-olds were asked to play a game putting colored toys into particular colored boxes. The instructor not only showed what he

Pictures may make memorizing easier.

was doing but also described it. This strategy worked so well that
the younger children remembered as well as the older group
(Corsini 1969).

Most research on memory has been done with young subjects. Children's recall performance seems to improve with age,
perhaps as part of the process of cognitive development. Or the
reverse might be true: maybe cognitive development depends on
a person's ability to develop memory strategies (Neimark, Slotnick, and Ulrich 1971).

Memory styles and devices   Very likely, encoding or memory styles differ from one person to another. Most of us have visual minds. We need to look at a page in order to remember what it says. But others do better by hearing the words. Some of us have a "good sense of direction." Driven to a place once, we can find our way back easily by ourselves. Others have trouble remembering even after going the same route half-a-dozen times. We have not learned to pay attention and picture the way in our minds. Others cannot manage unless they see the route on a map. Motivation, practice, and attention are all elements in the ability to remember, as well as the particular memory strategies with which each person feels comfortable. Whether you are conscious of it or not, your own memory depends on using elaborate visual coding and rehearsal strategies (Morrison, Holmes, and Haith 1974).

Different *mnemonic devices*—strategies to help memory— are often used as cues to help people recall information. Rhymes like "Thirty days hath September . . ." are one example. Acronyms are another device, frequently employed by advertisers and public relations people. They use the initial letters of a string of words in order to help people remember them, like NOW for National Organization of Women, or Nabisco, for National Biscuit Company. Associating images with words is a common mnemonic strategy. Many people work out a visual association with a person's name in order to remember someone they have just met.

Mnemonic device: a scheme for remembering and recalling information

Each child or adult has his or her own best strategy for encoding. Those who are visually oriented are better off memorizing by forming mental pictures. The people who "think best with their ears" can most efficiently use sounds as aids to memory.

One student, visually oriented and not very sensitive to music, used a deliberate encoding strategy to pass a music appreciation course. She played records and conjured up pictures in her mind that she associated with the titles. When the selections were played on exam day, she closed her eyes, summoned up the images and then the corresponding titles—and managed to get a perfect score.

Learning and memory theories and scholars' hypotheses still do not explain everything there is to know about learning. Some mysteries are yet to be plumbed. So far no theorist has given a logical description of what causes insight, or creativity, or original ideas, or inventions. The genius of Beethoven, Einstein, Rembrandt, and Edison, among countless others, is still not explained by learning theory. Nor is ordinary problem-solving truly understood. (See also Box 7–4).

For care-givers, parents, and teachers, what matters most, perhaps, are the practical ways in which learning and memory theory can be applied to improve the ability of children and young people to take advantage of the stores of practical knowledge with which our modern world is filled to overflowing.

Applying Learning Theory

Infant Learning

Learning when to be hungry Even a new baby who has just come home to the family has already started to learn. Now the parents can begin to teach the infant on purpose. That first

---

Box 7–4 Learning Hemispheres

Scientists are concluding that both right and left hemispheres of the brain are involved in the learning process but that their functions are somewhat different. Experiments in recent years seem to disprove the previous notion that only the left hemisphere is the "real" learning center.

A typical investigation leading to this conclusion was one in which different messages were sent, via earphones, to each ear of a young subject. The child's answers gave the researcher clues about how each side of the brain handles information. This study, among others, now leads to the belief that there are two different, although parallel, ways in which the brain processes information.

In most people, the left hemisphere of the brain seems to use verbal skills and step-by-step reasoning. The right hemisphere, in contrast, specializes in mental pictures and global, or holistic, problem-solving. In some people, one side of the brain dominates the learning process; in others, the other side is stronger. The result is that school problems that involve directions that require thinking by a person's stronger side could lead to better learning. But if the teacher's methods stress the "wrong" side for a particular individual, he or she is apt to perform more poorly.

These findings are still tentative. Scientists are still working on the fascinating problem of how the brain learns (Jaroslovsky 1979). (See also Box 4–3, page 140.)

frightening problem—how do I know when the baby should eat?—can be eased by applying simple learning theory. The fact is that the dispute about whether a baby should be fed on demand or on a particular schedule really depends on whether the parents are inclined to teach their baby or let nature take its course.

Infants demonstrate early learning through operant conditioning when they acquire or adapt to a particular feeding schedule. Infants only days or weeks old are able to learn to adjust to the particular conditions of their environment, with only one important limit: what they are asked to do must be already within the baby's "behavioral repertoire" (Bandura 1965b, pages 312–313).

Babies on a demand schedule, it has been found, usually become hungry in about three-and-a-half hours. But experimenters discovered that the rewarding presentation of breast or bottle at a particular interval—three hours, four hours—can train the baby that this is when the pangs of hunger should be felt. If infants are trained to wait only three hours, they will begin to fuss at close to three-hour intervals. If they are trained to a four-hour schedule, the fussing will not begin until close to their accustomed feeding time (Marquis 1941).

Exploratory learning The more things a baby has to see, hear, try out, explore, poke at, push, squeeze, taste—the more opportunities for learning. Variety in the environment facilitiates exploratory behavior and early learning. Babies learn from pain as well as from pleasure. They learn what to enjoy, what will bring a smile or a dry diaper or arms that will hold, and they learn what does not feel good, what will bring a frown or a harsh tone. They learn through trial and error, by imitating, by taking part in the activity of the household (Murphy 1967).

The urge to explore and to learn is very strong. Even a year-old baby notices and is attracted to "what's new." A group of babies were given a choice between a new room with new toys and a familiar room with familiar toys. They chose the unfamiliar (Ross, Rheingold, and Eckerman 1972).

But sights and sounds and things are not all there is to environment. The attitudes of early "teachers" can either encourage or inhibit exploratory behavior. For example, children attending a demonstration nursery school were presented with two different adults. One was friendly and approving, the other aloof and critical. The critical, aloof "parent" seemed to inhibit the children.

Exploratory learning!

They explored less, waited longer before starting to examine their surroundings, were less likely to guess the identity of objects. Fear of criticism by the standoffish adult seemed to hold them back (Moore and Bulbulian 1976). Evidently, adult encouragement is important if children are to take full advantage of the opportunity to learn from their surroundings. Curiosity is dampened by a disapproving adult (Coie 1974).

Toilet-training Toilet-training relies on reinforcement procedures. Take the common problem of night-time training. Most children can be trained without mechanical devices. Nor is it necessary to refuse that before-bedtime drink of milk or water. Techniques of operant conditioning like affection or praise speed training, provided the child is physiologically ready.

Box 7–5 Fast Potty-Training

Two psychologists who apply the principles taught by learning theorist B. F. Skinner worked out a system of fast potty-training for children who are physiologically ready to use the toilet. The procedure used by Nathan Azrin and Richard Foxx involves a combination of reward, repetition, and modeling. The rewards include food, lavish praise, and love. The models are a doll that urinates in a potty, Santa Claus ("Does Santa pee-pee in his pants?"), and the policeman ("Does the policeman wet his pants?")

The psychologists demonstrated with two three-year-old boy twins. They brought to the children's home two potty chairs and cotton training pants. They made friends with the children, in part by giving them all the soda they wanted. Then the special doll got a drink of water and was made to urinate in the potty.

The children were urged to reward the doll with a potato chip, because the doll had acted "like a big girl." When the child himself used the potty successfully, he was applauded, hugged, and given potato chips too. In the course of the session, the trainers asked leading questions about how Santa and the policeman went to the toilet. Checking the children's pants frequently and rewarding dryness each time with potato chips, drinks, and praise was part of the system.

"These kids can get more love when they're dry," Foxx commented.

While the training session took only a few hours, parents must follow up in a consistent manner for as many days or weeks as it takes to transform the lesson into established habit (Foxx and Azrin 1973).

When a child is dry in the morning, a parent can say something like, "I'm so proud of you—you kept your pants dry all by yourself!" A hug or kiss seals the bargain. Changing from diapers to "grown-up" pajamas with no diapers is another useful reinforcement for learning to stay dry (Benjamin, Serdahely, and Geppert 1971). It has been shown that it is possible to train a physiologically ready child in less than a day using techniques of observational learning and operant conditioning (Foxx and Azrin 1973). (See Box 7–5.)

A successful device currently used to train bedwetters relies on classical conditioning. The "Mowrer sheet," named after O. H. Mowrer, a learning theorist, is wired to a buzzer, which goes off when the sheet becomes moist. The child wakes up when the buzzer sounds. But eventually the bladder tension that becomes associated with the buzzer leads to waking up and going to the toilet before it is too late (Mowrer and Mowrer 1938).

Discipline: time-out Employing the principles of extinction can be effective in changing behavior. The *time-out* system is one version of extinction. In effect, it removes the child from social reinforcement—being with people. Withholding reinforcement seems to be a good way of teaching a child to behave more acceptably, like not hitting a baby brother. A little girl barely over two was put into five-minute isolation every time she attacked her 11-month-old sibling. By the time ten days had elapsed, this time-out system, faithfully followed, had wiped out the little girl's belligerency. It is important to note that the desired behavior lapsed somewhat when the system was dropped during the next ten days. But the child quickly resumed more desirable behavior when the time-out device was reinstated. An extra bonus was that the once feisty little girl played better with her brother, was more affectionate with him as well as with her parents, and behaved more amiably in general (Allison and Allison 1971).

Time-out: temporary removal of social reinforcement

Shaping Parents can also make practical use of reinforcement by *shaping:* reinforcing successive approximations of desired behavior. Suppose you want to teach a child how to ride a bicycle. You would certainly not wait until the youngster happens to get on a bike and tries to ride. Rather, through shaping, you would introduce the bicycle to the child, encourage him or her to sit on

Shaping: reinforcing successive approximations of desired behavior

the seat, reinforce the proper movements with praise and encouragement. As the youngster is introduced to each step in the technique of bicycle riding, you would applaud and praise the right responses until the technique of bike-riding was learned. (See also Box 7–6.)

Classroom learning

The most obvious place to apply learning theory is in the classroom. Research has demonstrated many ways in which pupils can be induced to learn, using the principles of operant condition-

Box 7–6 Drown-proofing Infants

Alice Hipsley is in the business of drown-proofing infants. Most of her students haven't even begun to walk. "You can't really teach one who is six or seven months old to swim the breast stroke, backstroke, or freestyle," she says, "but you can certainly teach infants the ability to maintain themselves for an appropriate distance to get them out of the danger area when they get into trouble."

First Ms. Hipsley holds the child in her arms and bounces it up and down to get it used to the water. Then the chin goes in the water. "We do everything to a three count. And after 45 minutes of saying 1–2–3 . . . it's amazing to see that they know what's going on. They know that on the count of three, something is going to happen."

Next the baby is placed on its back and taught to paddle, with the parent (who is in the water too) repeating, "Paddle, paddle, paddle." After that the infant goes under water. Young children, says Hipsley, will automatically hold their breath under water. "The minute you dunk them, their mouths go closed."

An important part of this teacher's method is her sensitivity to a baby's fears. "If I sense that there is an apprehension, I keep them very close to my face. And I'm constantly talking to them. It really doesn't matter what I'm saying."

Throughout, the parent takes part in the lesson and learns how to continue after the course is finished.

"It's all rather like training a new puppy," the swim teacher concludes (Robins 1977).

Hipsley's success is no miracle. She has simply taken splendid advantage of most of the "facts of life" about learning. Some learning starts very early in life. Often, early learning depends on reflex responses. Learning comes from environmental stimulation, but it depends on developmental readiness. Motivation, attention, and repetition are important factors in learning. So is reinforcement. Observation is an important means of learning, and habituation, also, plays a part in the process.

ing and observational learning, as well as other findings relating to memory.

Teacher as model All adults remember one or more teachers who made a lasting impression on our lives. Teacher-as-model is a prime stimulus for observational learning.

However, no one, not even a teacher, can take imitation for granted as a means of teaching young children. A child's cognitive level has to be considered. A five-year-old is obviously too young, cognitively speaking, to imitate a physics experiment. On the other hand, some developmentally advanced eight-year-olds may be less inclined to learn from a model. Motivation becomes a strong factor. (See Chapter 11, page 436.) They have "minds of their own" and are able to pick and choose what they want to learn. Thus, there may be an optimum age for the modeling method of teaching (Fouts and Liikanen 1975). Also, older children and some adults sometimes have the notion that copying is a form of cheating.

Other variables affect whether children will learn by imitation. Attention to the model is an important factor. The more attention, the more children will be able to recall what was taught. The better the instructions that direct attention, the better both attention and recall. Without such instruction, the prospect of reward or punishment may be helpful in fixing a pupil's attention on a lesson. Older children are more likely to pay attention and recall what was learned (Yussen 1974).

How a model (teacher) arranges the lesson also affects how well the task will be learned. Modeling accompanied by verbal explanation facilitates observational learning. A group of six-year-olds were presented with a problem that involved sorting a group of objects in logical fashion. Three different kinds of teaching strategy were used. The most successful model explained the whys and wherefores of the sorting system while illustrating it at the same time: actually showing what was done while explaining it. A previous effort without the explanation did not work at all (Denney, Denney, and Ziobrowski 1973).

Feedback from teachers With rewards ranging from gold stars to smiles to A's on the report card, teachers have traditionally reinforced their students for their efforts. Feedback from instructors may provide information as well as reinforcement. But some kinds of feedback are more helpful than others.

For example, first graders, faced with a simple problem of identifying figures on flash cards, were given one of three different kinds of responses: Some children were told "right" or "wrong" with each card. Others were told only if they were wrong. Others were told only "right" or given no comment. The best spur to learning was to tell the children whether they were right or wrong in so many words. However, no comment or "wrong" worked better than "right" or no comment.

This experiment may have implications for the programmed teaching devices that are supposed to aid learning by reinforcing pupils just when they are right. It seems that the most effective reinforcement comes from having the information that one is *either* right or wrong (Schroth 1970).

Mere exposure to the environment has only limited value in promoting concept formation. It is the teacher, providing feedback and reinforcement, who makes the difference between learning and not learning. The quality as well as the quantity of stimulation is important. Kindergartners in a highly stimulating physical environment did no better in organizing new information and making use of current information than children in an ordinary classroom. But children did learn to express new concepts from a teacher who explained, elaborated, and praised (Mann and Taylor 1973).

Also, as we saw previously, children learn better when they are taught to put cues into words. Language—verbal labeling and verbal mediation—is a distinctly useful tool in teaching and learning (Milgram and Noce 1968). (See also Chapter 6, page 233.)

Developmental limitations   Good teachers are always aware of the cognitive limitations of pupils. As children grow older they use more learning strategies, and their strategies become more complex. Some kinds of problems are almost impossible for a five-year-old, simple for a ten-year-old. For example, children of various ages were shown a cartoon in which the main character lost a toy. They were then asked to plan a search for the toy. Five-year-olds did not realize that the toy would logically be found somewhere in the path of the character who was carrying it. Not until the ages of 7 or 8 did children readily infer that there was a particular plausible area where the toy might be (Drozdal and Flavell 1975).

In a similar test, kindergartners through fifth graders were questioned about how they would go about finding a lost jacket at school. About a third of the fifth graders answered that they would try to remember where they had last had it and would try to work forward through their activities after that time. Very few of the younger children were able to map out such a strategy (Kreutzer, Leonard, and Flavell 1975).

The natural impulsiveness of young children is another factor that is related to ability to learn. For instance, the game of "Simon Says" depends on waiting for the right cue word before one makes a move. In an experiment with this game, first graders made far more impulsive mistakes than third graders. Practice improved the ability of third graders, first graders, and kindergarten girls. But kindergarten boys and preschoolers did not improve with practice (Strommen 1973).

The age of the child is also related to ability to formulate a hypothesis and try it out in attempting to solve a problem. (See Chapter 5, page 186.) For example, kindergartners, second graders, and fourth graders were challenged with a game of putting wooden pegs into the correct trays. If the children found the right tray they found a candy. The clues were small and large circles, colors, and position. To work out the "code" they would have had to formulate a hypothesis about which cues would be right for the candy slots. After repeated trials, it appeared that a much larger percentage of the older children worked out hypotheses to solve the problem. Such organized behavior was beyond the ability of the younger pupils (Rieber 1969).

Machines and programmed teaching The theory of operant conditioning has been directly responsible for the recent wave of teaching machines and *programmed teaching* for modern classrooms. Teaching machines were designed to let each student work at the student's own pace. They give immediate feedback on the pupil's answers to questions, and they provide reinforcement for the right replies. A major reason for using such machines is to save teachers time so that they can work individually with each child, as needed.

Programmed teaching: sequential presentation of material and feedback

But in actual use, teaching machines have not been as effective as the inventors had hoped, evidently because they are boring. So children do not learn any better than with traditional teaching methods, and learning time is no shorter.

Programmed texts have also been only moderately successful. They break up information into component parts, so that the student learns in a stepwise progression. But they are also boring. Such texts are most useful for drills or repetitive exercises, to supplement tried-and-true classroom methods.

Behavior modification Like almost any scientific advance, modern learning theory can have two faces—for good, and for ill. "Brainwashers" also use learning theory. Newspaper stories have reported cases of "conversions" of political prisoners through forced conditioning. It is also charged that brainwashing is used by some religious sects in proselytizing new converts. But employing the principles of conditioning and modeling is not only respectable but useful in the classroom and in the home.

Modeling has been used to curb impulsive school children. As children grow older, they are most responsive to models who are like themselves. Impulsive fourth and sixth graders who were given a chance to observe classmates working out a problem in a reflective, considered manner learned to copy the models. The system worked even better for boys than for girls (Cohen and Przybycien 1974).

A model need not be actually present. Children can also learn by having a model's behavior described. In a *behavior modification* experiment, fourth and fifth graders were subjected both to live models and to descriptions of what an adult would do. Some of the children were the type who find it hard to wait for a reward. They would settle for 25 cents today rather than wait a week for 35 cents. Others were willing to wait. The result was that both kinds of models had a real effect in changing the accustomed behavior of these children (Bandura and Mischel 1965).

Behavior modification is currently a popular technique for solving behavioral problems, not only in the classroom but also in the home. The method does seem to be a promising alternative to spanking and other forms of force that may be counterproductive because by their very use parents are modeling undesirable behavior.

Behavior modification: the use of modeling and reinforcement techniques to change behavior

Learning from films and television

The ultimate model in modern American society is the much criticized "idiot box." It is estimated that the average child spends a total of 23 hours and 16 minutes a week being spoon-fed by "the tube." According to the Census Bureau more than 95 out of 100 American households have at least one television set. Forty-five percent have two or more. Television, it is feared, is THE teacher. And yet, schools make enormous use of films as teaching devices, with the aid and implied blessing of large amounts of government help. Just how effective (or destructive) are filmed models?

Benefits Accumulated research in the last decade suggests that film models are an effective teaching tool. Yet films and TV are

TV is a learning asset, also a liability.

both an asset and a liability to impressionable children. The benefits are varied and well documented. Behavior can be changed through observational learning. For example, fears can be reduced or eliminated and altruistic behavior can be increased.

Teachers say youngsters who have been regulars in the "Sesame Street" audience appear to be better prepared for school, with no adverse effects on the viewers' interest in real school. The program may even be having a good effect on vocabulary and IQ scores (Bogatz and Ball 1971).

A program in the "Lassie" series taught children to be compassionate to animals even at the expense of abandoning a rewarding game (Sprafkin, Liebert, and Poulos 1975). Cognitive style, too, may be modified by watching a model in a film. Impulsive children became less so, and made fewer mistakes, after they had been exposed to a reflective model (Ridberg, Parke, and Hetherington 1971).

One of the problems of observational learning is that exactly what is learned may not always be regulated by anyone other than the learner. Viewers learn from films whether they are supposed to or not. In fact, third, sixth, seventh, and ninth graders who were shown a film that they enjoyed learned a great deal, even when the information was only incidental to the plot (Collins 1970; Collins et al. 1978). (See Chapter 10, page 423.)

Necessary conditions   To use television and film effectively as teaching tools, it is probably necessary to supplement them with various other techniques, such as putting the "moral" into words or having children role-play what they have seen. Verbal labeling seems to be more important if the children are intended to learn the content of a film. Abstract issues and values may also be learned more effectively through verbal labeling than by example alone. But if children are supposed to learn some sort of behavior—like helping other children who are in trouble—then role-playing may be more useful (Friedrich and Stein 1975). (See also Box 7–7.)

Films' usefulness is affected by the fact that learning often depends on the pupil's attitude, orientation, and relationship to the model. Viewers of a film tend to learn more from a film character with whom they can identify: someone of the same sex, or someone in a social class to which the viewer aspires. (See also Chapter 9, page 372.) But they do not remember everything the film model does. They seem to pick out what is especially relevant. Boys, for example, are apt to remember aggressive content, provided it was a boy-hero who was the aggressor. In the past, girls have identified with and remembered the boy–girl situations in a movie, whenever the girl was the heroine (Maccoby and Wilson 1957). The more similar the film's hero to the viewer, the more the preadolescent is likely to imitate and learn (Rosekrans 1967).

Age has a great deal to do with how much a child can learn from a film. Cognitive range also has to be considered. With increasing age and more developed cognitive abilities, a youngster is better able to remember the sequence of events in a film that is meant to be entertaining. The older the child, the better able to understand the characters' feelings and motivations. Children appear to be as telegraphic in their observational learning as they are in language. Complexities beyond their understanding at four become accessible at ten. Many of the things they see in the media, or witness in real life, are over their heads (Leifer et al. 1971).

Adult tastes may be poor criteria for judging a film's effectiveness for teaching children. The very touches that make grown-ups say "Now there's a well-done program!" are often the least effective. Children miss asides, whether they are visual or verbal or humorous. They will follow the general line of a program and fail to pick up factual statements that adults have "cleverly" slipped into a story. What an adult finds attractive

Box 7–7 Home TV-Viewing as a Learning Tool

Parents can help children make practical learning use of all their TV-viewing, according to a New York City education specialist, Raymond Coppola. He says talking to a child about what is being seen on the little screen can develop communication and thinking ability.

Encourage conversation during the commercials, says Coppola. Discuss the show, the characters, what has been seen. Ask leading questions about what the child might do in the same situation. At the end, ask the young viewer to tell all about the program. The commercials should be discussed, too, so that children can be led to watch and listen more critically.

Programs like news programs should be discussed beforehand as well, so that children will be alerted to what they are going to see. Youngsters might be asked to discuss their own lives that day, the news events of the day before, or be encouraged to predict what the program will show. News broadcasts on two different stations might be compared, to show either similarities or differences. Weather reports are a good subject for discussion, particularly since they are so closely connected to the child's own experience.

Other possibilities for children: Look up some of the program subjects in the encyclopedia. Take notes. Write down new words and look them up. Keep score for sports programs. Use the time of TV programs to help learn how to tell time. Write a critical review of some programs or commercials. Write to favorite performers. Make up a story or a scene for a favorite program. To promote reading, read books based on TV programs. As appropriate, discuss careers portrayed in programs and daily life in the past as shown on TV. Get relevant books at the library. (Of course, the parent has to watch TV along with the child in order to do all this.) (Coppola 1978.)

may seem irrelevant or incomprehensible to a child, or it may just slide by unnoticed. True, today's children are used to television and also ready and willing to learn from TV and films. But some presentations are simply beyond their cognitive level (Friedlander, Wetstone, and Scott 1974).

Television advertisers are very much aware of children's cognitive level when they try to "teach" young viewers to ask for certain products. Many people think it is unfair to use learning techniques to promote foods and toys that may be costly or harmful to health, or both. Research on the effects of commercials on children is fairly new. However, some evidence suggests that children become easily habituated to commercials. Therefore, their attention may wander when the commercial is on (Zuckerman, Ziegler, and Stevenson 1978).

There is so much television in modern children's lives that some people tend to attribute all learning problems to TV. But the most important and certainly the earliest influences on children and their ability to learn are still the home, parents, and other care-givers.

Environmental Differences

Belva Davis, a black woman who is a well-known television journalist, told an interviewer that until she entered high school, she was still sleeping on a pallet on the floor. Her family's three-room apartment was shared by 11 family members, including cousins, uncles, and aunts. But, she said, "we were not psychologically poor. I never felt poor, never felt deprived. There was a lot of love, closeness, sharing, encouragement, and pulling together" (Belva Davis—Channel 9, 1978). At the time of the interview, Ms. Davis was the anchorwoman for the public TV station in her area, noted for her charm, warmth, and intelligence.

The Davis story blasts the old but now dying stereotype that black children are somehow inferior, doomed by their racial background and upbringing to be poorer students and poorer achievers. Her description of her home also illustrates the fact that a child can have a good learning atmosphere *regardless* of socioeconomic status (and can grow up to teach others). Research confirms that families that encourage children to be curious and independent promote their children's learning ability. Therefore, a great deal of emphasis is currently being placed on how to repair apparent damage to children whose home environment and consequent impetus to learn in school are poor. (See Box 7–8.)

It is important to note that most of the data on children's learning ability come from tests given in school, in terms of school-related tasks. These tests relate to concept formation, knowledge of subject matter, organizing and encoding skills. Measuring these abilities depends mostly on "proper school language" and on specific orientation to school-type achievements. Thus, all studies of learning differences between children of different socioeconomic classes have a built-in middle-class bias. In fact, what the existing research shows is only that *what* children learn may be a function of their background. The evidence does not necessarily show that *ability* to learn differs on a "class" basis. Slum children learn very well what their environment de-

Box 7–8 Mothers Play, Children Learn

A program that taught low-income mothers how to play with their preschool children led to better learning achievement years later. Psychologist Phyllis Levenstein established her continuing project with considerable help, both financial and otherwise, in a large number of communities beginning in the 1960s. The purpose was to try to eliminate the difference between middle-income and low-income children in verbal and other skills important to academic achievement. The program was conceived as an alternative to Head Start, which offers special classes to low-income children during the preschool years.

In Dr. Levenstein's project, a "toy demonstrator," goes into homes to demonstrate toys and books to the preschoolers and their parents. The mother is taught how to play with the child, using the toys, in order to stimulate the youngster's ability to think and to learn. For example, a two-year-old plays with a toy vending machine and is coached by the parent to name the colors of the objects that pop out of the slots and to count the number of discs used to make the machine operate.

After a dozen years' experience with this "verbal interaction project," tests compared 78 third graders who had taken part in the program as two- to four-year-olds with 51 children who had not had the mother–child play practice. The experimental group out-performed the control group by a margin of about ten percentage points in both reading and arithmetic. The children in the experimental group were performing at the national average while the control group was below average.

The key to the program's success, according to its originator, is that the mothers were trained to expose their children to kinds of language and concepts that would not otherwise have been heard in their homes (Fiske 1979).

mands, such as basic survival skills. Still, if one assumes that all children must grow up to cope with a world dominated by middle-class values, it may be important to find ways of helping them learn better in middle-class–dominated classrooms.

Home environments vary

A study of the interaction of parents and preschool children in low socioeconomic areas showed that the good learners came from families where parents encouraged them to be "curious adventurers." The children's urges to be creative and independent were fostered. Conflicts were minimized and there was lots of conversation between parent and child (Swan and Stavros 1973). However, some homes provide surroundings that seem to have negative effects on youngsters' ability to learn.

Overstimulation   Overstimulation in the home tends to prevent children from differentiating among stimuli. *Quality* and *not quantity* of stimulation is what is important to learning. These conclusions come from a number of investigations.

A group of infants tested at the ages of 7, 11, 15, 18, and 22 months showed distinct deficiencies in psychological development. They were from homes with too much stimulation, a veritable bombardment, an inescapable jumble of too much going on, too loudly, a chaos of words and sounds and comings and goings. At the same time, in such homes there is too little stimulation of a different kind: no one person deliberately concentrating on the children to give them words for things, activities, events, relationships. Children raised under such conditions have trouble distinguishing one word from another. They learn to be inattentive. This adds up to scanty learning as well as poor learning habits (Wachs, Uzgiris, and Hunt 1971; Deutsch 1964). (See also Chapter 6, page 243.)

Verbal learning problems   Among other evidence of the effect of early environment on learning is a study of two-year-olds, half of whom were reared by college-graduate mothers, the other half by mothers who had gone no further than high school. In nonverbal or sensorimotor tasks, there were no differences in learning ability. But for verbal learning the differences were significant. The gap appeared between the ages of a year-and-a-half and three, when language becomes important for learning (Golden, Bridger, and Montare 1974).

Among four- to five-year-olds attending day-care centers, there was little evidence that children from middle- and lower-income homes think differently. Again the only differences seemed to center around verbal ability. The children from low-income homes had more trouble understanding what they were asked to do, needed more instructions, and were bored by some of the tasks (Stevenson, Williams, and Coleman 1971).

Without intervention, the verbal deficit of children with inadequate early learning opportunities may continue throughout the school years. The tendency for some children to duck the verbal and concentrate on what can be seen can also be found in older children from lower socioeconomic backgrounds. Given classifying tasks related to mathematics, fifth, eighth, and eleventh graders relied on perceptible likenesses and differences, rather than defining the differences or using the names of the concepts (Nelson and Klausmeier 1974). "Disadvantaged" students, whether they come from Appalachia or a city slum, seem to

Box 7–9   Teaching Reading to the "Disadvantaged"

Every September, Deborah Reddy faces the challenge of teaching reading to 26 or 27 six-year-olds, most of whom have never consciously seen a book or a magazine. Her pupils are mostly members of Spanish-speaking families in a farming community in the southwestern part of the United States. Many speak little or no English. By June, almost all her pupils are reading sentences in books, writing words, and are even able to tell the class a story. How does she do it?

First Deborah teaches her pupils what a word is. The first word is the child's name. Each is taught to write his or her name. But the child's friends' names are also words. Each discusses the names of favorite things to eat or do: more words (which happen to be key

vocabulary words). Deborah writes out every child's favorite words, each one on a piece of colored construction paper, linked like keys on a large binder ring. This is the child's own personal vocabulary. The teacher points out that some of these favorite words have the same letters as the child's name.

Now the instructor shows the children sentences. See, each is made up of words! The sentence, she points out, is like a line of children. Each word in a sentence, like each child, is different. Understanding this concept makes it possible for pupils to expand their "own" words into sentences. This is the child's exposure to the common "service" words.

The transition from words to reading comes when the pupil dictates

be less able to draw inferences and to make generalizations than students brought up in middle-class suburbs (Wulff 1974).

Remedial possibilities Special training can compensate for learning deficits related to an inappropriate learning environment. (See Box 7–9.) But it may be that remedial programs like Head Start attack the problem when the children are already too old. If developmental inadequacy shows up during the first year of life, some kind of help may be needed at that time (Wachs, Uzgiris, and Hunt 1971).

Psychologists are still struggling with the question of whether, in the light of the importance of verbal ability, it would help all children learn better if they were taught reading and writing as early as possible. Perhaps they should be taught in the years before conventional schools begin. Maybe the fact that older, brighter children who are culturally advantaged are more verbal causes them to be more advanced cognitively—rather

stories, happenings, dreams, hopes, fears, or wishes to the teacher. These are recorded in individual books for the child to read. From these stories, children select more favorite words to be added to their own word banks. Now the favorite words become flashcards for the child to use with a friend, or alone for creative sentence writing. At the same time, the teacher is conducting individual conferences and small group instruction. Some of the new words, drawn from the children themselves, are part of group discussion.

Very soon phonic instruction begins, intertwined with spelling, writing, and reading. Sounds are taught not in isolation but as the beginnings, endings, and middles of words. Now the pupils are finding their own words in stories and books.

At this point Deborah Reddy's children are ready for a basic reader. But some go right to "real" books. The teacher knows who is ready for what, and when.

Prizes rank high in Deborah's first-grade classes. She scrounges sacks full of everyday items to reward progress. Besides, each prize is a new word.

In her seven years of teaching, Deborah has found that any child with normal cognitive ability, no matter how "disadvantaged," can be taught to read. Some become excellent readers. She creates the necessary environment and provides the necessary stimuli.

than the other way around (Kohlberg 1968). Language and thought are certainly interdependent. But do they or do they not depend on intelligence? This controversy will be discussed further in the next chapter.

Summary

Modern learning theorists, notably B. F. Skinner, believe that almost all human behavior can be explained by a person's learned responses to the environment, which provides the necessary stimuli. The simplest form of learning is classical conditioning: the reflex response originally caused by one stimulus can be caused by a different stimulus, provided the new stimulus has been repeatedly paired with the original stimulus.

Operant, or instrumental, conditioning is another form of learning. Reinforcement is the motivating factor. The more frequent the reinforcement of a particular response, the more frequent the response. When the response has been reinforced all the time, the behavior is easier to extinguish than when reinforcement has been intermitten or partial.

Social, or observational, learning consists of lessons absorbed by observing models, including parents, friends, associates, teachers, television, movies. Observational learning can be an important method of formal teaching. Albert Bandura is a leading exponent of this learning theory. Sex, age, and cognitive level are important factors in observational learning. The younger the child, the more likely to imitate adults. Attention and motivation are factors.

The information-processing theory of learning proposes that sensory stimulation impinges on the senses, leading to arousal because of discrepancy, complexity, ambiguity, or incongruity of the stimulus. The resultant attention causes the information to be received into short-term memory. Long-term memory depends on a person's use of deliberate strategies.

Habituation is evidence of memory. Memory depends partly on developmental and cognitive level, partly on motivation, and partly on strategies used by individuals or their teachers. Images are more easily remembered than words. Encoding or memory styles differ among individuals.

Learning strategies are useful to parents and teachers at every stage of life. The richer the environment, the more learning. Children born into environments that provide inadequate stimulation for the learning required in middle-class schools show these learning deficiencies in the first few years of life. Remedial programs probably should begin in very early childhood, since learning differences between disadvantaged and middle-class children appear between the ages of one-and-a-half and three, when language becomes important for learning. Learning differences between socioeconomic classes appear to center about verbal ability, which is partly a product of environment.

Chronological Overview

Newborn
early memory: habituates to repetitive sounds, odors, and sights

Infancy
can be conditioned to a feeding schedule by operant conditioning

exploratory learning

Preschool
memory relies on concrete rather than abstract cues

no mental strategies for memorization

observational learning

operant conditioning useful for toilet training; behavior shaping

Childhood
uses pictorial but not verbal encoding strategy

observational learning with teacher as model, verbal explanation, and reinforcement

number and complexity of learning strategies increase with age

impulsive errors gradually decrease

increasing ability to formulate a hypothesis

imitation of models close to same age and of same sex

increasing ability to understand feelings and motivation

learning depends on cognitive level

Applying Your Knowledge

1. How do parents sometimes misuse reinforcement principles while training their children?
2. Give an example of how teachers employ learning principles in the classroom.
3. Why can't novel behavior be explained by current learning theories?

Further Readings

Azrin, Nathan H., and Foxx, Richard M. *Toilet training in less than a day.* New York: Simon and Schuster, 1974. Description of a professionally tested method for successful toilet training, using the principles of operant conditioning.
Paperback.

Cohen, Dorothy H. *The learning child: guidelines for parents and teachers.* New York: Vintage Books, 1973. Description of how children learn, especially from ages five to eleven.
Paperback.

Good, Thomas L.; Biddle, Bruce J.; and Brophy, Jere E. *Teachers make a difference.* New York: Holt, Rinehart and Winston, 1975. Documents the impact of teachers and schools on the educational progress of students.
Paperback.

Smith, Frank. *Comprehension and learning: a conceptual framework for teachers.* New York: Holt, Rinehart and Winston, 1975. A thorough account of comprehension as the basis for learning.
Paperback.

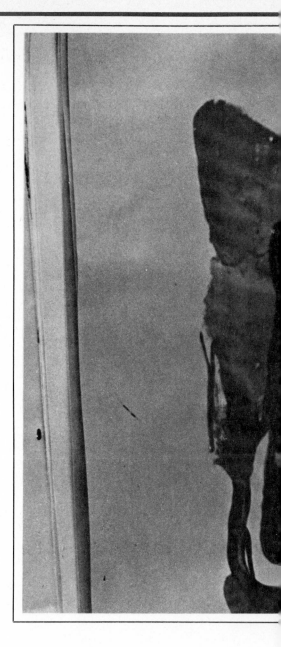

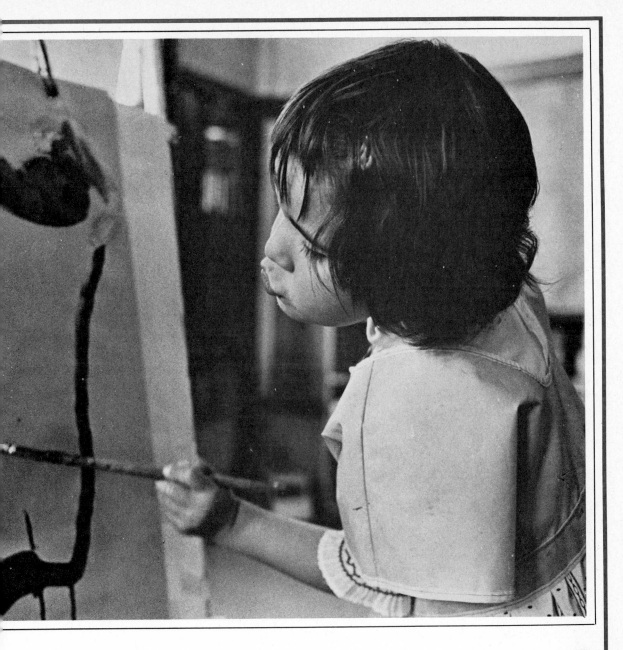

Chapter **8**

Intelligence, Aptitude, Achievement

Carl Flegal used to be the mayor of Fremont, California, a city of about 60,000. He has also been president of the Philharmonic Society in that area. In fact, he has been president of several other civic organizations too. He makes an excellent living as a certified public accountant and heads his own firm. Now he is in his sixties, happily married for over 35 years, the father of five and the grandfather of six.

What makes Flegal really different from most other men his age is that he has been part of a landmark study in a controversial area related to psychological development: *intelligence* and *IQ (intelligence quotient) scores*. In 1922 Carl Flegal was chosen, along with 1469 other public school children with IQ scores of 140 and over, to be studied over a long period of time. The head of the investigation was psychologist Lewis M. Terman of Stanford University.

Meaning of Intelligence

The Terman study

Terman's remarkable project has been carried on for over half a century by the major investigator, his staff, and his successors, through periodic reinvestigation of the original subjects and their spouses. The double purpose of this *longitudinal research* was to find out what traits characterize boys and girls with high IQs and to discover how they turn out as adults.

Longitudinal research: periodic study of a particular group over a long period of time

The results show that not only did these children do better in school, but their health, physique, and social adjustment tended to be above average (Terman et al. 1925; Terman 1954). As for their eventual success in life (at least as our society defines success), it was impressive.

Flegal's story is typical for this group. In spite of the fact that they grew up during the Great Depression, nine out of ten subjects went to college and seven out of ten stayed through to graduation. Thirty percent of the graduates won honors; two-thirds went on to graduate school. At the same time, a great many of them earned half or more of their college expenses, plus hundreds of thousands of dollars of scholarships and fellowships.

By the time they were 40 they had published countless books, articles, short stories, novels, plays, scripts; secured numerous technical patents; and achieved other kinds of occupational success and community accomplishment similar to Carl Flegal's. Many were listed in the *Who's Who* of their professions. In general, their accomplishments were 10 to 30 times as great as would have been expected for an equal number of people chosen at random from the general population (Terman 1954). (These achievements were chiefly among men, since few women embarked on careers in that era.)

Carl Flegal and his fellow "Termites" (as they call themselves) provide a vivid picture of what a high IQ seems to do for a person. However, the study leaves other important questions unanswered.

Major issues

Just what *is* intelligence? Do intelligent people learn better? Is intelligence the same as IQ? Can intelligence be accurately and reliably tested? Does intelligence depend mostly on genes inherited from parents and ancestors, or is intelligence a product of how we are brought up, how we are taught in school, and the rest of life's experiences? Does age affect intelligence—is it developmental? What is the relationship, if any, between intelligence and learning, cognitive ability, creativity, and genius? Can anyone deliberately plan to improve the intelligence of an individual or a group? And, most explosive question of all, are some races or groups naturally more intelligent than others?

These issues are not just theoretical. They go to the heart of our democratic society. The answers not only matter to scholars and educators but are also of deep interest to almost everybody.

Definitions Nobody has yet succeeded in defining intelligence to everyone's satisfaction. Many have tried. Samples:

"Intelligence is the summation of the learning experiences of the individual" (Wesman 1968, page 267).

"Intelligence is the aggregate or global capacity of the individual to act purposefully, to think rationally, and to deal effectively with his environment" (Wechsler 1944, page 1).

"Intelligence is defined by a consensus among psychologists. It is the repertoire of intellectual skills and knowledge available to a person at any one period of time" (Humphreys 1969, page 167).

Assumptions Commonly, *intelligence* is thought to refer to skill in problem-solving, to insight, and to ability to deal with abstract ideas. We also tend to associate good memory with intelligence. Thus, intelligence is considered to involve intellectual skills and cognitive ability. Not necessarily equated with intelligence are

Intelligence: insight, skill in problem-solving, and mental ability

A test: put the pieces together.

athletic, musical, and artistic ability. Nor is a person who has accumulated a great deal of factual knowledge or trivia necessarily considered to be intelligent.

Scholars' position on the question is that intelligence and IQ may not be the same thing, even though some psychologists half jokingly dismiss the matter by saying that "intelligence is what the intelligence test measures." However, the IQ does represent a *measurable facet* of intelligence. Therefore, it is important to an understanding of human development to learn the history of IQ-testing and other tests of mental ability and the controversial questions raised by their use.

Mental Tests

Stanford–Binet, individual testing

History   Alfred Binet devised the first test that was later known as an "intelligence test." Binet was a psychologist who had been given a practical problem by the French government in the 1890s. The authorities were concerned about overcrowded schools. They wanted a way of selecting children who would benefit most from formal education. Therefore, Binet and his collaborator, Henri Simon, designed a test that would predict an individual's ability to be successful in school.

The Binet examination, put into use in 1905, with revisions in 1908 and 1911, is the grandparent of today's intelligence tests. Some years later, in 1916, Professor Terman at Stanford University adapted the French test for American children, renaming it the Terman–Binet and eventually the Stanford–Binet. Later, other psychologists devised similar tests, all to similar ends: to predict how well people would do in school, in college or graduate school, or even in jobs or military service.

Meaning of "IQ"   The famous *IQ—intelligence quotient—*is the method of measurement of the Binet tests. Other standardized intelligence tests are designed to yield scores comparable to the Binet. However, only the Stanford–Binet test scores are a real quotient: *mental age (MA) divided by chronological age (CA) times 100 = IQ.* The reason for multiplying by 100 was to avoid using fractions, so that intelligence could be expressed as a whole number. The scores of other, later intelligence tests are converted to equivalent numbers, although they do not necessarily measure the relationship between mental age and chronological age.

IQ (intelligence quotient) score: a measure of intelligence, established by testing; mental age divided by chronological age times 100

Mental age: level of mental development typical for a particular chronological age

How it works A woman who is now in her thirties vividly remembers an incident from her kindergarten days in a public school near Stanford University. She was taken in a taxi with four other puzzled children to a room on the Stanford campus. There she waited till called into a smaller room by a male adult, who may have been a professor, or perhaps a graduate student. As she remembers, he asked strange questions, such as: "The sun shines during the day and the moon at . . . ?" He wanted her to repeat some numbers backwards. And he also asked the difference between a bird and a dog. Sometimes she hesitated in her answers because she was wondering, "Why doesn't this man know these simple things? Why does he ask *me?*"

What that "ignorant" man was doing, of course, was administering the Stanford–Binet test to find out her mental age. Presumably, someone had chosen the children in that kindergarten class who seemed the brightest, to discover how their ability might be reflected on an IQ test.

The Stanford–Binet test is based on the premise that mental ability is developmental—increases with age through childhood—but that an intelligence quotient is relatively stable. The two major assumptions are (a) that from birth through adolescence we grow increasingly able through maturation and experience and (b) that at any given chronological age children vary in their degree of mental competence. Thus, a chart of any normal child's increase in mental ability would be a *parabola,* rising from the lowest level at birth, ending in a plateau beginning around the age of 15. But from early adolescence on, both mental ability and IQ score would ordinarily be stable.

Parabola: a graphed curve that increases along the vertical axis and levels off parallel to horizontal axis

For the IQ score to remain the same over time, the mental age of the individual must increase in step with chronological age. However, the term *mental age* (level of mental ability typical of a particular age) is not applicable past adolescence, since intellectual ability is usually fully developed by that time. Note that adult learning involves the accumulation of new knowledge or information, not the skills or abilities that make it possible to acquire knowledge. Thus, the Binet test—which is sensitive only to increases in intellectual ability—and the Binet quotient are not applicable as chronological age continues into the adult years. (See Box 8–1 and Figure 8–1.)

Binet worked out 54 tests, for different age levels. The easiest questions, which are presented first in the test, are those that an average two-year-old can answer. The questions grow increasingly difficult. The hardest would be difficult for the average adult to answer correctly. The questions do not rely on what is learned in school. Rather, they are tests of memory, reasoning power, ability to understand, time orientation, facility in using number concepts, ability to combine ideas into a meaningful whole, perceptual ability, knowledge of common objects. In general, they measure cognitive abilities (Terman 1916). (See Box 8–2.)

The Binet test items are *standardized*—ranked according to age level and average ability expected for each age level. Binet

Standardized: using norms established according to some criteria

---

Box 8–1   IQs Are Not Always Stable

Binet's original testing program and later research by Terman, Wechsler, and other specialists show that mental age is normally developmental—it increases year by year—until the age of about 15. After that, chronological age continues to increase, of course, but mental ability remains relatively stable. IQ is a number that results from the relationship between mental age (MA) and chronological age (CA).

For example, suppose a child's mental age tests at the level that is normal for a seven-year-old. If that child is actually seven years old, the IQ (MA divided by CA times 100) is 100. Tested at eight, the child's mental age will probably be eight. So the IQ remains the same— stable—because mental age and chronological age have progressed together.

But chronological and mental ages do not always work in perfect tandem. Special circumstances can make mental age develop more slowly or faster than

chronological age, thus causing IQ to rise or fall, as the case may be.

A different long-term study followed the mental progress of a large group of children, every third child born in one city during one half-year period. Tests were given regularly to these 252 youngsters, from the age of 21 months to 18 years. In general, the results showed that the IQs of these children fluctuated very little over the long term. But there were many fluctuations over short periods, particularly at times when there were disturbing factors in the lives of individual youngsters. (See Figure 8–1.) Therefore, the researchers caution against using a single IQ test score, or even two scores, to predict a child's future performance. They add: "This finding seems of especial importance since many plans for individual children are made by schools, juvenile courts, and mental hygiene clinics on the basis of a single mental test score" (Honzik, Macfarlane, and Allen 1948, page 315).

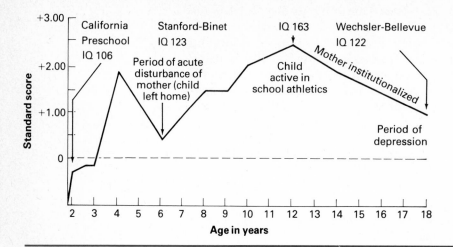

FIG. 8–1 Mental test performance of one boy. *Source:* M. P. Honzik, J. W. Macfarlane, and L. Allen, The stability of mental test performance between two and eighteen years, *Journal of Experimental Education,* 1948, *17,* 320.

assembled his questions for each age level by trying them out on many children. Thus he was able to determine which questions were most likely to be answered correctly by most children of each age. For example, if a particular set of questions got right answers from two out of three eight-year-olds, those questions were considered appropriate for that age level.

Once Binet had standardized his test in this way, he was able to pass it on to examiners.* They would start by asking their subjects to answer the easy questions, well below the child's presumed age level ability. Then the questions moved on up the age scale until the child made errors consistently: missed seven out of ten questions. If an eight-year-old, for example, successfully replied to the questions on the eight-year-old level, but no better, the pupil would be assigned a mental age of eight. But if the child's limit was questions on the seven-year level, the mental age would be seven. Figuring the intelligence quotient was a simple matter of dividing mental age by chronological age and multiplying by 100. So the eight-year-old with a mental age of seven has an IQ of 87.

---

*There are actually two different but equivalent forms of the Binet tests: "L" and "M," named for *L*ewis Terman and his collaborator, *M*aude James (Sears 1979).

After Binet's tests were applied to large groups of children, the accumulated statistics showed scores for the general population produce a graph in the shape of a *bell-shaped curve*, with a score of 100 as the average. Most people's mental age and chronological age are the same, so for a normal curve the *median* and *mean* IQ are *both* 100. The farther away from the mean or median (100) on either side of the scale, the fewer people. So both the highest and lowest IQs are rarest. (See Appendix, pages 526–527.)

The Stanford–Binet, best known and most like Binet's pioneering test, is most often given orally by a single examiner to

Bell-shaped curve: a normal distribution with an equal number of cases falling on either side of the mean

Median: middle-most score of a group of scores

Mean: mathematical average of scores (the sum of the scores divided by the number of scores)

Box 8–2   Sample Criteria from the Stanford–Binet Scale

Mental age	Ability
2	Identifies objects by name Builds a tower of blocks from a model Obeys the command, "Give me the dog"
3	Identifies pictures of common objects Sorts buttons according to color Copies a circle
4	Identifies objects, such as, "Which one gives us milk?" Names objects from memory
5	Copies a square Can define three common objects
6	Describes an orange Tells the difference between a slipper and a boot Can select a given number of blocks
7	Copies a diamond Tells how wood and coal are alike
8	Names the days of the week Tells similarities and differences between objects
9	Repeats four digits in reverse order Draws designs from memory
10	Defines abstract words Names at least 28 words in a minute

Source: Compiled from L. M. Terman and M. A. Merrill, *Stanford–Binet Intelligence Scale,* Manual for the third revision, Form L-M (Boston: Houghton Mifflin, 1960).

a single subject. It is an *individual* test, which permits the tester to assess the subject's emotional and physical state and to adjust timing and number of questions accordingly. Consequently, individual testing is usually considered to be a more precise instrument. However, in the interests of economy and efficiency, many of the other tests developed later for this country, and now in wider use, are designed to be given to *groups* by one examiner. Group tests rely on the subjects' ability to read and do arithmetic. Thus, they reflect schooling. And the examiner has no information on the state of mind or health of the individual who is being tested.

Other IQ tests

Wechsler scales   Aside from the Binet, among the leading current tests are the Wechsler Adult Intelligence Scale (WAIS), the Wechsler Intelligence Scale for Children (WISC—ages 7 to 16), and the Wechsler Preschool Primary Scale of Intelligence (WPPSI—ages 4 to 6½). David Wechsler was a clinical psychologist at Bellevue, a hospital in New York City, when he devised his first test. His purpose was to analyze adult patients—many of whom were derelicts, psychotics, illiterates—in order to find out whether there was a mental component in their problems. Since he believed that adults and children are different in their intellectual capacities, he decided that he needed a different examination from Binet's, which was originally designed for children. Yet the technique used in the Wechsler scales is now also popular for testing children. It is equally ironic that Binet's test, designed to identify individuals of low capacity, turned out to be the basis of Terman's famous long-term study of very bright children (Cronbach 1970).

For example, the Digital Symbol subtest shows a series of numbers, each with a special symbol. Then follows a group of numbers, but without their symbols. The pupil must fill in the

Wechsler and Binet did not differ in their concept of mental ability. But Wechsler wished to break up intellectual performance into several separate components. He worked out ten or more subtests that differed for the various age levels. Since the original Wechsler tests, new ones have been prepared along the same lines. The items have been improved, forms have been standardized, and the preschool level is now covered. Each of the subtests deals with one kind of task.

For example, the Digital Symbol subtest shows a series of numbers, each with a special symbol. Then follows a group of numbers, but without their symbols. The pupil must fill in the right symbol from the code. Motor ability to copy symbols quickly is involved, as well as ability to use the code correctly. A Picture Arrangement test asks the pupil to rearrange several cartoon panels in the right order to make a rational sequence. These performance tasks rely very little on verbal ability and are useful for children who are not at home with formal school activities (Cronbach 1970).

The Wechsler tests yield both a *verbal score* and a *performance score*. The single IQ scores that result indicate the subjects' ability in relation to the ability of others in the same age group. The Wechsler IQ scores are highly correlated with the Binet scores. The *correlation* coefficient is .80, which indicates on a scale of 0 to 1.00 the degree to which the two sets of scores are related to one another (Cronbach 1970). This high correlation indicates that both tests are measuring very nearly the same quality. Therefore, we can rely on either measure to test intelligence. Both Binet's test and the Wechsler tests have been adapted for use all over the globe.

Verbal score: score in language skills

Performance score: score in manual tasks

Correlation: degree of similarity or correspondence between two or more variables

Goodenough Yet another kind of intelligence test that, like the others, produces an IQ score, is the Goodenough Draw-a-Man (or -a-Woman) Test. The Goodenough is a measure of intellectual and conceptual maturity, which is based on the assumption that the ability to form concepts is the major sign of intelligence. Thus, the more complex the concept demonstrated, the higher the intellectual development. Florence Goodenough's premise is that the way a child draws a familiar object—not artistic skill but the number of *critical features* included—will reveal the child's conception of that object. The drawing will show ability to perceive likenesses and differences; ability to abstract, or to classify objects according to likenesses and differences; and ability to generalize, or to assign a newly experienced object to a class according to its attributes (Harris 1963).

Goodenough tests intelligence through children's drawings of people (rather than animals or inanimate objects) because it is assumed that, irrespective of background, children are most familiar with the human figure. Figure 8–2 shows how a five-year-old conceptualizes a man and a woman and how much more detailed are the six-, nine-, and ten-year-olds' drawings (Harris 1963).

The Goodenough test is valid up to the age of about 15. Since it measures concrete thinking, it is useful only for children who

FIG. 8–2 Examples of the Goodenough Draw-a-Man, Draw-a-Woman Test. *Source: Children's Drawings as Measures of Intellectual Maturity* by Dale B. Harris, © 1963 by Harcourt Brace Jovanovich, Inc. Reproduced by permission of the publisher.

Man, by boy, 5 years old

Woman, by same boy

Woman, by boy, 6 years old

Woman, by boy, 9
years old

Woman, by boy, 10
years old

Woman, by boy, 10
years old

have not reached the stage of abstract thought, or Piaget's formal operations period. (See Chapter 5, pages 186–189.)

Aptitude and achievement tests

Anyone reading this book has long since left intelligence tests behind. But another kind of testing, for aptitude or achievement, is similar in some respects. These tests are not only used frequently in the grade school years but are also widely employed by colleges and industry. *Aptitude* and *achievement tests* are employed either to predict individual occupational or academic success or to measure the success of teachers or schools.

Aptitude test: test that measures ability to perform a task

Achievement tests   Achievement tests are not intended to determine *ability* to learn, but rather *how much* has been learned. Often they are used to measure how well the school is doing in teaching, as well as what individual pupils have accomplished. For example, some states have a statewide achievement testing program every year. Tests in reading, writing, spelling, and mathematics are given to pupils on every level in all school districts throughout the state. Test results for the various grades are compared from district to district, to determine whether each school and each district are doing a better job than last year and to determine which districts are doing best.

Achievement test: test that measures current performance or learning

Achievement tests can also help in assessing the progress of an individual pupil. But their value for comparison from year to year and from school to school is mixed. Schools are never exactly comparable. Student bodies vary in ethnic background and in socioeconomic status. Some schools have a large number of pupils whose families move a great deal and whose past educational background is spotty. For these and other reasons, achievement test comparisons must be used with caution.

Aptitude tests: SAT, ACT   Applicants for admission to colleges or postgraduate schools are usually required to take an aptitude test. Aptitude tests are intended to measure *ability* to do well in the college program (or a job), not just accumulated knowledge. Most private colleges and universities use the Scholastic Aptitude Test (SAT) of the College Entrance Examination Board. SAT scores play an important part in admissions decisions by these schools, since there are a limited number of places for a large number of would-be students. The American College Testing Program administers a test known as ACT, which is used chiefly by public colleges and universities.

ACT and SAT are similar, although ACT puts more emphasis on what the student has previously learned. ACT also samples skills and knowledge that will be needed in college. For example, ACT asks questions designed to discover the student's reasoning in doing basic math. Reading matter must be corrected to improve clarity and to show the subject's knowledge of grammar. The person being examined must also be able to evaluate scientific reports and material dealing with social science and other kinds of reading.

The SAT tests are in two parts, verbal and mathematical. The verbal score depends mostly on reading comprehension, using college material. The math score asks the student to demonstrate reasoning and ability to draw conclusions from tables. These are *skills* needed in order to do college work. The test is not intended to assess what was learned in high school.

However, some authorities contend that so-called aptitude tests are achievement tests in disguise, since these group tests rely on reading and arithmetic, taught in all schools. Consequently, aptitude and achievement almost inevitably overlap, since it is difficult to distinguish aptitude from what has been learned in school (Cronbach 1970).

Value of group tests Aptitude and achievement tests are currently somewhat controversial. It is claimed that minority applicants are being discriminated against when test scores are given great weight in determining who will be admitted to colleges and graduate schools. It is said that true aptitude is not being measured by ACT and SAT. Rather, it is argued, results of these tests reflect previous environment and education, which may not conform to middle-class standards.

Group tests like SAT and ACT, as well as group IQ tests, are also criticized because they are primarily used to provide a numerical score and give no opportunity to judge the *quality* of the subject's performance. Group tests are invalid for subjects who are not trying to do their best or are not feeling well, and they are not appropriate for children with reading problems.

In contrast, individual tests, which do not rely on time limits, can reveal psychological subtleties about the person being tested. They give the examiner a chance to produce a rating regardless of whether the subject understands the test and wants to do well.

Individual tests can be fine-tuned instruments, but unfortunately they are often not practical in situations where many individuals must be tested (Cronbach 1970). This argument about group testing is related to the whole question of just how useful mental tests are in judging and predicting children's intellectual ability.

Value of Testing

Test predictability

Test predictability: capacity of a test to predict future abilities or performance

Someone brought baby Jon (then not quite two years old) a jigsaw puzzle. The toy had been produced by a well-known manufacturer and was marked "suitable for ages three to five." Jon seemed enchanted by the puzzle and within a very short time he had succeeded in putting the five large pieces together to make the complete picture—whereupon his parents immodestly decided that their child was certainly very intelligent, if not a genius.

Many parents do think the first baby in the family is a genius. Right or wrong, their testing methods are crude, as well as distinctly biased. But in their ability to forecast an infant's future intellectual ability, psychologists do not fare much better.

Preschool years It is difficult, if not impossible, to give an intelligence test to a baby who is not yet talking. Intelligence testing relies mostly on words: instructions or commands from an examiner, ability of a subject to understand those words and to act or reply accordingly. Thus, those who try to rate infant intelligence are really studying spontaneous behavior. But early sensorimotor behavior is not predictive of later intelligence (Lewis and McGurk 1972; Lewis 1973). Besides, infant development is unstable and a baby's performance will vary from day to day. Intellectual functioning, too, fluctuates until the second year. Only at that stage does it begin to be possible to predict later ability. Intellectual status does not become fixed until some time in the late preschool years (Bayley 1965).

Even at somewhat later ages in the preschool period, and using well-designed intelligence tests constructed by specialists, predictability is far from perfect. Performance on intelligence tests of children under school age is not highly predictive of intelligence test performance in the school years.

One group of experimenters followed 252 children from 21 months of age to 18 years old. The shorter the time interval between tests, the greater the ability to predict performance on later IQ tests. Many children who did either very well or very poorly before they entered school have performed very differently in later years. The variability of intelligence test performance seems to be related to life experiences. Health problems, emotional strains, and personality difficulties may play a part in the variation of these IQ scores, especially very early in life (Honzik, Macfarlane, and Allen 1948).

Disturbances in early development may predict later problems. Therefore, intelligence tests given at 20 months, specially devised for young children and used in combination with the ratings of a knowledgeable pediatrician, have been shown to be possible forecasts of school achievement at the age of ten (Werner, Honzik, and Smith 1968).

Some psychologists argue that the fact that early intelligence tests do not necessarily predict children's school-age intelligence test performance means that something crucial happens to their intellectual development in the early years. These preschool years, they contend, are a critical period for environmental stimulation, a time when IQ can be fixed at a higher or lower level (Bloom 1964), a time when the human "clay" is still malleable because it has not yet hardened into its eventual intellectual form.

But others argue that the lack of predictability of intelligence test performance in the early years may merely reflect the test's inability to measure mental development at that age. Perhaps "baby tests" fail to assess the factors that are important in intellectual functioning. Intelligence has many inherited components, which may show up later in ways that simply cannot be reduced to a test for young children (Kohlberg 1968).

School years There seems to be little question that intelligence tests during the school years are genuinely predictive. Predictability from intelligence tests increases with age. An adolescent's test score is likely to be very much the same as the adult IQ for the same person. The correlation between the two is around .80 (Bradway and Thompson 1962). The majority of Terman's gifted group, chosen from a variety of schools and a variety of backgrounds just on the basis of IQ scores from their early school years, did just what we now expect from people with superior IQs, not only in school but also in their subsequent careers.

Success as adults Still, while many of the Terman group did have successful careers, their success was not as spectacular as one might have forecast, given their unusually high IQs. The probable reason is that capacity is not the only factor in career success. Motivation and the many unforeseeable circumstances in life are among other important determinants. As for those Terman subjects who did fulfill their early promise, it is important to recognize that individuals' socioeconomic environment can help them to be "test-wise" and to score well. The same circumstances also cause individuals to be achievement-oriented.

For these reasons Terman's classic study has been criticized. He did not isolate "intelligence" from a number of environmental factors, many of which could have been related to career success (McClelland 1973).

Remedial uses

Aside from the question of their usefulness in forecasting career success, good tests are reasonably reliable in predicting ability to cope with formal schooling. Such forecasts are helpful not only for schools that must be selective in admission plans but also for guidance counselors. The tests can help single out children who may need special aid or enrichment. They may flag those whose development is not proceeding according to expectations. If school administrators know which children have low IQ scores, they can analyze weak areas, pinpoint learning disabilities, and be prepared to give special assistance as needed (Ames 1968). (However, some experts argue that foreknowledge of IQ scores can be a booby-trap. As we shall see in Chapter 11, such information may unconsciously prejudice a teacher, with negative effects on the pupil.)

Intelligence test scores can sometimes serve as an early warning system for emotional problems. One investigation discovered that children who are filled with anxiety, for whatever reason, tend to do poorly on IQ tests (Feldhusen and Klausmeier 1962). So it may be reasonable to conclude that if these children's anxiety were alleviated, their intellectual and cognitive ability would leap upward.

On the other hand, a child with a low IQ, failing in school, is not necessarily full of personality and emotional problems. A study of a group of boys at varied grade levels in a working-class community, all with IQs of 80 to 90, all of whom had failing grades in at least one school year, showed that they did not have a low self-concept. Nor did they lack career plans, have family problems, or fit into similar stereotypes (Opie and Lemasters, 1975).

Still, many mental health professionals can and do help parents of children with low intelligence scores to plan realistic goals for their children. Often the children themselves are aided by discussion of their difficulties, problems, and emotions. At the very least, children may benefit from a chance to talk things over, either through individual counseling or in a group (Opie and Lemasters 1975).

Of course, it does not necessarily take a professional to guide an unusually low or high IQ child. Parents who know they have an "exceptional" offspring are often able to help the child cope with limited cognitive ability or make the most of genius potential.

Criticisms

Pros and cons Regardless of the usefulness that many find in IQ scores, IQ testing has been dropped by some school districts. The reasons given are that IQ scores reflect characteristics other than intelligence, that they are biased in favor of the middle class, and that they may also be biased against blacks and other ethnic minority children. Some scholars contend that the tests are seriously flawed because they do not take into account variables like previous environment, schooling, and motivation.

In rebuttal, the advocates of continued IQ testing maintain that even if the tests are (perhaps inevitably) culturally biased, they are needed to serve Binet's original purpose: to predict ability to deal with school work and thus to make it possible to plan programs for students at their own levels. Most American schools are designed for a white middle-class society and "the tests are intended to measure what is important to success in twentieth century American society" (Gage and Berliner 1975, page 229). Regardless of what "causes" intelligence, IQ scores single out many of the children who will do well in school and also many of those who will do poorly (Rieber and Womack 1968).

Another argument for retaining IQ tests is that many employers are particularly interested in prospective employees' intelligence level and school history. While IQ scores may not directly predict occupational success, they probably predict trainability. One notion is that more education and higher IQ reduce the time needed to train the new employee (Thurow 1972).

A moderate point of view is that tests should be retained but the results should be interpreted with caution. The variables that may affect IQ test results—as we shall see, they include socioeconomic status, race, motivation, and other individual differences—must not be overlooked. IQ scores are being misused when they lead to the assumption that IQ reflects a fixed level of innate ability that cannot be altered during the course of life.

Some opposition to continued IQ testing stems from the fact that Binet's original objective, to limit school attendance to the fittest, is inappropriate in a democratic society like ours, which mandates education for all. Besides, IQ tests are not very useful in predicting many kinds of job success, like the skills needed to become a factory worker, bank teller, or air traffic controller (Berg, 1970). Ability to give the answer to questions like "Tell me the name of an animal that rhymes with fair" has nothing to do with everyday life (Stanford-Binet Scale, 1960, for Year 9).

One scholar, David McClelland (1973), notes ironically that those who demonstrate excellence in IQ test "games" are the ones who are selected for further education. He asks, "Why keep the best education for those who are already doing well at the games?" This investigator compared his best students with less able pupils, 20 years after they left college. Although the best students had been admitted to top medical and law schools, they could not be distinguished in terms of career success from those who attended "second rate" graduate schools.

Many other kinds of tests—aptitude, achievement, and various vocational tests—have more practical value than IQ tests. Nevertheless, American society does value "intelligence." While intelligence is hard to define and its origins continue to be debatable, we all continue to judge others at least partly on the basis of whether they are "bright" or "stupid." Careers that presumably demand high intelligence—college teaching, medicine, the law—have high status.

Creativity not tested Another criticism of IQ tests is that they are useless in predicting or even identifying *creativity*. A long list of famous creative people were considered stupid, lazy, or mediocre as youths. Some were drop-outs or even flunk-outs. They include, to name only a few, Isaac Newton, Leo Tolstoy, Winston Churchill, Frank Lloyd Wright, Frederic Chopin, Albert Einstein, Ivan Turgenev, Pablo Picasso, William Faulkner, and John Steinbeck, and even psychologist John Watson. Quite a few notable businessmen and inventors could be included, like Edwin Land, the creator of the Polaroid camera (Pang 1968).

Creativity: originality and novel insight

Creativity.

Many who have risen to eminence in their fields were graded mediocre or worse in school classes in those very fields. Some did badly in everything except one subject. Some did poorly across the board and flunked out. The ones we know about eventually did well in their fields in spite of their discouraging history. But what about those creative people who were lost to society precisely because they were put down early in life in conventional schools with conventional expectations (Pang 1968)?

Creativity and intelligence do not necessarily go hand in hand. Intelligence and achievement tests are designed to measure the ability of those who conform to accepted ideas and ways of thinking. But creative individuals are—by very definition—rule-breakers. There are no tests yet to ferret out such children.

While failure of intelligence tests to identify the creative is a regrettable flaw, a more serious criticism is that the tests tend to lead to the easy conclusion that intelligence is purely genetic and therefore "set in concrete" from the day of birth. Once intelligence is measured, critics charge, the person is forever pigeonholed at that level and treated accordingly. But some scholars believe that intelligence is, at least in part, a product of environment and thus subject to change.

This nature–nurture controversy has engulfed the question of intelligence testing in recent years. Authorities do not agree about where intelligence comes from, the genes or the environment. Yet the answer to the question is important, because it can affect the whole course of education and social policy. Must each of us take what intelligence we are born with and learn to live with it? Or can better homes and better schools make us more intelligent and thus more successful? Considerable research has been done on these questions and more is undoubtedly to come.

Heredity, Environment, and IQ

Nature and nurture: two case histories

Like Carl Flegal, Bernie Siner was a member of the Terman group of gifted children. Both of Siner's parents were non-English-speaking immigrants. The father died when the boy was 18 months old. The mother, who had five years of schooling, brought up her family in the direst poverty. Financial help came partly from an uncle who was a pawnbroker, partly from the several children in the family, who got jobs as early as the law permitted.

Bernie did reasonably well in school, but the school principal lectured him for underachievement in the light of his high IQ. The boy explained that studying was difficult, because he was working as well as going to school. Eventually the principal himself paid the young man's $17 public college registration fee so that he could go on to higher education.

After Siner worked his way through four years of college, graduate school was not financially feasible. So he opened a pawn shop like his uncle and prospered over the years. Still, the hunger to do something else remained. At 40, Siner entered law school and within a few years became a successful international lawyer.

Currently he is also active in local political affairs and has a stable family life.

Obviously, no scientific conclusions can be drawn from one man's history, no matter how provocative. But it does seem that Siner's early environment was mostly against him. One might guess, therefore, that heredity must have been by far the most telling factor in his high intelligence and ability to achieve.

But the case of Carl Flegal (who opened this chapter) might easily lead to a different conclusion. As a minister's son, his home was far above average. His mother was a college graduate as well as a school teacher. He was given every encouragement and every intellectual advantage. He, too, worked his way through college, but so did most of his generation. He, too, has been successful in middle-class terms. The environment in the Flegal home evidently also favored Carl's four brothers. The family was unique in the Terman group. All five brothers were individually singled out for the study because their teachers independently sent their names to the Stanford researchers as "the brightest in the class."

May one fairly assume that environment was an important factor in the Flegals' intellectual history? May one assume that heredity was the overwhelming element for Siner? What is the magic combination? Which accounts most for a person's intelligence—heredity or environment?

Drawing on studies done more than half a century ago, some psychologists decided that heredity was 75–80% responsible for an individual's level of intelligence (Burks 1928; Leahy 1935). However, their conclusions have since been called into question.

Twin studies

Value of studies A different and perhaps more conclusive way of discovering the relationship between child and parent intelligence is by studying twins. Analyzing the IQ scores of identical and fraternal twins reared together or apart can help to determine the relative influences of heredity and environment. Therefore, certain investigators sought out both identical and fraternal twins, some brought up by their own parents, some reared separately by foster or adoptive parents.

Identical twins, as we have already seen, are a product of the same ovum and the same sperm, and thus have exactly the same genetic makeup. They are alike in physical appearance, in other physical traits, and presumably in intelligence. Fraternal twins, in contrast, are the product of two different ova and two different sperm and, genetically, are only as like as any other siblings. Fraternal twins, like other siblings, share the *gene pool* of their parents. But since each child gets a different combination of the parental genes, the physical characteristics of fraternal twins are apt to be different. If intelligence is inherited, it, too, may be different.

Gene pool: hereditary factors common to a family or group and thus capable of being inherited by any one individual in the group

The value of twin studies in which environment does or does not differ is that they can provide the closest possible measurement of how much environment affects intelligence (or, at least, the IQ score). Did the separated identical twins remain as alike as the identicals who stayed together? Did the fraternal twins who stayed in the same environment become more alike than the fraternals separated by different homes?

One early study of this kind was done by Sir Cyril Burt, a noted British psychologist. In the 1950s and 1960s he published convincing data on identical twins who were reared together and some who were reared apart. His conclusion was that heredity was clearly more important than environment in contributing to IQ differences. At the time these findings were published, Burt's work was accepted as a significant contribution to the genetic theory of the origin of intelligence. Since then (an illustration of the strong emotional overtones in the nature–nurture issue), his work has been seriously questioned, to the point that some are convinced that the data were fabricated to support a particular theoretical position (Dorfman 1978). (See Box 8–3.)

Not genes alone   The results of later twin studies suggest that heredity and environment *both* influence IQ. Under normal circumstances, identical twins reared together are more similar in IQ than identical twins raised apart. In contrast, unseparated fraternal twins grow more mentally dissimilar as they become older, perhaps because they make their own individual, differing environments depending on their personalities, just as other siblings lead somewhat different lives (Newman, Freeman, and Holzinger 1937).

One investigation concluded that "if the environment differs greatly as compared with heredity, the share of environment in determining traits which are susceptible to environmental influence is large. If, on the other hand, there is large genetic difference and small environmental difference, the share of heredity is relatively large" (Newman, Freeman, and Holzinger 1937, page 35).

Similarity of identical twins Still, it is impressive that the majority of separated identical twins came out with such small IQ differences. The correlation was nearly as high as the IQ correlation of identicals reared together. This indicates the relatively strong influence of heredity. It does seem that even though differences in environment can cause substantial differences in IQ, the more fundamental differences from one individual to another do appear to be caused by genetic inheritance (Woodworth 1941). However, a counterargument is that identical twins reared apart may well have been placed in homes that were similar both socially and environmentally. If so, the environmental factor in their IQ similarity cannot be discounted.

This argument for some environmental influence seems to be borne out by the finding that the IQ test performance of fraternal

---

Box 8–3 Tracking a Statistical Crime

A scandal in the world of psychological science that broke in the late 1970s illustrates the importance of statistics, not only in carrying out research but also in judging its validity. Sir Cyril Burt, who died in 1971, was the British founder of educational psychology and the author of landmark work on the relationship between IQ and heredity. His studies presented data from intelligence tests that provided impressive proof that:

- IQ is inherited and fixed at birth;
- lower-class people have low IQs and upper-class people have high IQs;
- separating identical twins and bringing them up in different families has no effect on their intelligence;
- men are more intelligent than women.

The implications of Burt's findings had a strong influence on educational practices in Great Britain as well as elsewhere in the world.

But scholars who later studied the Englishman's data detected statistical peculiarities. They became convinced that he had "cooked" his information to satisfy his prejudices. Some information in Burt's 1961 study seemed to be identical to figures published over 30 years before. These earlier figures came from a different study. The IQ data seemed to have been deliberately selected to conform to a bell-shaped curve, even though it is now known that IQ distributions rarely result in a perfect bell-shaped curve. Other statistical peculiarities in Burt's figures led to some authorities' conclusion that the eminent psychologist was, in effect, guilty of a scientific crime. But some others believe Burt was merely careless, and they think his basic conclusions about IQ and heredity are still valid (Dorfman 1978).

twins resembles one another more closely than singletons in the same family. This statistic points strongly to an environmental factor in IQ because fraternal twins share a more similar upbringing than siblings of different ages (Erlenmeyer-Kimling and Jarvik 1963). Still, genetic influence is by no means ruled out.

Family genetic correlations

Siblings and parents   We can be reasonably sure that each of us gets a substantial part of our intelligence (at least, as expressed in the IQ score) from our parents' genes. Studies of parents and of siblings show that the closer the genetic relationship between two people, the greater the correlation in their IQ scores. The correlation is .50 for parents and their own children; .49 for siblings brought up together; .53 for fraternal twins, regardless of whether they are of the same or different sex; .87 for identical twins brought up together and .75 for thos reared apart. The results for identical twins reared together are no different from what might be found on successive tests of the same person.

In contrast, there is no relationship between the IQs of any two people selected at random and brought up separately. As for unrelated individuals reared together, as in institutions or in foster homes, the correlation is only .23 in intelligence scores (Erlenmeyer-Kimling and Jarvik 1963). (See Figure 8–3.)

Foster children   Analysis of the IQs of *foster* and natural children sheds additional light on the heredity-versus-environment puzzle. Comparisons have been made between children reared by their natural parents and children placed in foster homes before they were a year old. The investigators found a positive correlation (.45–.51) between the IQ of parents and their own children. But there was a weaker relationship (.07–.20) between the IQ of foster children and their foster parents (Burks 1928; Leahy 1935). (See Figure 8–4.) Thus, natural children's intelligence scores are more closely related to their parents' scores than those of foster children to their foster parents. So it appears that genetic influences (which also affect the home environment) are strong, if not controlling. Still, there is a certain amount of shift for adopted or foster children toward the intelligence level of their foster parents. The effects of environment certainly cannot be ruled out (Jones 1946).

One flaw in foster child studies, as in twin studies, comes from the practice of placing children in homes that are more or

Foster child: child reared by, but not the offspring of, the care-giver

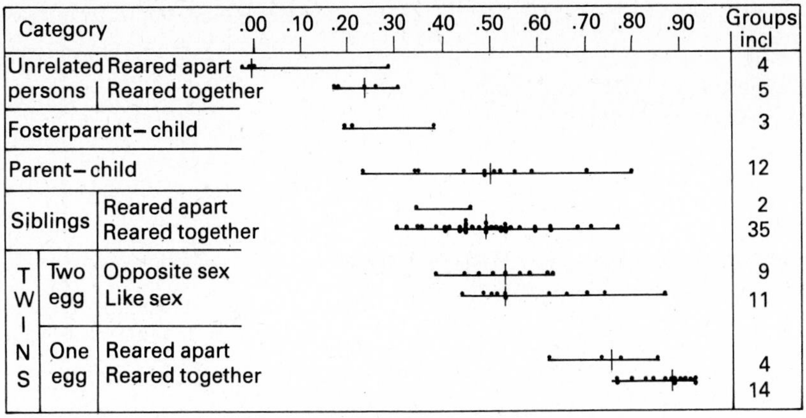

Category	.00 .10 .20 .30 .40 .50 .60 .70 .80 .90	Groups incl
Unrelated Reared apart		4
persons Reared together		5
Fosterparent—child		3
Parent—child		12
Siblings Reared apart		2
Reared together		35
TWINS Two egg Opposite sex		9
Like sex		11
One egg Reared apart		4
Reared together		14

FIG. 8–3 Correlation coefficients for "intelligence" test scores from 52 studies. *Source:* L. Erlenmeyer-Kimling and L. F. Jarvik, Genetics and intelligence: a review, *Science,* 1963, *142,* 1478. Copyright 1963 by the American Association for the Advancement of Science.

less on the same economic and cultural level as the homes of their natural parents. As a result, environmental differences are minimized. Another difficulty is the variation in the age at which children are moved from their own homes to foster homes. The older the child when homes are changed, the more mixed the environmental influence.

Another approach to measuring the relative influences of heredity and environment has been to trace the intellectual development of parent and child, by comparing children reared from early infancy by their own parents with those brought up by foster parents. Since it had already been found that the older they become, the more children's IQs resemble their parents', a study of two such groups promised to measure environmental factors more closely. Testing for both groups began at 21 months and continued into adolescence.

The investigators found that the mental ability of adopted children was more similar to their natural mothers' than to the foster mothers who had reared them. At the age of two, the adopted children's mental ability showed hardly any correlation with the natural mother's mental ability. But by the time the adopted children were four, the correlations had risen to about .3 and were considered statistically significant. Yet there was no relationship *at any age* between the intelligence of these children and that of the foster parents who reared them (Skodak and Skeels 1949).

As for the children who stayed with their own mothers, there was the same rise in IQ correlation over the first few years, from

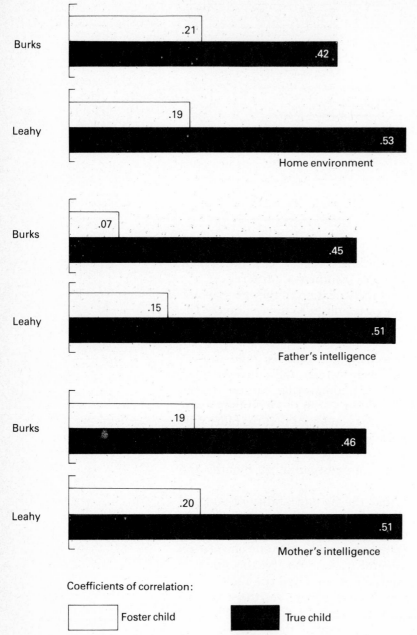

FIG. 8–4 A comparison of foster child and true child correlations: Burks and Leahy data. *Source:* Harold E. Jones, Environmental influences on mental development, in L. Carmichael (ed.), *Manual of child psychology,* p. 622 (New York: Wiley, 1946). Copyright © 1946 by John Wiley & Sons, Inc. Reprinted by permission of John Wiley & Sons, Inc.

zero to about .3 at age four. Parents' education seemed to have no particular influence on this correlation, supporting the contention that individual differences in measurable intelligence are largely genetic (Honzik 1957). (See Figure 8–5.)

Evidently even the *rate* of IQ growth is related to heredity. Identical twins, for example, reach the degree of maturity necessary for reliable intelligence testing at ages more similar to one another than fraternal twins (Wilson 1974).

Variability factor   There is probably not much point in trying to pin down to the last decimal how much heredity and environment contribute to intelligence or IQ. In any case, the relative importance of heredity and environment depends upon the amount of variability in each when two groups are being compared. If all children came from middle-class suburban homes, with schools to match, much IQ variation would obviously be genetic. But if environment differs a great deal, then one must pay serious attention to that influence (Kohlberg 1968).

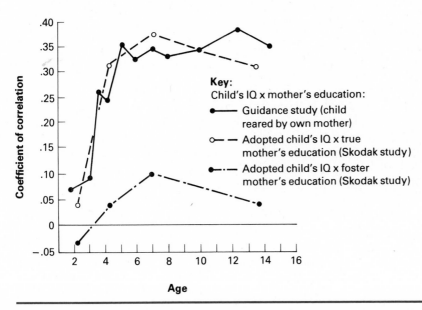

FIG. 8–5 Summary of three studies showing the education of mother in relation to child's IQ. *Source:* Majorie P. Honzik, Developmental studies of parent–child resemblance in intelligence, *Child Development,* 1957, *28*(2), 219. © The Society for Research in Child Development, Inc.

From a practical standpoint, since environmental influences are more easily controlled by society than are genetic factors, greater attention must be paid to the environmental factors that may influence intelligence. Besides, Western moral standards do not permit us to interfere with the genetic bases of intelligence. Nobody seriously considers forbidding or encouraging people to have children on genetic grounds alone. But environment is a different story: there our mores tell us that we have a clear duty to advise and in some cases to intervene. So it is entirely proper to try to discover what particular characteristics of the environment may add to or subtract from a person's inherited intellectual abilities.

Influence of environment

We do not know the precise influence on Bernie Siner of his im-poverished home and his ill-educated mother. Nor do we know how effective were his public school teachers. But all of them could conceivably have made a real difference in his intellectual development, impossible to measure 40 or 50 years later. Studies relating to the intellectual development of children on any socioeconomic level show that characteristics encouraged by parents and teachers may influence children's mental develop-ment. Any mother, father, or care-giver can make an important difference in a child's intellectual level. These adults influence children to achieve, to be active, to be intellectually curious, to be independent—or the reverse (Marjoribanks 1972).

Importance of early stimulation   Research bears out the wisdom of giving infants a certain amount of social life to develop their intellectual potential. Early social stimulation is conducive to intellectual growth. No matter how rich or poor the parent, no matter how well or poorly educated, the important thing is how they treat the baby, how they expose the child to the world. Do they let the baby explore the house? Do they talk to the child, touch the infant, introduce the youngster to other people? Chil-dren treated this way will flourish. Their minds and motor skills can increase, at least according to the tests now available for the youngest age group (Beckwith 1971).

All this should happen as early as possible in a child's life, since the "plasticity of intelligence" seems to decrease as the child grows older. Those formative years are probably crucial.

Even children with superior intellectual potential can be stunted, their later intellectual growth slowed, if they are not given the chance to develop through environmental opportunities and stimulation in the first few years.

Institutionalization   It is now known that isolation or institutionalization can result in inferior intellectual development. The longer children stay in institutions, or with parents who are mentally retarded, or in isolated homes in any restricted environment, the less chance they have to develop their perceptual skills. They lose their native ability to learn from adults. Their language acquisition suffers. They fail to gather essential basic information and concepts about the world. Their intelligence test scores actually drop. Conversely, if children are taken early enough from a nonstimulating environment their intellectual level rises. A mass of research makes these conclusions almost inescapable (Ausubel 1964).

Investigators made a striking discovery in 1939 of the effect of social interaction on normal intellectual development. A group of infant orphans who showed distinct signs of mental retardation had been placed by a court in a mental institution. There they were "adopted" by some of the older and brighter mentally retarded girls. At the same time, a similar group had been placed in a depersonalized orphanage. The investigators found that the infants reared with the mental retardates developed more normally in intellectual abilities than those brought up in the more socially sterile orphanage. Apparently the social interaction, close personal attention, and resulting stimulation that the older retardates offered were crucial factors. The infants received a reasonable facsimile of a "normal" upbringing, at least as close as an institutional setting could provide (Skeels and Dye 1939).

When these babies were grown up, there was a follow-up study. Those in the experimental group—reared by the retarded girls—had become self-supporting adults. In contrast, many of those who had grown up in the sterile orphanage had remained institutionalized (Skeels 1966). (See Box 8–4; see also Chapter 12, pages 485–487.)

Family influences   Young adults who blame their parents for an assortment of mistakes in their upbringing (the thanks tend to come much later) have a point, according to psychological re-

Box 8–4   What Happened to Skeels's Orphans

Case no.	Subject's occupation	Spouse's occupation	Female subject's occupation previous to marriage
Experimental group:			
1[a]	Staff sergeant	Dental technician	. . .
2	Housewife	Laborer	Nurses' aide
3	Housewife	Mechanic	Elementary school teacher
4	Nursing instructor	Unemployed	Registered nurse
5	Housewife	Semiskilled laborer	No work history
6	Waitress	Mechanic, semiskilled	Beauty operator
7	Housewife	Flight engineer	Dining room hostess
8	Housewife	Foreman, construction	No work history
9	Domestic service	Unmarried	. . .
10[a]	Real estate sales	Housewife	. . .
11[a]	Vocational counselor	Advertising copy writer[b]	. . .
12	Gift shop sales[c]	Unmarried	. . .
13	Housewife	Pressman-printer	Office-clerical
Contrast group:			
14	Institutional inmate	Unmarried	. . .
15	Dishwasher	Unmarried	. . .
16	Deceased	. . .	. . .
17[a]	Dishwasher	Unmarried	. . .
18[a]	Institutional inmate	Unmarried	. . .
19[a]	Compositor and typesetter	Housewife	. . .
20[a]	Institutional inmate	Unmarried	. . .
21[a]	Dishwasher	Unmarried	. . .
22[a]	Floater	Divorced	. . .
23	Cafeteria (part time)	Unmarried	. . .
24[a]	Institutional gardener's assistant	Unmarried	. . .
25[a]	Institutional inmate	Unmarried	. . .

[a]Male

[b]B.A. degree

[c]Previously had worked as a licensed practical nurse

Source: H. M. Skeels, Adult status of children with contrasting life experiences, *Monographs of the Society for Research in Child Development*, 1966, *31* (ser. no. 105), 33. © The Society for Research in Child Development, Inc.

search. Family influences on intelligence, aside from the influence of heredity, are innumerable.

Birth order may have an effect on mental development. Family influence may start with whoever is lucky enough (or unlucky, depending on how you look at it) to be the eldest in the family. (See also Chapter 9, page 362.) First children generally get more attention, which means that their environment is inevitably different from the environment of the children who come later. One result may be that they tend to score better in mathematical and verbal ability than later siblings (Marjoribanks and Walberg 1975).

Mothers' influence on their children can hardly be minimized, since they are usually the prime care-givers. Mothers also have a greater influence than fathers on the intellectual functioning of their teenage children. Young people who get high scores on tests generally have mothers who score higher than their husbands (Willerman and Stafford 1972).

As for fathers, their relationship to their children's intelligence seems to be complex, depending on the sex of the child and the family's socioeconomic status. Nurturance, social class, and level of father's education are related to positive intellectual growth. One study showed a relationship between sons' IQ scores and the amount of warmth and affection received from their fathers. No significant relationship has been shown between fathers' nurturance and their daughters' IQ scores. However, daughters of middle-class fathers had higher IQ scores than daughters of lower-class fathers (Jordan, Radin, and Epstein 1975).

An Israeli study found that mothers' education and preference for working outside the home also seemed to have a beneficial effect on children's mental level (Kohen-Raz 1968). Similarly, an Iranian investigation suggests that intelligence test scores of older adolescents may rise along with their fathers' educational level, but may be adversely affected by increased family size (Mehryar 1972). In American black families, the more highly educated the parents, the higher the children's intelligence test scores. The relationship is shown more strongly around the age of four than later, possibly indicating the strength of the dependency relationship between parent and child (Little, Kenny, and Middleton 1973).

Parents themselves are not the only ones who can provide the early environmental stimulation needed to boost a young child's intellectual ability. Group care, as in Israeli kibbutzim (communal colonies), can have the same beneficial effect (Moyles and Wolins 1971). Children reared in a kibbutz do as well as children brought up by mothers in a private Israeli home. But the kind of group care makes a difference. Group care in a poorly staffed institution may be harmful: children in Israeli institutions become as retarded as those in American institutions.

Early deprivation   Many studies indicate that intellectual harm can result from being reared in an impoverished atmosphere. But the effects of a deprived environment on intellectual growth may not be apparent until a child begins to speak (Southern and Plant 1971). Social and economic impoverishment does not seem to affect cognitive style during the earliest months, the sensorimotor period. But somewhere between a year-and-a-half and three years, when language becomes important, the effect of deprivation on intellectual development becomes apparent (Golden and Birns 1971; Bayley 1965).

Middle-class white preschoolers and socially disadvantaged Puerto Rican preschoolers in the United States were compared in one investigation. The deprived youngsters' IQ scores were well established by the time they were three and stayed at the same level thereafter. But the middle-class children had a typical gain in IQ scores between the ages of three and six (Hertzig and Birch 1971).

Exactly why the Puerto Ricans' IQ scores failed to rise is not clear. Is it possible that the nursery school experience of the middle-class youngsters, not provided for the Puerto Rican group, was responsible for the middle-class IQ gains? If this is so, then the investigators believe that compensatory education might help the deprived children (Hertzig and Birch 1971).

Race and IQ

Not all scholars agree that improved environment, in the form of better schooling or any other changes, can materially remedy intellectual deficiencies. Particularly in recent years, a few have argued that genetic influences on intelligence are so overwhelming that little can be done for those whose IQs are below average.

Jensen's theory   One psychologist in particular touched off a controversy in scientific circles, and even in the political arena, over the relationship between race and intelligence. Arthur R.

Jensen, a highly respected educational psychologist, published an article in the *Harvard Educational Review* (1969*a*) that concluded that blacks are genetically inferior in intelligence.

Jensen's closely reasoned discussion, aired at the height of the civil rights movement in the United States, was titled, "How Much Can We Boost IQ and Scholastic Achievement?" He contended that compensatory education has failed because the intellectual difference between whites and blacks is 80% due to heredity. He argued that no amount of educational enrichment can push children above their innate potential.

Jensen believes that the varying geographic origins of Jews, blacks, and Orientals (for example), their different social and economic histories, the different pressures to which they have been subjected over centuries of history all have created anatomical and biological characteristics different from one another. Color of skin is the most obvious. Other outward physiological differences are almost equally apparent. Why, then, argue against differences in intelligence (Jensen 1969*b*)?

Jensen's ideas have been seriously questioned by other scholars. Some deem the intellectual differences between whites and blacks to be small (MacDonald, Hines, and Kenoyer 1974). Others think any such discrepancies can disappear in the course of time. They point out that racial and social class groups will inevitably share distinctive traits, different from one group to another. The reason is that their genetic inheritance and environmental influences have been different, a result of selective survival and breeding over many centuries (Scarr-Salapatek 1971). To change such differences, intelligence included, built up over cultural and historical generations, can take many more generations, but it can be done (Sarason 1973).

Environmental influences on blacks   In effect Jensen's argument about blacks' native intellectual inferiority rests on his basic contention that intelligence is four-fifths genetic, only one-fifth environmental. These figures he deduces from others' studies of twins placed in foster homes and of unrelated children brought up in the same home. To this Jensen argument a strong rebuttal comes from psychologists who point out that studies of separated twins are inconclusive, since separated twins are most often placed into homes very much like the one that would have been provided by their natural parents. Thus, who can know the real reason for the twins' continued intellectual similarity, since

Pomfila Watson, a physically and mentally advanced two-year-old.

both their heredity *and* their environment continue to be more or less the same (Bronfenbrenner 1975)?

Moreover, as we have seen, even children brought up in the same home do not have identical environments. (See also Chapter 9, page 361.) Parents, teachers, siblings, peers—all treat each child differently whether they realize it or not. Similarly, the effect of environment on blacks cannot be ignored. Many are severely deprived not only socioeconomically but also as a result of bias in school and in the world in general. With another environment, who can tell how their intelligence might blossom (Bronfenbrenner 1975)? Striking evidence comes from an investigation of the children of interracial marriages. Four-year-olds brought up by white mothers (with black fathers) scored "significantly" higher than children brought up by black mothers (with white fathers). Assuming that the mother is the one who does the major part of child-rearing, the advantaged white mother (better educated, with "white" cultural background) may be able to use better child-rearing practices and to pass on the benefits to her children (Willerman, Naylor, and Myrianthopoulos 1970).

An analysis of 130 black and interracial children adopted by advantaged white families revealed that even though their natural parents were of only average IQ, the adopted children scored above the average of whites in the general population. However, the biological children of the adoptive parents scored even higher. Even when black children are reared in a white household, they cannot escape the effects of prejudice in the world outside their homes. The conclusion is that IQ is a malleable factor, influenced by racist attitudes toward blacks as well as by school (Scarr and Weinberg 1976).

The tendency to blame low intelligence for the behavioral problems of some black children is also condemned as a "pernicious double-standard way of thinking" (Sarason 1973, page 971). For example, if a child with a low IQ score strangled a dog, intelligence would probably be blamed. But if a child with a genius IQ level did the same thing, some other cause would probably be suspected (Sarason 1973).

Effects of schooling Different schooling may have a similar selective effect on blacks and whites. A group of black, Latin-American, and Anglo preschoolers, all from the lowest income families, were given an intelligence test. Income, educational level of parents, size of family, and whether the mother was employed were closely related to IQ scores. After only five weeks in a Head Start program, the children were retested and all showed "significant improvement" (Rieber and Womack 1968, page 609). (See Box 8–5 and Figure 8–6.)

Some authorities maintain that it is important to recognize how demoralizing school can be to environmentally deprived children. The curriculum may be too demanding and the child may become frustrated, confused, resentful. Self-confidence plummets. In contrast, properly planned programs in schools may provide disadvantaged children with the environment necessary to foster healthy intellectual growth. It has been suggested that children should start with lessons geared to their state of readiness. They must be helped to master one lesson at a time, before some other task is piled on their frail shoulders. Learning materials must be structured in a carefully planned, sequential way.

Box 8–5 Effectiveness of Head Start

If children from "deprived" backgrounds get special compensatory early education considerably before the time they would normally start going to public school, can their ultimate achievement be helped? Head Start, begun in the 1960s, and still continuing in many parts of the country, is the most notable such program but there are others.

Educational researchers all over the country have tried to discover what happened to the children who were part of the first compensatory education programs. For example, a long-term project chose children from low-income homes for special summer training (Gray and Klaus 1970). One group had a ten-week preschool program over a period of three summers. Another group was given similar training, but it lasted only two summers. A third and fourth group had no special training. The intervention program stressed methods of improving the children's aptitude and attitudes toward school achievement. The major finding was that average IQ scores of the "compensated" children rose higher than those of a similar group who did not attend special early classes. (See Figure 8–6.)

Another finding was that the special educated children were 40% less likely than a control group to have been assigned to special public school classes for slower children. In contrast, the control children were 20% more likely to have failed to be promoted in at least one grade. The sooner a child was put into compensatory education, the more professionals who were helping, and the more parents who were involved, the better the results, according to the investigators.

However, two of the researchers in the consortium group got different results when they studied local projects. A Kentucky study and a Florida study reported no advantage for children in their early-intervention programs. Nevertheless, the majority of the studies discovered not only IQ improvement in the children with special early education but also improved scores in reading and mathematics achievement.

Research on the effects of compensatory education is continuing. The investigators urge that "the merits of the research being examined be debated after the data are in. The issue is too important to ask the jury to reach a verdict before all the evidence is presented" (Michalak 1978).

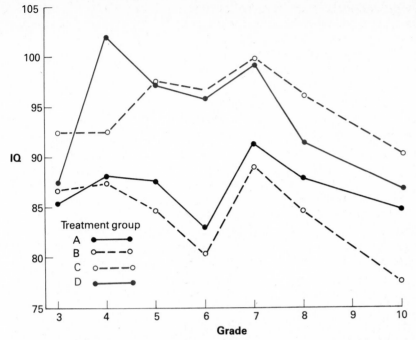

FIG. 8–6 Effect of preschool programs on IQ scores. The average Stanford-Binet IQ scores of four groups are being compared: groups A and B had no summer preschool programs; group C had two summer preschool programs; and group D had three summer preschool programs. *Source:* Compiled from S. Gray and R. A. Klaus, The early training project: a seventh year report, *Child Development,* 1970, *41,* 913, table 2.

In an article published in 1977, Jensen himself is willing to attribute some IQ differences to environment, rather than race. A study of blacks in Georgia and in California showed that the children in rural Georgia scored lower than blacks reared in better circumstances in California. He notes that if there had been a genetically based racial influence the effect should have been reflected in both groups.

Are IQ tests biased?   In fact, it may be teachers who are having an inordinate effect on how black children do on IQ tests. One experiment gave preschoolers (both black and white, middle and lower class) test-taking practice prior to giving them IQ tests. But a similar group was familiarized in advance with middle-class adults similar to those who would be giving the intelligence tests. This second group was also familiarized with the particular kind of language and materials used on the intelligence tests. It was the latter group, regardless of their background, who were helped to raise their IQ scores (Kinnie and Sternlof 1971).

Many investigations have revealed large differences in the distribution of intelligence quotients between black and white Americans. Average reported differences between the mean IQ (where most of the scores cluster) of whites and blacks are between 10 and 20 IQ points. But the difference is less for Northern blacks than for Southern blacks. So environment is obviously a factor in these test results. One study showed that blacks from some states in the northern part of this country scored better than whites from some states in the South. Still, when whites and blacks in the same state are tested, the whites generally do better (Bodmer and Cavalli-Sforza 1970).

A four-year analysis of arithmetic, reading, and verbal achievement of black and white children in one state showed that the gap between the two groups' achievement grew wider as the children progressed through school. Surprisingly enough, however, the differences were greatest on the test items that would have had the least cultural bias, such as arithmetic (Osborne 1960). What happened? Was the quality of schooling at fault? Motivation? Was the problem developmental?

A strong argument has been made that blacks do poorly on IQ tests because the questions deal with concepts that are encountered in a white world but not necessarily in the daily lives of many blacks. Yet testing black children on both culturally suspect tests and tests specially designed to eliminate such factors produces virtually the same scores. An attempt to test subjects in black "non-standard dialect" and also in standard English produced similar results. The resulting IQ was the same, regardless (Quay 1974). In any case, the tests that have removed verbal items—because verbal questions are apt to be culturally tainted—are also less useful in predicting school success. Can we conceive of intelligence apart from culture? Bright black children do well on either *culture-fair* tests or the standard IQ tests; the slower black children do poorly on either (Willard 1968).

Culture-fair: not biased in favor of any particular group

The last word has certainly not been said on the explosive question of black IQ. It may take generations, and years of social change, before anyone—scientist or living room theorist—can know the answer. Nevertheless, anyone who cares about the future of a democratic society in the United States cannot afford to write off the environmental factor as an influence on the well-being—intellectual or otherwise—of our children. Environment is the one element in all our lives that *can* be changed. We must assume that it is within our control to benefit the development of all children, whatever their racial origin.

Summary

Psychologists have been unable to agree on a definition of intelligence. The closest approach is the intelligence quotient (IQ), a product of tests that measure ability to do well in school. Binet originated the intelligence tests, which determined the subject's mental age, and then calculated the IQ by this formula: mental age divided by the chronological age times 100. More recent intelligence tests produce equivalent scores, also called IQ, though they do not necessarily measure mental age. The American adaptation is the Stanford–Binet.

A generally accepted premise is that mental ability is developmental but that intelligence is relatively constant. Thus, increases in mental ability may be graphed as a parabola, ending in a plateau around the age of 15. In the general population, IQs cluster around 100. The farther away from 100 on either side of the scale, the fewer people.

Other widely used intelligence tests were designed by Wechsler and Goodenough. Aptitude tests are somewhat similar to intelligence tests and are used to judge probable ability to do well in college or graduate school. Achievement tests are used to discover what has been learned in school.

"Baby" intelligence tests and preschool tests are not reliable predictors, except in the case of the severely retarded. As age increases, predictability becomes more reliable. Early uncertainties may be due to the malleability of human intelligence in the early years, or they may be due to imperfect testing devices.

Terman's landmark longitudinal study of high-IQ children demonstrated that they are superior not only in intelligence but also in scholastic, social, and physical activities, as well as body build.

An important unsettled question is the degree to which intelligence is genetically and environmentally influenced. Heredity probably accounts for the largest part of intelligence, but environment is also important. For example, the amount of stimulation early in life can improve or depress intelligence. Early deficits can probably be overcome by skilled teaching. Family influences on intelligence are also numerous and important.

Social class differences do not appear to affect intelligence during the sensorimotor period. But when language becomes important, the effect of deprivation on IQ becomes apparent.

Recently a controversy has arisen over the relative intelligence of blacks and whites. An average difference of between 10 and 20 IQ points appears to be somewhat related to economic factors and racism. Some psychologists contend that different racial stocks vary in intelligence, but others contend that improved environment can result in intellectual improvement over the long run. The quality of teaching, the identity of the examiner, and racism in the community have also been suggested as causes of inferior performance of some blacks on IQ tests.

Chronological overview

Infancy	scales for testing infant intelligence after the age of 2
Preschool to adolescence	intelligence testing with Stanford–Binet, Wechsler, and Goodenough scales
	aptitude tests
	achievement tests

Applying Your Knowledge

1. In what ways would it be helpful to a parent to know a child's IQ score? How could such information be harmful?

2. As a teacher, how could your students' IQ scores help you assess their abilities and performance?

3. Suggest some other useful information that the Terman group might ask in a follow-up of their study.

Further Readings

Muller, Phillippe. *The tasks of childhood*. New York: McGraw-Hill, 1970. Review of child psychology. Evaluation of methods and results in the testing of intelligence. Paperback.

Piaget, Jean. *Psychology of intelligence*. Totowa, N.J.: Littlefield, Adams, 1966. Critique of main theories of intelligence and their relation to Piagetian theory. Paperback.

PART 4

The Social Person

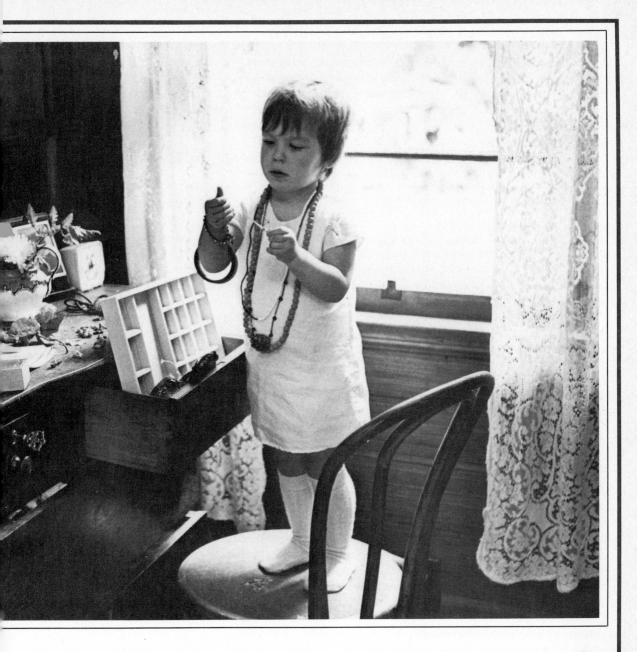

Chapter 9

Personality Development

Steve, Eric, and Michael are brothers, young adults who share the same parents but who are strikingly different in personality. Their counterparts may be found in any college classroom. Steve would be the one who sits next to the wall, a shy, studious type who seldom speaks. Eric would be the student in the front row, constantly asking questions or telling about personal experiences. And somewhere in the middle of the classroom, Michael would be striking up a friendship with a pretty girl and paying scant attention to the lecturer.

What Is Personality?

What made those three young men so different? What causes the personalities of us all to be so various? Can the fact that one baby is happy and seldom cries while another is hard to manage be traced to what the parents did or were they "just born that way"?

Speculating about these questions can be enjoyable gossip. But to psychologists these are particularly serious matters, the basis of complex theories and a great deal of research. To know what circumstances create personality differences, especially personality difficulties, might help to cure many individual psychological problems. But one stumbling block is the difficulty of defining personality, let alone stating the conditions that influence its development.

Definitions vary

Gordon Allport found no less than 49 different definitions of personality in scholarly literature. He then proposed his own: "Personality is the dynamic organization within the individual of those psycho-physical systems that determine his characteristic behavior and thought." Significantly, he added that "the evidence . . . does not depict man as a reactive robot" (Allport 1961, page 28). In other words, personality cannot be reduced to a simple formula.

A matter of individual differences   What many definitions of personality have in common is that they use the word *personality* to identify a particular theoretical concept that describes a person's behavior (McClelland 1951). But no matter what their theoretical bias, and regardless of their particular definition, all the researchers study individual differences and thus learn something

Personality: behavior that reflects the characteristics unique to an individual

about personality. Thus, a working definition is that personality reflects the behavioral characteristics unique to an individual.

Personality is the sum total of each of us—those attributes that make us unique and distinctive. Personality encompasses temperament, mood, character traits (like honesty, dependability, independence), and physical appearance and behavior. Personality also involves ability to interact with others as well as modes of adjustment to life changes. An individual's level of aspiration, motivation, intelligence, and creativity are also part of the total personality. In addition, personality has to do with *self-concept*, how one thinks about and perceives oneself; *self-esteem*, how one feels about oneself; and *self-image*, how one thinks others see oneself.

Self-concept: sum total of one's self-perceptions

Self-esteem: feelings about oneself

Self-image: how one visualizes oneself

Environment plus stages Psychologists generally agree that personality is shaped at least in part by an individual's experiences within the environment. Some of the most influential theorists, notably Freud and Erikson, also argue that personality development comes in stages and that during the earliest of those stages, mothers, fathers, and primary care-givers play decisive roles in determining how an individual's personality will eventually turn out.

Major Personality Theorists

Freud

Sigmund Freud, a Viennese neurologist of the late nineteenth century, developed the basic theories that trace personality to the interaction of biological drives and early family influences. Most current personality hypotheses have their origin in his immensely important work.

Three dynamic systems Through *psychoanalysis*, Freud explored his patients' hidden conflicts and past experiences. Their histories convinced Freud that personality has biological roots derived from instincts linked with survival. He theorized that each individual's behavior is determined by three dynamic, interacting psychological forces, which he called the *id*, the *ego*, and the *superego*.

Psychoananysis: form of psychotherapy that involves intensive exploration of an individual's conscious and unconscious feelings and experiences

The *id* is a person's basic animal nature. It is primarily unconscious and is characterized by a desire for immediate pleasure

Id: impulsive psychological force; the source of libido

and gratification. The id supplies what Freud calls *libido*—the supply of psychic energy born within each individual. Libido powers the satisfaction of biological drives, the animal impulses of the id. Libido is also the energy supply for the other two forces, the ego and the superego.

The second force in the personality, the *ego*, is the primary agent for an individual's day-to-day actions. The ego deals with the outside world in a conscious fashion. The third force, the *superego*, is also involved in the actions performed through the ego. The superego is the *conscience* that censors or modifies the raw impulses flowing from the id. The superego is partly conscious, partly unconscious: when we feel guilty, for instance, we sometimes realize why, but sometimes not.

According to Freud, these three forces interact throughout life, as a person seeks sensual gratification through five *psychosexual* developmental stages. The stages are called psychosexual (*psyche* means "individual"; *sexual* means "pleasurable") since they relate to the individual's continuing pleasure-seeking impulses.

One of the body's *erogenous zones*—areas that provide pleasurable sensation—is the primary focus of each stage. The

Libido: psychic energy

Ego: psychological force that is in touch with reality and mediates between the id and the superego

Superego: psychological force that embodies an individual's moral code

Psychosexual: pertaining to the individual's sensuality and sexual development, both mental and somatic

Erogenous zones: body areas that provide pleasurable sensation

Box 9–1 Freud's Stages of Psychosexual Development

Stage	Age range	Erogenous zone	Sexual activity
oral	0–18 months	mouth, lips, tongue, teeth	sucking, swallowing, chewing, biting
anal	8 months–4 years	anus, buttocks	expulsion and retention of waste products
phallic (Oedipus complex)	3–7 years	genitals	masturbation
latent	5–12 years	. . .	. . .
genital (Oedipus complex)	12–20 years	genitals	masturbation, sexual intercourse, feelings for others

According to Freud, the Oedipus complex (term derived from the Greek tragedy by Sophocles, *Oedipus Rex*) appears in boys beginning with the phallic stage, when sons have an incestuous desire to have intercourse with their mothers. The corresponding dynamic in girls—when girls have incestuous feelings toward their fathers—is called the Electra complex.

erogenous zones include mouth, lips, tongue, anus, and genitals. The stages overlap somewhat: the oral stage spans, roughly, the first 18 months of life; the anal stage starts at about eight months and ends at age four; the phallic stage spans ages three to seven; a latency period occurs from five to twelve; and the genital period starts around adolescence. (See Box 9–1.)

The crux of Freud's theory is that each individual must successfully resolve the needs and conflicts of each stage in order to pass successfully into the succeeding stage. The problem, however, according to Freud, is that many people do not reach the fulfillment of the genital stage. If they have not successfully mastered the challenges of the earlier stages, they are prey to a variety of emotional symptoms and personality problems.

Even though many authorities today do not accept Freud's ideas word for word, his concepts have been immensely influential. They are the foundation of the work of many present-day psychoanalytic practitioners and theorists. (See Box 9–2.)

Erikson

Ego psychology Erik Erikson is a *neo-Freudian*. He is an important theorist on human personality and behavior whose work is based on Freud's. He expanded Freud's developmental stages to eight, to cover the entire life span, instead of stopping at adolescence. He also broadened Freud's approach and added flexibility by allowing for cultural and social factors as well as biological influences. Erikson is the foremost proponent of *ego psychology*, the psychoanalytic study of the self. His stress is not on emotional illness but on the individual's opportunities to triumph over the psychological hazards of daily life.

Neo-Freudian: pertaining to an extension of Freud's teachings

Ego psychology: theory that emphasizes the study of the self, particularly an individual's self-concept

According to Erikson, life crises are important for healthy personal development. In every personal and social crisis an individual may find elements that are conducive to growth because by nature people are both creative and adaptive.

Erikson says newborns come into the world with the potential for unique personality development. The sexes have different developmental experiences, particularly since environment heavily influences individual development. However, individuals are active participants in forming their own psychological destiny throughout their lives.

A succession of crises Like Freud, Erikson teaches that psychological development is a continuous process, each phase or stage a part of a continuum. Each developmental stage presents a problem or crisis that the individual must face and master. These *psychosocial crises* are conflicts between a person and society or social institutions. They are the motivating forces behind the individual's behavior. Resolution of each life crisis enhances a person's ability to meet the next crisis.

Psychosocial crises: tension between the self and social institutions

Box 9–2 Sigmund Freud

Sigmund Freud, the man who so profoundly influenced the understanding of human psychology, was born in 1856 in Austria. He died, an exile, in 1939 in London, a victim of both Hitler and cancer. The son of a middle-class Jewish businessman and his youthful second wife, Freud studied medicine at the University of Vienna and later received, almost by accident, a grant to do special work with Dr. Jean Martin Charcot, a Parisian neurologist.

In France, Freud was exposed to a group of psychiatrists who used hypnosis to treat mental illness. The hypnotized patients revealed early memories that appeared to be connected to their symptoms. Many were cured by talking with their doctors and reliving those past traumatic experiences and feelings.

Later, back in Vienna, Freud adopted the "talking cure" and eventually discarded hypnosis altogether. His psychoanalytic method involved long, intensive exploration of his patients' memories and childhood experiences. By gaining an understanding of the roots of their difficulties, the sufferers were generally able to come to terms with their conflicts and to lose physical as well as emotional symptoms.

Freud, whose name is linked with theories of sexuality, lived an exemplary personal life, typical of the Victorian era. He married in 1886 and remained married to the same woman till he died. One of his six children, his daughter Anna, is a well-known psychoanalyst who has relied on his theories in working with children.

Freud's epochal contribution to human understanding was that individual personality development is deeply influenced by forces originating in the unconscious. These forces affect every area of behavior, including both accomplishment and failure. His books include *Studies in Hysteria* (1895), with Josef Breuer, and *The Interpretation of Dreams* (1900), which was eventually published in 44 editions throughout the world. *The Psychopathology of Everyday Life* was published in 1904; *Jokes and their Relation to the Unconscious*, in 1905; *Three Essays on the Theory of Sexuality*, in 1905. *Totem and Taboo*, an application of psychoanalytic technique to anthropology, was published in 1913. These were only the earliest of an enormous output of scientific writings. His last publication, *An Outline of Psychoanalysis*, summarizing his work, was published in 1940, after Freud's death (Cohen 1969).

What concerns Erikson are the ways in which people think their way through these successive crises in order to adapt themselves to physical and social reality. He maintains that it is necessary to master the challenge of each stage in order to pass on to the next stage. The process is somewhat like building a house; each stage is the foundation for the next.

Eight stages Erikson's stages emphasize the importance of social relationships in personality development. The first five are roughly comparable to Freud's, although Erikson's stages are psychosocial: focusing on the self in relation to the demands of society and of other people. (Freud's psychosexual stages center on the self in relation to sensual and biological urges.)

Erikson calls the first stage *basic sense of trust versus basic sense of mistrust*. This period is chiefly concerned with feeding and oral gratification. Seeking satisfaction of these needs is the basis of the trust–mistrust crisis.

Stage two, *basic sense of autonomy versus basic sense of shame and doubt*, involves discovery of self-control and self-assertiveness. This stage is characteristic of ages one to two years.

The third stage, *basic sense of initiative versus basic sense of guilt*, covers the preschool years. Children gain a sense of initiative when the environment presents new activities and new tasks to master, but a concurrent sense of guilt stems from conflicts when the child's activities intrude on others.

Basic sense of industry versus basic sense of inferiority follows, during the school years. Motivation and productivity are challenged by fear of failure. Learning is an important part of Erikson's fourth stage.

Erikson's fifth stage, *basic sense of identity versus identity diffusion*, takes place during the adolescent years, which are characterized by the need to achieve a stable sense of self.

Erikson extends his developmental scheme beyond Freud's with three additional periods in the adult years. His sixth stage, *basic sense of intimacy versus basic sense of isolation*, relates to the capacity to commit oneself to permanent relationships and partnerships. The seventh stage ordinarily takes place in the middle years. The crisis involves *basic sense of generativity* (concern for succeeding generations) *versus basic sense of stagnation*. The final (eighth) stage, late in life, pits *basic sense of integrity against basic sense of despair*, a feeling of life satisfaction or a sense that fulfillment has not been attained. (See Box 9–3.)

Not everyone goes through Erikson's eight stages as he has described them, any more than everyone conforms to Freud's five. Erikson himself notes that *foreclosure*—shutting off—or *moratorium*—suspension—in a previous stage may prevent an individual's passing into the next psychosocial period. Critics of his theories make a special point of the fact that many people never attain the later stages—or pass through the stages much earlier or later than Erikson suggests.

Foreclosure: shutting off

Moratorium: temporary suspension of activity

Box 9–3   Erikson's Psychosocial Crises

Psychosocial crisis	Age range	Positive outcome
1. Basic sense of trust vs. basic sense of mistrust (derived from the oral stage)	Infancy	Physical comfort and security
2. Basic sense of autonomy vs. basic sense of shame and doubt (derived from the anal stage)	Toddlerhood	Ability to hold on (dependency) and to let go (autonomy)
3. Basic sense of initiative vs. basic sense of guilt (derived from the phallic stage)	Preschool years	Initiative to master new tasks
4. Basic sense of industry vs. basic sense of inferiority (derived from the latent stage)	School years	Productivity and mastery of skills
5. Basic sense of identity vs. basic sense of identity diffusion (derived from the genital stage)	Adolescence	Ability to be oneself
6. Basic sense of intimacy vs. basic sense of isolation	Early adulthood	Capacity for affiliation and love
7. Basic sense of generativity vs. basic sense of stagnation	Middle adulthood	Concern for the succeeding generation
8. Basic sense of integrity vs. basic sense of despair	Late adulthood	Sense of fulfillment with one's life

Source: Modified from Erik H. Erikson, *Childhood and society,* 2d ed. (New York: W. W. Norton, 1963).

Humanistic theories: Maslow and Rogers

Yet another approach to personality theory is *humanistic*. Scholars who advance the humanistic view see individuals as all-important entities, endowed with the potential to be self-directed and responsible for their own destiny.

Maslow and Rogers are two leading humanistic psychologists. Both believe that everybody has a drive toward *self-actualization*, which is the ultimate motivating force for all ages. Both take the position that whatever has happened to a person in the past, no matter how unfortunate, need not necessarily spell doom to later efforts to realize potentialities. They hold that past experiences are important only to the extent that they directly influence today. People's current situation depends even more on what they seek for themselves in the future (Rappoport 1972).

Maslow believes that attainment of the ultimate step in personality development—self-actualization—is unlikely unless other basic needs are satisfied first. Food and water are primary necessities. Next come safety and security. After that, one needs love and affection. Self-esteem is the next prerequisite. Only if all those needs are met, according to Maslow, can self-actualization be achieved. (Maslow's theory of motivation and his hierarchy of needs will be explained at greater length in Chapter 11, which deals with motivation.)

Rogers has a slightly different approach. He holds that everybody has an overwhelming, biologically based drive to realize his or her own potential. This drive transcends everything else. According to Rogers, self-actualization is a biological fact for all living things. Unlike Maslow, Rogers holds that there are no indispensable prerequisites. For example, a woman who is a good mother realizes an important physiological potential (Rappoport 1972). So there are no insurmountable barriers to self-actualization. All one needs is to keep one's eye on the future.

People want to feel good about themselves, to increase self-regard, according to Rogers. In some cases, the approval of an audience is necessary. But the pleasure of self-actualization can also be realized all alone: by shooting a dozen baskets in solitary practice, writing a poem, even cleaning a house till it shines. Someone with a strong drive toward fulfillment can overcome past problems by concentrating on the goal.

Maslow, Rogers, Erikson, and Freud proposed personality theories that have many similarities as well as differences. One

Humanistic: centering on human interests and values and the capacity of individuals to fulfill their potential

Self-actualization: fulfilling one's ultimate potential

common thread is the importance of heredity and early parental influence in shaping the development of any individual's personality.

The Origins of Personality

When Steve (one of the three brothers introduced earlier) was an infant, he seemed exceptionally undemanding. This was a relief to his mother, who was preoccupied with Steve's older brother, Eric, a lively, mischievous child who seemed to need a great deal of her attention. As long as Steve was fed—and he woke, ravenously hungry, earlier than everyone else in the family—he gave very little trouble. As a youngster, Steve had few friends; he spent his out-of-school time with his brothers, books, and records. And it was Steve who sat near the wall in college classes, painfully shy.

Genetic influences on temperament

Personality theorists might trace Steve's distinctive personality at least in part to his own inborn traits. While scholars generally agree that family upbringing is an important influence on personality development (Looft 1971a), children's *temperaments* seem to differ from the moment of birth, and perhaps even before birth.

Temperament: disposition; psychological makeup

Twins Several recent studies confirm these innate personality differences, which are also seen in a less scientific way by any parents of more than one child. Although some environmentalists do not agree, children do seem to emerge from the womb with unique characteristics that can largely be attributed to genetic inheritance.

The personalities of 61 pairs of twin girls, some identical, some fraternal, aged six to ten, were studied with particular respect to *introversion* versus *extroversion:* characteristics like social apprehension versus friendliness and likeableness. These traits were selected because they seem to be key differences in how particular personalities deal with the world. The investigators found that the identical twins were far more similar in this respect than the fraternal twins. The findings can be attributed primarily to genetic differences, since the environment of all twins living together is substantially the same. The manifestations of introversion and extroversion continued to be seen over a

Introversion: inward-directedness

Extroversion: outward-directedness

long period. Such differences between one individual and another may be observed not only in the first five years of life but also over the years of development that follow (Scarr 1969; Thomas, Chess, and Birch 1970; Owen and Sines 1970).

Earliest manifestations   When a baby smiles at someone or shies away from a stranger, that child is revealing important aspects of the basic temperament and personality that will distinguish the individual throughout life. Both the smiles and the fear are important forerunners of later behavior. A smile is a human being's first expression of pleasure with another person. And an infant's fear of strangers seems to be the earliest manifestation of a human's fear of those who are different (Freedman 1965).

The genetic bases of personality are illustrated by differences between ethnic groups. For example, infants with European-American background become excited more easily and waver back and forth between being contented and being upset. In contrast, Chinese-American babies are calmer and steadier. Six ethnic groups were studied. While there were more similarities than differences, the temperament of each group was unique in some respects (Freedman 1971).

Interaction of nature and nurture   An important study of personality by Alexander Thomas, Stella Chess, and Herbert Birch (1970) followed 100 children for over ten years, leading to the conclusion that personality is formed by the constant interaction of innate temperament with upbringing and environment. The investigators started when each child was two or three months old. Parents gave periodic detailed descriptions of their children's behavior. The researchers sketched each child's behavioral profile by rating the child on nine separate three-point scales.

The children were distinctly individual in the first few weeks after they were born. These characteristics seemed to have nothing to do with the way their parents handled them. In most children, those same characteristics could be seen over the years of the study. Most children seemed to fall into one of three personality groups: the "easy" child, the "difficult" child, and the "slow-to-warm-up" child. Parents of "easy" children had very few problems with them over the years, in contrast to the "difficult" children. Those who were "slow to warm up" had trouble adapting to new circumstances and tended to be moody and negative. The relatively few children who defied categorization had a mixture of traits. (See Box 9–4.)

Box 9–4   Personality Types and Temperament

Type of child	Activity level	Rhythmicity	Distractibility	Approach Withdrawal	Adaptability
	(the proportion of active periods to inactive ones)	(regularity of hunger, excretion, sleep, and wakefulness)	(the degree to which extraneous stimuli alter behavior)	(the response to a new object or person)	(the ease with which a child adapts to changes in his environment)
"Easy"	Low to moderate	Very regular	Varies	Positive approach	Very adaptable
"Slow to Warm Up"	Varies	Varies	Varies	Initial withdrawal	Slowly adaptable
"Difficult"	Varies	Irregular	Varies	Withdrawal	Slowly adaptable

Type of child	Attention span and persistence	Intensity of Reaction	Threshold of responsiveness	Quality of mood
	(the amount of time devoted to an activity, and the effect of distraction on the activity)	(the energy of response, regardless of its quality or direction)	(the intensity of stimulation required to evoke a discernible response)	(the amount of friendly, pleasant, joyful behavior as contrasted with unpleasant, unfriendly behavior)
"Easy"	High or low	Low or mild	High or low	Positive
"Slow to Warm Up"	High or low	Mild	High or low	Slightly negative
"Difficult"	High or low	Intense	High or low	Negative

Temperament of a child allows classification as "easy," "slow to warm up," or "difficult" according to the rating in certain key categories in the nine-point personality index. The categories are only a general guide to temperament. Of the 141 subjects 65% could be categorized, but 35% displayed a mixture of traits. Such a child might, for example, be rated "easy" in some ways and "difficult" in others.

Source: A. Thomas, S. Chess, and H. G. Birch, The origin of personality, *Scientific American,* 1970, 223(2), 106–107.

The investigators concluded that when parents or any others make demands on a child that conflict too much with that child's personality and ability, the child is put under stress that might be unbearable. Therefore, they advise that parents keep in mind all the facets of their children's unique characteristics in order to tailor the way they deal with them. In this way, many behavioral problems could be avoided. Harmonizing the environment with the child's nature leads to healthy development, these scholars contend. There is no one "right" way to rear all children (Thomas, Chess, and Birch 1970).

Variations in parent–child relationships

Innate personality differences are often intensified by interaction with the home environment. A baby's temperament almost inevitably affects the way parents treat the child. Other influences on parental treatment are the child's sex, position in the family (first-born, second-born, "only" child), the size of the family, and the family's economic or social circumstances. The parents' child-rearing "style" will also influence the development of the child. Each parent is different, each child is different. And so the "mix" is different.

A mother or father does not even treat the same child the same way all the time. For example, a mother expects her baby to behave in a certain fashion, whether she realizes it or not. If the infant or toddler or the school-age child fails to conform to this pattern, the parent will change her own behavior in order to make the child "fit." The effort may or may not succeed, but the child's behavior and personality development will be somehow affected. The relationship changes all the time (Kagan and Moss 1962).

Temperament Some babies seem to be standoffish almost from birth, others the reverse (Schaffer and Emerson 1964a, b). The result is that the infant who likes to be cuddled and caressed will elicit different responses from a parent than a child who flinches from physical affection. A baby who likes to be cuddled will encourage a parent to give more of the same. The aloof child will probably be treated accordingly (Yarrow, Waxler, and Scott 1971; Osofsky and Danzger 1974). Independent individuals tend to fend off parental controls (Osofsky and O'Connell 1972). Likewise, the more a child responds to an adult's attention, the more attention the youngster is likely to receive (Yarrow, Waxler, and Scott 1971). A stubborn child is reared differently from either a dependent child or an independent child (Osofsky 1970).

Mothers, particularly, seem quick to respond to a dependent child's call for help, by giving reassurance, affection, approval. So the tendency is to make a dependent child even more dependent (Marcus 1975).

Even a baby's appearance may elicit special treatment from a parent. A wide-eyed, bright-looking infant who makes searching movements looks intelligent to the care-giver, a determination that may be made within the baby's first week or two. The parent will deal with the child accordingly, with subtle, long-lasting effects on the child's personality (Bennett 1971).

Birth order Parents treat their children differently according to birth order, with consequent effects on personality. To be a first-born is to be in a special class all one's own. Mothers spend more time with their first-born babies, give them more stimulation in general (Thoman, Leiderman, and Olson 1972; Jacobs and Moss 1976). They pressure them more to achieve. They are more anxious about them and tend to become more involved with them (Rothbart 1971). Thus, many first-born children turn out to be more high-powered than second children, if one considers "bossiness" to be the index (Sutton-Smith and Rosenberg 1968). The lists of high achievers always have more eldest children (Altus 1966).

To be second-born, particularly in a two-child family, often results in behavior patterns that are the opposite of those of the older child, perhaps because the younger is trying to avoid competing (Leventhal 1970). The birth of a sibling also has a major effect on both the older child and the mother. Children were observed in a play situation before and after the birth of a new baby. The mother's relationship with the older child is less nurturant after a sibling is born (Taylor and Kogan 1973).

Family size Personality characteristics may also be influenced by family size, though the effects are not clear-cut. Larger families seem to have more school problems (poor school work, truancy, cheating) and antisocial behavior (stealing, delinquency) than smaller families. On the other hand, there seems to be less anxiety and neurotic behavior in the larger families (Tuckman and Regan 1967). But other investigators have discovered advantages in smaller families, in terms of the children's emotional security and general social adjustment. In the smaller families parents and children may have a better chance to be closer to one another emotionally and in the give-and-take of daily life (Odom, Seeman, and Newbrough 1971).

Parental style The child-rearing techniques that are in vogue are another influence on a child's personality development. Many parents now emphasize self-actualization rather than conformity. The current generation of middle-class parents especially tend to adopt a humanistic, individualistic approach. They also aim to foster their children's social relationships by helping them to develop a sense of trust in other adult care-givers. The trend is away from trying to raise children to fit into a mold. Instead, many youngsters are being encouraged to find themselves according to their own particular inner nature (Bigner 1972).

An investigator who studied nursery school children and the way their parents treated them identified three distinct parental styles. She found very different effects on the children's behavior and personality, as a result of the varying methods of rearing (Baumrind 1971). (See Box 9–5.)

Nevertheless, generalizations about the effect of child-rearing techniques on personality are impossible to formulate. As Erikson and others have emphasized, an individual's eventual total personality depends on a subtle interplay of inheritance and environment. Since the parent (in most cases) is an essential part of the environment, it is important for mothers and fathers to know how to deal with the unique individual who is their child. As Thomas, Chess, and Birch (1970) pointed out, to harmonize child-rearing techniques with a child's special personality requirements is to give the developing individual a better chance of growing up with a minimum of emotional or adjustment problems. What works with one could be a disaster with another.

Attachment

Feeding

An act that is basic to the growth of human infants—feeding—is also basic in the development of personality. Feeding means more than absorbing nourishment. The feeding situation also develops affectionate bonds between the infant and specific persons, thus creating *attachment*, which is essential to the acquisition of basic trust or mistrust (in Erikson's terms).

Attachment: emotional dependence on or attraction to a particular person; affectionate bond

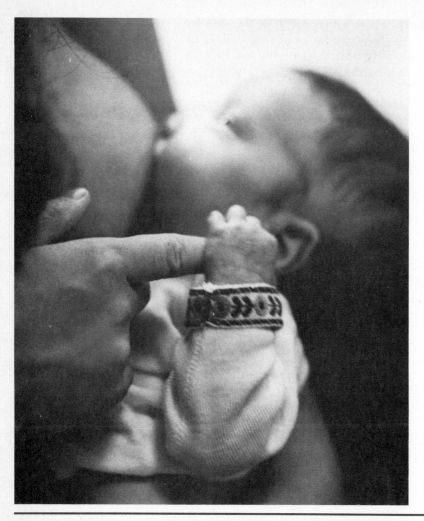

Feeding creates attachment.

Harlow monkeys Harry and Margaret Harlow undertook what turned out to be a landmark experiment in an effort to examine the basis of attachment. They used monkeys, which closely resemble humans. Not only do monkeys look uncannily like us, but in many ways they behave like us. These investigators took advantage of an important difference between monkeys and people—the fact that experiments can be performed on monkeys that would be unthinkable if used on humans. It was their goal to discover the basic elements of the parent–child relationship, which normally builds from the day of birth.

The Harlows reared a group of infant monkeys using only inanimate substitute mothers. One set of "mothers" was made of wire; the other set was made of sponge rubber and soft terry cloth and was heated by hidden bulbs. Both kinds of "mothers" had

How do you bring up a child to be "competent"? This, in effect, was the question Diana Baumrind was trying to answer when she studied 146 nursery school children and their parents (1971). She divided the parents into three groups, after carefully observing and charting their behavior with their children at home.

1. The *authoritarian* parent tries to impose absolute standards of conduct, stresses obedience, and favors using force, if necessary, to make the child conform to the parent's values.

2. The *authoritative* parent tries to direct the child but in a rational way, allowing discussion and reasoning. Control is used but the child is not hemmed in with restrictions. The youngster's own qualities are accepted, but standards are set for future conduct.

3. The *permissive* parent is nonpunitive, accepting, and affirmative. Family policy comes from parent–child consultation. Rules are explained. The parent makes few demands on the child for household responsibility and allows the child to make most decisions about what to do. Control is avoided. Reasoning, not use of power, is the parent's method of dealing with the youngster.

Detailed study of the children's behavior, both at home and in nursery school, led to the investigator's conclusion that authoritative parents are the most likely to succeed in developing "competent" children—children who behave both responsibly and independently. These parents are warm, loving, reasonable, firm, conscientious. But they make it clear that they expect their children to behave in a mature fashion. What they give their children for support in behaving competently is love and approval. These parents also serve as models of correct behavior. They themselves are mature, reasonable, decisive—in effect, competent.

Baumrind found that authoritarian parents tend to have children who are rather dependent, passive, submissive, and lack a sense of responsibility. As for permissive parents, the effect is likely to be children who are not very competent, resist the authority of teachers, and disregard social norms. However, the investigator found that parents generally do not conform in every way to a particular pattern. Many variations in parental style lead to many variations in the way children behave.

bottle-holders to permit nursing. Various feeding conditions were imposed on different groups of animals. Some were fed by wire mothers, some by cloth mothers, some had access to both but were fed by only one.

Regardless of the particular circumstances, all the baby monkeys who could reach the cloth mothers spent more time with those mothers, fled to them for protection and comfort, and seemed to gain courage from their presence. Those with only a wire mother to turn to, however, became highly emotional individuals, quite unlike the monkeys who had had access to a cloth mother. The ultimate effects of these experiments showed how different from that of normal monkeys was the adult behavior of the animals who had had surrogate mothers. The surrogate-reared monkeys could not socialize or get along with other monkeys. And when they were frightened, they sought comfort from terry-cloth-covered mothers rather than from other monkeys (Harlow 1959; Harlow and Harlow 1962).

Tactile comfort   The Harlow studies show the importance of *tactile comfort* in infant attachment. (Also see Chapter 3, page 107.) The studies also disprove the conditioning theory of infant-to-parent attachment, the previously held notion that attachment between a mother and child comes from the stark fact that the mother is the source of food. On the contrary, it appears that early bodily contact and immediate comfort are vital elements affecting the mother–child bond.

Tactile comfort: comfort from touching

Nursing seems to be important to both monkey and human babies for two reasons. The first, of course, is that the baby receives nourishment. But the second reason is that the process provides frequent intimate contact between infant and mother. Thus is created attachment, the emotional bond that is the basis of an individual's ability to develop normally.

Feeding time is when the relationship between mother and child is reciprocally cemented. As the mother helps the baby nurse or suck, she gives both nourishment and oral experience. The baby's satisfaction makes the mother feel satisfied and motivated to do more for the infant: she talks, coos, smiles, pats, hugs (O'Grady 1971). Before long, the baby is smiling at Mother, an indication of a normal emotional relationship (Spitz 1946a).

Both breast-fed and bottle-fed babies probably develop essentially the same way, psychologically speaking. What is important is the warmth and stimulation the baby gets while being fed (Sears, Maccoby, and Levin 1957).

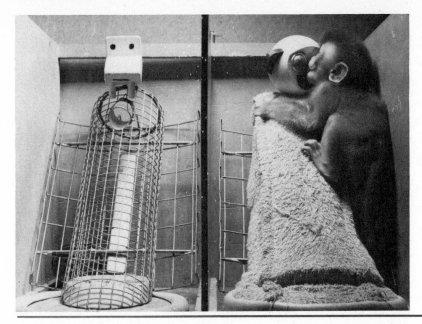

Harlow's monkey turns to the terry cloth "mother" for tactile comfort.

Recent stress on individuality and personality development has caused most mothers to be more flexible and relaxed than they used to be 30 or more years ago about infant feeding and weaning (Bronfenbrenner 1958). Excessively strict schedules and fixed timetables for weaning are out of style, because mothers and fathers have come to realize that a warm relationship with a primary care-giver is vital to the child's eventual emotional well-being.

Mother's voice Attachment to a mother or any primary care-giver comes from many other seemingly inconsequential influences, including all the variables experienced by the infant in the parent–child relationship. The very sound of a mother's voice can be a factor in attachment. She may not realize that her voice may be as important as her warmth, her touch, the food she is providing. What may seem (to a detached onlooker) like a silly conversation between a mother and her infant—her meaningless talk, his coos and sighs and noises, her imitations of the sounds he makes, the face-to-face interchanges between the two—all this is a subtle form of communication. It is the basis of an important relationship, which will later broaden into positive social ties with other people (Tulkin and Cohler 1973).

Attachment behavior

Seeking the care-giver Attachment causes infants to seek their care-givers when separated from them. This kind of behavior may be the result of an instinct to seek protection from danger (Bowlby 1951). A child shows a need for a mother's or care-giver's presence in myriad little ways. For example, it is easy to spot attachment behavior in ten-month-old infants. If a mother goes out of eye range, the child may cry, search in the direction of her disappearance, try to follow (Coates, Anderson, and Hartup 1972).

Children a year-and-a-half to two-and-a-half, playing with toys, are likely to leave the toys to put themselves where they can see their mothers. If the mother is safely within their view they go on playing contentedly. For humans, and perhaps for primates in general, face-to-face contact has a matchless potential for information and for emotional meaning (Carr, Dabbs, and Carr 1975).

In spite of the relatively limited amount of time many fathers spend with their infants, ten-month-old babies show distinct attachment responses to fathers as well as mothers. Babies will travel toward the father rather than toward a stranger—though, given a choice between the two parents, infants tend to move in the mother's direction (Cohen and Campos 1974; Weinraub and Frankel 1977).

While one-year-olds are commonly more attached to their mothers, a two-year-old in a stressful situation will run to either parent for help (Lamb 1976). These early father–child links may grow even stronger as more and more couples practice joint baby-tending.

Interaction varies Only the vast range of human differences can account for the fact that mother–infant interaction can go so well in some cases and so poorly in others. Each tries to influence the other, the one by crying, the other by picking up, feeding, changing the diaper. In most instances, the baby will stop crying when attention is paid. But not always. Other needs may complicate matters (Thoman 1974).

Nurturant care-givers appear to be the most effective. They are the ones who feed their infants on a demand schedule, pick up the crying baby rather than letting the child "cry it out." They are generally relaxed and somewhat permissive and are apt to start toilet-training somewhat later than average. In nursery school, the children of such mothers tend to choose adult dolls to play

Nurturant: warm; caring; need-satisfying

with and are more apt to identify with their mothers. Presumably these children grow up to be better adjusted in their adult roles (Levin 1963).

Stranger anxiety Can one overdo attachment? Some conscientious mothers, influenced by the current vogue for independence training, worry about causing their babies to become too attached to them. But their concern may relate to a phenomenon that is common for many—but not all—babies: *stranger anxiety*, recognition of a discrepancy between a familiar and unfamiliar person. Typically, at about eight months, a baby suddenly shies away from strangers, cries at the sight of a new person, or looks fearfully away. These reactions often come in the latter months of a child's first year (Greenberg, Hillman, and Grice 1973).

Stranger anxiety: apprehensive or fearful response to strangers

Stranger anxiety seems to be related not only to attachment but also to cognitive development. As we saw in Chapter 5 (page 174), at a certain point a child attains the ability to formulate a mental scheme of a person—usually the mother—and is able to keep that person in mind even though she may have disappeared from view. Children differ in the time they achieve object or person permanence and in their ability to become habituated to familiar objects or attentive to new sights. Thus, the most fearful nine- and ten-month-olds may be showing more maturity in terms of cognitive development than others their own age (Paradise and Curcio 1974).

object/person permanence

Attachment in young children may be gauged by the way they behave when a stranger is present. In a laboratory setting, a group of 18-month-olds were with both their mothers and fathers. They involved their fathers in play more than their mothers. But when a stranger arrived, they turned to their mothers. It was Mother to whom they were most closely attached and who represented a refuge from danger (Lamb 1976).

By the end of a baby's first year, stranger anxiety typically declines. As children grow older and better equipped to identify their experiences, strangers no longer distress them. It should be noted that the absence of stranger anxiety does not mean that attachment has not occurred. Some infants show different signs of attachment without exhibiting stranger anxiety.

Separation anxiety As frequent a development as stranger anxiety is *separation anxiety*, which may replace it as a "problem" for parents: children start to be upset about being left. But separa-

Separation anxiety: apprehensive or fearful response to being left by the accustomed care-giver

tion anxiety, too, is a product of both attachment and cognitive development. Separation anxiety is an indication that a baby recognizes a discrepant event—separation from the parent. Increasing cognitive maturity enables a child to become well aware of the difference between being cared for by Mother or Father and being tended by someone else.

A child who has had a great deal of attention from the father, in addition to the usual maternal care, seems to be more amenable to being left behind. Apparently the more experience a baby has with more people, the better the child's developing mental ability to understand and cope with the circumstances of separation (Spelke et al. 1973). When children feel secure in their attachment to their parents, they are less likely to suffer from separation anxiety. A child who has a confident relationship with Mother feels freer to venture away from her and is apt to use her as a "launching pad" for exploring the world (Ainsworth 1975).

How early in life a baby shows separation anxiety may be related to the intensity of parental attention. In Uganda, babies as young as six months become disturbed when the mother is absent. The probable reason is that in Uganda a baby is usually strapped to the mother's body and accompanies her everywhere. Loss of this stable element is more readily noticeable (Ainsworth 1967).

Similarly, in Guatemala, where most families live in a one-room rancho and constant contact is a fact of life, for a baby to be separated from care-givers is so unusual that it becomes painful very early. Protest appears at nine months (Lester et al. 1975).

Contrast this with the usual age of onset of separation anxiety—12 months—for American infants. Here most of our babies spend many hours in bassinets, cribs, playpens, often in a different room from their care-givers. It takes a greater degree of cognitive maturity and experience for our children to realize that the parent is a stable presence in their lives. Therefore they react to separation later.

Not only are separation and stranger anxiety normal, and probably signs of cognitive development, but the basic cause—attachment to a parent—is essential to healthy personality development. The Harlows report that monkeys raised in isolation for the first six months were permanently impaired in their future social relationships with other monkeys. Six months in a monkey's life is equivalent to two or three years in a human life. This has dire implications for institutionalized infants, who lose the advantages of early maternal care (Harlow and Harlow 1962).

Separation anxiety generally lasts through the second year. Then increased cognitive maturity helps a child understand that the separation is temporary.

Day care and attachment

What happens to the attachment process when small children spend a great deal of time away from their mothers? According to the Bureau of Labor Statistics, six million or more preschoolers in this country are left in the care of other adults while their mothers or fathers work at jobs outside the home.

Recent studies suggest that this kind of upbringing probably has scant ill effects on the essential progress of attachment and thus negligible negative influence on the children's personality or intellectual development (Belsky and Steinberg 1978; Rubenstein and Howes 1979). One investigation compared the attachment behavior of 35 middle-class three-and-a-half to four-year-olds. One group had been cared for in the conventional fashion, at home by their mothers. Another group had been enrolled in group day care after they were three. A third group was cared for by another family at a year old and moved to group day care about two years after. The investigators found that day care seemed to have no significant effect on the attachment patterns of these children, girls and boys alike (Portnoy and Simmons 1978).

Another research study observed 23 infants and toddlers who had been placed in day care. The situation was designed to reveal whether attachment behavior was stronger to the mother or to the day-care teacher. Both mothers and day-care teacher were in the room. All the children turned to their mothers, not their teachers, for reassurance or help under stress. And most of the children seemed to have developed a strong enough relationship to their mothers to permit them to feel secure and able to detach themselves and explore novel surroundings (Farran and Ramey 1977).

More support for the conclusion that day care does not hurt attachment to a mother came from comparison of two groups of three-and-a-half-year-old boys and girls, one with no group day-care experience and one with about six months of day care. The two groups behaved about the same. But the boys' attachment behavior did show some differences. Those who had been reared only at home tended to cling more to their mothers, tried more to avoid strangers. The day-care boys were more apt to explore and manipulate new toys (Moskowitz, Schwarz, and Corsini 1977).

Another study involved three dozen children, half Caucasian and half Chinese, who received day care from the age of three-and-a-half months until two-and-a-half. The children were carefully watched with respect to how they played, their language and cognitive development, and their social interaction. Compared with children of similar backgrounds reared at home, day care did not seem to influence their attachment to their mothers, nor did it change the way they related to other children (Kagan, Kearsley, and Zelazo 1978).

All these reports seem to show that attachment between mother and child normally develops whether or not the mother spends most of her time with her young child. But there is another essential element in personality development, identification, the process whereby children adopt the motives, values, and personal characteristics of a meaningful model. It is important to know how child-rearing affects the development of identification, because it involves not only personality but how an individual functions in society.

Identification

When Steve was about two-and-a-half, he told a neighbor: "I have a cold. So Mommy doesn't want me to play with Danny. He might catch my cold and his mommy would be angry."

But Steve's mother had said not a word to him about staying away from Danny. The boy had clearly adopted his mother's way of thinking. From mothers and fathers, children borrow motives, characteristics, ways of thinking and feeling, values, and the rules of behavior. They identify with them.

The identification process

Learning is involved *Identification* is not the same as imitation. True, we may dress or walk or gesture like somebody else. But to identify is to behave, react, and feel like that somebody. The whole process of identification is closely related to learning (see Chapter 7, pages 269–273). Children use their parents as models, imitating their behavior and adopting their attitudes. Parental approval reinforces this behavior.

In this way, children adopt the values of their parents. It is a cumulative result of learning and identification. They learn how to act like their parents and they also learn to think like them. Children usually share the political, religious, and moral beliefs

Identification: associating oneself closely with another person's characteristics, attitudes, and rules of behavior

Father-son identification.

of their parents. Republican parents tend to have Republican children. These are aspects of socialization that will be discussed further in Chapter 10.

Reasons for identifying   When a very young child identifies, the unconscious motive might be expressed this way: "This person has what I want. The more I behave like this person, the more likely I am to command the same abilities, the same pleasures, the same mastery over my surroundings. And in this way, too, I will be sure of having love and affection" (Kagan 1958; Sears, Rau, and Alpert 1965).

Another probable motive for identification learning is that children feel as if they are gaining higher status as a result of their parents' positive reactions. Thus, there is an intrinsic reward in identifying with parents—an increase in the child's self-esteem.

Children identify with their parents also because parents fulfill dependency needs and provide affection. When parents give children love, warmth, security, food, pleasure, stimulation, they are creating the conditions for establishing the child's identity. They are unconsciously encouraging children to grow up in their own image. By becoming like the parent and pleasing the parent, children seem to be trying to make sure that their needs will be met. A child is more likely to identify with a parent when there is a warm relationship, one in which the child wants to remain close to Mother or Father (Kagan 1958; Sears, Maccoby, and Levin 1957).

A sign that self-identity has been established comes when the child, at around three or four, starts to use the words *I* and *me;* Now the youngster realizes fully that he or she is a being who has an independent existence.

As each of us grows older, the need to identify with someone else decreases. We realize that we ourselves now possess the means for gratifying our desires (Kagan 1958). But in the beginning, we seize the identities of those who seem to control the whole world, our parents.

Self-concept

Who am I? Do I like myself?

In the process of child-rearing, parents create the answers to those two questions for their children. But these questions are likely to be asked over and over again at various times in our lives. People who are groping, unsure, or unhappy about themselves are the most likely to make trouble for themselves and for those around them. And the converse may also be true. Individuals who have a clear idea about their place in the scheme of things and are reasonably content with that identity have a better chance of living a good productive life with benefits for themselves, their families, and the community at large.

All this relates to *self-concept*, individuals' basic perception of themselves, what the world is like, and how they fit into it in terms of personal abilities and deficiencies. Through the process of identification a child begins to formulate a self-concept. Those with a positive picture of themselves experience *self-esteem*, a feeling of worth and a high level of personal confidence. Behavior, a sense of identity, self-concept—the basic characteristics that constitute an individual—all these personal aspects are molded by parents until the age of 10 or 11 (Emmerich, Goldman, and Shore 1971).

Self-esteem Self-esteem plays a significant role in a child's level of aspiration and achievement. Youngsters with high self-esteem tend to be active people who are both academically and socially

Who am I? I like myself!

successful. They feel secure about their eventual success in whatever they try to do. In contrast, those with low self-esteem feel inferior and are afraid in their dealings with others. They desperately try to find social approval but generally feel discouraged and depressed. How high one aspires is directly related to how much one values oneself (Coopersmith 1968).

The self-concept that originates in the parent–child relationship may well remain with the individual, sometimes virtually unchanged, all through life. In one study, for example, sixth graders who did well in reading and arithmetic were found to be first or second children with positive self-concepts who had been brought up in small families by warm, loving parents (Sears

1970). However, while self-concept may affect academic performance, teachers may have it within their power to make some change in a student's attitude and achievement (Samuels 1973). (See also Chapter 11, pages 459–463.)

Experiences both in and outside the home contribute to identity and self-esteem. Self-esteem suffers its greatest challenge around the age of 12. Children then are more self-conscious, have more problems with their self-image, more worries about what other people think. But difficulties also may come from something as simple as moving into junior high school. It is the new school that brings on the problem, not the individual's chronological age (Simmons, Rosenberg, and Rosenberg 1973).

A youngster's self-regard is closely related to the mother's child-rearing attitudes, and mothers generally play a more influential role than fathers during the troubled adolescent years. Both girls and boys confide more in their mothers than in their fathers, although girls tend to disclose more than boys (Rivenbark 1971).

However, fathers also exert demonstrable influence on both sons and daughters as they reach their teens. Fathers who are positively involved in their daughters' upbringing have been shown to have a good effect on the girls' adjustment in college. The girls who feel rejected by their fathers often have personality problems (Fish and Biller 1973). Boys who have been able to identify closely with their fathers are apt to have their fathers' educational and vocational goals (Crites 1962).

Identification with both mother and father seems to be strongest if a young person perceives the parents' marriage as egalitarian. If the husband is dominated by his wife, the father is less likely to be looked upon as a role model for the children (Bowerman and Bahr 1973). Children who mature late and are not very well adjusted tend to have inadequate self-concepts that stem from poor parent–child relationships and strong feelings of dependency (Jones and Mussen 1958).

In time, friends, classmates, teachers, and peers slowly displace mothers and fathers as molders of self-concept. Decisions and behavior are increasingly determined by what other important figures think (Utech and Hoving 1969).

Socioeconomic differences Socioeconomic class is apt to have a great deal to do with a child's sense of being somebody worthwhile. But not every child from an impoverished family has a poor self-concept, nor does every middle-class child have a good self-concept (Samuels 1973). One study showed that better-educated mothers probably add to feelings of confidence and self-worth, even in boys who are brought up in ghettos. But the environmental effects may dominate if there is no compensating influence of such a mother (T. Miller 1975).

Often, the self-concept of children brought up under unusual or deprived conditions deteriorates as the children grow older. They may go to school ill-prepared by attitude and environment for learning and success. They may fail to find scholastic success. Thus, their opinion of themselves goes down, particularly beginning at the third-grade level. This is when many such children start to have really serious learning problems (Brown and Renz 1973).

What these youngsters need is experience with success, which breeds self-confidence and more success. Special preschool programs like Head Start do not yet seem to be providing the answer. The apparent benefits of attending nursery school, in terms of improved self-concept or better achievements, seem to melt away by the time children reach the early grades in school (Baker 1973). Teacher training on all levels should probably include ways of dealing with children who start out expecting very little of themselves (Andrews 1966).

Sex roles

All human beings inevitably think of themselves as either male or female, a realization which comes around the age of three (Kagan 1964*b*; Thompson 1975). This *sex-role* concept is an obvious controlling element in everyone's life and everyone's personality.

Sex role: differing behaviors expected of and considered appropriate for males and females

What boys and girls learn about their sex roles as little children marks them all their lives, and not only in terms of their relationships with eventual lovers, husbands, and wives. As we shall see in Chapters 10 and 11, academic performance, career aspirations, and ability to function as a socially competent individual are also affected.

Early sex-typing Mothers and fathers are the prime sources of sex-role learning and *sex-typing*—learning the behavior that is conventionally appropriate for one's sex. Almost from the time the blanketed bundle is put into a mother's arms, the baby's sex affects how the parent will go about the task of child-rearing. Many young wives still probably feel a special pride in producing sons (Mitchell 1973). The mother is apt to spend more time feeding a boy. But if it is a girl, she will probably do more talking and

Sex-typing: learning a conventional sex role

true

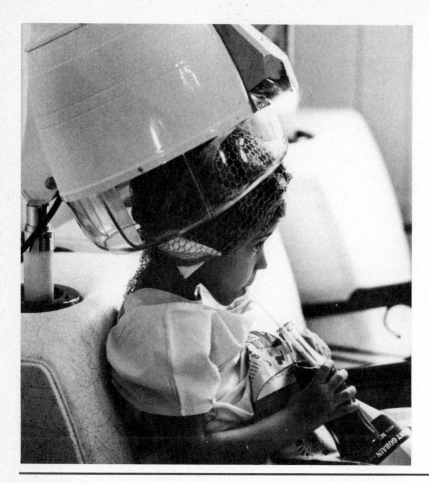

Children learn sex roles early.

smiling (Thoman, Leiderman, and Olson 1972). Male infants are generally rubbed, patted, touched, rocked more than girls (Brown et al. 1975).

Bedroom furnishings usually clearly reflect parents' ideas about what is appropriate to the two sexes. Boys' rooms have more vehicles, more sports equipment, toy animals, machinery, military toys, while girls' rooms run to ruffles, dolls, and domestic toys (Rheingold and Cook 1975).

Since it has generally been the mother who has done most of the early child care, both sexes have usually identified with their mothers in early years. As a result, boys must make an identity switch-over as they grow older. Earlier, however, both boys and girls behave like Steve, who modeled himself on Mommy, because it was she who provided care and most of the gratification he required when very young. Only thus would food, comfort, and love continue to flow (Sears, Rau, and Alpert 1965).

While children normally begin to identify with the parent of the same sex at around three, they will not do so unless the same-sex parent seems to be loving, caring, powerful, and competent in areas that seem important to the child (Kagan 1958). Children have usually learned to avoid acting like the opposite sex by the time they enter nursery school, and they pay increasing attention during the preschool period to learning how their own sex behaves (Connor and Serbin 1977; Fagot 1977).

Stereotypes Boys will be boys, says society indulgently. Male children are influenced very early to be aggressive, according to the male stereotype. Boys are also made aware of how girls behave, if only to avoid such inappropriate behavior themselves. Girls learn, for their part, that they are supposed to be anything but aggressive, either verbally or physically.

The traditional male sex role stresses aggressiveness, independence, and physical abilities. The traditional female sex role stresses passivity, dependency, conformity, warmth, and affection. Sex-role perceptions influence both behavior and self-concept.

Some boys and girls start to learn sex-appropriate behavior even before they have begun to toddle. Certainly as they become aware of their physical similarities to Father or Mother (around three), they catch on to the fact that they are expected to behave like others of their own sex (Slaby and Frey 1975). They think of themselves as masculine or feminine and acquire a sex role identity (Kagan 1964*b*).

Even children as young as two have acquired considerable knowledge of the sex-role stereotypes that prevail in the adult world. A high positive correlation has been found between children's understanding that their own gender is fixed and unchangeable and their knowledge of sex-role stereotypes (Kuhn, Nash, and Brucken 1978). Since most children learn early that men have most of the power in our society, both girls and boys have good reason to learn how a male behaves. A boy finds an obvious model in the male. But even though a girl identifies with women's behavior, she also observes men's behavior. It is important to learn how to deal with men if they are perceived to be in control of the world (Perry and Perry 1975).

Sex differences in play Mothers seem to promote the differences in how boys and girls play from the earliest days of their lives, by the ways in which they treat sons and daughters differently (Goldberg and Lewis 1969). When toddlers and parents were observed in their homes, investigators noted that parents had a significantly more favorable reaction when their children played in a "same-sex-preferred" way. Girls who engaged in gross motor activity (using large muscles) got a negative parental response, but the reaction was positive when the girls' behavior was dependent and adult-oriented. Nevertheless, aggressive behavior by boys and girls got the same negative response from parents (Fagot 1978).

Girls realize that females are expected to take care of others (their dolls, to begin with), to demonstrate warmth and affection. Boys understand that such behavior is for "sissies" (Kagan and Moss 1960; Kagan 1964*b*; Nadelman 1974). However, girls' perceptions of the kind of play that is appropriate seem to be changing. Even in the late 1950s, a study found that girls' interests had already widened to include many games that were formerly considered to be strictly masculine. But the investigators found no such interest in "girls' games" on the part of boys (Rosenberg and Sutton-Smith 1960).

Opposite-sex effect In the average home, the mother and the father convey differing sex role messages to their children. At some ages, mothers have more influence; at other ages, fathers seem to dominate. Even the consequences of the same kind of parental treatment may vary, depending on whether the child is male or female (Marcus and Corsini 1978).

Parents tend to be more lenient with their opposite-sex children. For example, fathers play a more active role in disciplining sons. But where daughters are concerned they are apt to express affection and praise and generally act more permissively. Indeed, a girl who has had less rigid sex role requirements has been more likely to bask in praise from both parents (Stinnett, Farris, and Walters 1974).

On the other hand, mothers generally are more lenient with their sons. Parents probably tend to identify with a child of the same sex and are punishing or being severe with their own unhappy memories as much as with the child for whom they are now responsible. A parent may also have a more kindly attitude toward a child who resembles husband or wife, but may have an unconscious feeling of rivalry with the same-sex child (Rothbart and Maccoby 1966).

Children could learn behavior from the opposite-sex parent that might create problems for them in a still strongly sex-oriented world. A boy who closely identifies with his mother might become passive, anxious, and feel inadequate with his peers. A girl who identifies completely with her father might feel unattractive to boys as she grows older and have a sense of strain in thinking of herself as a woman (Kagan 1964b).

The Freudian interpretation of why a boy normally behaves like his father is that only in this way can he make himself feel more comfortable about his Oedipal attraction to his mother. The boy admires his father, wants to be like him, but also would like to eliminate him as a rival for Mother's affection. Taking on Father's characteristics makes him pleasing to both parents at the same time (Sears, Rau, and Alpert 1965).

During the latter part of the preschool period, boys often become hostile toward their fathers, possibly because they see them as rivals for Mother's affection. Expecting counter-hostility and fearing retaliation, a boy's defense might be to adopt a "father's role" (Sears, Maccoby, and Levin 1957). Thus, a dominant father is a stronger identity model and leads to a boy's greater masculine self-perception (Biller 1969).

Girls and boys in adolescence A father's treatment seems to affect an adolescent girl's feelings about herself as a woman. He can encourage her to value her feminity, or he may subtly reject her because she does not measure up to his idea of how a woman should look or behave. Girls who have good relationships with their fathers are more likely to enjoy a good marital relationship (Biller 1971).

In the teen years girls may have special problems as they come to realize that females are often considered inferior to males in our society and that they must either accept this devalued sex role or break away from negative stereotyping (Bohan 1973). But boys' self-esteem is rising at this age, particularly when they are able to master specific skills that are socially valued, like swimming (Koocher 1971).

Girls seem to rely on other people's reactions, for they are the mirror in which girls see themselves as attractive, poised, acceptable. Thus, a girl can practice being feminine only with the aid of others. But boys' sex-role identity is far less dependent on such mirrors. They can develop "masculine" skills by themselves: by practicing shooting baskets, lifting weights, learning to fix a car (Kagan 1964*b*).

Adolescents themselves, both boys and girls, devalue the achievements of females (Etaugh and Rose 1975). Thus, most males who share the typical adolescent lack of self-confidence and self-esteem still emerge into adulthood feeling good about themselves. But the same does not necessarily happen to girls, who move from low prestige as teenagers to the same low prestige as grown women (Lyell 1973).

Effect of father absence   Sex role identification can be affected if a father is absent from the home, but boys and girls react differently. A boy who has only a mother with whom to identify might become passive, anxious, and feel inadequate with his peers (Kagan 1964*b*).

Boys' masculine identification may be particularly affected by the absence of a male parent before the age of five (Biller and Bahm 1971). Their cognitive style tends to be "feminine." They have better verbal scores and weaker math scores in College Board examinations. If these boys come from stable families that emphasize intellectual and academic pursuits, they have no trouble entering suitable professions, but they may feel less secure about their roles as adult men (Carlsmith 1973).

As for girls, an absent father may cost them the essential reflection of themselves in a man's eyes and the opportunity of learning what men are like. Girls who grow up without fathers may have different attitudes toward the opposite sex and sexual behavior, as compared with girls who have both parents. They may have trouble knowing how to act with boys.

For example, when interviewed by female interviewers, daughters of widows behaved the same as other girls. But when the interviewer was male, they had less speech and eye contact. They avoided being close to the interviewer. Their bodies were rigid. The earlier the separation from fathers, the greater the effects on their daughters. Probably these girls were suffering from lost opportunities for dealing with a loving, attentive man and they became apprehensive and clumsy in male relationships.

In contrast, daughters of divorcées behaved in a much more friendly manner toward male interviewers. These divorcées' daughters dated more and earlier and had sexual intercourse earlier than the relatively inhibited daughters of widows. But in other ways divorcées' daughters may be at a disadvantage compared to widows' daughters. The daughters of divorcées reflect their mothers' critical attitudes toward the father. But the girls who lost their fathers to death tend to have only happy memories.

Why the differences between the daughters of divorcées and girls whose fathers had died? One speculation is that children of divorce might perceive their mothers' single lives to be unsatisfying. Therefore, they feel they must find a man as soon as possible to ensure their own happiness. Another possibility is that these girls are in a hurry to leave a home dominated by a dissatisfied, anxious mother. In contrast, the girls who lost their fathers to death may have been brought up with excessive reverence for the lost parent, transmuted into excessive diffidence with all males (Hetherington 1972). It should be noted that later investigators found few differences in attitudes toward sex roles or romantic love between "father present" and "father absent" college women (Hainline and Feig 1978).

Changing the stereotypes No discussion of sex roles can ignore the fact that many women and quite a few men would now like to change sexual stereotypes. Both the women's movement and its natural counterpart, "men's lib," are new factors that may be having their effects on boys' and girls' perceptions of their sex roles. However, in the media, especially in television commercials, the old stereotypes often persist, even though some of the presentations have become a little subtler. Since sex-role learning depends in large part on observational learning, what is seen on television could possibly modify the efforts of some parents to present an entirely different sort of model.

In any case, to young people, sex roles are not usually seen as a problem in the early school years. They take themselves for granted. But during adolescence they typically begin to worry not only about various aspects of their masculinity or femininity but also about all the other facets of their identity. (See also Chapter 11, pages 451–459, a discussion of sex roles and motivation.)

Adolescent identity crisis

A newspaper tells the story of Sonia Soto, aged 20, who started life as Jane Doe, a four-day-old baby found abandoned in a station wagon. Sonia was trying to find her "real mother." She told a reporter, "I get that feeling that I don't know who I am. And she's the only one who could have some answers for me."

Sonia's *identity crisis*—a term coined by Erikson—occurred in spite of the fact that she had been brought up with love and

Identity crisis: confusion about the nature of one's true self, usually during adolescence

devotion by Rosa and Victor Soto, along with the Sotos' own sons and daughters (Hernandez 1976).

Even if Sonia did find her "real" mother, what she would learn from her probably would not answer Sonia's questions. We have seen that one's true identity is much more than that of the newborn infant who emerges from the womb, a product of two parents' genes. Rather, a person's identity is a collection of responses and kinds of behavior mostly absorbed from the people and circumstances of one's life. The Sotos could tell Sonia much about herself; her classmates and friends some more; her "real mother" very little.

Ambivalence Sonia's identity crisis came relatively late. She was experiencing confusion about the nature of her "true self," which generally happens around the time of puberty. The problems are developmental and may be unavoidable, though some adolescents suffer more than others.

Consider the adolescent's uncertainties. The body is changing fast. The person is no longer a child, but has not yet been physically transformed into an adult. The individual is of two minds about what he or she wants. Adult privileges? Certainly! But how to handle the responsibilities that go along with those privileges? (Stone and Church 1973). At the same time, the teenager also has a lingering wish for the prerogatives of childhood (Carroll 1968–1969).

Parents are also of two minds. They also have difficulty deciding whether the youngster is a child or an adult. In our society, parents often try to spur their adolescents toward at least some independence, but it is practically impossible for most young people to be self-sustaining, either emotionally or financially. Moreover, parents have a contradictory desire to hang on for their own emotional reasons. As a result, the combination of ambivalent parent and ambivalent adolescent is frequently explosive (Salzman 1973).

Role-playing The mother and father are helpless spectators at an identity-crisis drama. The morals, values, beliefs, and relationships so painstakingly instilled during earlier years are now all called into question. The adolescent is "trying on for size" all sorts of possible new roles, looking for an answer to the question, "Who am I?"

No matter how absurd the play-acting appears, the parents have to keep a straight face. Daughter as "femme fatale," tomboy, sage, wit; son as long-distance runner, big-man-on-campus, stud—it is often agony to observe, difficult to know when to intervene, hard to determine what is serious and what is transitory or unimportant.

It seems that all this posturing and changing is necessary, even vital. The adolescent is in the midst of a complex developmental task: to establish new relationships with parents, teachers, and peers based on a newly developing status; to work

Trying on a role.

out new and more appropriate ways of communicating with adults; to thread a way through all the possible identities until the right persona is found (Carroll 1968–1969).

Some people have problems during adolescence because they have not fully solved the developmental problems of earlier stages. They are still immature, still working out childish difficulties with parents, teachers, school work, schoolmates (Moore 1969). But some tend to reject their parents, particularly their mothers, no matter what the previous relationship had been. They turn against the whole culture as a consequence of perceiving their parents as hostile and as attempting inordinate control through psychological means (Rode 1971). They see their parents as not "on my side" (Wiggins 1973). In contrast, those adolescents who accept themselves and have the least trouble in adjustment see their parents as loving, rather than as neglectful or rejecting (Medinnus 1965).

Diffusion and confusion   The adolescent's world is fractured into two separate compartments: family and other adults, and friends and peers (Emmerich, Goldman, and Shore 1971). It seems to be peculiar to our society that young people are torn between their parents' goals for them and the influences of their adolescent subculture (Razavieh and Hoisseini 1972). Nevertheless, even during these often troubled teenage years, parents are generally a more important influence than peers. Deviant behavior is the exception, rather than the rule (Won, Yomamura, and Ikeda 1969).

Erikson's view is that in most cases *identity diffusion*—not necessarily confusion—is taking place in adolescence. New experiences in the areas of sex, friendship, and accomplishment provide added dimensions to the self-concept. Identity confusion occurs only when young people feel they have a number of different identities, and assume them the way a chameleon changes the color of its skin (Erikson 1970).

Identity diffusion: lacking direction, specificity, and integration

An adolescent who is suffering from identity confusion may have trouble in a variety of areas. It is hard to make a commitment to physical intimacy, difficult to make a vocational decision, hard to "see" oneself in any particular role (Bunt 1968). People who constantly are changing their majors in college are likely to be among the confused.

Resolving the crisis   In order to avoid confusion and to develop ego identity, an adolescent must somehow develop a realistic self-concept and a realistic idea of what others think of her or him as a person. A youngster can be helped by warm, sympathetic, understanding parents or teachers. Real communication between the adolescent and significant adults is evidently a *must* (Bunt 1968; Matteson 1974).

Experiences outside the home are significant. In college, for example, people have many chances to see themselves in a variety of situations, most of which are not so crucial that failure would be devastating. During those experiences they may be learning as much about themselves as they are learning substantive information in college courses. By the time they are seniors, they have a much clearer idea of who they are than when they were freshmen (Stark and Traxler 1974). College thus has its value in letting people grow up, and it is not just a matter of allowing four years to pass.

Not every adolescent has to have an identity crisis. Some theorists believe that the identity crisis is not even common in adolescence, that adolescent problems are greatly exaggerated. Instead, they see only a certain amount of rebellion, although in most instances there are good relationships between parents and teenagers. According to this view, most teenagers have good feelings about themselves (King 1972).

Although when Erikson coined the term *identity crisis* he was thinking particularly about adolescents and their problems, he did not say that all young people must suffer in the normal course of development. Rather, he stressed that adolescence is a time when in one way or another a young person develops a new self-concept: an idea of what kind of adult he or she is turning out to be. That is the major developmental challenge of these teenage years (Bohan 1973).

Summary

Personality is difficult to define, but scholars agree that it reflects the behavioral characteristics unique to an individual. Freud developed basic theories that trace personality to the interaction of biological drives and early family influences. Erikson, the foremost proponent of ego psychology, expanded Freud's three developmental stages to eight and allowed for cultural and social factors. Erikson believes life crises and their resolution are normal for healthy personal development. Maslow and Rogers, who are humanists, view individuals as endowed with the potential to be self-directed, able to triumph over past problems in the drive to meet biological and psychological needs, such as food, security, love, esteem, and self-actualization.

The basis of personality is probably genetic, since differences are evident among twins and various ethnic groups. Three early personality patterns are "easy," "difficult," and "slow-to-warm up." Environmental influences may intensify differences as care-givers respond to a child's particular temperament.

Child-rearing techniques affect a child's personality development. Current emphasis is on self-actualization rather than conformity. Parental practices are influenced by the child's age and temperament.

Personality development depends first on attachment, forming affectionate bonds between infant and adults. Harlow's studies of monkeys showed that feeding helps develop attachment through tactile comfort. Maternal warmth and nurturance in general develop attachment. Babies demonstrate attachment behavior when they seek care-givers, show stranger anxiety (at about eight months), and develop separation anxiety (at about a year). Children reared partly in day care show normal attachment to their mothers.

Personality is also developed through identification with parents or other care-givers. Identification is a learning process, whereby children adopt the values of their parents through modeling and reinforcement. Self-concept and self-esteem are developed through identification and play a life-time role in aspiration and achievement. Self-concept is also affected by socioeconomic class, the mother's level of education, the sex of the child and the respective sex of the parents. Self-concept continues to be affected by traditional sex-role stereotypes, though slow changes may be taking place.

The adolescent identity crisis is a common development, which results partly from the conflict between physiological maturation and lingering childhood behavior patterns. The adolescent is trying to establish new relationships with adults and peers and to find an appropriate sense of self. As maturity is reached, most young adults share the basic concepts of their parents.

Chronological Overview

Newborn	beginning of sex-typing through parents' response to child's sex
	temperamental characteristics are apparent soon after birth
Infancy	focus on feeding, attachment, oral gratification
0–6 months:	stranger anxiety appears
1 year:	stranger anxiety declines
	separation anxiety appears
2 years:	discovery of autonomy
	sensitivity to sex-role stereotyping

Preschool   desire to master tasks
jealousy and rivalry with siblings and peers
identification with meaningful model

Childhood   productivity
conflict due to feelings of inferiority
challenges to self-concept and self-esteem

Adolescence   struggle for identity
identity crisis

Applying Your Knowledge

1. Why should parents be sensitive to their children's differences in temperament?

2. How can teachers best explain to parents their children's separation protest when left at school? What advice might the teacher give the parent in dealing with the problem?

3. What might be some ways of studying the attachment bond between child and parent?

Further Readings

Bettelheim, Bruno. *The uses of enchantment: the meaning and importance of fairy tales.* New York: Knopf, 1976. A fascinating analysis of how fairy tales facilitate healthy personality and emotional development.
Hardback.

Bowlby, John. *Maternal care and mental health.* New York: Schocken, 1966. Bowlby's classic work, which was presented to the World Health Organization and was the impetus for major policy action protecting the welfare of homeless children.
Paperback.

Brazelton, T. Berry, M.D. *Toddlers and parents.* New York: Dell, 1974. A description of young children's typical struggles for independence and self-mastery and the critical time for both parents and children.
Paperback.

Erikson, Erik H. *Identity: youth and crisis.* New York: W. W. Norton, 1968. Review and reevaluation of the identity crisis of youth.
Paperback.

Kagan, Jerome. *Personality development.* New York: Harcourt Brace Jovanovich, 1969. An overview highlighting the major areas of personality development.
Paperback.

Chapter **10**
Socialization

When Michael, the youngest of three brothers, was four years old, he seized a carton of milk and threw it at his oldest brother, Eric, aged eight. Aside from the mess that someone had to clean up, did this incident have a deeper meaning? Did Michael learn such behavior on television? Did it show that the boy's parents had taught him by their example that violence pays? Was it an early warning sign of later delinquency? Did it mean that boys are aggressive or violent by nature?

The Process of Socialization

Definition

The process of *socialization*—learning the acceptable values and behavior of society—plays an important part in the developing personality. One observer put it this way:

> Twenty years is all we have to accomplish the task of civilizing the infants who are born into our midst each year. These savages know nothing of our language, our culture, our religion, our values . . . communism, fascism, democracy, civil liberties, the rights of the minority . . . respect, decency, honesty, customs, conventions, and manners . . . . (A. Siegel 1973, page 1).

Socialization: learning the acceptable values and behavior of the society to which one belongs

Learning all these things—successful socialization—affects an individual's realization of his or her own humanity. Humanity involves respect for others, which is impossible without self-respect. Thus, socialization is far more than learning a set of rules. Rules are part of socialization, but developing a positive self-concept is the other essential part. And, as we saw in the last chapter, identifying with an adult who is a constructive model is an important means of attaining a good self-concept.

Theories of social and moral development

Social (observational) learning According to social learning theory (see Chapters 7 and 9), children acquire most of their social concepts—the rules by which they live—from models whom they observe in the course of daily life, particularly parents, care-givers, teachers, peers. Part of this learning includes developing a conscience and also becoming (psychologically) male or female. They learn to develop and/or control dependence, independence, achievement, aggression, sexuality. Attachment is also part of the process (Lavatelli and Stendler 1972).

There is no hard-and-fast distinction between the subtle processes of identification and socialization. All the available models are the sources of socialization, and they teach children how to behave in the particular part of the world in which they live. Much of this teaching by modeling may not be explicit. Rules of behavior are absorbed as the personality is shaped. Thus, a parent who spanks is modeling and implicitly teaching aggression, even though the spanking is explicitly intended to stop a child's aggressive behavior.

Some children are more receptive than others to the influence of a model, depending on their personality. For instance, if they have a low opinion of themselves, or have a strong need for others' approval, children are more likely to imitate. According to the social learning theory, the models most likely to be imitated are those who are nurturant—warm, rewarding, and affectionate—like a mother or care-giver (Lavatelli and Stendler 1972).

But learning from a model is only part (although a major part) of socialization. Cognition—understanding what is learned through modeling—is necessary if an individual is to develop a moral code of behavior, to translate actions into ideas of right and wrong. Theorists generally agree that cognitive development is a factor in how children come to understand from models the rules that are supposed to govern their actions. Ability to grasp certain concepts depends on reaching appropriate levels of maturity. And yet no social or moral development can take place unless a child has a chance to interact with others (Kohlberg 1964).

Piaget's six dimensions Piaget, the leading theorist of cognitive development (see Chapter 5), recognized the link between cognitive and moral development and theorized that there are at least six major dimensions of moral development. For example, the cognitive limitations of a child who is between the ages of three and eight lead to confusion between moral rules and physical rules. Such a child sees the rules of behavior as fixed, immutable. Right is right and wrong is wrong and there is nothing in between. These rules appear to the youngster to be imposed from outside, like the rising and setting of the sun, not subject to human judgments (Piaget 1932).

Here are six of Piaget's dimensions of moral development:

1. *Intentionality in judgment.* A child of four is apt to judge an act in terms of physical consequences; an older child (aged

Intentionality: conscious motivation leading to action

nine) is likely to judge *intent* to do harm. For example, younger children think accidentally breaking five cups is more reprehensible than breaking one cup in the process of stealing some jam. Older children take the reverse position.

2. *Relativism in judgment.* A young child sees an action as either totally right or totally wrong and thinks everyone has the same view. In case of conflict, the adult's view is considered right. But older children accept the possibility that opinions differ.

Relativism: perceptions that include several points of view

3. *Independence of sanctions* Younger children judge an act bad because it will be punished. Older children judge actions without regard to sanctions: they deem an act to be bad because it violates a rule or harms other people.

Sanctions: punishment

4. *Use of reciprocity* "Do unto others" is not understood by younger children, and reciprocity is not their reason for giving consideration to other people. Not until about ten do children have the idea that they should treat others as they have been treated. When this idea does take shape, however, it is likely to be acted out concretely, as in hitting back. Somewhat later, between 11 and 13, the idea of putting oneself in the place of others emerges.

Reciprocity: mutual actions

5. *Use of punishment as restitution and reform.* Severe punishment is a young child's idea of making up for wrongdoing. As the individual grows older, the child is more likely to favor milder punishment, redress in the form of restitution, or attempts to reform the wrongdoer.

Restitution: restoration or reimbursement

6. *Naturalistic views of misfortune.* A younger child is likely to consider accidents that follow misdeeds as punishments from God. But older children have a more sophisticated attitude.

Naturalistic: pertaining to matters that are beyond human control

All six aspects of moral judgment seem to reflect cognitive development, and all are related to IQ as well as to age (Kohlberg 1964). An illustration of Piaget's findings comes from a study of 75 first, third, and fifth graders, who were asked to judge various questions (Lockhart, Abrahams, and Osherson 1977). Four groups of questions related to conventionality, a fifth group dealt with moral rules, and a sixth with physical laws. *Social convention*, in this context, relates to meanings of words, rules of a game, laws of the state, and rules of etiquette. Physical laws relate to such matters as gravity. Moral laws relate to problems like taking things that belong to somebody else.

Social convention: agreed-upon customs and practices of a cohesive group of people

The study showed that children's ability to distinguish between social convention and physical law increases with age. But before the distinction is made, children evidently pass through an intermediate stage in which they believe that both physical laws and social conventions can be changed. In the last stage, they become aware that society can change conventions—for example, eating with a fork instead of fingers is a social practice, which could be altered—but the law of gravity cannot be repealed. Children's willingness to change social conventions through mutual consent also increases with age, but they find some conventions more difficult to change than others. They are most reluctant to change moral rules.

Kohlberg's stages Lawrence Kohlberg's theory of social and moral development is somewhat similar to Piaget's. He, too, sees a clear relationship to cognitive development. But Kohlberg divides moral development into six stages, which appear to be the same in at least eight different societies. Each stage is related to cognitive development. The stages are divided into three levels: preconventional, conventional, and postconventional (Kohlberg 1964).

The first two stages, which include the childhood years through early puberty, are on the *preconventional* level. Moral judgments depend on considerations like punishment and unquestioning deference to authority. This level of judgment involves not so much morality as practical convenience. In the first stage, until about ten, a child simply does what is required to keep out of trouble with parents. For example: "Watch out! If you take your brother's cake, Mommy will spank you!" This is the *punishment and obedience orientation*.

The second stage—the *instrumental–relativist orientation*—is almost equally pragmatic. A child considers an act right if it satisfies his or her own needs (instrumental orientation) or occasionally someone else's (relativist orientation).

The two next stages, on the *conventional* level, begin in late adolescence, around 16, and continue into adulthood. Respect for authority governs this moral period. In the third stage a person behaves well simply to please other people. A high school student stays away from a rough crowd because parents would certainly disapprove. This is the *good-boy–nice-girl orientation*.

A slightly more elevated stance comes in stage four, when the individual begins to think about the needs of society as a whole

Preconventional morality: moral judgments that reflect a concern for physical consequences and personal needs

Conventional morality: moral judgment governed by adherence to authority and strives to live up to social rules for their own sake. The orientation is toward *law and order*. Mercy killing would be condemned because the law and religious teachings frown on euthanasia.

A very small proportion of adults reach the third, or *postconventional*, level described by Kohlberg: belief in higher principles of justice independent of personal consequences. Those who are at stage five, the *social contract–legalistic orientation*, take the position that society depends on a complex network of agreed-upon rules and modes of conduct. Even if one does not agree personally with those rules, still one has an obligation to conform and to work to secure change through the means provided by the

Postconventional morality: moral judgments independent of personal consequences and social convention; belief in higher principles of justice

---

Box 10–1 How Kohlberg Graded Moral Development

Motivation for Moral Action

Stage 1: Punishment—Danny, age 10: (Should Joe tell on his older brother to his father?) "In one way it would be right to tell on his brother or his father might get mad at him and spank him. In another way it would be right to keep quiet or his brother might beat him up."

Stage 2: Exchange and Reward—Jimmy, age 13: (Should Joe tell on his older brother to his father?) "I think he should keep quiet. He might want to go someplace like that, and if he squeals on Alex, Alex might squeal on him."

Stage 3: Disapproval Concern—Andy, age 16: (Should Joe keep quiet about what his brother did?) "If my father finds out later, he won't trust me. My brother wouldn't either, but I wouldn't have a *conscience* that he (my

brother) didn't." "I try to do things for my parents; they've always done things for me. I try to do everything my mother says; I try to please her. Like she wants me to be a doctor, and I want to, too, and she's helping me to get up there."

Stage 6: Self-condemnation Concern—Bill, age 16: (Should the husband steal the expensive black market drug needed to save his wife's life?) "Lawfully no, but morally speaking I think I would have done it. It would be awfully hard to live with myself afterward, knowing that I could have done something which would have saved her life and yet didn't for fear of punishment to myself."

Basis of Moral Worth of a Human Life

Stage 1: Life's Value Based on Physical and Status Aspects—Tommy, age 10: (Why should the druggist give the drug

Source: Review of Child Development, ed. by M. L. and L. W. Hoffman, © 1964 by Russell Sage Foundation, New York.

system. Individuals who operate on this level might allow themselves to be drafted to fight a war with which they are not in sympathy, but would bend every effort, within legal bounds, to end the war.

Stage six, Kohlberg's highest stage, is oriented toward *universal ethical principles*, moral standards common to all societies. One's own conscience is the sole criterion of right conduct. But the individual has strict standards: logical, comprehensive, universal, consistent. In effect, the law is considered subordinate to higher principles of justice. Some would break the law in favor of these higher principles and accept the legal consequences. (See Box 10–1.)

to the dying woman when her husband couldn't pay for it?) "If someone important is in a plane and is allergic to heights and the stewardess won't give him medicine because she's only got enough for one and she's got a sick one, a friend, in back, they'd probably put the stewardess in a lady's jail because she didn't help the important one."

(Is it better to save the life of one important person or a lot of unimportant people?) "All the people that aren't important because one man just has one house, maybe a lot of furniture, but a whole bunch of people have an awful lot of furniture and some of these poor people might have a lot of money and it doesn't look it."

Stage 2: Life's Value as Instrumental to Need-Satisfaction—Tommy at age 13: (Should the doctor "mercy-kill" a fatally ill woman requesting death because of her pain?) "Maybe it would be good to put her out of her pain, she'd be better off

that way. But the husband wouldn't want it, it's not like an animal. If a pet dies you can get along without it—it isn't something you really need. Well, you can get a new wife, but it's not really the same."

Stage 4: Life Sacred Because of a Social and Religious Order—John, age 16: (Should the doctor "mercy-kill" the woman?) "The doctor wouldn't have the right to take a life, no human has the right. He can't create life, he shouldn't destroy it."

Stage 6: Life's Value as Expressing the Sacredness of the Individual—Steve, age 16: (Should the husband steal the expensive drug to save his wife?) "By the law of society he was wrong but by the law of nature or of God the druggist was wrong and the husband was justified. Human life is above financial gain. Regardless of who was dying, if it was a total stranger, man has a duty to save him from dying."

Progression from one of these stages to the next depends not only on a person's cognitive development but also on opportunities to be exposed to new ideas and new experiences. For example, individuals generally do not pass from stage four to stage five until late adolescence or early adulthood. By then they have been subjected to a great many different individual and cultural values, which lead them to believe that stage four is inadequate. People move from stage to stage by a process of rejection and construction. They realize the contradictions of their previous beliefs, see that those ideas are illogical, and move on to a new stance (Turiel 1974).

Guilt and conscience theories   Guilt goes along with conscience at any stage, since none of us meets our own standards all the time. Developmental theory suggests that conscience and its component, guilt, stem directly from parents. A strong conscience and strong guilt feelings depend on how close the relationship has been between parent and child. Warmth and love, childish dependence, discipline that relies on *love withdrawal*, strong par-

Love withdrawal: expressing disappointment in or disapproval of an individual

Box 10–2   Cheating

Can children be taught to be honest? If so, who should do the teaching? A pioneering study, designed to answer questions relating to character and moral behavior in general, was conducted with a large number of New York school children in the 1920s. The findings are still of considerable interest today.

The investigators worked out various "character" tests. In attempting to measure honesty, they devised 14 situations that might reveal who would cheat in school, in athletics, in games, at parties, and in school homework. For example, in the classroom they gave pupils an opportunity to copy test answers from a sheet that was supposed to be used for corrections only *after* the examination. In

another situation, they determined which students added answers to a test after time was called. They also discovered who violated rules in solving a puzzle and which children opened their eyes when doing a stunt that was supposed to be performed with eyes closed. In each situation, the investigators devised hidden ways of discovering who had cheated.

The results were surprising. Evidently there are no totally honest children and no totally dishonest children. Very few cheated 23 times in 23 chances. Very few were honest 23 times in 23 chances. Most of the subjects were honest sometimes and dishonest sometimes.

No connection was found between

ental role-modeling and high expectations for the child: all these are factors in building both conscience and guilt.

Some theorize that a parent who is perceived as powerful both inside and outside the family circle is an especially potent source of conscience and guilt. Psychoanalytic theories suggest additional reasons for feelings of guilt; some people may harbor these feelings as a form of self-punishment. Freud's explanation relates to the existence of a superego—reflector of parental conscience and societal rules—distinct from the rest of the personality (Kohlberg 1963). (See Chapter 9, page 352.) Almost all the theories about guilt, however, are connected with early rearing and parent–child relationships. In fact, theorists agree that the entire process of socialization starts at home. (See Box 10–2.)

Family and Discipline

Parents' role

Many a parent has longed for a child-raising manual like a cookbook, which would give precise instructions on how to socialize a

cheating and a child's "moral code." Both cheaters and noncheaters had the same conventional ideas about what was right and what was wrong. Nor was there any correlation between age and conduct, although the older ones were a little more inclined to cheat than the younger ones. And boys and girls were equally likely to cheat.

Children who regularly attended Sunday school were no more honest than children who rarely went. However, there was some connection between the very fact of Sunday school enrollment and a better level of conduct. The investigators suggest that this may mean that families with higher standards at least try to send their children to religious school classes. In effect, family training may be the responsible factor, rather than formal religious schooling.

In fact, the only strong correlation the researchers found was in a comparison of the homes of the 50 most honest and the 50 most dishonest children. The cheaters' homes were full of discord, there was no discipline, and the family economic and social situation tended to be chaotic or changing. The attitudes of schoolteachers also seemed influential. The pupils of cooperative, sympathetic teachers were likely to be more honest than students in classes where teachers were arbitrary and dictatorial (Hartshorne and May 1928, 1930; Hartshorne, May, and Shuttleworth 1930).

child. B. F. Skinner, the noted behaviorist, complained wryly that the trouble with the family is that "the instruction book doesn't come with the baby" (Conversation with B. F. Skinner 1977, page 56).

No job, whether paid or unpaid, could be more frustrating and unpredictable than parenthood. (However, being a parent's child runs a close second.) For no other vocation is the preparation so catch-as-catch-can, if not entirely nonexistent. Parenthood may be the prime unskilled occupation in our society. At a time when special training, education, and experience are required for almost every other vocation, there are no educational requirements or restrictions for people who, whether by design or inadvertence, become fathers and mothers. Nevertheless, the kind of job done by these untrained mentors of the next generation can have far-reaching consequences.

A changing responsibility   The guidelines for parents change all the time, not only as society changes but also as particular parents and their children grow older. Family influences are not the same as they used to be. We live differently and the trends affect our children.

In years past, two parents used to be the usual number. No more. Besides the increasing number of one-parent families, many families in effect have more than two "parents," as more people marry more than once.

Another important change is the greater involvement of fathers in day-to-day child care. However, most of the research continues to concentrate on mothers, since it is the female who bears the child. And in most instances it is still the woman who has the major role in the upbringing of infants and preschoolers, a period that psychologists agree is crucial in determining how a person will develop. Nevertheless, many parents aspire to eliminate sexism in the upbringing of their sons and daughters. They would like to blur old-fashioned distinctions between how girls and boys should behave. But they do not necessarily know how to pull off this complicated maneuver in a society that continues to be deeply divided along sexist lines (Eiduson, Cohen, and Alexander 1973).

Another goal for some present-day parents is to do away with what they consider to be artificial taboos concerning sexuality, intimacy, and nudity. Earlier sophistication, earlier personal decision-making are encouraged. Competition is frowned upon. Sensory impressions are emphasized. Many parents insist that their children ought to develop as individuals and should not adopt them as role models. Yet those same parents cannot help fostering some of their own values (Eiduson, Cohen, and Alexander 1973).

Parents' questions Principles aside, parents continue to be in doubt about the specifics of child-rearing. Middle-class mothers of preteenagers listed no less than 12 specific areas in which they would have liked to have guidance (Guerney and Drake 1973). Discipline and training, particularly for preschoolers—and especially for two-and-a-half-year-old boys—bothered mothers the most. Many of their questions were of the "how to" variety. For example: What to do when a child refuses to go to school? How to woo a child from his pacifier (or thumb, or blanket)?

When was a key word in another important group of concerns: When should a child be expected to do thus or so? When will my son or daughter be able to understand how someone else feels? And *how much:* How much discipline is appropriate before, say, the age of three?

But authorities cannot give hard-and-fast answers about the consequences of the various child-rearing styles. A variety of studies done in the past 40 years do link disciplinary techniques with children's behavior and personality. But all the findings are tentative and hedged with many *ifs*, *ands*, and *buts*.

Love versus power Research seems to show that it is overly simplistic to group parents into two camps: permissive versus nonpermissive. *How* discipline is applied seems to be crucial. A parent who is *love-oriented* will generally use a combination of positive methods, like praise and reasoning, with negative methods that threaten the withdrawal of love by showing disappointment and disapproval. In contrast, some parents use *power-assertive techniques:* physical punishment, threats, yelling. However, even new-style parents may be ambivalent about using violence. They often let their children work out their own arguments without adult interference. But they may intervene in the interests of safety, and at times they resort to old-fashioned physical discipline (Eiduson, Cohen, and Alexander 1973).

Psychologists suspect that different approaches to discipline may have very different results. The child who has been disciplined with love will grow up with a conscience. That individual will in effect be trying to please Mother and Father and will feel guilty when behavior does not measure up to what was taught.

Love-oriented discipline: use of approval and/or disapproval to instill behavioral standards

Power-assertive techniques: strong and authoritarian disciplinary behavior

ambivalent

All this adds up to feelings of responsibility. Such a person will also be more likely to have cooperative relationships with other people, an extension of the desire to please.

In contrast, those people reared by the assertion of power will have learned only the uses of power and as a result will behave aggressively, less cooperatively, and perhaps with hostility. Both restrictive and permissive parents may be either warm or hostile. Their attitudes may make as much difference in the human product as their basic standards. A comprehensive study of child-rearing techniques showed that parents who use psychological methods of discipline rather than physical punishment with overly aggressive preschoolers get the best results (Sears, Maccoby, and Levin 1957).

In general, restrictiveness seems to cause children to be controlled but also fearful and dependent. Their intellectual drives may be dulled. They may conceal feelings of hostility. Children brought up permissively may turn out to be outgoing, social, striving, and yet may be less persistent, more aggressive (Becker 1964).

Positive and negative reinforcement   Positive and negative reinforcement are useful disciplinary tools. For example, in an obedience training program for mothers and nursery school children, the mother moved away if the child disobeyed (Toepfer, Reuter, and Maurer 1972). It was demonstrated that for preschoolers mother's presence can be an effective reward for obedience. This is an illustration of the power of reinforcement in social learning. (See also Chapter 7, pages 271–272.)

Verbal explanations are more effective than physical punishment. Older children, as young as first and second graders, are more amenable to reasoning than to reproaches (Leizer and Rogers 1974). Similarly, youngsters seem to learn best how to control their own behavior if the parents explain in so many words what the child has done wrong, what happened to lead up to the wrongdoing, and the bad consequences of the action both for the child and for other people (Aronfreed and Reber 1965). What happens is this: the child identifies with a loving model (mother or father); the child adopts the values of that model; when the child transgresses, the model shows displeasure and the child feels guilt. So in order to keep the affection of the model (parent), the child behaves without being forced to do so (Parke 1967).

If the model–parent had relied solely on spanking or some other external punishment, the "bad feeling" might be associated with the punishment and not the wrongdoing. In fact, in some cases spanking can do the opposite of what is intended. When aggression of some kind is being punished, spanking gives the child a model of the very activity that the parents wish to suppress. In contrast, a care-giver's signs of displeasure—in effect, a temporary withdrawal of love—activate conscience and the internal controls of conduct.

Whatever the punishment, it serves the purpose only if applied immediately. Waiting "till Daddy comes home" destroys the link between an act and its consequences. The lesson is lost (Aronfreed and Reber 1965).

Parents' temperament   The parent's own temperament will influence child-rearing techniques and their ultimate consequences. For example, a domineering mother may create in her child feelings of hostility and a craving for power, which are reflected in the way the child deals with peers and people in authority. A father's influence may be felt more indirectly. How he treats his wife may color her actions toward their children (Hoffman 1960). Some mothers are particularly strict because they feel their children are extensions of themselves and they feel overly responsible for their children's achievements and behavior (Halverson and Waldrop 1970).

A mother who has provided acceptance and affection during the early school years is likely to produce an adolescent boy who will conform to the standards she has instilled. As for girls, their eventual conformity and dependence seem to be connected with how severe and restrictive their mothers have been during the ages of four to seven (Kagan and Freeman 1963). However, as a child becomes older—and is increasingly emancipated from both parents—both praise and blame seem less immediate and crucial (Guardo and Meisels 1971).

Maturity factor   In any event, parental techniques must change as the child matures. What is effective in dealing with an eight-month-old who is in the midst of Erikson's trust–mistrust crisis may not work with an 18-month-old who has passed into the stage of autonomy versus shame and doubt. The degree of parental control must vary accordingly. Overcontrol can keep a child dependent too long, personality development and socialization

stalled. Mother or father goes on doing things for son or daughter after the child should really be able to do those things unaided.

But overcontrol can produce a different unfortunate effect. Parents who go on supervising too long get into the habit. They cannot easily stop. Instead of giving children responsibility, they think for them. Where to draw the line? Everything depends on the child's maturity level (Millar 1968).

Fathers

The father of our country became an instant parent when he married a widow with two children. Washington once wrote that he thought a father has "only two things principally to consider, the improvement of his son, and the finances to do it with."

This old-fashioned attitude is not uncommon in this day and age. Many people still think fathers' usefulness is limited to providing money for the household and laying down the law to adolescent sons. But lately researchers have made efforts to find out how important fathers are as compared with mothers and how the male parent affects the socialization and personality development of his son or daughter, even in the most conventional household (Lamb 1975).

Early influence   During early infancy, Father's role is minimal and indirect—or at least so it has been assumed, though not proven. It is now thought that fathers are extremely influential later on in the developmental process, although this, too, is not extensively documented (Lamb 1976).

There does seem to be some evidence that even in a family where the father goes to work and the mother stays home and tends the infant, the father makes some difference in a baby's life. Though most mothers take care of the endless physical needs of babies, most fathers also hold them and play with them. Babies obviously love it when fathers toss them in the air, a cheerful way of launching the process of socialization (Lamb 1975).

In any case, as the baby grows a little older, paternal roughhousing is common. By excited laughter at the "pretend" falls the infant shows enormous pleasure in father's attention. Before long, Daddy's arrival is an event to be anticipated with real excitement (Burlingham 1973).

Perhaps the very novelty of the father's attention gives him special value to a child. Children tend to take their mothers for granted, but anything a father says or does acquires such importance that it is more likely to be remembered, perhaps for years. In many homes, a father does not *have* to change diapers; what he does for his offspring is up to him. He can be free to do the parenting job according to his own particular style and inclination (Pedersen and Robson 1969).

Different masculine approach   Whether by masculine inclination or simply through lack of opportunity, fathers "talk" to their infants very little, much less than mothers do. In the first three months, even the fathers who do the most vocalizing spend only about ten minutes a day making sounds to their babies (Rebelsky and Hanks 1971).

A recent study of the interaction of 20 18-month-olds with their mothers, and an equal number with their fathers, shows that both the babies and their fathers related very differently from the mother–baby combinations. For example, parents talked to and tended to play more with the same sex than with opposite-sex infants. The mothers and fathers had different styles of dealing with their children. When the babies were close to the mothers, the mothers were more likely to look, talk to them, touch, sit on the floor, and play with their children. Mothers had a greater tendency to respond to children's vocalizations by looking at them or talking to them (Weinraub and Frankel 1977).

But later on fathers loom ever more important as socializing agents. Children commonly view their fathers as formidable figures, potential punishers, the source of household law. In contrast, the mothers are seen as "nicer," more likely to give presents (Kagan and Lemkin 1960). One study showed that both boys and girls think that daddies are smarter than mommies (Howe 1971).

Consequently, a father's praise and scolding both appear to be and actually may be more important and more effective than the mother's. But a father who is a habitual punisher causes the child to feel psychologically distant (Guardo and Meisels 1971).

Six- to eight-year-olds see their fathers as stronger, larger, darker, dirtier, more angular, and more dangerous than their mothers (Kagan, Hosken, and Watson 1961). These perceptions are not necessarily related to reality. When Michael, as a grade schooler, watched his mother discard old clothes, he called one of his father's shirts the "spanking shirt." But in that family, the corporal punishment had actually been done by the mother.

Both mothers' and fathers' influence on their children's behavior varies according to the age of the child. As children grow older, their perceptions of their parents commonly undergo a developmental change. For example, one study discovered that second graders saw their mothers as more accepting than their fathers. But children viewed their parents as progressively less accepting from grades two through four for fathers and from grades three to four for mothers. Mothers were considered more controlling than fathers, but at each higher grade children's assessment of the degree of control dropped significantly. The reason for the change in attitude may be that children spend less and less time with parents as they grow older, and parents expect children to be more independent as time goes on (Burger, Lamp, and Rogers 1975).

Father absence Children without fathers may have a harder time growing up to function successfully in the world as we know it today (Duncan and Duncan 1969). To be fatherless even during the first two years of life might have later consequences in terms of a child's socialization and personality development. By the time the child is ten, detrimental characteristics could appear (Santrock 1970). This finding supports Erikson's contention that building basic trust in the first stage of life is an essential foundation for later stages. (As we saw in Chapter 9, personality development is intimately involved with the models provided by both parents.)

There is also such a thing as psychological absence. A father can be away for most practical purposes even if he is living in the home but takes hardly any part in child-rearing or decision-making. This kind of neglect can be hard on both boys and girls (Rosen and Teague 1974).

A boy who has had too little attention and affection from his father is apt to feel rejected. He may have a sense of alienation from his family and the world at large, may be less happy, less achievement-oriented, may have a greater need to manipulate and control other people. In contrast, an affectionate father is more likely to be his son's confidant, a source of identification and direction (Mussen et al. 1963).

Some statistics show that many delinquents have been brought up without a father. A father's absence when the child is between the ages of four and seven seems to be most significant. A boy who has had the advantage of positive fathering by a substitute or a stepfather may be less likely to find himself in the toils of the law during adolescence (Anderson 1968; Chapman 1977). Other factors may also compensate for the absence of a male parent. It might be an older male sibling (Wohlford et al. 1971) or a well-adjusted, optimistic, not overly permissive mother (Kopf 1970).

The reasons why the father has been absent also may have something to do with the effect on children. Psychological profiles of children whose fathers have been in jail resemble those of juvenile delinquents. It is possible, of course, that troubled family relationships before the father left could have been the cause (Moerk 1973). Boys seem to be more affected than girls. Without an appropriate sex-role model in the home, at least around the ages of 9 to 11, boys may have adjustment problems (LeCorgne and Laosa 1976; Hoffman 1971). (See also Chapter 9, pages 377–384.)

Not every investigator agrees that fatherlessness necessarily leads to children's antisocial behavior (Atkinson and Ogston

1974). It may be that the youngsters without fathers are the ones more likely to be arrested. Studies of large groups of juveniles showed that the number arrested does not indicate the actual number involved in illegal actions. Many violators remain undiscovered (Hoover 1965). Therefore, the absent father–juvenile delinquency data may be suspect because they come only from statistics on young people who have actually been apprehended.

Mothers

Working mothers Not too long ago, American society would have equated a working mother with an absent father in terms of the damage done to children. But research fails to support the notion that children's socialization suffers if their mothers are employed outside the home. Rather, *satisfied* mothers, whether or not they work at paid jobs, appear to have the best-adjusted children (Banducci 1967; Etaugh 1974). The assumption that mothers at work leave their children unsupervised, and that therefore those children become delinquent, is also struck down by recent studies. True, insufficient supervision is often related to delinquency—but that happens regardless of the mother's employment status. Working mothers do not have more delinquency among their children than nonworking mothers (Hoffman 1974).

What seems to matter most is the *stability* of the home environment and the mother's own attitude toward her work. Delinquency has been found to occur more often where mothers were occasionally employed than in homes where the mother had a regular job. The occasionally employed mother may be a sign of an unstable home with an inadequate or frequently absent father or male figure and/or an unstable marriage (Glueck and Glueck 1957).

The psychological harm that can come to children when the mother works outside the home usually develops if there is no good substitute child care, or if the home is filled with tensions because the parents have not succeeded in coming to terms with their life-style. Maternal outside employment alone does not seem to be linked to problems for the children. The stability of the home seems to be the key (Woods 1972).

Social class and cultural differences

When George Bernard Shaw's Professor Higgins undertook to make a lady out of slum-reared Eliza, he had to teach her far more than how to avoid dropping her *h*'s. In this country we like to think we are narrowing social class differences. But in reality, differences in child-rearing and socialization practices do exist, depending on socioeconomic status and the parents' educational level.

Education   Middle-class mothers are much more verbal in dealing with their children. However, no matter what their status, all mothers tend to give children the same degree of physical attention (Tulkin and Kagan 1972). Higher-status, better-educated mothers have a greater tendency to be warmer, more understanding and accepting (Bayley and Schaefer 1960; Aronfreed and Reber 1965). They are less intrusive and prohibitive with little children (Minton, Kagan, and Levine 1971).

Lower-class mothers are apt to take a severe, punitive approach to toilet-training, modesty, sex play, and aggression. They may spank or use other physical methods of control. Verbal reasoning and praise are more often preferred by better-educated parents (Maccoby and Gibbs 1964).

Lower-class mothers try to teach their children respectability. Middle-class mothers may try to instill standards that will be a general guide to conduct or teach children to make the most of their attributes (Kohn 1959). Many of these differences obviously stem from the parents' previous education (Busse and Busse 1972).

A study of middle-class and lower-class families with sons aged 11 and 16 revealed an interesting power struggle among fathers, mothers, and sons. In the middle-class families, the father's power and influence were relatively secure no matter what the children's ages. In contrast, in the lower-class families, the father tended to lose influence to his adolescent son (Jacob 1974).

Culture   Socialization goals and practices also vary with the values and beliefs of a family's culture or subculture. For example, American mothers' care-giving style produces active, vocal babies, in contrast with the quiet, contented infants of Japanese families (Caudill and Weinstein 1969). Close-knit Chinese families, which provide plenty of care, security, and trust, develop children who are less prone to delinquency and aggression. But *assimilation* into the American mainstream and use of American child-rearing methods tend to cause these differences to disappear (Sollenberger 1968).

Assimilation (cultural): becoming part of a group by adopting its customs and practices

The varying classroom behavior of children from different cultural groups can probably be related to different child-rearing styles. Mexican-American and Chinese-American mothers teach obedience and respect for older people. In school, these children are more likely to accept what they are taught without much question. In contrast, Anglo children usually come from child-centered homes, and their freedom is reflected in how they act in school (Steward and Steward 1973).

It appears that Chinese children in Taiwan generally behave better than American children because Chinese parents typically use more reasoning and less physical punishment. Chinese mothers try to help their children understand, discuss motives, explain, point out consequences of aggressive behavior, and suggest other ways of solving conflicts (Niem and Collard 1972).

Mothers of the various groups have described the attitudes that result in the varied humans they send to school. The Chinese mother thinks teaching is an important part of her role. She gives regular formal instruction to her preschoolers. In contrast, the Chicana takes the position that she is the mother, not the teacher; teaching is the school's job. The Anglo is ambivalent. This mother sees teaching as only one of several roles.

A typical consequence of these varying maternal attitudes is that Chinese mothers ask the kindergarten teacher to call them if the child does not learn. Mothers of Mexican-American children want to be called if their children misbehave (Steward and Steward 1973).

Cultural differences in mothers' attitudes may be the reason why some minority groups have trouble becoming assimilated into the dominant Anglo society in this country. Cultural differences may also have something to do with the difficulty the various groups have in understanding one another (Caudill and Weinstein 1969). The children have simply been socialized differently.

However, assimilation has its own problems. For instance, the Chinese communities in this country used to have exceptionally low delinquency rates, presumably because of their close-knit family lives and conscientious rearing by warm, caring mothers. But the more the groups become assimilated, the fewer differences between their behavior and the behavior of the community at large (Sollenberger 1968).

Communal child-rearing Children are affected in still other ways by the unique child-rearing practices of a *kibbutz*. A small

Kibbutz: Israeli communal settlement

percentage of Israelis live in these communal, partly agricultural communities, which give children the benefit of group rearing part of the day and parental care the rest of the time. The kibbutz system has been eyed by some Americans as a possible solution for our own child-rearing problems. They hope that a similar system in this country might be a creative way not only to solve the baby-sitting problem for working mothers but also perhaps to eliminate troublesome "youth problems."

Psychologists who have studied the kibbutzim report that children's lives there are distinctly different from life in a nuclear American family. These collectives vary in size, up to several hundred families. Children live apart from their parents and are reared in age groups, each group in the charge of a *metapelet*—nurse, teacher, care-giver. The parents continue to be the primary nurturers, although parent–child contact is less constant than in our society and also less than in Israeli nuclear families.

In the kibbutz, children have much to do with their peers, spend very little time totally alone, and become accustomed very early to being separated from their parents for a day or two. The result is that kibbutz children learn independence much earlier than American children.

The metapelet is usually the children's disciplinarian, so the parents are free to represent only warmth and nurturance to their children. Children have a much greater circle of loved ones than ours do. Peers and the metapelet may well be included among those to whom they go for warmth and security.

Another striking difference from our ways is that kibbutz children are not economically dependent on parents. All, children and adults alike, take their sustenance from the commune. Therefore, kibbutz children tend to be more independent and autonomous.

The result of this new kind of upbringing is that kibbutz adolescents do not seem to have the same conflicts with parents as American teenagers. They do not have to fight for their freedom. They already have it.

Day care   Would such a system work in this country? Obviously, our current economic and social situation would make kibbutz-type rearing difficult. While we do have some communal living groups in the United States, they have yet to be studied in any significant way. A more frequent approach to outside-the-home rearing in this country are day-care centers for preschoolers. We have already noted that day care seems to have little effect on the attachment behavior of young children (see Chapter 9, page 371). As for the effects of nursery school or day care on children's socialization, the findings are not clear-cut.

One investigator reported that very young children in high-quality day care differ very little from children reared at home (Doyle 1975). But another study showed that three- and four-year-olds in day care from infancy became more aggressive, more active, less cooperative with adults, leading to the conclusion that such children acquire adult cultural values more slowly than others (Schwarz, Strickland, and Krolick 1974). It may be that the age at which children start in day care and the quality of the day care are factors.

Peers and Socialization

Children reveal their developing socialization in the games they play, in the way they treat other people, in their fears, and in the way they live up to the rules at home and in school. A parent or teacher who watches children with understanding and sympathy can often deduce what influences have been socializing the immature individual and perhaps even what kind of adult the child will become.

Play

Play has an important role in a child's psychological and social development. Through play children test acceptable behavior, learn from their companions, and expand their socialization. "Child's play," an expression that usually means something trivial and unimportant, is nothing of the kind, according to Freud. He called play a child's first great cultural and psychological achievement.

A link with the real world   Play is a child's language, a way of communicating, of mastering the world, and of asserting oneself. Fantasy or imaginative play seems to be a link between what goes on inside us and the real world outside. The "rules" of play are a child's own rules, a chance to make life according to the child's own design. But when play runs into the limits imposed by reality—as when a tower of blocks falls down—the child realizes it is necessary to yield to what is (Bettelheim 1972).

Play is an important learning activity and form of self-expression. Play is said to be "the natural work of children," a

natural work
of children
form of self-expression

symbolic expression of their personalities. When a child is free to play without the interference of chaotic or dangerous surroundings (as in a ghetto area), the youngster has a better chance of learning and coping with later experiences; sensual and perceptive "pores" seem to be open and receptive (Borowitz, Hirsch, and Costello 1970).

As we saw in Chapter 5, Piaget believed play was a demonstration of a child's intelligence, an indication of what the child knows or guesses about the world. In effect, the youngster is enjoying the pleasure of mastery. Part of play is imitation, mimicking adults, whether it is a six-month-old clapping hands like Mother, or a three-year-old pretending to talk on the phone like Daddy.

Exploration and experimentation   Another component of play is exploration. A baby plays with its own hands and finds out what they look like and what they can do. A 14-month-old empties all the cupboards to find out what is inside. A three-year-old manipulates toys to discover their properties: will they fall down, like blocks? break, like a plastic doll?

Destructive play often seems to be an innocent effort to get a new effect. The child is trying to find out whether a particular effort will have the expected result. By building or constructing, too, a child has a chance to find out what it is possible to do, and what is not possible (Sutton-Smith 1971).

Playing with peers   Wear a pot as a hat? Only the most whimsical of mothers or fathers would think of doing such a thing. But an 18-month-old toddler might use a pot that way, and the toddler's companion of the same age would probably do likewise. Even very young children can have friends whom they imitate and who give them new notions about using their toys (Rubenstein and Howes 1979). Peers—contemporaries—are influential at every stage of social development except earliest infancy.

Play, of course, is a prime means of learning how to get along with other people. At first, socializing is beyond the infant. Up to the age of a year, the baby is *solitary* and plays alone. Then, by 18 months, there may be a playing partner, usually a child the same age. But it is usually *parallel play*. Children may be side-by-side, they enjoy one another's company, but their play projects are generally quite separate. However, parallel play paves the way for social interaction. It provides valuable preliminary experience in dealing with others (Mueller and Brenner 1977).

Solitary play: playing alone

Parallel play: playing alongside a peer

Social interaction.

At four, play is usually *associative.* Two children may be playing at the same activity, but there is probably no interchange; they are not actually helping one another. *Cooperative play* does not usually begin until about the age of five, when there is real mutuality: rules are followed, ideas are exchanged.

As we saw in Chapter 9, boys' and girls' play are generally quite different, as a result of early sex-role stereotyping. Social class also seems to be related to the way children play with one another, again perhaps because of parents' differing socialization efforts. For instance, middle-class preschoolers are less likely to play in parallel fashion, more apt to cooperate with playmates and to embark on building projects of one kind or another (Rubin, Maioni, and Hornung 1976).

Associative play: playing at the same activity, but independently

Cooperative play: playing with a peer, exchanging ideas

Even television has an effect on play. One example is the nationally televised "Mister Rogers' Neighborhood," which has been shown to increase helping behavior in children who view it (Singer and Singer 1973).

Friends and associates

Influence in school   Just as peers are influential in toddlers' play, so are they agents of socialization for all age groups. Sociability seems to be a personality characteristic that appears relatively early in life.

Even in nursery school it is possible to rate a child's *sociometric status* and to see a pattern that is relatively stable through the first few grades of elementary school. Often by the time children are in kindergarten it is clear that some are more capable of making and keeping friends than others (Northway 1968; Waldrop and Halverson 1975).

Sociometric status: an individual's level of acceptance or rejection by members of a group

The reasons are uncertain. Is it because of the child's early relationships with adults? Experiences with other children? Some kind of genetic predisposition? No one yet knows the answer for sure, but probably all three influences play a part (Northway 1968).

Status   Social status and popularity appear in relatively young age groups. Studies have given some clues about what qualities children look for in their peers. Classmates almost always choose as their leaders children who are socially adept. And it develops that those children are usually healthier, more intelligent, higher achievers, and better adjusted (Harrison, Rawls, and Rawls 1971).

Fourth graders like classmates who are kind, who share toys and books, who invite everybody to their parties, who follow the rules of the game and take their turn as they should. They do not admire bullies, screamers, children who insist on having their own way (Smith 1950). On the other side of the equation, it seems that unpopular children fail to understand what it takes to attract friendship. Their social skills are undeveloped (Gottman, Gonson, and Rasmussen 1975).

Prejudice   As early as the beginning school years children show signs of prejudice and *ethnocentrism*—clannishness, chauvinism, a tendency to glorify their own "in" group and to reject those who

Ethnocentrism: believing one's own ethnic group is superior to others

seem weak or different. Their socialization appears to be related to such prejudices. Only a quarter of 1500 children aged 11 to 17 who were surveyed were found to be generally unprejudiced or "liberal" (Frenkel-Brunswik 1948).

Evidently the way children are treated by their parents is a critical factor. The liberal child is more likely than the ethnocentric child to have been treated as an equal by the parents, to have been given a chance to express feelings of rebellion or disagreement. The parents of prejudiced children are very much concerned with status. These parents are harsher disciplinarians. Their rigid standards are of the "do as I say or else" variety. Family relationships are often devoid of genuine affection. These prejudiced children sometimes feel neglected, rejected, unfairly punished. In general, they are pressured at home to conform to parental authority and parental social standards. They have no way of showing hostility. All this tends to create narrow, rigid personalities (Frenkel-Brunswik 1948).

From society's point of view, the most important problem posed by these prejudiced children is their rigid attitude toward authority. People who are forced to submit to their parents' domination to such an extreme probably conform only on the surface. Their simplistic antagonism to people who are different might turn into eventual blind destructiveness. Perhaps children with such tendencies might be helped to be less dogmatic in their social attitudes if they are somehow drawn into democratic participation in school. If they are exposed to a mix of permissiveness and guidance they might have a better chance of developing a genuine identification with society, and a chance for the international understanding that is in the best interests of us all (Frenkel-Brunswik 1948).

None of this necessarily means that the "liberal" child is perfectly adjusted. That group seems to have more open anxieties, more feelings of insecurity, more conflicts. But the young person is aware of them and, most important, does not tend to blame others (Frenkel-Brunswick 1948).

It would be unfair to charge parents alone for the simple racial stereotypes children pick up: blacks are thus-and-so, Germans are thus-and-so. These ideas are rife in society, and children absorb them regardless (Masangkay et al. 1972). Youngsters start very early to form a clear idea of the group to which they belong. Black preschoolers, for example, were asked to answer the question "Which one is you?" by selecting appropriate pictures. Some of the three-year-olds chose pictures of animals. But four-year-olds all selected pictures of children, usually black children (Clark and Clark 1939). To identify with one's own race seems to be a function of the socialization process.

But awareness of what one is does not necessarily mean liking oneself. A dramatic illustration of how social attitudes can affect children's personal attitudes comes from similar studies, done many years apart. Given a choice of black and white dolls and asked to choose which were "nice" and which looked "bad," in the late 1940s black children preferred white dolls and rejected the black ones (Clark and Clark 1947). But a generation later, after many changes in American society, a similar investigation determined that most of the black children preferred black dolls. Black had become beautiful (Hraba and Grant 1970; Harris and Braun 1971).

Young children's racial prejudices can be changed. Using standard training techniques, emphasizing reinforcement, white preschoolers learned to associate dark-skinned human figures with positive attributes, replacing previous negative connections (McMurtry and Williams 1972). The television program "Sesame Street," which included inserts showing nonwhites, was also effective in influencing three- to five-year-old white children to wish to play with nonwhites (Gorn, Goldberg, and Kanugo 1976).

Later social problems

Aggression   Just as prejudice is learned in the process of socialization, so do individuals learn to control aggression in the course of becoming socialized. Or, they can be socialized in the direction of violence.

The evidence seems to show that there are developmental stages, especially between the ages of two and four, when children normally tend toward violent expression of their feelings and may even experiment with cruelty. Theorists believe that how parents and care-givers cope with these childish impulses will determine whether aggressiveness will become a way of life or will instead be channeled into more constructive expression (Lourie 1973).

The obvious way to diminish childish aggression is for a parent to disapprove. After Michael threw the milk carton (in the beginning of this chapter), he was probably feeling guilty about having given in to such an impulse. He had learned full well in that particular household that such acts would not be tolerated. As Erikson explained, it is in the preschool years that children learn (usually from parents) to curb certain kinds of initiative. They suffer guilt feelings when they fail to meet the standards parents have been teaching. Later on, it is the responsibility of teachers to intervene when somebody tries to commit mayhem on the playground. But if teachers ignore or do not see what is happening, classmates are apt to encourage the aggressor (Smith and Green 1975). Aggressive children give themselves away by the way they fight. They will not stop pummeling an opponent until the victim shows clearly that he is hurt (Perry and Perry 1974).

The older the child, the longer the exposure to society's rules, the more effective are the internal brakes on antisocial conduct. For instance, 12-year-olds are less likely to respond aggressively if

Socialized by television?

someone provokes them. But seven-year-olds make no distinction between intentional and accidental provocation (Shantz and Voydanoff 1973).

Television influence Many people blame television for socializing today's children to be aggressive. Federal committees and agencies have issued official reports charging that violence on television teaches violence, that viewers are more aggressive immediately following a violent program, and that those who watch a great deal of violent programming will be more violent years later. It has even been claimed in court cases that brutal behavior by adolescents was caused by viewing similar behavior on television.

A number of studies have demonstrated a carry-over from television violence into children's lives. Using a special device to measure emotional arousal, investigators tested four- and five-year-olds' reactions to four short televised films. Two contained violent actions, one a cartoon, the other with human actors. Two others showed no violence at all. The violent episodes provoked the most reaction, particularly the one with human actors, and it was remembered in more detail than the others a week later (Osborn and Endsley 1971).

Another study followed a group of boys and girls for a decade, between the ages of 8 and 18. Boys who had preferred violent programs at 8 seemed to be more aggressive and delinquent at 18. The girls showed the same tendency, though less strongly. Perhaps the television programs caused the antisocial behavior. On the other hand, perhaps the kinds of programs children like to watch are a symptom of a problem personality in the making (Murray 1973).

It does seem that children who watch a great deal of television may become *desensitized* or used to violence in general, according to an investigation that tested their reactions with a device that measures emotions (Cline, Croft, and Courrier 1972). There is also evidence that children who see aggression films do behave more aggressively on the playground (Lovaas 1961; Liebert and Baron 1972). (Also see Chapter 7, pages 271, 291.)

Desensitize: to make less sensitive or reactive

Many factors seem to determine whether violence will be imitated, and whether it will have a lasting effect. Apparently, what is learned from film depends on the novelty of the content and a child's own interests. A new situation, an unfamiliar kind of behavior, may be imitated. But when a film depicts a situation already familiar to a child, there is less imitation. It may be that children who will be most strongly influenced by films are those who have few interests of their own (Kniveton and Stephenson 1970).

Cognitive level also has a bearing on how much learning children will absorb from a violent television program. What unsophisticated children may be learning from television is only the violence that they see modeled before their eyes. They are probably not learning the motives that lie behind the violence, the intent to cause harm (Collins et al. 1978). Those intentions are fortunately much harder to model and less likely to be acted out. Thus they are not transmitted to the viewer. "Bang-bang" on the playground, copied from yesterday's television program, will not necessarily carry over into teenage mayhem. It undoubtedly takes other influences in a child's life besides television to produce a bully or a murderer.

Still, it is safer to protect children from watching wrongdoing in the movies or on television, even though children exposed to lawbreaking episodes will probably not go out and rob a bank. However, they might learn from the models *how* to rob a bank. And one day they could use the information "should the environmental contingencies ever unambiguously favor their occurrence" (Liebert and Fernandez 1970, page 852).

One argument in the continuing debate on television violence is that watching violence can get hostile impulses out of the viewer's system, an illustration of Aristotle's concept of catharsis, or purgation. But other authorities argue that films that show violence could be training schools for delinquency. Children may not realize the difference between the make-believe on the little screen and the real world. At least for a short time after seeing a program that shows violence, the viewer may feel justified in going out and committing violence against playmates who have been the source of frustration (Berkowitz 1964).

But it is a far cry from fighting in the school yard to attacking an old lady on the street and snatching her purse. Some authorities maintain that their studies of adolescents prove "rather conclusively" that television violence is not the only or even the chief cause of aggressive behavior. Television, according to this body of opinion, may indeed be a factor in delinquency, but it is only one of many (Chaffee 1971). Watching television is not the only way for young people to learn wrongdoing. Violence can be modeled at school and in the neighborhood as well as in the home. Worse, in those places the models are people with whom adolescents may identify.

Adolescent Behavior

Parental role

Violence, delinquency, experimentation with sex and drugs—all of these are behavior problems that can sometimes appear in adolescence. The teenage years are a period when parents and society in general seem to be reaping the results of children's earlier socialization. But what many parents seem not to realize is that much adolescent behavior is a temporary phenomenon, a

Sexual awareness is natural.

developmental stage. If they could see into the future they would realize that the standards of behavior their growing children eventually adopt are generally their parents' standards. Early socialization bears appropriate fruit later on.

Some teenage problems—drinking, use of drugs, sexual promiscuity—have been found to be negatively correlated with the mother's level of traditional beliefs. That is, mothers who are basically conservative and have traditional attitudes toward God, right and wrong, lying, stealing, drugs, and sex tend to have junior and high school age children who are relatively free from adolescent problems in those areas. Apparently, the mother's beliefs influence the way she socializes her child, and she offers rewards for behavior consistent with her values. She probably even influences her child's selection of friends and peers—those the child chooses are likely to support behavior consistent with the mother's beliefs (Jessor and Jessor 1974).

Father is particularly important during adolescence since that is the time when children are especially open to outside influence. In the traditional family, the father is the ambassador from the real world beyond the home. He is also the internal prototype of authority. In a family where the father does not function in this way, anti-authoritarian attitudes are more likely to develop (van Mannen 1968).

The parents of adolescents must make peace with developmental realities. Naked power is not an appropriate child-rearing tool at this stage of development. Rather, dealing with adolescents must rely on reasoning, persuasion, across-the-table negotiation. This is only proper, in view of the greater experience and the higher cognitive level of these young adults (LaVoie 1973; Baumrind 1968). Development is the key word: a 16-year-old is not a 6-year-old.

Sexual behavior

Some behavioral questions that are particularly troublesome in adolescence relate to sex, independence, and conformity. Teenagers who break the rules they have been taught inevitably suffer from guilt. They feel guilty about sexual experimentation, about trying to break away from clinging parents, about any deviation from parental standards. Now, too, they are old enough to be aware of the double standards they have been absorbing, both in sexual behavior and in everyday situations where lying or cheating are condoned in one context and condemned in another (Mitchell 1974).

Sex play *Sexuality* is not a problem that appears out of the blue in adolescence. Sexual awareness is natural all through childhood. Up to about the age of ten, boys and girls indulge in about the same amount of sex play. But then girls appear to suppress such activity, while boys seem to do more of it throughout their adolescent years (Maddock 1973).

Sexuality: sexual capacity and behavior

Development of the genital organs and secondary sex characteristics enhances an adolescent's awareness of his or her sex and sexuality. A maturing boy cannot help realizing that his penis has become functional and its use pleasurable. But the most obvious biological development for a maturing female is her breasts. Thus, adolescent petting often mainly involves breast manipulation. Not only are the breasts readily available but they are a focus of new sexual awareness (Maddock 1973).

One of the normal experiences of *puberty* is *masturbation*. Both sexes do it. But not until Kinsey's classic pioneering study was it known how widespread and frequent the practice is. Kinsey's 1953 data still have high status in research circles. He reported that masturbation in boys had its highest incidence between the ages of 12 and 15; in girls, not until 20 (Kinsey, Pomeroy, and Martin 1948). Another Kinsey study (Kinsey et al. 1953) revealed that adolescent and young adult males were more active, perhaps twice as active as females, in masturbation, premarital petting, and *coitus*.

Puberty: period when reproductive organs first become functional, till onset of adulthood

Masturbation: self-stimulation of the sex organs

Coitus: act of sexual intercourse

Change in mores   Adults are almost always viewing adolescent sexuality with alarm. But not all teenagers' behavior is different from that of previous generations. Most normal adolescents probably move more slowly toward sexual experience than one would suppose from reading the newspapers or watching television (Offer 1971). Much depends on the particular segment of society in which one is growing up.

The really dramatic change in modern American sexual *mores* may have begun in the 1920s. The avowed standards of those who were young then were "looser." But those who remember those days maintain that the sexual revolution was more a matter of words than of deeds. Even in the late twenties Karl Menninger (1927) suggested that the newspapers were greatly exaggerating young people's heterosexual activity. The lack of reliable birth control and cures for venereal disease were practical deterrents. Since those years, adolescent sexual expresssion has increased only gradually, although steadily.

Mores: ethical customs

Kinsey reported that 2% of women born before 1900 had premarital intercourse before the age of 16, 8% before 20, and 14% before 25. Corresponding figures for women who are middle-aged now are 4%, 21% and 37% (Kinsey, Pomeroy, and Martin 1948; Kinsey et al. 1953). The data for today's teenagers show that 44% of boys and 30% of girls have had sexual intercourse before 16. By age 19, the figures were 72% and 57%, respectively (Sorenson 1973).

The changes between the generations are dramatic for women but less so for men (Maddock 1973). For the generation of the fathers of the male teenagers surveyed, 39% had engaged in intercourse by 16, and 72% by 19. The rate of increase may have been somewhat greater among girls than among boys (Maddock 1973) because of peer pressure: "Everybody does it."

Even though 52% of young Americans between 13 and 19 say they have engaged in sexual intercourse, that leaves 48% who have not. Even within these two groups generalizations are dangerous. Behavior varies among individuals and social groups, and also within the span of only a few years. For example, younger adolescents' attitudes and behavior as of 1973 seemed more conservative than the mores of boys and girls who might have been their older siblings (Sorenson 1973). Different groups have different expectations, different rules for playing the dating game, different moral requirements (Salzman 1973). College youth seem to be less conservative than noncollege contemporaries. Differences between some groups of young people are even wider than differences in attitudes between most youth and most adults.

In general, a new moral code seems to be emerging among today's adolescents: more openness, more honesty, greater mutual respect, less exploitation, a more "natural" attitude in general (Conger 1975). A study dated 1970 reported that 80% of adolescent boys and 72% of girls agree that intercourse is "all right" without marriage only if there is love (Packard 1970). And most are opposed to intercourse only for physical enjoyment or between people too young to understand the consequences (Sorenson 1973). Nevertheless, modern adolescent sexuality does present social and psychological problems among youngsters who fall victim to their own immaturity and ignorance. (See Box 10–3.)

Living together   Evidence that the old double standard of sexual behavior is far from dead comes from a survey of college students. The males still associate dating success with sexual permissiveness. But girls do not. Permissiveness adds to a male's self-esteem. It has no such relationship for a female (Berman and Osborn 1975).

"Living together" also seems to have different connotations for the two sexes. A 1971 survey at one northeastern university showed that, at least among males, the arrangement was not regarded as a substitute for marriage but as a means of sexual gratification. But most of the females hoped that it would be a step in the direction of marriage.

Perhaps living together will eventually become a universal stage in the life cycle of young adults. Or it may turn out to be a substitute for marriage for adults of all ages. At least for the time being, it is neither. Most parents disapprove of the arrangement, even though they may do nothing about it because they are afraid of alienating their children (Arafat and Yorburg 1973).

Box 10–3   Problems of Teenage Sexuality

Precise statistics on the extent of sexual activity, pregnancy, and venereal disease among teenagers in the 1980s are not available at this writing. But many teachers, social workers, religious leaders, and others who are particularly concerned about youthful sexuality are convinced that the most serious problem is many youngsters' ignorance about what used to be called the facts of life. The sophistication that adults attribute to young people who have entered puberty is entirely superficial, according to these authorities.

One teacher who spent several years teaching sex education classes to sophomores and seniors in a public high school found that many boys and girls have no real knowledge about the mechanics of intercourse and its consequences. They live by absurd and often dangerous myths about the chances of becoming pregnant or acquiring venereal disease. They do not know the facts about the relationship of the menstrual cycle to fertility, the nature of male ejaculation and its seminal content, and the practical means of preventing pregnancy and disease. They do not understand abortion and where to obtain counseling about abortion. They lack information about

the use and danger of various birth control devices and how best to prevent pregnancy. Nobody has ever taught them the positive value of self-control and abstinence.

According to one point of view, sex education may be the answer to teenage sexual problems. But whether parents can provide it is doubtful. One reason is the normal distance that develops between adolescents and their parents. Youngsters are reluctant to discuss sex with their parents. And mothers and fathers still find it difficult to broach these matters to their seemingly knowledgeable children.

Public school or church classes are considered by many authorities to be the best possible source of sex education. Some school districts now offer such classes on either a mandatory or optional basis, usually taught separately to boys and girls. Parental permission is often required. One problem is that few teachers are trained to teach the subject. Also, some parents believe the prerogative is theirs. Unfortunately, as matters now stand, neither parents, nor church, nor school seems to be doing the job (Dolloff and Resnick 1972; Project on Human Sexual Development 1978).

The values of adolescents

Activists To some parents, an adolescent development as troubling as sexuality is political activism. If conscience is basically acquired from parents, how is it that so many young activists seem to have sprung from conventional middle-class homes? This question troubles almost every generation, not only the parents who reared the student marchers of the 1960s. There are young activists in almost every era and in every nation in modern Western society.

A survey of the Vietnam antiwar and antidraft demonstrators discovered that these young people were not repudiating their parents' values at all. In fact, they were acting out the values they had been taught. Their protests were an overt demonstration of sympathy for those whom they deemed oppressed. The world-changers often have found their models at home. Even as a young adult, exposed most of the time to outside influences, an individual shows he or she is still very much the parents' child (Troll, Neugarten, and Kraines 1969).

In contrast were the *culturally alienated* youth of the same era, who were not usually to be found on picket lines but who dropped out altogether, to become "flower children" or members of the drug culture. These young people were indeed rejecting their parents' values. They usually saw their fathers as having "sold out" and were determined to live better lives themselves. The alienated youths were more sympathetic to their mothers, whom they were apt to see as victims, something they were determined not to be (Keniston 1967).

Culturally alienated: estranged from the society to which one belongs

Activists are not necessarily those who have reached Kohlberg's higher stages of moral development. In fact, most Americans remain at the conventional stage. However, a majority of a group of college activists surveyed were impelled by postconventional moralistic feelings. But many others had less elevated motives for joining the campus protesters. Among nonprotesters, an overwhelming number were in the conventional stage; they wanted to be "good boys" and "good girls" (Keniston 1970).

Generation gap People who are bracing themselves to deal with maturing children can console themselves with one apparent truth. The celebrated generation gap probably does not really exist. A recent study found no significant differences on basic concepts, like marriage, leisure, friends, parents, among three generations: college-age adolescents, their parents, and their grandparents.

This bears out other findings concerning the deep influence of parents on their children's socialization and psychological development from the very beginning of their lives. That influence continues during adolescence. Children continue to borrow basic aspects of their behavior from those who have reared them (Armstrong and Scotzin 1974).

As far as psychologists have been able to discover, the so-called youth culture is only a superficial phenomenon. Most young people are basically stable, bent on worthwhile goals, at one with their families and the community. At least one researcher feels that adolescents who take drugs, behave promiscuously, are "alienated," are actually disturbed individuals who need special treatment for what amounts to a psychological illness (Weiner 1971).

Summary

Socialization, acquiring the acceptable values and behavior of society, is a combination of learning rules of behavior and developing a positive self-concept. Children absorb most of their social concepts and their conscience from parental models and early rearing. Cognitive development is a factor in children's ability to learn these standards.

Piaget theorizes six major dimensions of moral development, related to cognitive level, intelligence, and age. Kohlberg divides moral development into three levels, which appear to be the same in many societies: preconventional, conventional, and postconventional. Progress depends on age, cognitive development, and environmental exposure.

In disciplining and socializing their children, parents' standards change as society changes and as children grow older. Love-oriented discipline may be most effective, compared to power-assertive techniques. Positive reinforcement, verbal explanation, and praise are effective socializing practices.

Mothers and fathers have different effects on socialization. Father absence may have a negative influence, possibly related to later delinquency, but father substitutes are effective. The employment of mothers has no adverse effect on children's socialization, provided the home environment is stable and the mother is satisfied with her situation.

Child-rearing practices and socialization differ among social classes, between more- or less-educated parents, and among cultural and ethnic groups. Concerning day care, its quality appears to be the important factor in socialization.

Play has an important role in social development. Through play and peer relationships children test acceptable behavior, expand socialization, explore, and experiment. Friends and associates are agents of socialization for all age groups.

Parental rearing practices are the link to children's prejudice and ethnocentrism. These attitudes appear early. Training may modify prejudice. The ideas now prevalent in society are major influences.

Violence and aggression are products of development and of certain parental disciplinary practices. Disapproval, leading to guilt, is effective in curbing such behavior. Televised violence does not necessarily lead to viewer violence; however, the viewer may become desensitized to violence.

Sexual behavior in adolescence reflects normal postpubertal development and current moral standards. Behavior varies among individuals and social groups and also within the span of a few years. A new moral code does seem to be emerging among adolescents, more open, more honest, stressing greater mutual respect and less exploitation.

Adolescent activists are not necessarily repudiating parents' values but often acting out values they have been taught. Some are at Kohlberg's conventional stage, although most activists are impelled by postconventional moralistic feelings. However, young adults for the most part behave according to the standards of those who have reared them.

Chronological Overview

Infancy

1 year	solitary play
1½ years	parallel play
Preschool	begins to control impulses and curb aggression; toilet-training; moral judgments based on consequences of the act
3 years	aware of own race
4 years	associative play
5 years	cooperative play

Childhood	moral judgments depend on threat of punishment and deference to authority
Adolescence	emergence of overt sexuality, later for boys than for girls
	moral judgments depend on desire to avoid censure by others

Applying Your Knowledge

1. How can a single parent compensate for the absence of a spouse to minimize negative effects on children?
2. How does school act as a socializing agent for children?
3. Suggest a research project that would throw further light on the influence of television on aggression.

Further Readings

Bjorklund, Gail. *Planning for play: a developmental approach.* Columbus, Ohio: Charles E. Merrill, 1978. A multimedia instructional program examining aspects of play as part of child development.
Paperback.

Maccoby, Eleanor E., and Jacklin, Carol Nagy. *The psychology of sex differences*, Vol. 1, text. Stanford, Calif.: Stanford University Press, 1978. One of the most comprehensive reviews of the research on psychological sex differences.
Paperback.

Mussen, Paul, and Eisenberg-Berg, Nancy. *Roots of caring, sharing, and helping.* San Francisco: W. H. Freeman, 1977. A review of the development of prosocial behaviors, such as altruism, generosity, personal consideration, and sharing.
Paperback.

Ribal, Joseph E. *Learning sex roles.* San Francisco: Canfield, 1973.
A cross-cultural study of sex-role learning.
Paperback.

Tavris, Carol, and Offir, Carole. *The longest war: sex differences in perspective.* New York: Harcourt Brace Jovanovich, 1977.
A lively and very interesting account of sex differences and sex roles.
Paperback.

Motivation Powers Development

What is motivation?

Kinds of Motivation

Physiological motivation
Mastery–competence
Achievement
Intrinsic motivation and curiosity
Anxiety
Maslow's hierarchy of needs

Motivation in the Home

Genetic influence
Early family interaction

Sex Differences

Mothers versus fathers
Sex roles in school
Occupational motivation
Changing sex-related motivation

Teachers and Motivation

Teaching techniques
Racial influence

Motivation and Socioeconomic Status

Values
School problems
Intervention programs
What teachers can do
Drop-outs

Chapter **11**
Motivation and Achievement

"B+!" roared the cartoon father. "That's not good enough for a Fitzgerald!"

The sketch, which showed a fierce-looking adult and a cowed-looking little boy with report card in hand, once appeared in a popular magazine. Many of us can chuckle ruefully. That is often how it was. If, as children, we were achievers or frustrated underachievers, we tend to trace our *motivation*, or lack of it, to our parents.

Motivation: incentive to goal-directed behavior

Motivation Powers Development

What is motivation?

Why do some of us strive for A's in school, for more money, for the manager's job, for social justice NOW, for a perfect tone on the violin? And why, conversely, do some of us give up—never really learn to read, drop out of school, settle for a job that is beneath our ability? Is the responsibility our own or can it be attributed to the influence of teachers or parents?

Definition   Motivation is a cause of action and behavior, "the energizing of behavior . . . especially the sources of energy in a particular set of responses that keep them temporarily dominant over others and account for continuity and direction in behavior" (Hebb 1955, page 244).

In most aspects of human development—cognition, language, perceptual awareness, learning—motivation plays a continuing role. Motivation is evident almost from the beginning of life. Even infant behavior shows the effects of motivation. Babies are motivated to suck hungrily at the breast or the bottle, to grab for a toy, to pull themselves up in the playpen, to cling to Mama, to demand milk in the language of their people.

The question of causes   What is the secret of motivation? A psychologist puts the question this way: "(a) Why does an organism or person become active? (b) Why does the organism or person act one way rather than another? (c) How do you get the organism or person to change his behavior to something conceived to be more desirable or appropriate?" (Hunt 1960, page 490).

In other words, what is the origin of the forces that impel individuals to learn, to strive, to excel? Why do those forces, or motives, seem so strong in some people, so weak in others? More important, can motivation be deliberately created? If we could learn what motivates people and what turns them off, parents might conceivably foster "better" children, schools might produce better learners, society could reap better contributors to industry, culture, science.

Various scholars have theories about the nature of motivation. They do not agree in all respects, but each sheds useful light on what makes human beings either strive or give up. Some answers have come from investigation and experimentation with children, adults, and animals. We now know enough to provide a rough guide for the fictional Mr. Fitzgerald and his B+ son.

Kinds of Motivation

Physiological motivation

For convenience, scholars have divided motivation into two basic categories: physiological motivation, usually called *drive*, and various kinds of psychological motivation. To investigate physiological motivation, they have made extensive use of animals. The assumption is that both rats and humans seek food, drink, sexual release, and physical pleasure because they have built-in motivators (drives) located in identifiable areas of the brain. These areas direct certain activities from the time of birth.

Drive: physiological basis of motivation

One experimenter discovered that hungry rats would forego food and choose instead to have the *hypothalamus* region of their brain stimulated. (This was done by an electrode implanted in the rat's skull.) Apparently the electrical stimulation was more satisfying than food (Olds and Milner 1954). This finding suggests that there are physiological centers for motivation, such as the hypothalamus.

Hypothalamus: the part of the brain that controls hunger, thirst, and other visceral functions

But psychological motivation is not so easy to isolate experimentally. However, scholars theorize that there are several different types of motivation, including mastery–competence, achievement, and intrinsic motivation. Curiosity and anxiety are also motivating forces.

Mastery–competence

An enthralled little group of relatives watched while eight-month-old Abigail, who had recently learned to crawl, headed toward the three steps going up from her grandparents' living

A built-in need to deal with the environment.

room to their dining room. Stairs were new to her. From a kneeling position, grasping the first step was easy. But then she stopped, pushed, and moved her feet on the floor, this way, that way. Nothing happened. Then she raised a knee. But the stair's riser was too deep for her. The knee came down. She tried again. Still no success. On the third try, with immense effort, the knee made it, landed on the next step. She grinned, raised the other knee, and arrived at the second step. The relatives started to cheer. She rested a moment, gathered herself together, and repeated the process. Now she had reached the top. Everybody was audibly delighted. But none more than Abigail herself.

What made her try? Her answer might have been the same as the classic mountain-climber's retort: because it's there!

Need to deal with environment According to some theorists, humans and animals have a built-in need to deal with the environment, to develop skills and abilities—a need for *mastery*, or *competence*. Mastery motivation, or competence motivation, is the desire to achieve proficiency in or to master a set of behaviors. Such behavior is selective, directed, and persistent. It builds slowly through the developmental phases of human growth, giving each individual a chance to learn what he or she needs to know about the world.

Mastery–competence motivation: desire to achieve proficiency in a set of behaviors

An illustration comes from an investigation that devised a game for children. Rewards were offered for choosing correct answers. Two groups of youngsters, aged four and ten, were given the option of playing the game for as long as they wished. The experimenter found that both groups, especially boys, played chiefly for the satisfaction of mastering the task. Prizes did not seem important to them (Harter 1975). The popularity of puzzles and games at all ages illustrates the same point.

Not physiological or maturational According to Robert White (1959), the urge to achieve competence cannot be explained by physical drives and instincts. It was not merely Abigail's age and state of development that caused her to work till she had mastered stair-climbing. Nor did development motivate the four- and ten-year-olds who played the experimenter's game. Rather, "we need a different kind of motivational idea to account fully for the fact that man and the higher mammals develop a competence in dealing with the environment which they . . . certainly do not arrive at simply through maturation" (White 1959, page 297).

Obviously, the mastery motive is useful, if not crucial, for success in school or in life. Mastery motivation appears to be somewhat stable from childhood to adulthood. In a group of individuals followed from the age of six through early adulthood, those who strove for intellectual mastery in the earliest school years were apt to be still striving for such achievement as adults (Moss and Kagan 1961). Evidently, if ways can be found to retain children's natural will to conquer the environment, the effort will pay off throughout their lives.

Achievement

What makes children try to get A's instead of B's? Why did Jimmy Carter want to be president? *Achievement motivation* involves striving for excellence. This concept, described by David McClelland, among others, suggests that individuals perceive performance or competence in terms of standards of excellence (McClelland et al. 1953). If they deviate, they feel bad. If they measure up, they feel good about their achievement.

Achievement motivation: desire to strive for excellence, recognition, and approval

Need for approval   Another definition of achievement behavior is behavior that aims for approval (or to avoid disapproval) from oneself or from other people. This motivation relates to how one performs in situations where standards of excellence can be applied. Achievement behavior is an effort to accomplish something better or faster (Crandall, Katkovsky, and Preston 1960).

When does it begin?   Signs of achievement motivation may be seen at least by the school years, and possibly earlier. But nobody is sure just when children are able to judge the excellence of their own behavior. Some think it starts between the ages of 18 months and three-and-a-half years (Crandall 1972). Certainly individual differences in the amount of effort put forth can be detected during the first three years, but it may be that only at three or a little later can children be said to impose standards on what they do and strive to achieve (Crandall, Katkovsky, and Preston 1960). Other theorists think the achievement motive is not formed until the early school years, somewhere between the ages of five and nine (McClelland 1958). At that age level it is comparatively easy to identify high achievers.

Children with high achievement motivation display types of behavior different from those with low achievement motivation. For instance, one investigator gave fifth and sixth graders a puzzle to solve. The higher achievers worked longer than those who were less motivated (Ollendick 1974). Teachers have said that highly motivated children seem to show more personal responsibility and persistence than children with low achievement goals (Hermans, ter Laak, and Maes 1972).

Selectivity   Actually, achievement is not a single motive but a complex set of motives. For example, someone might have the will to achieve intellectually, but no interest in grades in school. Everyone has run into at least one person like that—a bookworm

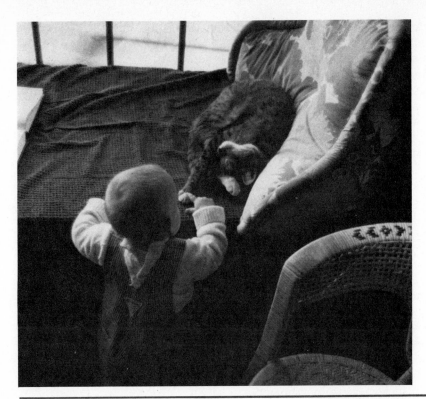

Curiosity.

or science enthusiast who acts as if other school subjects are beneath notice (Crandall et al. 1964). Another example is the young adult who works hard in a campus group to halt nuclear development but cares very little about doing well in math.

The selectivity of the achievement motive seems to be influenced by how individuals perceive their chances of success, the value they put on a particular task, personal standards, and belief in their own competence (Crandall et al. 1964). Some high school students spend hours at tennis but don't crack a book in English—or vice versa.

Intrinsic motivation and curiosity

Still to be explained is *intrinsic motivation*, which causes people to seek knowledge or to do a task for its own sake. This kind of urge may have animated an Edison. It could also send a teenager to the library to read every book on space and satellites. To foster this motive in culturally deprived children might be especially

Intrinsic motivation: desire to behave in a particular fashion because the behavior itself provides a sense of fulfillment

helpful in getting them through schoolwork that may seem irrelevant to real life (Ausubel 1964).

Curiosity is somewhat similar to intrinsic motivation. It activates individuals to seek answers to questions. Animals as well as humans show curiosity. An experiment with monkeys showed that they would even turn away from food in order to push levers that gave them a view of the comings and goings in a corridor outside their cages (Butler 1954).

Curiosity: desire to understand the unknown

Abigail, at seven months, sitting in a high chair in an unfamiliar kitchen, turned 30 degrees away from her food to look at a loudly ticking kitchen clock. Poles away, but a demonstration of the same motive, were Louis and Mary Leakey, who spent thirty years digging tirelessly before they found evidence of the existence of man millions of years ago in a remote part of Africa.

Anxiety

Anxiety is not precisely a motive, but it is an emotional state that can activate certain behavior. For example, anxiety over failure can "motivate" efforts for success. However, the level of anxiety is critical. Low or mild anxiety results in much more productive behavior than does high anxiety.

Anxiety: state of emotional tension

One might think that a student concerned about succeeding would try to improve. Often such concern has the opposite effect. Anxious children have been found to perform poorly because of motivational difficulties, not learning deficiencies (Hill and Eaton 1977). Fourth graders who were full of fears of failure and disapproval were compared with a group with low anxiety. An experimenter tested them using novel material and a colored light machine. Subjects were supposed to learn which button turned off each light. As in similar studies using adults, the highly motivated, anxious students made significantly *more* errors (Palermo, Castaneda, and McCandless 1956).

Anxiety is a factor that can affect achievement throughout life. Studies of college students show that anxiety has a material effect on performance in the classroom. Anxious students see achievement in terms of finishing reading assignments and passing tests. They actually need these markers to relieve their feelings. Under such conditions, anxiety is a powerful motivator. But if the markers are missing, anxious pupils may actually be hindered from doing their best (McKeachie 1951).

Overly fearful individuals may adjust their goals to suit their perceived abilities. They lower their sights. A study of 67 male undergraduates revealed that as fear of failure increased, the students aspired to less prestigious occupations (Burnstein 1963).

Maslow's hierarchy of needs

Another way of looking at motivation comes from Abraham Maslow, who has evolved a set of theories as a result of his clinical experiences as a psychiatrist. He has influenced the thinking of many psychologists. Maslow's *hierarchy of needs* sets up a ladder of motivating forces, beginning with physical needs, followed by *affective* needs, and ending with needs for self-fulfillment.

Hierarchy of needs: developmental progression of motivating needs

Affective: relating to feelings and emotions

Life essentials   On the first rung of Maslow's ladder are *survival needs*—needs that must be satisfied in order to maintain life. The most basic is hunger. When a person is hungry, that need is the overwhelming motive; nothing else seems important. Along with food are other survival needs, like the need for air to breathe.

Safety and security   If physiological needs are fairly well satisfied, then new needs and motives emerge: *need for safety, security, and protection*—that is, freedom from fear, and stability in general. Education, says Maslow, serves these needs by neutralizing apparent dangers through knowledge. His example: "I am not afraid of thunder because I know something about it" (Maslow 1970, page 39).

In children, the need for safety is shown by a preference for routine. Children can feel anxious and unsafe when parents treat them inconsistently or too permissively. A chaotic family situation—divorce, quarrels, death—terrifies children and creates anxiety. An experience in a hospital can have the same effect.

The safety motive may be shown in adults' striving for job security, insurance, money in the bank. Maslow attributes people's acceptance of dictatorship or military rule to their reaction to extreme domestic chaos. Their safety motivation causes them to embrace order at whatever cost.

Belongingness and love   Once these more basic needs are satisfied, according to Maslow, people are motivated to seek *belongingness and love*. Maslow makes a sharp distinction between the physiological sex drive and the need for love and affection. Belongingness and love involve both giving and receiving, he

maintains, while sex is just receiving. The quest for belongingness accounts for adolescent cliques, clubs, gangs, and romances,
as well as for adult family relationships and the multitude of
groups many of us join.

Achievement and prestige Next and higher still in Maslow's
hierarchy are the *needs for achievement and prestige.* People try to
satisfy these motives in order to feel self-confident and strong. If
they are frustrated in seeking achievement they feel weak and
inferior and can actually become emotionally sick.

Self-actualization At the top of Maslow's list of human motives
is the *need for self-actualization*—individuals' need to do what
they are uniquely suited to do, whether it is to paint pictures,
write stories, tend the sick, be a creative housekeeper or parent.
This is the urge "to become everything that one is capable of
becoming" (Maslow 1970, page 46).

Self-actualization: fulfilling
one's ultimate potential

Seemingly successful people abruptly change careers in mid-
life in the quest for self-actualization. A case in point is a man
who had been a stockbroker, married, with 7 children and 23
grandchildren. His wife died. At the age of 65 he was ordained a
Roman Catholic priest. "It may sound corny, but I wanted to
have more self-fulfillment. I just wanted a different type of life. I
wanted to serve Christ and my fellow man" (Grandpa's a Catholic
priest now 1977, page 1).

Everyone has his or her own version of self-actualization. But
all the lesser needs in the hierarchy must usually be satisfied
before individuals can concentrate on the motive to be fully
themselves.

Aesthetic need Another motive that Maslow has identified in
some individuals is a basic aesthetic need. He sees an appreciation of beauty in almost all healthy children. Evidences of aesthetic needs are seen in every culture in every age—as far back as the
prehistoric decorated abodes of the cavemen. Perhaps the aesthetic motive is connected with the need for order, as when somebody has an irresistible impulse to shut open bureau drawers or
straighten a crooked picture on the wall.

Exceptions Maslow's hierarchy may not apply to everyone. Depending on an individual's experiences, one level of needs may
dominate others. Some people must be creative at the expense of
every other value. Others, scarred by economic problems early in
life, are obsessed forever after with the quest for food or security,

even long after they have actually achieved a full measure of both. And circumstances in the home or in school can forever blot out curiosity or self-esteem. Satisfaction or lack of satisfaction of needs can have a cumulative effect on later motivation.

Once one motive is satisfied it is not necessarily gone forever, giving way to the next in the hierarchy. Normal people are "partially satisfied in all their basic needs and partially unsatisfied in all their basic needs at the same time" (Maslow 1970, page 54). The motives are often unconscious. Still, most of what we achieve can be attributed to all these various motivations, whatever label we place on them. And when we fail to achieve, it means that our motives have been somehow damaged by what has happened to us at one stage or another in our lives. (See Box 11–1.)

Motivation in the Home

When Steve entered fifth grade, the previously bright pupil was mysteriously transformed into a boy who sat uncooperatively and unresponsively at his desk. It seemed that his motivation to do school work had disappeared. The teacher notified his parents. But after both parents and teacher had spent weeks trying various remedies, Steve remained uninterested. Eventually, a move to another school roused him from his torpor, and he was again a high achiever.

Nobody really knows what caused Steve's motivational slump. In retrospect, the parents guess that the problem might have stemmed from the extra attention being given at that time to his older brother, who had become a leader in the sixth grade and on the playground as well. Or perhaps Steve and the teacher were incompatible. No specialists were consulted and the answer will never be known. But this little real-life drama illustrates the complexity of family and environmental influences on students' motivation to learn.

Genetic influence

What our parents give us at conception—not only how they treat us during the early years—has been shown to affect motivation and will to achieve throughout life. The basis for motivation may be genetic; heredity is a parent's first and most basic contribution.

Activity level Investigators believe that motivation, as well as personality, is reflected in activity level during infancy. As we saw in Chapter 9 (page 358), individual differences in activity level seem to be genetic, as shown by a study of 61 pairs of twin girls. The investigator found a link between activity and motivation, which was defined as "persistent and recurring states of arousal leading to interactions with the environment" (Scarr 1966, page 664). The results indicated a "moderate" inheritance factor for activity.

Individual developmental rate Another motivational influence that has a genetic basis, in a sense, is an individual's own peculiar developmental schedule. Maturation rate is genetically influ-

---

Box 11–1 Motivational Storms in Later Life

Striving does not suddenly stop when someone has finished school or college. Maslow's hierarchy of needs applies to adults too. Gail Sheehy, the author of *Passages* (1976), translated Maslow into real middle-class people who usually go through several periodic crises in their lives as their goals and motivations change. Sometimes these passages can be stormy. They may involve change of jobs or of mates, as individuals realize that what they want today is not what they strove for ten years ago. The author calls these the predictable crises of adulthood.

Sheehy interviewed people who changed careers in their thirties because they moved from one rung of the motivational ladder to another. Another crisis may come in the forties or fifties, when a different motivational stage is reached. Many fortunate people find still another kind of life arrangement in their sixties as they "get it all together" and at last succeed in doing what gives them a feeling of self-actualization.

The Terman study of exceptional children, which followed individuals with high IQs for over half a century, discovered that those who reported satisfaction with their work or their retirement past the age of sixty were the same ones who had shown drive thirty years earlier. Making a great deal of money did not seem to be the criterion. Rather, there appeared to be a correlation between feelings of optimism, an enjoyment of "occupational combat," and a feeling of self-worth (Sears 1977).

However, for people in the lower socioeconomic groups, the happy ending seems less likely. They become stuck on the "security" rung of Maslow's ladder. Many appear to worry all through their lives about falling off. Lillian Rubin, the author of *Worlds of pain: life in the working class family* (1977), maintains that the happy, affluent worker is a myth: "People aren't going to have the good life if they have to work 60 hours a week to pay the bills."

enced, and in terms of achievement, it makes a difference if one is a late or an early maturer. "Late bloomers" seem to have stronger drives for social acceptance, perhaps because of earlier feelings of insecurity and dependence. They are apt to express those drives in attention-getting social techniques (Mussen and Jones 1958).

Early family interaction

Maslow's hierarchy demonstrated Genetic factors aside, parents' influence on a child's later will to achieve may begin, literally, in the cradle. Some theorists believe that care-givers may effectively block a child's eventual desire to satisfy Maslow's higher order of needs—for information, for understanding, for beauty, for self-actualization—if they have not routinely satisfied the infant's "lower" needs—for physiological satisfaction, safety, belongingness and love, importance, respect, self-esteem, independence.

But a care-giver can go too far in the opposite direction: protectiveness, if overdone, can have negative results in terms of motivation. Immediate gratification of every want in childhood could cause an individual to focus on similar gratification always. When belongingness, love, and self-respect depend on conforming to strict household rules and always being dependent on parents, a youngster may be discouraged from ever trying to find self-actualization.

Maslow's hierarchy may suggest a reason for the comparative lack of motivation of economically disadvantaged pupils. These children are motivated, but at a "lower" level (Blackbourn and Summerlin 1974). Maslow pointed out that the "higher" goals, such as understanding, beauty, and self-actualization, are not strong factors in the lives of those who are concentrating on survival.

Parental reinforcement Children with learning problems may have come from a home where circumstances failed to foster motivation to do well in school. Many studies have been made of the early backgrounds of children with learning problems. Young children especially need parental reinforcement. For example, the performance of four-year-olds in a simple task improved significantly when adults were there and praised the children (Meddock, Parsons, and Hill 1971). A study of nursery school children showed that a child's attempts to do new things seems to depend on how much achievement behavior is rewarded at home and how much the child has been praised for trying (Crandall 1972).

The mothers of high achievers are generally warm and loving. The positive effects of their attitude can be seen in how well their children do in school. Investigators observed black and white mothers and children of low socioeconomic status in their homes (Radin 1971). A strong correlation was found between the warmth of the mothers' relationships with their children and the child's IQ, motivation, and behavior in a preschool compensatory education program. A correlation was also found with IQ gain in preschool, teacher ratings of academic motivation, and motivation as judged by the tester in the testing situation. Thus, maternal child-rearing practices are "significantly" related to children's response. However, another investigator suggests that mothers who expect independence and achievement too early may foster anxiety and fear of failure (Teevan and McGhee 1972).

Parents' aspirations Parents' aspirations for their children have an obvious effect on their children's motivation. There seems to be a high correlation between parents' educational and occupational hopes for their children and the children's own goals. This is true, at least, among most white families and among higher socioeconomic-level black families (Brook et al. 1974).

Parents can actually set out to produce children who aspire to high achievement. It has been suggested that the age at which a child enters school may be a time when children are receptive to what parents expect. Children are influenced not only by what they are told but also by an environment that fosters independence, curiosity, achievement, and mastery. Also helpful are parental support and a moderate amount of control (Berens 1972). The parents of high-achiever boys are more competitive, more involved, pleased, interested, and concerned with their sons' performance. They expect more and show appreciation for achievement (Rosen and D'Andrade 1959).

But excessive parental involvement and criticism might be counterproductive. Children seem to need to be bolstered in self-confidence, expectation of success, and sense of competence. The more positive the parent's feedback after the fact, the more the expectation of future success. But too much praise seems to get diminishing returns. On the other hand, ignoring what a child does seems like criticism whether it is intended as such or not (Crandall, Katovsky, and Preston 1960).

Motivation can begin at home.

Home atmosphere   The home life of high achievers clearly differs from the home life of low achievers. The good students' "home atmosphere is pleasant. Parents show interest, affection, and pride in their children. Children respond by being happy, respectful, and eager to please their parents" (Kurtz and Swenson 1951, page 478).

Fostering independence and self-reliance early in life provides the foundation for later motivation. Parents should probably offer to help their children, although it may be a healthy sign for a higher achiever to refuse aid. Anxious children seem to have parents who did not react to their expressions of insecurity and failed to express appreciation for success (Hermans, ter Laak, and Maes 1972).

It may also be that the care-givers of problem learners are more restrictive. They may discourage energetic activities like climbing, jumping, sports. They may fail to express affection in words: they may spank rather than reprimand (Austin 1970).

Children from homes that induce anxiety and insecurity can also fail to develop adequate motivation for learning. Problem situations include heavy exposure to traumatic events or violence during the first six years of life; the threat of being abandoned or deserted by one or both parents (or actual desertion); death or fear of the death of significant family members; instability in the home; weakness or illness, threatened or actual, their own or in others close to them; deprivation, defeat, exposure to slurs and taunts. In effect, these children carry a high overload of anxiety, with devastating effects on their school performance (Gardner 1971).

Some low achievers' homes seem to lack affection. Their parents appear to expect little of them. Nor do the children seem anxious to please. High achievers often make friends with other high achievers. Low achievers may have no friends at all, or friends whose standards are equally low (Kurtz and Swenson 1951).

Parental influence may also tend to cause pessimism. Some youngsters automatically expect failure in situations where adults are concerned. Children who have had many early experiences in which they are physically or verbally punished for doing poorly carry their negative attitudes to school (Ryback 1970).

Birth order   A significant family influence on motivation may be birth order. First-born children tend to be high achievers. Statistics show that first-born children are greatly overrepresented in the college population, regardless of family size and social class (Greene and Clark 1968). Parents tend to concentrate their hopes and aspirations on the first child, to invest more of themselves in the process of training and socialization. The "movers and shakers" of this world are apt to be first children or only children.

Adolescent motivation   Popular impressions to the contrary notwithstanding, teenage goals and motives are similar to those their parents hold for them. Teenagers' feelings about becoming successful in their parents' terms have been shown to become stronger with increasing age. They become more self-confident and their fear of failure diminishes (Distefano, Pryer, and Rice 1970). And their educational goals are more apt to match what the mother wants for them than what the best school friend wants. Parents' desires are a more important influence on the child's educational plans than the social class in which the youngster mixes. Parents may sometimes doubt it, but what they want for their children really does usually carry more weight than the opinions of the gang in the cafeteria (Kandel and Lesser 1969).

Sex Differences

It will come as no surprise to feminists that, thus far at least, a person's sex makes a difference in motivation. How many girls dream of becoming president of IBM or shop steward of a union? It is easy to guess that there are few. Boys' ambitions generally soar beyond those of girls. Is it because they were born ambitious? Or did their upbringing, the media, school, make them that way?

It is also well known that girls tend to do better in school, at least in the early years. Why the seeming contradiction between their lack of will to go far vocationally and their initial desire to perform well academically? The motivational differences between the sexes have been repeatedly demonstrated. But the basic reasons are far less clear. We still do not know for certain whether our culture alone makes the difference or whether it is also true that men and women are born that way.

As we saw in Chapter 9, sex roles, which influence personality, are taught by parents, teachers, and society almost from the moment a child is born. Motivation is intimately bound up with one's perception of what is expected of one's sex. A girl is taught to strive for what is girlish or womanly, and a boy is taught to "be a man." (See Box 11–2.)

Mothers versus fathers

At least until recently, mothers and fathers have had contrasting influences on their children's motivation. While both parents provide achievement and independence training, fathers seem to have been more influential in these areas than mothers, at least with sons. Fathers have given hints, allowing their sons more of a sense of initiative; mothers have tended to be more "pushy," issuing explicit directions. (Learning to be independent requires opportunity to practice.) A more dominating father may "crush" his son, but a mother who dominates seems not to have had quite so negative an effect (Rosen and D'Andrade 1959).

Girls A 1963 study showed that sex differences in parental effects on motivation appear as early as the nursery school years. As far as girls are concerned, different forms of dependency have been related to the degree of parental permissiveness and parents' involvement in child-rearing. Girls who were "negative attention seeking"—disobedient or irritable—usually had parents who made few demands on them and imposed few restrictions.

Among the girls who sought positive attention were those who were relatively passive and who needed physical reassurance. They needed to be near adults or other children, to be touched and helped; sometimes they were "clinging." These were children whose fathers did not participate much in their upbringing and who were not subjected to many demands or restrictions by either parent.

Box 11–2 Male versus Female

Aside from the obvious differences between the sexual characteristics of men and women, are there other significant differences that should keep women out of certain vocations? Psychologists' review of thousands of research papers revealed only four areas in which sex differences seem unmistakable: males are more aggressive; they are better in math; they are better at tasks that require a person to coordinate visual and spatial ability; but women have better verbal ability.

Whether these differences are inborn or encouraged by the way boys and girls are reared is another matter. Nobody knows for sure. But the evidence so far seems to suggest that environment is the controlling influence in most sex differences. As early as the 1930s, the famous anthropologist, Margaret Mead, studied sex and temperament in three different New Guinea tribes. She found varying sex-linked behavioral characteristics among the tribes, obviously a result of training and tribal goals.

More recently, Dr. Helen H. Lambert, a feminist who specializes in brain hormones, stated: "You can't deny that there are certain biological differences. These may extend to behavior as well." Among the important genetic differ-

Source: Compiled from Gilder 1979 and Rensberger 1978.

The girls whose dependency behavior was considered more "mature" were those who actively sought and were satisfied by verbal approval. It appeared that their mothers had devoted themselves relatively little to taking care of them in infancy. These girls were being reared strictly and taught not to be aggressive. In sum, most girls had been brought up to be dependent (Sears 1963).

Boys The effects of parental treatment on boys are not as clear. However, investigation showed that less highly motivated boys appear to have had mothers and fathers who gave them little freedom and little incentive for rapid maturing (Sears 1963). In a group of four-year-olds, boys whose fathers were helpful, encouraging, and interested seemed to be motivated to do well on a test of intellectual performance. Restrictive fathers hindered their sons' achievement. Fathers' influence on four-year-old daughters was not so marked (Epstein and Radin 1975).

ences, Lambert believes, is males' superior visual–spatial ability and their more frequently expressed aggression. Aggression, she says, is not "hostility" but "an active, assertive, dominating approach to the world."

Greater male aggression has been found in all human societies—early in life before environment has had a chance to operate. The same sex differences in aggression are seen in subhuman primates. Evidently there is a relationship between aggression and levels of sex hormones.

Some authorities argue that there is no society in human history where women rule or where they have final authority. Males are alleged to have a combination of traits—aggressiveness, larger physical stature, and a need to dominate related to the sex act—that make them natural leaders in society.

Physical differences between men and women have been used as a major argument against using women in military combat. One study concluded that women have two-thirds the endurance of men and little more than half the muscular strength of males. Also, even when men and women are the same size, women are only 80% as strong. A West Point study found that with the same training, women's strength improved less than half as much as men's strength. The suggested reason is the combined effect of testosterone (the hormone of the male sex drive), of aggression, and of protein synthesis.

Opposite-sex effect At a slightly later age, however, fathers' attitudes related to daughters' motivation. The second-, third-, and fourth-grade girls who did best academically were those who got more frequent praise from their fathers and less frequent criticism (Crandall et al. 1964). Mothers' attitudes may have an opposite effect on their daughters. Mothers who were "less affectionate and less nurturant" seemed to produce academically more competent girls.

In the same study, mothers' evaluation of and satisfaction with how well their children did seemed to be closely tied in with how well the children performed. The fathers' attitudes were apparently not similarly related (Crandall et al. 1964). It may be that less affectionate, less doting mothers are themselves career women who provide a model for how their daughters should turn out (Crandall 1972).

The differential effects of parents' treatment have been evident throughout the school years. Typically, mothers of boys have begun earlier to expect their sons to behave more independently and to do well on their own. Their expectations for their daughters have come later. But girls who are high achievers in the fifth grade have tended to be those on whom mastery demands were made earlier (Berens 1972).

Sex roles in school

A "feminine" place School activities seem to suit the feminine sex role. The girl who has learned that it is appropriate for her to please other people does well in school in the early years. Also, the female sex role has been passive and school seems to be a passive sort of activity.

An equal number of girls and boys from kindergarten, second, and fourth grades were asked to tell whether boys or girls used various school-related objects. Shown ten objects, neither sex in kindergarten thought the objects were clearly sex-related. But by the fourth grade, most of the items were seen as feminine by the girls, and the boys' consensus became much more split (Hill, Hubbs, and Verble 1974).

Another study asked second and third graders to identify objects commonly found in school—chalkboard, book, desk, page of arithmetic problems—as masculine or feminine. The children more frequently called them feminine. School evidently seems to be a place for females, and boys are not motivated to do well there (Kagan 1964*a*).

Self-fulfilling prophecies   Under normal conditions, girls and boys seem to be acting out self-fulfilling prophecies in terms of what they expect of their sex. Given tasks that they thought were supposed to test ability in "boys'" and "girls'" subjects, sixth graders spent less time on the tests labeled not appropriate to their sex, and they did relatively poorly on those tasks (Stein, Pohly, and Mueller 1971).

Mechanical, athletic, math, reading, artistic, and social skills have had distinct connotations as appropriate for one sex or the other. The older the children, the more firmly do those standards seem to be established. Ninth graders are even more influenced by sex-typing than sixth graders (Stein, Pohly, and Mueller 1971).

By the time girls and boys are in junior high and high school, they have learned some other important lessons about the differences between males and females and where each sex ought to fit. Middle-class ninth graders, asked to rate themselves in a variety of ways, differed distinctly in how they saw their status, depending on their sex. In general, boys rated themselves significantly higher than girls in terms of "desired academic aspirations" and "expected academic aspirations." Boys were more confident in sports and science, less so in English. Girls' self-ratings were exactly opposite. Also, girls saw themselves as better in their relationships with school, teachers, and other people, perhaps because girls mature earlier than boys and are encouraged earlier to develop social skills (Wiggins 1973).

Occupational motivation

Early perceptions   The way the sexes have been reared has given them a clear perception of the occupational opportunities open to them, even early in childhood. Studies thus far show that only boys perceive a wide range of choices (Looft 1971b). Sex-role expectations for adult occupations may be acquired as early as six to eight. Girls learn that they should aspire to a much more limited variety of eventual vocations. Boys' horizons broaden with age; girls' horizons narrow (Hewitt 1975).

To measure the relative aspirations of boys and girls, second graders were asked to choose occupations. Boys chose twice as many as girls did. Also, boys were more likely than girls to know what their fathers did for a living. But even the girls who knew the nature of their father's work were not likely to select the occupation for themselves (C. L. Siegel 1973). Obviously, people have been learning their assigned places in society very early.

Fathers and careers   Fathers have had special influence on the career orientation of both sons and daughters. Teenage boys who strive the most have been likely to come from homes with fathers whose work is in some way managerial, whether middle or working class. Fathers have passed on to their boys the values and psychological disposition that make them try to become supervisors, decision-makers, managers (Turner 1970). Sons who identified closely with their fathers have tended to be more strongly oriented toward education and vocational goals than nonidentifying boys (Crites 1962).

Career women also seem to have been influenced by fathers. Career-oriented college girls often remember their fathers as having pressed them for achievement. The homemaker types appear to have identified with their mothers, while their fathers accepted them as they were. Young women who say they want only a stop-gap job, pending marriage, but whose tests show the motivational pattern of the career-oriented, might be redirected by counselors who recognize the implicit conflict (Oliver 1975).

Changing sex-related motivation

Are today's American homes now reflecting the new feminism? Early returns from current research suggest that the changes most of us perceive are already affecting the motivational patterns of tomorrow's adults.

Employed mothers   A recent study of the sex-role concepts, personality adjustment, and academic achievement of 223 ten-year-old boys and girls compared those whose mothers had full-time jobs outside the home with those whose mothers stayed at home. The families were from various socioeconomic strata. The youngsters with the most egalitarian sex-role concepts were those with employed mothers, a correlation that seemed to stem from the mothers' greater satisfaction with their lives (Gold and Andres 1978).

What changes when Mother goes out to work is her image but not her emotional support for her children. Daughters of mothers who stay at home are more likely to see their mothers as dishwashers and their fathers as money-earners (S. Miller 1975). But a woman employed outside the home provides a multifaceted model for her children. She shows them that Mother is not just cook, maid, chauffeur, but possibly attorney, physician, teacher, chief or co-equal breadwinner. Equally important, modern mothers are not necessarily dependent, passive, unassertive—the stereotype female. Rather, they may be independent, active, assertive. Kindergarten daughters of working mothers are now more likely than the daughters of housewives to choose Mother as the person they would most like to be "when I grow up" (S. Miller 1975).

Children of employed mothers also tend to achieve more academically and to have higher aspirations than children of nonworking mothers (Banducci 1967; Hoffman 1974). Modeling themselves on Mother, the daughters also envision careers for themselves (Hoffman 1977). Particularly if the mother has made a success of her dual role, both boys and girls learn to accept and even favor a more egalitarian family style (Etaugh 1974).

New roles for men   In many homes today, children are also seeing new male sex roles. Husbands of working mothers are apt to help with household chores and child care. Many boys and girls now see fathers who are more than breadwinners—and they may also see more of their fathers. Children of working mothers tend to rate men and women as equally competent (Hoffman 1974).

Research done so far seems to lead to the conclusion that the chief consequence of outside jobs for mothers is that the socialization experiences of boys and girls are becoming more alike, and thus sex differences are likely to decrease. The girls are receiving more independence training and more occupational orientation.

Could new problems arise?   All these changes raise questions for the future. Will girls become more competitive and aggressive? Will either sex draw the necessary encouragement to develop nurturance, warmth, and expressiveness? Will boys become more drawn to parenting as girls are more drawn to holding jobs? Will new child-rearing practices develop to readjust the traditional balance between mothering and fathering? No one knows yet (Hoffman 1977).

Certainly the real world is beginning to look very different to children from what it used to be. Abigail sees a mother who goes to work every day and prepares meals only every other week. She also sees a father who changes diapers at least half the time and is often the one who collects her from her daytime baby-sitter (a

Children are beginning to see new male sex roles.

woman). What will Abigail and many of her contemporaries learn about their sex roles?

Reeducating the sexes   Vast changes in sex stereotypes probably have not taken place yet. A few years ago, in 1978, a study on co-education and sex roles questioned over 3000 undergraduates at seven well-known colleges about their aspirations. The conclusion was that the women had lower self-esteem and lower aspirations than men, even though their grades were similar.

   Research shows that if society wishes to do so, children's minds can be deliberately changed about what women and men may dare to do. Just providing storybooks that propagandize a more egalitarian way of life can modify stereotypes (Flerx, Fidler, and Rogers 1976).

Training and reinforcement can produce changes in the sex-typed aspirations of young girls, according to one study (Barclay 1974). Short exposure—only three 15-minute lessons dealing with women's careers—affected kindergarten girls' perceptions of the possibilities open to them. Evidently a few books, judiciously used, could make a difference in how girls see themselves and their future in society.

Special reinforcement works on children as young as eight or nine. If an adult provides appropriate feedback, girls respond even more than boys (Hill and Dusek 1969). This finding suggests that girls are being starved for the encouragement to do the kinds of things that society has been reserving for males.

Teachers and Motivation

Teaching techniques

Both authors of this book vividly remember their first-grade teachers, what they looked like, what they said, much of what happened in their classrooms. The strength of these memories is not unusual. Second only to parents—in some instances more important than parents—are teachers. They influence not only the aspirations of their pupils but also their immediate achievements. Along with mother and father, a teacher is a *soliciting agent* who can elicit a response from children. Sometimes a teacher is an inspiration, sometimes a source of discouragement. Teachers' attitudes can influence not only classroom activities but children's behavior and their perceptions of school as well. Some teachers can even produce an anxiety-arousing environment (Halperin 1976).

Soliciting agent: someone who elicits a response

An "ideal" teacher What would an ideal teacher be like? From school boards to college education departments to psychologists to students themselves—everyone has been trying for years to pin down the characteristics of an ideal teacher.

One typical attempt to sketch such a person called for a warm, orderly, systematic individual, able to influence pupils indirectly through question-asking, a good organizer of the material to be learned (Gage 1965). But it may well be impossible to

A teacher can be an inspiration.

draw a picture of an academic savior. Talented, effective teachers are in abundance, but the chances are that they are all somewhat different. In fact, different teachers may well be effective with different children. Given those provisos, we nevertheless know a great deal about how various kinds of teacher behavior affect children.

Approval–disapproval   A teacher's approval or disapproval can have a significant effect on motivation, though more for first graders than for fifth graders. A child may be afraid to speak out in the classroom not because of lack of knowledge but because of fear of criticism. Praise has the opposite effect (Spear 1970).

Disapproval may hinder both motivation and learning. In one study, children receiving criticism were slower to answer, made more mistakes, were less likely to do their best on a task than children who were praised, or at least got no feedback at all from the teacher. The younger the child—especially boys—the more affected by disapproval (Allen, Spear, and Lucke 1971).

Competition versus praise   Praise—if it is specific, or "labeled," telling children just what they are being praised for—helps performance (Bernhardt and Forehand 1975). Praise is a more effective motivator than competition. Competition seems to be effective in the classroom chiefly if the tasks are boring (Senior and Brophy 1973). But constant use of competitive situations in school can be habit-forming, a lifetime influence. Spelling bees, seating in the classroom according to how well pupils do on tests, games played to win—these make a motivational pattern that some people never break. Habitual losers may feel like losers throughout their lives, and they may stop trying altogether. Winners want to win in every situation, from card games to marital arguments. Perhaps Americans are competition-happy because of the methods used by our teachers during our early schooling. Certainly competition may have a place in pedagogy, but its results may be mixed.

Using curiosity   Skilled teachers can make use of normal curiosity as a motive to help children learn. A child who is having trouble with reading might be inveigled into the effort if interest is aroused by a new and stimulating reader. On the other hand, arousing too much curiosity can be detrimental to learning. If a classroom is full of colorful posters, people walking in from the outside, or playground noises drifting through open windows, children's curiosity may distract them from the task at hand. It has been suggested that teachers should try to recognize the "preferred level of arousal" of each child, the level at which he or she functions best (Day 1968).

Mitigating anxiety   A teacher's behavior can also make a difference when a pupil's motivation is endangered by anxiety. In one investigation of anxiety in preschoolers, two different teachers were involved. One was pleasant, responsive, complimentary. The other was aloof, businesslike, unsmiling, indifferent. Some of the children, aroused by a scary film, had become anxious. They were then asked to perform a particular task—a marble game.

The anxious children performed better with the nonresponsive teacher than with the responsive teacher. Apparently the children were motivated by a desire to escape punishment, which they expected would be more likely to be meted out by the indifferent teacher. But with less anxious children, the pleasant, complimentary adult was more effective. These children were evidently interested in rewards, and the responsive adult was seen as potentially more rewarding (Lepper 1970).

A study of older children also deals with the question of teacher impact. It suggests that students' perceptions of teachers may be related to student performance. The investigators maintain that students who thought the teacher was "warm" and "affable" were typically overachievers. In contrast, underachievers thought the teacher was "cold" and "unapproachable." The implication is that if a teacher tries to make children "feel good" about what is going on in the classroom, students might try harder to do well (White and Dekle 1966).

Teachers and sex roles Teachers tend to reward children who adopt their own sex-role behavior. Thus they, too, are agents of socialization and influence sex-typed motivation through reinforcement (Etaugh, Collins, and Gerson 1975; Fagot 1977). During the early school years, boys identify with the men who are part of their lives and also with males they know not at all, like show business figures and athletes. The sex of the model seems to be more important for boys than for girls. Girls are apt to select both male and female role models, including entertainment personalities and men and women in history. Some psychologists have concluded that it is especially important for more men to become elementary school teachers, since both boys and girls seem to find male teachers more psychologically rewarding (Forslund and Hull 1972).

Teachers' expectations A controversy began more than a decade ago over the question of whether a teacher's preconceived expectations can have an effect on IQ or how well a pupil learns. A widely publicized study by Robert Rosenthal and Lenore Jacobsen (1966, 1968) set out to test the existence of the self-fulfilling prophecy.

At the end of a school year in grades kindergarten through five in a San Francisco area school, all the children were given an intelligence test that was new to the teachers in the school. The following year, the teachers were told, seemingly casually, which children in their new classes had done well in the test. What the teachers did not know is that the pupils' names had been chosen haphazardly and bore no necessary relationship to the real scores. Later, when all the children were retested, the results were startling. The children labeled as promising seemed to make greater gains on IQ tests than the other children in the class.

The Rosenthal–Jacobsen study was later discredited. Critics charged that the statistics were inappropriately used and that erroneous conclusions had been drawn (Snow 1969). However, a review of the literature on the effect of teachers' expectations does indicate that these attitudes consistently influence pupils' behavior and achievement, as well the behavior of teachers themselves. But no relationship between IQ scores and teachers' expectations has been found (Baker and Crist 1971).

Some authorities point out that there is a subtle difference between teachers' biases and teachers' expectations. A teacher who is prejudiced for or against a student does not necessarily influence that pupil's performance. However, teachers do harbor legitimate expectations based on students' ability and these expectations may be influential (Dusek and O'Connell 1973).

Racial influence

Teachers' attitudes The whole question of school integration may be closely tied in with teachers' attitudes—not their feelings about whether schools should be integrated, but less obvious attitudes about children of a different race. Studies indicate that the racial background of teacher and student may interact in such a way as to influence student performance.

One investigation involved black elementary school pupils and both black and white examiners. What the investigators expected came out in the results of the experiment. The black pupils did better when the black examiner administered the verbal learning tests. The subjects seem to have perceived the black teachers as being "more nurturant" (Katz, Henchy, and Allen 1968). The same results came out of a reverse study. White pupils did better in a test administered by white experimenters than a similar group given the same test by persons of a different race (Turner 1971).

Findings like this could mean that it makes as much difference who teaches a black child as who sits in the next seat in the classroom. But being taught by whites is not the only reason that black children's motivation in school generally seems to be weaker than white children's.

Student aspirations   Children's educational goals and occupational goals may not necessarily coincide, and a racial factor appears to be involved. Comparing the educational and occupational aspirations of black, Mexican-American, and white pupils in elementary school, blacks, it appears, have the highest educational goals, the whites the next highest. Mexican-Americans aspire to the least education (Hindelang 1970).

But in terms of occupational hopes, it seems to be the white and Mexican-American pupils who have the most desire for the better occupations. Perhaps the reason is that black children gird themselves against the inevitable disappointments in the real world after school ends (Hindelang 1970).

This attitude may explain the difference between black and white children with respect to goals, attitudes toward school success, and orientation to the future. White and black fifth graders were asked their views regarding the relative importance of ability, effort, task difficulty, and luck, in school success. White children replied that ability and effort were most significant. But the blacks, seemingly giving up on themselves, judged the difficulty of a task to be most important. Both groups saw themselves as putting similar amounts of ability and effort into their work. But the whites were more likely to blame themselves for failure. This was true no matter what the socioeconomic level of their homes (Friend and Neale 1972).

Even as early as three and six years old, black children's vocational aspirations come to bitter terms with reality as they perceive it. A comparison of white and black children in those two age groups showed that the black children were not as advanced as the whites in seeing themselves as adults and in a job. The black girls foreclosed their options even earlier than the boys. They hoped to be "parents." The boys did speak of being grown up and what that would entail (Vondracek and Kirchner 1974).

Something obviously happens to black children during the early school years that sends them on the path either to postsecondary education or to nonacademic activities. The IQ histories of black college graduates, all of low socioeconomic status, were analyzed. When they were in the second grade, their scores were no different from the scores of control groups. But by the eighth grade, the future college graduates' IQ scores were "significantly higher" than the control group scores. If research could pin down just what blunted the motivation of the control groups, and what fired the aspirations of the college graduates, it could be a real breakthrough in educational psychology (Lane 1973).

Motivation and Socioeconomic Status

Like most textbooks, this one has an inevitable middle-class orientation—written by middle-class authors; edited by members of the middle class; used as a teaching adjunct by middle-class educators who lecture to middle-class students. Having reached the status of author, editor, professor, college student—whatever their race or family background—all these people are necessarily now by income and occupation in the middle class.

Thus, as a result of its middle-class point of view, this book has been emphasizing motivation in middle-class terms: the will to do well in school; ambition for higher education; active efforts to prepare for a challenging vocation. But it must be acknowledged that not everyone aspires to be college-educated or a reader of books and that the lack of motivation in those areas should not necessarily be considered a fault to be corrected.

Still, research does suggest that the motivational development of some children in any terms, middle-class or otherwise, may be severely affected by their early environment. We have already seen that, no matter how the various types of motivation are labeled, they are all kindled in the preschool years, chiefly in the home.

Values

Children of the lower socioeconomic class evidently perceive their future as more limited than middle-class students. They come to school already programmed for different goals—lesser ones, by middle-class standards (Marcus and Corsini 1978). They develop an alternative set of values based on their perception of their own reduced possibilities for material achievement (Rodman 1963). If the home is poverty-stricken, all the family members are likely to focus on the lower rungs of Maslow's motivational ladder. They are interested in survival, not self actualization (Blackbourn an Summerlin 1974).

Add to that the fact that these children's experiences may have already taught them that life holds very little for them in the way of conventional accomplishment. One study of high school seniors from low socioeconomic backgrounds clearly illustrated this built-in defeatism. Asked what occupation they would like to have at ages 25 to 30, the students' goals were modest and directly correlated with their fathers' accomplishments, both educational and vocational (Caro and Pihlblad 1965).

An investigation of the aspirations of male high school juniors in St. Paul, Minnesota, bears out this hypothesis. Interviews were conducted with students whose fathers were unskilled or semiskilled workers and who were not high school graduates. These students were compared with boys whose fathers were professionals, semiprofessionals, or managers and who were at least high school graduates. All the boys were asked to picture themselves in the future, after high school graduation, in terms of educational and occupational alternatives.

All preferred the high-prestige occupations that were suggested to them. All believed that college was the best path to those desirable positions. But their emphasis differed. The lower-class students were flexible about their occupational aspirations; they would clearly settle for less. The middle-class boys would not. But the middle-class students also clearly perceived that they had greater access to college, seemed to see college as an end in itself.

In contrast, the boys of lower socioeconomic background did not seem too attracted to the idea of college for themselves and were able to visualize themselves doing various other things after high school. Evidently they downgraded the desirability of what they deemed unattainable and upgraded what seemed to be within their reach. The influence comes, according to the investigator, "from the person's subculture" and from parents who have tried to shield their children by encouraging them to accept a more limited future (Caro 1966).

School problems

The difficulties of non-middle-class children in a middle-class-dominated world become evident as soon as they enter school. Children who live with little parental interaction or in minimum-care institutions lack the encouragement that might prepare them for the demands and expectations of their teachers. The values of those teachers may be in sharp conflict with values learned earlier. Teachers may be unconsciously prejudiced against these children. They neither look nor act nor speak the way a promising pupil is supposed to look, act, or speak. The teacher might give up on them before the first day of school is over (Cheyney 1966).

To these children, school may seem so different from home in attitudes and demands that they are like people dumped into a foreign country with inexplicable customs and a strange language. Almost immediately, "the school becomes a place which makes puzzling demands, and where failure is frequent and feelings of competence are subsequently not generated. Motivation decreases, and the school loses its effectiveness" (Deutsch 1964, page 238).

Besides, these children often come to school already far behind their middle-class contemporaries in the skills related to school achievement. They start with failure. Their alienation increases. And the gap between them and middle-class children widens as the years pass.

The differences between the achievements of middle-class children and those from lower-class homes seem to be smallest in the first grade, but they increase through the grade school years. School is not at fault for the initial difference, but school can probably be blamed for not overcoming the problem and for letting it get worse (Deutsch 1964).

Intervention programs

Under these circumstances, how can the children of low socioeconomic status be motivated and equipped to succeed and move up in the American world? Somehow, they must be better prepared to meet school's demands before they accumulate failures and negative attitudes (Deutsch 1964). Since the early years are when a person is most malleable, intervention programs probably should begin at that time. Many believe that a "third environment"—a nursery school—to intervene between home and school, may help reconcile the differences between them.

Maria Montessori devised such an early enrichment program for slum children in Italy. (Ironically, the rather costly American nursery schools that use Montessori's methods are much in favor with upper-middle-class parents.) Head Start is a preschool program that was government-funded in the 1960s to compensate for some of the educational and motivational differences between middle-class children and children from less favored backgrounds. Such compensatory programs have been more or less successful, yielding some long-term effects, two to seven years after intervention (Deutsch 1963, 1969; Gray and Klaus 1965;

Box 11–3 Montessori Method of Motivation

Early in the twentieth century, Maria Montessori, the first Italian woman to earn a medical degree, began her experimental schools for slum children. Her methods worked so well that they became popular elsewhere, especially for preschoolers in this country.

Montessori's techniques take advantage of the human being's need for mastery–competence and for achievement. The system also draws on a child's natural curiosity and on the intrinsic motivation that causes people to seek knowledge for its own sake. Her methods pointedly omit more destructive motivational factors, like anxiety. Nor does she stress the need for adult approval.

This pioneer created a prepared environment in which young children could work at their own level. Natural materials were abundant, the kinds of things found at home. Learning to use these materials gave her charges the experience of mastering their own environment. Children were exposed to the "exercises of practical life." This was particularly helpful for children with learning problems, who could get satisfaction from conquering their environ-

ment. Moreover, using the Montessori materials improves coordination and prepares pupils for later school work.

Montessori materials include such things as bricks or blocks and boards to make storage shelves, all the objects necessary for personal grooming, cleaning implements, flowers, and plants. Children are encouraged to master simple activities just for the joy of the activity. Everyone sets his or her own pace. Doing things for others is also stressed. Exercises for muscular coordination particularly help those who are developmentally retarded to feel that they are as competent as others. Recognizing that young children think concretely, Montessori developed a method that provides sandpaper letters, movable cardboard alphabets, and other materials that are tangible and speak to the child's senses. The children experience success with the concrete before they must deal with the abstract. According to the Montessori philosophy, children with learning difficulties should be developing feelings of competence and worth, instead of having to compete, possibly fail, and thus give up (Gitter 1967).

Klaus and Gray 1968; and Gray and Klaus 1970). But even in the more successful programs, the increases in school achievement were small over long periods of time. (See Box 11–3, and Chapter 8, pages 339–340.)

What teachers can do

Part of the solution to children's special motivational problems may well rest with teachers. We have already noted the enormous influence of teachers' attitudes on pupils in general. The teacher's treatment matters to all children, but especially to those who are receiving minimal support and encouragement at home.

Middle-class teachers of the disadvantaged have to learn to cope with their own biases. (Even teachers who start out disadvantaged themselves have become middle class by virtue of their income and professional standing.) The qualities that work best begin with respect for the pupil. Patience, understanding, sensitivity, good judgment, and a sense of humor are all important. In fact, special training is usually necessary for teachers who deal with disadvantaged children (Cheyney 1966). In effect, these teachers must learn to cope with a different culture and in some cases with a different language.

Drop-outs

Not everyone can or should aspire to be a lawyer, doctor, or corporation president. However, Americans are fairly well agreed (note our mandatory education laws) that a high school education is probably important for everybody, regardless of capacity or background. So it is important to know what motivational failures account for the drop-out, the girl or boy who never finishes high school and who, in our system, almost inevitably becomes a marginal person—earning little, low on the social scale, burdened by a larger than average family to support, and even apt to turn to crime (Hathaway, Reynolds, and Monachesi 1969).

Family influences Dropping out is probably caused by family and early school influences. Some drop-outs miss the normal emotional support and closeness of mothers and fathers: "My mother doesn't understand me. She just don't have time to understand me . . . I can take care of myself." "It seems when I was little I was always left out."

Typically, drop-outs' homes also lack stability. Communication is minimal. The drop-out is often socially inept and has a poor self-image. Drop-outs may feel that they have little encouragement at home—or else that they are pressured and nagged beyond endurance. They may lack companionship from their families: "I can't sit down and talk to my father about what I should do. And my brother and I don't even speak." Rarely do the families "do things" together. Their homes are seen as unhappy homes.

As a result, the potential drop-out lacks a strong self-image and may feel worthless. There has been little chance to practice the communication skills that come from talking to sympathetic parents or family members, no practice in social interaction. This

Box 11–4   Using Rewards to Motivate Learning

An educational psychologist and a county juvenile probation officer collaborated on an experiment involving a 14-year-old delinquent boy from a large, culturally and economically deprived family. In all his school years the boy had never passed any of his courses. In effect, the school had promoted him just to get rid of him. He misbehaved constantly in class and had been in trouble with the police many times. When the experiment began, he was reading at a second-grade level.

The system the researchers used was to give the boy individual tutoring in reading. At the same time, he was rewarded for right answers and attentive behavior with tokens that had varying monetary value. The training lasted for 40 hours over a period of four-and-a-half months, while the boy continued to attend school as usual. By the end of that time, the youngster had learned and retained 430 new words, thus progressing to a fourth-grade reading level. In school he passed all his courses for the first time in his life. He also stopped behaving disruptively. And the rewards he gained during the experiment totaled $20.31 (in 1965 dollars), enabling him to acquire, among other things, shoes, hair pomade, a phonograph record, an ice cream sundae, a ticket to a school function, and money to send to a brother in reform school.

In reporting on their work, the investigators point out that children like this boy do not typically acquire "reinforcer systems" from their home surroundings. Good grades in school would have received no parental praise. What the researchers did was to supply some of the missing motivation for learning and for good behavior (Staats and Butterfield 1965).

is a formula for school failure, according to several scholars. In fact, one writer maintains that the family is so pivotal that if the background of a child of average intelligence were analyzed on the first day of school, one could predict the pupil's chances for eventual success or failures (Cervantes 1965).

Other indicators Among the indicators for a potential drop-out are early school failure, poor family background, and little family emphasis on schooling. In the elementary grades the typical future drop-out's school achievement is below grade level; the family has a low income; and the parents have not gone very far in school themselves. The pupil is apt to participate very little in extracurricular activities. By the time the girl or boy gets to high school it may be too late. So the most promising remedy may be found in the first three grades (Dentler 1964).

Many specialists who are concerned about the problem stress social forces, especially the collision of different subcultures, as a prime reason for dropping out of high school. Not included in this analysis, of course, are students who have left involuntarily: those who become sick or disabled, the retarded who are not up to high school work, and those who are forced out because of special circumstances, like pregnancy or delinquency. The drop-out problem relates, rather, to those who are intellectually capable but who drop out anyway.

The reason seems to be that they come from a background where manners and mores are so different from the school's middle-class standards that they feel they can never do well in school. They suffer from "status deprivation." Their values, attitudes, vocabulary, the way they express themselves, even their clothing, are "different." Their middle-class teachers automatically disapprove of their behavior because the teachers were employed to foster middle-class standards. These potential drop-outs cannot seem to play the game according to the established rules. If they have associates—friends, brothers or sisters—who have already dropped out, dropping out does not seem like such a horrendous alternative to permanent inferiority at school (Elliott, Voss, and Wendling 1966). Besides, many of the families of drop-outs do not insist on school accomplishments. Their values may emphasize getting a job instead (Bertrand 1962; Reich and Young 1975). (See Box 11-4.)

It is easier to describe the drop-out problem than to solve it. Perhaps the solution rests with teachers and principals who can somehow surmount their middle-class backgrounds and make some attempt to understand and help young people who are struggling to keep their balance with their feet in two different worlds.

Summary

Motivation does not necessarily depend on maturation. But motivation does play a role in development from the beginning of life. Scholars theorize that there are two categories of motivation: physiological motivation, usually called drive, and various kinds of psychological motivation.

Physiological drive is responsible for efforts to find food, drink, sexual release, and physical pleasure. Psychological motives include the desire for mastery–competence, the desire for achievement, and intrinsic motivation, as in the search for knowledge and learning for its own sake. Curiosity and anxiety also play a part in motivation.

Maslow's hierarchy of needs explains motivation in another way. He believes the need to satisfy hunger is the most basic need. After physiological needs are satisfied come desires for safety, security, and protection; for freedom from fear; and for stability in general. Education can sometimes satisfy these needs by neutralizing dangers through knowledge. Next comes the motivation to seek belongingness and love. After that people strive for achievement and prestige. At the top of the Maslow list is the desire for self-actualization. All the lesser needs in the hierarchy must usually be satisfied before self-actualization can be sought. One motive may dominate the others in particular individuals. But most people are concerned with most of these drives all their lives.

Parents exert a strong influence on children's motivation. There may be a moderate hereditary factor as well. Overprotectiveness, stimulation in the environment, praise, lack of affection or encouragement, parental aspirations, the quality of the home atmosphere—all may have an effect on a child's will to achieve. Sex-typing and birth order also affect motivation.

The motivation of girls and boys differs greatly, but cultural influences are probably responsible. Girls' aspirations are generally more limited than boys', but girls seem to respond more readily than boys to efforts to broaden their horizons. Sex-role standards are clearly seen in school, where girls do better than boys because school is evidently seen as feminine. The sexes appear to act out self-fulfilling prophecies in terms of what achievements they expect of their sex. Current social change may eventually blur the distinctions in motivation between the sexes.

Teachers are soliciting agents—they can elicit responses and can influence children's achievement motives. Effective teachers can motivate children through warm attitudes, approval, and praise. A teacher's preconceptions about a pupil's ability also may affect achievement.

Children from lower-class backgrounds and some minority children appear to have low school and/or career motivation, perhaps because of the reduced possibilities they perceive in middle-class schools and the world in general. Being taught by middle-class teachers with different values may also affect their will to achieve. School drop-outs also represent motivational failure, probably caused by early home and school influences.

Chronological Overview

Motivation begins in the cradle and continues throughout life, but not according to any developmental sequence. Motivation plays a role in most aspects of development, notably cognition, language, perceptual awareness, and learning. Fostering independence and self-reliance early in life provides the foundation for later motivation.

Applying Your Knowledge

1. Suggest ways in which parents might motivate their children to achieve in school.

2. What types of teaching styles could improve children's motivation to learn?

3. Why is motivation a difficult area to study?

Further Reading

Maslow, Abraham H. *Motivation and personality*, 2d ed. New York: Harper and Row, 1970. A general theory of motivation emphasizing the psychology of health and self-actualization. Paperback.

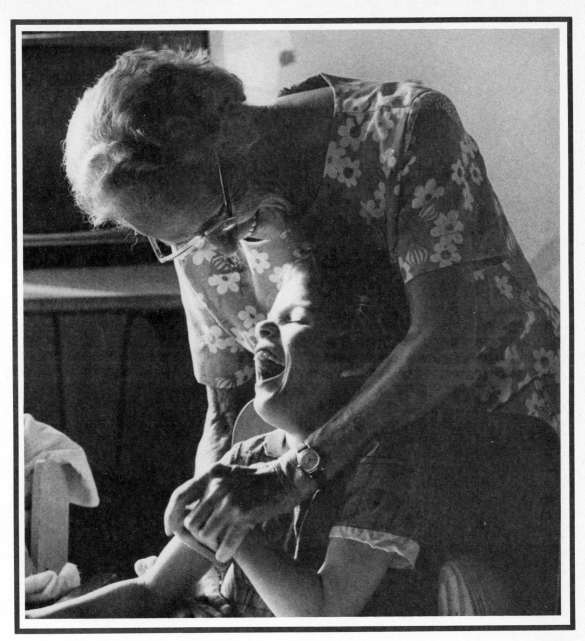

PART 5

Abnormal Development

Chapter **12**
Atypical Development

Only the name Sybil is fiction. But the facts are true. One day a young woman with puzzling emotional symptoms came to a psychiatrist for help. She was disturbed and unhappy, aware that something was wrong with her. But what? The psychiatrist had no immediate answer. But in the course of therapy, it became slowly evident that Sybil was a person who had no less than 16 different psychological selves. Each one had a distinct personality, distinctive dress, even a different name. Most of the selves were unaware of the others' existence.

In this bizarre case, a caring, skilled analyst was able to help Sybil remember the traumatic events that had caused her development to go awry and her personality to become so tragically fragmented. The result was that she was cured and was able thereafter to live a normal life as a single personality (Schreiber 1973).

The Normal–Abnormal Continuum

A difficult distinction

Sybil's emotional illness was a problem that obviously called for psychiatric treatment. But in most instances of *abnormal* psychological development, it is far from easy to determine what kind of behavior is normal and what is abnormal, who needs a doctor, and who will "get over it" or "outgrow it."

Abnormal: atypical or deviant, as distinguished from the average

Consider Michael's problem at the time he started kindergarten. He was finding it necessary to go to the boys' room to urinate half a dozen times in the few hours of the school session. The teacher sent home a note suggesting that his parents take Michael to a doctor because she thought the boy must have some sort of bladder problem. But Michael's parents felt he was probably just nervous about going to school. They decided to wait and see. It turned out that they were right. Within a week or so, Michael got used to kindergarten and stopped needing to run to the toilet.

Drawing the line Both Sybil's case and Michael's case illustrate a major principle: *normal* and *abnormal* are relative terms, part of a continuum of behavior. Some behavior is so exaggerated or inappropriate—so far from usual—that it is clearly at one end of the scale. Other behavior, however, may not be so easily categorized. When to draw the line and call behavior abnormal?

Not only teachers and parents, but even doctors and researchers have trouble drawing that line. However, by the time parents have become so alarmed about a child's behavior that they seek professional help, the task of identifying some sort of abnormality has been accomplished (Kessler 1966). Now it is apparent to the specialist that whatever the nature of the problem, it is certainly causing difficulties at home, or in school, in the neighborhood, or in the community. Diagnosis and treatment can go on from there.

The statistical approach One common way of deciding what is normal is to use a statistical approach. Normal behavior—behavior that adapts to society's needs—is defined by means of *statistical frequency*. Whatever the largest group in the population does is usually considered normal. People who laugh occasionally are normal; people who laugh all the time are not.

Statistical frequency: numerical tabulation of the frequency of a behavior

But society's standards are not usually so clear-cut. Certainly, not *all* behavior differences are abnormal. In fact, if we were all tied to the average, we would confine our geniuses and our political dissidents to asylums (as has evidently been done in some totalitarian countries) (Jahoda 1955). So normal adjustment must be carefully defined. It implies a practical balance between what an individual wants to do and what social conditions require (Kessler 1966). Society must take a reasonably broad view.

Still, the statistical approach often works well. Age norms are an example. Research has given us a fairly complete description of how a three-year-old behaves. When a 12-year-old acts that way, it is clear that the 12-year-old is showing abnormality (Kessler 1966). Behavior is abnormal, too, when it is clearly not appropriate to the circumstances.

Certainly individual differences must be taken into account. Everyone acts "abnormally" at times. One survey of a large group of children, ranging in age from two to seven, showed that almost every one of the 239 had two or more of 18 "symptoms" of abnormality, including daydreaming, laziness, and restlessness (Cummings 1944).

This does not mean that "normally abnormal" behavior should necessarily be ignored (Kessler 1966). If the symptoms get in the way and make life difficult, someone should pay attention. People are not usually hospitalized for a cold in the head, but the cold is not ignored, either.

Causes and cures

Illness or psychosocial problem? What causes abnormal behavior and how should it be treated? *Psychopathology*, the science dealing with behavioral deviation, takes varying approaches. One viewpoint assumes that emotional or psychological problems are forms of *mental illness*. Some experts believe that mental illness is a result of poor heredity or some kind of disease. A doctor would have to treat people so afflicted. A variation on this hypothesis is that some forms of abnormal behavior result from *biochemical imbalances* in the brain. An outgrowth of the mental illness hypothesis is the profession of psychiatry; psychiatrists are medical doctors who specialize in the treatment of mental and emotional disorders.

Psychopathology: study of behavioral deviation

Mental illness: any serious behavioral disorder that requires professional treatment

Biochemical imbalance: a condition in which the biochemical elements in the brain are not of normal proportions

The mental illness approach is denounced by Thomas Szasz, an authority who is himself a psychiatrist, and by George Albee, a well-known psychologist. Their contention is that most abnormal behavior comes from what is learned during socialization; it is neither an affliction nor an infection (Szasz 1961; Albee 1968). Thus, in their view, abnormal behavior is a *psychosocial* problem. Like normal behavior, abnormal behavior arises in the course of development. Szasz and Albee believe that people who are abnormal may have learned the wrong things or had bad experiences during their developmental years. The psychosocial approach holds that medical treatment is not required. Rather, the sufferer must be guided through the process of *psychotherapy* to be reeducated (Davids 1973).

Psychosocial: pertaining to the self in relation to other people and society

Psychotherapy: treatment of mental or emotional disorders by psychiatric or psychological means

However, even those who lean to the psychosocial orientation readily concede that some specific behavioral disorders have been clearly identified as genetic or physical in origin. Therefore, the prevention or cure of such problems is sometimes, though not always, a case for medical science.

Many affected Between 20 and 32 million Americans need treatment for a wide variety of mental and emotional problems, according to the President's Commission on Mental Health (1978). The commission maintains that psychological illness is not limited to people who are obviously disabled. Also included are those who suffer from alcohol and drug abuse, social isolation, poverty, discrimination, anger, depression, anxiety, fear, physical handicaps. All these conditions, the commission says, involve emotional distress.

Not specifically mentioned by the commission is the large number of Americans who are "abnormal" in another respect: those who commit serious crimes. More than half of the individuals apprehended are 14- to 24-year-olds, mostly males.

Add those who are afflicted from birth by illnesses that affect mental and emotional development. Add also the children who cannot learn. If all these are considered, the number of abnormal individuals could comprise a large proportion of the population of the United States.

In the pages that follow, we will limit our discussion to the most common mental and emotional problems that can arise in the course of child development. We will consider the causes of these abnormalities and what, if anything, psychologists and physicians believe can be done to prevent or cure them.

Genetic Disorders

Almost every pregnant woman worries about whether her baby will be normal. Most infants are. But aside from the possible physical problems that can harm the fetus, a baby may be born with a mental or emotional abnormality.

Inherited and genetic

Some psychological abnormalities originate in the genes passed on by the two parents. These conditions are genetic. (See Chapter 2, page 39.) But this does not mean that they are necessarily inherited from "tainted" ancestors. Some genes are noninherited mutations—genes that are defective due to chance or because of environmental factors to which mother or father were exposed, like radiation, illness, drugs. All inherited abnormalities are genetic, but not all genetic characteristics are inherited.

As we saw in Chapter 2, twin studies have helped investigators trace the origin of some serious genetically based abnormalities. Identical twins, the result of a single fertilized ovum and sperm, share precisely the same genes. Thus, if they have the same psychological abnormality even though subjected to different environments while being reared, it is reasonably clear that the abnormality is inherited.

Fraternal twins, in contrast, result from the fertilization of two different ova by two different sperm. These twins' genes are apt to be quite different—as different as those of any two siblings. So when fraternal twins turn out to have the same abnormality, it could be caused by shared environment.

A caring teacher and a child suffering from Down's syndrome.

Inherited: PKU   An example of an inherited disorder is *phenylketonuria (PKU)*. One person in 70 carries the recessive gene that causes PKU, an enzyme deficiency. And one in 10,000 children is born with this disease, a consequence of receiving the same recessive gene from each parent (Apgar and Beck 1973). Without the enzyme, a toxic quantity of certain amino acids accumulates in the body. The result is brain and spinal cord damage during the growing years, causing mental retardation and physical problems that could be severe.

Fortunately, there appears to be an effective treatment for PKU. But it must be started immediately after birth. A diet that limits the intake of protein (like meat and eggs) to the precise amount normally used by the body prevents the accumulation of

PKU: inherited enzyme deficiency that causes a toxic accumulation of amino acids and results in retardation

amino acids. It is thought that the treatment must continue through adolescence or longer.

It is impossible to look at a newborn and see whether or not the baby has PKU. But a simple blood test will reveal the problem. In many states, that test is now legally required for all babies born in hospitals. There is also a urine test for PKU, which pediatricians may use when infants go for the first postnatal checkup.

Genetic counseling can now identify PKU carriers and predict their chances of giving the disease to their children (Apgar and Beck 1973). If both parents are carriers, chances are one in four that they will produce a child with PKU.

Genetic only　One in 600 babies is born with *Down's syndrome*, a genetic but not inherited disorder that affects a child who inexplicably has three number 21 chromosomes instead of two. Such an infant has poor muscle tone, a large tongue, abnormal palm and foot prints, heart defects, mental retardation, and slanted, Oriental-looking eyes. The latter characteristic is responsible for the unfortunate name *mongolism,* which is sometimes given to this disease. The disorder can usually be diagnosed at birth. These children are usually sterile and cannot pass the disease on to another generation (Apgar and Beck 1973).

Women who become pregnant after 35 seem to be in the greatest danger of producing infants with Down's syndrome, perhaps because their ova are aged and "spoiled." The risk is one in 3000 for mothers under 30. It rises to one in 600 for women between 30 and 34; increases still further to one in 280 in the next five years; and is one in 80 for women who give birth between 40 and 44 (Apgar and Beck 1973). The age of the father seems to be irrelevant.

An irregular number of sex chromosomes causes *Turner's syndrome* in females. Instead of the normal two chromosomes, only one X chromosome is present. These babies have few secondary sex characteristics. When mature they tend to be exceptionally short, do not menstruate, and are sterile (Redding and Hirschhorn 1968).

Some chromosomal anomalies affect only males. *Klinefelter's syndrome* is the consequence of an XXY combination. At puberty, such a boy is generally normal-looking but sterile. He has small testes, a high-pitched voice, possibly abnormal breast development, and is often mentally retarded (Redding and Hirschhorn 1968).

Down's syndrome (mongolism): a genetic disorder caused by an extra number 21 chromosome

Turner's syndrome: a female genetic disorder caused by the absence of a sex chromosome

Klinefelter's syndrome: a male genetic disorder caused by one or more extra X sex chromosomes

Prevention

Counseling   Nobody can control the genes that make a baby, although eliminating known environmental hazards may limit possible harm. But advance planning, counseling, and testing may guide decisions involving the conception and birth of infants who will probably be born with certain genetic disorders. The abnormalities that have been described underline the importance of genetic counseling for couples who believe they may be at risk. Chromosomal studies and family history are the clues that can give a qualified genetic counselor the basis for advising a pair who are thinking about having children.

Amniocentesis   An analysis called *amniocentesis* may be performed after pregnancy has begun in cases where counseling suggests the possibility of genetic disease. The test shows whether or not the fetus has defective or abnormal chromosomes. Submitting to the procedure permits the birth of wanted children to couples who would not ordinarily try to conceive because of the possibility of producing a handicapped infant. Depending on the results of amniocentesis, the pregnancy may be either aborted or permitted to proceed.

Amniocentesis: medical procedure that extracts amniotic fluid from the uterus and tests for chromosomal abnormality

Amniocentesis may be performed as early as the twelfth or thirteenth week of pregnancy but no later than the sixteenth week. A hollow needle is inserted into the uterus and a fluid is withdrawn from the amniotic sac that surrounds the fetus. Since the test is delicate and involves a certain risk to the fetus if improperly performed, it is done only when abnormality is a real possibility. (See Figure 12–1.)

Amniocentesis is coming into wider use. One of the subjects was Princess Anne of Britain, whose doctors must have suspected the possibility of genes carrying familial abnormality. The pregnancy proceeded and a healthy son was born. A by-product of amniocentesis is that the test can also reveal the fetus' sex-determining chromosomes. But the princess did not share the information with the public at the time.

Environmental Disorders

Many parents go right on worrying even after they have brought a normal baby home. However, the chances are good that caring mothers and fathers will be able to bring up a child who will develop without serious mental or emotional problems. Still, no

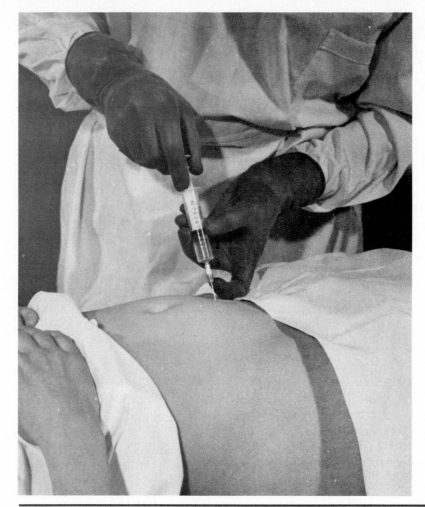

FIG. 12–1 Amniocentesis. A hypodermic needle, guided by ultrasound, is used to take a sample of amniotic fluid from the pregnant woman's uterus. The fluid contains cells sloughed off by the fetus. These cells are tested for biochemical and chromosomal defects.

society is perfect. Environmentalists contend that the conditions under which individuals grow up account for many, if not most, of the illnesses and deviations that affect mental health, both in this country and elsewhere.

Institutional deprivation

Dennis Smith, 17, came to public attention when he sued public authorities for half-a-million dollars in damages because he had been shunted from foster home to institution to foster home 16 times during his life. The teenager said: "It's like a scar on your brain" (Moskowitz 1976, page 4). This was one case when the sufferer himself diagnosed the cause of his problems.

Inadequate mothering   In Chapters 9 and 10, we pointed out the importance of early close relationships with parents, and later with peers and other people. Implied is the risk of abnormal development when children suffer social deprivation. Lack of mothering is a critical variable in early abnormal development. The consequences have been strikingly illustrated by many studies of institutionalized children.

One important investigation compared 15 three-year-old children who had been institutionalized since early infancy with a group of children who had been in a foster home for their first three years (Goldfarb 1945*a*, *b*). Tests showed that the foster home children were within average intelligence range. But the institutionalized youngsters were below normal in tests of both verbal and nonverbal performance. Their reaction to the examiner was cold and distant. They showed an insatiable need for affection. Their conceptual development was impaired, compared with the other group. They were less likely to think abstractly or to generalize. They had trouble with time and space concepts. They could not follow rules of behavior.

What the institutionalized children lacked, compared with the foster home children, was handling, physical and verbal stimulation, someone to play with them and talk to them. Even after six months in a foster home, the previously institutionalized children lagged behind children who had spent all their lives in foster homes. Being deprived of normal "tender loving care" by a mother and a father seemed to have condemned these youngsters to possibly permanent emotional and conceptual damage (Goldfarb 1945*a*, *b*).

A different analysis showed abnormal development in infants reared in an institution where physical needs were met but adequate mothering was not provided. Evaluation of their progress at the ages of three to four showed that their emotional relationships to people were poor. They were attached to no one person. They never developed a sense of trust in their adult care-givers. They rarely sought out adults for help, comfort, or pleasure. Their speech was retarded and they had noticeable difficulty in communicating with others. They had no names for either people or things. They did not even use noises to express their feelings or show what they wanted. They played poorly, without joy, and without showing many ideas of what to do while playing (Provence and Lipton 1962).

Substitute mothers One investigator played "mother" to a group of institutionalized infants, while a second group remained under the routine care of the institution's staff. After two months, the mothered group was noticeably ahead of the untreated group in social responsiveness. They reacted to strangers and smiled at people (Rheingold 1956). Even such a seemingly small difference in rearing seems to be important for an individual's later years. A child who gets a solid grounding in emotional relationships from a primary care-giver appears to have a sound basis for emotional relationships and social attachments later on.

An unusual comparison of two different groups of mentally retarded babies also showed the importance of almost any kind of consistent mothering. One group was in an orphanage where the mothering was clearly inadequate. The other group was placed in a different institution whose population was mentally retarded. Mentally retarded older girls took care of the infants. This group of babies emerged with distinctly higher IQ scores than their orphanage counterparts (Skeels 1966). (See Chapter 8, pages 333–334.) Evidently, mothering can compensate for some of the adverse effects of institutionalization. It is better for a child to have some kind of personal attention than no mothering at all.

Foster grandparents seem to be an effective substitute for natural mothers. This conclusion comes from a comparison of two groups of institutionalized children over a four-year period. One group had part-time mothering by elderly individuals while the other did not. There was a significant IQ difference between the two groups. Not only were the "grandmothered" children helped but so were the grandmothers, who had found a new function (Saltz 1971).

Foster grandparents: older adults who give substitute mothering

Findings like these have motivated important changes in medical and social practices in recent years. Babies and children who, for one reason or another, cannot be cared for by parents are usually placed in a foster home as soon as possible. Institutions try to supply a single care-giver for a child instead of many (Rheingold 1956). Some programs for deprived children have enlisted the help of older adults to serve as foster grandparents (Saltz 1971). In some areas, foster grandparent programs are now supported by public funds. Well-run public agencies also try to avoid shunting a child from one home to another, to prevent the kind of psychological damage suffered by Dennis Smith.

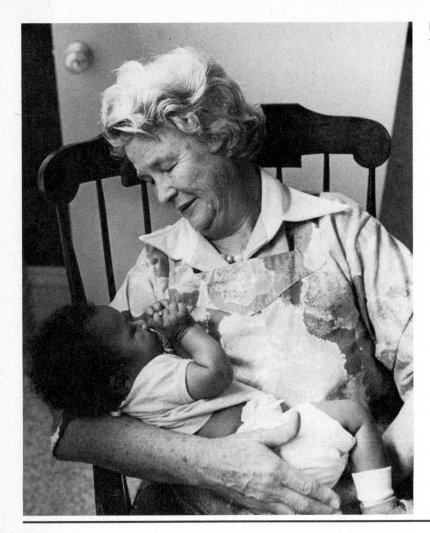

Foster grandparents may be female . . .

Damaged home environment

Separation   A child need not be institutionalized to be damaged by inadequate mothering. When an infant is separated from parents for a long time, whatever the reason, it may cause emotional harm. A child may display "grief and mourning" (Bowlby 1960), become depressed, and even behave autistically—lose the power to relate to anyone (Spitz 1946*a,b*). Babies who suffer from lack of affection and stimulation in the first three to six months may

. . . or male.

never achieve adequate psychological development (Freedman 1968).

Even to be separated from the mother for a short time in the early weeks after birth—as in the case of premature babies who spend days or weeks in an isolette—may have untoward consequences in terms of later development. When a premature baby is finally given to the mother, she tends to feel less adequate, smiles and handles the infant less than the mother of a full-term baby (Leifer et al. 1972).

Neglect Rich or poor, institutionalized or brought up at home—these are not necessarily clear-cut criteria of whether children are being reared to be normal. Differences in emotional support and affection might be called psychological class differences, with consequences for a child's emotional health (Stone and Kestenbaum 1974).

Consider the case of Jane V., the daughter of a family of immense wealth and social prominence. She turned up in a psychiatrist's office at the age of 19, suffering from vomiting, depression, and apathy. In spite of her intelligence, she was doing poorly in college, had little sense of purpose and very little self-discipline. She hardly remembered her parents from her early childhood. What she did recall was neglect, lack of affection, harsh reprimands. Her three brothers seemed to have been the favorites. As a child she had been in the habit of finding lonely refuge in a cave on the family estate where she read comics and downed soft drinks (Stone and Kestenbaum 1974).

Many other cases of apparent maternal deprivation among wealthy families come to psychiatrists. These damaged children and adults might be considered to be in the same psychological class as children brought up in institutions. The loss of adequate parenting seems to be the key to their problems.

Child abuse Both children and parents may be considered the victims in what has been called the *battered child syndrome*. Child abuse is an environmental disease that is a major cause of infant mortality in our society. Parents who abuse their children tend to be dissatisfied with their own marriage and life-style. Many have had poor home environments when they were children and may themselves have been abused.

Battered child syndrome: child abuse and the social and psychological factors related to it

Child-abusers are typically young, lonely, rejected, and financially insecure. The children who are abused were very likely unwanted. Or they were wanted for the wrong reason: to supply the love that the mother's or father's own parents had failed to give and that the youthful mate is also unable to provide. When a baby acts like a baby—refuses to eat, cries, gets into mischief—the parent experiences feelings of rejection all over again. The child is beaten out of feelings of frustration and inadequacy (Joint Commission on Mental Health of Children 1970). Economic stress is a factor in more than one out of three child-abuse cases, according to a New York study (Garbarino 1976).

In some child-abuse cases, there is a history of difficult pregnancy, delivery problems, early ill health of mother or child or both, or parental separation in the first six months after birth. Perhaps better, more thoughtful treatment of the parents by doctors, nurses, or social workers during these difficult pre- and postnatal months could be a preventive measure (Lynch 1975).

Psychoneuroses

Nature of the problem

Blaming parents—especially mothers—for children's emotional difficulties is so common in our society that (just on general principles) some conscientious middle-class parents live with a constant and usually unwarranted feeling of guilt. But while parents often do play a part in the emotional disturbances of children and adults, not all problems stem from parent–child difficulties.

Defense against anxiety Betty S., a bright first grader, refused to go to school and vomited every morning. Jim B., a 12-year-old, was always worried about catching a disease. He kept washing his hands until they were raw and red. Mark K., in the third grade, developed the habit of constantly blinking his eyes.

All three of these children had caring parents and seemingly good homes. Yet they were all suffering from different varieties of emotional disturbance—psychoneuroses. *Psychoneurosis* is a functional (as opposed to organic) disorder that involves intense feelings of anxiety.

Psychoneurosis: functional (psychological) disorder involving intense anxiety

Psychoneurosis is not the same as psychosis, a much more severe emotional problem (see page 497). It must also be distinguished from organic behavior disorders, which have a physical or physiological basis (Kessler 1966).*

Parents and teachers are constantly being faced with behavioral problems that may really be neurotic reactions. "Unconscious and habitual ways of dealing with anxiety" are a sign of neurosis (Engel 1972, page 96). Children may unconsciously try to protect themselves from guilt, anxiety, or shame by resorting to various kinds of *defense mechanisms*, behavior that, in effect,

Defense mechanism: behavior that protects the psyche from guilt, anxiety, or shame

---

*The American Psychiatric Association has been considering the possibility of dropping the term *neurosis* and using instead descriptions of specific disorders.

hides them from their own feelings. By distorting or denying certain aspects of their lives they feel less threatened. (See Box 12–1.)

Children do not usually develop psychoneuroses until they are of school age, because such internalized conflicts depend on a certain minimum level of cognitive ability. Neuroses are fairly common, and they are the least serious of psychological disturbances. A good therapist can usually cure the sufferer, sometimes very quickly, because the underlying causes are generally relatively easy for an expert to discover (Kessler 1966).

From the behavioral point of view, all anxieties and neuroses are learned, and so are all the various coping mechanisms—behavior adopted by the sufferer to reduce anxiety. According to the psychoanalytic view, deriving from Freud, the neurosis stems from unconscious causes.

Box 12–1   Defense Mechanisms

When people are coping with anxiety, they often try to reduce tension by setting up defense mechanisms as a protection against feared dangers. But at the same time, these techniques distort or deny certain aspects of reality.

Freud laid great stress on sexuality as the basis of anxiety and consequent defense mechanisms. In the Victorian era, when Freud was developing his theories, the repression of sexuality was widespread. But today psychiatrists and psychologists recognize that there may be other kinds of anxiety that lead to neurotic behavior (Engel 1972).

Repression is a defense mechanism that totally banishes from awareness an event, feeling, or idea. An example is the compulsive hand-washer who has an exaggerated fear of disease. The youngster is repressing some underlying anxiety, maybe guilt over masturbation. But now the guilt becomes dirt on the hands, relieved by washing. Freud believed that such suppression is conscious and deliberate, but the current theory is that it is unconscious.

Reaction formation is the term used to describe behavior unconsciously designed to be the opposite of behavior that is being repressed. An example is the cleanliness fanatic who may actually be a "dirty person"—someone who has repressed the enjoyment of making a mess.

Rationalization is another common neurotic device. People work out elaborate false justifications for their behavior to hide their basic anxiety-provoking

Kinds of neuroses

Phobia A typical form of childhood neurosis is *phobia*: an un-reasonable preoccupation with an object or situation—a fear so intense that it can be disabling. Fears of school, transportation, or animals are common. But not all such fears are phobias. The child who is afraid of dogs may be upset only if a dog is nearby. But if the child is so afraid of dogs that the fear makes going to school or playing with friends or even going outside the house frightening, a phobia has developed (Kessler 1966).

Phobia: excessive fear of an object or situation

In 1909, Freud reported a classic study of phobia (Freud 1953). Five-year-old Hans was neurotically afraid of a horse. According to Freud, the boy's excessive fear did not really relate to the horse but to his own frightening impulses, which had been repressed. He would have liked to attack his father but projected this unacceptable impulse on the father: he felt that his parent

motivation and save face in their own eyes. This kind of rationalization makes it possible to go on functioning until the time when the anxiety-producing situation can be resolved.

Projection—casting blame on someone else, or attributing to others a quality one may not wish to acknowledge in oneself—is a common neurotic habit. "You're immature!" when, in fact, *I* am.

Regression is a neurotic retreat to an earlier developmental level because of fear. Toilet-trained toddlers frequently regress and start to soil themselves again in the face of disruption, like a move to a new house or the birth of a sibling.

Disassociation or *denial* is a neurotic repression of unpleasant memories. Sybil's form of disassociation was to assume multiple personalities, to permit her to separate herself from unpleasant memories or feelings. Some people develop amnesia.

Displacement is the practice of substituting a nonthreatening target for a threatening one. In everyday life, we might kick the door instead of kicking Mother. "Hate" groups take it out on the Jews or the blacks or the "Commies"—but deep down they may really hate what happened to them in childhood.

Sublimation is a device to save a person from an anxiety-provoking situation by diverting the energy in a socially acceptable way. For example, boys used to be urged to sublimate their sexual urges by going in for strenuous sports.

wished to attack him. The "solution" was displacement. He believed the horse was dangerous, not his father. In this way he solved his conflict, which was loving and hating Father at the same time. The solution was practical, too: a boy has to see his father every day, but the horse can be avoided just by staying indoors (Kessler 1966).

Common fears   For a young child to have fears is common and ordinarily not neurotic. Fear of loud noises is common in infants. And stranger anxiety is a normal development (see Chapter 9, page 369).

Fear of noises and of strange people declines as children grow older. But many grow increasingly afraid of imagined, anticipated, and supernatural dangers (Jersild and Holmes 1935–36). Then, when they reach school age, children begin to have less trouble with imaginary fears, like ghosts and monsters. But new, more realistic concerns take their place, such as worry over bodily injury and physical danger (Bauer 1976). Later on, around third grade, children start to worry about political dangers— wars, Communist take-over—seemingly as a consequence of television-watching and exposure to the media in general. But many continue to fear animals and supernatural phenomena, too (Croake 1969).

Children may be helped to lose their fears in the same way they are taught other lessons: by conditioning. A parent can encourage a child to become more familiar with whatever is frightening. Learning theory (see Chapter 7) may be used to eliminate fears, as well as to teach school subjects (Jersild and Holmes 1935–36).

A group of children who were afraid of dogs was shown a series of movies in which models were playing with dogs without fear and with increasingly intimate contact. The children who saw even one model playing with a dog became less fearful themselves. Better still, those who saw a number of people harmlessly playing with dogs learned to do it themselves without apparent fear. The lesson was even transferred to other previously fearsome objects (Bandura and Menlove 1968; Woody 1969).

Similarly, in a program at Stanford University individuals were taught to conquer their fear of snakes. They were systematically desensitized by being subjected to a hierarchy of anxiety-producing situations, starting with a mild situation and then working up gradually to more frightening encounters with the dreaded object.

Parents often coax terrified children into the ocean or a pool in the same fashion. The child is induced to put toes in first. Then ankles. Then the youngster moves in a few more inches, holding tightly to the parent. Eventually, the child's face is in the water and swimming lessons can begin. All this is operant conditioning, whether or not the teacher–parent realizes it, with a dollop of modeling thrown in.

Some parents worry that television may cause neurotic fear. Should youngsters be allowed to look at fairy-tale films like Snow White or the Wizard of Oz? At least one child therapist believes fairy tales contribute to healthy personality development (Bettleheim 1976). It has also been suggested that television programs may be useful in showing parents how to play with their children and how to cope with their youthful fears (Singer and Singer 1973).

School phobia   School phobia is an extremely common problem in our society. Betty S., who vomited every morning to avoid going to school, was really frightened that her mother would disappear while she was gone. One day her mother had, in fact, been late coming back from marketing. Betty returned to an unoccupied house and was terrified by her apparent abandonment. But the reason for the phobia came out only after a psychologist saw the child several times.

School phobias seldom have anything to do with real fear of failing in school. There is usually some other reason, like fear of the teacher, or the cafeteria, or the trip to school, or some home situation. In any case, how long the phobia lasts and how severe it becomes often depends on the parent's reaction. Parents who overreact with their own anxiety can make the situation worse (Kessler 1966). (See also Box 12–2.)

Obsessive–compulsive behavior   Also common in childhood is *obsessive–compulsive behavior*. The child has thoughts or ideas that will not go away. The result is compulsive behavior, which is ritualistically repeated, reflecting the obsessive anxiety. Examples might be compulsive hand-washing or continually checking all the locks on the doors and windows. Minor compulsive behavior, such as avoiding the cracks in the sidewalk, is normal in the

Obsessive–compulsive behavior: ritualistic, repetitive behavior resulting from continually recurring thoughts

course of development. Such behavior is neurotic only when it is so important that the child becomes extremely upset and anxious when the ritual cannot be carried out.

Hysteria   A child struggling unsuccessfully with anxiety may also manifest signs of *hysteria*. There may be excessive involuntary movements of parts of the body: twitches, tics, jerky movements. Another form of hysteria is psychological inability to use some part of the body that is physically healthy: loss of the voice, inability to eat or to go to the toilet. Usually the conflicts that cause hysteria in children go away without any intervention (Kessler 1966).

Hysteria: excessive involuntary movement or loss of a bodily function

Whatever the neurosis, a therapist would have to make sure that a child's behavior is truly abnormal, and not just a result of reasonable anxiety. Maybe there really is a fierce dog next door. But if there is no real danger, and a child still worries all the time

---

Box 12–2   School Phobia

When a child wants to stay home with Mother instead of going to school, the problem is called *school phobia*. It is not the same as truancy, when the simple object is to do something more pleasurable than going to school (Eisenberg 1958).

Not all authorities agree that the real basis of school phobia is separation anxiety. Some contend that the cause may be an unrealistically high self-image. When the realities of school threaten a child's feeling of superiority, the pupil prefers to retreat to the safety of home (Leventhal and Sills 1964).

More girls than boys have school phobia, although boy clients outnumber girls in child guidance clinics. While school phobia may happen at any age, it is more common in the lower grades. Even when the symptoms develop later, the source can usually be found in the early school years.

Some therapists treat school phobia by trying to resolve conflicts between mother and child. Others think the most important thing is to get the youngster back to school by any means short of physical force. Both systems seem to work (Davids 1973). In any case, collaboration of mother, child, and teacher is necessary for a cure. Learning theory may help. Using classical and operant conditioning, a child can be systematically desensitized to going to school by being taken back for short visits, and also by being given rewards for going to school. (See Chapter 7, pages 265–269.) At the same time, the parents should treat the child with sympathy, understanding, and a minimum of anxiety (Kessler 1966).

---

to the point of neurosis, then the sufferer must be helped to get over the underlying worry (Engel 1972).

Most of us have had experience with neurotic behavior, our own or someone else's. It probably would not occur to us to want to confine a neurotic person to a hospital. People with a neurosis can usually continue to function in daily life, although sometimes rather poorly.

Psychosis

Unlike neurotics, some individuals are so disturbed they are more or less out of touch with reality. They are *psychotic*—severely upset, not only emotionally but also sometimes in their perceptions of what is happening, in their movements, in their speech, in their thoughts, in their sense of themselves as individuals.

Psychosis: organic disorder involving separation from reality

Manifestations

Psychoses may be manifested in children in the following ways:

1. *Affect*—strange ways of expressing feelings; temper tantrums for no reason; wildly inappropriate emotions, or no feelings at all.
2. *Perception*—gross misinterpretations of what is seen or heard, like hallucinations or disorientation.
3. *Motility*—peculiar mannerisms, like *severe* head-banging (many normal children are crib-rockers) or other repeated physical movements that could be dangerous.
4. *Speech*—not speaking at all, or constantly making odd, meaningless noises.
5. *Individuation*—being "fused" to the mother both physically and emotionally; inability to differentiate between own body and someone else's; no sense of identity as separate from other people.
6. *Thought*—bizarre thoughts; inability to control thoughts; illogical or peculiarly symbolic thoughts.

Age has a great deal to do with whether a child is adjudged to be severely ill. If a behavior is inappropriate for a particular age level, it may be merely a sign of immaturity or it may be a sign of emotional disturbance. Some kinds of behavior, at first appearing only immature, may in fact turn out to be psychotic (Engel 1972).

Nobody is sure what causes psychoses. Some authorities believe the origin could be genetic. Others suggest body chemistry may be at fault. Early upbringing is another possibility. Failing definitive answers, it is still useful to consider the *etiology* of certain specific psychoses: the complex, varied circumstances that appear to be associated with their occurrence.

Etiology: study of possible causes or circumstances associated with the onset of a disorder

Autism

Children suffering from *autism*, a psychosis characterized by primitive and repetitive behavior, are not usually diagnosed until the ages of three or four, when the symptoms become obvious. But the condition seems to be present from birth.

Autism: a psychotic disorder characterized by extreme preoccupation with one's own thoughts and repetitive, ritualistic behavior

The causes of autism are controversial and debatable. Some investigators feel autism is related to the sex chromosomes, because more boys than girls are diagnosed as autistic. Others feel that the cause is environmental, that a cold, rejecting home life can be responsible. Still others subscribe to the theory that autism is due to a biochemical imbalance in the brain. A recent review of the literature concludes that autism is possibly the result of central nervous system impairment caused by trauma before or during birth (Suran and Rizzo 1979).

Autistic children are out of touch with reality, isolated, alone, extremely preoccupied with their own thoughts. When handled, they make no anticipatory gestures (Kanner 1943). They insist on sameness: walking in straight lines, wearing the same clothes, eating the same foods. They cannot learn new things or establish new routines. Their behavior is characteristically repetitive and ritualistic: they may rock, wiggle their fingers, tap, walk on tiptoes. Behavior is primitive: they scream, bite, kick (Chambers 1969). Their communication system is poor. They may be mute; they may merely echo what they hear; or they may react to some sounds but appear deaf to others. They may fear harmless things, yet be impervious to real danger. Overactivity is common—repetitive jumping, spinning (Chambers 1969; Kanner 1943).

All this behavior might be normal if it were transitory, but in autistic children it goes on indefinitely. While autistic children do outgrow some of these symptoms, they continue to be totally self-centered.

Autistic children are not unintelligent. They may be able to function at their own age level academically, but their classmates are not people to whom they relate. On the other hand, they may talk to strangers as if they know them without realizing they are not part of their daily lives (Kessler 1966). While unable to relate to people, autistic children establish good relations to objects. These children are physically healthy, look alert, are bright and serious-minded, and often are from very intelligent families (Chambers 1969). What happens to autistic children as they grow toward adulthood seems to depend on their own inherent nature, plus whatever the parents are able to contribute to the relationship.

Schizophrenia

Comparison with autism Childhood *schizophrenia* starts later than autism and the factors that seem to influence it are somewhat different, but the two disorders share some of the same symptoms (Chambers 1969). Autism becomes apparent early in life, usually around the ages of three and four; schizophrenia appears after a period of apparently normal development (Suran and Rizzo 1979). Schizophrenics seem to have more physical and neurological problems than the autistic, who are usually healthy and have good motor development.

Schizophrenia: general name for a group of psychotic reactions

Schizophrenia seems to involve even more complex personality and emotional problems than autism. However, not all authorities feel that it is valid to differentiate between the two, since there are so many similarities (Kessler 1966). Schizophrenics behave much the same way as autistic children, though they are also apt to have hallucinations and delusions.

Causes Schizophrenic children are like normal children in basic physical characteristics but below par in neurological functions. So it is possible that neurological defects can cause schizophrenia. However, abnormal rearing could also be at fault. It may be that there are really two kinds of schizophrenics: those who have a neurological defect from brain damage and those who have severely abnormal upbringing (Goldfarb 1961). It is also possible that the two causes may work together to produce the symptoms.

A classic study by Franz Kallman (1946) demonstrated that individuals may become schizophrenic because of a *genetic predisposition*. If one identical twin develops the disease, the other has an eight in ten chance of developing it too. The incidence of both identical twins suffering from schizophrenia is eight times as great as for fraternal twins. But even fraternal twins and siblings (who have somewhat similar genetic relationships) are

Genetic predisposition: tendency to a behavior or condition linked to inheritance

more likely to share the disease than unrelated people. Their chances are one in ten.

Comparisons between the relatives of schizophrenics and the general population have shown that the closer the biological relationship to a schizophrenic, the more likely it is that an individual will have the same illness (Suran and Rizzo 1979). In one study, nearly one in ten of the children of schizophrenic parents became schizophrenic, even when brought up by adoptive or foster parents. In contrast, none of the offspring of nonschizophrenics developed the disease (Wender 1969).

However, studies done later than Kallman's dispute the exceptionally high incidence of schizophrenia for both identical twins. Based on more stringent blood tests and more closely controlled sample populations, the new finding is that the chance of both identical twins suffering from schizophrenia is only two to four times as great as for fraternal twins. The genetic cause is not denied, but it appears that there are probably also both prenatal and postnatal environmental influences that will determine whether any individual will actually become emotionally ill (Stabenau 1968; Kringlen 1966). Thus, environmental factors do seem to contribute to the occurrence of the disease. If they did not, then *both* identical twins would always become schizophrenic.

The premise that the illness had a genetic basis seemed to preclude any hope of treatment. But since it seems that the genetic weakness is a problem of metabolism, there is a real possibility that someone will discover a remedy that will reverse schizophrenia. In a way, this is a more hopeful prospect than if it were true that environment is the sole cause (Karlsson 1967).

Delinquency

Obviously, the most serious consequences of neuroses and psychoses fall upon the afflicted person and the immediate family (although almost all illnesses have social costs as well). But there are other personality problems that unquestionably and inevitably endanger society as a whole. In this category are the characteristics that cause criminal behavior.

Who are the delinquents?

Society puts the label "delinquent" on acts that depart more or less seriously from legally established norms. Delinquents are

individuals who have inadequate control over their behavior. They cannot wait to gratify their desires and are unable to impose society's standards on themselves or to resist temptation (Ross 1974).

Delinquents have inadequate control over their own behavior.

More than 2% of the American population between 10 and 17 shows up in juvenile court every year. The proportion has been going up year by year. Most likely to be arrested and prosecuted are boys, particularly those from the lowest socioeconomic levels (Davids 1973).

Predicting delinquency   Studies show that it may be possible to predict in the early school years who will eventually be among those in trouble with the law. Juvenile delinquents tend to have distinctive childhood histories. These little children, from kindergarten to the third grade, already are behaving unacceptably, they already have more academic problems, they already seem emotionally disturbed (Davids 1973).

They seem to care less than others about the rights and feelings of their classmates. They seem less aware of the need to accept responsibility for their obligations, either as individuals or as members of a group. They have poor attitudes toward authority; they do not seem to understand the need for rules and why they have to abide by them. They have trouble getting along with others, are discourteous, tactless, unable to be fair in their dealings. All this leads to their being disliked and not accepted by their peers (Conger, Miller, and Walsmith 1965).

Several years ago, one public figure was so impressed by the possibility of nipping delinquency in the bud by screening young children that he proposed that the government embark on a formal program of early testing. But the idea created a political uproar. Opponents pointed out that such a project would amount to conviction without trial. Besides, it might unjustly tag many innocent youngsters for life.

A case history A lengthy probation report presented to the juvenile department of a state court provides a vivid picture of the background of a 19-year-old who had been in repeated trouble. "John Doe" was born and brought up in a small town. He left high school as early as the law permitted. In the meantime, his list of offenses included shoplifting, burglary of a church, bicycle theft, receiving stolen property, malicious mischief, truancy, petty theft, drunkenness, threatening telephone calls, arson: a total of 15 brushes with the law.

The Doe family includes eight children, all delinquent. Their home was described as poorly maintained, cluttered, dirty. According to the probation officer, the family "only receives barely enough money to get by." The father had been unemployed for years and "claims to be totally disabled because of a bad back and bleeding ulcers . . . his daily routine often includes sleeping until noon, watching television all day, and yelling at the children." Mr. Doe "has always allowed his children to come and go as they please as long as they do not bother him. He has become extremely irate in the past whenever his children have been arrested or questioned by the police. . . . Although [the father] has not been arrested for several years, in the past he was arrested for being drunk in public and on one occasion for a peace disturbance in which he beat up his wife."

As for the mother, she "has always kept in the background and allowed her husband to dominate every situation where this department was involved. She has always been very subservient to [Mr. Doe] and she has always bailed him out of jail, even on an occasion when he beat her up."

According to an employer, John Doe was "very unreliable, keeping irregular hours and requesting to leave work early complaining of numerous ailments. After he talked to [John] regarding his poor work habits, the subject failed to report for work any further."

Causes of delinquency

Undeveloped conscience   John Doe's case illustrates most of the characteristics and causes of delinquency. Delinquency, a character disorder, appears to be a result of a poorly developed conscience, failure to learn controls, and inadequate parent–child relationships. The delinquent's conscience—superego, in Freudian terms—is functioning poorly for one or more reasons: early neglect or deprivation by care-givers; failure to establish meaningful relationships early in life; identification with socially inadequate models and adoption of their antisocial values; parents who permit antisocial behavior even though they have said it is wrong. These conditions can occur in any level of society, among the educated well-to-do as well as among the poverty-stricken.

Delinquents give in to their instinctual desires even though they know what they are doing is not right. Some push their consciences aside and break the law as a way of punishing their parents, or punishing themselves because of unconscious guilt feelings (Kessler 1966).

Failure to learn control   Juvenile delinquents do not usually learn how to be delinquent. What they do seldom requires skills, like counterfeiting. Rather, they are demonstrating a *failure to learn* how to control their behavior, which is a "skill" acquired by most people as they grow up. Delinquents have not learned how to delay gratification of their desires. In Freudian terms, they are still governed by the infantile id, which operates primarily on impulses (Ross 1974).

John Doe vividly illustrates factors often associated with potential delinquency: too strict or erratic discipline by father; unsuitable supervision by mother; father's and mother's indifference or hostility; lack of family cohesiveness—weak ties, few shared interests (Glueck and Glueck 1959).

Home environment   Arrest records suggest that, in urban areas, delinquency occurs more frequently in families low on the socioeconomic scale, but in rural and urban communities taken together the delinquency rate is not so much a function of social class as of neighborhood, family structure, and the youngster's social group (Short and Strodtbeck 1965; Clark and Wenninger 1962; Erickson and Empey 1965). Also, the delinquent from the lower socioeconomic group is likely to be placed on probation or in a reformatory. But the middle- or upper-class delinquent is apt to be returned to parents, who may consult a specialist on child or adolescent behavior (Joint Commission on Mental Health of Children 1973). Therefore, statistics may lead to a possibly false conclusion that poor children commit more crimes than richer children.

One frequent assumption is that when a mother goes out to work, her children will become delinquents. Studies do not bear out this conclusion. While there is evidence that insufficient supervision is related to delinquency, a child may go astray regardless of the mother's employment. Working mothers do not have more delinquency in their families than nonworking mothers (Hoffman 1974). (See Chapter 10, page 410.)

What seems to matter most is the stability of the home environment and the mother's attitude toward her work. In poor families, delinquency happens more often where mothers are "occasionally employed" than in homes where the mother has a regular job. The occasionally employed mother often reflects an unstable home environment with an inadequate or frequently absent father or male figure and/or a rocky marriage (Glueck and Glueck 1957).

Delinquency is frequently associated with father absence (Anderson 1968). It has been shown that a fatherless home, or one in which the father has little influence, is apt to produce children who rebel against all authority (van Mannen 1968). Juvenile crime rates are lowest when fathers are warm or at least passive (McCord and McCord 1959).

However, the mere fact that a home has only one parent does not necessarily cause the children to become delinquents, even though one-parent households do more frequently breed lawbreakers. Two large groups of boys were compared, delinquents in one group, nondelinquents in the other. One in three of the delinquents came from homes with only one parent. Only one in five of the law-abiding youngsters was being raised by one parent (Glueck and Glueck 1959).

However, single-parent homes are the norm from the outset in some cultural groups. The children have no sense of dissension or disruption as they do in families where the father has died or the parents have had a stormy relationship before the marriage ended. The conditions that breed delinquency are so varied there is no way to determine for sure which combination will contribute to behavioral problems (Ross 1974).

It appears that the *quality* of the home life and family interaction are important determinants of delinquency. What seems to make the difference is whether or not the home is happy or unhappy; how poor the family is; whether there are recreational and educational opportunities, and whether there are neighborhood gangs or delinquents that may influence the children. The only generalization that may safely be made about the cause of delinquency is that a child's early environment does influence later behavior and ability to suppress antisocial impulses (Ross 1974).

Cognitive Abnormality

Some social theorists believe that the way children are reared creates mental as well as emotional deficiency. But investigators have determined that there are both genetic and other environmental factors which lead to mental retardation and learning disabilities.

Mental retardation

Definition Who is mentally retarded? The accepted definition of *mental retardation* is subaverage intellectual functioning that is associated with impaired adaptive behavior (Heber 1959; Kessler 1966).

Mental retardation: subaverage intellectual ability

If one relies on IQ tests, some 16% of the American population may be said to be mentally retarded. The most commonly used demarcation between retarded and normal is an IQ of 70 on the Stanford-Binet scale. (See Chapter 8, pages 307, 311.) Below that score, and sometimes even several points above, children are usually placed in special public school classes.

Causes   Some causes of retardation are present at birth. They are either inherited or due to conditions that affect the pregnancy or the birth: Down's syndrome, prenatal infections, prematurity, difficult delivery, anatomically abnormal brain structure, metabolic defects. Certain childhood accidents and diseases may also result in mental retardation (Kessler 1966).

Environmentalists attribute mental retardation to inadequacies in the environment, since many children score low on intelligence tests without any apparent physical cause. Numerous black children are in this category. Most psychologists believe this kind of retardation is environmental and cultural, a function of poverty: poor living conditions, inadequate health care, faulty upbringing (Robinson and Robinson 1965). Among poor blacks, there are also more premature births and complications of pregnancy (Davids 1973).

Natural versus learned competence   Jerome Kagan is one of those psychologists who stress the distinction between natural intellectual competence and culturally acquired ability. Almost all children will eventually attain some intellectual abilities because they are basic to humans: perception, speech, memory, reasoning. But most children will not acquire cultural abilities—like arithmetic, reading, science—unless they are specifically taught. Kagan maintains that the distinction is important in defining mental retardation since "society has made relative retardation in culturally arbitrary skills synonymous with absolute retardation in basic intellectual skills" (Kagan 1973, page 11).

In other words, some children are called retarded merely because they have not had an opportunity to learn. Unfortunately, the functional definition of retardation lumps together all those who are mentally and socially inadequate to the demands of society and who cannot compete with others the same age (Kessler 1966). Since retardation is often diagnosed only after a child reaches school, such retardation may be chiefly a reflection of community standards (Robinson and Robinson 1965). This culturally based retardation caused by deficiencies in the environment could be reversed by education, the earlier the better (Kagan 1973). George Albee, another authority, suggests that insufficient efforts to train the retarded to become self-sufficient may be due to the tragic misconception that all retardation is a disease that has no remedy (Davids 1973).

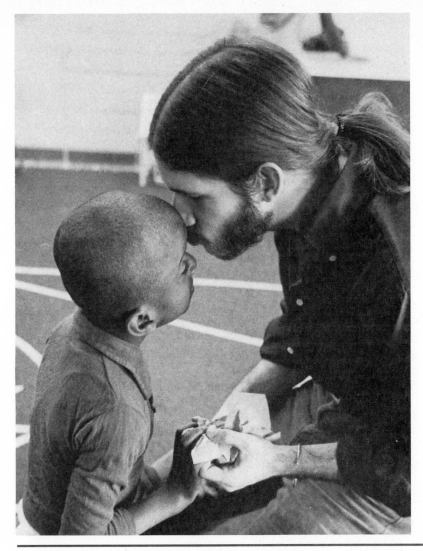

Even severely damaged children may be helped by loving care.

Remedies Until relatively recent years, the mentally retarded were indeed considered hopeless and many were "warehoused" in institutions. But now there is a concerted effort by schools to separate the trainable and the untrainable. The trainable are taught simple reading and arithmetic and other basic skills. The object is to help them develop ways of taking care of themselves.

They may never become financially or socially independent, but at least the attention they need will be minimized.

Some parents have discovered in their own way that even severely retarded children may be helped by loving care. A note written by a dying father when he left his seven-year-old retarded daughter at a Catholic school provides a touching example: "She is visibly alert, usually happy and coyly smiling or laughing to secure the attention she successfully obtains—she is to me irresistible. [Once] she ignored social stimula and just paced and wandered unwilling to concentrate on any object or person. How blessed I felt when she began finally to respond to the kisses and stroking she has received" (A merciful child desertion 1977).

Learning disability

"Johnny can't read" became a catchword in recent years, a symbol of allegedly poor educational methods. But poor reading ability may also be the result of learning disabilities. *Learning disabilities* refer to perceptual or communication difficulties that affect a child's ability to absorb or deal with information.

Children with learning disabilities are not retarded. Their inability to conform to currently acceptable academic norms may be caused by poor health or some kind of sensory problem. Perhaps scholastic requirements are too high for them or the teaching not good enough. Learning disabilities were once considered a sign of emotional problems (Kessler 1966). However, the more recent view is that the term *learning disabilities* should not be used to describe learning problems caused by special conditions like emotional disturbance or mental retardation (Suran and Rizzo 1979).

Diagnosing the problem Strictly speaking, the diagnosis of learning disability should be limited to a *specific* incapacity or disorder in one or more of the processes of speech, language, perception, reading, spelling, writing, or arithmetic. In other words, in children with learning disability the retardation is not general, even though a retarded child could also have a particular learning disability (Kirk 1964; Suran and Rizzo 1979).

Sometimes children are pegged as having a reading disability merely because reading is so important to our educational system that it overshadows everything else. Many cases of reading disability are actually cases of learning disability in general. Some of these children may suffer from a form of retardation.

Learning disabilities: perceptual or communication difficulties that hinder the ability to obtain or process information

Others may have an emotional disorder, brain damage, physical handicaps, or sensory defects (Kessler 1966; Davids 1973).

Major kinds of disability   Aphasia, dyslexia, and hyperkinesis are three of the better known kinds of learning disability.

Aphasia is a language disorder, the result of a defect in the central nervous system. It is not the same as problems that come from hearing loss, paralysis, retardation, or emotional disturbance (Agranowitz 1964; Kleffner 1959; Weisenburg and McBride 1964). An aphasic child usually has severe difficulty both in understanding language and in speaking.

Aphasia: partial or complete inability to use language

A child who is suffering from *expressive (motor) aphasia* can understand speech but cannot repeat sound patterns or sequences. Language, when it is used, is ungrammatical, vocabulary is limited, sentences are short. *Receptive aphasics* are those who neither understand speech nor use it (Mordock 1975).

Dyslexia is a disorder that relates specifically to reading. Children with dyslexia have extreme difficulty in reading and in understanding what they read; they have poor spelling ability, may reverse the order of letters or words, and make many mispronunciations. Intelligence is unrelated to the problem. Former U.S. Vice-President Nelson Rockefeller was one of those who suffered from dyslexia as a child.

Dyslexia: impairment of reading ability

The causes of dyslexia are still not known, although many theories exist. Some believe the brain of a child with this problem may have matured more slowly than normal, particularly the left hemisphere of the brain, which governs reading ability. Another theory is that insufficient memory development is a cause. Reading, which is visual, nevertheless depends on auditory learning, and dyslectics may fail to remember the connection (Mordock 1975).

Hyperkinesis in schoolchildren has had considerable public attention in recent years, particularly since there have been reports that as many as one child in ten is being given drugs to control the problem. Characteristics of this disorder are short attention span, poor power of concentration, impulsiveness, inability to wait, irritability, explosiveness. Children who behave this way cannot learn well and they also disrupt the classroom (Davids 1973).

Hyperkinesis: high level of movement; hyperactivity

What to do about the hyperactivity problem depends partly on what causes it, a matter that is still in doubt. One pediatric allergist believes food additives and dyes cause an allergic reaction in the form of hyperactivity. His solution is diet to eliminate the harmful substances (Feingold 1975). This theory may be supported by a finding that hyperactivity is "simply not a familiar problem" in China, where food is presumably entirely natural (Kessen 1975, page 144). Many mothers of hyper children also subscribe to the notion that food is the cause of the problem. However, the allergy theory is still hotly contested in the scientific community.

Drug therapy for hyperactivity has been a popular remedy for years, ever since the discovery in the 1930s that amphetamines, which work as stimulants on normal adults, have a reverse effect on hyperkinetic children (Davids 1973). This treatment is controversial. Not all children respond. There may be side-effects. And the children's civil liberties are said to be invaded. Some opponents also argue that adults have no right to restrict behavior through medication over which the individual has no control.

The opposite viewpoint is that neither do adults have a right to withhold a medication that may help children function better in school and learn what they need to become useful members of society. Research still has a way to go to discover just what biochemical mechanisms are involved when the drugs do work and what their long-term effects might be (Davids 1973).

Treating the Abnormal

Desperate problems often provoke desperate solutions. In attempts to cure the abnormal, people sometimes try powerful drugs, faith healers, violent therapy featuring physical or emotional abuse. The most bizarre methods occasionally seem to work, at least temporarily. Frequently they do not.

While much remains to be learned about the causes and cure of mental and emotional abnormality, enough is known now to produce remissions, partial remedies, and even complete cures in some cases.

Diagnosis and referral

The first step for anyone who is responsible for a "problem" child is to determine whether the child is abnormal and needs help and to find out just what the trouble is. How does one detect the need for treatment?

According to Anna Freud, a child's drastic failure to develop more or less in step with peers could be a sign that something is wrong (Freud 1962). Once it has become clear to a teacher or pediatrician that a child needs help, the parent must be convinced. Tact and genuine concern must be expressed, so that the mother and father do not get the impression that the teacher merely wants to get rid of a nuisance (Kessler 1966). Specialists should be consulted for diagnosis. After diagnosis, some problems with a functional or physiological cause might be treated by drugs, diet, or intensive training, under the direction of a specialist. Problems that are emotional have a chance of being modified or even cured by some form of psychotherapy. (See Box 12–3.)

Box 12–3 Is It Normal?

How does a parent or teacher decide whether a child's behavior is truly abnormal and whether the child needs professional help? Seven criteria have been suggested:

1. *Age discrepancy.* Is this behavior common at this age or is the habit one that should have been outgrown?

2. *Frequency.* Occasional symptomatic behavior is not ordinarily a serious problem. Emotional or physical stress can cause regression to previous patterns, like wetting the bed. But if only a little stress causes the behavior, and if it happens often, the problem is more serious.

3. *Number of symptoms.* A great many behavioral problems cause added difficulties, making it even more urgent school phobia, could also need expert help.

4. *Degree of social disadvantage.* Some behavioral problems cause added dif-

ficulties, making it even more urgent to get at the root of what is happening. For example, overly aggressive behavior may cause the youngster to become so unpopular that the repercussions can last a long time.

5. *Inner suffering.* The shame a child feels about neurotic behavior can itself be disabling, making it worthwhile to get help.

6. *Intractable behavior.* When children continue to act in a difficult manner in spite of all efforts to get them to change, they are, in effect, crying out for assistance.

7. *General personality appraisal.* The whole child must be considered, not just a symptom or two. If the child's general adjustment to family and school life is poor, the parent or teacher should probably look for professional advice (Kessler 1966).

Psychoanalysis

Emotional difficulties and personality conflicts that are non-organic—have no physiological cause—are sometimes referred for a form of psychotherapy called *psychoanalysis.* This is the best known treatment for anxiety and conflict. The method is essentially Freud's, based on his theory that the roots of these problems are generally unconscious, derived from childhood conflicts. While therapists' methods depend partly on the specific theories they follow, all are influenced to one degree or another by Freudian doctrine. Freud made the crucial point that child-rearing practices and cultural values have a strong effect on personality. He stressed that emotional problems were rooted in sexual repression, a common condition in the Victorian era.

But today psychiatrists and psychologists recognize that other kinds of anxiety may lead to abnormal behavior (Engel 1972). For example, Freud's analysis of Hans' fear of the horse (see page 493) would be disputed by current learning theorists. They hold that irrational ideas and behavior are learned the same way as all other behavior is learned in the course of socialization. Thus, a learning theorist would assume that Hans had really been frightened by horses.

The analytic process A notable example of the psychoanalytic process at work was Sybil, the young woman with 16 personalities. She required 11 years of therapy to discover the childhood roots of her problems and to relearn integrated behavior as a single personality.

What happens when a person goes to a psychoanalyst? First the analyst must gain the patient's confidence. Then the sufferer is guided to say anything that comes to mind: *free association.* At the same time, the therapist is steering the patient's revelations into channels that may reveal unconscious emotions. During treatment, the patient may transfer feelings about others to the therapist: *transference.* The analyst is always nonpunitive and accepting in responding. In the course of the treatment, some physician–analysts may also prescribe anxiety-reducing medication. Eventually, the patient is helped to break down unfortunate behavioral patterns and is reeducated.

Few analysts work with the very young because children must be mature enough and verbal enough to benefit by treatment and able to endure the intense, anxiety-provoking relationship with the physician. However, psychoanalysis is only one

Psychoanalysis: a form of psychotherapy that involves intensive exploration of an individual's conscious and unconscious thoughts and feelings

Free association: random reminiscence

Transference: transfer of an individual's feelings and emotions about others to the therapist

form of psychotherapy. Psychiatrists use various methods to help their patients understand and deal with their problems.

Play therapy

Therapists who deal with young children face a special challenge in trying to uncover the child's buried anxieties. It is usually not possible to have one-to-one give-and-take discussions, as with teenagers and adults. A useful means of communicating with a child is to watch the child play, to play with the child, or to take part in the child's flights of imagination.

Play therapy offers a medium for children's self-expression. What a child does with a doll—put it in jail, spank it, talk to it in a particular way—may give an alert therapist valuable clues to underlying problems. The play in itself is not a therapy, but playing situations arranged by an expert carry valuable messages that might lead to a cure (Engel 1972). A trained therapist studies the play situation and decodes the hidden messages that the child may be expressing. They are hidden because they are too painful to deal with directly. The therapist determines the treatment method after the cause of the problem is uncovered.

Play therapy: treating children's emotional problems through insights gained as they play

Psychodrama   A kind of play therapy on a more mature level is the technique of *psychodrama* and role-playing. Therapists treating more than one individual at a time may ask them to act out particular roles in a "drama." They are told what role to assume, but the dialog and action are up to the participants to make up as they go along. As in play therapy, the psychologist gets valuable clues to what is bothering the person from the way the role is played.

Psychodrama: role-playing to gain psychological insight

Group therapy

Psychodrama is one of the tools sometimes used in group therapy. One advantage of group therapy is that it is less expensive than private treatment. Another plus is that in a group situation a skilled therapist may guide discussion among people with similar problems in such a way that they gain insight into their own emotional difficulties by being exposed to others' problems. All kinds of feelings and attitudes that are not usually expressed—hostility, sadness, anger—may be freely displayed in an atmoshere where nobody is blamed or punished. The participants' sense of self-worth is increased. A feeling of being socially accept-able is built up. Egos are strengthened, conflicts diminished, ways of handling problems are learned.

Family therapy   Often, emotional problems revolve around a family situation, and the family itself becomes a group. Some of the family members may have individual therapy also. This system assumes that mother, father, and children are part of a single emotional system. Change for any one inevitably changes the others. Problems of any one are derived from the others and may even be mutual problems with different facets. When a child is having emotional difficulties, most therapists generally call in the parents, either together or singly, for separate therapeutic sessions.

Behavior therapy

Bandura: social learning   Albert Bandura, who is a major exponent of social learning theory (see Chapter 7, pages 269–273), contends that abnormal behavior is a consequence of learning inappropriate ways of coping with problems and conflicts. He believes that the cure for emotional ailments is to reverse faulty learning by developing constructive alternative ways of behaving. The right way to behave is modeled; the subject imitates; the result is modified behavior (Bandura 1968).

Behavior therapy employs the principles of conditioning to modify behavior. As we saw in Chapter 7, conditioning may produce new, learned behavior. *Operant conditioning* reinforces the student when correct behavior is copied (see pages 264–268). When this kind of learning is used therapeutically, rewards are given for self-sufficiency, improved social relationships, and progress in vocational training.

Counterconditioning takes place when behavior learned through conditioning is reversed or modified by new conditioning. Depending on whether a particular kind of behavior is to be encouraged or discouraged, strong positive or adversive responses are deliberately induced in the subject to counter the effects of previous conditioning. A child who has learned to be afraid of dogs may be counterconditioned if reinforced with praise and affection when in the presence of dogs.

Counterconditioning: use of conditioning principles to modify a response originally acquired through conditioning

Behavior therapy (conditioning) has had dramatic results with some severely disturbed children. In several controversial experiments, autistic and schizophrenic children were treated with painful electric shock, in an attempt to get their attention.

They learned to approach adults in order to avoid shock. They stopped damaging themselves. Tantrums ended. They became affectionate toward adults who were connected with reducing the shocks. Nontalkers began to talk normally after several months of treatment. Some nonsleepers began to sleep through the night.

The experimenters stress that their treatment is no panacea, just a last-ditch method to be used with children who have responded to nothing else, or an emergency means of keeping children from inflicting bodily harm on themselves (Lovaas et al. 1973; Lovaas, Schaeffer, and Simmons 1965). A much milder way of dealing with undesirable behavior is *time-out:* temporarily removing the child from the presence of loving adults. But when that method fails to work, more drastic treatment may be necessary (Ross 1974).

Time-out: temporary removal of social reinforcement

Conditioning therapy can also help delinquents. One project taught 18-year-old delinquent boys employment skills along with the social attitudes necessary to hold jobs. A follow-up after three years showed that the arrest record of the trained group was half that of a comparable group of delinquents who got no training.

In working with delinquents, conditioning methods must use positive reinforcement. Punishment for failing to perform does not succeed as it might with nondelinquents (Schlichter and Ratliff 1971). Attempts to use psychotherapy to cure delinquency have also failed (McCord and McCord 1959; Toby 1965). (See Box 12–4.)

Parent "therapists" An advantage of behavior therapy is that nonprofessionals, like a mother or father, can function as therapists. Aside from the problem of cost, professional therapists are relatively few. For every 8000 troubled children, it was recently estimated, there is only one professional therapist (Miller et al. 1971). In cases where behavior therapy could be useful, the techniques may be described and taught simply and quickly to people who are not members of the mental health professions, particularly parents. Besides, if behavior is to be modified, the remedy must be applied when and where the undesirable behavior is taking place, usually at home, or at least when a parent is present. Therapy works best in the natural environment (Tharp and Wetzel 1969).

For the more severe emotional disturbances and for chronic delinquency, the "state of the art" of healing is still far from advanced. Much remains to be learned. Even when therapists are available, they are not infallible. One elaborate test showed how vulnerable mental health practitioners can be.

Eight normal adults volunteered to be hospitalized in mental health institutions. They told the admissions officers they were hearing voices. All during their stay and treatment (an average of 19 days), although they were now acting normally, the treatment

---

Box 12–4 Behavior Modification

Learning theory that uses the reward principle has been the basis of some notable efforts to cure serious behavior problems. In some applications the method is controversial because it may seem morally offensive. In extreme form, behavior modification could also be called brain-washing, which is abhorrent by most standards. Ethical choices must be made when such methods are used. Even though the technique is controversial, it does appear to be successful in changing kinds of behavior that are socially undesirable.

A desperation method of dealing with autistic children uses electric shock. When the autistic child fails to respond to an adult, shock is applied. Then the adult "rescues" the child from the shock, thus forcing the child to perceive the adult as a positive reinforcer. In this way, the child learns to relate to the adult. A child shocked in this fashion is very reluctant to return to the situation that caused so much distress (Lovaas, Schaeffer, and Simmons 1965). Another method that works with some autistic children is using food as a reward. They are taught to respond to the adult who rescues them from hunger.

An elaborate system of rewards has been successful in teaching retarded children. One institution's program for the developmentally disabled uses a full-blown token economy, with a point system for class attendance, participation, and output. In another state hospital, tokens are the rewards that teach the mentally retarded simple language, like "Look at me!" The chits can be used to buy treats.

These methods are not really so different from what happens in many normal families. Spankings are noxious stimuli, intended to prevent undesirable behavior. And rewards are also given for good behavior: parental approval, food, treats, allowances, clothing, toys.

On an adult level, alcoholics have been cured, or at least controlled, by methods that are essentially behavior modification. Some clinics countercondition alcohol abusers by giving them a drug which, when combined with an alcoholic drink, causes violent temporary illness. The stimulus, alcohol, becomes associated with an extremely noxious result, and thus the drinking behavior is inhibited. This treatment does not solve the alcoholic's real life problems but may prevent the person from turning to alcohol for relief and making the problems even worse. Some drug clinics operate on the same principle.

staffs continued to be convinced the "patients" were schizo-phrenic. When they were discharged, they were labeled "in remission"—not cured. The only ones who suspected that the pseudopatients were not really ill were the real patients in the various hospitals (Rosenhan 1973).

The investigators in this experiment did not necessarily question the basic competence of clinical psychologists or psychiatrists. But they noted that an initial diagnosis tends to prejudice treatment, perhaps indefinitely. It may well be that in treating abnormal children there is a much larger place for par-ents, teachers, and intimates who really know the patients. What lay people need is basic knowledge of how normal individuals develop in the course of their lives, plus guidance in what to do when abnormal symptoms appear.

Happily, the behavior of the vast majority of children is within normal limits. This does not mean that normal develop-ment is uneventful and trouble-free. People are as different from one another as their fingerprints. And every life history is differ-ent, starting at conception and continuing through the life span. One important value of a knowledge of child development, for those who rear, teach, or treat children, is that they become aware of both the similarities and the vast range of normal differ-ences among individuals. That kind of understanding provides a vital perspective on our basic national treasure: America's children.

Summary

Normal and abnormal behavior are part of a continuum. Soci-ety's standards must be flexible enough to include individual dif-ferences. Treatment depends on whether abnormality is consid-ered to be an illness or a case of faulty education.

Some disorders are genetic or result from prenatal damage. Birth of genetically abnormal children may sometimes be averted by prepregnancy counseling and/or testing during pregnancy.

Some abnormality is caused by lack of adequate mothering, a problem seen at all socioeconomic levels. Child abuse is also an environmental disease.

Psychoneuroses are manifested by unusual behavior which is an unconscious, habitual way of dealing with anxiety. The underlying causes are usually relatively easy to discover and treat. Included are phobias, unreasonable preoccupation with a frightening object or situation. Obsessive–compulsive behavior and hysteria are other childhood neuroses. Many childhood fears are transitory or may be dispelled by conditioning.

Psychoses, such as autism or schizophrenia, are serious emotional illnesses involving loss of touch with reality and manifested by bizarre behavior. Causes are doubtful and treatment is often difficult or impossible. Schizophrenia may arise from genetic predisposition, possibly metabolic and thus possibly reversible.

Delinquency is a character disorder found in all social classes, probably environmentally caused. A poorly developed conscience results from failure to learn controls and from an inadequate parent–child relationship.

Cognitive abnormality may have either genetic or environmental causes. Mental retardation begins early in development, usually caused by defective genes or conditions affecting pregnancy and birth. Early lack of opportunity to learn may cause cultural retardation, shown by low IQ scores. Learning disabilities involving difficulty in perception or communication include aphasia, dyslexia, and hyperkinesis, caused either by slow maturation of the brain or by metabolic or chemical problems.

Treating the abnormal requires accurate diagnosis, since appropriate treatment depends on the cause. Some problems need medical help, some require psychotherapy, others are helped by environmental change, and some respond to retraining and education. Sometimes parents can be taught how to help their abnormal children, with good results.

Applying Your Knowledge

1. What advice should be given to a couple who are contemplating pregnancy and whose family history includes a genetic disorder?

2. What steps could be taken by a teacher who becomes aware that a pupil may have symptoms of atypical development? What are some symptoms to watch for?

3. What critical variables should be controlled when gathering statistics on delinquency?

Further Readings

Axline, Virginia M. *Dibs: in search of self*. New York: Random House, 1964. A case history of a withdrawn five-year-old boy and his struggle for identity through play therapy. Paperback.

Bettelheim, Bruno. *The empty fortress*. New York: Free Press, 1967. An in-depth look at infantile autism through three case histories. Paperback.

Braun, Samuel J., and Lasher, Miriam G. *Are you ready to mainstream? Helping preschoolers with learning and behavior problems*. Columbus, Ohio: Charles E. Merrill, 1978. A good overview of early childhood intervention programs and practical suggestions for program planning. Paperback.

Engel, Mary. *Psychopathology in childhood*. New York: Harcourt Brace Jovanovich, 1972. A brief overview of the social, diagnostic, and therapeutic aspects of childhood psychopathology. Paperback.

O'Neil, Sally M.; McLaughlin, Barbara N.; and Knapp, Mary Beth. *Behavioral approaches to children with developmental delays*. St. Louis: C. V. Mosby, 1977. A case-oriented experiential approach using the concepts of child development and behavior modification. Paperback.

Appendix

A Guide to Psychological Research

Almost all the information in this book has come from research projects conducted by qualified investigators. In order to understand the conclusions reached by these scholars, it is useful to understand the accepted scientific rules and concepts that underlie those projects. Equally useful would be a student's own research project: learning by doing.

In the following pages are:

1. An outline provided by a teacher of child development for students assigned to conduct their own investigation.

2. A brief account of operational definitions and sampling methods used in research.

3. A summary of major statistical concepts employed in gathering information.

4. An explanation of important tests of statistical significance used to judge the results of a research project.

5. Guidelines for a consent form.

This material supplements the more general information on research terms and methods in Chapter 1.

Pointers for Students Planning a Research Project

Problem:

What is your problem?

Is it worth researching?

What is the background or relevant literature on the problem?

State the problem in terms of a hypothesis.

Is your hypothesis provable?

What are the variables—independent, dependent, intervening?

How are the variables and problem operationally defined?

How is the dependent variable(s) to be measured?

What controls are necessary?

Method:

What is the procedure to be followed?

Describe exactly what you plan to do.

How is the sample selected?

How are the data collected?

How should the results be analyzed?

Results:

Review the research design.

What are the expected results?

How would the results support or refute your hypothesis?

What unplanned occurrences might be present, and which of these might affect your results?

Discussion:

What are some possible conclusions? Why?

What are some of the implications of these conclusions?

Criticize and discuss the project.

Summary:

Summarize your research and conclusions in one or two short paragraphs.

References:

Cite all your references.

Some Important Elements in Psychological Research

Hypothesis

The *hypothesis*—the suggested answer to a problem—is both the beginning and the end of a research project. It is a proposition that is to be tested to determine whether it is valid, whether it can be proved or supported by the facts.

An ideal hypothesis is simple. It should avoid ambiguity or vagueness. A well-worded hypothesis is a declarative sentence that proposes an answer to a specific problem. The hypothesis will be either verified or refuted by the results of the investigation. If the hypothesis is either clearly accepted or clearly rejected, the research has been successful.

Operational definitions

Because the goal of scientific research is to make it possible to abstract information and form generalizations, precise *operational definitions* are a must in designing a research project. These arbitrary definitions clearly describe the areas to be investigated, the specific conditions under which the work is to be carried out, the criteria to be used, and the kinds of groups to be studied. If one defines what one is looking for, one can recognize it when it is found. Without such definitions, the meaning of the research results would be in doubt.

Variables

Basic to any experiment are the *relevant variables*. These include *independent variables*, those conditions that are manipulated by the experimenter; *dependent variables*, those conditions that are a function of the independent variable; and *intervening variables*, which may affect the dependent variable but are not manipulated by the experimenter.

Another term for the dependent variable is the *response:* any response that is presumably related to the independent variable. One could measure *latency* of the response (reaction time); *intensity (amplitude)* of the response; *frequency (rate)* of response; or *duration* of the response (how long it lasted). How many of these dependent variables are measured will depend on the particular experiment, but a good researcher looks for as many dependent variables as possible, especially when the outcome of the investigation has been difficult to predict.

The investigator's task is to determine the amount of change in the dependent variable as a function of the manipulation of the independent variable.

Sampling

Experiments in psychology usually hope to be able to generalize, to an entire population, results that are produced by testing a relatively small group. The researcher would like to make inferences on the basis of the statistics and thus be able to predict what would or will happen in the population at large. Public opinion polling is an example.

The ability to draw inferences from research depends almost entirely on the researcher's ability to construct a *representative sample*. Ideally each individual in the total population under study would have an equal chance of being included in the sample. In other words, the sample would be *random*. Statistical tables have been worked out as a guide to constructing representative random samples.

However, it is not always possible or practical to obtain a random sample of the entire population under study, so other types of sample selection are used. A *stratified sample,* which is more selective than a random sample, is the kind used by the Gallup poll and other well-known public opinion pollsters. The characteristics of the total population under study are determined, in terms of the proportion of people in various categories: such as age group, race, geographic area, income bracket, educational level. Then the sample is selected to conform to those proportions and those characteristics.

Matched pair samples are usually split into experimental and control groups. But matched pairs may also be constructed by sampling individuals who are similar—for example, twins, or subjects matched on the basis of IQ, age, income, education, nationality, etc.

The *experimental* groups are those in which the independent variable is manipulated. The *control* groups are those in which the independent variable is absent. Without a control group, any changes in the experimental group could not be attributed to the experimental variables. Intervening variables, such as passage of time, would be controlled by the use of the control group.

Research projects often compare identical twins and fraternal twins because nature has already controlled important variables. Heredity is absolutely controlled for the identicals, who share the same genes. But fraternals' genes are as varied as those of any siblings. Thus, important conclusions may be reached in correlational studies relating to the influence of heredity and environment.

The various sampling methods are not mutually exclusive. Often two or more approaches, such as random and cross-sectional (see Chapter 1, pages 14–15) by age, are combined to suit the purposes of an investigation.

The problem of experimenter bias

All research projects run the danger of yielding inaccurate results because of the *experimenter's bias* in relation to the subjects of the investigation. In fact, the goal of a well-known study was to determine the consequences of prejudice on the part of an experimenter who has advance knowledge of the capabilities of subjects (Rosenthal and Jacobsen 1966, 1968). The "Rosenthal effect" was the bias shown by teachers who were given false information about the IQs of their pupils. The children who were thought to be more intelligent (but whose real IQs did not match the teachers' information) benefited more from instruction than the pupils who were thought to be less intelligent (see Chapter 11, page 462). This study showed the importance of avoiding *contamination* of the hypothesis by the experimenter.

Experimenter bias could also affect public opinion polls. The questioner must not only avoid asking "loaded" questions, which lead the respondent into certain kinds of answers, but must also be strictly neutral in manner. Investigators who deal with children must be particularly careful to be evenhanded, since children are more vulnerable to adults' attitudes and position of authority.

Statistical Concepts in Research

Reliability and validity

The product of most research projects is raw data—a collection of numbers. What makes those numbers mean something is grouping them in such a way that they provide a convincing summary of the research results. Thus, it is important to grasp the basic statistical concepts that underlie research projects.

Proper use of statistics makes it possible to fulfill the basic goal of psychological research: to generalize about some facet of human development. Every research project depends, in the end, on being able to prove that the research results are, indeed, valid and reliable. Would it be possible to get the same results another time with different subjects? Does the test really measure whatever was supposed to be measured? Would a different experimenter or observer get the same result?

All these questions relate to *reliability* and *validity*. Unless research is both reliable and valid, it fails to accomplish its purpose. For example, an IQ test may be said to be valid if it can be shown that it really measures intelligence, rather than just vocabulary. And the test is *reliable* if different testers would get the same results for the same subjects within a reasonable length of time, thus showing that the examination is both consistent and stable. Both reliability and validity depend on a properly designed project, but they can only be proved statistically.

Descriptive statistics

A basic function of statistical analysis is to *describe* a research study and its results. There are three kinds of descriptive statistics: those that show central tendency, those that indicate variability, and those that involve relationship.

Central tendency *Central tendency* is a score that is *typical* for the group tested in a particular study. But there are different ways of computing what is typical.

The *mean* is another term for the average. It is arrived at by adding all scores and dividing by the number of subjects. The mean reflects the full range of scores, both the very high and the very low, including "outliers," which are very much above or below most of the other scores. In IQ testing, the tests are designed to yield a mean score of 100, the average IQ for the entire population.

The *median* is the score that falls exactly in the middle of a whole group of scores. For example, if a test is administered to 100 people, the score that turns out to be fiftieth from the highest and the lowest would be the median. The median score is most useful when there are a great many scores that are very high or very low. In such cases, a simple average of all the scores would mask the true meaning of the results. The median is less influenced by unusual extremes.

The *mode* is the particular score that occurs most frequently in any distribution of scores. Questionnaire or survey results often employ the mode (rather than the mean or median) to establish the most frequently occurring responses.

Variability It is obviously necessary to find out how typical the mean or the median is in any test or research project. Are there many scores bunched around the mean or the median? Only a few? Are many at either the upper or the lower end? Various measures of *variability* have been devised.

The *range* is the difference between the highest and lowest scores. But to determine the range without other information is to show very little, because the range is changeable. It depends on only two values, the highest and lowest scores. Another run of the same test could change the range materially if either the highest or lowest score changes. It would still not reveal a great deal about the many scores in between. However, a school principal might be very much interested in the range of IQ scores in a school in order to plan class composition and teacher assignment.

In most research, a meaningful measure of variability within a range is the *standard deviation*, which describes how scores are spread above and below the mean. The symbols used for standard deviation include *SD*, *s*, or *σ*. A large standard deviation means that the scores vary a good deal around the mean. When there is a small standard deviation, the differences from the mean among individual scores are slight. The standard deviation is calculated by taking all the scores into account. Therefore it is considered far more stable than the range, which is determined by only two values, the highest and the lowest scores. For instance, if the standard deviation is 5, and the mean is 50, then a score of 35 is three standard deviations below the mean.

The *variance* is the standard deviation squared. It is used to show how wide the spread of scores is. See Figure A–1 for an illustration of different spreads.

The shape of a distribution of scores is also meaningful to researchers in interpreting the results of an experiment. As the sketches in Figure A–2 show, the way the scores are distributed can produce an *asymmetrical*, or *skewed*, graph—many scores at one end of the distribution. Or, the scores can cluster in the middle, with gradually decreasing numbers on both sides of the mean. This is a *bell-shaped distribution*, which may have either a high peak (small *SD*) or a gentler peak (large *SD*).

Relationship   Quite often the variables are associated with one another and can be expressed in terms of a statistical relationship. The statistic for expressing the strength of a relationship is the *correlation coefficient*, which has the symbol *r*. Coefficients are on a scale of +1.00 to −1.00. A perfect positive correlation is indicated by the coefficient +1.00 and means that a second variable is always *present* with the first variable. A perfect negative correlation is indicated by the coefficient −1.00 and means that a second variable is always *absent* when the first variable is present. A coefficient of 0.00 means that there is no relationship and

correlation coefficient: number or value indicating the degree of similarity or correspondence between two variables

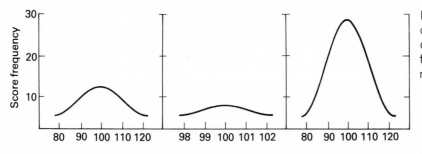

FIG. A-1 Three bell-shaped, or normal, distributions with different spreads and therefore different values for the mean and standard deviation.

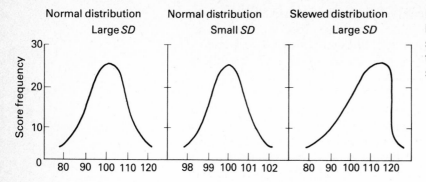

the two variables under study are not associated with one another. While correlation coefficients indicate the strength of a relationship, they do not determine cause and effect.

In comparing two correlation coefficients, it is important to realize that the relationship is not like simple arithmetic. One compares the *square* of the two coefficients: thus, a correlation of $+.40$ is four times as good as a correlation of $+.20$.

Correlations are especially useful in comparing the judgment of two different sets of observers. For example, if observers are looking through a one-way window at children playing in a room, rating them for specific characteristics, and their ratings have a high correlation, then the observers' ratings would be considered reliable.

Correlations are also used to compare the performance of a particular individual on two parts of a test or on the same test at different times, to determine *stability* (or *internal consistency*) and *reliability* of the test.

Tests of statistical significance

A major objective of research is to permit valid generalizations concerning groups far larger than those used in the experiment. Therefore, statisticians have devised rules that make it possible to work out the likelihood, or *probability*, that the differences or relationships found by the study are due to chance or accident. Thus, probability is the heart of *inferential statistics*.

Tests of statistical significance state probability this way: $p < .05$ or $p < .01$. The first expression means that the probability is less than 5 in 100 that the results are pure chance. Another way of stating it is that there are 95 chances in 100 that the results are due to the experiment. The second expression means that chances are less than 1 in 100 that the findings are a result of chance—in other words, 99 chances out of 100 the results flow from the experimental conditions. The accepted cut-off for significance is anything that is .05 or less. Statistical tests are employed to determine the probability levels.

Guidelines for a Consent Form

This is a typical outline given to researchers who seek approval to engage in medical, psychological, or sociological research involving human subjects at a large public hospital in a Western city. It illustrates the precautions that are necessary in conducting investigations of human behavior.

GUIDELINES FOR A CONSENT FORM

The format suggested below is sufficiently flexible to cover the majority of research studies and is designed to comply with the minimum requirements of the DHEW regulations and state law. The format may be modified or expanded, depending upon the nature of the particular study involved, but *the consent form is to contain all elements included below.* Existing consent forms, regardless of approval elsewhere, will not be accepted unless they include these elements. *Please use language which the average person is likely to understand.*

INSTITUTE FOR MEDICAL RESEARCH
Name of responsible physician
Address
Telephone
Name of Cooperating Hospital
Name(s) and telephone number(s) of co-investigator(s)

1. Give a clear explanation to the participant (in non-technical language) of the procedures to be followed and their purpose, including identification of any procedures which are experimental.
2. Drug(s) to be used in this study—identify generic name(s), trade name(s) and manufacturer(s).
3. Describe any associated discomforts and/or risks that can reasonably be expected.
4. Describe any benefits that can reasonably be expected, to the subject, society or both.
5. List alternative procedures, if any, that might be advantageous.
6. State that any data under the investigator's control will be disclosed in a manner that does not reveal the participant's identity. (If applicable, state the persons or agencies to whom the information will be furnished, the nature of that information, and the purpose of the disclosure).
7. Describe any compensation to the subject, the amount and nature. If there is the possibility of additional cost to the subject because of participation, describe such.

The remainder of the consent form should be copied as follows:

8. I give permission to discuss with my nearest available relative my participation in this study as outlined in this form. (   ) YES   (   ) NO

9. I understand that I am free to withdraw my consent and discontinue participation in the project at any time without prejudice to me or effect on my medical care. All my questions regarding this project have been answered. I agree to participate in the project as described above.

_____ _____
Signature of Witness   Signature of Subject

_____
Date Signed

10. I have discussed with this subject the procedure(s) described above and the risks involved, and I believe he/she understands the contents of the consent form.*

_____ _____
Signature of Responsible Physician   Date Signed

11. I certify that the above subject is competent to give informed consent to participate in this study.**

_____ _____
Signature of physician not associated with the project or under the   Date Signed
direction of any physician involved in the project.

12. If you are not satisified with the manner in which this study is being conducted, you may report (anonymously if you so choose) any complaints to the Institute for Medical Research.

13. A COPY OF THIS FORM IS AVAILABLE UPON REQUEST.

*For subjects whose physical or mental condition does not allow them to give informed consent, substitute the following:

"I have discussed with this subject (or, if the subject cannot comprehend or respond, with the subject's spouse, parent, or guardian the procedures described above and the risks involved, and I believe he/she understands the consent form."

**In cases of experimental drug use, this item should read, "I certify that the above subject is competent to give informed consent for the administration of the experimental drug."

Glossary

abnormal   atypical or deviant, as distinguished from the average   (478)

abstract   pertaining to a general idea or notion   (232)

accommodation   modification of one's repertoire of behavior to include new experiences   (169)

achievement motivation   desire to strive for excellence, recognition, and approval   (440)

achievement test   test that measures current performance or learning   (316)

acuity   sharpness of perception   (87)

adaptation   reaction to new experiences through assimilation and accommodation   (169)

adaptive behavior   behavior that helps an individual adjust to the environment   (268)

affective   relating to feelings and emotions   (443)

amniocentesis   medical procedure that extracts amniotic fluid from the uterus to test for chromosomal abnormality   (39)

amniotic sac   fluid-filled sac that surrounds the fetus   (49)

anoxia   oxygen deficiency   (52)

anxiety   state of emotional tension   (442)

aphasia   partial or complete inability to use language   (509)

apnea   temporary cessation of breathing   (69)

aptitude test   test that measures ability to perform a task   (316)

assimilation   inclusion of new experiences into existing repertoire of behavior   (169)

assimilation (cultural)   becoming part of a group by adopting its customs and practices   (411)

associative play   playing at the same activity, but independently   (416)

attachment   emotional dependence on or attraction to a particular person   (95)

autism   a psychotic disorder characterized by extreme preoccupation with one's own thoughts and repetitive, ritualistic behavior   (498)

battered child syndrome   child abuse and the social and psychological factors related to it   (490)

behaviorism   explanation of human actions in terms of learned responses to the environment   (269)

behavior modification   the use of modeling and reinforcement techniques to change behavior   (289)

bell-shaped curve   a normal distribution with an equal number of cases falling on either side of the mean   (311)

biochemical imbalance   a condition in which the biochemical elements in the brain are not of normal proportions   (480)

blink response   involuntary (reflexive) shutting and opening of the eyes as a result of a stimulus   (96)

breech birth   when the newborn emerges feet or buttocks first   (69)

caesarian section   delivering the baby through an incision in the mother's abdomen   (69)

cell   the basic unit of life, capable of reproducing itself   (28)

cephalocaudal   head-to-toe   (121)

child development   the physical, mental, emotional, and social growth of the child   (4)

chromosomes   rodlike structures that contain the genetic material of cells   (29)

classical conditioning   learning elicited by associating a neutral stimulus with a stimulus that produces a reflex (unlearned) response   (262)

classification   division of a category into component parts or the grouping of objects according to a criterion   (178)

clinical   involving investigation of background factors, family relations, and test results for a diagnosis   (14)

cognition   ability to think and reason logically and to understand abstract principles   (162)

cognitive ability   ability to think, reason, understand   (96)

cognitive dissonance   conflict between expectation and the reality of the situation   (176)

cognitive style   an individual's unique way of thinking or problem-solving   (201)

cohort   a group of individuals with a certain factor in common, such as age   (16)

coitus   act of sexual intercourse   (426)

combinatorial thought   ability to combine elements in a systematic, methodical way   (187)

compensatory programs organized efforts to make up for inadequacies in previous experience (244)

concept an idea or notion, usually represented by a word or symbol (233)

conception the union of the sperm and ovum to produce a zygote (36)

conceptual tempo pace in solving problems (203)

concrete pertaining to a specific instance or object (232)

concrete operational thought logical reasoning (184)

conditioned learned (263)

congenital present at birth (35)

conservation ability to understand that change in appearance only does not necessarily imply change in quantity (177)

control group subjects not exposed to special conditions (13)

conventional morality moral judgment governed by adherence to authority (397)

cooperative play playing with a peer, exchanging ideas (416)

coordination of secondary circular reactions goal-oriented activities (175)

correlation degree of similarity or correspondence between two variables (14)

correlation coefficient number or value indicating the degree of similarity or correspondence between two or more variables (527)

counterconditioning use of conditioning principles to modify a response originally acquired through conditioning (514)

creativity originality and novel insight (322)

cross-cultural relating to the differences among peoples in the world (16)

crossing-over process that mixes the genetic content of chromosomes (32)

cross-sectional study comparison of behavior of individuals in a group similar in all except one characteristic (15)

culturally alienated estranged from the society to which one belongs (429)

culture-fair not biased in favor of any particular group (342)

curiosity desire to understand the unknown (442)

decenter to become aware of other points of view than one's own (167)

defense mechanism behavior that protects the psyche from guilt, anxiety, or shame (491)

desensitize to make less sensitive or reactive (422)

development growth and behavior that reflect maturation and learning (120)

developmental related to maturation and experience (82)

developmental psychology the branch of psychology that studies the processes of growth and maturation and the effects of experience (9)

developmental task skills, achievements, or competencies that are considered important at certain ages for normal development (93)

differentiated separated into finer parts; discriminated into parts (83)

differentiation specialization of cell functions (28)

discrimination ability to perceive differences, to make distinctions (97)

distinctive features attributes or characteristics essential for discriminating one object from another (83)

dizygotic twins developed from two zygotes (41)

DNA a double-helix structure in chromosomes that carries the genetic code (29)

dominant traits governed by genes that ordinarily prevail over recessive genes, producing an individual's observable characteristics (35)

Down's syndrome (mongolism) a genetic disorder caught by an extra number 21 chromosome (483)

drive physiological basis of motivation (437)

dyslexia impairment of reading ability (509)

echolalia repetition and imitation of sounds or words (221)

ego psychological force that is in touch with reality and mediates between the id and the superego (352)

egocentric having perceptions based on one's own view, or focusing on only one aspect of a situation (167)

egocentric speech self-centered speech that shows no concern for the listener (229)

ego psychology theory that emphasizes the study of the self, particularly an individual's self-concept (353)

ejaculation release of sperm, usually in intercourse or masturbation (143)

embryo fertilized ovum in the second to eighth week of development (47)

enactive action-oriented (192)

encoding transformation of information into a set of cues (275)

environment all the conditions and forces that surround and influence the individual (6)

equilibration tendency to function at a higher, more complex, level (168)

erogenous zones body areas that provide pleasurable sensation (352)

ethnocentrism believing one's own ethnic group is superior to others (417)

etiology study of possible causes or circumstances associated with the onset of a disorder (498)

events activities involving the senses and movement, according to Piaget (171)

experimental group subjects exposed to conditions whose effect is to be tested (13)

extinction gradual decline in rate of response because reinforcement is withheld (265)

extroversion outward-directedness (358)

fertilization the penetration of the ovum by the sperm (36)

fetus unborn child from third through ninth month (49)

forceps delivery using a surgical instrument to ease the newborn out of the birth canal (69)

foreclosure shutting off (356)

formal operational thought logical and abstract reasoning (186)

foster child child reared by but not the offspring of the caregiver (328)

foster grandparents older adults who give substitute mothering (487)

free association random reminiscence (512)

functional pertaining to use (232)

gene pool hereditary factors common to a family or group and thus capable of being inherited by any one individual in the group (326)

genes the elementary units of heredity (11)

genetic predisposition tendency to a behavior or condition linked to inheritance (499)

germ cell cell from which a sperm or ovum is generated (31)

gestation period length of prenatal development (127)

global, holistic relating to the whole, or entirety, rather than the parts (83)

glottis the opening between the lower pair of vocal cords in the larynx (220)

grammar classes of words and their functions in sentences (215)

graphemes nonsense forms that resemble letters of the alphabet (99)

habituation adaptation to a stimulus so that it no longer elicits a response (91)

haptic perception perception through touch (84)

heredity characteristics passed on from parents to children (29)

hierarchy of needs developmental progression of motivating needs (443)

holophrase one-word sentence (223)

humanistic centering on human interests and values and the capacity of individuals to fulfill their potential (357)

hyperkinesis high level of movement; hyperactivity (509)

hypothalamus the part of the brain that controls hunger, thirst, and other visceral functions (437)

hypothesis a proposition that must be tested to determine its validity (13)

hysteria excessive involuntary movement or loss of a bodily function (496)

iconic image-oriented (193)

id impulsive psychological force; the source of libido (351)

identification associating oneself closely with another person's characteristics, attitudes, and rules of behavior (372)

identity crisis confusion about the nature of one's true self, usually during adolescence (384)

identity diffusion lacking direction, specificity, and integration (387)

information processing the mind accepts experiences as input and translates the data into behavior (output) and/or memory (274)

innate present at birth; inborn (82)

instrumental-relativist moral orientation doing the right thing to serve someone's particular need (397)

intelligence insight, skill in problem-solving, and mental ability (305)

intentionality conscious motivation leading to action (395)

intervening variable a variable that may affect the dependent variable but is not manipulated by the experimenter (523)

intrinsic motivation desire to behave in a particular fashion because the behavior itself provides a sense of fulfillment (441)

introversion inward-directedness (358)

IQ (intelligence quotient) score a measure of intelligence, established by testing; mental age divided by chronological age times 100 (307)

irreversibility inability to mentally return a transformed event to its original condition (167)

kibbutz Israeli communal settlement (412)

Klinefelter's syndrome a male genetic disorder caused by one or more extra X sex chromosomes (483)

Lamaze childbirth method using relaxation exercises (67)

Language Acquisition Device (LAD) a hypothetical innate mechanism in the brain that acquires language (217)

learning acquisition of knowledge, skills, or habits through experience (82)

learning disabilities perceptual or communication difficulties that hinder the ability to obtain or process information (508)

libido psychic energy (352)

longitudinal research periodic study of a particular group over a long period of time (15)

long-term memory (LTM) storage of information for an indefinite period of time (274)

love-oriented discipline use of approval and/or disapproval to instill behavioral standards (403)

love withdrawal expressing disappointment in or disapproval of an individual (400)

mastery–competence motivation desire to achieve proficiency in a set of behaviors (439)

masturbation self-stimulation of the sex organs (426)

maturation physical and mental growth and development, governed by heredity (82)

mean mathematical average of scores (the sum of the scores divided by the number of scores) (311)

median middle-most score of a group of scores (311)

meiosis cell division into either sperm or ova, containing 23 chromosomes each; the key to sexual reproduction (31)

memory ability to retain and recall learned material (172)

menarche first menstruation (274)

menstruation discharge of blood and uterine material in monthly cycles (143)

mental age level of mental development typical for a particular chronological age (307)

mental combinations using the mind to put together ideas (schemes) (177)

mental illness any serious behavioral disorder that requires professional treatment (480)

mental retardation subaverage intellectual ability (505)

metapelet nurse, teacher, care-giver in a kibbutz (413)

miscarriage death of the embryo (48)

mitosis cell reproduction into "daughter" cells, identical to the parent cell, with 46 chromosomes each; the key to growth and development (31)

mnemonic device a scheme for remembering and recalling information (278)

model someone who exhibits any kind of observable behavior (13)

monozygotic twins developed from one zygote (41)

moratorium temporary suspension of activity (356)

mores ethical customs (426)

morpheme smallest unit of meaningful sound (223)

motivation incentive to goal-directed behavior (261)

naturalistic pertaining to matters that are beyond human control (396)

nature inherited characteristics (11)

nature–nurture issue the problem of deciding the relative influences of heredity and environment on development (11)

negative reinforcement escape from or avoidance of unpleasantness (265)

neo-Freudian pertaining to an extension of Freud's teachings (353)

neonate newborn baby (74)

norms standards or measurements of behavior or development (9)

nucleus a subunit of the cell that carries the structures of heredity (28)

nurturant warm; caring; need-satisfying (368)

nurture environmental factors (11)

object permanence awareness that a thing continues to exist although not in view (171)

object recognition ability to identify a familiar thing (171)

obsessive–compulsive behavior ritualistic, repetitive behavior resulting from continually recurring thoughts (495)

ontogeny the development of the individual (11)

operant (instrumental) conditioning learning through reinforcement (264)

operational definition a definition relating to the way in which a particular experimental condition will be measured (523)

operations events that have an end point but can be returned to the starting point; reversible events (167)

organization combination of schemes (168)

orientation position in space (98)

ovulation release of a mature egg from the ovaries (36)

ovum female sex cell (28)

parabola a graphed curve that increases along the vertical axis and then levels off parallel to the horizontal axis (224)

parallel play playing alongside a peer (415)

perception ability to organize and interpret sensory stimulation in the light of previous experience (82)

perceptual logic ability to add up parts (of anything) to make a whole (100)

performance score score in manual tasks (313)

personality behavior that reflects the characteristics unique to an individual (350)

phobia excessive fear of an object or situation (493)

phoneme basic language sound (220)

phylogenetic research study of nonhuman behavior in order to relate findings to humans (15)

phylogeny the development or evolution of the species (11)

pivot word a word used repeatedly in the same position in several sentences (226)

PKU (phenylketonuria) inherited enzyme deficiency that causes a toxic accumulation of amino acids and results in retardation (482)

placenta an organ that nourishes the fetus by transmitting food products and metabolic wastes between the blood of the mother and the fetus   (49)

play therapy   treating children's emotional problems through insights gained as they play   (513)

population   the entire group of people under study, from which a sample is taken   (13)

positive reinforcement   a reward   (265)

postconventional morality   moral judgments independent of personal consequences and social convention; belief in higher principles of justice   (397)

power-assertive techniques   strong and authoritarian disciplinary behavior   (403)

preconventional morality   moral judgments that reflect a concern for physical consequences and personal needs   (397)

prematurity   when a newborn weighs less than 5 pounds   (70)

preoperational thought   illogical reasoning   (177)

primipara   a first-time mother   (60)

primary circular reactions   purposeless repetitive behavior oriented toward the body   (171)

primary reinforcers   things or events that satisfy survival needs   (265)

progesterone   a female sex hormone that inhibits muscle contractions in the uterus during pregnancy   (48)

programmed teaching   sequential presentation of material and feedback   (288)

proximodistal   from the center of the body to fingertips or most distant points   (121)

psychoanalysis   form of psychotherapy that involves intensive exploration of an individual's conscious and unconscious thoughts and feelings   (351)

psychodrama   role-playing to gain psychological insight   (513)

psychoneurosis   functional (psychological) disorder involving intense anxiety   (491)

psychopathology   study of behavioral deviation   (480)

psychosexual   pertaining to the individual's sensuality and sexual development, both mental and somatic   (352)

psychosis   organic disorder involving separation from reality   (497)

psychosocial   pertaining to the self in relation to other people and society   (352)

psychosocial crises   tension between the self and social institutions   (354)

psychotherapy treatment of mental or emotional disorders by psychiatric or psychological means (480)

puberty period when reproductive organs first become functional, till onset of adulthood (141)

qualitative related to distinctive traits or activities (120)

quantitative related to measurable portions (120)

random drawn by chance (14)

recessive traits governed by genes that produce an observable characteristic only when a dominant gene for the same characteristic is not present (35)

reciprocity mutual actions (396)

reduplicated monosyllable single syllable sound repeated to form a word (223)

reflexes unlearned motor responses (127)

reinforcement anything that increases the frequency of a response (264)

reinforcement theory a response is learned when it is strengthened by a desirable outcome (216)

relativism perceptions that include several points of view (167)

response any behavior or psychological reaction produced by a stimulus (261)

response generalization responses similar to the originally learned response are produced by the same stimulus (269)

restitution restoration or reimbursement (396)

Rh factor substance in most people's red blood cells that may cause neonatal problem when mother alone lacks it (70)

sample a group of people, representative of a larger group (population), who are studied in order to gain information about the entire population (13)

sanctions punishment (396)

scheme fundamental unit of images, thoughts, or actions; an outline or mental sketch (95)

schizophrenia general name for a group of psychotic reactions (499)

secondary circular reactions activities repeated because of their interesting effects (173)

secondary reinforcers things or events that are satisfying but not essential to survival (265)

secular trend patterns of evolutionary growth related to heredity and environment (122)

selective attention   focused attention   (101)

selective imitation   learning particular aspects of a language, such as its structure   (218)

selective perception   focused perception   (104)

self-actualization   fulfilling one's ultimate potential   (357)

self-concept   sum total of one's self-perceptions   (237)

self-esteem   feelings about oneself   (351)

self-image   how one visualizes oneself   (351)

semantics   meaning in language   (229)

seminal emission   involuntary release of sperm, usually during sleep   (143)

sensorimotor coordination   the harmonious working together of sensory and motor responses   (130)

sensorimotor period   developmental level dominated by the senses and movement   (171)

sensory   pertaining to the sense organs   (82)

separation anxiety   apprehensive or fearful response to being left by the accustomed care-giver   (369)

sex role   differing behaviors expected of and considered appropriate for males and females   (377)

sex-typing   learning a conventional sex role   (377)

sexuality   sexual capacity and behavior   (425)

shaping   reinforcing successive approximations of desired behavior   (283)

short-term memory (STM)   storage of information for a few seconds or minutes   (274)

social contract–legalistic moral orientation   acting within society's rules and modes of conduct   (398)

social convention   agreed-upon customs and practices of a cohesive group of people   (396)

socialization   learning the acceptable values and behavior of the society to which one belongs   (394)

socialized speech   speech that takes the listener into consideration   (229)

social (observational) learning   learning from models   (269)

sociometric status   an individual's level of acceptance or rejection by members of a group   (417)

soliciting agent   someone who elicits a response   (459)

solitary play   playing alone   (415)

spatial localization   locating an object or event in space   (103)

spatial visualization forming a mental picture of an object in space (110)

sperm male sex cell (28)

standardized using norms established according to some criteria (309)

state a person's mental, emotional, or physical condition (106)

statistical frequency numerical tabulation of the frequency of a behavior (479)

stimulus something that provokes a response (84)

stimulus generalization stimuli similar to the original stimulus that caused a learned response produce the same response (269)

stranger anxiety apprehensive or fearful response to strangers (95)

subject person being studied (14)

superego psychological force that embodies an individual's moral code (352)

symbolic symbol-oriented (193)

syntax the way in which words are put together to form phrases and sentences (215)

tactile ability ability to perceive by sense of touch (104)

tactile comfort comfort from touching (366)

telegraphic speech abbreviated sentences containing only the words essential to convey meaning (223)

temperament disposition; psychological makeup (358)

tertiary circular reactions exploratory behavior and trial-and-error experimentation (176)

test predictability capacity of a test to predict future abilities or performance (318)

theory a general principle that attempts to explain the relationship of a set of facts of behaviors (13)

time-out temporary removal of social reinforcement (283)

transference transfer of an individual's feelings and emotions about others to the therapist (512)

Turner's syndrome a female genetic disorder caused by the absence of a sex chromosome (483)

ultrasound technique using sound waves to detect the size, shape, and position of the fetus (59)

unconditioned unlearned (263)

universal common to all persons or cultures or groups (16)

universal ethical principles moral standards common to all societies (16)

universal sounds sounds common to all languages (216)

uterus saclike, muscular organ in a woman's pelvic area (45)

variables influencing factors in a given situation (13)

verbal mediation use of language to direct thought and action (233)

verbal score score in language skills (313)

visual accommodation changes in the lens of the eye to focus on near and far objects (96)

zygote the single cell produced by conception (36)

Bibliography

Abravenal, Eugene. Intersensory integration of spatial position during early childhood. *Perceptual and Motor Skills*, 1968, *26*(1), 251–256. 98

Acheson, R. M. Maturation of the skeleton. In F. Falkner (ed.), *Human development*, pp. 465–502. Philadelphia: Saunders, 1966. 141

Agranowitz, A. *Aphasia handbook.* Springfield, Ill.: C. C. Thomas, 1964. 509

Ainsworth, Mary D. S. *Infancy in Uganda.* Baltimore: Johns Hopkins University Press, 1967. 370

——. The development of infant-mother attachment. In Bettye Caldwell and Henry N. Riccioti (eds.), *Review of child development research*, Vol. 3. Chicago: University of Chicago Press, 1975. 370

Albee, George W. Models, myths, and manpower. *Mental Hygiene*, 1968, *52*, 168–180. 480

Aleksandrowicz, M. K. The effect of pain-relieving drugs administered during labor and delivery on the behavior of the newborn: a review. *Merrill-Palmer Quarterly*, 1974, *20*, 121–141. 64, 65

Alexander, Tom. Psychologists are rediscovering the mind. *Fortune*, November 1970, pp. 108–111. 86

Al-Issa, Ishan. The development of word definition in children. *Journal of Genetic Psychology*, 1969, *114*, 25–28. 232

Allen, Sara A.; Spear, Paul S.; and Lucke, Jon R. Effects of social reinforcement on learning and retention in children. *Developmental Psychology*, 1971, *5*(1), 73–80. 461

Allison, Tom S., and Allison, Sharon L. Time-out from reinforcement: effect on sibling aggression. *Psychological Record*, 1971, *21*(1), 81–86. 283

Allport, G. W. *Pattern and growth in personality.* New York: Holt, Rinehart and Winston, 1961. 350

Altus, W. D. Birth order and its sequelae. *Science*, 1966, *151*, 44–49. 362

A merciful child desertion: poignant plea to nuns. *San Francisco Chronicle*, November 5, 1977. 508

Ames, Louise B. A low intelligence quotient often not recognized as the chief cause of many learning difficulties. *Journal of Learning Disabilities*, 1968, *1*(2), 735–739. 320

Amidon, Arlene, and Carey, Peter. Why five-year-olds cannot understand before and after. *Journal of Verbal Learning and Verbal Behavior*, 1972, *11*, 417–423. 230

Andersen, Elaine S. Cups and glasses: learning that boundaries are vague. *Journal of Child Language*, 1975, *2*, 79–103. 232

Anderson, Robert E. Where's dad? Paternal deprivation and delinquency. *Archives of General Psychiatry*, 1968 *18*(6), 641–649. 409, 504

Andrews, R. J. The self-concept and pupils with learning difficulties. *Slow Learning Child*, 1966, *13*, 47–54. 377

Apgar, Virginia, and Beck, Joan. *Is my baby all right?* New York: Simon and Schuster, 1973. 55, 58

Apgar, Virginia, and Stickle, Gabriel. Birth defects. *Journal of the American Medical Association*, 1968, *204*(5), 371–374. 74

Arafat, Ibithaj, and Yorburg, Betty. On living together without marriage. *Journal of Sex Research*, 1973, *9*(2), 97–106. 428

Aries, P. *Centuries of childhood.* New York: Knopf, 1962. 5

Armstrong, Barbara N., and Scotzin, Martha M. Intergenerational comparison of attitudes toward basic life concepts. *Journal of Psychology*, 1974, *87*(2), 293–304. 430

Arnold, Richard D., and Wist, Anne H. Auditory discrimination abilities of disadvantaged Anglo- and Mexican-American children. *Elementary School Journal*, 1970, *70*(6), 295–299. 112

Aronfreed, Justin, and Reber, Arthur. Internalized behavioral suppression and the timing of social punishment. *Journal of Personality and Social Psychology*, 1965, *1*, 3–16. 404, 405, 411

Aronson, Eric, and Rosenbloom, Shelley. Space perception in early infancy: perception within a common auditory-visual space. *Science*, 1971, *172*(3988), 1161–1163. 103

Asher, James J. Children learning another language: a developmental hypothesis. *Child Development*, 1977, *48*, 1040–1048. 253

Atkinson, Brian R., and Ogston, Donald G. The effect of father absence on male children in the home and school. *Journal of School Psychology*, 1974, *12*(3), 213–221. 409

Austin, Alice. Maternal attitudes and the development of learning disabilities in black children. *Smith College Studies in Social Work*, 1970, *40*(3), 198–210. 450

Ausubel, D. P. How reversible are the cognitive and motivational effects of cultural deprivation? Implications for teaching the culturally deprived child. *Urban Education*, 1964, *1*, 16–38. 333, 442

Awa, A. A.; Bloom, A. D.; Yoshida, M. C.; Neriishi, S.; and Archer, P. G. Cytogenetic study of the offspring of atom bomb survivors. *Nature*, 1968, *218*(5139), 367–368. 55

Azrin, Nathan H., and Foxx, Richard M. *Toilet training in less than a day.* New York: Simon and Schuster, 1974. 134

Baby vision is highly developed. *Science News*, 1979, *115*(10), 152. 90

Baker, Georgia P. The effectiveness of nursery school on affective and con-

---

* The numbers in color indicate where the references appear in the text.

ceptual development of disadvantaged and nondisadvantaged children. *Developmental Psychology*, 1973, *9*(1), 140. 377

Baker, J. Phillip, and Crist, Janet L. Teacher expectancies: a review of the literature. In J. D. Elashoff and R. E. Snow (eds.), *Pygmalion reconsidered*, pp. 48–64. Worthington, Ohio: Charles A. Jones, 1971. 463

Bakwin, Harry. Body-weight regulation in twins. *Developmental Medicine and Child Neurology*, 1973, *15*(2), 178–183. 139

Ball, William, and Tronick, Edward. Infant responses to impending collision: optical and real. *Science*, 1971, *171*(3973), 818–820. 91

Banducci, Raymond. The effect of mother's employment on the achievement, aspirations, and expectations of the child. *Personnel and Guidance Journal*, 1967, *46*(3), 263 263–267, 410, 457

Bandura, A. Influence of models' reinforcement contingencies on the acquisition of imitative responses. *Journal of Personality and Social Psychology*, 1965*a*, *1*, 589–595. 271

——. Behavioral modification through modeling procedures. In L. Krasner and L. P. Ullman (eds.), *Research in behavior modification*. New York: Holt, Rinehart and Winston, 1965*a*. 280

——. A social learning interpretation of psychological dysfunctions. In P. London and D. Rosenhan (eds.), *Foundations of abnormal psychology*. New York: Holt, Rinehart and Winston, 1968. 514

——. *Social learning theory*. Morristown, N.J.: General Learning Press, 1971. 272

Bandura, A., and Menlove, F. L. Factors determining vicarious extinction of avoidance behavior through symbolic modeling. *Journal of Personality and Social Psychology*, 1968, *8*, 99–108. 494

Bandura, A., and Mischel, W. Modification of self-imposed delay of reward through exposure to live and symbolic models. *Journal of Personality and Social Psychology*, 1965, *2*, 698–705. 289

Bandura, A.; Ross, Dorothea; and Ross, Sheila A. Transmission of aggression through imitation of aggressive models. *Journal of Abnormal and Social Psychology*, 1961, *63*, 575–582. 13, 271, 272

——. Imitation of film-mediated aggressive models. *Journal of Abnor-*

mal and Social Psychology, 1963*a*, *66*, 3–11. 13, 271

——. Vicarious reinforcement and imitative learning. *Journal of Abnormal and Social Psychology*, 1963*b*, *67*, 601–607. 13, 271

Barclay, J. Richard, and Comalli, Peter E., Jr. Age differences in perceptual learning on the Müller-Lyer illusion. *Psychonomic Science*, 1970, *19*(6), 323–325. 102

Barclay, Lisa K. The emergence of vocational expectations in preschool children. *Journal of Vocational Behavior*, 1974, *4*(1), 1–14. 459

Barrie-Blackley, Sandie. Six-year-old children's understanding of sentences adjoined with time adverbs. *Journal of Psycholinguistic Research*, 1973, *2*(2), 153–165. 230

Barstis, Susan Weiss, and Ford, LeRoy H., Jr. Reflection-impulsivity, conservation, and the development of ability to control cognitive tempo. *Child Development*, 1977, *48*, 953–959. 204

Bauer, David H. An exploratory study of developmental changes in children's fears. *Journal of Child Psychology and Psychiatry and Allied Disciplines*, 1976, *17*(1), 69–74. 494

Baumrind, Diana. Authoritarian vs. authoritative parental control. *Adolescence*, 1968, *3*(11), 255–272. 425

——. Current patterns of parental authority. *Developmental Psychology Monograph*, 1971, *4*(1, Part 2). 363, 365

Bay, E. Ontogeny of stable speech area in the human brain. In E. Lenneberg (ed.), *Foundations of language development*, vol. 2, pp. 21–29. New York: Academic Press, 1975. 219

Bayley, N., and Schaefer, E. S. Relationships between socio-economic variables and the behavior of mothers toward young children. *Journal of Genetic Psychology*, 1960, *96*, 61–77. 134

——. Comparisons of mental and motor test scores for ages 1–15 months by sex, birth order, race, geographical location, and education of parents. *Child Development*, 1965, *36*, 379–411. 125, 147, 318

Bayley, N., and Schaefer, E. S. Relationships between socioeconomic variables and the behavior of mothers toward young children. *Journal of Genetic Psychology*, 1960, *96*, 61/77. 411

Beard, Ruth M. *An outline of Piaget's developmental psychology for students and teachers*. New York:

Basic Books, 1969. 198

Becker, W. C. Consequences of rent kinds of parental discipline. In M. L. Hoffman and L. W. Hoffman (eds.), *Review of child development*, Vol. 1. New York: Russell Sage Foundation, 1964. 404

Beckwith, Leila. Relationships between attributes of mothers and their infants' IQ scores. *Child Development*, 1971, *42*(4), 1083–1097. 332

Bee, Helen L.; Van Egeren, Lawrence F.; Streissguth, Ann Pytkowicz; Nyman, Barry A.; and Leckie, Maxine S. Social class differences in maternal teaching strategies and speech patterns. *Developmental Psychology*, 1969, *1*(6), 726–734. 243

Bell, Sylvia M. The development of the concept of object as related to infant-mother attachment. *Child Development*, 1970, *41*(2), 292–311. 175, 205

Belsky, Jay, and Steinberg, Laurence D. The effects of day care: a critical review. *Child Development*, 1978, *49*, 929–949. 371

Belva Davis–Channel 9. *San Francisco Examiner–Chronicle*, December 10, 1978. 293

Benjamin, Lorna S. The beginning of thumbsucking. *Child Development*, 1967, *38*(4), 1065–1078. 129

Benjamin, Lorna S.; Serdahely, William: and Geppert, Thomas V. Night training through parents' implicit use of operant conditioning. *Child Development*, 1971, *42*(3), 963–966. 283

Bennett, Stephen. Infant-caretaker interactions. *Journal of the American Academy of Child Psychiatry*, 1971, *10*(2), 321–335. 362

Ben-Zeev, Sandra. The influence of bilingualism on cognitive strategy and cognitive development. *Child Development*, 1977, *48*, 1009–1018. 252

Berens, Anne E. The socialization of need for achievement in boys and girls. *Proceedings of the Annual Convention of the American Psychological Association*, 1972, *7*(Part 1), 273–274. 448, 454

Berg, Ivar. *Education and jobs: the great training robbery*. New York: Praeger, 1970. 322

Berko, Jean. The child's learning of English morphology. *Word*, 1958, *14*, 150–177. 226

Berko, Jean, and Brown, R. Psycholinguistic research methods. In P. H. Mussen (ed.), *Handbook of research methods in child development*, pp. 517–557. New York: Wiley, 1960. 180

Berkowitz, Leonard. The effects of

observing violence. *Scientific American*, 1964, *20*(2), 35–41. 423

Berman, John, and Osborn, Don. Specific self-esteem and sexual permissiveness. *Psychological Reports*, 1975, *36*(1), 323–326. 427

Bernard, John A., and Ramey, Craig T. Visual regard of familiar and unfamiliar persons in the first six months of infancy. *Merrill-Palmer Quarterly*, 1977, *23*(2), 121–127. 95

Bernhardt, Alan J., and Forehand, Rex. The effects of labeled and unlabeled praise upon lower and middle class children. *Journal of Experimental Child Psychology*, 1975, *19*(3), 536–543. 461

Bernstein, Anne C., and Cowan, Philip A. Children's concepts of how people get babies. *Child Development*, 1975, *46*(1), 77–91. 197, 199

Bernstein, B. Social class, linguistic codes and grammatical elements. *Language and Speech*, 1962, *5*, 221–240. 243

Bertrand A. L. School attendance and attainment: function and dysfunction of school and family social systems. *Social Forces*, 1962, *40*, 228–233. 471

Berzonsky, Michael D.; Weiner, Alan S.; and Raphael, Dennis. Interdependence of formal reasoning. *Developmental Psychology*, 1975, *11*(2), 258. 192

Bettelheim, Bruno. Play and education. *School Review*, 1972, *81*(1), 1–13. 414

——. *The uses of enchantment*. New York: Knopf, 1976. 495

Bigner, Jerry J. Parent education in popular literature: 1950–1970. *Family Coordinator*, 1972, *21*(3), 313–319. 363

Biller, Henry B. Father dominance and sex-role development in kindergarten-age boys. *Developmental Psychology*, 1969, *1*(2), 87–94. 382

——. Fathering and female sexual development. *Medical Aspects of Human Sexuality*, 1971, *5*(11), 126–138. 382

Biller, Henry B., and Bahm, Robert M. Father absence, perceived maternal behavior, and masculinity of self-concept among junior high school boys. *Developmental Psychology*, 1971, *4*(2), 178–181. 383

Bing, Elizabeth. Six practical lessons for an easier childbirth. New York: Bantam Books, 1969. 62

Blackbourn, Joe M., and Summerlin, Curtis G. Need occurrence in disadvantaged and non-disadvantaged.

Adolescence, 1974, *9*(34), 233–236. 447, 465

Blank, M., and Solomon, F. A tutorial language program to develop abstract thinking in socially disadvantaged preschool children. *Child Development*, 1968, *39*(2), 379–389. 250

Blankfield, Adele. Natural childbirth: its origins, aims, and implications. *Medical Journal of Australia*, 1968, *1*(24), 1064–1067. 66

Bloom, B. *Stability and change in human characteristics*. New York: Wiley, 1964. 319

Bloom, Kathleen. Social elicitation of infant vocal behavior. *Journal of Experimental Child Psychology*, 1975, *20*(1), 51–58. 240

Bodmer, Walter F., and Cavalli-Sforza, Luigi Luca. Intelligence and Race. *Scientific American*, 1970, *233*(4), 19–29. 342

Bogatz, Gerry Ann, and Ball, Samuel. A summary of the major findings in "The Second Year of Sesame Street: A Continuing Evaluation." Princeton, N.J.: Educational Testing Service, November 1971. 290

Bohan, Janis S. Age and sex differences in the self-concept. *Adolescence*, 1973, *8*(31), 379–384. 382, 388

Boring, E. G.; Langfeld, H. S.; Werner, H.; and Yerkes, R. M. (eds.). A history of psychology in autobiography. Worcester, Mass.: Clark University Press, 1952. 165

Bornstein, Marc H. Qualities of color vision in infancy. *Journal of Experimental Child Psychology*, 1975, *19*(3), 401–419. 90

Bornstein, Marc H.; Kessen, William; and Weiskopf, Sally. Color vision and hue categorization in young human infants. *Journal of Experimental Psychology: Human Perception and Performance*, 1976, *2*(1), 115–129. 84

Borowitz, Gene H.; Hirsch, Jay G.; and Costello, Joan. Play behavior and competence in ghetto four-year-olds. *Journal of Special Education*, 1970, *4*(2), 215–221. 415

Bower, T. G. R. The object in the world of the infant. *Scientific American*, 1971, *225*, 30–38. 91

——. Repetitive process in child development. *Scientific American*, 1976, *235*(5), 38–47. 104, 173

Bower, T. G. R.; Broughton, J.; and Moore, M. K. Development of object concept as manifested in changes in tracking behavior of infants between 7 and 20 weeks of age. *Journal of Experimental Child Psychology*, 1971, *11*, 182–193. 91, 175

Bower, T. G. R., and Wishart, Jennifer G. The effects of motor skill on object permanence in infants. *Cognition*, 1972, *1*(2–3), 165–172. 172

Bowerman, Charles E., and Bahr, Stephen J. Conjugal power and adolescent identification with parents. *Sociometry*, 1973, *36*(3), 366–377, 376

Bowlby, John. Maternal care and mental health. *Bulletin of the World Health Organization*, 1951, *3*, 355–534. 368

——. Separation anxiety. *International Journal of Psychoanalysis*, 1960, *41*, 89–113. 488

Brackbill, Yvonne. Cumulative effects of continuous stimulation on arousal level in infants. *Child Development*, 1971, *42*(1), 17–26. 105

Bradway, K. P., and Thompson, C. W. Intelligence at adulthood: a twenty-five year follow-up. *Journal of Educational Psychology*, 1962, *53*, 1–14. 319

Braine, M. D. S. The ontogeny of English phrase structure: the first phase. *Language*, 1963, *39*, 1–13.

Braine, M. D. S.; Heimer, C. B.; Wortis, H.; and Freedman, A. M. Factors associated with impairment of the early development of prematures. *Monographs of the Society for Research in Child Development*, 1966, *31*(106), 1–92. 226

Brainerd, Charles J., and Allen, Terry W. Training and generalization of density conservation: effects of feedback and consecutive similar stimuli. *Child Development*, 1971, *42*(3), 693–704. 196

Brazelton, T. Berry. Effect of prenatal drugs on the behavior of the neonate. *American Journal of Psychiatry*, 1970, *126*(9), 1261–1266. 53

Brennan, W. M.; Ames, E. W.; and Moore, E. W. Age differences in infant's attention to patterns of different complexities. *Science*, 1966, *151*, 354–356. 90

Brodbeck, Arthur J., and Irwin, Orvis C. The speech behavior of infants without families. *Child Development*, 1946, *17*, 145–156. 247

Bronfenbrenner, Urie. Socialization and social class through time and space. In E. E. Maccoby; T. M. Newcomb; and E. L. Hartley (eds.), *Readings in social psychology*, 3d ed. pp. 400–425. New York: Holt, Rinehart and Winston, 1958. 367

——. Is 80% of intelligence genetically determined? In Urie Bronfenbrenner and M. A. Mahoney (eds.), *Influences on human development*, 2d ed., pp.

91–100. Hinsdale, Ill.: Dryden Press, 1975. 338

Brook, Judith S.; Whiteman, Martin: Peisach, Estelle; and Deutsch, Martin. Aspiration levels of and for children: age, sex, race, and socioeconomic correlates. *Journal of Genetic Psychology*, 1974, *124*(1), 3–16. 448

Brown, Josephine V.; Bakeman, Roger; Snyder, Patricia A.; Fredrickson, W. Timm; Morgan, Sharon T.; and Hepler, Ruth. Interactions of black inner-city mothers with their newborn infants. *Child Development*, 1975, *46*(3), 677–686. 378

Brown, Nina W., and Renz, Paul. Altering the reality self-concept of seventh grade culturally deprived girls in the inner city. *Adolescence*, 1973, *8*(32), 463–474. 377

Brown, Roger. *Words and things*. Glencoe, Ill.: Free Press, 1958. 234

——. Development of the first language in the human species. *American Psychologist*, 1973, *28*(2), 97–106. 217, 228

Brown, R., and Bellugi, U. Three processes in the child's acquisition of syntax. *Harvard Educational Review*, 1964, *34*, 133–151. 242

Brown, R.; Cazden, C. B.; and Bellugi, U. The child's grammar from I to III. In J. P. Hill (ed.), *Minnesota symposium on child development*, Vol. 2, pp. 28–73. Minneapolis: University of Minnesota Press, 1968. 241

Bruner, Jerome S. *Toward a theory of instruction*. Cambridge, Mass.: Harvard University Press, 1966. 193

——. Organization of early skilled action. *Child Development*, 1973, *44*(1), 1–11. 130

Bruner, Jerome S., and Bruner, B. M. On voluntary action and its hierarchical structure. Presented at the Symposium on New Perspective in the Sciences of Man, Alpbach, Austria, 1968. 129

Bruner, Jerome S.; Olver, R.; Greenfield, M.; Hornsby, J.; Kenney, H.; Maccoby, M.; Modiano, N.; Mosher, F.; Olson, D.; Potter, M.; Reich, L.; Sonstroem, A. *Studies in cognitive growth*. New York: Wiley, 1966. 180, 194, 195

Buhler, C., and Hetzer, H. *Testing children's development from birth to school age*. New York: Farrar and Rinehart, 1935. 222

Bunt, Miriam E. Ego identity: its relationship to the discrepancy between how an adolescent views himself and how he perceives that others view him. *Psychology*, 1968, *5*(3),

14–25. 387

Burger, Gary K.; Lamp, Robert E.; and Rogers, Donald. Developmental trends in children's perceptions of parental child-rearing behavior. *Developmental Psychology*, 1975, *11*(3), 391. 408

Burke, B. S.; Beal, V. A.; Kirkwood, S. B.; and Stuart, H. C. The influence of nutrition during pregnancy upon the conditions of the infant at birth. *Journal of Nutrition*, 1943, *26*, 569–583. 52

Burks, B. S. The relative influence of nature and nurture upon mental development: a comparative study of foster parent–foster child resemblance and true parent–true child resemblance. In *Child psychology*, 27th Yearbook of the National Society for Studies in Education, Part 1, pp. 219–319. Chicago: University of Chicago Press, 1928. 325, 328

Burlingham, Dorothy, The preoedipal infant-father relationship. *Psychoanalytic Study of the Child*, 1973, *28*, 23–47. 407

Burnstein, E. Fear of failure, achievement motivation, and aspiring to prestigeful occupations. *Journal of Abnormal Social Psychology*, 1963, *67*, 189–193.

Burt, C. The genetic determination of differences in intelligence: a study of monozygotic twins reared together and apart. *British Journal of Psychology*, 1966, *57*, 137–153. 326

Busse, Thomas V., and Busse, Pauline. Negro parental behavior and social class variables. *Journal of Genetic Psychology*, 1972, *120*(2), 287–294. 327

Butler, Robert A. Curiosity in monkeys. *Scientific American*, 1954, *190*(2), 70–75. 442

Caldwell, Edward C., and Hall, Vernon C. Concept learning in the discrimination tasks. *Developmental Psychology*, 1970, *2*(1), 41–48. 98

Caputo, Daniel V., and Mandell Wallace. Consequence of low birth weight. *Developmental Psychology*, 1970, *3*(3, Part 1), 363–383. 72

Carlsmith, Lyn. Some personality characteristics of boys separated from their fathers during World War II. *Ethos*, 1973, *1*(4), 466–477. 383

Carlson, J. S. Children's probability judgments as related to age, intelligence, socio-economic level, and sex. *Human Development*, 1969, *12*(3), 192–203. 200

Carmichael, L.; Hogan, H. P.; and Walter, A. A. An experimental study

of the effect of language on the reproduction of visually perceived form. *Journal of Experimental Psychology*, 1932, *15*, 73–86. 234

Caro, F. G. Social class and attitudes of young relevant for the realization of adult goals. *Social Forces*, 1966, *44*, 492–498. 466

Caro, F. G., and Pihlblad, C. T. Aspirations and expectations: a reexamination of the bases for social class differences in the occupational orientations of male high school students. *Sociology and Social Research*, 1965, *49*, 465–475. 466

Carr, Suzanne J.; Dabbs, James M., Jr.; and Carr, Timothy S. Mother-infant attachment: the importance of the mother's visual field. *Child Development*, 1975, *45*(2), 331–338. 368

Carroll, Jerome F. Understanding adolescent needs. *Adolescence*, 1968–1969, *3*(12), 381–394. 385, 386

Carroll, John B. *Language and thought*. Englewood Cliffs, N.J.: Prentice-Hall, 1964. 233

Caudill, William, and Weinstein, Helen. Maternal care and infant behavior in Japan and America. *Psychiatry*, 1969, *32*, 12–43. 411, 412

Cervantes, L. F. Family background, primary relationships, and the high school dropout. *Journal of Marriage and Family*, 1965, *5*, 218–223. 471

Chaffee, Steven H. Television and adolescent aggressiveness (overview). In G. A. Comstock and E. A. Rubenstein (eds.), *Television and social behavior*, Vol. 3. Report of the U.S. Department of Health, Education, and Welfare, 1971. 423

Chambers, Charles H. Leo Kanner's concept of early infantile autism. *British Journal of Medical Psychology*, 1969, *42*(1), 51–54. 498, 499

Chapman, Michael. Father absence, stepfathers, and the cognitive performance of college students. *Child Development*, 1977, *48*, 1155–1158. 409

Chapman, Robert H. The development of children's understanding of proportions. *Child Development*, 1975, *46*(1), 141–148. 189

Chase, H. Peter, and Martin, Harold P. Undernutrition and child development. *New England Journal of Medicine*, 1970, *282*(17), 933–939. 151

Chen, H. P., and Irwin, O. C. Infant speech: vowel and consonant types. *Journal of Speech Disorders*, 1946, *11*, 27–29. 224

Cherry, Louise, and Lewis, Michael. Mothers and two-year-olds: a study of sex-differentiated aspects of verbal interaction. *Developmental Psychology*, 1976, *12*(4), 278–282. 238

Cheyney, A. B. Teachers of the culturally disadvantaged. *Exceptional Children*, 1966, *33*, 83–88. 467, 469

Chomsky, Noam. *Syntactic structures.* The Hague: Mouton, 1957. 217

Cicirelli, Victor G. Effects of mother and older sibling on the problem-solving behavior of the younger child. *Developmental Psychology*, 1975, *11*(6), 749–756. 206

Clarke, Eve V. On the acquisition of the meaning of before and after. *Journal of Verbal Learning and Verbal Behavior*, 1971, *10*(3), 266–275. 230

———. On the child's acquisition of antonyms in two semantic fields. *Journal of Verbal Learning and Verbal Behavior*, 1972, *11*(6), 750–758. 231

Clark, J. P., and Wenninger, E. P. Socio-economic class and area as correlates of illegal behavior among juveniles. *American Sociological Review*, 1962, *27*, 826–834. 504

Clark, K. B., and Clark, M. K. The development of consciousness of self in the emergence of racial identification in Negro preschool children. *Journal of Social Psychology*, 1939, *10*, 591–599. 419

———. Racial identification and preference in Negro children. In T. Newcomb and E. Hartley (eds.), *Readings in Social Psychology*, New York: Holt, 1947. 419

Clarke, Anne E., and Ruble, Diane N. Young adolescents' beliefs concerning menstruation. *Child Development*, 1978, *49*, 231–234. 146

Clarke-Stewart, K. Alison. Popular primers for parents. *American Psychologist*, 1978, *33*(4), 359–369. 4

Clifford, Edward. Body satisfaction in adolescence. *Perceptual and Motor Skills*, 1971, *33*(1), 119–125. 145

Cline, Victor B.; Croft, Roger, G.; and Courrier, Steven. The desensitization of children to television violence. *Proceedings of the Annual Convention of the American Psychological Association*, 1972, 7(Part 1), 99–100. 422

Coates, Brian; Anderson, Elizabeth P.; and Hartup, Willard W. Interrelationships in the attachment behavior of human infants. *Developmental Psychology*, 1972, *6*(2), 218–230. 368

Cobb, H. V. Role wishes and general wishes of children and adolescents. *Child Development*, 1954, *25*, 161–171. 145

Cohen, Jozef. *Personality dynamics.* Chicago: Rand McNally, 1969. 354

Cohen, Leslie Jordan, and Campos, Joseph J. Father, mother, and stranger as elicitors of attachment behaviors in infancy. *Developmental Psychology*, 1974, *10*(1), 146–154. 368

Cohen, Sarale E. Developmental differences in infants' attentional responses to face-voice incongruity of mother and stranger. *Child Development*, 1974, *45*(4), 1155–1158. 103

Cohen, Sarale E., and Beckwith, Leila. Maternal language in infancy. *Developmental Psychology*, 1976 *12*(4), 371–372. 241

Cohen, Stewart, and Przybycien, Colette A. Some effects of sociometrically selected peer models on the cognitive styles of impulsive children. *Journal of Genetic Psychology*, 1974, *124*(2), 213–220. 289

Coie, John D. An evaluation of the cross-situational stability of children's curiosity. *Journal of Personality*, 1974, *42*(1), 93–116. 282

Collins, W. Andrew. Learning of media content: a developmental study. *Child Development*, 1970, *41*(4), 1133–1142. 291

Collins, W. Andrew; Wellman, Henry; Keniston, Allen H.; and Westby, Sally D. Age-related aspects of comprehension and inference from a televised dramatic narrative. *Child Development*, 1978, *49*, 389–399. 291, 422

Colman, Arthur D., and Colman, Libby Lee. *Pregnancy: the psychological experience.* New York: Seabury press, 1973. 56

Condon, William S., and Sander, Louis W. Synchrony demonstrated between movements of the neonate and adult speech. *Child Development*, 1974, *45*(2), 456–462. 222

Conger, John Janeway. Sexual attitudes and behavior of contemporary adolescents. In John Janeway Conger (ed.), *Contemporary issues in adolescent development*. New York: Harper and Row, 1975. 427

Conger, John Janeway; Miller, W. C.; and Walsmith, C. R. Antecedents of delinquency, personality, social class and intelligence. In P. H. Mussen, John Janeway Conger, and J. Kagan (eds.), *Readings in child development and personality*, pp. 565–588. New York: Harper and Row, 1965. 502

Connor, Jane M., and Serbin, Lisa A. Behaviorally based masculine-and-feminine-activity-preference scales for preschoolers: correlates with other classroom behaviors and cognitive tests. *Child Development*, 1977,

48, 1411–1416. 379

Conversation with B. F. Skinner, *Harvard Magazine*, July–August 1977, p. 56. 402

Coopersmith, Stanley. Studies in self-esteem. *Scientific American*, 1968, *218*(2), 96–106. 375

Coppola, Raymond. What if Wonder Woman teamed up with the Hulk? *TV Guide*, December 30, 1978. 292

Corah, N. L.; Anthony, E. J.; Painter, P.; Stern, J. A.; and Thurston, D. Effects of perinatal anoxia after 7 years. *Psychological Monographs*, 1965, *79*, 1–34. 65

Cornell, Edward H., and Gottfried, Allen W. Intervention with premature human infants. *Child Development*, 1976, *47*, 32–39. 148

Corsini, David A. Developmental changes in the effect of nonverbal cues on retention. *Developmental Psychology*, 1969, *1*(4), 425–435. 276, 277

Corter, Carl M. The nature of the mother's absence and the infant's response to brief separations. *Developmental Psychology*, 1976, *12*(5), 428–434. 95

Cottle, Thomas J.; Howard, Peter; and Pleck, Joseph. Adolescent perceptions of time: the effect of age, sex, and social class. *Journal of Personality*, 1969, *37*(4), 636–650. 192

Cox, M. V. Perspective ability: the conditions of change. *Child Development*, 1977, *48*, 1724–1727. 181

Crandall, Virginia C. The Fels study: some contributions to personality development and achievement in childhood and adulthood. *Seminars in Psychiatry*, 1972, *4*(4), 383–397 440, 448, 454

Crandall, V. J.; Dewey, R.; Katovsky, W.; and Preston, A. Parents' attitudes and behaviors and grade school children's academic achievement. *Journal of Genetic Psychology*, 1964, *104*, 53–66. 441, 45

Crandall, V.; Katovsky, W.; and Preston, A. A conceptual formulation for some research on children's achievement development. *Child Development*, 1960, *31*, 787. 440, 448

Crites, J. O. Parental identification in relation to vocational interest development. *Journal of Educational Psychology*, 1962, *53*, 262–270. 376, 456

Croake, J. W. Fears of children. *Human Development*, 1969, *12*(4), 239–247. 494

Cronbach, L. J. *Essentials of psychological testing.* 3d ed. New York:

Harper and Row, 1970. 312, 313

Cronenwett, Linda R., and Newmark, Lucy L. Fathers' responses to childbirth. *Nursing Research*, 1974, *23*(3), 210–217. 68

Cummings, J. E. Incidence of emotional symptoms in school children. *British Journal of Educational Psychology*, 1944, *14*, 151–161. 479

Dales, Ruth J. Motor and language development of twins during the first three years. *Journal of Genetic Psychology*, 1969, *114*(2), 263–271. 241

Dasen, Pierre R. Cross-cultural Piagetian research: a summary. *Journal of Cross-Cultural Psychology*, 1972, *3*(1), 23–40. 206

Davids, Anthony. A research design for studying maternal emotionality before childbirth and after social interaction with the child. *Merrill-Palmer Quarterly*, 1968, *14*(4), 344–354. 56

——. ed. *Issues in abnormal child psychology*. Monterey, Calif.: Brooks-Cole, 1973. 480, 496

Davids, Anthony; De Vault, S.; and Talmadge, M. Anxiety, pregnancy and childbirth abnormalities. *Journal of Consulting Psychology*, 1961, *25*, 74–77. 56

Davison, A. N., and Dobbing, J. Myelinization as a vulnerable period in brain development. *British Medical Bulletin*, 1966, *22*, 40–45. 52

Day, H. I. The importance of arousal as a motivational factor in learning to read. *Canadian Psychologist*, 1968, *9*(2), 154–161. 461

de Hirsch, Katrina. A review of early language development. *Developmental Medicine and Child Neurology*, 1970, *12*, 87–97. 219, 221

de Lemos, Marion M. The development of conservation in aboriginal children. *International Journal of Psychology*, 1969, *4*(4), 255–269. 197, 206

De Mause, Lloyd. The evolution of childhood: a symposium. *History of Childhood Quarterly*, 1974, *1*(4), 503–. 123

Denner, Bruce. Representational and syntactic competence of problem readers. *Child Development*, 1970, *41*, 881–887. 244

Denney, Douglas R.; Denney, Nancy Wadsworth; and Ziobrowski, Martin J. Alterations in the information-processing strategies of young children following observation of adult models. *Developmental Psychology*, 1973, *8*(2), 202–208. 286

Dennis, W. Infant development under conditions of restricted practice and of minimum social stimulation. *Genetic Psychological Monographs*, 1941, *23*, 143–191. 152

——. Causes of retardation among institutional children: Iran. *Journal of Genetic Psychology*, 1960, *96*, 47–59. 152

Dentler, R. A. Dropouts, automation, and the cities. *Teachers College Record*, 1964, *65*, 475–483. 471

Desmond, M. M.; Franklin, R. R.; Vallbona, C.; Hilt, R. H.; Plumb, R.; Arnold, H.; and Watts, J. The clinical behavior of the newly born. *Journal of Pediatrics*, 1963, *62*, 307–325. 75

Desor, J. A.; Maller, Owen; and Turner, Robert E. Taste in acceptance of sugars by human infants. *Journal of Comparative and Physiological Psychology*, 1973, *84*(3), 496–501. 109

DeStefano, Johanna S. Register: social variation in language use. *Elementary School Journal*, 1972, *72*(4), 189–194. 246

Deutsch, M. The disadvantaged child and the learning process. In A. H. Passow (ed.), *Education in depressed areas*, pp. 163–179. New York: Columbia University Press, 1963. 469

——. Social and psychological perspectives on the development of the disadvantaged learner. *Journal of Negro Education*, 1964, *33*, 232–244. 295, 467

——. Happenings on the way back to the forum: social science, IQ and race differences revisited. *Harvard Educational Review*, 1969, *39*, 523–527. 469

deVilliers, Jill G., and deVilliers, Peter A. *Language acquisition*. Cambridge, Mass.: Harvard University Press, 1978. 217, 218

DeVries, Rheta. Relationships among Piagetian, IQ, and achievement assessments. *Child Development*, 1974, *45*(3), 746–756. 200

Distefano, M. K., Jr.; Pryer, Margaret W.; and Rice, David P. Changes in success-failure attitudes during adolescence. *Journal of Genetic Psychology*, 1970, *116*(1), 11–13. 450

Distel, Dave. The eyes have it. *San Francisco Chronicle–Examiner*, August 15, 1976. 102

Dollinger, Stephen J., and Thelen, Mark H. Anticipated model consequences, model affect, and imitation. *Developmental Psychology*, 1975, *11*(3), 390. 272

Dolloff, Phyllis, and Resnick, Miriam. *Patterns of life*. Columbus, Ohio: Charles E. Merrill, 1972. 428

Dorfman, D. D. The Cyril Burt question: new findings. *Science*, 1978, *201*(4362), 1177–1186. 326, 327

Downing, John; Ollila, Lloyd; and Oliver, Peter. Concepts of language in children from differing socioeconomic backgrounds. *Journal of Educational Research*, 1977, *70*(5), 277–281. 244

Doyle, Anna-Beth. Infant development in day care. *Developmental Psychology*, 1975, *11*(5), 655–656. 414

Drake, William E. *The American school in transition*. Englewood Cliffs, N.J.: Prentice-Hall, 1955. 8

Drillien, C. M., and Ellis, R. W. B. *The growth and development of the prematurely born infant*. Baltimore: Williams and Wilkins, 1964. 72

Drillien, C. M., and Richmond, F. Prematurity in Edinburgh. *Archives of Disturbances in Childhood*, 1956, *31*, 390. 51

Drozdal, John G., Jr.; and Flavell, John H. A developmental study of logical search behavior. *Child Development*, 1975, *46*(1), 389–393. 287

Dubignon, Judith, and Campbell, Dugal. Discrimination between nutriments by the human neonate. *Psychonomic Science*, 1969, *16*(4), 186–187. 109

Duncan, Beverly, and Duncan, Otis D. Family stability and occupational success. *Social Problems*, 1969, *16*(3), 273–285. 409

Dusek, Jerome B., and O'Connell, Edward J. Teacher expectancy effects on the achievement test performance of elementary school children. *Journal of Educational Psychology*, 1973, *65*(3), 371–377. 463

Dwyer, Johanna, and Mayer, Jean. Psychological effects of variations in physical appearance during adolescence. *Adolescence*, 1968–69, *3*, 353–386. 145

Ebbs, J. H.; Brown, A.; Tisdall, F. F.; Moyle, W. J.; and Bell, M. The influence of improved prenatal nutrition upon the infant. *Canadian Medical Association Journal*, 1942, *46*(1), 1–6. 52

Edwards, Nancy. The relationship between physical condition immediately after birth and mental and motor performance at age four. *Genetic Psychology Monographs*, 1968, *78*(2), 257–289. 127, 129

Eichorn, Dorothy H. Variations in growth rate. *Childhood Education*, 1968, *44*(5), 286–291. 137, 141

Eiduson, Bernice T.; Cohen, Jerome; and Alexander, Jannette. Alternatives in child-rearing in the 1970s. *American Journal of Orthopsychiatry*, 1973, *43*(5), 720–731. 402, 403

Eisenberg, Leon. School phobia: A study in the communication of anxiety. *American Journal of Psychiatry*, 1958, *114*, 712–718. 496

Elardo, Richard; Bradley, Robert; and Caldwell, Bettye M. A longitudinal study of the relation of infants' home environments to language development at age three. *Child Development*, 1977, *48*(2), 595–603. 240

Elkind, David. Quantity conceptions in junior and senior high school students. *Child Development*, 1961, *32*, 551–560. 186, 187

——. Egocentrism in adolescence. *Child Development*, 1967, *38*, 1025–1034. 190, 191

——. *Children and adolescents*. 2d ed. New York: Oxford University Press, 1974. 179

Elkind, David; Anagnostopoulou, Rena; and Malone, Susan. Determinants of part-whole perception in children. *Child Development*, 1970, *41*(2), 391–397. 100

Elkind, David; Koegler, R. R.; and Go, E. Studies in perceptual development. *Child Development*, 1964, *35*, 81–90. 83

Elliott, D. S.; Voss, H. L.; and Wendling, A. Dropout and the social milieu of the high school: a preliminary analysis. *American Journal of Orthopsychiatry*, 1966, *36*, 808–817. 471

Emmerich, Walter; Goldman, Karla, S.; and Shore, Roy E. Differentiation and development of social norms. *Journal of Personality and Social Psychology*, 1971, *18*(3), 323–353. 374, 387

Endsley, Richard C., and Clarey, Susan A. Answering young children's questions as a determinant of their subsequent question-asking behavior. *Developmental Psychology*, 1975, *11*(6), 863. 242

Engel, Mary. *Psychopathology in childhood: social, diagnostic, and therapeutic aspects*. New York: Harcourt Brace Jovanovich, 1972. 491, 492, 497

Engen, Trygg, and Lipsitt, Lewis P. Decrement and recovery of responses to olfactory stimuli in the human neonate. *Journal of Comparative and Physiological Psychology*, 1965, *59*, 312–316. 110

Engen, Trygg; Lipsitt, Lewis P.; and Peck, Marjorie B. Ability of newborn infants to discriminate sapid substances. *Development Psychology*,

1974, *10*(5) 741–744. 109

Ennis, Robert H. Conditional logic and primary school children: a developmental study. *Interchange*, 1971, *2*(2), 126–132. 171

Entwisle, Doris R., and Huggins, W. H. Iconic memory in children. *Child Development*, 1973, *44*(2), 392–394. 276

Epstein, Ann S., and Radin, Norma. Motivational components related to father behavior and cognitive functioning in preschoolers. *Child Development*, 1975, *46*(4), 831–839. 453

Erickson, M. L., and Empey, L. T. Class position, peers and delinquency. *Sociology and Social Research*, 1965, *49*, 268–282. 504

Erikson, Erik H. *Childhood and society*, 2d ed. New York: W. W. Norton, 1963. 356

——. Reflections on the dissent of contemporary youth. *Daedalus*, 1970, *99*(1), 154–176. 387

Erlenmeyer-Kimling, L., and Jarvik, L. F. Genetics and intelligence. *Science*, 1963, *142*, 1477–1479. 328

Ernhart, C. B.; Graham, F. K., and Thurston, D. Relationship of neonatal apnea to development at three years. *Archives of Neurology*, 1960, *2*, 504–510. 64

Ervin, S. M., and Miller, W. R. Language development. In H. W. Stevenson (ed.), *Child psychology*, 62nd yearbook of the National Society for Studies in Education, Part 1, pp. 108–143. Chicago: University of Chicago Press, 1963. 227

Etaugh, Claire. Effects of maternal employment on children: a review of recent research. *Merrill-Palmer Quarterly*, 1974, *20*(2), 71–98. 410, 457

Etaugh, Claire; Collins, Gene; and Gerson, Arene. Reinforcement of sex-typed behaviors of two-year-old children in a nursery school setting. *Developmental Psychology*, 1975, *11*(2), 255. 462

Etaugh, Claire, and Rose, Suzanne. Adolescents' sex bias in the evaluation of performance. *Developmental Psychology*, 1975, *11* (5), 663–664. 382

Etzel, Barbara C., and Gewirtz, Jacob L. Experimental modification of caretaker-maintained high-rate operant crying in a 6- and a 20-week-old infant (Infans tyrannotearus): extinction of crying with reinforcement of eye contact and smiling. *Journal of Experimental Child Psychology*, 1967, *5*, 303–317. 266

Fagan, Joseph F. Infant color percep-

tion. *Science*, 1974, *183*(4128), 973–975. 90

Fagot, Beverly I. Consequences of moderate cross-gender behavior in preschool children. *Child Development*, 1977, *48*, 902–907. 379, 462

——. The influence of sex of child on parental reactions to toddler children. *Child Development*, 1978, *49*, 459–465. 381

Fantz, Robert L. The origin of form perception. *Scientific American*, 1961, *204*(5), 66–72.

——. Visual experience in infants: decreased attention to familiar patterns relative to novel ones. *Science*, 1964, *146*, 668–670. 83, 88

Fantz, Robert L., and Fagan, Joseph F., III. Visual attention to size and number of pattern details by term and preterm infants during the first six months. *Child Development*, 1975, *46*, 3–18. 90

Farran, Dale C., and Ramey, Craig T. Infant day care and attachment behaviors toward mothers and teachers. *Child Development*, 1977, *48*, 1112–116. 371

Farrell, Margaret A. The formal stage: a review of the research. *Journal of Research and Development in Education*, 1969, *3*(1), 111–118. 184

Fein, Greta G. The effect of chronological age and model reward on imitative behavior. *Developmental Psychology*, 1973, *9*(3), 283–289. 282

——. Children's sensitivity to social contexts at 18 months of age. *Developmental Psychology*, 1975, *11*(6), 853–854. 227

Feingold, Robert. *Why your child is hyperactive*. New York: Random House, 1975. 510

Feldhusen, J. F., and Klausmeier, H. J. Anxiety, intelligence, and achievement in children of low, average, and high intelligence. *Child Development*, 1962, *33*, 403–409. 320

Feldman, Sarah S. Children's understanding of negation as a logical operation in a classification task. *Dissertation Abstracts*, 1969, *29*(7-B), 2626–2617. 104, 231

Field, Jeffrey. Coordination of vision and prehension in young infants. *Child Development*, 1977, *48*(1), 97–103. 88

Fish, Kathleen D., and Biller, Henry B. Perceived childhood paternal relationships and college females' personal adjustment. *Adolescence*, 1973, *8*(31), 415–420. 376

Fiske, Edward B. Toys can polish preschooler skills. *New York Times*, February 20, 1979. 294

Flavell, J. H. *The developmental psychology of Jean Piaget.* Princeton, N.J.: Van Nostrand, 1963. 185

Forslund, Morris A., and Hull, Ronald E. Sex-role identification in preadolescence. *Psychology in the Schools*, 1972, *9*(4), 413–417. 462

Fouts, Gregory, and Liikanen, Pirkko. The effects of age and developmental level on imitation in children. *Child Development*, 1975, *46*(2), 555–558. 286

Foxx, R. M., and Azrin, N. H. Dry pants: a rapid method of toilet training children. *Behaviour Research and Therapy*, 1973, *11*(4), 435–442. 282, 283

Frazier, A., and Lisonbee, L. K. Adolescent concerns with physique. *School Review*, 1950, *58*, 397–405. 145

Fredrickson, W. Timm, and Brown, Josephine V. Posture as a determinant of visual behavior in newborns. *Child Development*, 1975, *46*, 579–582. 85

Freedman, D. An ethological approach to the genetic study of human behavior. In S. G. Vandenberg (ed.), *Methods and goals in human behavior genetics*, pp. 141–161. New York: Academic Press, 1965. 359

Freedman, David A. The influence of congenital and perinatal sensory deprivations on later development. *Psychosomatics*, 1968, *9*,(5), 272–277. 489

Freedman, David A.; Fox-Kolenda, B. J.; Margileth, D. A.; and Miller, D. H. The development of the use of sound as a guide to affective and cognitive behavior: a two-phase process. *Child Development*, 1969, *40*(4), 1099–1105. 103

Freedman, D. G. An evolutionary approach to research on the life cycle. *Human Development*, 1971, *14*(2), 87–99. 359

Frenkel-Brunswik, E. A study of prejudice in children. *Human Relations*, 1948, *1*, 295–306. 418, 419

Freud, Anna. Assessment of childhood disturbances. *Psychoanalytic study of the child*, Vol. 18. New York: International Universities Press, 1962. 511

Freud, S. *Analysis of a phobia in a five-year-old boy (1909).* Standard edition, Vol. 10, edited and translated by James Strachey. London: Hogarth Press, 1953. 493

Friedlander, Bernard Z. The effect of speaker identity, voice inflection, vocabulary and message redundancy on infants' selection of vocal rein-

forcement. *Journal of Experimental Child Psychology*, 1968, *6*, 443–459. 222

Friedlander, Bernard Z.; Wetstone, Harriet S.; and Scott, Christopher S. Suburban preschool children's comprehension of an age-appropriate informational television program. *Child Development*, 1974, *45*(2), 561–565. 293

Friedrich, Lynette K., and Stein, Aletha H. Prosocial television and young children: the effects of verbal labeling and role playing on learning and behavior. *Child Development*, 1975, *46*(1), 27–38. 291

Friend, Ronald M., and Neale, John M. Children's perceptions of success and failure: an attributional analysis of the effects of race and social class. *Developmental Psychology*, 1972, 7(2), 124–128. 464

Furth, H. G. Piaget, IQ and the nature-nurture controversy. *Human Development*, 1973, *16*(1–2), 61–73. 200

Gaensbauer, Theodore J., and Emde, Robert N. Wakefulness and feeding in human newborns. *Archives of General Psychiatry*, 1973, *28*(6), 894–897. 105

Gage, N. L. Desirable behaviors of teachers. *Urban Education*, 1965, *1*, 85–95. 459

Gage, N. L., and Berliner, David C. *Educational psychology*, Chicago: Rand McNally, 1975. 321

Garbarino, James. A preliminary study of some ecological correlates of child abuse: the impact of socioeconomic stress on mothers. *Child Development*, 1976, *47*(1), 178–185. 490

Gardner, George E. Aggression and violence: the enemies of precision learning in children. *American Journal of Psychiatry*, 1971, *128*(4), 445–450. 450

Garn, S. M. Body size and its implications. In L. W. Hoffman and M. L. Hoffman (eds.), *Review of child development research*, Vol. 2, pp. 540–561. New York: Russell Sage Foundation, 1966. 137, 141, 150

Garn, S. M.; Clark, A.; Landkof, Lina; and Newell, Laura. Parental body build and developmental progress in the offspring. *Science*, 1960, *132*, 1555–1556. 41

Genshaft, Judy L., and Hirt, Michael. Language differences between black children and white children. *Developmental Psychology*, 1974, *10*(3), 451–456. 246

Gesell, A. The ontogenesis of infant behavior. In L. Carmichael (ed.), *Manu-

al of child psychology*, 2d ed., pp. 355–373. New York: Wiley, 1954. 128

Gesell, A.; Halverson, H. M.; Thompson, H.; Ilg, F. L.; Castner, B. M.; Ames, L. B.; and Amatruda, C. S. *The first five years of life: a guide to the study of the preschool child.* New York: Harper and Row, 1940. 131

Gesell, A.; Ilg, F. L.; and Ames, L. B. *Youth: the years from ten to sixteen.* New York: Harper and Row, 1956. 142

Gesell, A., and Thompson, Helen. Learning and maturation in identical twins: an experimental analysis by the method of co-twin control. *Genetic Psychology Monographs*, 1929, *6*, 5–124. 123, 125, 138

Gibson, Eleanor J. Perceptual development. In H. W. Stevenson (ed.), *Child psychology*, 62nd yearbook of the National Society for Studies in Education, Part 1, pp. 144–195. Chicago: University of Chicago Press, 1963*a*. 82, 84

——. Development of perception: discrimination of depth compared with discrimination of graphic symbols. In J. C. Wright and J. Kagan (ed.), Basic cognitive processes in children. *Monographs of the Society for Research in Child Development*, 1963*b*, *28*(2), 5–32. 84

——. *Principles of perceptual learning and development.* New York: Appleton-Century-Crofts, 1969. 99

Gibson, Eleanor J.; Gibson, James J.; Pick, Anne D.; and Osser, Harry. A developmental study of the discrimination of letter-like forms. *Journal of Comparative and Physiological Psychology*, 1962, *55*(6), 897–906. 99

Gibson, Eleanor J., and Walk, Richard D. The "visual cliff." *Scientific American*, 1960, *202*, 64–71. 91

Gibson, J. J., and Gibson, Eleanor J. Perceptual learning: differentiation or enrichment? *Psychological Review*, 1955, *62*, 32–41. 83, 99

Gilder, George. The case against women in combat. *New York Times Magazine*, January 28, 1979, pp. 29–30, 44–46. 452

Gitter, Lena L. The promise of Montessori for special education. *Journal of Special Education*, 1967, *2*(1), 5–13. 468

Glantz, Leonard H.; Annas, George J.; and Katz, Barbara F. Scientific research with children: legal incapacity and proxy consent. *Family Law Quarterly*, 1977, *11*(3), 253–295. 18, 19

Gliner, Cynthia R. Tactual discrimination thresholds for shape and texture in young children. *Journal of Experimental Child Psychology*, 1967, *5*(4), 536–547. 108

Glueck, S., and Glueck, E. Working mothers and delinquency. *Mental Hygiene*, 1957, *41*, 327–352. 410, 504
——. *Predicting delinquency and crime.* Cambridge, Mass.: Harvard University Press, 1959. 504, 505

Gold, Dolores, and Andres, David. Developmental comparisons between ten-year-old children with employed and nonemployed mothers. *Child Development*, 1978, *49*, 75–84. 456

Goldberg, Susan. Infant care and growth in urban Zambia. *Human Development*, 1972, *15*(2), 77–89. 150

Goldberg, Susan, and Lewis, Michael. Play behavior in the year-old infant: early sex differences. *Child Development*, 1969, *40*(1), 21–31. 380

Golden, Mark, and Birns, Beverly. Social class, intelligence, and cognitive style in infancy. *Child Development*, 1971, *42*(6), 2114–2116. 336

Golden, Mark; Bridger, Wagner H.; and Montare, Albert. Social class differences in the ability of young children to use verbal information to facilitate learning. *American Journal of Orthopsychiatry*, 1974, *44*(1), 86–91. 295

Golden, Mark; Montare, Alberto; and Bridger, Wagner. Verbal control of delay behavior in two-year-old boys as a function of social class. *Child Development*, 1977, *48*, 1107–1111. 235

Golden, Nancy E., and Steiner, Sharon R. Auditory and visual functions in good and poor readers. *Journal of Learning Disabilities*, 1969, *2*(9), 476–481. 236

Goldfarb, W. Infant rearing and problem behavior. *American Journal of Orthopsychiatry*, 1943, *13*, 249–266. 247
——. Effects of psychological deprivation in infancy and subsequent stimulation. *American Journal of Psychiatry*, 1945*a*, *102*, 18–33. 246, 286
——. Psychological privation in infancy and subsequent adjustment. *American Journal of Orthopsychiatry*, 1945 *b*, *15*, 79–85. 499
——. *Childhood schizophrenia.* Cambridge, Mass.: Harvard University Press, 1961. 499

Goldman, Ronald, and Sanders, Jay W. Cultural factors and hearing. *Exceptional Children*, 1969, *35*(6), 489–490. 112

Goldschmid, Marcel L. Different types

of conservation and nonconservation and their relation to age, sex, IQ, MA, and vocabulary. *Child Development*, 1967, *38*,(4), 1229–1246. 200

Gorn, Gerald J.; Goldberg, Marvin E.; and Kanungo, Kabindra N. The role of educational television in changing the intergroup attitudes of children. *Child Development*, 1976, *47*(1), 277–280. 420

Gottman, John; Gonson, Jonni; and Rasmussen, Brian. Social interaction, social competence, and friendship in children. *Child Development*, 1975, *46*(3), 709–718. 417

Govatos, Louis A. Relationships and age differences in growth measures and motor skills. *Child Development*, *30*, 1959, 333–340. 142

Grandpa's a Catholic priest now. *San Jose* (Calif.) *Mercury*, April 3, 1977. 444

Gratch, Gerald, and Landers, William F. Stage IV of Piaget's theory of infant's object concepts: a longitudinal study. *Child Development*, 1971, *42*(2), 359–372. 175

Graves, Michael F., and Koziol, Stephen. Noun plural development in primary grade children. *Child Development*, 1971, *42*(4), 1165–1173. 227

Gray, Susan W., and Klaus, R. A. An experimental preschool program for culturally deprived children. *Child Development*, 1965, *36*(4), 887–898. 469
——. The early training project: a seventh-year report. *Child Development*, 1970, *41*, 909–924. 340, 469

Greenberg, David J., and Blue, Sima Z. Visual complexity in infancy: contour or numerosity? *Child Development*, 1975, *46*, 357–363. 90

Greenberg, David J.; Hillman, Donald; and Grice, Dean. Infant and stranger variables related to stranger anxiety in the first year of life. *Developmental Psychology*, 1973, *9*(2), 207–212. 95, 369

Greenberg, David J.; O'Donnell, William J.; and Crawford, Daniel. Complexity levels, habituation, and individual differences in early infancy. *Child Development*, 1973, *44*(3), 569–574. 97

Greenberg, David J.; Uzgiris, Ina C.; and Hunt, J. M. Hastening the development of the blink-response with looking. *Journal of Genetic Psychology*, 1968, *113*(2), 167–176. 96, 97, 114

Greenberg, M.; Pelliteri, O.; and Barton, J. Frequency of defects in infants whose mothers had rubella during

pregnancy. *Journal of the American Medical Association*, 1957, *165*, 675–678. 48

Greene, Roger L., and Clark, John R. Birth order and college attendance in a cross-cultural setting. *Journal of Social Psychology*, 1968, *75*(2), 289–290. 450

Guardo, Carol J., and Miesels, Murray. Child-parent spatial patterns under praise and reproof. *Developmental Psychology*, 1971, *5*(2), 365. 405, 408

Guerney, Bernard G., and Drake, Ann. An exploratory survey on maternal child-rearing concerns and help seeking. *Child Psychiatry and Human Development*, 1973, *3*(3), 165–178. 403

Haaf, Robert A. Visual response to complex facelike patterns by 15- and 20-week-old infants. *Developmental Psychology*, 1977, *13*(1), 77–78. 95

Haaf, Robert A., and Bell, Richard Q. A facial dimension in visual discrimination by human infants. *Child Development*, 1967, *38*, 893–899. 95

Hainline, Louise, and Feig, Ellen. The correlates of childhood father absence in college-aged women. *Child Development*, 1978, *49*, 37–42. 384

Haith, M. M. The response of the human newborn to visual movement. *Journal of Experimental Child Psychology*, 1966, *3*, 235–243. 84
——. Development changes in visual information processing and short-term visual memory. *Human Development*, 1971, *14*(4), 249–261. 276

Hall, G. S. *Adolescence*. New York: Appleton, 1904. 11

Halperin, Marcia S. First-grade teachers' goals and children's developing perceptions of school. *Journal of Educational Psychology*, 1976, *68*(5), 636–648. 459

Halverson, Charles F., and Waldrop, Mary F. Maternal behavior toward own and other preschool children: the problem of "ownness." *Child Development*, 1970, *41*(3), 839–845. 405

Halverson, H. M. An experimental study of prehension in infants by means of systematic cinema records. *Genetic Psychology Monographs*, 1931, *10*, 107–286. 130

Hardy, Janet B. Birth weight and subsequent physical and intellectual development. *New England Journal of Medicine*, 1973, *289*(18), 973–974. 127

Harlen, W. The development of scientific concepts in young children. *Educational Research*, 1968, *11*(1), 4–13. 195

Harlow, Harry F. Love in infant monkeys. *Scientific American*, 1959, *200*(6), 68/74. 107, 366

Harlow, Harry F., and Harlow, Margaret Kuenne. Social deprivation in monkeys. *Scientific American*, November 1962. 366, 370

Harris, Dale B. *Children's drawings as measures of intellectual maturity*. New York: Harcourt, Brace and World, 1963. 313

Harris, Susan, and Braun, John R. Self-esteem and racial preference in black children. *Proceedings of the Annual Convention of the American Psychological Association*, 1971, *6*(Part 1), 259–260. 419

Harrison, C. Wade; Rawls, James R.; and Rawls, Donna J. Differences between leaders and nonleaders in six-to eleven-year-old children. *Journal of Social Psychology*, 1971, *84*(2), 269–272. 417

Harter, Susan. Developmental differences in the manifestation of mastery motivation on problem-solving tasks. *Child Development*, 1975, *46*(2), 370–378. 439

Hartig, Monika, and Kanfer, Frederik H. The role of verbal self-instruction in children's resistance to temptation. *Journal of Personality and Social Psychology*, 1973, *25*(2), 259–267. 235

Hartshorne, Hugh, and May, Mark A. *Studies in the nature of character studies in deceit*. Book 1. New York: Macmillan, 1928. 401

——. A summary of the work of the character education inquiry. *Religious Education*, 1930, *25*. 401

Hartshorne, Hugh; May, Mark A.; and Shuttleworth, F. K. *Studies in the organization of character*. New York: Macmillan, 1930. 401

Hatch, Evelyn. The young child's comprehension of time connectives. *Child Development*, 1971, *42*(6), 2111–2113. 230

Hathaway, Starke R.; Reynolds, Phyllis C.; and Monachesi, Elio D. Follow-up of the later careers and lives of 1,000 boys who dropped out of high school. *Journal of Consulting and Clinical Psychology*, 1969, *33*(3), 370–380. 469

Haugan, Gertrude M., and McIntire, Roger W. Comparisons of vocal imitation, tactile stimulation, and food as reinforcers for infant vocalizations. *Developmental Psychology*, 1972, *6*(2), 201–209. 240

Haynes, H.; White, B. L.; and Held, R. Visual accommodation in human infants. *Science*, 1965, *148*, 528–530. 84

Hazlett, William H. The male factor in

obstetrics. *Child and Family*, 1967, *6*(4), 3–11. 68

Hebb, D. O. Drives and the CNS (conceptual nervous system). *Psychological Review*, 1955, *62*, 243–254. 436

Heber, Rick. A manual on terminology and classification in mental retardation. *Monograph Supplements to American Journal of Mental Deficiency*, 1959, *64*(2). 505

Henkin, Robert I. Taste loss in aging. In J. M. Hsu, Robert L. Davis, and A. Neithamer (eds.), *The biomedical role of trace elements in aging*. St. Petersburg, Fla.: Eckerd College Gerontology Center, 1976. 110

Hermans, Hubert J.; ter Laak, Jan J.; and Maes, Piet C. Achievement motivation and fear of failure in family and school. *Developmental Psychology*, 1972, *6*(3), 520–528. 440, 449

Hernandez, Marita. Sonia hunts a lost part of her life. *San Jose* (Calif.) *Mercury*, November 26, 1976. 384

Hershenson, M. Visual discrimination in the human newborn. *Journal of Comparative and Physiological Psychology*, 1964, *58*, 270–276. 84

Hertzig, Margaret E., and Birch, Herbert G. Longitudinal course of measured intelligence in preschool children of different social and ethnic backgrounds. *American Journal of Orthopsychiatry*, 1971, *41*(3), 416–426. 336

Hess, Robert D., and Shipman, Virginia. Early experience and the socialization of cognitive modes in children. *Child Development*, 1965, *36*, 869–886. 243

Hetherington, E. M. Effects of father absence on personality development in adolescent daughters. *Developmental Psychology*, 1972, 7(3), 313–326. 384

Hewitt, Lynn S. Age and sex differences in the vocational aspirations of elementary school children. *Journal of Social Psychology*, 1975, *96*(2), 173–177. 455

Hill, Clara E.; Hubbs, Mary A.; and Verble, Charla. A developmental analysis of the sex-role identification of school-related objects. *Journal of Educational Research*, 1974, *67*(5), 205–206. 454

Hill, Kennedy T., and Dusek, Jerome B. Children's social achievement expectations as a function of social reinforcement, sex of subject, and text anxiety. *Child Development*, 1969, *40*(2), 547–557. 459

Hill, Kennedy T., and Eaton, Warren O. The interaction of test anxiety and

success-failure experiences in determining children's arithmetic performance. *Developmental Psychology*, 1977, *13*(3), 205–211. 442

Hindelang, Michael. Educational and occupational aspirations among working class Negro, Mexican-American and white elementary school children. *Journal of Negro Education*, 1970, *39*(4), 351–353. 464

Hoffman, Lois Wladis. Effects of maternal employment on the child—a review of the research. *Developmental Psychology*, 1974, *10*(2), 204–228. 410, 457, 504

——. Changes in family roles, socialization and sex differences. *American Psychologist*, 1977, *32*(8), 644–657. 457

Hoffman, Martin L. Power assertion by the parent and its impact on the child. *Child Development*, 1960, *31*, 129–143. 405

——. Father absence and conscience development. *Developmental Psychology*, 1971, *4*(3), 400–406. 409

Holland, V. Melissa, and Palermo, David S. On learning "less": language and cognitive development. *Child Development*, 1975, *46*(2), 437–443. 181

Honzik, Marjorie P. Developmental studies of parent-child resemblance in intelligence. *Child Development*, 1957, *28*, 215–228. 331

Honzik, M. P.; Macfarlane, J. W.; and Allen, L. The stability of mental test performance between two and eighteen years. *Journal of Experimental Education*, 1948, *17*, 309–324. 309, 319

Hoover, J. E. *Uniform crime reports—1965*, pp. 104, 116. Washington, D.C.: U.S. Department of Justice. 410

Hopwood, Howard H., and Van Iden, Starr S. Scholastic underachievement as related to sub-par physical growth. *Journal of School Health*, 1965, *35*, 337–349. 138

Horrocks, John E. The adolescent. In L. Carmichael (ed.), *Manual of child psychology*, 2d ed., pp. 697–734. New York: Wiley, 1954. 141, 142

Houston, Susan H. A reexamination of some assumptions about the language of the disadvantaged child. *Child Development*, 1970, *41*, 947–963. 246

Howe, Florence. Sexual stereotypes start early. *Saturday Review*, October 16, 1971, pp. 79–93. 408

Hraba, Joseph, and Grant, Geoffrey. Black is beautiful: a reexamination of racial preference and identification. *Journal of Personality and Social Psychology*, 1970, *16*(3), 398–402. 419

Hughes, J. G.; Ehmann, B.; and Brown, U. A. Electroencephalography of the newborn. *American Journal of Diseases of Children*, 1948, *76*, 626–633. 53

Hulsebus, Robert C. An interaction between vertical dimension and age in children's judgments of size. *Perceptual and Motor Skills*, 1969, *28*(3), 841–842. 65

Humphreys, L. Letters. *Science*, 1969, *166*(3902), 167. 305

Hunt, J. McVicker. Experience in the development of motivation: some reinterpretations. *Child Development*, 1960, *31* 489–504. 436

Hunt, J. McVicker; Kirk, Girvin E.; and Volkmar, Fred. Social class and preschool language skill. Part 3, Semantic mastery of position information. *Genetic Psychology Monographs*, 1975, *91*(2), 317–337. 247

Inhelder, B., and Piaget, J. The growth of logical thinking from childhood through adolescence. New York: Basic Books, 1958. 190

——. *The early growth of logic in the child.* New York: Harper and Row, 1964. 181

Irwin, O. C. Infant speech. *Scientific American*, 1949, *181*(3), 22–24. 220

Irwin, O. C., and Curry, F. Vowel elements in the crying vocalization of infants under ten days of age. *Child Development*, 1941, *12*, 99–109. 220

Jacob, Theodore. Patterns of family conflict and dominance as a function of child age and social class. *Developmental Psychology*, 1974, *10*(1), 1–12. 411

Jacobs, Blanche S., and Moss, Howard A. Birth order and sex of sibling as determinants of mother-infant interaction. *Child Development*, 1976, *47*(2), 315–322. 362

Jahoda, Gustva, and McGurk, Henry. Development of pictorial depth perception: cross-cultural replications. *Child Development*, 1974 *45*(4), 1042–1047. 93

Jahoda, Marie. Toward a social psychology of mental health. In Ruth Kolinsky and Helen Witmer (eds.), *Community problems for mental health.* Cambridge, Mass.: Harvard University Press, 1955.

Jakobson (1941). Cited in G. A. Miller (ed.), *Language and communication*, p. 146. New York: McGraw-Hill, 1951. 479

Jaroslovsky, Rich. Brain hemispheres seen as vital factor in way we learn.

Wall Street Journal, March 30, 1979. 279

Jensen, A. R. How much can we boost IQ and scholastic achievement? *Harvard Educational Review*, 1969a, *39*, 1–123. 336

——. Input–Arthur Jensen replies. *Psychology Today*, 1969b, *3*(5), 4. 337

——. Cumulative deficit in IQ of blacks in the rural south. *Developmental Psychology*, 1977, *13*(3), 184–191. 341

Jensen, K. Differential reactions to taste and temperature stimuli in newborn infants. *Genetic Psychology Monographs*, 1932, *12*, 363–479. 109,110

Jersild, A. T., and Holmes, F. B. Methods of overcoming children's fears. *Journal of Psychology*, 1935–36, *1*, 75–104. 494

Jessor, Shirley L., and Jessor, Richard. Maternal ideology and adolescent problem behavior. *Developmental Psychology*, 1974, *10*(2), 246–254. 425

Johnston, Francis E. Individual variation in the rate of skeletal maturation between five and eighteen years. *Child Development*, 1964, *35*, 75–80. 127

Joint Commission on Mental Health of Children. *Crises in child mental health: challenge for the 1970's.* New York: Harper and Row, 1970. 490, 504

——. *Mental health: from infancy through adolescence.* New York: Harper and Row, 1973.

Jones, H. E. Environmental influence on mental development. In L. Carmichael (ed.), *Manual of child psychology*, pp. 582–632. New York: Wiley, 1946. 490

Jones, K. L.; Smith, D. W.; Ulleland, C. N.; and Streissguth, A. P. Pattern of malformation in offspring of chronic alcoholic mothers. *Lancet*, 1973, *1*(7815), 1267–1271. 54

Jones, M. C. The later career of boys who were early or late maturing. *Child Development*, 1957, *28*, 113–128. 145

Jones, M. C., and Mussen, P. H. Self conceptions, motivations and interpersonal attitudes of early and late maturing girls. *Child Development*, 1958, *29*, 491–501. 376

Jones, Pauline A. Formal operational reasoning and the use of tentative statements. *Cognitive Psychology*, 1972a, *3*(3), 467–471. 181

——. Home environment and the development of verbal ability. *Child Development*, 1972b, *43*(3), 1081–1086. 244

Jordan, Bonnie E.; Radin, Norma; and

Epstein, Ann. Paternal behavior and intellectual functioning in preschool boys and girls. *Developmental Psychology*, 1975, *11*(3), 407–408. 335

Jost, H., and Sontag, L. W. The genetic factors in autonomic nervous system function. *Psychosomatic Medicine*, 1944, *6*, 308–310. 40, 139

Kagan, Jerome. The concept of identification. *Psychological Review*, 1958, *65*, 296–305. 373, 374

——. The child's sex role classification of school objects. *Child Development*, 1964a, *35*, 1051–1056. 373

——. Acquisition and significance of sex typing and sex role identity. In M. L. Hoffman and L. W. Hoffman (eds.), *Review of child development research*, Vol. 1, pp. 137–168. New York: Russel Sage Foundation, 1964b. 377, 379, 381, 382

——. Impulsive and reflective children. In J. Krumboltz (ed.), *Learning and the educational process.* Chicago: Rand McNally, 1965. 203

——. Generality and dynamics of conceptual temp. *Journal of Abnormal Psychology*, 1966, *71*, 17–24. 201, 203

——. The determinants of attention in the infant. *American Scientist*, 1970, *58*, 298–306. 176

——. Letter to the editor, *APA Monitor*, 1973, *4*(6), 11. 206

Kagan, Jerome, and Freeman, Marion. Relation of childhood intelligence, maternal behaviors, and social class to behavior during adolescence. *Child Development*, 1963, *34*, 899–911. 405

Kagan, Jerome; Hosken, B.; and Watson, S. The child's symbolic conceptualization of the parents. *Child Development*, 1961, *32*, 625 408

Kagan, Jerome; Kearsley, Richard B.; and Zelazo, Philip R. *Infancy: its place in human development.* Cambridge, Mass.: Harvard University Press, 1978. 372

Kagan, Jerome; Klein, Robert E.; and Haith, Marshall M. Memory and meaning in two cultures. *Child Development*, 1973, *44*(1), 221–223. 276

Kagan, Jerome, and Lemkin, J. The child's differential perception of parental attributes. *Journal of Abnormal Social Psychology*, 1960, *61*, 440–447. 408

Kagan, Jerome, and Moss, H. A. The stability of passive and dependent behavior from childhood through adulthood. *Child Development*, 1960, *31*, 577–591. 381

——. *Birth to maturity: a study in psychological development.* New

York: Wiley, 1962. 361

Kagan, Jerome; Moss, H. A.; and Sigel, I. E. Psychological significance of styles of conceptualization. In J. C. Wright and Jerome Kagan (eds.), Basic cognitive processes in children. *Monographs of the Society for Research in Child Development*, 1963, *28*(2), 73–112. 201, 202, 204

Kagan, Jerome; Pearson, L.; and Welch, L. The modifiability of an impulsive temp. *Journal of Educational Psychology*, 1966*a*, *57*, 359–365. 204

——. Conceptual impulsivity and inductive reasoning. *Child Development*, 1966*b*, *37*(3), 583–594. 202

Kallmann, F. J. The genetic theory of schizophrenia. *American Journal of Psychiatry*, 1946, *103*, 309–322. 499

Kallmann, F. J., and Sander, G. Twin studies on aging and longevity. *Journal of Heredity*, 1948, *39*, 349–357. 42

Kandel, Denise B., and Lesser, Gerald S. Parental and peer influences on educational plans of adolescents. *American Sociological Review*, 1969, *34*(2), 213–223. 451

Kanner, Leo. Autistic disturbances of affective contact. *The Nervous Child*, 1943, *2*, 217–250. 498

Karlsson, Jon L. Evidence for hereditary transmission of schizophrenia. *Journal of Schizophrenia*, 1967, *1*(4), 239–256. 500

Karnes, Merle B.; Hodgins, Audrey S.; Stoneburner, Robert L.; Studley, William M.; and Teska, James A. Effects of a highly structured program of language development on intellectual functioning and psycholinguistic development of culturally disadvantaged three year olds. *Journal of Special Education*, 1968, *2*(4), 405–412. 247

Katz, Irwin; Henchy, Thomas; and Allen, Harvey. Effects of race of tester, approval-disproval, and need on Negro children's learning. *Journal of Personality and Social Psychology*, 1968, *8*(1, Part 1), 38–42. 463

Kearsley, Richard B. The newborn's response to auditory stimulation: a demonstration of orienting and defensive behavior. *Child Development*, 1973, *44*, 582–590. 103

Keating, Daniel P. Precocious cognitive development at the level of formal operations. *Child Development*, 1975, *46*(1), 276–280. 200

Kendler, T. S.; Kendler, H. H.; and Wells, D. Reversal and nonreversal shifts in nursery school children. *Journal of Comparative and Physiological Psychology*, 1960, *53*, 83–87. 234

Keniston, Kenneth. The sources of student dissent. *Journal of Social Issues*, 1967, *23*(3), 108–137. 429

——. Student activism, moral development, and morality. *American Journal of Orthopsychiatry*, 1970, *40*(4), 577–592. 429

Kennell, John H.; Jerauld, Richard; Wolfe, Harriet; Chesler, David; Kreger, Nancy C.; Alpine, Willie; Steffa, Meredith; and Klaus, Marshall H. Maternal behavior one year after early and extended post-partum contact. *Developmental Medicine and Child Neurology*, 1974, *16*(2), 172–179. 73, 76

Keogh, Barbara. Pattern copying under three conditions of an expanded spatial field. *Developmental Psychology*, 1971, *4*(1), 25–31. 111

Kessen, William. *The child*. New York: Wiley, 1965. 8

——. ed. *Child in China*. London: Yale University Press, 1975. 510

Kessler, Jane W. *Psychopathology of childhood*. Englewood Cliffs, N.J.: Prentice-Hall, 1966. 479

King, Stanley H. Coping and growth in adolescence. *Seminars in Psychiatry*, 1972, *4*(4), 355–366. 388

Kingsley, Benedict. Survey of advances in diagnostic ultrasound. *Medical Electronics and Data*, 1975, *6*(4), 83–84. 59

Kinnie, Ernest J., and Sternlof, Richard E. The influence of nonintellective factors on the IQ scores of middle- and lower-class children. *Child Development*, 1971, *42*(6), 1989–1995. 341

Kinsey, A. C.; Pomeroy, W. B.; and Martin, C. E. *Sexual behavior in the human male*. Philadelphia: Saunders, 1948. 426

Kinsey, A. C.; Pomeroy, W. B.; Martin, C. E.; and Gebhard, P. H. *Sexual behavior in the human female*. Philadelphia: Saunders, 1953. 426

Kirk, Girvin, E., and Hunt, J. McVicker. Social class and preschool language skill. Part 1, Introduction. *Genetic Psychology Monographs*, 1975, *92*(2), 281–298. 244

Kirk, S. A. Research in education. In H. A. Stevens and R. Heber (eds.), *Mental retardation*. Chicago: University of Chicago Press, 1964. 508

Kivowitz, Alexandra L. Letter to the editor. *Ms. Magazine*, August 1976. 41

Klapper, Zelda S., and Birch, Herbert G. Perceptual and action equivalence to objects and photographs in children. *Perceptual and Motor Skills*,

1969, *29*(3), 763–771. 101

Klaus, R. A., and Gray, S. W. The early training project for disadvantaged children: a report after five years. *Monographs of the Society for Research in Child Development*, 1968, *33*(4). 469

Kleffner, F. R. Teaching aphasic children. *Education*, 1959, *79*, 413–418. 509

Klusman, Lawrence E. Reduction of pain in childbirth by the alleviation of anxiety during pregnancy. *Journal of Clinical and Consulting Psychology*, 1975, *43*(2), 162–165. 66

Kniveton, Bromley H. and Stephenson, Geoffrey M. The effect of pre-experience on imitation of an aggressive film model. *British Journal of Social and Clinical Psychology*, 1970, *9*(1), 31–36. 422

Knop, C. A. The dynamics of newly born babies. *Journal of Pediatrics*, 1946, *29*, 721–728. 141

Koenigsberg, Riki Sharfman. Evaluation of procedures for improvement of orientation discrimination in preschool children. *Proceedings of the Annual Convention of the American Psychological Association*, 1971, *6*(Part 1), 183–184. 98

——. An evaluation of visual versus sensorimotor methods for improving orientation discrimination of letter reversals by preschool children. *Child Development*, 1973, *44*(4), 764–769. 98

Kohen-Raz, Reuven. Mental and motor development of kibbutz, institutionalized, and home-reared infants in Israel. *Child Development*, 1968, *39*(2), 489–504. 125, 153, 335

Kohlberg, Lawrence. Moral development and identification. In H. W. Stevenson (eds.), *Child psychology*, 62nd yearbook of the National Society for Studies in Education, pp. 277–332. Chicago: University of Chicago Press, 1963. 401

——. Development of moral character and moral ideology. In M. L. Hoffman and L. W. Hoffman (eds.), *Child development research*, Vol. 1. New York: Russell Sage Foundation, 1964. 395, 396, 397

——. Early education: cognitive-development, view. *Child Development*, 1968, *39*(4), 1013–1062. 232, 298

Kohlberg, Lawrence; Yaeger, Judy; and Hjertholm, Else. Private speech: four studies and a review of theories. *Child Development*, 1968, *39*, 691–736. 232

Kohn, M. L. Social class and parental values. *American Journal of Sociology*, 1959, *64*, 337–351.411

Koocher, Gerald P. Swimming, competence, and personality change. *Journal of Personality and Social Psychology*, 1971, *18*(3), 275–278.382

Kopf, Katherine E. Family variables and school adjustment of eighth grade father-absent boys. *Family Coordinator*, 1970, *19*(2), 145–150. 409

Korner, Anneliese F.; and Beason, Lynn M. Association of two congenitally organized behavior patterns in the newborn: hand-mouth coordination and looking. *Perceptual and Motor Skills*, 1972, *35*(1), 115–118.85

Korner, Anneliese F.; Chuck, Bernadine; and Dontchors, Soula. Organismic determinants of spontaneous oral behavior in neonates. *Child Development*, 1968, *39*(4), 1145–1157. 75, 76

Korner, Anneliese F., and Thoman, Evelyn B. Visual alertness in neonates as evoked by maternal care. *Journal of Experimental Child Psychology*, 1970, *10*(1), 67–78.85

Kossuth, Gina L.; Carroll, Wayne R.; and Rogers, Cecil A. Free recall of words and objects. *Developmental Psychology*, 1971, *4*(3), 480.276

Kotelchuck, M. The nature of the child's tie to his father. *Proceedings of the meeting of the Society for Research in Child Development*, 1973.176

Kotelchuck, M.; Zelazo, P.; Kagan, J.; and Spelke, E. Infant reaction to parental separations when left with familiar and unfamiliar adult. *Journal of Genetic Psychology*, 1975, *126*, 255–262.176

Kraynak, Audrey R., and Raskin, Larry M. The influence of age and stimulus dimensionality on form perception by preschool children. *Developmental Psychology*, 1971, *4*(3), 389–393.107

Kreutzer, M. A.; Leonard, C.; and Flavell, J. H. An interview study of children's knowledge about memory. *Monographs of the Society for Research in Child Development*, 1975, *40*(1).287

Kringlen, I. Schizophrenia in twins. *Psychiatry*, 1966, *29*, 172–184.500

Kuczaj, Stan A., II, and Maratsos, Michael P. On the acquisition of front, back, and side. *Child Development*, 1975, *46*(1), 202–210.231

Kuhn, Deanna; Nash, Sharon Chumin; and Brucken, Laura. Sex role concepts of two- and three-year-olds.

Child Development, 1978, *49*, 445–451.379

Kuhn, Deanna, and Phelps, Henry. The development of children's comprehension of causal direction. *Child Development*, 1976, *47*(1), 248–251. 231

Kurtz, J. J., and Swenson, E. G. Factors related to overachievement and underachievement in school. *School Review*, 1951, *59*, 472–480.449, 450

LaBarbera, J. D.; Izard, C. E.; Vietze, P.; and Parisi, S. A. Four- and six-month-old infants' visual responses to joy, anger, and neutral expressions. *Child Development*, 1976, *47*, 535–538.94

Lagerspetz, Kirsti; Nygard, Margaretha; and Strandvik, Christina. The effects of training in crawling on the motor and mental development of infants. *Scandinavian Journal of Psychology*, 1971, *12*(3), 192–197.150

Lamb, Michael E. Fathers: forgotten contributors to child development. *Human Development*, 1975, *18*(4), 245–266.407

——. Effects of stress and cohort on mother- and father-infant interaction. *Developmental Psychology*, 1976, *12*(5), 435–443.368, 369

Lane, Ellen A. Childhood characteristics of black college graduates reared in poverty. *Developmental Psychology*, 1973, *8*(1), 42–45.465

LaPointe, Karen, and O'Donnell, James P. Number conservation in children below age six: its relationship to age, perceptual dimensions, and language comprehension. *Developmental Psychology*, 1974, *10*(3), 422–428.183

Lavatelli, Celia Stendler, and Stendler, Faith. *Readings in child behavior and development*, 3d ed. New York: Harcourt Brace Jovanovich, 1972. 394, 395

LaVoie, Joseph C. Punishment and adolescent self-control. *Developmental Psychology*, 1973, *8*(1), 16–24.425

Leahy, A. M. Nature-nurture and intelligence. *Genetic Psychology Monographs*, 1935, *17*, 235–308.325, 328

LeCorgne, Lyle L., and Laosa, Luis M. Father absence in low-income Mexican-American families: children's social adjustment and conceptual differentiation of sex role attributes. *Developmental Psychology*, 1976, *12*(5), 470–471.409

Lee, L. C.; Kagan, J.; and Rabson, A. Influence of a preference for analytic categorization upon concept acquisition. *Child Development*, 1963, *34*,

433–442.201

Lehman, Gerd. Family composition and its influence on the language development of the 18–34 month-old child in the American lower and middle class family. *Journal of Behavioral Science*, 1971, *1*(3), 125–130.241

Leifer, Aimee D.; Collins, W. Andrew; Gross, Barbara M.; Taylor, Peter H.; Andrews, Lewis; and Blackmer, Elizabeth R. Developmental aspects of variables relevant to observational learning. *Child Development*, 1971, *42*, 1509–1516.292

Leifer, Aimee D.; Leiderman, P. H.; Barnett, C. R.; and Williams, J. A. Effects of mother-infant separation on maternal attachment behavior. *Child Development*, 1972, *43*(4), 1203–1218.73, 489

Leithwood, K. A., and Fowler, W. Complex motor learning in four-year-olds. *Child Development*, 1971, *42*(3), 781–792.150

Leizer, Joseph I., and Rogers, Ronald W. Effects of method of discipline, timing of punishment, and timing of test on resistance to temptation. *Child Development*, 1974, *45*(3), 790–793.404

Lenneberg, Eric H. The natural history of language. In F. Smith and G. A. Miller (eds.), *The genesis of language*. Cambridge, Mass.: M.I.T. Press, 1966.213, 215, 224

Lepper, Mark R. Anxiety and experimenter valence as determinants of social reinforcer effectiveness. *Journal of Personality and Social Psychology*, 1970, *16*(4), 704–709.462

Lessor, Harvey, and Drouin, Carol. Training in the use of double-function terms. *Journal of Psycholinguistic Research*, 1975, *4*(4), 285–302.231

Lester, Barry M. Spectrum analysis of the cry sounds of well-nourished and malnourished infants. *Child Development*, 1976, *47*, 237–241.151

Lester, Barry M.; Kotelchuck, Milton; Spelke, Elizabeth; Sellers, Martha Julia; Klein, Robert E. Separation protest in Guatamalan infants: cross-cultural and cognitive findings. *Developmental Psychology*, 1975, *10*(1), 79–85.370

Levenstein, Phyllis. Cognitive growth in pre-schoolers through verbal interaction with mothers. *American Journal of Orthopsychiatry*, 1970, *40*(3), 426–432.207

Leventhal, Gerald S. Influence of brothers and sisters on sex-role behavior. *Journal of Personality and So-*

cial Psychology, 1970, 16(3), 452–465. 362

Leventhal, T., and Sills, M. Self-image in school phobia. American Journal of Orthopsychiatry, 1964, 34, 685–695. 496

Levin, Harry. Permissive child rearing and adult role behavior. Paper delivered at the Eastern Psychological Association, Atlantic City, March 28, 1952. In D. E. Dulany; R. L. De-Valois; D. C. Beardsley; and M. R. Winterbottom (eds.), Contributions to modern psychology, pp. 351–355. New York: Oxford University Press, 1963. 369

Lewis, Michael. Infant intelligence tests: their use and misuse. Human Development, 1973, 16(1–2), 108–118. 318

Lewis, Michael, and McGurk, Harry. Evaluation of infant intelligence: infant intelligence scores–true or false? Science, 1972, 178(4066), 1174–1177. 318

Lewis, Michael; Martels, B.; Campbell, H.; and Goldberg, S. Individual differences in attention. American Journal of Diseases of Children, 1967, 113, 461–465. 74

Lewis, Michael, and Wilson, Cornelia D. Infant development in lower-class American families. Human Development, 1972, 15(2), 112–127. 243

Liebenberg, Beatrice. Expectant fathers. Child and Family, 1969, 8(3), 265–277. 69

Lieberman, P. Intonation, perception and language. Cambridge, Mass.: M.I.T. Press, 1967. 219

Liebert, Robert M., and Baron, Robert A. Some immediate effects of televised violence on children's behavior. Developmental Psychology, 1972, 6(3), 469–475. 422

Liebert, Robert M., and Fernandez, Luis E. Effects of vicarious consequences on imitative performance. Child Development, 1970, 41(3), 847–852. 272, 423

Liedtke, Werner W., and Nelson, L. Doyal. Concept formation and bilingualism. Alberta Journal of Educational Research, 1968, 14(4), 225–232. 251

Ling, Daniel, and Ling, Agnes H. Communication development in the first three years of life. Journal of Speech and Hearing Research, 1974, 17(1), 146–159. 240, 241

Lipsitt, Lewis P. Learning processes of newborns. Merrill-Palmer Quarterly, 1966, 12, 45–71. 84

——. Learning in the human infant. In H. W. Stevenson; E. H. Hess; and H. L. Rheingold (eds.), Early behavior, pp. 225–247. New York: Wiley, 1967. 275

Lipsitt, Lewis P., and Levy, Nissim. Electrotactual threshold in the neonate. Child Development, 1959, 30, 547–554. 111

Little, Audrey. A longitudinal study of cognitive development in young children. Child Development, 1972, 43(3), 1024–1034. 200

Little, William B.; Kenny, Charles T.; and Middleton, Morris C. Differences in intelligence among low socioeconomic class Negro children as a function of sex, age, educational level of parents, and home stability. Journal of Genetic Psychology, 1973, 123(2), 241–250. 335

Locke, John L. Phonetic mediation in four-year-old children. Psychonomic Science, 1971, 23(6), 409. 235

Locke, John L., and Locke, Virginia L. Recall of phonetically and semantically similar words by 3-year-old children. Psychonomic Science, 1971, 24(4), 189–190. 235

Lockhart, Kristi L.; Abrahams, Barbara; Osherson, Daniel N. Children's understanding of uniformity in the environment. Child Development, 1977, 48, 1521–1531. 396

Looft, William R. Perceptions across the life span of important informational sources for children and adolescents. Journal of Psychology, 1971a, 78, 207–211. 358

——. Sex differences in the expression of vocational aspirations by elementary school children. Developmental Psychology, 1971b, 5(2), 366. 455

——. Egocentrism and social interaction across the life span. Psychological Bulletin, 1972, 78(2), 73–92. 171

Looft, William R., and Charles, Don C. Modification of the life concept in children. Developmental Psychology, 1969, 1(4), 445. 171

Lourie, Reginald S. The roots of violence: an essay on its nature and early developmental determinants. Early Child Development and Care, 1973, 2(1), 1–12. 420

Lovaas, O. Ivar. Effect of exposure to symbolic aggression on aggressive behavior. Child Development, 1961, 32, 37–44. 422

Lovaas, O. Ivar; Koegel, R.; Simmons, J. Q.; and Long, J. S. Some generalization and follow-up measures on autistic children in behavior therapy. Journal of Applied Behavior Analysis, 1973, 6, 131–166. 515

Lovaas, O. Ivar; Schaeffer, Benson; Simmons, James Q. Building social behavior in autistic children by use of electric shock. Journal of Experimental Research in Personality, 1965, 1, 99–109. 515, 516

Lugo, James O., and Hershey, Gerald L. Human development. New York: Macmillan, 1974. 97

Lumsden, Ernest A., Jr., and Poteat, Barbara W. The salience of the vertical dimension in the concept of "bigger" in five- and six-year-olds. Journal of Verbal Learning and Verbal Behavior, 1968, 7(2), 404–408. 180

Luria, A. R. The role of language in the formation of temporary connections. In B. Simon (ed.), Psychology in the Soviet Union. Stanford, Calif.: Stanford University Press, 1957. 229, 232, 233

Lyell, Ruth G. Adolescent and adult self-esteem as related to cultural values. Adolescence, 1973, 8(29), 85–92. 382

Lynch, Margaret A. Ill health and child abuse. Lancet, 1975, 2(7929), 317–319. 491

McCall, Robert B.; Kennedy, Cindy Bellows; and Applebaum, Mark I. Magnitude of discrepancy and the distribution of attention in infants. Child Development, 1977, 48, 772–785. 90

McClelland, D. C. Personality. New York: Dryden Press, 1951. 350

——. Methods of measuring human motivation. In J. W. Atkinson (ed.), Motives in fantasy, action, and society. Princeton, N.J.: Van Nostrand, 1958. 440

——. Testing for competence rather than for "intelligence." American Psychologist, 1973, 28, 1–14, 201–2, 225, 230. 320, 322

McClelland, D.; Atkinson, J.; Clark, R.; and Lowell, E. The achievement motive. New York: Appleton-Century-Crofts, 1953. 440

Maccoby, E. E. Selective auditory attention in children. In L. P. Lipsitt and C. C. Spiker (eds.), Advances in child development and behavior, pp. 99–124. New York: Academic Press, 1967. 411

Maccoby, E. E.; Gibbs, P. K.; and the staff of the Laboratory of Human Development, Harvard University. Methods of child-rearing in two social classes. In W. E. Martin and C. B. Stendler (eds.), Readings in child development, pp. 272–287. New York: Harcourt, Brace and World, 1964. 411

Maccoby, E. E., and Jacklin, Carol Nagy. The psychology of sex differences. Stanford, Calif.: Stanford University Press, 1974. 204, 205

Maccoby, E. E., and Wilson, W. C. Identification and observational learning from film. *Journal of Abnormal Social Psychology*, 1957, *55*, 76. 291

McCord, W., and McCord, J. *Origins of crime: a new evaluation of the Cambridge–Somerville Youth Study.* New York: Columbia University Press, 1959. 504, 515

MacDonald, Randolph; Hines, Brainard; and Kenoyer, Charles. Socioeconomic status as related to two levels of conceptual attainment. *Journal of Genetic Psychology*, 1974, *125*(2), 195–199. 337

McKeachie, W. J. Anxiety in the college classroom. *Journal of Educational Research*, 1951, *55*, 153–160. 442

McKinney, James D. Problem-solving strategies in impulsive and reflective second graders. *Developmental Psychology*, 1973, *8*(1), 145. 203

McMurtry, C. Allen, and Williams, John E. Evaluation dimension of the affective meaning system of the preschool child. *Developmental Psychology*, 1972, *6*(2), 238–246. 420

MacNamara, John. Cognitive basis of language learning in infants. *Psychological Review*, 1972, 79(1). 228

McNeill, D. The development of language. In P. Mussen (ed.), *Manual of child psychology*, 3d ed., pp. 1061–1162. New York: Wiley, 1970. 215, 223, 226

McQueen, Robert. Larry: case history of a mistake. *Saturday Review*, September 12, 1970. 251

Maddock, James W. Sex in adolescence: its meaning and its future *Adolescence*, 1973, *8*(31), 325–342. 146, 425

Mann, Marlis, and Taylor, Anne. The effects of multi-sensory learning systems on the concept formation of young children. *Journal of Research and Development in Education*, 1973, *6*(3), 35–43. 287

Maratsos, Michael P. Decrease in the understanding of the word "big" in preschool children. *Child Development*, 1973, *44*(4), 747–752. 180, 181

Marcus, Robert F. The child as elicitor of parental sanctions for independent and dependent behavior: a simulation of parent-child interaction. *Developmental Psychology*, 1975, *4*, 443–452. 362

Marcus, Terri L., and Corsini, David A. Parental expectations of preschool children as related to child gender and socioeconomic status. *Child Development*, 1978, *49*, 243–246. 381, 465

Maresh, M. M. Changes in tissue widths during growth. *American Journal of Diseases of Children*, 1966, *3*, 142–155. 136

Marjoribanks, Kevin. Environment, social class, and mental abilities. *Journal of Educational Psychology*, 1972, *63*, 103–109. 332

Marjoribanks, Kevin, and Walberg, Herbert J. Ordinal position, family environment, and mental abilities. *Journal of Social Psychology*, 1975, *95*(1), 77–84. 335

Marquis, D. P. Learning in the neonate. The modification of behavior under three feeding schedules. *Journal of Experimental Psychology*, 1941, *29*, 263–282. 280

Martin, Felix. Questioning skills among advantaged and disadvantaged children in first grade. *Psychological Reports*, 1970, *27*, 617–618. 244

Martorano, Suzanne C. A developmental analysis of performance on Piaget's formal operations task. *Developmental Psychology*, 1977, *13*(6), 666–672. 171

Marvick, Elizabeth W. Childhood history and decisions of state: the case of Louis XIII. *History of Childhood Quarterly: The Journal of Psychohistory*, 1974, *2*(2), 135–180. 8

Masangkay, Z. S.; Villorente, F. F.; Somcio, R. S.; Reyes, E. S.; and Taylor, D. M. The development of ethnic group perception. *Journal of Genetic Psychology*, 1972, *121*, 263–270. 419

Maslow, Abraham. *Motivation and personality*, 2d ed. New York: Harper and Row, 1970. 443, 444

Matheny, Adam P., and Brown, Anne M. Activity, motor coordination and attention: individual differences in twins. *Perceptual and Motor Skills*, 1971, *32*(1), 151–158. 136

Matteson, Roberta. Adolescent self-esteem, family communication, and marital satisfaction. *Journal of Psychology*, 1974, *86*(1), 35–47. 387

Maurer, Daphne, and Salapatek, Philip. Developmental changes in the scanning of faces by young infants. *Child Development*, 1976, *47*, 523–527. 95

Mecham, Merlin J. Measurement of verbal listening accuracy in children. *Journal of Learning Disabilities*, 1971, *4*(5), 257–259. 104

Meddock, Terry D.; Parsons, Joseph A.; and Hill, Kennedy T. Effects of an adult's presence and praise on young children's performance. *Journal of Experimental Child Psychology*, 1971,

12(2), 197–211. 447

Medinnus, G. R. Adolescents' self-acceptance and perceptions of their parents. *Journal of Consulting Psychology*, 1965, *29*, 150–154. 387

Mehryar, Amir H. Father's education, family size and children's intelligence and academic performance in Iran. *International Journal of Psychology*, 1972, *7*(1), 47–50. 335

Meichenbaum, D. H., and Goodman, J. Training impulsive children to talk to themselves: a means of developing self-control. *Journal of Abnormal Psychology*, 1971, 77(2), 115–126. 235

Menig-Peterson, Carole L. The modification of communicative behavior in preschool-aged children as a function of the listener's perspective. *Child Development*, 1975, *46*(4), 1015–1018. 229

Menninger, Karl. Adaptation difficulties in college students. *Mental Hygiene*, 1927, *2*, t19. 426

Menyuk, P. The role of distinctive features in children's acquisition of phonology. *Journal of Speech Research*, 1958, *11*, 138. 221

Meredith, Howard V. Change in the structure and body weight of North American boys during the last 80 years. In L. Lipsett and C. Spiker (eds.), *Advances in child development and behavior*, Vol. 1, pp. 69–114. New York: Academic Press, 1963. 123

——. Body size of contemporary groups of preschool children studied in different parts of the world. *Child Development*, 1968, *39*(2), 335–377. 148

——. Body size of contemporary groups of one year old infants studied in different parts of the world. *Child Development*, 1970, *41*, 551–600. 148

Merskey, H. Pain, learning and memory. *Journal of Psychosomatic Research*, 1975, *19*(5–6), 319–324. 108

Michalak, Joseph. Head Start–type programs get second look. *New York Times*, April 30, 1978.

Milgram, Norman A., and Noce, James S. Relevant and irrelevant verbalization in discrimination and reversal learning by normal and retarded children. *Journal of Educational Psychology*, 1968, *59*(3), 169–175. 287

Millar, T. P. Limit setting and psychological maturation. *Archives of General Psychiatry*, 1968, *18*(2), 214–221. 406

Miller, G. A. *Language and communication.* New York: McGraw-Hill, 1951. 215, 219

Miller, L. C.; Hampe, E.; Barrett, C. L.; and Noble, H. Children's deviant behavior within the general population. *Journal of Clinical and Consulting Psychology*, 1971, *37*, 16–22. 515

Miller, Patricia H. Attention to stimulus dimensions in the conservation of liquid quantity. *Child Development*, 1973, *44*(1), 129–136. 180

Miller, Patricia H.; Grabowski, Teddy L.; and Heldmeyer, Karen H. The role of stimulus dimensions in the conservation of substance. *Child Development*, 1973, *44*(4), 646–650. 181

Miller, Shirley M. Effects of maternal employment on sex role perception, interests, and self-esteem in kindergarten children. *Developmental Psychology*, 1975, *11*(3), 405–406. 456, 457

Miller, Thomas W. Effects of maternal age, education, and employment status on the self-esteem of the child. *Journal of Social Psychology*, 1975, *95*(1), 141–142. 377

Minton, Cheryl; Kagan, Jerome; and Levine, Janet A. Maternal control and obedience in the two-year-old. *Child Development*, 1971, *42*(6), 1873–1894. 411

Miranda, Simon B. Visual abilities and pattern preferences of premature infants and full-term neonates. *Journal of Experimental Child Psychology*, 1970, *10*(2), 189–205. 90

Mitchell, Edna. The learning of sex roles through toys and books: a woman's view. *Young Children*, 1973, *28*(4), 226–231. 377

Mitchell, John J. Moral dilemmas of early adolescence. *School Counselor*, 1974, *22*(1), 16–22. 425

Mittler, Peter. Biological and social aspects of language development in twins. *Developmental Medicine and Child Nuerology*, 1970, *12*(6), 741–757. 241

Moerk, Ernst L. Like father, like son: imprisonment of fathers and the psychological adjustment of sons. *Journal of Youth and Adolescence*, 1973, *2*(4), 303–312. 409

——. Changes in verbal child-mother interactions with increasing language skills of the child. *Journal of Psycholinguistic Research*, 1974, *3*(2), 101–116. 240, 242

Moffitt, Alan R. Consonant cue perception by twenty- to twenty-four-week-old infants. *Child Development*, 1971, *42*, 717–731. 222

Montagu, M. F. A. Constitutional and prenatal factors in infant and child health. In M. J. E. Senn (ed.), *Symposium on the healthy personality*, pp. 148–169. New York: Josiah Macy, Jr., Foundation, 1950. 51, 55

——. *Life before birth*. New York: New American Library, 1964. 47

Moore, Shirley G., and Bulbulian, K. Naomi. The effects of contrasting styles of adult-child interaction on children's curiosity. *Developmental Psychology*, 1976, *12*(2), 171–172. 282

Moore, Terence. Language and intelligence: a longitudinal study of the first eight years. *Human Development*, 1967, *10*, 88–106. 237

——. Stress in normal childhood. *Human Relations*, 1969, *22*(3), 235–250. 386

Mordock, John B. *The other children: an introduction to exceptionality*. New York: Harper and Row, 1975. 509

Morrison, Frederick J.; Holmes, Deborah L.; and Haith, Marshall M. A developmental study of the effect of familiarity on short-term visual memory. *Journal of Experimental Child Psychology*, 1974, *18*(3), 412–425. 278

Morrison, Frederick J.; Yarborough, Charles; Klein, Robert E.; and Lasky, Robert. Cognitive style in rural preschool Guatemalan children: a serendipitous finding. *Journal of Genetic Psychology*, 1977, *130*(2), 221–228. 204

Moskowitz, Debbie S.; Schwarz, J. Conrad; and Corsini, David A. Initiating day care of three years of age: effects on attachment. *Child Development*, 1977, *48*, 1271–1276. 371

Moskowitz, Ronald D. Foster child's mental scars. *San Francisco Chronicle*, November 15, 1976. 486

Moss, H. A., and Kagan, Jerome. The stability of achievement and recognition seeking behaviors. *Journal of Abnormal Social Psychology*, 1961, *52*, 504–513 439

Mowbray, Carol T., and Luria, Zella. Effects of labeling on children's visual imagery. *Developmental Psychology*, 1973, *9*(1), 1–8. 276

Mowrer, O. H., and Mowrer, W. M. Enuresis: a method for its study and treatment. *American Journal of Orthopsychiatry*, 1938, *8*, 359–436. 283

Moyles, E. William, and Wolins, Martin. Group care and intellectual development. *Developmental Psychology*, 1971, *4*(3), 370–380. 336

Mueller, Edward, and Brenner, Jeffrey. The origins of social skills and interaction among playgroup toddlers. *Child Development*, 1977, *48*, 854–861. 415

Murphy, Lois B. Spontaneous ways of learning in young children. *Children*,

1967, *14*(6), 210–216. 280

Murray, John P. Television and violence: implications of the Surgeon General's research program. *American Psychologist*, 1973, *28*(6), 472–478. 422

Mussen, P. H., and Jones, M. C. Self conceptions, motivations, and interpersonal attitudes of late and early maturing boys. *Child Development*, 1957, *28*, 243–256. 145

——. The behavior-inferred motivations of late and early maturing boys. *Child Development*, 1958, *29*, 61–67. 447

Mussen, P. H.; Young, H. B.; Gaddini, R.; and Morante, L. The influence of father-son relationships on adolescent personality and attitudes. *Journal of Child Psychology and Psychiatry*, 1963, *4*, 3–16. 409

Muuss, Rolf E. Adolescent development and the secular trend. *Adolescence*, 1970, *5*, 267–284. 146

Nadelman, Lorraine. Sex identity in American children: memory, knowledge, and preference tests. *Developmental Psychology*, 1974, *10*(3), 413–417. 381

Neimark, Edith; Slotnick, Nan S.; and Ulrich, Thomas. Development of memorization strategies. *Developmental Psychology*, 1971, *5*(3), 427–43. 277

Nelson, A. K. A study of taste, smell and temperature in infants. Cited in K. Jensen, Differential reactions to taste and temperature stimuli and newborn infants. *Genetic Psychology Monographs*, 1932, *12*, 363–479. 109

Nelson, Gordon K., and Klausmeier, Herbert J. Classificatory behaviors of low socioeconomic-status children. *Journal of Educational Psychology*, 1974, *66*(3), 432–438. 296

Nelson, Katherine. Structure and strategy in learning to talk. *Monographs of the Society for Research in Child Development*, 1973, *38*(1–2). 241

Newman, H. H.; Freeman, R. N.; and Holzinger, K. J. *Twins: a study of heredity and environment*. Chicago: University of Chicago Press, 1937. 326

Nicholas, Karen B.; McCarter, Robert E.; and Heckel, Robert V. Imitation of adult and peer television models by white and Negro children. *Journal of Social Psychology*, 1971, *85*(2), 317–318. 272

Niem, Tien-ing Chyou, and Collard, Robert R. Parental discipline of aggressive behaviors in four-year-old Chinese and American children. *Pro-*

ceedings of the Annual Convention of the American Psychological Association, 1972, 7(Part 1), 95–96. 412

Nisbett, Richard E., and Gurwitz, Sharon B. Weight, sex, and the eating behavior of human newborns. *Journal of Comparative and Physiological Psychology*, 1970, *73*(2), 245–253. 111

Northway, Mary L. The stability of young children's social relations. *Educational Research*, 1968, *11*(1), 54–57. 417

Odom, Linda; Seeman, Julius; and Newbrough, J. R. A study of family communication patterns and personality integration in children. *Child Psychiatry and Human Development*, 1971, *1*(4), 275–285. 363

Offer, Daniel. Sexual behavior of a group of normal adolescents. *Medical Aspects of Human Sexuality*, 1971, *5*(9), 40–49. 426

O'Grady, Roberta. Feeding behavior in infants. *American Journal of Nursing*, 1971, *71*(4), 736–739. 366

Olds, J., and Milner, P. Positive reinforcement produced by electrical stimulation of septal area and other regions of the rat brain. *Journal of Comparative and Physiological Psychology*, 1954, *47*, 419–427. 437

Oliver, Laurel W. The relationships of parental attitudes and parent identification to career and homemaking orientation in college women. *Journal of Vocational Behavior*, 1975, *7*(1), 1–12. 456

Ollendick, Thomas H. Level of N achievement and persistence behavior in children. *Developmental Psychology*, 1974, *10*(3), 457. 440

Opie, Nancy, and Lemasters, Grace. Do boys with a low-average IQ actually have a low self-esteem? *Journal of School Health*, 1975, *45*(7), 381–385. 321

Osborn, D. K., and Endsley, R. C. Emotional reactions of young children to TV violence. *Child Development*, 1971, *42*(1), 321–331. 422

Osborne, R. T. Racial differences in mental growth and school achievement: a longitudinal study. *Psychological Reports*, 1960, *7*, 233–239. 342

Osgood, Shirley W., and Thomas, Georgelle. Verticality as the cue for "bigger" in tactile and visual tasks. *Psychonomic Science*, 1971, *25*(2), 65–66. 180

Osofsky, Joy D. The shaping of mother's behavior by children. *Journal of Marriage and the Family*, 1970, *32*(3), 400–405. 362

Osofsky, Joy D., and Danzger, Bar-

bara. Relationships between neonatal characteristics and mother-infant interaction. *Developmental Psychology*, 1974, *10*(1), 124–130. 361

Osofsky, Joy D., and O'Connell, Edward J. Parent-child interaction: daughters' effects upon mothers' and fathers' behaviors. *Developmental Psychology*, 1972, *7*(2), 157–168. 361

Owen, David R., and Sines, Jacob O. Heritability of personality in children. *Behavior Genetics*, 1970, *1*(3–4), 235–248. 359

Packard, V. *The sexual wilderness: the contemporary upheaval in male-female relationships*. New York: Pocket Books, 1970. 427

Palermo, D. S.; Castaneda, A.; and McCandless, B. R. The relationships of anxiety in children to performance in a complex learning task. *Child Development*, 1956, *27*, 333–337. 442

Pang, Harry. Undistinguished school experiences of distinguished persons. *Adolescence*, 1968, *3*(11), 319–326. 322, 323

Paradise, Eleanor B., and Curcio, Frank. Relationship of cognitive and affective behaviors to fear of strangers in male infants. *Developmental Psychology*, 1974, *10*(4), 476–483. 369

Parke, Ross D. Nurturance, nurturance withdrawals and resistance to deviation. *Child Development*, 1967, *38*(4), 1101–1110. 404

Parke, Ross D.; O'Leary, Sandra E.; and West, Stephen. Mother-father-newborn interaction: effects of maternal medication, labor and sex of infant. *Proceedings of the Annual Convention of the American Psychological Association*, 1972, 7(Part 1), 85–86. 68

Peatman, J. G., and Higgons, R. A. Relation of infants' weight and body build to locomotor development. *American Journal of Orthopsychiatry*, 1942, *12*, 234–240. 127

Pedersen, Frank A., and Robson, Kenneth S. Father participation in infancy. *American Journal of Orthopsychiatry*, 1969, *39*(3), 466–472. 407

Perry, David G., and Perry, Louise C. Denial of suffering in the victim as a stimulus to violence in aggressive boys. *Child Development*, 1974, *45*(1), 55–62. 420

——. Observational learning in children: effects of sex of model and subject's sex-role behavior. *Journal of Personality and Social Psychology*, 1975, *31*(6), 1083–1088. 379

Phillips, John L., Jr. *The origins of intellect: Piaget's theory*. San Francisco:

W. H. Freeman, 1969 (2d ed., 1975). 179, 184

Phye, Gary, and Tenbrink, Terry. Stimulus position and functional direction: confounds in the concept of "bigger" in 5- and 6-year-olds. *Psychonomic Science*, 1972, *29*(6-A), 357–359. 180

Piaget, J. *The language and thought of the child*. London: Routledge and Kegan Paul, 1926. 162-189

——. *The child's conception of physical causality*. London: Routledge and Kegan Paul, 1930. 162-189

——. *The moral judgment of the child*. London: Routledge and Kegan Paul, 1932. 395

——. *Play, dreams, and imitation in childhood*. New York: W. W. Norton, 1951. 162-189

——. *The construction of reality in the child*. New York: Basic Books, 1954. 162-189

——. *Logic and psychology*. New York: Basic Books, 1957. 162-189

——. *Origins of intelligence in children*. New York: W. W. Norton, 1963. 172

——. *Six psychological studies*. Edited by D. Elkind. New York: Random House, Vintage Books, 1968. 162-189

——. Intellectual evolution from adolescence to adulthood. *Human Development*, 1972, *15*(1), 1–12. 162, 189

Piaget, J., and Inhelder, B. *The child's conception of space*. London: Routledge and Kegan Paul, 1956. 179

——. *The psychology of the child*. New York: Basic Books, 1969. 174

Piaget, J., and Szeminska, Alina. *Child's conception of number*. New York: Humanities Press, 1952. 162-189

Pick, Anne D.; Christy, Monica D.; and Frankel, Gusti W. A developmental study of visual selective attention. *Journal of Experimental Child Psychology*, 1972, *14*(2), 165–175. 101

Pikler, Emmi. Some contributions to the study of the gross motor development of children. *Journal of Genetic Psychology*, 1968, *113*(1), 27–39. 125, 134, 153

Pipp, Sandra L., and Haith, Marshall M. Infant visual scanning of two- and three-dimensional forms. *Child Development*, 1977, *48*, 1640–1644. 90, 91

Plummer, G. Anomalies occurring in children exposed in utero to the atomic bomb in Hiroshima. *Pediatrics*, 1952, *10*, 687–693. 54

Politzer, Robert L., and Weiss, Louis. Developmental aspects of auditory discrimination, echo response, and recall. *Modern Language Journal*, 1969, *53*(2), 75–85. 253

Pollack, Dorothy, and Halpern, Harvey. An analysis of the babbling stage of institutionalized infants. *Journal of Communication Disorders*, 1971, *4*, 302–309. 215

Portnoy, Fern C., and Simmons, Carolyn H. Day care and attachment. *Child Development*, 1978, *49*, 239–242. 371

Prawat, Richard S., and Jones, Herman. A longitudinal study of language development in children at different levels of cognitive development. *Merrill-Palmer Quarterly*, 1977, *23*(2), 115–120. 233

President's Commission on Mental Health. *Report and recommendations to the president*, Vol. 1, 1978. 480

Project on Human Sexual Development. *Family life and sexual learning*. Cambridge, Mass.: Harvard University Press, 1978. 428

Provence, S., and Lipton, R. C. *Infants in institutions*. New York: International Universities Press, 1962. 487

Quay, Lorene C. Language dialect, age, and intelligence-test performance in disadvantaged black children. *Child Development*, 1974, *45*(2), 463–468. 342

Radin, Norma. Maternal warmth, achievement motivation, and cognitive functioning in lower-class preschool children. *Child Development*, 1971, *42*(5), 1560–1565. 448

Rappaport, Leon. *Personality development: the chronology of experience*. Glenview, Ill.: Scott, Foresman, 1972. 357

Razavieh, A. A., and Hosseini, A. A. Family, peer, and academic orientation of Iranian adolescents. *Journal of Psychology*, 1972, *80*(2), 337–344. 387

Rebelsky, Freda, and Hanks, Cheryl. Fathers' verbal interaction with infants in the first three months of life. *Child Development*, 1971, *42*(1), 63–68. 407

Redding, Audrey, and Hirschhorn, Kurt. Guide to human chromosome defects. *Birth Defects Original Article Series*, 1968, *4*(4). 483

Reich, Carol, and Young, Vivienne. Patterns of dropping out. *Interchange*, 1975, *6*(4), 6–15. 471

Renner, J. W.; Stafford, D. G.; Lawson, A. E.; McKinnon; J. W.; Friot, F. Elizabeth; and Kellogg, D. H. *Research, teaching, and learning with the Piaget model*. Norman, Okla.: University of Oklahoma Press, 1976. 199

Rensberger, Boyce. Behavior is shaped largely by culture. *New York Times*, December 19, 1978, pp. C1–C2. 452

Rheingold, H. L. The modification of social responsiveness in institutional babies. *Monographs of the Society for Research in Child Development*, 1956, *21*(2). 487

Rheingold, Harriet L., and Cook, Kaye V. The contents of boys' and girls' rooms as an index of parents' behavior. *Child Development*, 1975, *46*(2), 459–463. 378

Rice, Ruth Dianne. Neurophysiological development in premature infants following stimulation. *Developmental Psychology*, 1977, *13*(1), 69–76. 72, 73

Ridberg, Eugene H.; Parke, Ross D.; and Hetherington, E. Mavis. Modification of impulsive and reflective cognitive styles through observation of film-mediated models. *Developmental Psychology*, 1971, *5*(3), 369–377. 291

Rieber, Morton. Hypothesis testing in children as a function of age. *Developmental Psychology*, 1969, *1*(4), 389–395. 288

Rieber, Morton, and Womack, Marceleete. The intelligence of preschool children as related to ethnic and demographic variables. *Exceptional Children*, 1968, *34*(8), 609–614. 321, 339

Rivenbark, W. H. Self-disclosure patterns among adolescents. *Psychological Reports*, 1971, *28*(1), 35–42. 376

Roberts, Beverly, and Campbell, Dugal. Activity in newborns and the sound of a human heart. *Psychonomic Science*, 1967, *9*(6), 339–340. 103

Robins, Cynthia. Teaching life-saving skills to the youngest swimmers. *San Francisco Examiner–Chronicle*, May 15, 1977. 284

Robinson, H. B., and Robinson, N. M. *The mentally retarded child: a psychological approach*. New York: McGraw-Hill, 1965. 506

Rode, Alex. Perceptions of parental behavior among alienated adolescents. *Adolescence*, 1971, *6*(21), 19–38. 386

Rodman, Hyman. The lower class value stretch. *Social Forces*, 1963, *42*, 205–215. 465

Roffwarg, H. P.; Muzio, J. N.; and Dement, W. C. Ontogenetic development of the human sleep-dream cycle. *Science*, 1966, *152*, 604–619. 106

Rogers, Carl R. *Counseling and psychotherapy*. Boston: Houghton Mifflin, 1942. 357

——. *Client-centered therapy*. Boston: Houghton Mifflin, 1951. 357

——. *On becoming a person*. Boston: Houghton Mifflin, 1961. 357

Rorvik, David M., and Shettles, Landrum B. *Your baby's sex: now you can choose*. New York: Dodd, Mead, and Co., 1970. 37

Rose, Susan Ann. Infant's transfer of response between two-dimensional and three-dimensional stimuli. *Child Development*, 1977, *48*, 1086–1091. 91

Rosekrans, Mary A. Imitation in children as a function of perceived similarity to a social model and vicarious reinforcement. *Journal of Personality and Social Psychology*, 1967, 7(3, Part 1), 307–315. 291

Rosen, Alexander C., and Teague, James. Case studies in development of masculinity and femininity in male children. *Psychological Reports*, 1974, *34*(3, Part 1), 971–983. 409

Rosen, B. D., and D'Andrade, R. The psychosocial origins of achievement motivation. *Sociometry*, 1959, *22*, 185–218. 448, 452

Rosenberg, B. G., and Sutton-Smith, B. A. A revised conception of masculine feminine differences in play activities. *Journal of Genetic Psychology*, 1960, *96*, 165–170. 381

Rosenhan, D. L. On being sane in insane places. *Science*, 1973, *179*, 250–258. 517

Rosenthal, Bernard G. Attitude toward money, need, and methods of presentation as determinants of perception of coins from 6 to 10 years of age. *Journal of General Psychology*, 1968, *78*(1), 85–103. 109

Rosenthal, Robert, and Jacobsen, Lenore. Teacher expectancies: determinants of pupils' IQ gains. *Psychological Reports*, 1966, *19*, 115–118. 462

——. Teacher expectations for the disadvantaged. *Scientific American*, 1968, *218*(4), 19–28. 462

Ross, Alan O. *Psychological disorders of children: a behavioral approach to theory, research, and therapy*. New York: McGraw-Hill, 1974. 501, 503, 505

Ross, Hildy S., and Balzer, Rita H. Determinants and consequences of children's questions. *Child Development*, 1975, *46*(2), 536–539. 242

Ross, Hildy S.; Rheingold, Harriet L.; and Eckerman, Carol O. Approach and exploration of a novel alternative by 12-month-old infants. *Journal of Experimental Child Psychology*, 1972, *13*(1), 85–93. 280

Rothbart, Mary K. Birth order and mother-child interaction in an achievement situation. *Journal of Personality and Social Psychology*, 1971, *17*(2), 113–120. 362

Rothbart, Mary K., and Maccoby, E. E. Parents' differential reactions to sons and daughters. *Journal of Personality and Social Psychology*, 1966, *3*, 237–243. 381

Rubenstein, Judith. Maternal attentiveness and subsequent exploratory behavior in the infant. *Child Development*, 1967, *38*(4), 1089–1100. 153

——. A concordance of visual and manipulative responsiveness to novel and familiar stimuli in six-month-old infants. *Child Development*, 1974, *45*(1), 194–195. 130

Rubenstein, Judith L., and Howes, Carollee. Caregiving and infant behavior in day care and in homes. *Developmental Psychology*, 1979, *15*(1), 1–24. 371

Rubin, Ernest. The sex ratio at birth. *American Statistician*, 1967, *21*(4), 45–48. 37

Rubin, Kenneth H.; Maioni, Terrence L.; and Hornung, Margaret. Free play behaviors in middle- and lower-class preschoolers: Parten and Piaget revisited. *Child Development*, 1976, *47*(2), 414–419. 416

Rubin, Lillian. *Worlds of pain: life in the working class family*. New York: Basic Books, 1977. 446

Ruff, Holly A. Development changes in the infant's attention to pattern detail. *Perceptual and Motor Skills*, 1976, *43*(2), 351–358. 90

Ruff, Holly A., and Turkewitz, Gerald. Developmental changes in the effectiveness of stimulus intensity on infant visual attention. *Developmental Psychology*, 1975, *11*(6), 705–710. 90

Ryback, David. Optimism-pessimism as a consequence of success or failure in children. *Psychological Reports*, 1970, *26*(2), 385. 450

Sagi, Abraham, and Hoffman, Martin L. Emphatic distress in the newborn. *Developmental Psychology*, 1976, *12*(2), 175–176. 103

Saltz, Rosalynn. Aging persons as child-care workers in a foster-grandparent program: psychosocial effects and work performance. *Aging and Human Development*, 1971, *2*, 314–340. 487

Salzman, Leon. Adolescence: epoch or disease? *Adolescence*, 1973, *8*(30), 247–256. 385, 427

Samuels, Shirley C. An investigation into the self-concepts of lower- and middle-class black and white kindergarten children. *Journal of Negro Education*, 1973, *42*(4), 467–472. 376, 377

Santrock, John W. Influence of onset and type of paternal absence on the first four Eriksonian developmental crises. *Developmental Psychology*, 1970, *3*(2), 273–274. 409

Sarason, Seymour B. Jewishness, blackishness, and the nature-nurture controversy. *American Psychologist*, 1973, *28*(11), 962–971. 337, 339

Scarr, Sandra. Genetic factors in activity motivation. *Child Development*, 1966, *37*, 663–673. 446

——. Social introversion-extroversion. *Child Development*, 1969, *40*, 823–832. 359

Scarr, Sandra and Weinberg, Richard A. IQ test performance of black children adopted by white families. *American Psychologist*, 1976, *31*(10), 726–739. 339

Scarr-Salapatek, Sandra. Race, social class, and IQ. *Science*, 1971, *174*(4016), 1285–1295. 337

Scarr-Salapatek, Sandra, and Williams, M. L. The effects of early stimulation on low-birthweight infants. *Child Development*, 1973, *4r*(1), 94–101. 114, 149

Schaar, Karen. What's right about being left-handed. *American Psychological Association Monitor*, 1974, *5*(12). 140

Schaffer, H. R., and Emerson, P. E. Patterns of response to physical contact in early human development. *Journal of Child Psychology and Psychiatry*, 1964a, *5*, 1–13. 361

——. The development of social attachment in infancy. *Monographs of the Society for Research in Child Development*, 1964b, *29*(3). 361

Schaffer, H. R., and Parry, M. H. Perceptual-motor behavior in infancy as a function of age and stimulus familiarity. *British Journal of Psychology*, 1969, *60*(1), 1–9. 93

Schlichter, K. J., and Ratliff, R. G. Discrimination learning in juvenile delinquents. *Journal of Abnormal Psychology*, 1971, *77*, 46–48. 515

Schonfeld, W. A. Primary and secondary sexual characteristics: study of their development in males from birth through maturity, with biometric study of penis and testes. *American Journal of the Disturbed Child*, 1943, *65*, 535–549. 144

Schreiber, Flora Rheta. *Sybil*. New York: Warner Books, 1973. 478

Schroth, Marvin L. The effect of informative feedback on problem solving. *Child Development*, 1970, *41*(3), 831–837. 287

Schuster, D., and Schuster, L. Speculative mechanisms affecting sex ratio. *Journal of Genetic Psychology*, 1972, *121*(2), 245–254. 37

Schwartz, Andrew N.; Campos, Joseph J.; and Baisel, Edward J. The visual cliff: cardiac and behavioral responses on the deep and shallow sides at five and nine months of age. *Journal of Experimental Child Psychology*, 1973, *15*(1), 86–99. 93

Schwartz, J. Conrad; Strickland, Robert G.; and Krolock, George. Infant day care: behavioral effects at preschool age. *Developmental Psychology*, 1974, *10*(4), 502–506. 414

Schwebel, Milton. Formal operations in first-year college students. *Journal of Psychology*, 1975, *91*(1), 133–141. 200

Sears, Robert R. Dependency motivation. In M. R. Jones (ed.), *Nebraska symposium on motivation*. Lincoln: University of Nebraska Press, 1963. 453

——. Relation of early socialization experiences to self-concepts and gender role in middle childhood. *Child Development* 1970, *41*(2), 267–289. 375

——. Sources of life satisfactions of the Terman gifted men. *American Psychologist*, 1977, *32*(2), 119–128. 446

——. Maud Merrill James (1888–1978). *American Psychologist*, 1979, *34*(2), 176. 310

Sears, Robert R.; Maccoby, Eleanor E.; and Levin, Henry *Patterns of child rearing*. New York: Harper and Row, 1957. 134, 366

Sears, Robert R.; Rau, Lucy; and Alpert, Richard. *Identification and child rearing*. Stanford, Calif.: Stanford University Press, 1965. 373, 379

Seitz, Sue, and Stewart, Catherine. Imitation and expansions: some developmental aspects of mother-child communications. *Developmental Psychology*, 1975, *11*(6), 763–768. 240

Sellers, Martha J.; Klein, Robert E.; Kagan, Jerome; and Minton, Cheryl. Developmental determinants of attention: a cross-cultural replication. *Developmental Psychology*, 1972, *6*(1), 185. 93

Senior, Kathleen, and Brophy, Jere. Praise and group competition as motivating incentives for children. *Psychological Reports*, 1973, 32(3, pf. 1)., 951–958. 461

Serunian, Sally A., and Broman, Sarah H. Relationships of Apgar scores and Bayley mental and motor scores. *Child Development*, 1975, *46*, 696–700. 127

Shantz, David W., and Voydanoff, Douglas A. Situational effects on retaliatory aggression at three age levels. *Child Development*, 1973, *44*(1), 149–153. 421

Shatz, Marilyn, and Gelman, Rachel. The development of communication skills: modifications in the speech of young children as a function of listener. *Monographs of the Society for Research in Child Development*, 1973, *38*(5), 1–37. 229

Shaw, Jon; Wheeler, Peggy; and Morgan, Donald W. Mother-infant relationship and weight gain in the first month of life. *Journal of the American Academy of Child Psychiatry*, 1970, *9*(3), 428–444. 148

Sheehy, Gail. *Passages*. New York: E. P. Dutton, 1976. 446

Sheppard, John L. Conservation of part and whole in the acquisition of class inclusion. *Child Development*, 1973, *44*(2), 380–383. 196

Shettles, Landrum B. Conception and birth sex ratios: a review. *Obstetrics and Gynecology*, 1961, *18*, 122–130. 38

Shine, Denise, and Walsh, John F. Developmental trends in the use of logical connectives. *Psychonomic Science*, 1971, *23*(2), 171–172. 231

Shirley, M. M. *The first two years: a study of twenty-five babies*. Vol. 1, *Postural and locomotor development*. Institute of Child Welfare Monographs, Serial No. 6. Minneapolis: University of Minnesota Press, 1933. 121

Short, J. F., and Strodtbeck, F. L. *Group process and gang delinquency*. Chicago: University of Chicago Press, 1965. 504

Siegel, Alberta. Only 20 years left, baby. *Stanford Observer*, October 1973, p. 1. 394

Siegel, Claire L. Sex differences in the occupational choices of second graders. *Journal of Vocational Behavior*. 1973, *3*(1), 15–19. 455

Silverman, Irwin, and Schneider, Dale S. A study of the development of conservation by a nonverbal method. *Journal of Genetic Psychology*, 1968, *112*(2), 287–291. 181

Simmons, Roberta G.; Rosenberg, Florence; and Rosenberg, Morris. Disturbance in the self-image at adolescence. *American Sociological Review*, 1973, *38*(5), 553–568. 376

Singer, J. L., and Singer, D. G. Experimental studies of imaginative

and sociodramatic play. *Division 8 Newsletter*, American Psychological Association, July 1973. 417, 495

Skeels, H. M. Adult status of children with contrasting early life experiences: a follow-up study. *Monographs of the Society for Research in Child Development*, 1966, *31*(3), 27–65. 333, 334, 487

Skeels, H. M., and Dye, H. B. A study of the effects of differential stimulation on mentally retarded children. *Proceedings and Addresses of the American Association on Mental Deficiency*, 1939, *44*, 114–136. 333

Skodak, Marie, and Skeels, H. M. A final follow-up study of one hundred adopted children. *Journal of Genetic Psychology*, 1949, *75*, 85–125. 329

Slaby, Ronald G., and Frey, Karin S. Development of gender constancy and selective attention to same-sex models. *Child Development*, 1975, *46*(4), 849–856. 379

Slater, Alan M., and Findlay, John M. Binocular fixation in the newborn baby. *Journal of Experimental Child Psychology*, 1975, *20*(2), 248–273. 84

Slobin, Dan I. They learn the same way all around the world. *Psychology Today*, July 1972, pp. 261–264. 214

——. Cognitive prerequisites for development of grammar. In C. A. Ferguson and D. I. Slobin (eds.), *Studies of child language development*, pp. 175–208. New York: Holt, Rinehart and Winston, 1973. 226

——. On the nature of talk to children. In E. Lenneberg and E. Lenneberg (eds.), *Foundations of language development: a multidisciplinary approach*, Vol. 1, pp. 283–297. New York: Academic Press, 1975. 217, 241, 242

Slovin-Ela, Susan, and Kohen-Raz, R. Developmental differences in primary reaching responses of young infants from varying social backgrounds. *Child Development*, 1978, *49*, 132–140. 153

Smart, Mollie S., and Smart, Russell C. *Infants: development and relationships*. New York: Macmillan, 1973. 108

Smedslund, Jan. The acquisition of conservation of substance and weight in children. *Scandinavian Journal of Psychology*, 1961, *2*, 71–84. 195

Smith, Frank. The relation between spoken and written language. In E. Lenneberg and E. Lenneberg (eds.), *Foundations of language development*, Vol. 2, pp. 347–360. New York:

Academic Press, 1975. 101, 204

Smith, G. H. Sociometric study of best-liked and least-liked children. *Elementary School Journal*, 1950, *51*, 77–85. 417

Smith, Peter K., and Green, Maureen. Aggressive behavior in English nurseries and play groups: sex differences and response of adults. *Child Development*, 1975, *46*(1), 211–214. 420

Smoking and health. *H.E.W. Report*, January 1979. 54

Snow, Catherine E. Mother's speech to children learning language. *Child Development*, 1972, *43*(2), 549–565. 240

Snow, Richard E. Unfinished pygmalion. *Contemporary Psychology*, 1969, *14*(4), 197–199. 463

Solkoff, N.; Yaffe, S.; Weintraub, D.; and Blase, B. Effects of handling on the subsequent development of premature infants. *Developmental Psychology*, 1969, *1*, 765–768. 148

Sollenberger, Richard T. Chinese-American child-rearing practices and juvenile delinquency. *Journal of Social Psychology*, 1968, *74*, 13–23. 411, 412

Sontag, L. W. The significance of fetal environmental differences. *American Journal of Obstetrics and Gynecology*, 1941, *42*, 996–1003. 44, 55

——. Differences in modifiability of fetal behavior and physiology. *Psychosomatic Medicine*, 1944, *6*, 151–154. 55

Sorenson, R. C. *Adolescent sexuality in contemporary America: personal values and sexual behavior ages*. New York: World, 1973. 426, 427

Southern, Mara L., and Plant, Walter T. Differential cognitive development within and between racial and ethnic groups of disadvantaged preschool and kindergarten children. *Journal of Genetic Psychology*, 1971, *119*(2), 259–266. 336

Spear, Paul S. Motivational effects of praise and criticism on children's learning. *Developmental Psychology*, 1970, *3*(1), 124–132. 460

Spectorman, Arlette R.; Shulman, Tamara; and Ernhart, Claire B. The influence of concept and orientation training on letter discrimination. *Journal of Genetic Psychology*, 1977, *130*(1), i153–154. 236

Spelke, Elizabeth; Zelazo, Philip; Kagan, Jerome; and Kotelchuck, Milton. Father interaction and separation protest. *Developmental Psychology*, 1973, *9*(1), 83–90. 370

Spelt, D. K. The conditioning of the

human fetus in utero. *Journal of Experimental Psychology*, 1948, *38*, 338–346. 261

Spencer, W. P. Heredity: facts and fallacies. In M. Fishbein and R. J. R. Kennedy (eds.), *Modern marriage and family living*, pp. 341–356. New York: Oxford University Press, 1957. 38, 55

Spitz, René A. The smiling response: a contribution to the ontogenesis of social relations. *Genetic Psychology Monographs*, 1946a, *34*, 57–125. 488

—. Anaclitic depression: an inquiry into the genesis of psychiatric conditions in early childhood. In A. Freud et al (eds.), *The psychoanalytic study of the child*, Vol. 2. New York: International Universities Press, 1946b. 488

Sprafkin, Joyce N.; Liebert, Robert M.; and Poulos, Rita. Effects of a prosocial televised example on children's helping. *Journal of Experimental Psychology*, 1975, *20*(1), 119–126. 290

Staats, A. W., and Butterfield, W. H. Treatment of nonreading in a culturally deprived juvenile delinquent: an application of reinforcement principles. *Child Development*, 1965, *36*, 925–942. 470

Stabenau, James R. Heredity and environment in schizophrenia: the contribution of twin studies. *Archives of General Psychiatry*, 1968, *18*(4), 458–463. 500

Stark, Patricia A., and Traxler, Anthony J. Empirical validation of Erikson's theory of identity crises in late adolescence. *Journal of Psychology*, 1974, *86*(1), 25–33. 388

Stechler, G. Newborn attention as affection by medication during labor. *Science*, 1964a, *144*, 315–317. 64

—. A longitudinal follow-up of neonatal apnea. *Child Development*, 1964b, *35*, 333–348. 69

Stedman's Medical Dictionary. Baltimore: Williams and Wilkins, 1972. 70

Stein, Aletha H.; Pohly, Sheila R.; and Mueller, Edward. The influence of masculine, feminine, and neutral tasks on children's achievement behavior, expectancies of success, and attainment values. *Child Development*, 1971, *42*(1), 195–207. 455

Stevenson, Harold W.; Williams, Anne M.; and Coleman, Edgar. Interrelations among learning and performance tasks in disadvantaged children. *Journal of Educational Psychology*, 1971, *62*(3), 179–184. 296

Steward, Margaret, and Steward, David. The observation of Anglo-, Mexican-, and Chinese-American mothers teaching their young sons. *Child Development*, 1973, *44*(2), 329–337. 412

Stinnett, Nick; Farris, Joe A.; and Walters, James. Parent-child relationships of male and female high school students. *Journal of Genetic Psychology*, 1974, *125*(1), 99–106. 381

Stone, L. Joseph, and Church, Joseph. *Childhood and adolescence*, 3d. ed. New York: Random House, 1973. 385

Stone, Michael H., and Kestenbaum, Clarice J. Maternal deprivation in children of the wealthy: a paradox in socioeconomic vs. psychological class. *History of Childhood Quarterly: The Journal of Psychohistory*, 1974, *2*(1), 79–106. 490

Strayer (1930). Cited in G. A. Miller (ed.), *Language and communication*, pp. 140–141. New York: McGraw-Hill, 1951. 213

Strommen, Ellen A. Verbal self-regulation in a children's game: impulsive errors on "Simon says." *Child Development*, 1973, *44*(4), 849–853. 288

Suran, Bernard G., and Rizzo, Joseph V. *Special children: an integrative approach*. Glenview, Ill.: Scott, Foresman, 1979. 498, 499

Sutton-Smith, Brian. Child's play: very serious business. *Psychology Today*, 1971, *5*(7), 66–69, 87. 415

Sutton-Smith, Brian, and Rosenberg, B. G. Sibling consensus on power tactics. *Journal of Genetic Psychology*, 1968, *112*, 63–72. 362

Swan, Raymond W., and Stavros, Helen. Child-rearing practices associated with the development of cognitive skills of children in low socioeconomic areas. *Early Child Development and Care*, 1973, *2*(1), 23–38. 295

Szasz, T. S. *The myth of mental illness*. New York: Hoeber-Harper, 1961. 480

Tanner, J. M. *Education and physical growth*. London: University of London Press, 1961. 148

—. The adolescent growth: spurt and developmental age. In G. A. Harrison; J. S. Weiner; J. M. Tanner; and N. A. Barnicot, *Human biology: an introduction to human evolution, variation and growth*, pp. 321–339. Oxford: Clarendon Press, 1964. 121, 141

—. Earlier maturation in man. *Scientific American*, 1968, *218*, 21–27. 122, 123

—. Growing up. *Scientific American*, 1973, *229*(3), 34–43. 139

Taylor, Ann. Institutionalized infants: concept formation ability. *American Journal of Orthopsychiatry*, 1968, *38*(1), 110–115.

—. Followup of institutionalized infants' concept formation ability at age 12. American Journal of Orthopsychiatry, 1970, *40*(3), 441–447. 206

Taylor, John A., and Wales, Roger J. A developmental study of form discrimination in pre-school children. *Quarterly Journal of Experimental Psychology*, 1970, *22*(4), 720–734. 98

Taylor, Muriel K., and Kogan, Kate L. Effects of birth of a sibling on mother-child interactions. *Child Psychiatry and Human Development*, 1973, *4*(1), 53–58. 362

Teevan, Richard C., and McGhee, Paul E. Childhood development of fear of failure and motivation. *Journal of Personality and Social Psychology*, 1972, *21*(3), 345–348. 448

Terman, Lewis M. *The measurement of intelligence*. Boston: Houghton Mifflin, 1916. 309

—. The discovery and encouragement of exceptional talent. *American Psychologist*, 1954, *9*, 221–230. 304, 305

Terman, Lewis M., et al. Mental and physical traits of a thousand gifted children. In L. M. Terman, (ed.), *Genetic Studies of Genius*, Vol. 1. Stanford: Stanford University Press, 1925. 304

Terman, Lewis M., and Merrill, Maud A. *Stanford-Binet intelligence scale*. Boston: Houghton Mifflin, 1960. 311

Ter Vrugt, Dick, and Pederson, David R. The effects of vertical rocking frequencies on the arousal level in two-month-old infants. *Child Development*, 1973, *44*(1), 205–209. 105

Tharp, R. G., and Wetzel, R. J. *Behavior modification in the natural environment*. New York: Academic Press, 1969. 265, 515

Thoman, Evelyn. Some consequences of early infant-mother-infant interaction. *Early Child Development and Care*, 1974, *3*(3), 249–261. 368

Thoman, Evelyn B.; Leiderman, P. Herbert; and Olson, Joan P. Neonate-mother interaction during breast-feeding. *Developmental Psychology*, 1972, *6*(1), 110–118. 362, 378

Thomas, Alexander; Chess, Stella; and Birch, Herbert G. The origin of personality. *Scientific American*, 1970, *223*(2), 102–109. 359, 360

Thompson, Helen. Physical growth. In L. Carmichael (ed.), *Manual of child psychology*, pp. 292–334. New York: Wiley, 1954. 126, 131

Thompson, Spencer K. Gender labels and early sex role development. *Child Development*, 1975, *46*(2), 339–347. 377

Thoms, Herbert, and Blevin, Bruce, Jr. Life before birth. *McCall's Magazine*, February 1958. 45

Thornburg, Kathy R., and Fisher, Virginia L. Discrimination of 2-D letters by children after play with 2- or 3-dimensional letter forms. *Perceptual and Motor Skills*, 1970, *30*(3), 979–986. 107

Thurow, Lester. Education and economic equality. *The Public Interest*, Summer 1972, pp. 66–81. 321

Toby, J. An evaluation of early identification and intensive treatment programs for pre-delinquents. *Social Problems*, 1965, *13*, 160–175. 515

Toepfer, Caroline; Reuter, Jeannette; and Maurer, Charles. Design and evaluation of an obedience training program for mothers of preschool children. *Journal of Consulting and Clinical Psychology*, 1972, *39*(2), 194–198. 404

Tompkins, W. T. The clinical significance of nutritional deficiencies in pregnancy. *Bulletin, New York Academy of Medicine*, 1948, *24*, 376–388. 52

Troll, Lillian E.; Neugarten, Bernice L.; and Kraines, Ruth J. Similarities in values and other personality characteristics in college students and their parents. *Merrill-Palmer Quarterly*, 1969, *15*(4), 323–336. 429

Tuckman, Jacob, and Regan, Richard A. Size of family and behavioral problems in children. *Journal of Genetic Psychology*, 1967, *111*(2), 151–160. 362

Tulkin, Steven R., and Cohler, Bertram J. Child-rearing attitudes and mother-child interaction in the first year of life. *Merrill-Palmer Quarterly*, 1973, *19*(2), 95–106. 367

Tulkin, Steven R., and Kagan, Jerome. Mother-child interaction in the first year of life. *Child Development*, 1972, *43*(1), 31–41. 411

Turiel, Elliot. Conflict and transition in adolescent moral development. *Child Development*, 1974, *45*(1), 14–29. 400

Turner, Charles. Effects of race of tester and need for approval on children's learning. *Journal of Educational Psychology*, 1971, *62*(3), 240–244. 463

Turner, Jonetha H. Entrepreneurial environments and the emergence of achievement motivation in adoles-cent males. *Sociometry*, 1970, *33*(2), 147–165. 456

Turnure, James; Buium, Nissan; and Thurlow, Martha. The effectiveness of interrogatives for promoting verbal elaboration productivity in young children. *Child Development*, 1976, *47*, 851–855. 242

Tversky, Barbara. Pictorial and verbal encoding in preschool children. *Developmental Psychology*, 1973, *3*(3), 149–153. 276

Utech, David A., and Hoving, Kenneth L. Parents and peers as competing influences in the decisions of children of differing ages. *Journal of Social Psychology*, 1969, *78*(2), 267–274. 376

Vandenberg, Steven G. A twin study of spatial ability. *Multivariate Behavioral Research*, 1969, *4*(3), 273–294. 111

Van den Daele, Leland D., The modification of infant state through treatment in a rockerbox. *Journal of Psychology*, 1970, *74*(2), 161–165. 105

van Mannen, Gloria C. Father roles and adolescent socialization. *Adolescence*, 1968, *3*(1), 139–162. 425, 504

Vietze, Peter; Friedman, Steven; and Foster, Martha. Noncontingent stimulation: effects of stimulus movement on infants; visual and motor behavior. *Perceptual and Motor Skills*, 1974, *38*(1), 331–336. 105

Vondracek, Sarah I., and Kirchner, Elizabeth P. Vocational development in early childhood: an examination of young children's expressions of vocational aspirations. *Journal of Vocational Behavior*, 1974, *5*(2), 251–260. 464

Vygotsky, L. S. *Thought and language*. Cambridge, Mass.: M.I.T. Press, 1962. 232

Wachs, Theodore D. Utilization of a Piagetian approach in the investigation of early experience effects: a research strategy and some illustrative data. *Merrill-Palmer Quarterly*, 1976, *22*(1), 11–30. 205

Wachs, Theodore D.; Uzgiris, Ina C.; and Hunt, J. McV. Cognitive development in infants of different age levels and from different environmental backgrounds: an explanatory investigation. *Merrill-Palmer Quarterly*, 1971, *17*(4), 283–317. 243, 295, 297

Wald, Michael S. Legal policies affecting children: a lawyer's request for aid. *Child Development*, 1976, *47*, 1–5. 12

Waldrop, Mary F., and Halverson, Charles F., Jr. Intensive and extensive peer behavior: longitudinal and cross-sectional analyses. *Child Development*, 1975, *46*(1), 19–26. 417

Walters, C. Etta. Comparative development of Negro and white infants. *Journal of Genetic Psychology*, 1967, *110*, 243–251. 147

Wasik, Barbara H., and Wasik, John L. Performance of culturals deprived children on the concept assessment kit: conservation. *Child Development*, 1971, *45*(5), 1586–1590. 205

Wattenberg, W. W., and Clifford, C. Relation of self-concepts to beginning achievement in reading. *Child Development*, 1964, *35*, 461–467. 237

Webb, Roger A.; Oliveri, Mary Ellen; and O'Keeffe, Lynda. Investigations of the meaning of "different" in the language of young children. *Child Development*, 1974, *45*(4), 984–991. 230

Wechsler, David. *The measurement of adult intelligence*. Baltimore: Williams and Wilkins, 1939. 312

——. *The measurement of adult intelligence*. Baltimore: Williams and Wilkins, 1944. 305

——. *Wechsler intelligence scale for children*. New York: The Psychological Corporation, 1952. 312

Wei, Tam T.; Lavatelli, Celia B.; and Jones, R. Stewart. Piaget's concept of classification: a comparative study of socially disadvantaged and middle-class young children. *Child Development*, 1971, *42*(3), 919–927. 205

Weiner, Irving B. The generation gap: fact and fancy. *Adolescence*, 1971, *6*(22), 156–166. 430

Weinraub, Marsha, and Frankel, Jay. Sex differences in parent-infant interaction during free play, departure, and separation. *Child Development*, 1977, *48*, 1240–1249. 368, 408

Weisenburg, T., and McBride, K. *Aphasia: a clinical and psychological study*. New York: Hafner, 1964. 509

Weizmann, Frederic; Cohen, Leslie B.; and Pratt, R. Jeanene. Novelty, familiarity, and the development of infant attention. *Developmental Psychology*, 1971, *4*(2), 149–154. 97

Wellman, Henry M., and Lempers, Jacques D. The naturalistic communicative abilities of two-year-olds. *Child Development*, 1977, *48*, 1052–1057. 227

Wender, Paul H. The role of genetics in the etiology of the schizophrenias. *American Journal of Orthopsychiatry*, 1969, *39*(3), 447–458. 500

Werner, Emmy E.; Honzik, Marjorie P.; and Smith, Ruth S. Prediction of intelligence and achievement at ten years from twenty months pediatric and psychologic examinations. *Child Development*, 1968, *39*(4), 1063–1075. 319

Werner, Heinz. The concept of development from a comparative and organismic point of view. In D. Harris (ed.), *The concept of development: an issue in the study of human behavior*, pp. 125–148. Minneapolis: University of Minnesota Press, 1957. 83

Wesman, A. G. Intelligent testing. *American Psychologist*, 1968, *23*,(4), 267–274. 305

Wetherford, Margaret J., and Cohen, Leslie B. Developmental changes in infant visual preferences for novelty and familiarity. *Child Development*, 1973, *44*, 416–424. 97

Whipple, Dorothy V. Human growth through the ages. In Dorothy V. Whipple (ed.), *Dynamics of development: euthenic pediatrics*. New York: McGraw-Hill, 1966. 134

White, Burton L., and Held, Richard. Plasticity of sensorimotor development in the human infant. In J. F. Rosenblith and W. Allinsmith (eds.), *The causes of behavior: readings in child development and educational psycholgoy*, 2d ed., pp. 60–70. Boston: Allyn and Bacon, 1966. 97, 131, 149

White, Robert. Motivation reconsidered: the concept of competence. *Psychological Review*, 1959, *66*, 297–333. 439

White, W. F., and Dekle, O. T. Effect of teacher's motivational cues on achievement level in elementary grades. *Psychological Reports*, 1966, *18*, 351–356. 462

Whitehurst, Grover J., and Vasta, Ross. Is language acquired through imitation? *Journal of Psycholinguistic Research*, 1975, *4*(1), 37–59. 217, 218

Wiggins, R. Gene. Differences in self-perceptions of ninth grade boys and girls. *Adolescence*, 1973, *8*(32), 491–496. 387, 455

Wight, Byron W.; Gloniger, Margaret F.; and Keeve, J. Philip. Cultural deprivation: operational definition in terms of language development. *American Journal of Orthopsychiatry*, 1970, *40*(1) 77–86. 247

Willard, Louisa S. A comparison of culture fair test scores with group and individual intelligence test scores of disadvantaged Negro children. *Journal of Learning Disabilities*, 1968, *1*(10), 584–589 342

Willerman, Lee. Activity level and hyperactivity in twins. *Child Development*, 1973, *44*(2), 288–293. 339

Willerman, Lee; Naylor, Alfred F.; and Myrianthopoulos, Ntinos C. Intellectual development of children from interracial matings. *Science*, 1970, *170*(3964), 1329–1331. 140

Willerman, Lee, and Stafford, Richard E. Maternal effects on intellectual functioning. *Behavior Genetics*, 1972, *2*(4), 321–325. 335

Williams, Robert L. *The BITCH test: black intelligence test of cultural homogeneity*. Black Studies Program, Washington University, St. Louis, Mo., 1972. 248, 249

Wilson, Ronald S. Twins: mental development in the pre-school years. *Developmental Psychology*, 1974, *10*(4), 580–588. 331

Wilson, Ronald S., and Harpring, Eileen B. Mental and motor development in infant twins. *Developmental Psychology*, 1972, *7*(3), 277–287. 139

Winer, Gerald A. Conservation of different quantities among preschool children. *Child Development*, 1974, *45*(3), 839–842. 182

Wingerd, John. The relation of growth from birth to two years to sex, parental size and other factors, using Rao's method of transformed time scale. *Human Biology*, 1970, *42*(1), 105–131. 139

Winick, Myron; Meyer, Kharig; and Harris, Ruth C. Malnutrition and environmental enrichment by early adoption. *Science*, 1975, *190*(4220), 1173–1175. 152

Wohlford, Paul; Santrock, John W.; Berger, Stephen E.; and Liberman, D. Older brothers' influence on sex-typed, aggressive, and dependent behavior in father-absent children. *Developmental Psychology*, 1971, *4*(2), 124–134. 409

Wohlwill, J. F. Developmental studies of perception. *Psychological Bulletin*, 1960, *57*, 249–288. 83

Wolf, Willavene. Perception of visual displays. *Viewpoints*, 1971, *47*(4), 112–140. 101

Wolff, Peter H. The causes, controls and organization of behavior in the newborn. *Psychological Issues*, 1966, *5*(1), 80–86 106

Won, George Y.; Yomamura, Douglas S.; and Ikeda, Kiyoshi. The relation of communication with parents and peers to deviant behavior of youth. *Journal of Marriage and the Family*, 1969, *31*(1), 43–47. 387

Woodruff, M. Emerson. Observations on the visual acuity of children during the first five years of life. *American Journal of Optometry and Archives of the American Academy of Optometry*, 1972, *49*(3), 205–215. 94

Woods, Merilyn B. The unsupervised child of the working mother. *Developmental Psychology*, 1972, *6*(1), 14–25. 410

Woodworth, R. S. *Heredity and environment*, Research Council Bulletin, No. 47. New York: Social Science Research Council, 1941. 327

Woody, Robert H. Clinical suggestion and the video-taped vicarious desensitization method. *American Journal of Clinical Hypnosis*, 1969, *11*(4), 239–244. 494

World Health Organization. *Agents stimulating gonadal function in the human*. Technical Report Series No. 514. World Health Organization, 1973. 53

Wulff, K. R. Cognitive development in disadvantaged students. *Journal of Educational Research*, 1974, *67*(7), 307–310. 297

Yarrow, Marian R.; Waxler, Carolyn Z.; and Scott, Phyllis M. Child effects on adult behavior, *Developmental Psychology*, 1971, *5*(2), 300–311. 361

Yussen, Steven R. Determinants of visual attention and recall in observational learning by preschoolers and second graders. *Developmental Psychology*, 1974, *10*(1), 93–100. 286

Zelazo, N. A.; Zelazo, P. R.; and Kolb, S. Walking in the newborn. *Science*, 1972, *176*, 314–215. 129, 150

Zuckerman, Paul; Ziegler, Mark; and Stevenson, Harold W. Children's viewing of television and recognition memory of commercials. *Child Development*, 1978, *49*, 96–104. 293

Index

* Italic numbers refer to bibliographic entries

Lepper, M. R., *462*
Lessor, H., *231*
Lester, B. M., *151, 370*
Levenstein, P., *207, 294*
Leventhal, G. S., *362*
Leventhal, T., *496*
Levin, H., *369*
Lewis, M., *74, 243, 318*
Libido, 352
Liebenberg, B., *69*
Lieberman, P., *219*
Liebert, R. M., *272, 422, 423*
Liedtke, W. W., *251*
Life crisis, 353–56
Life span, 41
Ling, D., *240, 241*
Lipsitt, L. P., *84, 111, 275*
Little, A., *200*
Little, W. B., *335*
Living together, 427–28
Locke, J., 6–7, 9, *235*
Lockhart, K. L., *396*
Longitudinal (research) study, 15, 304
Long-term memory, 274–75
   See also Memory
Looft, W. R., *171, 358, 455*
Looking time research, 88–89
Lourie, R. S., *420*
Lovaas, O. I., *422, 515, 516*
Love-oriented discipline, 403
Love withdrawal, 400–401, 405
Lower class
   See Socioeconomic status
Lugo, J. O., *97*
Lumsden Jr., E. A., *180*
Luria, A. R., *229, 232, 233*
Lyell, R. G., *382*
Lynch, M. A., *491*

McCall, R. B., *90*
McClelland, D., *440*
McClelland, D. C., *320, 322, 350, 440*
Maccoby, E. E., *104, 204, 205, 291, 411*
McCord, W., *504, 515*
MacDonald, R., *337*
McKeachie, W. J., *442*

McKinney, J. D., *203*
McMurtry, C. A., *420*
MacNamara, J., *228*
McNeill, D., *215, 223, 226, 228*
McQueen, R., *251*
Maddock, J. W., *146, 425, 426, 427*
Male physical development
   See Physical development;
      Sexual development
Malnutrition, 150–52
   See also Nutrition
Manipulation, 121, 129–31, 136, 138, 153
Mann, M., *287*
Maratsos, M. P., *180, 181*
Marcus, R. F., *362*
Marcus, T. L., *381, 465*
Maresh, M. M., *136, 141*
Marjoribanks, K., *332, 335*
Marquis, D. P., *280*
Martin, F., *244*
Martorano, S. C., *171*
Marvick, E. W., *8*
Masangkay, Z. S., *419*
Maslow, A., 9, 357, *443–45*, 446, 447, *465*
Mastery-competence motivation, 437–39
Masturbation, 426
Matched pair, 524
Maternal influence
   See Environmental influence;
      Working mothers
Mathematical ability, 335
Matheny, A. P., *136*
Matteson, R., *387*
Maturation:
   in cognition, 193
   defined, 82, 120
   in language acquisition, 213–15, 228
   in learning, 260, 261
   in motivation, 439, 446–47
   in perceptual development, 83ff
   in physical and motor
      development, 120–26, 138–39, 144–46
   prenatal, 45–51
   and socialization, 395, 397, 405–6, 420
Maurer, D., *95*

Mead, M., 452
Mean (definition), 311
Mecham, M. J., *104*
Meddock, T. D., *447*
Median (definition), 311
Medinnus, G. R., *387*
Mehryar, A. H., *335*
Meichenbaum, D. H., *235*
Meiosis, 30–34
Memory, 172, 173, 235, 262, 274–79, 305, 309
Menarche, 143, 147
Mendel, G., 35, 43
Menig-Peterson, C. L., *229*
Menninger, K., *426*
Menstruation, 46, 122, 142, 145–46
Mental age, 307–10
Mental combinations, 177
Mental health
   See Atypical development
Mental illness (definition), 480
Mental retardation, 333, 334, 482, 483, 487, 505–8, 516
   See also Down's syndrome
Menyuk, P., *221*
Meredith, H. V., *123, 148*
Merskey, H., *108*
Metabolism, 500, 506
Metapelet, 413
Mexican-Americans, 296, 412, 464
Michalak, J., *340*
Middle Ages, 4–5
Middle class
   See Socioeconomic status
Midwives, 65
Milgram, N. A., *287*
Millar, T. P., *406*
Miller, G. A., *215, 219, 222, 223, 227, 228, 229*
Miller, L. C., *515*
Miller, P. H., *180, 181*
Miller, S. M., *456, 457*
Miller, T. W., *377*
Minton, C., *411*
Miranda, S. B., *90*
Miscarriage, 48
"Mister Rogers' Neighborhood," 417

Mitchell, E., *377*
Mitchell, J. J., *425*
Mitosis, 30, 31, 47
Mnemonic devices, 278
Mode, 526
Model, modeling, 13, 269–73, 282,
  285–86, 289–93, 394–95, 403,
  404, 409, 423, 494–95, 503
  See also Identification;
  Observational learning
Moerk, E. L., *240, 242, 409*
Moffitt, A. R., *222*
Monkey experiments, 107, 364–67,
  370, 442
Monozygotic twins (definition), 41
  See also Identical twins
Montagu, M. F. A., *47, 51, 52, 54, 55,
  64, 71*
Montessori, M., 468
Montessori schools, 107, 467–68
Moore, S. G., *282*
Moore, T., *237, 386*
Moral development,
  Kohlberg's stages, 397–400
  Piaget's six dimensions, 395–96
  See also Socialization
Moratorium, 356
Mordock, J. B., *509*
Mores, 426
Morphemes, 223
Morrison, F. J., *204, 278*
Mortality rates, 141
Moskowitz, D. S., *371*
Moskowitz, R. D., *486*
Moss, H. A., *439*
Mothers
  See Environmental influence;
  Working mothers; specific
  subject headings
Mothering and atypical
  development, 486–91
Motion, effect on infants, 105
Motivation, 436–73
  and compensatory education,
    467–69
  definition, 261, 436
  and drop-outs, 469–72
  genetic influence on, 445–47
  kinds, 437–45
  and learning, 260–61, 275, 284

parental influence, 447–54
and personality development,
  354, 355, 357
racial differences, 463–65
sex differences, 439, 451–59
and socioeconomic status,
  465–67
teachers' influence, 459–64,
  469–70
Motor coordination and skills
  See Physical and motor
  development
Motor development, 120–54
  See also Physical and motor
  development
Mowbray, C. T., *276*
Mower, O. H., *283*
Moyles, E. W., *336*
Mueller, E., *415*
Murphy, L. B., *280*
Murray, J. P., *422*
Mussen, P. H., *145, 409, 447*
Muuss, R. E., *146*

Nadelman, L., *381*
Natural childbirth, 65–66
Natural goodness, 7
Naturalistic views of misfortune,
  396
Nature (definition), 11
Nature–nurture issue, 11, 43, 44,
  324–32, 359, 361
Negative reinforcement
  (definition), 265
Neglect, 490
Neimark, E., 277
Nelson, A. K., 109
Nelson, G. K., *296*
Nelson, K., *241*
Neo-Freudian (definition), 353
Neonate, 73–77, 83, 127–29, 353
Neurosis, Neurotic behavior, 362,
  492–97
Newhart, B., 69
Newman, H. H., *326*
Nicholas, K. B., *272*
Niem, T. C., *412*
Nisbett, R. E., *111*
Noise (during pregnancy), 55

Norms (definition), 120
  cognitive, 171ff
  physical and motor, 126–36,
    142–46
Northway, M. L., *417*
Nucleus (definition), 28
Nursing, 366–67
Nurturant (definition), 368
Nurture (definition), 11
Nutrition, 52, 150–52, 509–10,
  511

Object permanence, 171, 173, 174,
  175, 369
Object recognition, 171
Observational (social) learning,
  262, 269–73, 283, 284, 286,
  289–93, 384, 394–95, 404
Obsessive-compulsive behavior,
  495–96
Occupational motivation, 455–59
Oedipus complex, 352, 382
Odom, L., *363*
Offer, D., *426*
Office childbirth, 66
O'Grady, R., *366*
Olds, J., *437*
Oliver, L. W., *456*
Ollendick., T. H., *440*
On the Origin of Species, 8
Ontogeny, 11
Operant conditioning, 262
Operations (definition), 167
Operational definitions in
  research, 523
Opie, N., *321*
Opposite-sex effects, 381–82, 454
Oral stage, 353
Organization (definition), 168
Orientals, 337
Orientation (definition), 98
Osborn, D. K., *422*
Osborne, R. T., *342*
Osgood, S. W., *180*
Osofsky, J. D., *361, 362*
Overgeneralization, 231
Overstimulation, 97, 104, 295
Ovulation, ovaries, 36